# HANGING BY A THREAD

## Ronald W. Hull

Booklocker.com, Inc.
Ronald W. Hull
Houston, Texas USA
Ron's Place: http://ronhullauthor.com
2014

# Table of Contents

The coal-heated Victorian we lived in from 1949-54.
622 Jefferson Street, Wausau, Wisconsin.

Roger and I share twin kittens.

# Preface

Christopher Reeve is not the first person to suffer severe spinal cord injury, although he became an icon for it. The author was injured in1963, thirty-two years before Reeve. At that time there was no Americans with Disabilities Act, and little hope for improvement in a life that usually became highly restricted and limited by surgeries, disease and other health problems, resulting in early death. In others' eyes, Dr. Ron Hull often became just another polio victim. People called him *"blessed"* or *"courageous"* as a way of distancing themselves from his *"affliction."*

It would have been easier to stay home with his parents, like so many others did. But Ron could still walk and pass for normal, so he set out on his own, determined to be independent. As a result, his challenges and accomplishments were many.

What Ronald Hull learned was that the stigma of paralysis could not be overcome by persistence or ingenuity, and that there comes a time when you must depend on others to go on. Medical breakthroughs and *"just in time"* technologies do the rest.

With more and more young people being injured each year in active lifestyles, it is hoped that Ron's story will inspire others to reach out and achieve, regardless of their limitations and physical disabilities.

With my twin brother, Roger (dark shorts)
at the shack our parents rented.
Owen, Wisconsin. 1944

# Dedication

To my parents, who instilled in me the confidence and self-reliance that has sustained me in my quest for independence and a full life. And to my attendants who got me through many a painful, stressful night, got me out of bed and ready to work every single day, working long hours for low pay, keeping me active and healthy. And finally, to Beh, who came into my life as a bright star and stayed with me through thick and thin, becoming a true partner in everything.

Ron, Judy, Roger

A picnic with Mom, Me, Dad, Judy, Grandpa Wenzel, Roger. 1952

With Roger and Judy, dressed in our best. Wausau Wisconsin 1953

# 1

# Introduction

Once, I visited my younger brother, Tim, while he was in college. He generously gave me his bed for the night. His idea of decoration was to hang the grille of his junked '69 Austin America from the ceiling by fishing line. The grille hung directly overhead, its sharp corner pointing at me like a Sword of Damocles. No matter how I changed my position, I couldn't seem to get safe from the thought of that line breaking and the grille spearing me in the face. I didn't sleep much that night.

Now, it is I hanging from the thread. And I don't sleep much thinking of it breaking and my body falling into that numb nothingness that comes with a lack of communication between the brain and the body, that point where I will still think, but be unable to act on the thoughts.

This is not a heroic story of overcoming great odds. Rather it is the story of one man's efforts to try to lead a normal life when an accident changed its course.

It may have begun before I was born. I was an identical twin. My brother Roger and I came from the same egg. We may have been joined at the spine as we developed, causing a deficiency in my neck structure as we separated some time before birth. Whatever it was, it was not obvious as I grew up. Our mother was only seventeen, so our birth that cold December day in 1942 was not easy. My brother was born with a concussion, and I suffered from scarlet fever and pneumonia before I was four. There was that time at two when Roger and I didn't know that tipping over beehives would be a problem. I don't remember, but my teenage mom and little friend, Rags, took the brunt of the bees' rage. Still, I grew and thrived, with a few childhood setbacks caused by several bouts with measles, influenza, and almost chronic winter colds. I managed to lead as normal a childhood as one can when you're a "cute" twin, considered to be a "brain" by your classmates. I did take books home for show but never did any homework. I'd just drop the books off, and then head out to play the faddish games our gang was constantly into.

I was the dominant one. To overcome the stigma of *cuteness* fostered by dressing alike and being the center of feminine attention, I was always exploring the limits of my physical ability and taking my brother into dangerous territory.

One time when we were seven, I watched Roger try to outrun a pickup while crossing Sixth Street. He lost the race and was knocked down and out. After an ambulance ride and stay in the hospital for his second concussion, Roger was okay. They said he darted out between parked cars, but I saw him run down the street when the truck didn't stop. But, just like the crowd around Roger as he lay unconscious on the lawn where the driver had carried him from the street, nobody believed his brother, a *kid*. It was only when I ran down the block to get our dad that I got anyone's attention. I had to stay home with my little sister while my dad rode with Roger in the ambulance to the hospital.

I was small, and slow to develop. But I compensated by taking almost any dare and priding myself in my speed, agility, and endurance. Until I was eighteen, I never got a stitch, or even a bad cut. Except in Cub Scouts, while Sumo (I didn't know what it was—we just did it) wrestling squatting on a gym floor, I fell backward, stuck out my left arm and broke it above the elbow. I wore a metal splint that was easy to bend, and the break took a long time to heal. Later, in high school, I would break my left wrist. Both breaks healed quickly and I seemed indestructible. That would change, as all things eventually do.

## 2

# Reach for the Stars

I wanted to be an astronaut. I don't know when I decided to seek that goal, but somewhere in the '50s I found out that I was smart, fearless, and resourceful—a natural leader who aspired to do something great with my life.

To me, riding rockets would be as easy as riding bikes, driving cars, and all the other things I'd learned to do on the first try. I knew I was different from the other kids, but I didn't possess any special talent for math, sports, music, or anything else that set me apart. Still, many times I pulled together my resources and excelled where I wasn't supposed. I remember learning to ride my bike without hands, like a unicycle. This is no great feat, but I made it more interesting. We lived in an urban neighborhood with sidewalks, driveways, alleys, and narrow yards. I worked out a path all around the neighborhood that I could ride without hands and avoid all the curbs, holes, bumps, and other obstacles that would force me to grab the handlebars. I worked in a spot where I would pull up to a stop sign, stop, look both ways, and then take a right turn. I could do this regardless of pedestrian or car traffic, never putting my foot down or touching the handlebars. No other kid could do it, but I could ride for hours on that course without stopping. At family outings, we all showed off feats of physical prowess. My father could hang from a bar by his toes. When my foot muscles proved too weak to do that, I learned that I could hang by my heels. No one else I knew could do that. The high point was when my uncle filmed me one time, hanging upside down from my heels, smiling and waving, ever ready to duck inward if I should fall to avoid breaking my neck. I never fell.

I loved to climb and climbed every tree in sight. I enjoyed challenges and learned to climb where there were no branches by hugging the trunk like a bear. I respected trees and didn't damage them like other kids did, carving and cutting on them. We never nailed steps on a tree or built a tree house. Trees were living and growing and I just wanted to use them to get high for a moment. The trees must have respected me because I never fell from one. But then, I knew my body, and though I'd take a dare, I never tried anything that I couldn't do. By the time I was a teenager, I'd developed a technique that impressed the competition. I'd climb a young sapling twenty to thirty feet tall. By the time I'd get near the top, my weight would begin to get too heavy for the tree. By picking the side I was on and how high I climbed, the tree would bend to my will, usually to a clear spot without branches from other trees. The trunk would bend slowly at first, and then speed up as I headed toward the spot I'd picked. As the trunk bent horizontal I'd swing my legs free and hang from my hands until I gently reached the ground. Once there, I'd let go of the trunk and the tree would snap back into place, its top whipping back and forth, a little ruffled, a little over-stretched, but none the worse for wear. I especially liked this type of climb because the climb up was fast and easy and I didn't have to climb down. It sure beat sliding down a rough trunk, skinning up the insides of my arms and tearing up my jeans.

My first try at swimming was at the local YMCA in midwinter. I remember being very cold and unsuccessful on my first tries. I finally learned to swim when I was seven at the city pool in Wausau. I had almost no fat, so I couldn't float. Roger and I would go down to the pool, pay ten cents to enter, and spend the afternoon diving. I would dive into the two foot end of the pool, never touching the bottom except with my hands, and glide to where the water was about four feet deep. I would end up standing up to my chest in water. So, I learned to dive and swim under water first, and always found it more comfortable than trying to stay afloat. At nine, we took lessons, and I learned enough to swim twenty feet and pass the test. With enough ability to finally swim in the deep, ten foot, end of the pool, my first day out I headed for the high diving board. Since I didn't like the struggle to stay afloat, my time at pools was spent doing flips and other dives, and swimming great distances under water. I practiced holding my breath until I could stay under water for up to two minutes. Since I wouldn't float, even with air in my lungs, I enjoyed scaring people by swimming to the bottom and lying there, relaxed, until they became concerned that I was in trouble. Or I would enter the pool in a busy spot, swim under water to a distant side and sneak out, while observers couldn't see where I'd gone. It was fun to sneak back to where they were sitting and go to the pool's edge again where they'd seen me disappear into the water.

We started picking beans when we were nine. In July and August, Roger and I would meet school buses and cars at the school playground, ride fifteen to thirty miles to green and yellow string bean fields, and then pick beans for the farmer all day. Depending on the quality of the beans, I could pick 70 to 90 pounds in a day. We got paid up to 3 cents a pound and were happy for it. Although I usually picked more than Roger, I was envious of the 15 and 16 year old girls who often picked over 100 pounds. Finally when I was 13, the beans were especially good one day and I picked 105 pounds, not enough to beat the big girls but more than ever before. Then, one day that summer, the farmer offered a 50-cent bonus for the most beans picked. I tried my best that day and picked 100 pounds, more than anyone else, and proudly took home $3.50 for my ten-hour workday. Mom had us put the money in the bank in our savings account. It helped buy school clothes in the fall.

Bandura proposed a theory of single trial learning. Through experiments with monkeys and babies, he observed that only humans and monkeys possess the ability to learn a set of complex psychomotor motions by observation and imitation, and then repeat them in one try. Without lessons, that's how I learned to ride a bike, dive, water ski, and many other things. I built up a repertoire of psychomotor skills by the time I was nine or ten so that I could just do things that others required lessons to learn. From an early age, I stood on the seat behind my father and watched him drive. So, at the age of nine, when he let me drive his '54 Ford out in the hay field, I already knew how to drive. As I "soloed" my first time out, I waved at my grandfather when I passed him on his tractor. I had no difficulty with the car, but when I returned from my tour, I overheard my dad being chastised for, "...Letting those kids drive!" I had to wait after that until I was sixteen and had completed Drivers' Training before I got behind the wheel of the family car again. I tried hard enough in Boy Scouts to earn merit badges in swimming and life saving, but it wasn't until I took a required swimming course my freshman year in college that I learned how to swim. The instructor, Mr. Johnson, a strict disciplinarian who was also the athletic director and a sports legend, told us that no one would pass the course without learning to float. I tried and tried, but never floated. But I learned to swim. I left the course with an "A" and a new found sense of security in the water.

I hadn't let that bother me though. My mind always seemed more mature than my body. By the time we were fourteen, Roger and I were Explorer Scouts and spent a week at the wilderness explorer base on the Flambeau River. Part of the week was canoe training and a two-day, sixty-five mile trip down the river. It had rained a lot and the river was nearly at flood stage. We had a wet, wild ride, and water flew high over the bow many times as we dove over five foot drops, but we never swamped. I learned to avoid rocks and dangerous spots that would swamp or wreck a canoe. It was cold and wet and hard work, but we weren't afraid of the river. Our worst problem was sunburn.

The next summer we joined an elite group going to the Quietico-Superior wilderness area, a region of thousands of glacier-created lakes and rivers as primitive as it was when the first French voyagers came there in the 1600s. Our group consisted of an adult leader and six scouts in three canoes. Roger and I were the smallest, weighing in about 80 pounds each. One scout who was a year older and more mature-looking was elected the group leader. The guys paired off. Since our canoe was the lightest in the water, we got a rider and the heavy food pack. A route was charted that would take us in a loop extending 97 miles over six days. The first portage was the toughest, because we had never carried a seventy pound canoe before, but the food pack was a ninety pound killer too. Somehow, I managed to prop the canoe up against a tree, get under it, lift it to an unsteady balance on my shoulders, and walk unsteadily the hundred yards of rocky, sometimes muddy, trail to the next lake. Roger complained of the agonizing weight of the food pack. By the end of the trip the food pack was light and Roger was able to carry the canoe, unassisted, over a five-mile portage. I was proud of him; I couldn't do that.

The adult leader insisted that we rise at 5 am each morning. Most of us were reluctant to get up because we had spent the night in scout issue tents without mosquito netting. It was August and quite warm, and the mosquitoes would come up in clouds and attack us most of the night and sometimes during the day. Crawling down into our sleeping bags worked for some, but it was too hot and exposing hands or faces resulted in numerous bites. So, I came up with a solution. I dispensed with the tent and placed four tall stakes in a square pattern at the head of my sleeping bag. I put my spare wool blanket over the stakes, making a small tent over my head. It was still too hot, and the sound of thousands of mosquitoes buzzing just overhead above the blanket was unnerving, but soon everyone was following my lead. The adult leader had a pup tent with netting, so he didn't have problems sleeping.

Each morning was a race to see who would lead and the others would paddle way ahead. But both the adult and chosen leaders, capable of carrying their canoes and packs quickly over portages and paddling to the lead, got us lost the first couple of days. After that, they gave me the map, and I navigated from the physical characteristics of the landscape for the rest of the trip. We never got lost again and made good time with my estimates.

Starting so early and pushing so hard resulted in everyone stopping to rest about 2 pm. They literally fell out and went to sleep when we arrived at the chosen campsite. No one wanted to cook supper, so I took it upon myself to cook the meals. After I gathered wood, built a fire, and cooked a meal, they would get up one by one, and eat. We saw much evidence of bears, especially among wild blueberry patches. But we were spared a confrontation, perhaps because food was so plentiful for them that time of year.

The way we were traveling put us behind schedule. One day the wind was to our backs and we were on a thirty-mile long lake. I lashed a mast in camp. Everyone laughed at my crude attempt at sailing as they took off, way ahead of us. I rigged a sail made from a tarp. By holding the mast up with my feet in the front of the canoe, and holding ropes tied to the bottom of the tarp, I sat back and caught the wind while Roger ruddered with a canoe paddle in the rear. Soon, we overtook the others. The adult leader called us over, had us lash the three canoes together, put up another mast and a poncho for a second sail. We were off for a wild ride as the wind and waves increased. We had to lash canoe paddles together to keep them from bending to the breaking point as our tri-hulled sailing machine raced the shoreline. It was exhilarating and tiring, and when the cool wind blew away the mosquitoes, we slept well that night, dreaming of the thirty miles we'd made without paddling.

About the half way point of our trip, we camped with another group on a rocky island. We caught some fish and our leader cooked them. There was a cliff on the island and we started to use it to dive the thirty feet or so to the deep water below. I remember having to dive way out from the slightly sloping outcropping to avoid hitting rocks below, punching the water with a tremendous blow to my hands and head, coasting deep into the cool, clear water, swimming down twenty feet or so until it was dark, and then, without reaching bottom, swimming upward to the light of the surface. At one point I was standing on the edge watching someone below when one of the guys, I don't remember who, jokingly gave me a push. I couldn't dive from that place so I turned toward him. My feet slipped off the edge and I fell. I caught the ledge with my chest and outstretched arms and a chill ran up my spine. I remember yelling at the guy about how dangerous it was and pictured myself mangled on the sharp rocks below. We had no radio, and it was three days hard paddling to the nearest road. It was no place to be hurt. I didn't tell the leaders what happened, just told the guys not to horse around on those dangerous rocks. Except for sunburn, numerous mosquito bites, paddling blisters, overstrained young muscles, and an insatiable desire for hamburgers, we returned uninjured and better men. I knew I that I thrived on the opportunity and adversity the wilderness presented, and that I could lead, even though I had to accommodate those who were more experienced, older, or physically stronger.

In the beginning, I'd also wanted to be an architect. There was no conflict in my mind that I could be an astronaut and an architect, too. From an early age, many of us in Wisconsin had heard of Frank Lloyd Wright and we wanted to create a new modern world where vehicles and homes would burst the bounds of tradition and emerge into an image created by Buckminster Fuller, Walt Disney, and Werner von Braun. From grade school through high school, I expressed my desire to become an architect. It was safe and respectable. No one in our immediate family had gone to college, so architecture as a profession seemed to be more like a far off dream, unattainable without a special talent, or the backing necessary to enter a school like Wright's. I was good at drafting and, more important, I did well in all my studies: English, math, physics, and chemistry. Still, I possessed no special talent or accomplishment that would catch the eye of a good school or sponsor. Instead, by the end of high school, I was eleventh in a class of 129. I won a small two-year Kiwanis Club scholarship. I was advised to attend a small technical college where I was assured a good education and a good job after four years. College also provided a draft deferment most young men my age were seeking from the Vietnam War.

.

# 3

# The First Accident

The summer of '59 when we were sixteen, my brother and I were unable to get a summer job except as raspberry pickers for a local grower who had some plots in the middle of our town. We didn't start working every day until mid summer. Before that, we did some fishing in local streams and swimming in the afternoons.

The city pool was unheated and it was usually mid June before I could stand to stay in the shockingly cold 60° water very long. Our friends would stake out a warm bench in the sun where we could dry off between sessions of jumping or diving off the high and low diving boards. I perfected a single back flip and a forward one and a half off the low board. I also got pretty good with a lay out single flip off the high board, landing feet first with my toes pointing downward. I would slip all the way to the bottom, and then push off to whatever side of the pool I was headed. One day, in the middle of the flip, I decided to end the dive in a cannonball, hoping to surprise everyone with a big splash. Instead, the momentum created by bending at the waist brought me too far over, and my arms never made it to beneath my knees. I landed still rotating, my chest, face, and arms slapping the water's surface. My arms went numb and my face and chest burned in pain. I swam toward the ladder, but I couldn't feel the motion of my arms or the water against my skin. It was a strange thing I'd never felt before, but one I would come to expect and live with. The feeling soon returned to my arms, but my face and chest still stung from their violent slap with the water. I sat out for a while, maybe fifteen minutes, contemplating what I'd done wrong with the flip, and then I returned to the water.

About two weeks later, we were at the pool again, and joined by friends from our class, John, Wayne, and Jeff. We had developed an active, fun

9

game that we called "Dibble-Dabble." We played Dibble-Dabble by "burying" a Popsicle stick in 4 to 5 feet of water, and then finding it. All the players stood at the edge of the pool at the 5-foot level. The player in possession of the stick would dive in and, by swimming around near the bottom, try to "hide" where the stick was released. The stick, once released, floated slowly upward, invisible until it got close to the surface. The players on the edge would watch for the stick where they thought it was released. At about 3 feet, the stick could be seen, and the players would jump or dive in to grab it. The turbulence caused by so many people going in and out of the water made the stick hard to grab. Once a player grabbed it, he would swim to the surface and shout, "Dibble-Dabble." Everyone then would climb out of the pool and the player in possession would dive in and bury it again. No one kept score but everyone wanted to get the stick more than the other guy.

The game was very physical, and that kept us warm on cool days, but we purposely avoided hitting one another as we rushed in and out of the water, relying instead on strategy and skill in placing and catching the ever-elusive Popsicle stick. But collisions were unavoidable as each one of us vied for capturing the stick the most.

I was a good player, often jumping or diving to where I expected the stick was placed and relying on my underwater vision and swimming ability to find the stick before others saw it from the surface. This time I saw the stick and jumped in with my fingers outstretched as I slid rapidly to the bottom. The stick had eluded my fingers and was nowhere in sight as I crouched on my feet on the bottom for a moment. Then, I decided to propel myself upward to the edge of the pool where I would pull myself out in a single motion and reenter the game from above where I could see the stick again.

As I pushed off the bottom and started to straighten up, I entered a strange world where my mind was clear and thinking but my body was floating without feeling. My head was above water and I was slithering like a snake to the side of the pool, up over the edge, and to a bench about ten feet from the pool. While sitting on the bench, still amazed how I got there without moving a muscle, feeling came back to my limbs in the form of shooting pain running up and down from the tips of my fingers and toes, through every muscle to my shoulders.

The others were still engaged in the game. No one knew that I was hurt. And because I hadn't cried out or showed any signs of injury, acted in disbelief when I told them that I was seriously hurt and urged me to rejoin them in the game. Only Wayne showed any sympathy with what I told him, and sat with me while the others played on. It was the beginning of misunderstandings about this kind of injury that has plagued me ever since.

I don't think I ever played Dibble-Dabble again, at least that afternoon. Instead I sat there and felt sorry for myself, watching my brother and buddies play as my arms, hands, legs, chest, and feet suffered thousands of needle-sharp pricks of pain. This strange pain they could only see on my face, but not feel themselves. It was impossible for them to understand what I was going through.

I know now but I didn't know then that at least one of the fourth or fifth vertebrae in my cervical spine had been fractured. I believe that as I pushed off the bottom, one of my buddies saw the stick and jumped in. I believe that a foot or two below the surface, his heels hit me in the neck, causing the injury as I pushed up and he came down. While no one ever admitted to hitting me, I believe I know who did it. Perhaps, in the heat of the game, he actually doesn't remember the blow, or thinks he hit the bottom.

Later, when I refused to continue to play, Roger began to agree that I was hurt. We bicycled the usual two miles to home. I had no trouble doing that. After a couple of nights having difficulty sleeping because my skin kept having that prickly pain, especially against my sheets, my mother sent me to a doctor. The doctor was an osteopath and a distant relative who had a clinic in town. He took x-rays, gave me an "adjustment", and told me that if I took it easy, the pain would go away in a couple of weeks. It did.

Years later, I learned that the x-rays showed at least one hairline fracture and that the adjustment, a procedure used by chiropractors to stretch the muscles and ligaments of the spine by force, could have increased the injury I already had to ligaments, muscle, cartilage, bone, and disk. Fortunately, I didn't feel any worse after the adjustment, but I often wonder about the strange code of medical ethics that prevents a doctor from showing an intelligent sixteen-year-old his own x-rays. But then, withholding information from a patient is safer if there is misdiagnosis. No repercussions or malpractice if the patient never learns the facts.

George and Ron (bareback) sailing Lake Agnes at 16. Three canoes lashed together with sails made from a poncho and tarp. 1958

I lettered in wrestling, track, and Cross Country (right) in high school

# 4

# College Bound

I forgot the injury and got on with my busy life and my junior year of high school. Besides a heavy load of college preparatory classes, Roger and I both joined cross-country, wrestling, and track. Then, to earn spending money, we worked setting pins in a bowling alley four nights a week. We went to football and basketball games most Friday nights, hunted with our buddies on Saturdays and Sundays, and attended a youth church group on Sunday nights. We had to give up Explorer Scouts, but turned our attention to driving and dating on the few free nights we had. This heavy schedule was good for my grades and me, but it turned out to be hard on Roger.

In late October, we went pheasant hunting in the snow one Saturday. We crossed a storm-swollen icy stream up to our waists and were frozen, soaked, and miserable by the time we got back to the car. By Monday night I worked but Roger didn't. We both had developed bad colds. During gym class, one of the football players threw a basketball at Roger from the stage. His reaction was slowed by his cold, and not knowing that the ball was thrown to him, he failed to protect himself and the ball hit him in the chest. After that, Roger started experiencing chest pain and claimed that it was a broken or cracked rib from the ball. That Saturday we traveled 150 miles to a state cross-country meet. The car was overheating so the coaches turned off the heater that they thought was the source of the problem. Roger didn't run because of his cold and sore ribs, but I did. The ground was frozen and it was snowing lightly. After a mile or so running in thinclads, I was burning up on the inside from exertion and freezing where my skin was exposed. We didn't know about wind chill in those days, but I didn't react to the telltale sign I got either. As I ran full speed down a long hill on the golf course we were running, each stiff-legged step hammered my spine as I hit the frozen ground with as much cushion as I could muster with my foot's instep extended and my knees slightly bent. The numbing pain that hammered through me was excruciating. I didn't finish well and I didn't know that those shocks were different from what the other runners were feeling.

It was very cold going home. By the time we got there, Roger was doubled over in pain. Dad took him to the hospital. With one lung full of fluid, and the other half involved, he nearly died that night. We missed the telltale sign. The pain in his chest was pleurisy and not a cracked or broken rib. He carries scarred and weakened lungs as a legacy. In December he had to undergo major surgery to remove heavy scar tissue from his left lung.

In his weakened condition, even with a good recovery, Roger was no longer an identical match, pound for pound, muscle for muscle, from that to measure my strength. With our attention drawn to him, it took me longer to read the signs of my own condition.

And they were many. While I handled pins and sixteen-pound bowling balls with ease at the bowling alley, the first hint of weakness came in wrestling. Early in the wrestling season, the coach dropped in on a local country bar and caught the entire varsity above my weight class, mostly seniors, drinking beer. The coach kicked them all off the squad. This gave me more opportunity, even though there were still seniors at my weight. I was still learning all I could about wrestling, especially leg moves like the figure four and grapevine, and I was very good at takedowns. Still, I lacked the upper body strength to hold my opponents and the neck strength to get me out of trouble when I landed on my back. I thought that I just lacked muscle maturity, but the signs were already there. I lost some big matches that spring, but figured I'd do much better in my senior year. By turning to leg moves, I was already compensating.

The first meet of the track season was an indoor one at Stevens Point. I was a developing pole-vaulter and 440 yard sprinter. In my sophomore year, I had reached 10' 6" pole vaulting and hoped to make 13 to 14' by my senior year. My 440 times had been about 60 seconds, but I always felt that I could do much better. The pit for pole vaulting was filled with sand instead of the usual wood shavings. The runway was dirt instead of the usual cinders and the field house lights overhead were more distracting. We didn't have a field house so our track was still snowbound. I had only practiced in our gym, so I spent a lot of time practicing that night before the meet. I was having trouble turning and pushing off after clearing the bar with my legs. One time I fell headfirst and broke my fall with my left hand. I felt a sharp pain in my wrist, but shook it off as a muscle pull and continued to vault.

I don't think I made 9 feet that night. Things were worse in the 440. I got off to a good start, leading the pack. But, by the time I reached the fourth corner, I'd run out of gas and finished last. My consolation was that a spectator, a teacher whose twin sons were younger and "stars" for their ability in the 100, 220, and half mile, said, "You have the best form of all the runners." Intrinsically, I knew I had the best form, but I couldn't figure out why I couldn't push on past the pain in my tightening legs t o win.

My coach told me to have my wrist checked the next morning if the swelling didn't go down. It didn't, and X-rays showed that I had a green break in a small bone. The wrist was in a cast for twenty days. I continued to run and returned to pole vaulting late in the season, but I never regained the momentum of my sophomore year. I blamed my "weak" left arm and wrist to the two broken bones. I would continue to use that as an excuse for the next three years.

The summer after our junior year, Roger and I started working in a mobile home factory. The work, building wall framing, was not heavy. But it was fast-paced and we drove hundreds of eight-penny nails a day. My right wrist and arm were noticeably strengthened by all the exercise, but Roger, in spite of his weakened condition from his bout with pneumonia, continued to beat me in all contests of arm or wrist wrestling.

My senior year I did well in cross-country, but not as well as I expected and wanted. One teammate, a junior whose chest had been crushed when he was run over by a loaded hay wagon at thirteen, continually beat me when it came to the "kick" past the two-mile mark. Roger and I had quit riding our bicycles to school. So one night after cross-country practice, I accepted a ride for the two miles we usually walked home. As I got in the car my right thigh knotted in pain. I was told that it was a "Charley Horse". I had never heard of a Charley Horse or experienced a muscle spasm before. It was another sign that would become very familiar.

In wrestling, I was the "old man" now. But, I had to "wrestle-off" with my twin brother to make the team. Roger was too easy to beat, and I regretted that we were in the same weight class. He caught pneumonia again before Christmas, and never returned to practice. It was a relief for me because I hated to be pitted against him in his weakened condition. I did have a rival though. He was a strong sophomore whose older brother was a fellow senior in a lower weight class who had finished high in state tournament competition. We had to wrestle-off before every varsity match. By this time I was relying on my knowledge and agility rather than strength, and won half the wrestle-offs by using the grapevine or figure four. I learned how to arch my back and strengthened my neck trying to avoid being pinned by stronger opponents like him. It was undignified, but I avoided the worse indignity of being pinned. We shared the spotlight and both earned letters, but he got the big matches and got to complete in the tournaments. I taught him every thing I knew, and, two years later he was State Champion at 127 lbs.

When track season arrived, I couldn't pole vault well enough to make the team. Several times I was first out of the blocks and led the pack in the 440, only to tighten up in the home stretch when I should have won with ease. I blamed my pole-vaulting performance on my weakened left arm. My 440 performance was blamed on my starting out too fast and not "gutsing it out" in the stretch. My coach put me in the 100 yard dash to resolve the pulling-up problem, but even though I was usually first off the starting line, sophomores beat me at the tape.

That summer before college was spent working twelve-hour days at the mobile home factory so there wasn't much time for me to think about why I was failing in sports. I was making good money, enjoying my free time with my brother and other friends, and looking forward to college in the fall. We decided to visit a grade school friend, so went to see him one Sunday. Our friend lived on a lake and had bought a boat. He had water skiing gear and we spent the afternoon skiing. He didn't have a slalom ski, but after jumping the wake and other maneuvers, I tried a one-ski trick where I would bend my knee and lift one ski off the water while I slalomed across the wake with the other ski. I wasn't paying attention because the trick was quite easy. I let the front of the ski I was holding up drop, and, when its tip entered the water the sudden drag caused me to lose my grip on the rope as I cartwheeled forward violently.

I ended up floating in my life vest, numb from the neck down, just like the earlier swimming accident. I got into the boat with shooting pains in my arms and legs and decided not to ski any more that day. A little while later I changed my mind and skied for a half hour straight just to prove that I was only temporarily hurt. I didn't try that one ski trick again; I don't recall ever doing it again.

My freshman year in college, I went out for wrestling and track. Before that, I got my first stitches. One Saturday we were free swimming in the university pool. I enjoyed cannonballing one of the bigger football players who was twice my size. I would leap from the side or spring board and splash him thoroughly as he tried to swim away. To get even, he tried to get me too, but I would dive under water or dodge his splash. One time after he had missed, I started to swim away. He came up from the bottom and his head struck me in the chin. The force of the blow didn't knock me out, but it put my teeth through my lower lip. We went to the emergency room where I got stitched up, and then we stopped for hamburgers on the way back to the dorm. My lower lip felt like a ball of raw meat from the inside. The hamburger went down easily.

In college wrestling, I relied entirely on my leg moves and the strength of my neck. On the mat my opponents would easily pull away from me, so I specialized in takedowns and escapes that led to high-scoring matches. I often lost. In the weight room, I could easily squat lift or leg lift 350 lbs, more than some of the football players. My biggest concerns were weight control, colds, and my ears. I limited my diet and liquid intake to the point of dehydration. Over the Christmas Holidays, I reached 145 lbs. I wrestled that season at 130. I caught colds easily, and found "hitting the mat" caused painful sinus headaches. Large doses of vitamin C tablets helped eliminate the colds, but my ears presented another problem. Four years of punishment without headgear caused painful swelling. I decided to quit wrestling.

I don't remember much about that track season except that I didn't win anything and decided that I wasn't going to be a college athlete. My grades were good and I was participating in many activities, so I didn't miss sports and the time they took.

That summer I got a job as a draftsman for Praschak Machine, a local company that made concrete block machinery. The chief engineer had a drafting machine that I never used. Using a T-square and triangles, I became quite proficient at machine drafting.

It was a heady time to be in college. As freshmen, Roger and I had participated in the boycott of a local hangout that had refused to serve Black football players. At the alternative, a country bar for some reason called Alcatraz, we learned a new dance, the twist, and how to crowd the dance floor. There was a feed sack on a stage bearing a target from some turkey shoot, and one night a skunk under the floor made the place uninviting to all but the local regulars. In spite of this we mobbed the place on weekends and I became quite good at the new dances that seemed to be invented weekly. John Kennedy was president and we were going to the Moon. I wanted to be a part of everything: the Civil Rights Movement, the end to the Cold War, and the Space Program. I wrote to Christopher Craft, administrator for NASA in Houston, asking about working with the astronauts. He wrote back that I should get a good education. In spite of being in a school that didn't stress academics, I intended to.

One day in the early spring of 1963, Roger and I were working on drafting machines in an open lab. Always competing, Roger said that I was operating the drafting machine wrong. He showed me that I should be rotating the drawing edge knob with my left hand, leaving my right hand free to draw. While I was moving the drawing edge around the board with ease, when it came to rotating it to the 30 and 45-degree positions, I was using my right hand to assist my left to rotate the tool into position. He said, "See, the reason you can't do it is that you don't have any muscle on the back of your hand!" He compared his left hand to mine and he was right. His hand was filled in with muscle, while the tendons on the back of mine, leading to each knuckle stuck out from the hollow spaces between them. We compared right hands and they were okay. Suddenly it dawned on us why I always lost to him in arm and wrist wrestling. There was something wrong with my left hand. We didn't talk about it again that spring but it would come up again that summer.

A President's Commission on Physical Fitness had determined that America's youth were not physically fit. President Kennedy recommended walking as something almost everyone could participate in. He liked fifty-mile walks. Soon, walking fifty miles became a fad. An enterprising student at our college set up a walk from Menomonie, where our school was, to Eau Claire, the next, larger city with rival, Eau Claire State, and back, a distance of fifty miles. As a warm-up, his group walked twenty miles to a nearer town the Saturday before.

I was working on a term paper when the walkers came back into town that first Saturday. The paper was the best that I'd done, describing a closed ecological environment for interstellar space flight. It was a subject potentially interesting to scientists, engineers, and architects, but not necessarily to my Expository Writing professor. My graphic of the closed system was especially good, but I remember having trouble finding adequate source material in our library. I also remember having trouble with the "a" on our ancient Royal manual typewriter. I got cramps using the little finger on my bad left hand, and had to "force" the a each time I typed it.

Roger and our roommate, Bob Kraiss, had delayed their papers that were due the same time as mine. We all went to our second story apartment window to watch the walkers pass. I remember asking Bob what was going on and he told us that they were preparing for a fifty mile walk the next Saturday and that he was going to participate. My brother and I decided to join Bob on the walk. I turned in my paper early and made some preparations to walk further than I ever had before.

On Friday night I put together a lunch of sandwiches, cans of pop, and Hershey chocolate bars that was light and full of energy. The lunch would be carried out to us each hour by cars, so I planned to eat lightly all day and drink plenty of the pop. At the last minute, Roger and Bob backed out, claiming that they had to finish their papers that were due Monday morning.

Saturday morning at 6 am, nineteen of us showed up at the starting point: eight women and eleven men. I felt alone without my friends, and just watched the others talk about their new hiking boots and their plans for the walk. I was wearing my well-worn black high top "tennies" that my mother bought at J. C. Penney. The talk of expensive hiking boots by Seniors I didn't know was a bit intimidating, but I felt comfortable in those old shoes and knew they wouldn't bother me. I was worried though about a former track teammate who was tall and in good shape. He was a good half miler and I expected him to set the pace. The men did most of the talking, but I knew the women were going to have to be reckoned with too.

Everyone took off at a pace that belied a fifty-mile journey. I didn't want to tighten up so I settled into a fast, comfortable walk of about four miles an hour. After about two miles, I started passing some of those who started off too fast. Among them, the track star was limping, complaining of shin splints. I never saw him again, but he did finish.

It was one of those beautiful clear May days, when the sun and the pavement were not too hot, ideal for the walk. Most of the route was on lightly traveled County Road E with only an occasional speeding car and the hourly relief car with my cache of goodies. I started walking with a freshman girl from New York. She was athletic and tough, and annoyed me by wanting to "track it" down every downgrade. I would jog a bit, trying to avoid that jarring that came from running straight-legged downhill on pavement. I spent a lot of time catching up, but eventually we settled in to just walking.

There was a restaurant at the twenty-five mile point. Most of the walkers had not prepared adequate food for the walk, were hungry, and stopped to eat. We waited a half hour for some of them to eat before heading back. We started walking with a guy who had worn loafers. He had huge blisters on his heels and soon had to drop out at thirty miles. The ones with new boots all developed blisters and other foot problems and followed suit. I had to stop at about forty miles with my own foot problem. My little toenail on my left foot was too long, and, after miles of walking, started to dig into the toe next to it. I was lucky. Instead of having to stop in pain, I just sat down under a tree, took off my shoe and sock, broke off the offending toenail, put my sock and shoe back on, and resumed walking. By forty miles, we were walking with the lead couple. The woman said that she had to rest, and dropped back. The three of us walked on, my companions slowing and complaining. I was starting to tighten up badly, so I wanted to walk faster to stretch my legs. I wanted to walk on in with my newfound friends, but they wanted to rest. I knew that if I rested, I would have to ride in. So, I took off alone, leaving them resting their weary, sore feet under a tree. Walking faster again, I felt good, but it was strange walking alone on the main highway into town against the sun in the late afternoon. People coming into town who could see that I was tired and looked in need of assistance offered me rides. They knew nothing of the walk. I waved them off. I did stop for a few minutes to talk to a local radio reporter who tape-recorded an interview with me by the roadside. I was impatient and anxiously wanted to head on in. I'm not sure what I said, something about eating right and staying in shape, but I never heard the interview on the radio. Others told me they did.

I arrived at the starting point about 5 pm, eleven hours after we started. No one greeted me. After a half hour, the school photographer came by and we rode out in his car to see where the others were. They were strung out for twenty miles. The two I left under the tree arrived at about 6 pm and the others came straggling in after that. Finally, one woman, with the help of two cyclists carrying lights, was the eleventh and last one to finish. In all, six women and five men finished the walk. That day, I learned who was the toughest when it came to the superiority of the sexes.

Although I was dead tired, I couldn't sleep that night. If my feet hurt, I didn't know it, but every muscle in my legs cramped and knotted in pain. To add salt to my wounds, my brother and roommate skipped across the street as we left for church the next morning, forcing me to limp after them in pain.

That afternoon, I claimed my reward. The Rendezvous Bar offered a free large pizza with the "works'" to all who finished. It was my first pizza with the works and a bit overwhelming. Of course, my brother and friends helped me eat it, and my stomach hurt too much to eat much of it. My fellow walkers who finished and earned their own free pizzas were not there, all too sick and tired to accept their reward.

My paper, turned in early, got lost, but when the professor finally found it again, earned an "A".

The summer of 1963 was a busy one. Roger bought a 1935 Ford three window coupe that had been chopped and channeled, with a dropped front axle, Z-ed frame, and a 1949 Cadillac overhead valve V-8 engine. We paid $100 for coupe and it needed a lot of work. I bought my father's '57 Ford Fairlane 500 back from a local schoolteacher who had had it for a couple of years, and had the engine rebuilt. They no longer needed my drafting skills at Praschak Machine, so we went back to work at the mobile home factory, Rollohome. Early in the summer I started dating a secretary for the school superintendent. Doris was a recent high school graduate with no immediate plans for college, but intensely interested in marriage. She was engaged to the guy she dated before me, but ditched him after our first date. I was surprised when she asked me to marry her that very first date. Her directness caught me off guard. We dated steadily, but I wanted to finish college before assuming the responsibilities of marriage.

The '35 hot rod consumed much of my time. Working on and under that old car gave me a sense of accomplishment, and time to think that I relished. It was the kind of summer that should have gone on forever. I had been on the Dean's List four straight semesters; my father and mother were both working making good money. My grandmother shared a little trailer beside our house and helped my fifteen-year-old sister take care of our twin four-year-old brothers. I had a girlfriend, a great brother, a car to drive, and a car to play with. The summer of '63 was as close to Camelot as I got. It was a point of great beginnings. I wasn't sure what, but it marked the major turning point in my life. As the Kennedy family would suffer, so would mine. And through our unrelated suffering, we would struggle to regain that wholeness we once knew in summers when anything was possible.

Sometime that summer, Roger told my mother of the weakness he had found in my left hand. When we compared hands for her, she became concerned, and asked me to go back to the osteopath to try to see what was wrong.

I went to Dr. Middlestadt again. After examining me, he gave me an adjustment and determined that my weakness might be a muscle disease or a spinal problem caused by having one leg longer than the other. He gave me a series of niacin shots to improve my circulation, asked me to wear a lift in one shoe, and ordered me not to lift more than five pounds. Finally, my mother, dissatisfied with the diagnosis and treatment, asked him to refer me to the local clinic.

The Marshfield Clinic was associated with St. Joseph Hospital, had many specialists, and was considered to be second only to the Mayo Clinic in the entire region. Just before I went back to college, I got an appointment. The neurologist who examined me took one look at my left hand and immediately said that I had neurological damage. He took muscle tests. The grip test was the most telling. He said that a man of my age and stature should have a grip of 250 lbs in each hand. I could only squeeze 175 lbs with my right hand and 50 with my left. Clearly, something was wrong with my spine. He introduced me to a neurosurgeon, Dr. Salibi. Salibi wanted to do further tests in a hospital. When he learned that I was going back to college soon, Salibi said that he would schedule the tests for me at St. Joseph Hospital over the Thanksgiving break.

1935 Ford Coupe in October 1962, a year before I destroyed our work.

# 5

## The Accident Before the Accident

The fall of 1963 I had renewed concern for my future. I went to the career office and took the Strong Interest Blank. Later, I learned that the Strong Interest Blank was very valid and reliable for determining a person's interests, especially over time. The Interest Blank did this by comparing a person's interests with those of specific professions. My highest interest aligned with those of jet pilots, followed by chemists and production managers. What is significant is that my highest interest was not the same as an architect, and that my interest in being a teacher was quite low. From time to time, thoughts of these results would haunt me. But then, I decided to abandon my plan to go on the graduate school in architecture and instead focus on industrial technology and production management. The last thing on my mind was training to be a jet pilot in the Vietnam War, but at least two of my classmates did. One from my hometown rode home as a passenger in my car many weekends, became a Marine pilot after graduation, and died over Vietnam leaving his wife and child behind. The other, a math whiz and rival in physics classes, I don't know what happened to.

That fall, I was enrolled in an auto mechanics course. By the end of September, I brought the 35 Ford to the shop for repairs. I had been going home every weekend to see Doris. That weekend, Doris and the girlfriend of another freshman student, John Loveland, who left his car at home in Marshfield and rode in my car decided to come to Stout instead.

Friday night the girls arrived early in John's car. We toured the campus and arrived where the street dance would be, as it was turning dark. No one was there yet, so I suggested that we take a ride in the hot rod, parked nearby, outside the auto shop at Frykland Hall. I had just tuned it up and was interested in how it would run on the road. I picked a route that would lead out of town on a road where I could "open it up," then take a narrow, steep and curvy road back into town, a circuit of about seven miles that I'd taken the hot rod on a couple of nights before.

We drove west out of town, across the river and up a grade that would lead to top of the hill about three miles to the road I would take to the right. It was a smooth, wide asphalt state highway, with wide shoulders, and almost straight, perfect for testing the power of the newly tuned Cad V-8. I accelerated from the start, and we were laughing and talking as we enjoyed the exhilaration of acceleration. About two miles out and eighty miles an hour, John, in the back seat yelled, "Watch out!"

I saw a black or gray panel truck pulling into my lane from a street that angled onto the highway from the right. It was a '50s model Chevy panel van with one taillight and no signals. The driver, a 16 year old, said later that he pulled out because my low headlights were "dim and appeared far away." I think he probably never really looked but just pulled out onto the highway.

I hit the brakes and clutch with all my might. As the weight of the heavy engine and four passengers shifted forward, the rear of the light car came off the pavement, putting all the braking on the front tires. The car drifted to the left and I could not control it. We slid across the oncoming lane in the face of a terrified woman in an oncoming car. Fortunately, we continued off the road to the left with the rear of the car catching up on the left. Soon, the car was sideways and still going more than fifty miles an hour as we slid across the shoulder to the darkness of a steep down slope beyond. As the rubber reached the heavy grass of the bank, I said to myself, "Don't catch.... Don't catch...!"

But both front and rear left wheels dug into the soft dirt beyond the gravel shoulder. The car lurched downward to the left, we stopped momentarily, and then it was airborne, and rolling rapidly. It seemed like a long time before we touched ground again, but when we did, we rolled and rolled, and the hood and trunk lids flew up and both doors flew out. I was hitting the roof in one instant, and then the seat the next. I remember reaching up and out of the open door and grabbing the roof to keep from flying up and down. Suddenly, I sensed that my arm could be cut off if the door closed, and I pulled it in. At that point, I was forced out the door, my left knee caught up under the dash against the door as my face was pushed into grass and dirt and the car rolled one last time about three feet above me. It landed on its wheels and rolled backward to a stop at the bottom of the ditch. Its headlights were still shining on me. My left knee hurt, but I got up and yelled if anyone was hurt. John and his girlfriend in the back seat yelled back that they were OK, and I quickly found Doris lying on her back on the slope, head down. There was blood on her forehead and she said that she couldn't move her legs or arms.

There was a college bar nearby. Suddenly, there were a hundred people milling about. I don't remember an ambulance, but we all went to the emergency room. My friend had a badly bruised ankle. His girlfriend received a stitch on her eyelid. Doris received a couple of stitches for a head cut and a split finger tip, and some painkillers for her many bruises. I got eight stitches above my left knee for a puncture wound from the bottom edge of the dashboard. We were all very lucky.

We didn't get to the dance. Instead, I had to tell Roger that I'd totaled his car, and we drove my friend's car the 100 miles to get the girls home. For all its violence, I don't recall any injury to my neck in the wreck. Instead, my girl took a week off so that her bruises could heal and her finger could heal so she could type, and the rest of us returned to class Monday morning. Two months later, I was paralyzed.

My rendering of the completed car, to be painted a violent violet

Roger, Judy, Tom, Tim, and Ron.  Christmas 1962

Third from the right, I wrestled and ran track my freshman year.

# 6

# The Second Accident

T he neurosurgeon's office called and told me that Dr. Salibi wanted
me to check into St Joseph's Hospital Sunday night. Stout was strict
about the "no cut days" before holidays, so I had to get special
permission from the Dean of Students to take the entire
Thanksgiving week off for my tests. I was ready to go into the hospital,
feeling a bit sorry for myself.

Early in November, Doris was a bridesmaid for her cousin. I couldn't
attend the wedding because I was finishing replacing the fender on my '57
Ford. When I got to the reception I sat with her parents, but she was with
the wedding party and sat next to the best man and brother of the groom, a
submariner, stationed in North Carolina. She left with him. A week later he
returned to base and I heard that they were engaged. She wasn't the only
friend I lost. I soon found out how fragile friendships are.

Early that week, I had the tests. The only one I remember was the
myelogram on Monday morning. Dr. Salibi and a neurologist were present.
They placed me face down on a cold x-ray table. Then, after deadening an
area in the small of my back with Novocain, they explained that they were
injecting a heavy radioactive dye into my spinal fluid. They tilted the table
downward, allowing the fluid to flow along my spine toward my head,
observing its progress through a fluoroscope.

The doctors were saying, "That's a good one!", and stopping to take x-
rays, so I knew they had found something. I didn't know that they didn't
know what it was they were looking at until later that week.

I had to lie on my back in bed for 48 hours. I was told that air bubbles introduced into my spinal fluid when the dye was removed would cause terrible "myelogram headaches". Later, I would have the displeasure of experiencing them. It was hard for an active 20 year old to stay down, but I dutifully avoided getting up, even to urinate, and felt no headaches as my reward.

On Thanksgiving morning, my parents and I met with Dr. Salibi. He explained that the myelogram showed pressure on my spinal cord, but he couldn't tell what was causing it was without surgery. He said that it could be enlarged disks, bone spurs, or a sac of fluid from the earlier injury. Or it could be a tumor. Salibi considered that unlikely. We agreed to go ahead with the surgery, even though it meant that I wouldn't be going back to school after the holiday. Not until after Christmas. The surgery would take that long to heal. I remember him telling us that there was always a chance of paralysis, especially if it was a fluid sac or tumor. And death... I chose to ignore that prospect, but some would choose the freedom of death over the prospect of life confined to a body that does not move or function without help. I don't know what my parents thought, but I focused on enduring the pain of surgery so that I could return to school in a couple of weeks with the problem in my neck fixed. Since I never had experienced paralysis, I considered it a problem that I could overcome with healing and physical discipline. I was wrong.

I had a sinus infection so the neurosurgeon postponed an operation until he was assured that antibiotics had cleared it up. In the meantime, I explored the hospital, waiting for time and treatment to clear the infection and a date of surgery. I had a semi-private room. My first roommate was a German farmer in his 70s who was also a legendary deer hunter. I had hunted with gun and bow several seasons without seeing a buck I could shoot. I admired and envied these old timers who always got a deer, year after year. He was having a colostomy reversed. The year before, he had shot a deer, and then, without help, had tried to drag it back to camp, and in his words, "Busted his guts." He told me that he had a deal with his doctor to wait until after he got a deer this year before he would come in to have his colon reattached. He bragged that he never missed shooting a buck. In fact one year at his favorite stand he said that he shot six bucks and then waited for members of his hunting party to come by and tag them. This year, he got his buck the first day so he could get his operation over with.

I hung out in the patient lounge, playing pool with myself and watching television. I don't remember exactly when Jack Kennedy was shot. I must have been the only one in America. But I was watching when Oswald was brought out, only to see Jack Ruby shoot him, cutting short the frenzy that would have ensued, leaving only a dull emptiness that I was to feel more than most. My depression about losing Doris and my anxiety about the upcoming operation wrapped me in a cloak of doom.

There were loud screams that came from down the hall. Talk in the patient lounge was that a twenty-three year old woman had received too much anesthetic during a gall bladder operation. Her heart had stopped beating for eight minutes, causing brain damage. I don't know exactly what happened to her, but I had time to think of a young mother whose life had been changed forever by an accident during surgery to save her life.

My grandmother Hull had had a gall bladder operation. I remember her showing us a large stone in a jar, as if confirming the need for the operation. My next roommate was a big, strong middle-aged man who gave me a new respect for the gall bladder. He was brought in so sick that he thought that he was going to die. After his emergency operation, he acted as if he still was going to die, yellow bile oozing out of him in a river of pain. It made me think that I would never put off needed surgery like he did because I was too poor, busy, or afraid like he was.

I started to get a bad reputation on the ward. Here I was hanging around the halls with a sinus infection, while the nurses had to deal with an increased number of patients who always come with the stress and overeating of the holiday season. The head nurse, who was also a Nun, treated me with disdain. My nose was dry and irritated. When it bled as it always did in winter in those days, she grabbed me and squeezed my nose so hard it bled more before it stopped. I was used to stopping the bleeding myself by simply holding a handkerchief under it gently until it stopped. Her approach seemed violent and unnecessary—like she felt my hospital stay was. She soon learned why I was there. Once she heard, I didn't see her again.

Surgery was scheduled early on December 4th. My preparation involved shaving my head from my ears back. The intern who shaved me covered it with gauze that he attached with adhesive tape. When I was wheeled into a pre-operation room, I was given a shot and an intravenous tube with a yellow liquid that I think was sodium pentothal. The man then removed the tape using cotton soaked in a liquid I thought smelled of ether. I was quite relaxed but I remember breathing in those fumes to hasten sleep. I do not remember leaving that room.

I do remember waking up in the operating room, and looking up at Dr. Salibi, his face surrounded by bright light. He was saying, "Are you all right?"

At the same time I said, "Hi, Doc. Yes, I'm okay."

But I was not okay, I just felt that way. When I woke up in the room, I felt good. I was acutely aware of everything around me and reacting with a clear head that my sinus condition hadn't allowed before. I felt no pain from the surgery, only a, "tightness," in my neck where a stiff bandage was taped. I couldn't feel anything from my neck down, so I didn't try to move anything, not even my hands.

Everyone was so worried, but I wasn't. I knew the operation wasn't a success, but in my own naive way, I felt that I would walk out of the hospital in a couple of weeks. I was very talkative and buoyant and wanted to play chess or do calculus, but only in my head. If I could have put pen to paper, I think those brilliant thoughts would have evaporated, leaving only the garbled ramblings of an accelerated stream of consciousness. It was only the morphine talking. Still, I am grateful that the powerful drug spared me from the pain my body must have been going through.

Dr. Salibi came in. He ran a ballpoint pen up the bottom of my feet and poked my hands, feet, arms, and legs with a sharp pin. I felt nothing and moved nothing. He was not encouraged by the results, but said we'd have to wait for the swelling to go down where the five-inch incision had disrupted my spine.

Somehow I had avoided the recovery room and intensive care. But my mother, grandmother, and father took turns staying up all night with me. I didn't move, so I required little. I was hooked up to intravenous feeding and had a catheter for urine, so I just lay there with my thoughts. Nurses would come in and check my vital signs and give me hypos, but day blended to night as I lay there talking and thinking, and staring at the ceiling. Roger had returned to school after Thanksgiving, and was given the onerous task of withdrawing me from school. It was the first time he was alone. The first time he had to make decisions without conferring with me first. While I was coming to terms with my paralysis, Roger was coming to terms with a forced separation from a brother who determined the direction of his life. In some ways the accident was harder on him than it was on me.

In a couple of days, my feeling came back in my legs and feet, and, more encouragingly, movement. Now, when Dr. Salibi used his ballpoint, my toes curled downward in pain. Soon, the bottom of my feet had many blue lines from his tests. My arms and hands were harder to heal. It started in the neck muscles attached to my shoulders, a combination of itching and tingling, and then moved down my chest and through my shoulders and down my arms. For several days these sensations grew and grew, until at night it felt like, especially when I closed my eyes, like my arms were thrust into barrels of biting ants, swarming over and biting my skin nonstop. The tightness in my neck grew tighter, and only the activity of the day with people talking to me kept the demons away. Worse than the ebbing and flowing of my reawakening nerve endings was my lack of sleep. For ten days, I did not sleep. When I tried to relax, put the irritating sensations to a corner of my mind, and close my eyes, my head would pull downward violently toward the strong pull of my bandage, my rigid body would start to rotate backward, and my feet would float toward the ceiling in an accelerating backspin. I was falling backward faster than I had been thrown from the rolling car. The force was immense. Thoughts would rush into my head at the same time. This must have been Hell, and I would always wake up and open my eyes to keep from falling into it. Finally, late one night when I was really strung out and raving, Dr. Salibi appeared in front of me with a needle. As he pushed its contents into my arm, I went out as if hit in the head with a hammer, only to wake up a couple of hours later, at dawn.

Finally, Dr. Salibi sat down and told me what happened in surgery. Operations like mine were done with the patient sitting up in a special frame holding the body and head straight. He didn't tell me, but I always thought that I was given a gas as an anesthetic. A medical student at the Emory Clinic in 1980 told me that operations like mine, a cervical laminectomy, were done using a spinal anesthetic. He also said that the procedure caused many cardiac arrests. Salibi just said that, after he had my spinal cord exposed and was about to try to determine my problem, my heart rate had suddenly slowed, reducing blood pressure to my brain. They had to remove me from the frame, and as Dr. Salibi held my head and shoulders, lower me gently to the operating table. Lying flat on my back, my blood pressure was restored. But hemmorghing in the open incision was causing pressure on my spinal cord. Salibi stopped the bleeding and stitched me up, without ever completing the original exploratory operation. I don't know when it was that he allowed me to wake up on the operating table, but it seems to me he was checking to see if I had brain damage from the cardiac arrest.

He explained that he was going to keep me in the hospital and carefully monitor my progress before allowing me to attempt too much activity, eat, or urinate without the catheter. He gave me many vitamins and antibiotics, and gradually reduced the morphine.

I knew I was better when I started to complain. My skin had become so sensitive that the sheets bothered me a lot. One morning, I got a dressing gown that felt stiff, course, and scratchy. When the nurse checked it, my chest and neck were covered with a rash. Salibi declared it a reaction to penicillin. It was my first brush with an allergy. Later I would learn to live with many of them.

Gradually, I was put on a liquid diet. After a week without solid food, I longed for a hamburger. My throat was cracked and raw from stomach acid that came up from my empty stomach. Enemas the doctor prescribed did nothing but confirm that I had no food left in my system. Finally, he let me eat an evening meal. It was good, but not enough to satisfy the hole in my stomach. That night my mother brought me a big bowl of popcorn. As therapy, I decided to use the thumb and forefinger of my left hand to pick each kernel up one at a time. It took a long time to eat the popcorn that way and I never did it again. That was the first night I slept.

When the catheter was removed, I thought that I would return to normal urination. Instead, after two days, I developed an overly distended bladder and couldn't urinate at all. The doctor reinserted the catheter. A few days later, he removed the catheter again and I started to urinate frequently into a urinal kept by the bed.

The mean head nurse I spoke of earlier had disappeared. I heard later that some nurses, nurse aides, and orderlies had refused to work with me for fear of hurting me. Instead, several young, energetic nurses treated me with great care. On December 21st, also my 21st Birthday, my family was scheduled to visit at 2 pm. I had eaten lunch and decided to urinate before they came so that I wouldn't have to interrupt the visit. After I finished, I propped the urinal on my hip and reached for the call button that I grasped with my left hand and pushed against my chin to activate. The button was pinned near my head. Reaching for it I tipped over the urinal, soaking the bed and me. When a nurse answered the call, she found another nurse and they changed the bed and me in five minutes. They pulled the new sheets tight across my chest with my arms out on top. Before the nurses left, they decided to crank up my bed so that I'd be sitting up. The sheet was so tight that I was left hanging high by my armpits, unable to wiggle out, until my mother loosened the sheet and let me slide down to a more comfortable position. We laughed. I was relieved.

Later that night, some young people visited the young man who awaited surgery in the next bed. They offered me a drink from some liquor they were carrying. That was the closest I got to a party for my 21st Birthday. That Christmas was the hardest. I spent it in the hospital. This was my hometown, but few of my high school friends home from college visited. I got many cards. Some came from people I didn't know. Some came from friends who seemed no longer to be friends. Most said, "Get well soon." I kept explaining that I wasn't sick, only paralyzed. It annoyed me to think that many of my so-called "friends" would expect me to recover fully from some strange illness, but wouldn't rally to my side as I struggled to lead a new life. The hardest lesson I learned was that over half the young people I had reached out to and considered friends would, because of a surgical accident that was a result of nothing I did or deserved, abandon me forever. Some friends I reclaimed much later, like Ruth Kohs from my high school class whom I had chauffeured on dates. She even went with Roger to our Junior Prom, double-dating with my date and me. She was a nurse in the same hospital, but never stopped by to see me. Maybe it was a fear of seeing me "crippled" or maybe it was an awkwardness that many people feel around people with disabilities. Whatever it was, I vowed to go forward and make new friends. But inwardly the hurt remains. I remember lying there alone one day when a group of carolers came by. They stopped outside and sang a couple of beautiful Christmas carols. The music filled me up with emotion. I was so glad that I was still alive. I started to cry uncontrollably. At that moment my sister's best friend stopped by. Taken back by my crying, she almost left. I said, "Wait. Come back. I'm okay." She did, and we talked, but I'm not sure I convinced her that I was crying because I was happy.

My therapy consisted of stretches and forced movements by a physical therapist, accompanied by muscle shock therapy. The movements were painless and daily gave me a better sense of my muscles, their strength, and range of motion. The shock therapy consisted of running a 90-volt direct current through a muscle by attaching two electrode pads. The pads were soaked in a saline solution. The shock caused the muscle to flex, supposedly recreating normal nerve function and preventing muscle atrophy. Muscle atrophy, or a withering of the muscle, occurred in both my hands and arms within a day or two after the accident. While the muscles I still had control of seemed to respond to the therapy and other exercise, the muscles that atrophied reached that state quickly, and never returned to normal or changed after that. I began to hate the shock therapy. For all its benefits, I flinched at the cold, wet feel of the pads on my skin, the sharp sting of the shocks on my skin, and the burns that left red marks like an octopus all over my arms.

When my legs were ready, I started to sit up and eventually walk. After five weeks, I was released from the hospital. My therapy continued at home or as an outpatient for four months until that summer.

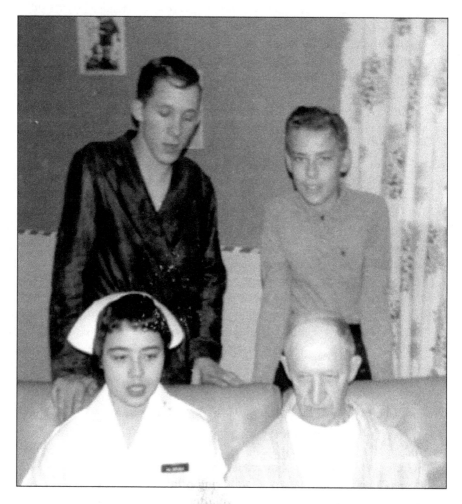

Ron at 20, awaiting surgery with a sinus infection, watching the John F. Kennedy assassination aftermath in the hospital lounge.

# 7

# Home Alone

It was strange being home. I sat and watched TV and thought. When the weather was good, I walked down to the river. No one came around and I went nowhere. I was depressed. I watched the ice go out on the river. It was as though I had dropped off the face of the Earth.

My grandmother gave me shock treatments twice a day with a portable battery-operated device. Three mornings a week she drove me into the clinic for exercise treatments. I enjoyed the sessions with the therapist. Miss Gray was my only contact with a world outside the lonely one at home. One Monday morning in March, we arrived home about 11 am from therapy to find my parents leaving for Menomonie where Roger was in college. They said that he had been diagnosed with polio and they had to get there soon because he was very sick. By that night he started having trouble breathing so the doctors decided to transport him 210 miles to the state hospital in Madison where he could get an iron lung. My parents returned home. Halfway home, the transmission on their 1960 Oldsmobile gave out. I don't know how they got home, but when they did, they asked to use my car to go the next day to see Roger in Madison. I felt helpless and worried that my parents would have two paralyzed sons to deal with. At least I felt good that my car, sitting since December, could be of help.

When Roger arrived at the state hospital, he was diagnosed with cellulitus instead of polio. He spent the next five weeks receiving massive doses of the antibiotic, stancillin, and returned to school after the infection was eliminated.

It seemed as though I was in another world. I wanted to get back to college, but I was sitting there all alone with no friends. Just the daily routine of therapy and watching TV. I started to take long walks in the afternoon, down to the river and beyond. I was depressed, but somehow those long periods alone helped me think through my recovery. I started riding my sister's bicycle. The girl's bike was easier for me because it was mid size and didn't have the cross bar to contend with.

The next farm beyond the river supported a large family. Amos Martin had arthritis and couldn't do farm work, so he put his wife and fourteen children to work after they "graduated" from the eighth grade of the Catholic school just up the road. The older children had had their fill of hard farm work and had left to find their own way. The current eldest son, Tom, was left to run the farm at 17. I started "dropping in" on the farm with all of its barnyard animals and children on my walks, and soon befriended Tom. He was like me, isolated from his age group by his circumstance. He was my first new friend after my life changed. We had been neighbors for four years, but, had I not slowed down my life during my recovery, I doubt if we would have ever met. As it was, Tom was my way out, and I was his. We started to take his father's '50 Ford two door out in the evenings, looking for girls and generally escaping from the dreary lives we both were captive to. He showed me that there were people who would accept a cripple as a friend. I hope I showed him that those of us with high educational expectations and too much schooling could understand the circumstances of those who have to drop out and helped give him the incentive to get more education. Later, he did.

This was the time when I began to test my limitations. Once in early spring, I was down by the river where the two branches came together at Ebbe Park. The south branch flowed over a small rocky outcropping into the north branch just below the bridge. A bank covered with mature White Pine overlooked the pool below the bridge at the outcropping. That day, I was standing on the bank admiring the scene, when I decided to slide down to the rocks below on the light covering of snow. I took the opportunity to walk across the river on the rocks, stepping from stone to stone. When I returned to the bank, I lifted my right leg and placed my foot to climb the three feet to the top of the bank. Instead, my foot slipped and I fell hard against the bank. Shoots of tingling pain ran up and down my body to my feet. Soon, I realized that I couldn't get up, that my leg wasn't strong enough to propel me up like it always had before. After some time, I managed to pull myself up by grabbing the roots of trees and combining it with thrusts of my feet. It was the first time I fell after being paralyzed, but not the last time, for falling, or for falling at that place.

My first break in boredom came in April. Jim Sternwize, the farmer who owned the land where our farmhouse sat, needed to drag the plowed fields in preparation for planting oats. Dragging broke up the heavy clay sod, hardened by snow and the plowing process. Jim had a new Oliver six cylinder tractor with an automatic transmission and power steering. He set the throttle at a medium speed and I drove it by shifting on the fly from neutral to drive, to low, or back to drive. I half stood, half sat to drive, and headed out across the field at about 15 miles per hour, my bent knees absorbing the shock as I bounced over the furrows. My neck brace absorbed the shocks to my neck as my head bobbed up and down. Steering was easy, but maintaining my balance wasn't, especially when I'd lurch over a bump and the front wheels would lift three feet off the ground. It was a wild ride, but exhilarating, as the powerful tractor ate up the field. I finished in a couple of days, didn't get stuck in the mud, and didn't tip it over. Dr. Salibi would have had a heart attack if he knew what I was doing. Later, I found out that tractors often tipped over, seriously injuring drivers. I was lucky that nothing happened. But the experience led me to believe that I could break free from the bounds of paralysis, if only under limited conditions.

By early summer, Dr. Salibi had an idea that I would benefit from a stay at the state hospital in Madison, the same hospital Roger stayed in recovering from cellulitus earlier. I was admitted as a welfare patient in a 14 patient ward with juvenile offenders, state prisoners, veterans, and other welfare patients. Aside from filming my hands in use, and occupational therapy that consisted of teaching me to make potholders by wrapping yarn around nails on boards, they did nothing for me. I found handicrafts extremely tedious for my paralyzed hands and told them that the best therapy for me was to get back to college and my books.

I spent my days in the hospital with two juveniles who were there for counseling and surgery. I kept them out of trouble and became somewhat of a big brother. We spent a lot of time bothering the nurses and roaming the halls. The only wards we didn't enter were the TB and maternity units. The high point of our time together was getting one of the nurses, a sexy lady we called Frenchy, to get us some hamburgers and fries from the lunch counter across the street from the hospital. One of the guys was being treated for teenage alcoholism. At fifteen, he had joined the crowds getting free beer at the Oktoberfest in his hometown, LaCrosse. After that, he couldn't stop drinking and getting into trouble. The other guy, at 15, was facing real problems with his masculinity. He had an operation to have his breasts reduced. We never communicated after our stay in the hospital together, so I don't know what happened to them.

Finally, the head neurosurgeon came by and angrily demanded to know what I was doing there. All I could tell him was that Dr Salibi had sent me and that I was waiting for some treatment he thought they could provide. After two months, I was finally sent home. Some good did come from my stay. In August, I was readmitted as an outpatient and stayed in a motel with my grandmother for two days while a special hand splint was made for me.

For two days, I watched in awe as an ex-Marine used stainless steel rods and thin plates to fashion a splint for my right hand. He had never done one before, but he had a left-handed version to use as a model. Using a lever arrangement, the splint converted an ability I still had to raise my wrist into a pincer action between my thumb and first two fingers. My fingers and thumb were held rigid by stainless steel rings. The splint was strapped to my arm with nylon Velcro straps. The finger rings were separate assembly and connected to the splint by a spring-loaded catch. I found that my fingers were flexible enough so that I could push them into the rings without removing the finger section from the splint, so I never used the catch. The splint enabled me to pick up objects with the fingers in my right hand, but because it was steel, wasn't of any use for heavy or hard objects. It didn't help with eating because tableware would slip on the metal surfaces of the splint. I could hold a pen, especially if it was encased in surgical tubing, but what good would writing do if I couldn't go to school?

By this time Roger was in summer school making up for classes he lost during his bout with cellulitus. I let him use my car. He put the '57 Ford to heavy use as a Fuller Brush man on a rural route. I wanted to drive and asked Dr. Salibi if he thought I could. His response was abrupt. He said that he would, "...take away..." my driver's license rather than let me drive. I talked it over with my physical therapist. Miss Gray thought it was a good idea, that driving would be good therapy for regaining use of my hands. I decided to prove the doctor wrong and retest my driving ability with proper authority.

The day of the driving test was hot, so I was nervous about taking the test with my grandmother's '56 Buick. It had power steering and brakes, and an automatic transmission that made it easy to drive, but that day I was afraid my sweaty hands would slip on the plastic and chrome steering wheel. Instead, the examiner spent the test telling me how he would convert a furnace into air conditioning to beat the heat. To my relief, he passed me without a second thought. My license was restricted to automatic transmission, power steering and power brakes, and I was on the road again. I couldn't drive the '57 Ford, so I put it up for sale.

I started driving to pick up my mother at work. When I got a date to go to the drive-in movie, my father insisted that the girl I was taking drive the car. I drove dad's '57 Buick station wagon to pick her up, but she was to drive it on the date. When we pulled out of our viewing spot after watching a drive-in movie, she cut the turn too short, and the speaker stand scraped the side of the car. Distrust of my ability to drive stayed with my father and haunted many others for as long as I drove. As if having paralyzed hands had impaired my judgment. She said that the big Buick didn't turn as easily as her family's small Falcon, but, as my truck-driving father knew, a good driver adjusts driving to accommodate each vehicle's turning radius. He should have trusted me rather than someone with good hands and unknown driving experience. I drove her and the Buick home and faced the music.

Tom and Tim home from school. Grandma Wenzel's 1956 Buick I took my driving test in August 1964. Received a restricted license.

Tom and Tim with Pete on the scooter I rode during the summer of 1964.

I drove Grandma, Tom and Tim to Lake of the Clouds in August 1965

# 8

# Back on Track

We learned that our county had a federally funded pilot rehabilitation program with three centers, the only one in the state. One office was in Marshfield, my hometown. I told the counselor that I wanted to return to college and he agreed, saying that they would support me financially. He worked out a budget for my room and board and tuition, and agreed to rent an electric typewriter. I was back in school, free from financial worry.

I had Roger put an ad in the newspaper in Menomonie asking for a room with assistance. The family of a former professor, Michael Jerry, responded. I had to eat in restaurants, but the room worked out well. Then came the hard part. At registration I was a stranger. After nine months, most of my friends had evaporated. It was surprising to have classmates call me by my brother's name. I walked through registration, but I didn't complete any of the forms. Roger did that for me. I was unsure how I was going to reenter my junior year with all that it entailed.

My advisor, Mr. Erickson, took one look at me and threw up his hands. A retired industry draftsman, Erickson viewed my paralyzed hands as a liability in the hands-on environment our school promoted. He sent me to the department head. Ironically, this same inadequate advisor was later made placement director. I often wonder if his inadequacy with me led to bad decisions about the employment of others from the school with disabilities.

The department head, Dr. Wesley S. Sommers, took me in. An intellectual trapped in a management role, he converted my one experience as one of his students in my sophomore year into an opportunity to be his understudy. Realistically, Dr. Sommers set up a light schedule that first semester. He also reduced the technical, hands-on, portion of my program in industrial technology by offering me independent study courses. My first independent study course was with him, and it gave me the time and individual attention I needed to feel confident about my ability to reenter the college mainstream.

The first day of class, I put my hand splint on and started writing. The electric typewriter really helped, and soon I was turning out papers with ease using only the tip of my middle finger on my right hand with the splint on to type and my left thumb to operate the shift, tab and other keys.

My social life had changed dramatically. Roger took on a night job dispatching and driving cab for two-cab company. Soon, he met a freshman who would later become his wife. Roger and Lin became inseparable, so I started to venture out on my own. I still could dance, and enjoyed the fall mixers, but it was clear to me that the girls were looking for husbands when they would dance and enjoy themselves, but not commit to a date with a cripple. It hurt at first, but I soon learned that there were a few ladies who would not be intimidated by my physical condition. One of my biggest problems was that I didn't behave like a person with a disability was supposed to; I was too forward and confident. It made some girls uneasy. I had to struggle with that a lot. People have a way of trying to define how I am supposed to behave. Somehow, God had defined my life and I was now "blessed" and supposed to behave like it. Many thought that my physical condition destined me to be a good follower, and I was to a point, but the leader in me wouldn't stand for it when I was forced to follow someone with less ability than me. I wanted to take charge, but I could no longer use my physical stature to do it. Appearance and body language are powerful diviners of authority.

Roger's circle of friends soon faded and I struck out on my own. I accepted the role of treasurer of a college religious club and soon had a girl friend. I quickly found out that she was suffering from severe psychological problems, so I let her down easy. I felt helpless to help her when I needed so much help myself. After that, I came across several people with psychological problems. Maybe it was my empathy that let them into my life. Maybe it was their perception of me as some kind of kindred spirit.

Maybe it is the nature of colleges to attract unstable people. Anyway, as a friend once put it, "Ron, you sure attract a lot of crazies."

Trying to fit in, I followed the college ritual of going to beer bars, even though I never drank beer. I practiced playing pool left handed, and found out that I could still play. It was difficult because I couldn't put any English on the cue ball or break balls with any force. One night, I was playing with a friend when we were challenged to a game of eight ball. I agreed. When we started to play, my friend asked if I'd bet a beer. When I told him, "Yes," he was quite concerned. When I sank the eight ball and won him two beers, he changed his mind. I never was timid about gambling with pool again.

Dealing with the coming winter was another matter. My manner of dressing had changed. I no longer wore t-shirts or long-sleeved shirts. I couldn't wear earmuffs or gloves. I had a rainproof trench coat with a zip-in lining and a couple of sweaters for warmth but that was all. I couldn't zip up my jackets or button the coat, so they were open unless someone was around to help me. I no longer attended football games or spent long periods out in the cold. I was summoned to the Dean of Student's office for a consultation one day. He wanted to know how I was getting along. I mentioned that I was doing okay, but was worried about the upcoming cold weather. He said his grandfather had died and left leather mittens that he would give to me if I could use them. I found that I could pull a mitt over my left hand with my fingers in a fist, and then snake my limp right fingers in the other mitt using my teeth. I could carry my leather notecase with my hand splint on top, pressed between my wrist and the notebook, while my left fingers in their permanent "flex" gripped the notebook. But I couldn't do that with the mittens on, so I used my pockets a lot. Still, those mittens were lifesavers and a most generous gift.

I often had to hurry from one warm spot to another in winter. In the morning I would walk six blocks from my room to Erv's Restaurant for breakfast, warm up, and then walk the remaining four blocks to campus. Erv was great. With his toothy grin and grease-stained apron, he catered to the regular morning crowd. He'd slice and dice French toast for me in a flourish. I only ate it a few times because it was so heavy it made me run to the restroom before I finished. One regular worth remembering was an old guy with part of his jaw gone from cancer who came in for coffee, to escape the Mrs. and swap fishing stories. I admired his zest for life.

One morning it was sixteen below zero and there was a wind off the frozen lake. When I arrived at the cafe, my left hand was numb as it often was on cold mornings. But this time it didn't warm up while I ate. After the walk to my physics class, it took over two hours for the feeling to return to those fingers. And they hurt, hurt like I remember from my frozen childhood. First the fingertips were red, and then they turned gray as the skin died. Finally, for several days they itched as the skin flaked off. After that case of frostbite, I made sure not to expose my skin too long to sub-freezing temperatures if I could help it.

Ice was another problem. My brain still hadn't learned that my left foot wouldn't always go where I thought. Walking on ice presented special problems, especially in street shoes. My first lesson came when I hit the porch at my brother's apartment after coming downstairs at a fast clip with some guys. The floor of the porch was covered with a thin coat of ice from frozen rain. Both of my feet flew straight out forward and the bumps on my spine bounced off the edge of each of the six steps before I landed flat on my back at the bottom. The force of the fall had thrown both of my shoes off and left me checking to see if my spine was injured further. Except for the familiar tingling sensations, it wasn't.

Then, one morning the next spring, I was on my way early to class when I came upon my brother's roommate crossing my path and said, "Hi." At 7:10 am, we were the only two there and he had gotten the first parking spot on Wilson Avenue across from Frykland Hall where I was headed. It was cold, but there was no snow. He was nearly a block away to my right when I reached the curb to cross the street to my classroom in Frykland. When I stepped off the curb I stepped on a small, unseen, patch of ice and suddenly both of my feet were high off the ground. I fell backward, landing only on the back of my head as it hit the street. There was a loud "crack!" that echoed off the brick buildings like a batter hitting a home run. I heard it and lay there, remaining totally conscious. My brother's roommate heard it too and came running back. Blood was pouring from the back of my head, so he got me a rag from his car, and with me holding that to the wound, rushed me to the hospital in his car.

The hospital was only a few blocks away. In the emergency room, I was told that they would shave my head and stitch up the split. I vainly protested, remembering how long it took for my half-shaved head to grow back. Dr. James, he was called "Jesse" for his wild manner, agreed to let it go without shaving. But, not before he warned me about infection and stuck his finger under the flap of skin, grabbed it, and shook my head back and forth to make the wound bleed again. I walked out with my hair and another eight stitches. I got to the lab one hour late, had a bad headache for the rest of the day, and couldn't sleep well on the stitches for a few days. I was lucky not to have a skull fracture, broken neck, or worse.

After that first semester, I gained confidence and took a full load of classes. Using independent studies, I was able to get technical credit for most of the "hands-on" courses. In others, I worked out arrangements with professors and lab partners to get the technical requirements out of the way. Often in a lab situation, I would learn the set up, specify the tools, materials, and procedures, monitor the work, and make any data recording, calculations, or reports required. Invariably my lab partners and I got "As" for our collaborative work, and whatever I could do, like use a screwdriver, wrench, or paintbrush, I did.

I became concerned about what a guy with my paralysis could do in the "real world" after college. Roger began interviewing with companies who wanted our school's graduates because they knew we could step in and do whatever work was required without further training. Stout graduates were particularly good at industrial engineering, project management, supervision, and the like. I wasn't sure that I could start out on the ground floor with a stopwatch and clipboard, so I set my sights on graduate school. An advisor suggested "human engineering", and it made sense. I'd always wanted to be an astronaut; maybe I could work with the astronauts. I wrote Christopher Craft, the director of NASA's manned space effort, asking if a handicapped student with a degree from a small state school had a chance being employed in the country's effort to go to the Moon. Craft responded with a letter that suggested that I continue my education.

I remembered what a Sunday school teacher, Earl Nelson, had once told us. Nelson, a successful businessman from our hometown, had gone to a local small college as a freshman. He was dissatisfied with the school and decided to do better. He listed, in order, the schools he wanted to go to, putting Harvard at the top of the list, and started writing to them. Harvard accepted him and provided financial aid. While at Harvard, he met his wife, obtained an MBA, and the confidence to return to his home community and establish several successful businesses. His lesson impressed me that nothing is gained if you don't try, and his experience fostered mine.

I made a list of schools that I felt had programs that would support a master's degree in this emerging field of human engineering. I researched catalogues and bulletins from other schools that were available in our library and graduate and placement offices, and wrote letters to department heads requesting information on financial aid and the availability of the type of program I had in mind. I wrote sixty letters in all, and received information back from most. Some sent applications and financial aid information and were encouraging. Some were not. Two of the best schools, the university of Wisconsin and Stanford, were most encouraging. The industrial technology degree was new and untested, and viewed with suspicion by engineering programs. Some schools, like MIT, responded that they had no knowledge of human engineering.

Another problem was that I would graduate in January. Most financial aid programs were locked into an academic year that meant that awards were only made in the spring for the following fall. I hoped to enter grad school immediately, but I wasn't sure how I'd pay for it.

By spring 1965, I was a senior, and needing more freedom, I decided to buy a car. During the Easter break, my father located a '57 DeSoto, that, although it had only 60,000 miles on it, was rusted out and a good buy at $100. I'm not sure if my rehabilitation counselor was pleased or not that I saved my rehab money to buy a car and get insurance. Anyway, I had proved to him that I could reenter school and do well. When I asked him about graduate school, it was a different matter. The program's mandate was to rehabilitate to the point of employment. For most, the mandate meant retraining, counseling, and guidance until the client had secured a job. I was an exception, one of the few being supported in going to college. To my counselor, graduation was the end of the program's responsibility. If I wanted to continue my studies, it would have to be on my own.

There was a big snowstorm as we drove back to school. Roger and Lin went ahead in his sports car because he was having trouble adjusting the carburetors and thought it might stall. I was to follow, confident that I could keep up and help out if he had trouble. My tires were worn, and it was hard for me to keep up. Finally, about forty miles out, in a deserted, wooded area, I slid off a curve in eight inches of new snow into a deep, muddy ditch. A local guy came by and took me to a nearby town. With the help of a milk truck he rounded up and a wrecker that finally came by, I got pulled out. My front wheels were buried to the hood ornament in mud and snow. The wrecker couldn't pull my car out alone. With the milk truck hooked to the front of the wrecker, my car came out with "whoosh" of air like a cow pulling its leg out of the mud. Roger had looked for me but had his own troubles with the road, his car, and traffic that night. He got Lin back to the dorm a half hour after the 10:30 pm curfew. I arrived a couple of hours late. Many times after that, whenever I had a flat or other car trouble by the road, there were always good people willing to help.

Roger was in the midst of interviews, making money on expenses by driving to most of them. He received six offers. He was scheduled to join a training program with Johns-Manville when he opted for Aluminum Specialty Company in Manitowoc to be close to his fiancée, Lin. Once he graduated and left school, our close relationship dissolved into one of occasional get-togethers, brought on by distance and our separate lives. The sudden change brought on by my paralysis had freed him to be his own man, but it had severed a close, day-to-day, relationship only identical twins know.

I attended summer school for the first time and enjoyed it. I parked the car most of the time and rode my sister's bicycle. The bike was medium-sized and fit conveniently in the DeSoto's cavernous trunk. I could carry my hand splint and books in the front basket, and I could park it anywhere in front of buildings without fear that it would be stolen. The last time I looked, the bike still had the 1965 Menomonie bike license plate hanging under the seat.

That summer, Stout was completing a new heating plant. Two men were completing the smokestack brick by brick, a few feet each day, until the stack towered two hundred feet over the school and surrounding houses. A friend, an older student, lived in a rooming house under the emerging stack. He had an old Harley "Hog" and I went riding with him some evenings. The bricklayers, an experienced tall structure worker and his young apprentice, had new Harleys, and we sometimes rode with them. I admired their skill and daring, doing work with ease that most men would avoid. Next year they would be gone, off to another smokestack in a distant place, unfettered from ordinary work and ordinary lives. I wanted to ride a motorcycle myself, but my hands wouldn't permit it, so I had to settle for riding my bike or with someone else. I knew that riding was dangerous, especially with my spine the way it was, but this guy and his Harley drove as steady as a family sedan. I was comfortable with that and rode with him without concern.

At the end of summer school, I went home. I was broke but had enough gas, or so I thought. Going through a little town halfway home, I felt the car lurch and die. I coasted into a gas station right to a pump. I hocked my electric alarm clock for two bucks worth of gas, enough to get me home.

Two weeks later, I traveled the same route to my brother's wedding. I gave the owner his two dollars, thanked him, and retrieved my clock from the top of a refrigerator. The wedding was a big sendoff for Roger. He avoided the draft and became a hard-working family man, while I remained the single student, hocking my clock for gas money. He enjoyed his new responsibility. I enjoyed my growing freedom.

I decided to take Tim and Tom fishing. We dug some worms, loaded our gear in the car, and drove down to the river. Once again, I was at the spot where the two branches came together at Ebbe Park where my legs had failed me the previous winter. In late August, the water was low and the bass were eager to bite in the pools. We just had to get to them. I rigged Tim up with a worm, and then picked him up and carried him, stepping rock to rock, out to an ideal spot where the side stream met the larger pool of the main stream. Once he was in place, I returned to set up Tom. I just got started when Tim yelled out that a fish had taken his worm. I put down Tom's rod and headed out to help Tim. Halfway to him, I extended my left foot to a rock that sloped away from me. I came up short of the top. My wet shoe slipped quickly down the rock's side to the water below as my momentum carried me forward. My shin caught the top of the rock, and I pivoted forward to smash my face in a hard cold blur of rocks and water on the other side. I struggled to my feet, somehow retrieved my glasses from the water, waded to Tim, picked him up, and waded back to the base of the bank. I told the guys to gather up our stuff and head for the car as I struggled up the bank that had thwarted me earlier. Tim said, dismayed, "Uuh. Ron, you're bleeding!"

I said, "I know, I know! Just get in the car and let's go."

When we got back to the house, I held a rag to my forehead and rushed upstairs to the bathroom; afraid my mother would see the damage and panic. As I washed the wound above my eye with water, I could see that it was deep but not serious, and I went downstairs to show Mom. She decided I needed stitches and had Grandma drive me to the emergency room at the hospital. When I was being stitched up, Dr. Salibi appeared and ran me through a battery of X-rays that showed no broken bones or other injuries. I had collected another 10 stitches and a realization that my left foot would often fail to reach where I thought it could.

An older student who had taken electronics class with me that summer was looking for a roommate. It was my next step toward independence. He was so happy to have me help with the rent that he gave me an offer I couldn't refuse. He gave up his bed in the one bedroom apartment to me and slept on the couch. He also did all the cooking and cleaning, including washing the dishes. It was one-sided, but I enjoyed the arrangement because it left me free from worry about day-to-day things. I especially enjoyed his Sunday chicken dinners after church. And I laughed when he quipped, "Whatsamatter, ya crippled or something?" I lost track of him after I left school, maybe because the only thing we had in common was this perfect business relationship. I did think of him though when a good friend of his from high school that he supported and campaigned for became Congressman David Obey from Wisconsin.

That fall semester was eventful, but I felt the loss of not graduating with my class. I became the president of our church group, and my cousin, Terry, started school as a freshman. With my required courses out of the way, I took elective courses like marriage and family and enjoyed them very much.

As a senior at the fall mixers on Friday nights, I met some freshman girls who were impressed with my dancing ability and my senior status. I walked them home to the girl's dorm and usually called for a date the next week. By early October, none of the three or four girls would accept a date, and I couldn't figure out why. Then, somehow, I learned that they were all from the same floor, and two were roommates. I guess they had compared dates as young ladies tend to do, and when they found out that they were dating the same man, declared me off limits! I was hurt, a victim of circumstance.

In late October, we had a weekend retreat with a Lutheran group at an old mansion owned by the Episcopal Church called the Bishop's House. I met a half German, half Swedish freshman whose intelligence, strong convictions, and good looks stole my heart. Karin was a heart breaker who romanticized "marrying late", or past thirty, like her parents had. One thing she said openly at that retreat stayed with me: "All my boyfriends are conscientious objectors."

This thought weighed heavy. At some point my draft classification had become "1Y" and my draft board forgot me. As a hunter, I had killed. As a leader and woodsman, I admired the heroic aspect of war. Above all, I hated the intimidation of the underdog and always stepped in, in defense. In spite of the anti-war rhetoric that insisted that the Vietnamese were in a civil war that we had no business meddling with, I saw ordinary people being overrun with tanks and forced to follow ideologies that robbed them of free choice. Many of the so-called "conscientious objectors" I knew were more concerned about maintaining their narrow, selfish way of life, unwilling to help a poor, defenseless country of people they didn't understand. Their objection would disappear if it were their parent's home that was being threatened. They were cowards when it came to putting their life on the line for others. As senseless as the war became, opting for cowardliness or dropping out when things got tough evidenced an immaturity I detested in my peers.

There were a few, true objectors who joined the Peace Corps or became missionaries. These people I admired and wanted to protect. The mistake this wonderful girl made was that because I was president of a church group and paralyzed, somehow I would fit her idea of a boyfriend. The reality of who I was didn't fit her expectation of me. Our relationship was stormy and short. Four years later, I heard that Karin was living with an artist who was an instructor at Stout. It caused a stir when he photographed, and then cast, her breasts in bronze.

After Christmas in 1965, I joined a group attending the Quadrennial Conference of the Methodist Church in Omaha. We rode by bus all night from Minneapolis and I got dehydrated and caught a bad cold. I shared a place on the floor in a motel room with seven ministers. By the middle of the week, my temperature had reached 102° and I stayed in bed until New Year's Eve when I finally got out to attend the address by Martin Luther King. His speech, boring at first by his monotone, preacher's delivery, moved me in the end to go out on the line for equality, even to my death. Unfortunately, he was the one targeted to die, and I never got the chance to stand by his side against injustice.

After school started in January, my cousin, Terry, and I had a skating date with two girls one evening. We had the Wilson Street rink to ourselves and were just getting started when I lost it going too fast. I remember flying through the air feet first, and then landing on my elbow to excruciating pain. Inspection showed that I had torn my bicep muscle in the middle, and there were red lines of blood under the skin to my shoulder, all of that turned red, and then blue, and then green and yellow, in a process of healing that took about four weeks. After the battery of x-rays I'd received from earlier falls, and the over concern of my neurosurgeon, I figured I couldn't tolerate a splint or cast, and decided to tough out the healing process with aspirin and rest. Rest meant avoiding any unnecessary strain on the limb. In time, it healed.

I had to take the Graduate Record Exam for entry into some graduate schools. The test was to be given at Eau Claire State College on Saturday. That Friday night, Terry had lined up six girls to ride with us out to a favorite nightspot seven miles from town. About 12:30 am we left because I had to get up at 6 am to take the test at 8 am. About a mile from the club we were all talking when I hit a patch of ice and we slid into deep snow in the ditch. Other cars came by and picked up the girls, and at least two other cars followed me into the ditch. By the time a wrecker came to pull us out, it was 3 am and 20° below zero. My radiator was so packed with snow the fan was jammed in it and had to be freed up.

The next morning, my radiator was now packed with ice and the car was front-heavy, but I made the thirty-mile drive to the test site on time. I was cold and tired, and it took me a long time to warm up in that big old, drafty room. In the afternoon, I took the engineering exam. I knew that I didn't do well on that. I'd often thought about how I would have done on that test had things been different, but I never took the GRE again. I made it a habit to do something once and accept the consequences. I was always interested in forging ahead rather than retracing my steps to try to do better on something I'd already done.

I spent most of the month of January taking aspirin to ward off the pain in my wrenched arm and shoulder. I was still in pain by the morning of my graduation late in the month. In spite of not graduating with my brother and class, it was rewarding to receive "high distinction" (magna cum laude) honors and have my parents, Terry, and two girlfriends present to send me off. One girl I don't remember. I'd met her the week before. The other, a friend from our church group, Pat Richardson, became a lifelong friend. I didn't know either was coming, and I was as surprised as Mom, who knew I was still mourning losing Karin.

I was accepted at the University of Wisconsin in Madison in the industrial engineering program. I left my apartment and Stout and headed straight there. True to form, I arrived out of gas late on a below zero Sunday to a drug store parking lot. I called a friend and he came with his Model A Ford and siphoned gas from the tank below his windshield into my car. To avoid conflict with my studies, I took up residence at the university YMCA where there was a lunch counter for breakfast and a dining hall for evening meals. My roommate was a straight-A sophomore studying French who was nocturnal. He stayed up all night most nights studying, and then slept during the day except when in class. It was dreary and confining staying there. I remember looking down in late winter to people on the dirty snow-covered streets while Simon and Garfunkle sang "I am a rock, a fortress steep and mighty..." in the background. I felt quite alone and often listened to the "sound of silence."

There were two of us in the graduate program from America: Bernie MacDonald, a guy from Columbus, Ohio, and me. The rest of the students were primarily from India and Pakistan. I had an assistantship working with the major professor, Dr. Gerald Nadler, on a project sponsored by the University Hospital to improve the quality of patient care. My assignment was to identify factors that would be used to develop a mathematical model of patient care. The model would be used to optimize the mix of services to patients and hopefully improve the quality of care.

I was entered in a joint Master's and PhD program. I took French to meet the language requirement. When I failed my first French reading test, it became obvious that all of my previous success in school would be tested. The Pakistani guys would use Urdu as their language and pass with ease. They also passed most mathematics and statistics courses with ease. But, some of them struggled with English and the American culture.

The results of my GRE exams were mixed. While I scored in the 98th percentile in the quantitative section, I only made the 45th percentile on the verbal side. My engineering score was only in the 23rd percentile. While some of my Indian friends had scored in only the 2nd or 4th percentile on their verbal scores, their quantitative and engineering scores were very high, often above 99%.

A friend explained it to me. The English did a good job of teaching their language to the people of the subcontinent before they abandoned colonial rule in 1947. After that, the teaching of English was forbidden in many schools as regional languages and dialects took over. English was still spoken and used widely, but formal training in the language was limited. As the people of this poorest part of the world viewed a way out of poverty, they saw it in the Western World's use of science and technology. Many sought training in mathematics, science, and engineering—unlike the U.S. where students of the fifties and sixties generally avoided these rigorous courses of study. Only the best were allowed to come to the United States to pursue graduate study. Many took engineering because it led directly to work with large U.S. corporations. So I was studying among the best of the best, the astronauts of their country—come to conquer America. And, they did.

But first they had to assimilate into American culture, and I helped out. I taught five or six of my fellow students how to drive and helped a couple buy cars. Appakutan promptly drove the Volkswagen Beetle I helped him buy to Milwaukee where he rolled it over trying to exit when road construction ended the freeway. Years later, I read about him being honored in Puerto Rico as the founder of a highway safety program credited with saving many lives during his tenure as a professor at the

University of Puerto Rico. I was a bit surprised because he told me that Douglas Aircraft was going to hire him as soon as he finished his doctorate.

I was in a doctoral track, but really only interested in a Master's Degree. In March, I received word that I'd received a Wheeler Engineering Fellowship at Stanford. The lure of California sunshine was too great. I told Dr. Nadler that I would enter Stanford in the fall. He was a leader in the field of industrial engineering, a former student of Lillian Moller Gilbreth, and one of the persons responsible for the emergence of Japanese prominence in productivity. I don't believe he ever forgave me for leaving. But I viewed going to California as another step in getting free from being paralyzed and more independent.

A fellow student from Bombay, Behram Randelia, who had a statistics class with me and stayed at the Y, too, started eating with me. We became friends. One day, he suggested that we get an apartment together. I hadn't thought about it, but agreed it would be a good idea. We found an apartment that an undergrad was subletting and moved in with him. I helped him buy a '58 DeSoto, and taught him to drive it.

A church group I joined was interested in canoeing. Although I could still paddle on the left side, I couldn't carry canoes anymore. We took one trip to the Little Wolf River where I helped ferry the canoes by car. We spent a lot of time running a five mile stretch, and I seem to remember running it too. Then, I helped plan a weekend trip down the Flambeau River. Behram took his car to help carry the canoes and ferry the canoers. He and I did the driving and didn't canoe the sixty-five mile journey. The water level was so low that the canoers had to walk the canoes a lot the first day. My fondest memory of that trip was driving through an area of virgin forest west of Phillips, Wisconsin. The trees towered high over the road, closing it in like a dark canopy overhead and blocking out the sun. There was something mysterious and special about driving among trees older than the country. These trees were destroyed in a downburst in July 1977. They are missed. One giant pine, like a huge pole with only a small topknot of foliage left after it struggled to grow to the sunshine high above, survived. It had little for the wind to get hold of. Now it stands as a lone reminder of the grandeur that forest was.

While scouting for a landing site on the Chippewa Flowage on the second day, Behram and I found a fully equipped cabin, complete with welcoming messages and a guest book. When the canoers arrived that night, we cooked on the wood stove, feasted, and ate all the food that I was accused of buying too much of. I could no longer be the first and boldest to run the rapids, but as a facilitator I could participate fully in the fun.

The engineering students wanted to have a party because there were few women in engineering and they wanted to meet some. One student was renting a small house on Lake Mendota and offered to have the party there. I remember much soliciting to get coeds to go to the party and we were somewhat successful in that. There was a canoe, so I asked a girl to paddle out on the lake with me. I put her in the back and we headed out. She had never been in a canoe before. She couldn't steer at all. I couldn't bring the canoe back by paddling only on the left front side. After circling around awhile, a guy came out in a boat and towed us in. That was one time I really wanted my old skill back. While I could have enjoyed romantically paddling a lovely lady on calm evening waters, I ended up having to be rescued, leaving a young lady in distress.

I was soon vindicated when a guy arrived with an underpowered speedboat with a pair of skis. Few of the engineers could water ski or even wanted to try. I expressed a desire to ski again, but thought that it would be impossible. The boat owner told me that he had started skiing with a rope and snow skis in the early fifties. He didn't know anyone who skied, so he just did what he saw others do in pictures. He said he'd like to try to get me up. I was afraid that I'd fail but eager to try at the same time.

I decided to hold the toe bar against my right wrist, just above my left hand clamped on my right wrist with all the strength my weakened fingers could muster. At first the driver took off too slowly, dragging me through the water. The pull seemed to try to yank my arms out of their sockets, and then pull my left hand from its grip on my wrist. After a few feet of trying to get up, I would have to let go when my hands flew apart from the pressure. Finally, I got him to take me up faster, and I made it up. There were no acrobatics or other tricks, I just hung on for dear life as the incessant pull of the rope tried to pull my left hand from its grip on my wrist and my arms out of their sockets. He made a loop, coming back to the dock, but didn't go in close. Instead, he headed back out, making another loop while I hung on, hoping I wouldn't lose the rope and fall, and hoping that he wouldn't go back around again. Finally, he headed in for the dock and I released the rope. I was exhilarated that I could still ski, and although my arms hurt, probably would have tried again if it hadn't been so late and getting dark.

# 9

# Venturing Out

At end of the summer, I headed for California. Not wanting to travel alone, I posted notices seeking riders. When I got no responses, I thought of my grandmothers, both of whom were living alone nearby. My mother told me that Grandma Hull had a heart condition, and that I shouldn't ask her. Grandma Wenzel was thrilled with the idea, and immediately made plans. School did not start until late September, so we had a couple of weeks to take a leisurely trip without the summer crowds.

I was enthralled with the majesty and history of the American West. We stayed in cheap motels and rooming houses, ate lunches my grandmother prepared by the roadside, and enjoyed the sights and the weather. We stopped at every park and national monument, often venturing off the main road to find them.

The first day out, in South Dakota, I ran out of gas. I hitched a ride while my grandma waited in the car. I got a can of gas and was going to hitch a ride back from the first gas station, about five miles away. I started to stick my thumb out when a guy at the station offered me a ride back to the car. I accepted. He tried to sell me a bug screen the whole way, saying that without it I couldn't drive any distance without overheating. When we got back to the station, I filled my car up and paid with a credit card, ignoring the guy's advice to get a bug screen. Back on the road, my grandma noticed an additional charge of $5.00 for the ride the guy had given me. I'd been ripped off. That incident taught me to watch what I was signing for with my credit card and never to expect a stranger to help out without pay. After that, I didn't stretch the gasoline and we didn't have any more bad experiences.

After seeing the sights in the Black Hills, we headed for Spearfish. Road signs said that there was "damaged road ahead". I expected to see potholes or other bad spots. Instead, for a few miles down a canyon, a flood had ripped out part of the road. Several times, the road was gone all the way to the centerline, and in some places, gravel had been put in where the road was completely washed out. I never saw anything like it before. Welcome to the Wild West.

My grandmother had a fear of mountain roads. In 1946, she had rolled over her car on an icy road in the Southern Nevada Mountains and she refused to drive in them again. After visiting Devil's Tower and the Little Big Horn battlefield, we approached the Big Horn Mountains. The road undulated over the high prairie, ending at a wall of mountains. I asked, "Are we going over that?" Thinking that maybe there was a way around.

She said, "No, I don't think so." in a voice as though she wanted to go back. She was right. Soon, we were climbing rapidly up the side of the mountain wall, snaking back and forth as we climbed. My DeSoto had a lot of power, but it labored at the altitude and climb. My grandmother closed her eyes. She missed much of the trip.

At Yellowstone, we saw about 500 bear. They were foraging everywhere, preparing for their winter hibernation. At Tower Falls, a parking area had been made from landslide debris from the earthquake a couple of years earlier. A bear was sitting ahead of the only open parking space, so we pulled up to it and got out. The bear was busy ransacking a snack bag. Later, a woman came up and held out a potato chip. The bear rolled back on its haunches and reached out with his tongue, flicking the chip out of the woman's fingers. So much for not feeding the bears.

There was a large bear near the entrance to a picnic area where we stopped to eat lunch. We ate thinking that the bear would burst in to spoil our lunch. Thankfully, it didn't. Instead, mountain jays and ground squirrels vied for every crumb, stealing our sandwiches and crackers, stocking up for the long winter to come. My biggest thrill came walking back into the woods to photograph a bull elk. He had a harem of about forty cows, so I was worried that he'd charge me. I got ready to run every time he lifted his head from eating. I got my photo and got out.

After seeing all the bears, we wanted to get a picture of one before we left the park. We stopped by one at the side of the road. He was in front of the car. I lured him around to the driver's side vent window with a cracker while Grandma got out the passenger side with the camera. The bear immediately ran around the car forcing grandma back inside. When he started back around to my side, she moved out again. Suddenly, he stood up and sprawled over the hood. Grandma took a quick shot. He came around to my side, slobbering all over the vent window. Grandma took another picture through the car of him doing that. Then, she jumped in and we took off before he would start to try to get in the car. In her excitement, my grandmother failed to advance the film, the resulting double exposure showed nothing of the bear.

We stopped at Craters of the Moon National Monument. Although the terrain was hilly and barren, it was not mountainous. I decided to climb a 500-foot cinder cone that lay before me. I ran up. By the time I reached the top, I was winded and the strength had gone out of my legs. At over 10,000 feet, it was the first time I'd felt the affects of altitude on my body.

Climbing to Merced Pass I killed three squirrels. They seemed bent on committing suicide as they ran under my wheels. I felt bad about that. At the top, remnants of the Oregon Trail were worn in the lava flows by many wagons. There was a lava tower with sighting holes to volcanoes, Rainier, Hood, St. Helens, a view that would have significance years later when the volcanic nature of this beautiful range would capture the world's attention when Mount St. Helens blew up.

The Willamette Valley was a cornucopia of fall harvest plenty. The roadside ditches were black with boysenberries and the fruit trees were laden with fruit of all kinds. At Florence, we took a wild ride on a dune buggy on the high dunes near the beach, and then drove down the avenue of giant redwoods to wine country.

Stanford provided a new set of challenges. My fellowship was generous, but I had to borrow from the school to complete the year. My advisor laid out a program of courses, but there was no close identification with the program that I'd had in my previous university experience. This hurt me without my knowing it.

California provided other distractions. At a center to identify roommates, a medical school student had located a small house to rent next to campus and needed a roommate. I was interested in joining him but opted instead to throw in with three other guys in a new two-bedroom apartment several miles from campus. There was a game room with a pool table and Olympic size pool. It was a mistake.

The four of us had nothing in common. We were from different backgrounds and had different programs of study, interests, and personalities. The pressure of going to Stanford was no help, and we split by the end of the semester. In the meantime, the pool was irresistible. I spent many afternoons out in the sun, trying to read, but too distracted and lulled to read with much comprehension.

I found myself in remedial undergraduate courses rather than rubbing elbows with great industrial engineering professors. My undergraduate coursework did not prepare me for the competitive, rigorous nature of the Stanford courses. The teachers, with a few exceptions, didn't teach. Rather, they paraded their latest theoretical research, challenging the brightest students to provide ideas and critique. Tests were usually not on the material presented in class. Tests were prepared and graded by graduate assistants. When the material was relevant and applied to real world situations it was easy to understand. But when it was theoretical and an exercise in mathematical gamesmanship, I was lost. Later, engineering programs changed when employers found that graduates had to be retrained to work in the day-to-day challenges of engineering, but I was a victim of the height of irrelevant theoretical engineerese. Where before, I'd always formed strong partnerships with professors and teams of students, now I only identified with other students, class by class, who were experiencing the same difficulties that I was.

Others were in full rebellion. Every morning on my way to class I walked past Ken Kesey's psychedelically painted Morris Minor and heard David Harris exhort the crowds in White Plaza. Others around me were tuning in to the new ethic of peace and love and dropping out of a society they considered bankrupt. I was tempted by the music and the need to be carefree, but I wouldn't and didn't have any part of the drugs that were part of the scene. I wanted to identify with something as real as a concern for the natural environment. But, I wanted no part of immature selfishness that permeated the rhetoric of most of the dropouts I met.

For the first time, I had no one to identify with but myself. All this contradictory information caused me to examine my own place in this milieu called California. I became atheist. I had taken a long time to come to this conclusion. I was tired of young people who spouted borrowed ideologies, as if they had no minds of their own, picking up a new one like a fad every time it suited them. Religion was no exception. Fundamentalists carried their dogma around like a shield, deflecting all ideas that didn't fit. Most people dragged out their religious shield when they were afraid, or when it was convenient. "Let us pray" was required if you were human and essential if you were afraid. People used it to justify all kinds of behavior. Belonging was important. If you didn't conform to the ideology, no matter how ridiculous, you didn't belong. I knew I would be ostracized for not conforming to the norm. But, as a person with an obvious deformity to my hands and physical ability, I was ostracized anyway.

So I was free. I perfected my eight ball game at the pool table in our game room. I took excursions to San Francisco, Santa Cruz, Stockton, and Monterey, and enjoyed the pool. I didn't worry too much about my grades, but they were bad. I worked on breath control, and soon I was able to swim from the shallow end to the deep, and back, a distance about a hundred yards, under water. All the other guys who tried it came up gasping. It was one area of physical prowess that I excelled in. I credited it to never smoking and my early physical training. I also dived a lot, perfecting a forward one and a half flip, a back flip, and various other dives. I wanted to do a splash less swan dive, but my right hand and left fist, once extended in front of me, would collapse when I hit the water, striking me in the face. I opted for keeping my arms tight to my sides, and entering the water head first, head down. It worked well, and I entered the water cleanly. I never worried about hitting the bottom with my head because I kept my eyes open and could always change direction once I was under the water.

The second semester, I shared an efficiency apartment with a Stanford sophomore I met at the apartment, Jim Cheek. Jim was a wrestler, but that's all we had in common. I found myself cooking and cleaning for him. He was a poor student from a rich family, and he undermined my attempts to do better in my schoolwork. When he became too much, I took a room with a middle-aged couple, Keith and Dory Clawson. I shared the room with their thirteen-year-old son, Daryl. Daryl had a paralyzed hand from a deep cut to his lower arm. Dory thought I'd be a good example for her son and took me in. Although it was nice to have someone cooking and cleaning for me again, the Clawsons were alcoholic and spent their evenings arguing about money until they had to go to bed early, drunk. I had no money for an apartment, but I wanted no more bad roommates, so I stuck it out.

I met a beautiful young woman by the pool one day. She nervously got up from her lounge and walked around me to flick the ash from her cigarette until I spoke and asked her to move the ashtray closer to her. Geisla Parker was too much of a distraction in her blue bikini. Geisla was from Germany and had met her husband in Paris. Tate worked at the airport and was an art student at Hayward, so he was almost never home. He had

59

told her to go down to the pool and meet someone because she was so homesick and lonely. I identified with that and eventually helped her learn to drive. She started working for a German travel agency and eventually they moved away into other apartments closer to the City. Tate was abusive and I was sympathetic to her concerns. She was only one of the married women I met during that period trapped in a bad marriage. Most of the single women I met were borderline crazy; some were stone cold crazy. I don't know what it was, but I had a hard time finding a normal woman that I wanted to spend time with who wasn't married.

There was this stewardess, blond, blue-eyed and a great personality that hung out by the pool. Her boyfriend was from El Paso with a big scar across his face and seemed to be a threat, so I avoided him. She extolled the virtues of marijuana. Much later, I learned that the reason she was so attractive was her dilated pupils, probably caused by excessive marijuana use.

Entering the apartment house one day, I saw a woman sitting on a couch in the living room through the openings in the slats of the patio fence next to the entrance. Soon after that a friendly, outgoing young woman appeared in the game room and started watching TV and playing pool with us. We found out that Beverly was newly arrived from Canada with a friend, Donna. They were nurses working at the Stanford Hospital and hadn't seen the Bay Area yet. My roommate suggested that we double date for the Chinese New Year. We drove Jim's red convertible up to San Francisco and took in everything the City had to offer, Grant Avenue, Pier 23, and the midnight underground movies.

My roommate, Jim Cheek, was much younger than the rest of us, so he quickly lost interest in Bev, but Donna intrigued me. It was winter and mostly rainy and cold. She was working revolving shifts in cardiac care, with some of the toughest cases in the country, including heart transplants. And, she was homesick. Donna was the one I had seen sitting on the couch, probably crying. Our date was her first time out.

I spent the next few months trying to cheer her up. But I had problems of my own. Ours was a dark relationship. Her grandmother had raised her. Her parents were divorced and she'd been separated from her brother. We were intimate, but she kept her distance, ever fearful of following her mother's path. There were other men, but she ended up with me. Not happily with me, just with me.

We took a long weekend trip to Tijuana. The first night out, we ate by the ocean in Malibu and found a motel at Venice. Donna insisted that I rent two rooms, so I did. The next morning, we stopped near Hamilton Beach, she took off her nylons, and we walked on the cold, windy beach. When we got to Tijuana, she wouldn't get out of the car, so I just drove around the streets. By nightfall, we were back in LA, and stayed at a cheap motel in Hollywood. It was cold that night, so she had to light my gas heater. We went to a premiere of the movie, "Grand Prix" at the Pacifica Theatre. Donna was upset because she couldn't find her nylons. No one in the theater saw, knew, or cared. I found them months later under the front seat where the wind on the beach had blown them.

I applied to all the major aerospace companies, but never got past the campus interview. Most of them were cutting back after major projects for the manned moon effort, so I didn't fault them for that. The students were outraged that the CIA was interviewing, but the idea of serving my country that way was intriguing, so I signed up. The grizzled old interviewer asked a tough question that I answered wrong. He asked me if I could decipher signals from a Soviet satellite. I was trying be positive and boldly said yes, knowing that I would work with a team of experts and use methods I would learn. I didn't elaborate and the look on his face told me that he thought I was just pretending to have the skills and lying to please him. Cracking codes was not a pastime of mine, but I had come up with unique solutions to difficult problems, usually with the help of tools and others. Code cracking is more a matter of persistence than brilliance. I certainly exhibited that. I believed like Arthur C. Clarke that unsolved problems can be solved if you have imagination and the nerve to act on them. At the end of the interview, he told me that he was very experienced, and that I was not CIA material. I didn't protest because I felt that I could never work with an organization that couldn't include me. Either he meant that my grades at Stanford were too low and my answer to the tough question was wrong, or that paraplegics didn't fit the image of a CIA agent. I think it may have been the later. I probably would have received the same treatment applying for the FBI or Marines. After all, in 1967 these organizations weren't hiring women for the same ill-conceived notions.

W. Grant Ireson, the department head, called me in told me that he had a job in quality control. It was at a local company I had never heard of. With no on site interviews in sight, I called them up and was asked to visit. The job was to assist the supervisor of inspectors with redesigning a computer system for in process quality control. The supervisor, Wilhelm Hemminghaus, was a German immigrant with a charm that enabled him to manage a team of inspectors who were mostly divorced women with children. Bill took me on a "cook's tour" of the plant. At the end of his tour, he asked me directly when I wanted to start work. I was hired.

Lenkurt, named for the first names of its founders, two electrical engineering graduates of Stanford, had started in a garage, grown through World War II as a provider of battlefield communication systems, and become a leader in products supporting voice, video, and data communications. In 1959, the owners sold the company to General Telephone and Electronics. Lenkurt retained its name in 1967 as a division of Sylvania. The company employed about 3000 people and produced about 100 products.

A week before graduation, I was called in to a review by the faculty. I had received 'pluses' in some of the graduate seminars so they were not counted in my grade point average. My GPA for all the courses, including those undergraduate remedial courses I hadn't done well in, was too low for graduation. They offered me a special project, worth six-quarter hours, that, if I did well on it, would be enough to obtain the degree. When I told the manager of quality assurance of my problem, he docked my pay, but agreed to allow me to use our workplace for my study.

I got an apartment near work, and my life changed. The project lasted six months, and shed light on the quality of visual inspection when the inspector is faced with high production rates. I found that the defect rate was somewhat affected by the quantity and complexity of the products presented for inspection and that inspectors were prone to miss visual defects on complex printed circuit boards. One of my conclusions, to use electronic visual templates and lasers to spot these defects, is widely practiced today.

With few exceptions, the men I worked with were World War II veterans who respected my education, youth, and new ideas. I was accepted and respected and felt like a part of the quality assurance team. Soon, another manager of quality assurance was named, and I became his assistant. I was also given responsibility for "system" quality assurance. I was responsible for "hot tests" of 12 to 64 line telephone communication systems we supplied to the military. Since I wasn't an electrical engineer, I had to rely heavily on my technicians to verify that our product was being produced to specifications. I worked on and developed the in-process quality monitoring system I was hired to do. It was installed after I left and used for at least five years after that. I joined the American Society for Quality Control and passed the first test administered to certify quality assurance engineers. I met and attended conferences with the "greats" in the field: Grant, Shewhart, and Demming. I attended the national conference with Bill in Los Angeles. On a tour, I observed how Rockwell used astronauts to inspect the components of the moon modules being built at Downy. The purpose was to educate workers about the real lives any defects they introduced would affect. I passed Walter Shirra in the hall and saw the Apollo 11 Command Module being outfitted in a large clean room with several sister ships. It was a heady time to be alive.

I saved my money to pay my loan at Stanford and get a better car. I was surprised to find a bill in the mail from Wisconsin welfare for $200 for my hand splint. I was glad to pay for the splint after all it had done for me. By this time, the catch holding the finger rings had to be held in place with a rubber band. The rubber band kept breaking and the catch kept coming apart. The prototype shop at the plant took the splint, ground off the catch, and welded the finger ring permanently to the splint.

The first two weeks in August, Lenkurt shut down for an annual plant-wide vacation. I asked Donna if she wanted me to drive her to Saskatchewan for a visit. A technician, Nick Hordin, told me he was going home to Rochester, New York, like he always did, and planned to take in Expo 67, Boston, New York City, and Washington, D.C. on the way. I asked how he could do that? Nick said that he drove straight through to the East Coast.

When I pressed her, Donna said that it wouldn't look right for us to travel together to Saskatoon. I was intrigued with Nick's plan, so I asked him if I could tag along. Glad for the company, he agreed. I left my car with Donna, and we left at dawn that Saturday morning.

Nick had a '62 Austin Healey Sprite that had made the trip several times. He was worried about its condition, especially a clutch that made noises and caused vibration at speed. I traveled light: two blankets, a small suitcase, and about $90 cash. Nick had less money, but we could rely on my credit card for gas.

The Sprite was a dirty white with a black vinyl top. The top was coming unglued from the bar that attached it to the windshield frame, but Nick had some tape he used to keep the road wind from pulling it apart.

Taking I-80 east, we made good time, 80 mph on the flat, that slowed to 50 mph as the little 4-cylinder engine struggled to take us up the long grades. Passing on grades was a problem, but the maneuverability and narrowness of the car kept us out of trouble in tight spots. I didn't drive and was sure I couldn't. I just rode along so low that I could have reached out and touched the ground. We arrived in Salt Lake City in time for their outdoor pageant of Mormon history. It seemed unreal to be there when we left the Bay only that morning.

But we didn't stop, just drove off into the night until we reached the Continental Divide about 2 am. We took a range road along the Divide to a high ridge, and I slept in the rocks and sagebrush. Nick slept in the car. I don't know how he could do it.

Before dawn, we were back on the road. We cleaned up at Little America. At Cheyenne, I missed a left turn, and, sixty miles down the road; I saw a sign welcoming us to Colorado. We turned around and returned. We tried to cut across on a range road to I-80, but the road soon went nowhere and became too rough. We stopped somewhere in cowboy country for lunch and heard "If You're Going to San Francisco" on the jukebox. We were high on the idea of traveling the country like hippies and claiming the "City by the Bay" as our home. Our euphoria was lost on the locals.

Nebraska goes on forever, especially if you've wasted a couple of hours on a side trip to Denver. Somewhere in the hot, buggy night we stopped to call Nick's girlfriend. I had no plans to call Donna. I was struggling to see after long hours of road exhaustion, heat, and grime. I stayed away from the phone booth Nick chose to call from; it was swarming with bugs of all description. I checked my glasses and found them covered with smashed bugs. No wonder I was having trouble seeing. They were coming through the crack between the top and the windshield frame and committing suicide on my glasses. By 3 or 4 am, I sprawled out on a picnic table in a park in Omaha for a brief sleep, only to be on the road again before dawn.

We drove cross-country through Iowa and Minnesota to Central Wisconsin and my parents' home, arriving in early afternoon. Dad gave Nick a new roll of duct tape to replace the tape he had, and they taped the top down well. We didn't stay, heading instead after supper to Manitowoc and Roger's place. After Nick took time to admire Roger's '58 Sprite, still in good condition, we left the next morning. We drove north to Sault St. Marie and Canada. I don't remember where or if we slept that night, but we drove from wilderness mining operations to quaint farming countryside. We stopped briefly in Ottawa and enjoyed the impressive gray stone and green copper roof government buildings, and at Hull, where we ate in a unique restaurant-grocery store.

We headed for Montreal. A young man on the street told us of $2 a night cots at a fraternity house basement. It was the kind of lodging we were looking for. After an elegant breakfast at a Hungarian restaurant, we took the subway to the venues of Expo '67. In two days, with carefully planned waits in the longest lines, we saw it all without wasting time in all the expensive restaurants—we ate waiting in line. I remember the thousands of TVs in the Russian pavilion. More TVs than in all of Russia? And eating my first microwaved apple there. And the chrome-plated satellites, too heavy to send to space, but great to look at. The USA's geodesic dome lacked TV sets. All of them must have been in our homes. The dome also leaked, leaving puddles in the gray carpet. We ventured seven stories high on rickety wood decking in France's flagship. We marveled at the art and artistry at the Czechoslovakian pavilion. I put my camera down for a moment to dance to a steel drum band and it was stolen. My mother gave me that camera, one she had used since 1940. Along with a family heirloom, I lost all the pictures I'd taken of that memorable trip.

We drove south to the U.S. Nick took me to Rochester, where his mother lived, and Behram drove up from Painted Post to pick me up. Gone was the idea of touring Boston, New York City, and Washington, D.C. We settled for a few days with friends and family. Behram had accepted a job with Ingersoll-Rand and was living with his wife, recently arrived from Bombay, in company housing just down the street from the famous Indian painted post marker for the town. I spent four days relaxing and touring the area with them.

Then Nick returned. The Sprite had no top. It had blown off in four pieces eighty miles back. He threw it in a rest area trash barrel. We set out on a rainy day without a top. In Western Pennsylvania we were slowed going through a small town, and it rained a little bit. On the road, a light rain was blown off over the windshield, but here, crawling through town, it dripped off trees down the back of my neck. It didn't rain again. But the wind on the back of my neck was brutal, beating me all day long. We stopped in the evening at a roadside diner. The waitress served us coffee immediately, but I was too road weary to order. Thinking that she had done something wrong, she asked Nick. He just told her that I was too tired to think about ordering. After that coffee and a trip to the restroom to wash the road grime from my face, I was able to order something to eat.

We drove out across Ohio in the night. We arrived at my cousin's house near Toledo about 11 pm. Kaye was there, but Keith wasn't. Kaye welcomed us in and gave us some chili. Keith had been out trying to hunt a bobcat that had been spotted in the area. He got back about 1 am to find two dirty "hippies" in his kitchen. He kept staring at us in disbelief, but finally mellowed out. We left again into the night. I had to wrap my wool army blanket around my neck to keep the cold night wind off.

Sometime near dawn and Indianapolis, we rested by the road for about an hour, but we were back on the road before first light. Nick was excited about stopping by the new arch in St. Louis, but when we got there about 11 am, things changed. In construction traffic on the Eads Bridge across the Mississippi, we heard a metal "pinging" sound of metal hitting the concrete, and Nick couldn't shift. The clutch wouldn't disengage. I got out and pushed the car. At a slow speed, Nick could get the car in first gear. I hopped in, and we jerked our way across the bridge into the city in search of a garage. Luckily, we found one. A pin used to operate the hydraulic clutch had fallen out. The mechanic fashioned one from a bolt. We then spent an hour locating a parts store where Nick bought a kit to rebuild the clutch mechanism.

As we left the outskirts of St. Louis and Nick shifted into fourth gear, we heard that "pinging" sound again, but we were going 70 mph and there was no stopping us now. Two hundred miles up the road, we were about to pull off the road and get gas when water suddenly hit the windshield. We were at a garage before the car overheated. No mechanic was on duty, but we had no money anyway, so we paid $5 to use the hoist. A heater-coupling gasket had given out. Nick cut off the bottom of an oil can and used it to seal off the leak in the coupling. It also shut water off to the heater, but it was August. The bolt pin had fallen out of its dashpot, and Nick repositioned it.

We drove west, reaching Kansas City in the evening. Nick visited his sister. She lived with her kids in a basement in a run-down part of town. I felt sorry for her having to live like that, but I didn't say anything, and Nick didn't talk about her. By noon the next day, we were in Denver. Wind and sun were taking their toll on my face. I needed to get in the shade a while. We stopped at a McDonald's, but it had an outside serving window and no shade. We went to a mid-town park, but there were no large trees for shade. We rested and talked to a kid who said he was from Mexico, didn't like Denver, and wanted to go to California with us. We left without him.

I wanted to take I-70 west out of Denver. Nick didn't. Somehow I persuaded him, and started driving. Gradually, throughout the trip, I had taken the wheel. First, I'd push in the clutch, and he'd shift, and then, I started shifting myself. I was game to do this drive, but a bit unsure. About five miles out, I was passing a truck when I needed to downshift to third gear. I missed the shift and had to pull to the side as we lost momentum and a truck and several cars struggled by. Nick took over and the pin dropped out again. We stopped at a garage at the top of the grade. Nick asked for the hoist again and rebuilt the clutch mechanism with the kit he bought in St. Louis. I wanted to continue on, but Nick took the wheel and we drove back to Denver.

After that, things became a blur. This time, Little America was a real oasis where I could get out of the sun and wind. Nick's face got darker. Mine got redder, and my skin started coming off. We got to Salt Lake City in the morning, and detoured to Sears where we bought two yards of canvas. Using the car's support rods, and Dad's duct tape, we made a makeshift top. Going across the Salt Flats, I half stood out the side window, constantly rubbing the tape that held the canvas to the windshield frame. The tape held, and soon I was enjoying the shade.

By nightfall, I was driving again and Nick was sleeping. I-80 was still being built, so there were stretches of four-lane highway, followed by segments of the old, two-lane road. I remember driving along, maybe 70 mph, when I woke up to see barricades rushing toward me in my headlights. I instinctually jerked the wheel to the right just in time to catch the transition road to the old highway. The violent motion of the car jostled Nick awake. He said, "Wha... what, you want me to drive?"

I said, "No, I'm awake now." I drove on for a couple more hours before I got drowsy again.

I got more than that. I got so tired of riding that I had to stop somewhere for the night. Instead, Nick stopped at a bar to check it out. Too tired to go in and too tired to sleep, I just sat in the car. Finally, he came out and we drove on to Dayton, former capitol city of Nevada. There was not a blade of grass to lie down on. At a ballpark, we found some rolls of chicken-wire fence. I balanced on the top of one and went to sleep. As usual, Nick slept sitting up in the driver's seat. I had nightmares that that roll of wire sheltered a nest of rattlesnakes. As far as I remember, I slept well.

We toured Virginia City, grabbed a cheap breakfast in Reno, headed up through Lake Tahoe, and coasted downhill to the Central Valley and home. My DeSoto was unmoved, with a dead battery. Donna had left the lights on the first day, and never drove it after that. Nick jump-started me, and I drove back to my apartment and everyday life. A week later, I passed Nick in the hall. He said, "Let's do it again!" We never did.

I bought a used 1966 Olds Toronado. It had power windows, seats, and other equipment that made it easy to drive. It was expensive to drive and maintain, but it was safe and fast, so fast that it satisfied my need for speed.

While I drove carefully and avoided unsafe situations, I liked to drive it to its limit, and the open highway provided a place to open it up.

Donna's dream was to travel around the world and visit romantic places. She got her wish. By the fall of 1968, she had saved up enough for a planned trip around the world. She was tired of the stress of working the Stanford Hospital and wanted to change direction. Where she was going didn't seem to include me. By September, she returned to Saskatchewan. In October she came back, on a Northwest Orient liner from Vancouver bound for Los Angeles and Hong Kong. Bev and I met her and her traveling companion at the dock in the City. We spent a few hours together and she was gone.

She called me from L.A. after Halloween, telling how friends from the boat were bored and decided to go "trick or treating" in Hollywood. They went to Lucille Ball's house and she surprised them by coming to the door and giving them water pistols. Later, she wrote about trying to give coins to all the kids of Hong Kong, being ripped off by cabbies there and about nursing in a quarantine station in Sydney. About not going to India because of what she learned in Bangkok about nursing conditions there. *And, about throwing my letter in Sydney Harbor.* I wrote to addresses Bev gave me, but she never wrote me again. Through Bev, I found out Donna traveled and worked a year. Then, after she returned to Saskatoon, married a former boyfriend, a schoolteacher, and settled in British Columbia.

One morning a year after I started to work at Lenkurt, I got an early morning call from Herb Anderson, the Dean of Industry and Technology at my alma mater. He said that they had heard that I had received my master's degree and that they had two positions open. I told him that I was flattered with the offer, but that I was happy where I was.

With Donna gone for good, I wasn't doing that well with the ladies. After two moves I settled into an efficiency in a small apartment house with a nice pool. The occupants were young business people. Opportunities to meet young women there were limited to those invited by other men. One young woman did appear at the pool often, but she was playing tennis and golf with a vengeance, a response to a bout with polio when she was a teenager. She was too busy denying her nerve damage to be dragged down by a disabled person like me. A short while later she announced her engagement to a guy I didn't even know she knew. I hope she left that fear of being physically inferior behind and hasn't suffered from post-polio syndrome in the years since.

Like so many others, I joined singles clubs to meet ladies. It was a disaster. I did not fit the idea of what most young women came to California for. I took out a devout Catholic girl living in San Francisco. She acted like a nun. I dated a Ph.D. candidate in history from Stanford. This spinster was crazy, either from scholastic pressure, poorly chosen previous friends, or too much intelligence. I suspect it was the later. She was interesting because she had a cherry black and white 56 Ford Crown Victoria her truck driver father bought from a "Little old lady from Pasadena." Her biggest thrill from our two dates was taking the Gold Bond gasoline stamps I'd collected in my glove compartment. Later, she sent me a note thanking me for the salad bowl set she got with them.

One night at a singles club dance, I met a beautiful, blond Swedish girl who was an identical twin like me. All the men seemed to be after Ingabrit, the dominant one, but I was instantly attracted to Gunabrit-Margaret. She worked at Stanford and I thought we had something in common. She took me to a local park in her red convertible for a quiet picnic. She liked books and read a lot, but seemed to be troubled with something. Then on a date to San Francisco she got falling-down drunk and called me "Eric". I wanted to help her through her problems, but after I took a week's vacation, her phone number changed and I couldn't contact her again.

I was a "square" in a suit, and although I identified with the laid back California lifestyle, I belonged to no group that would let me in. Perhaps it was me. I was no "joiner".

The high point of my singles madness was to take a ski trip to Tahoe. On the weekend before Thanksgiving, about sixty strangers boarded a bus with rented skis, bound for the gambling and winter sports Mecca. On the four hour ride up, pairing off began, and by the time we were assigned to a motel, almost everyone had plans to ski or stay with someone. With no knowledge of skiing gamesmanship, I picked up all the information I could, but was alone. I was assigned a roommate at the motel. He was an expert skier, newly arrived from the Netherlands, who felt the same way I did, and we decided to forget the girls and ski together.

We were skiing Heavenly Valley, a ski area that begins at 6,500 feet in the city of Lake Tahoe and rises to 10,500 feet. It rained all weekend at the base, but snowed above 8,000 feet. The lower slopes were icy, and most of them were advanced or expert, so we elected to ski from the top, an intermediate slope.

From previous experience, I rented short skis without poles. I couldn't hang on to poles and short skis enabled me to snowplow, turn, and side step easier. Slaloming and traversing was difficult because without poles for balance, it was difficult to make sharp turns, and my skis had poor edges. Inadvertently, I had chosen an approach that worked for me, but stumbled upon what later became the way beginners were taught to ski—short skis.

Getting to the top involved taking a lift in the rain to above the snow line, and then skiing about a half mile down a road to the next lift. The second lift took us to a point where it was snowing the heaviest, keeping the slopes covered with fresh, but heavy, snow. The third lift took us over an advanced slope past lightning-scarred trees to the tree line, and then to the top of the mountain, where the snow was lighter and more powdery.

Leaving the lift was difficult. I would jump off and try to regain my balance as I snowplowed to a stop. A couple of times, I ended up in a heap. And, a couple of times, I hit other skiers ahead of me. Most of the time my friend was along side of me, and he steadied me when he could.

We skied the intermediate slope, running along the ridge of the mountain in a long arc, eventually ending at the base of the last lift. The top of the run was windy and icy, and I would accelerate straight down the middle to a point where all I could do was hold my skis as parallel as possible and lean forward into the wind like a downhill racer. I could only steer in gradual turns and came close to hitting other skiers at 30 mph as they crossed my path traversing. Then, I would hit an area of deep new snow that would slow me down and offer more control. Still, in this stretch, there were steep, almost vertical, drops that often caused me to take violent spills as I lost control. My friend would always ski up, reclaim my boots to my skis, and then help me up. This happened countless times as I tried to learn the soft snow and steep areas. The last third of the run was more gradual, so I could relax and ski on to the lift.

My rented boots didn't fit right, and the front edge of the left boot top dug in with every maneuver. But I was having fun so I endured the pain and kept going. It wore a hole that took weeks to heal and left a scar. Having no ski clothes except an old ski jacket, I wore a sweater, the jacket, a bit waterproof, and corduroy jeans. It was so warm skiing hard that I sometimes had to unzip the coat for my runs. Falling in the snow kempt my jeans pretty wet, but it didn't bother me. What did bother me was the wet snow that kept coming down and would quickly cover my glasses. I had to put them in my pocket and ski blind. Every time I fell hard on that right hip, I worried that my glasses were smashed, but they survived both days and many falls.

The last lift was scary, maybe because I couldn't hang on with my paralyzed hands. We would sit on a plank with no seat belt or bar, our legs and skis dangling below, a below that at times seemed to be a hundred feet or more above tall tree tops. All you had to do to fall out was lean forward. This lift ascended above an advanced slope that started at the top. All day, I watched as toboggans and the ski patrol ferried injured skiers down this slope. I was having fun, but I didn't want to join them. My friend kept urging me to try that run, but I resisted, knowing that I was already over my head on the run we were on, and I didn't want a catastrophe to end our fun. Luckily, he didn't insist or abandon me, otherwise I would have had to stop skiing.

Back at work the next week, I heard that a fellow engineer had broken his leg on the ice on a bunny slope at the base of the mountain. I was glad that I'd gone right to the top.

Lenkurt offered stable employment. I survived a 10% cut in 1968, watching good friends with more experience and family get laid off in the name of cost cutting. There were no clear plans for me to advance, so I got restless. In late summer, I interviewed with Serendipity Associates, a consulting firm vying for design work on the Super Sonic Transport being planned by Boeing. They interviewed me for the layout of the console. I got the impression that they wanted a retired commercial pilot rather than a green human factors engineer for this job. I spent a week visiting Roger and Lin in Philadelphia and attending my cousin Terry's wedding in New York City, and when I returned there was no word from Serendipity. Either they didn't get the contract or they had disqualified me. I lost touch with Gunabrit at the same time.

In the spring of 1969, I called my Alma Mater back, and asked if they still had any openings. Dean Anderson said that one of the previous year's openings had been vacated, and I could take it if I wanted. My career in higher education had begun. I didn't know that I'd never be able to work in private industry again. I resigned Lenkurt effective August 1. My fellow engineers gave me a big sendoff party. They were all proud of me. At the company picnic, my boss, George Griffith, a rising star in the company who would later become a Vice president of GTE, told me that he was disappointed that I wanted to leave and that he and the company had plans for me.

Jack Swanson and I had become good friends. I started going to his house for dinner, served by Lois. Afterward, we'd play chess. I lost, but I learned. I think he had me in mind for his daughter, Lou Ann. He was very protective of her, and she was trying to break free. She made some great ceramic pieces, and I bought some. I wend to her graduation ceremony at Redwood City High. It was right out of the movies. While the valedictorian was spouting the credo of "we are going to save the world," the students were passing pot in the front row. Before the ceremony was over, a near riot broke out in the back and police carted off a student. A pall fell over Lou Ann's graduation party when she learned that a good friend who had epilepsy had drowned that day after a seizure in the pool. No one was there to save him.

Jack invited me over for breakfast in his backyard to watch Neil Armstrong step onto the moon. He regretted my leaving. Since we were all off for the plant shutdown, I decided to take him and his eldest son, Kevin, six at the time, to visit his father in Seattle. Since I was moving, Jack carefully packed my things in the trunk, leaving room for us in my car. While packing, I broke a ceramic bowl Lou Ann had made for me. I thought it was a loss, but Jack took it home with us and glued it back together the night before we left.

I let Jack drive. Soon, we were going 90 up I-5 to Shasta. His Rambler station wagon never went over 65in the Bay area. We spent a night with my Grandmother's cousins, Neil and Viola in Junction City, and then on to Seattle. Jack's father was wealthy from his inventions. In his eighties, he puttered in a garage shop, and had a factory to produce what he came up with, mostly improvements for sewing machines. At the time, he was making crystal chandeliers with brass and fine crystal from China. I got to glimpse hydroplane races as we crossed Lake Washington on the bridge. Soon, I headed for a tour of the Olympic Peninsula and Port Angeles.

I got to see some rain forest, but didn't have time to hike to a glacier. I ended up that night in Port Angeles, looking for an old buddy of Jack's. I found him in a bar, avoiding his wife. After a night of drinking with him, I ended up sleeping in the car, waiting for the first ferry to Victoria.

Victoria was beautiful. There were flowers everywhere, deer played with people in the parks, and even the crows were unafraid. It was such a peaceful place. I joined Lou Brewer and his family for a hockey game that night. The next morning, I was on the ferry to Vancouver. I didn't stop, just drove out of town. Not before I picked up two young ladies, hitch hiking.

Girls, was more like it. I think that they were thirteen and fourteen. Lou had encouraged me to go to Prince George and a new highway, just opened, to Jasper, so I offered to take the girls that way. They declined. They were from Thunder Bay. They had been working for the summer in Vancouver and needed to get back home. We drove through some spectacular scenery on Canada One, following the line of the Canadian National Railway for half a day, and then I headed north, dropping the girls off.

The heart of British Columbia was not as I'd expected. There were no mountains, lakes, or other features to the landscape, just a sea of trees. Prince George had the look of a boomtown. It was all new and bustling—like California. I could have driven to Dawson Creek and the Alcan Highway, but elected instead to take the new road to Jasper. The new road, a hundred and eighty miles of gravel, was also not as I expected. It was wide and straight. I was soon going eighty over gently rolling hills. The bridges weren't finished, but side roads forded the many dry streams. I hardly slowed down for them. I saw two hulking guys with huge packs hitching, and I stopped. Somehow, their pack fit in the back seat and they, alongside me on my Toronado's bench seat. Each of them toped six feet and 200 pounds.

They barely spoke English, but I got their story. They were refugees from the revolt in Prague in 1968. They got out with thousands during the turmoil. They had been working for a man, clearing brush, and showed me their bloody, blistered hands to prove it. They told me they were going to the CN station. I didn't know what it was, but would take them to Jasper. We passed Mount Robson, Canada's highest peak. It seemed puny compared to Colorado, at 12,500 feet.

When we arrived at Jasper, I pulled into a Chevron gas station, and offered to buy my riders dinner at a restaurant, next door. The Czechs declined, took their packs, and walked off. After dinner, I headed on down the road, eventually passing the Canadian National Railway Station. It finally dawned on me that the "CN" station they were speaking of was this one. I felt embarrassed that I couldn't figure out what they wanted and hadn't brought them there.

I drove on, south of Jasper, until, when it was getting dark; I pulled into a rest stop near some elk, grazing by the road. It was good to see wildlife again. My whole trip up the heart of BC, and my run on the new road hadn't produced even a bird. Wilderness can be barren, too. I parked the car and walked up the road in the growing darkness toward the elk.

It was only about fifty yards, but, by the time I reached the small group of, about 15, it was pitch dark. I could hear them moving, eating, and breathing right in front of me, but I couldn't see them. I could feel the heat from their massive bodies. It was eerie and a bit scary. I decided to head back to the car.

I slept well until dawn. When it was light, I cranked her up, flipped on the wipers to throw off the dew, and headed out on the highway. Something was drastically wrong. As the car dragged to the right shoulder, I could feel my right rear tire was flat. I was in the middle of nowhere at 5:30 in the morning. Not a good situation. A car pulled up in my rear view mirror. It was a black and white '57 Pontiac. The big guy who emerged from it wore glasses and a black beard. He cheerfully asked if he could be of any help. I told him that my spare was in the trunk under all my belongings and that I had room inside the car for them if he'd unpack. He just smiled and set to work. In a short time, he had my stuff in the car and my spare on, ready to go. He refused any money and went on his way—probably to work.

It was a hundred miles or so to the Athabasca Glacier. There was a service station by the hotel, so I dropped the car there to get the tire fixed while I ate breakfast in the hotel. I took the first tour of the day in a snowmobile, a tracked vehicle seating eight, powered by a Plymouth V8 engine. It was a half-mile up the valley before the receding glacier began, but then it was an exhilarating ride over ridges of ice, crevasses, and puddles of water. I don't remember much of the tour, just the snowmobile and the way it rode.

When I got back to the hotel, I had the car repacked and was on my way, making Lake Louise by evening. You could see grizzly bears at the Lake Louise dump, but I passed that up, and hundreds of hippie hitch hikers in the tourist trap, and headed back east on Canada 1

The next morning, I made a mistake. I picked up an old man who appeared to be a bum, carrying a paper bag. To my surprise, it was an old Indian, on his way to a local "doings", translated, rodeo. His lunch was in the paper bag. He told me that he'd been in a movie once. The director wanted them to paddle canoes. No one had been in a canoe before. They had to learn how to paddle and be convincing Indians. I dropped him off at the doings, where a crowd was gathering and declined his offer to join them.

Just outside Medicine Hat, I picked up a young couple, Ellie and Phil. Phillip Coolidge was a sophomore at Harvard. Ellie, his girlfriend, was a Vassar sophomore from Ohio. They were traveling for the summer, and decided to hitch home from Vancouver rather than take the bus. Ellie was so engaging, I was glad they had.

That night, we stopped at a park camp in Manitoba. We cooked by a campfire. Before long, Ellie had invited some guy, a stranger, to join us. Neither Phil nor I wanted him around. By the following evening, we pulled into my parents' house. They weren't home, so I drove us to the city park, where I thought my dad would be playing softball. We looked for my parents' car, but couldn't find it, so we went back to the house. Ellie made coffee. When Mom and Dad arrived, Ellie served them. Mom was shocked.

The next morning, I took them to visit Judy in Mazomanie, and then dropped them at Shot Tower State park. Phil wrote later that mosquitoes drove them out of their stay there.

Graduate engineering student, at Stanford with 2nd '57 DeSoto, Dec '66.

QC engineer Ron's used '66 Olds Toronado at Foothill College, Feb'68

Ron at the Golden Gate, Sept '66 Master's degree at Stanford, June '68

With Roger for my cousin, Terry and Tina Wenzel in NYC 6/8/68

# 10

# A New Career

I returned to Stout as an instructor of industrial management. I was welcomed heartily by my faculty colleagues, many of whom had recently been my professors. Housing was not that easy. Students had taken most of the rental housing in town. Finally, a senior student was offering to share his new mobile home, so I took him up on it. This turned out to be a mistake. Dewey, the student, was suffering severe emotional problems. I was more concerned about my work, so I concentrated on that and tried to ignore him.

It was scary to teach at first. But I had several sections of a basic industrial organization class with a standard workbook and tests, so it was easy. I also got to teach statistical quality control. Statistical QC was harder to develop meaningful examples and good tests for, but more interesting.

A Chinese student worked in the department as a student assistant. Margaret Ma was from Taipei, working on her master's degree in vocational rehabilitation. For some reason, she thought I was the department head. When the Thanksgiving holiday came, I learned that she was alone, so I offered to have her join me with my family over the weekend. My mother was, once again, surprised, but gracious as always. Margaret enjoyed her brief visit to Americana and my family enjoyed her quiet presence.

Margaret was having trouble with a roommate, also Chinese. Housing had assigned her to live with the girl, but they had nothing in common, so she moved in with seven American girls in a large apartment. During the

Christmas break, I was invited to join Roger and Lin and Lin's parents to celebrate New Year's Eve in nearby Eau Claire. I had been visiting my parents but returned to my room early so that I could attend the party. I expected Margaret to be visiting with one of her roommates for the holidays, but called her on a hunch. I was surprised to find her alone in the apartment. I asked her to the party. The older men at the party treated Margaret badly, leering and hanging around like she was some whore they met in Hong Kong. One guy had the gall to tell her that he'd killed a lot of people who looked like her in the war. What he didn't know was that her father had studied medicine at Johns Hopkins and was rich enough to buy the hotel where the party was. Still, she was undisturbed and enjoyed comparing our New Year celebration with the Chinese one. Margaret told me that her father was "pushing" her to go to school. But all she wanted was to be happily married like her sister. She graduated that January and went on to Ohio State for her doctorate. I heard later that she married another Chinese student there. So Margaret got her wish. At the time, I was interested in sharing cultures and helping her out, nothing romantic. Since then, I'd learned that Chinese women are indirect about their feelings, and I think now that her treating me like the department chairman and discussion of her desire to marry were evidence that she was in love with me. Unfortunately, I was too culturally blind to see it.

By January, Dewey, who had been a straight-A student and was one of the most talented artists I'd ever seen, was failing all of his classes and becoming more unstable with each passing day. I worked hard on my course preparation, stayed in my room, and avoided him. Then, one Saturday, without warning, Dewey came into my tiny room with his six foot, 200+ pound frame, shaking in anger, and threatened to throw me and my things out in the snow. I reported the incident to the police and moved out the next Monday. All I could find was a miserable little one-room efficiency, but it was a relief to get out of that situation.

I was socializing with young faculty members from my all male department, but they were all married. Our time together was confined to Friday night "seminars", playing pool and talking to students at a local bar. Then, one early spring evening I attended a discussion group and that changed. She was a young instructor of home management from Kentucky. Although Eva Gail Mayer had only started teaching when I did, her warm Southern charm, wit, and intelligence had won over most of the established faculty in short order. We were labeled a "couple" almost immediately, and started doing things together. What I didn't know was her secret. I would come to know it the hard way.

Gail was smart, probably one of the most intelligent people I'd met, and good looking. Several of the single male faculty had noticed her and she enjoyed putting them off by using me. Still, she kept me at a distance, and I couldn't tell why. She was very studious and committed to learning, so I thought maybe she just wanted to establish her career before settling down. I had conquered my paralysis and kept that brash, risk-taking attitude that I'd had all my life, taking chances, making mistakes, and suffering the consequences. While she enjoyed risky things, she would think things through until she was sure that she wouldn't make a mistake. In all our disagreements, she was never wrong. I took Gail to visit my family. My grandmother, being cared for by my mother and dying of cancer at the time, told my mother what she thought after we left. "She's too bossy," Grandma said.

When summer came, I had no classes, so I signed up for a federally funded program to provide education courses for early retirees from industry, designed to help them enter teaching. One other young guy and I joined all these old guys from many occupations who took the program. It was an intensive course but I breezed through it. The old guys, called "retreads", were an inspiration to me.

Gail was tied up too. She joined Helen Van Zante, a senior faculty member who was working on a revision of a textbook on home equipment. Working nonstop on the book, she didn't seem to have any time for me. Finally, I talked them both into taking a day off and we drove to Lake Superior. They enjoyed the break, but I didn't. The one thing that stands out about that day was that the whole shallow bay on west end of Superior was brown with pollution. Years later, I learned that the pollution we'd seen was asbestos mine tailings dumped for decades by Reserve Mining on the north side of the bay.

Finally, the book was finished and Gail entered a concentrated two-week course taught by a visiting architect from the Netherlands, Heinrich Van Lewan. Many parties accompanied the course in the evenings. I was invited to join Gail on these occasions. I got to know several faculty members better.

Then, Gail went home to Kentucky for the month of August. I had cast about for options to that hole I was living in. I considered a custom-built mobile home at one time. I'd happened on tract of land I liked, eight wooded acres on a hill top five miles southwest of town, and bought it on a land contract. I thought about putting a mobile home on it until I could afford a dream home of my own design.

A faculty member was leaving to pursue his doctorate and offered his one-year-old country A-frame on a lease-purchase option. It was a good offer so I abandoned my plans for my hilltop and rented the A-frame.

One of the retreads, J. R. Calloway Brown, a chemistry Ph.D. who had retired from Westinghouse, joined the faculty and took a room with me. Later, in his room, I saw his doctoral diploma from the University of Virginia. It was dated 1928. He was divorced, had had cataracts removed, and was suffering from hypertension that was aggravated by a secretive addiction to cigarettes. He kept in contact with his children by telephone, but I never saw them. I learned that he had been a part of the Manhattan Project. What part, I don't know. But I respected his privacy and never asked him. We led separate lives and didn't socialize or eat together.

The last week of the summer vacation I flew to Kentucky to visit Gail and her family. The trip consisted of short hops from Wausau to Milwaukee, and then from Milwaukee to Chicago and on to Paducah. On the Milwaukee leg to Chicago I sat behind an important-looking gentleman who sat with his recently hired French chef and his male secretary who took notes across the aisle. I eavesdropped while they discussed wines, condos in the Caribbean Islands, and what they would do at the Waldorf Astoria once they got to New York. I didn't introduce myself. It was only later that I learned that the man was Herbert Kohl, head of Kohl's supermarkets that later became Kohl's Department stores and Herb became the Senator from Wisconsin.

At O'Hare, my flight to Paducah left from Midway. There was a limousine service, but I'd never been on a helicopter, so I paid extra to take the short flight—thought that I'd see the skyline. It was interesting how the pilot hovered at the runway, making sure all was clear before crossing it on our way. Unfortunately, we flew low over miles of suburban sprawl without sighting any of the downtown skyscrapers. At Midway, we waited outside in the midday heat. I bought a vending machine brat whose pale skin and bland taste told me that I'd left Wisconsin.

There was a farm pond on the Mayer land, so I tried fishing. I could cast a bobber and worm out into the pond, and hook the small bass that quickly struck the bait, but I couldn't reel them in. Gail did that for me. She also had to bait the hook and release the fish, so it was no fun for her. Then a large water snake swam directly for the dock, raising its head six inches out of the water as it approached. She fled in horror. I couldn't persuade her to fish after that. We went to Mammoth Cave. I was okay, working my way through the passages. Until we reached an area called "fat man's agony". I was quite skinny, but I had a great deal of trouble squeezing in that narrow passage.

One afternoon, I watched Gail's family spray their beef cattle for pinkeye. As she wrestled a steer, Gail showed a rough side I hadn't seen before. Her other side showed too. We played Bridge with her parents. I was an experienced card player, but new at Bridge. I played in my usual fast reckless fashion, learning as I played. She was cautious, playing only when she was sure she had made the best play. She never made a mistake. I was upset with her because she slowed the play and she was upset with me because I was losing games with reckless play. Her parents were great, and seemed unconcerned about the tension between us. But I was concerned at her need to win, to be right.

Gail's father took us water skiing on the Ohio and Tennessee Rivers. Her younger brother was an expert skier and was towed for miles while he performed tricks. One trick was disturbing. He would put the tow bar behind his head and ski with his hands free. I was worried every time he did that we'd hit a submerged log or a boat wake and he'd fall and break his neck or strangle in the rope. I knew what an accident could do. He was young and immortal, oblivious to the danger he put himself in.

We stopped in a backwater and I tried skiing. Gail's mom was a nurse and wrapped my right wrist with elastic bandage to protect it from the bar and rope. I tried several techniques for hanging on, but the only one that worked was to grab my wrist with my left hand to hold the bar in place against my left wrist and let my wrists, elbows, and biceps do the work. After several tries, each one threatening to pull my arms out of my shoulder sockets, I made it up. I made two circles of that calm backwater, skirting debris that had left the main current. It was a pleasant little triumph of my trip to see Gail. It was the last time I'd ski, water or otherwise.

Trees mark the 8 acre home site I bought near Irvington, Wis. Dec 1970

A-frame that I rented to buy in August 1970

Fishing for bass in the Mayer pond. Gail had to reel in those I hooked.

# 11

# Turning Point

"You're limping." My mother said. I tried not to pay attention, but inherently I knew that I wasn't walking well, dragging my left foot a bit. I told everyone that my left foot would just get "stiff" after sitting for a long time. I was experiencing a loss in the fingers of my right hand that I used to help with zippers. Four years and California had intervened since I had last seen my doctor, so I made an appointment.

Dr. Salibi was alarmed. He said that my condition had deteriorated greatly and that he would have to operate again. If he didn't operate immediately, he said that I'd be "bedridden" in ten years. He blamed me for leaving his care and going to California. I told him that I had become independent and accomplished a lot in spite of my paralysis. I wasn't going to let him just operate and cause further damage. It was apparent to me but not to him that he was affected by my condition, a condition he had left me in and then tried to forget, his worst nightmare. He acted as though I were a child rather than a college instructor. It was disturbing. When I told him that I had a girlfriend and planned to marry, he said that my condition was congenital and that I should never marry. Finally, he told me that I was taking too much of his valuable time and assigned me to a colleague. I was hurt by the way he had treated me, ignoring my success for his singular pursuit of my undiagnosed problem. But, I understood his behavior as a shield he couldn't let down. He couldn't tolerate his own mistake and failure. It was easier to blame my problem on a "congenital" condition than accept the result of his mistake.

Dr. Ottensmeier, the neurosurgeon I was assigned to, was more tolerant. We arranged for a myelogram during the break between semesters in January to determine if anything surgical could be done to stop the deterioration. When I returned to school I arranged to enter the hospital at the close of the semester.

That fall went quickly. A former classmate, Steve Christianson, had come back to pursue his master's degree and stopped to talk to me. When I mentioned that I had an unfinished third bedroom in the loft of the A-frame, he jumped at the chance to rent it. Steve took over cleaning the house and we shared meals. Calloway still elected to eat alone or out. The arrangement worked out well for all of us.

That fall I had a student with cerebral palsy in production management. He pushed his wheelchair backward with one foot, could talk with some difficulty, and needed a student assistant to take notes and tests. He was somewhat of a celebrity, a partygoer, with a cadre of young ladies around to assist. My course required working on problems and it was not easy for him to take the tests. His assistant in my class was a brilliant young man who easily handled the work. It soon became obvious that the CP student wasn't able to solve the problems without help from the assistant. In the end, he earned a "C". His assistant earned an "A". I felt bad that I couldn't have helped him more. It was obvious that other instructors had given him good grades for his spunk and personality, feeling as inadequate as I had when it came to measuring his true ability.

While Gail liked my new house and the attention I gave her, she seemed less willing as time went on to spend time with me. She seemed preoccupied with the upcoming myelogram. A new movie, "Love Story," was playing in Minneapolis. One night, I took her to dinner and then on to the Twin Cities to see it. She sat, without commenting, through the last scene, and then we got up and walked out. I tried to ask her how she liked the movie, but she just got a strange look on her face, and said nothing. Then, before we left the theater, she started crying. She said something about, "That was us!" and sobbed uncontrollably the entire sixty-mile drive home. While it was a good, sad story, I couldn't identify with the heroine who dies of cancer just when she's falling in love. Gail could and did.

I spent the holiday season concentrating on finishing my courses and preparing myself for the hospital. One Sunday, I saw a lone adult Bald Eagle sitting in a tree across the road. The eagle sat there a long time. Then, just as I prepared to go out and get a closer look, it flew down behind a small hill across the road. After a while, I walked down to where I could see over the small hill. There was a dead calf in the valley, with many eagle tracks around it. I assumed the farmer who owned the land had dumped the calf out there after it died. I called the local game warden. He said that there were several adult eagles that wintered along the Red Cedar River. I was grateful to hear that eagles were still around after being decimated by insecticides. After I frightened the eagle, I didn't see it return. The warden said that they were very wary and would not return if disturbed from a feeding site.

I parked my car at the hospital, confident that I would drive away after two days of tests. The myelogram went well. Through a spinal tap in my lower back, a heavy, radioactive fluid was introduced into my spinal column to provide contrast for x-rays. This time, I was more comfortable, lying on my stomach with my head up. A monitor to my left recorded the flow of radioactive fluid as I was tilted downward, headfirst. After the procedure, I was required to lie flat on my back for 24 hours. I was only allowed to get up briefly to urinate. This urination was frequent and necessary, because it helped remove the fluid being absorbed by my system. It was necessary to lie down because minute bubbles of air, formed in the spinal fluid when the fluid is injected, can cause severe headaches. Myelogram headaches result when these bubbles float up the spinal column to the base of the brain when active or staying upright, and apply pressure to the brain.

I felt good after my rest and prepared a list of questions for Ottensmeier about what could be wrong and what procedures could be used to counter the problems. He answered them in writing, and then explained. Was it a tumor? All indications were that it wasn't. Was it a fluid sac requiring drainage? This was possible, but there was no imminent pressure, requiring immediate attention. The only way to know for sure would be to expose the cord with surgery. Was it enlarged disks, pressing against the cord? This condition, originally expected, did not appear to be the case. There was a lot of scar tissue left from the 1963 surgery but it wasn't causing any problem.

Surgery was recommended, but I could see no purpose to it except to cause further damage and paralysis. Ottensmeier and Salibi could provide no definite diagnosis. The idea of exploratory surgery did not make any sense. I elected to get a second opinion from the Mayo Clinic. I requested that an appointment be made at Mayo, and that my records be copied and sent to Mayo.

When I returned to work, I had already missed the first day of classes for the spring semester. My department head had assumed the worst and reassigned my classes to other instructors. My colleagues were glad to see me that Friday as they struggled with overloads of classes they hadn't intended to teach. I rested over the weekend, and was grateful that it was the beginning of the semester and my evening class work was light. The next week went quickly. I tried to eat and go to bed early because I was still tired from the strain of my hospital stay and demands of my lectures in the new classes. I wanted to avoid myelogram headaches and I could feel them coming on.

By Friday, I went home early with the feeling of a pending headache pursuing me. That evening the "Professor of Love," Leo Buscaglia, had come from Los Angeles and was speaking at the Field House. Although I protested and wanted to stay lying down, I agreed to go with Gail if she drove. We had to sit high in the bleachers because of the crowd. By the time he began speaking, I was in agony. A headache would come on like a railroad spike being driven between my eyes. Accompanying the headache was nausea that threatened instant rejection of the contents of my stomach. These feelings would subside as soon as I lowered my head. But there was no room to lie down on the bleachers. I excused myself and went below the bleachers where I found a rolled-up mat. I lay back on the mat and listened to the speech. Gail was upset that I had left her alone, but I assured her that it was the only thing I could do. Normally, we would go over to her apartment for a while. But this night I had her drive me straight home while I kept my head low. It was snowing.

The next day, I stayed in bed. Gail agreed to come over that evening to prepare my supper and keep me company. Calloway was gone and Steve had gone to his parents' for the weekend, so we were alone. Calloway came home about 7 pm and told us that the road was drifting shut. He had seen a car in the ditch before the main road and had had to fight his way through drifts to get home. He went to bed exhausted.

We had had about an inch of snow the night before. Late in the day a front had come through bringing strong winds and plummeting temperatures. Gail decided to go home and left about 8 pm. Twenty minutes later I heard something at the door and she was back. She was crying hysterically and her face showed the effects of the wind. She said that she had gotten stuck in a hard drift and passed a "hole" where another car had been stuck. She had walked back into the wind a quarter mile. I told her to stay the night, but in her state of mind all she wanted to do was get back to her apartment.

So, I decided to help her as best I could in my condition. I gave her a pair of my pants, my ski jacket, boots and mittens, my snow shovel, and a pail of sand. Then, I put her in my car and drove her as far as I could toward where her car was stuck. It was about twenty below and the wind was howling about 40 mph, causing blinding blowing snow. I crossed a couple of small, hard drifts to a place where the wind had blown the road clean to the old snow. I told her to dig her way through the drifts. If she got cold, she should get in her car and warm up, not try to walk back against the wind.

By that time, I was feeling a headache coming. I wanted to stay and help her, but I couldn't leave the car and I might get drifted in myself. So, she walked off into the snow, and I started to back the car up. As I turned around to reach over the seat and look back, a headache hit me. Nausea rose in my stomach and my whole body started to convulse. I dropped to the seat and it faded away. After five minutes, I would rise up carefully, back the car a few feet until the convulsions came again, and then stop, and lie down again. After a half hour or so, I drove up into my garage. I went back to bed and waited until 11 pm to call. When I called she had just arrived at her apartment after digging through several drifts to get to the main road. I was relieved because even though I was suffering from the headaches and she seemed unreasonable going out into the wind that night, everything had worked out for both of us. I spent the next day in bed. By Monday, the myelogram headaches were gone, but I'd developed a healthy respect for them.

Suddenly, Gail had no time for me. She told me that she loved me, but was seeing another man, another faculty member. By Valentine's Day she was seeing him every night. She said that she could work in the evenings with him, but not with me. But, she was willing to share, to spend one evening a week with me. I didn't consider one night a week sharing and felt closed out. I sought counseling from fellow faculty member, Dr. Rimel, a friend of Gail's and my former marriage and family instructor. Through Rimel, I found out that Gail had been seen with the other man before she met me, and was even named in his divorce. I stopped seeing Gail after that, but a hurt burned inside me when I thought that she had used me to divert attention from this other love.

One day in early February, I got up early and drove to the Mayo Clinic. The flights of geese near the city seemed strange in mid winter. Later I found out that Rochester had played a part in bringing Canadian Geese back from near extinction and fed a large resident flock that kept them nearby all winter.

The main waiting room was huge, dark, empty, and cold, a stone mausoleum to the massive image that was Mayo. They accepted the myelogram, but claimed that my x-rays, done on new equipment, were inferior. The battery of x-rays they took were taken on huge, ancient machines, and to my mind, inferior. A team of five or so doctors examined me. In the end, they agreed with me that the risk of another exploratory surgery outweighed the deterioration I was experiencing. I decided to take another look at it in a few years. Maybe the future would provide a precise diagnosis. Maybe it would provide a cure.

About a month later, Calloway disappeared. At first I wasn't worried, because he was always going somewhere; but when his friend, a business professor, called, I got concerned. Finally, I got a call from Calloway. He had checked himself into the hospital at the Mayo Clinic, the psychiatric ward. I gathered up a few things for him, that's when I saw his diploma, and drove back to Rochester. The ward was like a prison. I remember them searching his shaving kit and taking his razor. He returned after a few days. When the semester ended, Calloway loaded his car and disappeared forever, not leaving so much as a forwarding address.

I went through another depressed period. I started a book on my travels, but it didn't get very far. I just finished the semester. I wasn't sure where I was headed. The student with cerebral palsy came by my office. He was close to finishing his degree and had been interviewing for jobs. He was worried that his carefree college days would soon be over and he wouldn't be able to get a job. I felt helpless to help him when I knew of no work or anyone that was hiring. I never saw him again. I don't know what happened to him. There was a story of a young woman who had broken her neck and was quadriplegic in Life Magazine. It was one of those heroic stories of overcoming great odds. She was pictured with a special friend who was helping her overcome the trauma of being paralyzed. In my depression, I wrote to her. She wrote back that there were special people out there and one of them was a woman who would love me for who I was, not for my physical strength. I hoped what she said was true. It hadn't been my experience.

I did have a special friend during that period. Steve provided encouragement even though he wasn't female and lacked the spirit of adventure that I had. He was a good friend and I didn't give him the credit he deserved. The people who owned the house wrote that they would like to return in the fall and begged me to let them return to their house. I had no written contract and no special attachment to the house, so I agreed to leave it. Steve and I decided to stay together and lined up a log cabin on Tainter Lake to rent in the fall.

A crisis came at the end of the spring semester. I had given my final exams in four sections of production management on Tuesday and Wednesday. On Wednesday night, when I sat down to grade the tests that contained problems and required detailed grading, I discovered my hand splint had broken where the finger rings had been welded to the frame at Lenkurt two years earlier. The heat from the weld had weakened the ring and bending and fatigue had caused the tough stainless steel to fail. If I couldn't write, I couldn't grade the tests or finish my grades, due the following Monday.

Thursday morning after class, I went to the metals shop and a colleague of mine there helped me find some flat stock in stainless that was slightly thicker than my rings. He cut me a strip the width of the ring, long enough for two rings. Later that day, I located Michael Jerry, my former design professor, whose house I'd roomed in when I returned to school. I asked him to help, knowing that he had to get his grades in, too. Friday morning, I dropped my splint off with him and began to worry. I kept waiting for his call but it didn't come. I resisted calling him until I couldn't wait any more to find out if he could do it. Finally, at eleven o'clock on Saturday morning, I called. He said that he'd stayed up most of the night to finish it. He wouldn't take any money. I picked up my splint and spent the rest of the weekend grading. I got my grades in on time Monday morning and the exams back to the students. My splint was stronger than before.

I heard of a fellowship at West Virginia University from one of the Retreads and applied. That summer, 1971, I taught classes and planned a trip back to California after summer school. A high point was a weeklong visit by Tim and Tom who were eleven. They were very impressed by campus life, my house, and the computers at the office. While I worked, I put them in our little computer room. I showed Tom how to calculate the area of rings on our Wang 2000. He took to it with ease. Later, he chose computer science when he went to college.

A group from campus was going to "The Three Musketeers" at the Guthrie Theater in Minneapolis. I was afraid Gail and her friend would be on the bus. Fortunately, they weren't and I didn't have to do any explaining to my brothers.

In July, I got a call. It was Paul DeVore from West Virginia University. I hadn't won a University Fellowship, but he was offering an assistantship in a federally funded program. The handwriting was on the wall. If I was going to stay in higher education, I would need a doctorate. My colleagues all had plans. I decided to act. I went to Dean Anderson and asked for a leave of absence. He said that he couldn't grant me one, but would accept my resignation. I was struck by how little he seemed to value my determination to improve myself.

I put a notice up seeking riders to California. I told Steve to find another roommate and take the cabin in the fall. Two young student ladies needed a ride to California. I packed my bags and I was gone. I dropped off the students in Northern California. Coming into the Bay Area with the sun setting made me feel as if I was returning home.

After a week's stay in California, I returned to Wisconsin through Western Canada. In Medicine Hat I picked up a couple hitchhiking. Phil was a senior at Harvard and Ellie was a senior at Radcliff. Ellie was clearly in charge. I enjoyed their company. We arrived at my parents' in the evening and found no one home. We were tired, but drove to the park where my dad played softball, didn't find anyone, and returned to the house. Ellie made coffee. My parents arrived and Ellie served my mother some coffee. Mom didn't know what to expect. I was always driving off thousands of miles, and then arriving unexpectedly with strays I'd picked up. We stayed the night. The next day, I dropped Phil and Ellie off at Shot7 Tower State Park in Southern Wisconsin and visited my sister Judy. It was good to be a student and free again.

Crater Lake on a trip to California, June 1971

# 12

# Return to School

As I drove into Wheeling on I-80, the radio was playing John Denver's rendition of "Country Roads". It seemed appropriate, John's words were describing a place I hadn't seen or been, West Virginia. "Dark and dusty, painted on the sky, misty taste the Moon beam, teardrops in my eye."

After a brief stay in a rooming house, I located an efficiency apartment in student housing for the medical school. It was institutional and austere, but within walking distance of the office of the project and the "new" campus. From these confines, I planned to concentrate on study and finish my doctorate as soon as possible.

The federal project I was hired as a graduate assistant to work on was to transform the way teachers taught students about the technical world. The brainchild of Dr. Paul W. DeVore, the program focused on positive change. Most schools taught "shop", based on manual training in the crafts of drafting, woodworking, auto mechanics, and metal working, as an introduction to the world of work. These courses became the mainstay for students with poor academic achievement. A strong vocational training program was underway, funded by the federal government, to train these poor achievers in specific vocational crafts. In a rapidly changing technical world it was becoming increasingly difficult to train an individual in a skill that would provide a good paying job for a lifetime.

We developed a new curriculum designed to educate all secondary students about the opportunities and pitfalls of the technical world. We traveled throughout West Virginia and retrained the teachers in new ways to use their shops, tools, and skills to help the young people of West Virginia learn to master their changing world rather than focus on learning a single skill that may inevitably force them into unemployment and poverty.

There were no women in the program in the beginning. Most of the guys were married and former high school teachers. Two schools of thought evolved. One school favored local, small-scale, low impact technologies as a way for individuals and communities to grow. The second school, that I favored, focused on the "high" technologies evolving in electronics, medicine, transportation, and production. Computers will drive everything, so I became the computer advocate. The university had acquired the first big time-shared computer, an IBM 360, Model 67. It had terminals connected by telephone modems throughout campus. I learned a word processing program called WYLBUR and taught it to anyone willing to use it. WYLBUR had been developed at Stanford for the IBM 360, Model 65, the first time-shared computer. It had moved the Northern Illinois State University. Soon, I found that the word processor could be used to do graphics. From that evolved the concept that the computer could be used as a symbol processor. Up to that point, computers were used primarily to do massive calculations, difficult or too time consuming to do by hand. I saw computers as an extension of human thought, with the ability to process the symbols of our thoughts in highly creative and productive ways.

I had no social life except the frequent trips to the locations targeted for teacher training workshops and occasional departmental parties. I dove into my studies with a resolve I hadn't experienced before. My failure to get good grades at Stanford and brief stint as an instructor had changed my attitude toward learning. I wasn't passively absorbing what my professors taught any more. Rather, I was devouring knowledge and trying to create new understanding in each assignment.

That Fall, I did a little exploring by car, seeking out mountain retreats in the Appalachians. Cooper's Rock, overlooking the Cheat River Gorge, was nearby. One of my fellow students, Ray Beauregard, a self-styled mountain climber, and I went out to the Rock one day with the intention of hiking down to the river, fifteen hundred feet below. It was easy to go around the ends of the Rock on trails that led to the base of the Rock. It was interesting exploring the cliffs and fissures that characterized the base of the Rock, that soared over one hundred feet above.

As we started further down the side of the gorge, we first encountered loose rock on the slope that was difficult to walk on. I found myself reaching for small trees to keep from sliding. Finally, we came to a vertical drop of over ten feet that blocked our way down. I told Ray I couldn't continue and started back up.

The loose rock was now my enemy. With each step upward I slid back. Hooking higher trees with my arms helped some, but my progress was torturous. Ray had his climbing boots on and made good progress. I didn't. Finally, I stood on the slope exhausted, unable to move up or down, and my left leg started shaking violently. The shaking was new to me then, and I didn't know what it was, except that my leg muscle was tired. Later, these spasms would become common, like a friend releasing tension from my strained muscles. On the hillside, the spasming was dangerous. It was getting late and colder, and I felt as if I couldn't get off that mountain. Ray came to my rescue. He had a short rope that he tied around my waist. Then, working from footholds above, he literally pulled me up the mountain until we reached the trails and I could walk again. After that, I confined my exploration to roads and established trails.

After my first semester of classes, I concentrated on my program of study and the formation of my doctoral committee. One of my committee members appeared to be a problem from the start. But I heeded the advice of one of my colleagues at Stout, Frank Pershern, who had finished his doctorate just before I left. "Ron," Frank said, "do anything your committee asks." That advice stayed with me. When a member of my committee made an asinine or stupid request, I didn't argue. Instead, I'd enthusiastically head out and try to complete the request as quickly as possible. It worked, and I progressed. Some of my fellow students chose to argue with their committees or ignore requests. It took them far longer to finish than me.

The old 1950s style office typewriter that I'd bought after leaving rehabilitation in 1966 became my mainstay. With the knuckle of my left index finger on the shift key and the rigid tip of my thumb or index finger, braced by my hand splint, I hunted and pecked my way through reams of paper. Although I typed less than twenty words a minute, I tried to be accurate, taking my rough, handwritten draft and transforming it into finished copy while I typed. Except for drawings and sketches, I typed all my work. I became obsessed with form and format. My studies showed that the way information is presented is as important as the information itself. My human factors training showed that we are highly visual, absorbing 93% of the information our brain processes as color images received by our eyes. The placement of words on a page and the way we emphasize them contributes to how they are received and read. I spent a lot of time making drawings and diagrams because these nonverbal means of communication are more powerful than words in conveying meaning. Using color photos and colored markers, I made flip chart presentations that were most effective. The flip chart presentations were good for small groups. For larger groups I had the charts photographed and made into 35mm slides.

I decided to use PERT, program evaluation and review technique, to write my program proposal. My program was very well received and soon became a model for other students' proposals. With my committee and program approved, I was ready to select a topic.

Dr. DeVore was interested in educational philosophy. He believed that the philosophy of the teacher determines what is ultimately taught. I had never studied philosophy, but I was intrigued. We decided to develop a test that would help an individual determine his or her philosophy of education. A computer terminal and print out a profile would deliver the test after the test concluded. The test was designed to be interactive, unique to each user, and self-improving through the introduction of new questions by the users and elimination of questions through analysis of how valid each one was.

I read all the philosophy books I could find, extracting statements that represented a philosophical point of view, and built a base of 3000 statements from that to derive questions. The computer would randomly choose the questions and present them to the user. The user would select the answer he or she wanted from the list. I named the system ORACLE after the Oracle of Delphi who was propertied to foretell the future. I got the idea from the PLATO Project at the University of Illinois. Through interactive technology, PLATO was attempting to teach college courses on computer terminals. My system would teach the user philosophy while it explored the user's beliefs, but it was designed primarily to reveal the user's belief system.

ORACLE never reached the computer. I flow-charted the logic but the cost to program it, about $15,000, was too much. So, the system was never implemented. I often think of resurrecting it for today's interactive computers, but haven't yet.

I left the teacher training program to assist Dr. DeVore with proposals for funding project ideas he had. We got funding for an FAA training program. We had written a good proposal, and were guaranteed funding. Then, we were forced to alter our proposal to precisely match the FAA's requirements. I learned from that lesson that most funding was achieved politically, and that proposals were often written after the fact to meet the grantor's requirements.

Marion County had received just such a grant from Vocational Education. The School Superintendent sought out DeVore as principal investigator. Paul was too tied up with other projects, so he asked me to take it on. It was a study of needs and opportunities for the handicapped in a county in West Virginia. It was a labor of love for me. I put a lot into it. The project focused on training for employment. I traveled throughout the region with county officials to find model programs for the ones that would be used in Marion County. I also surveyed ten percent of the County's businesses to determine attitudes toward hiring disabled people. We put all the information we gathered in a book for planning the County's educational programs for the handicapped.

In retrospect, I failed to survey the recipients themselves, many of whom were probably confined to family homes and unable to avail of any education or training, let alone employment. A 1993 survey of individuals with spinal injuries showed that only 26% were employed, and half of those listed their employment as housewife or husband. While I don't want to disparage the value of keeping a home and caring for children, it brings no money in. For thirty years, I maintained my own household and worked paying jobs too. We define ourselves by what we do. Maintaining house and home is a necessary evil, and some people make a high science of it. But, unless the disabled person can make money from outside the home, like in a housecleaning or catering service, work at home, no matter how difficult, is not employment.

I finished my doctorate in two and one half years, earning "straight As" in the process. The other students began asking, "How did you do it?" My program plan and dissertation were in demand as a model for other students to follow. I counseled anyone who came to me, hoping to allay their fears, but some inevitably still made the mistakes I warned against and took years to finish.

My next challenge was to find employment. Engineering had reached a low point in higher education, so job opportunities teaching industrial engineering were almost nonexistent. I sent out a computer form letter to all the industrial engineering programs in the country. Responses were favorable, and the department head at Notre Dame was interested, but his funding fell through. Industrial arts programs were not so kind. These programs were tied up in an "old boy" network with many schisms and considerable skepticism about the "upstart" program at West Virginia. One department head from the old school wrote Dr. DeVore that he was offended by my form letter. It was obvious that he obtained his entire faculty by referral through the old boy network.

I got an interview at Middle Tennessee State. The interview went well, especially an evening with the family of a fellow industrial engineer on the staff. Driving back to the airport, the department head confessed that he couldn't hire me because he didn't think I was physically able to do the job.

I got an interview with Daniel Construction of Greenville, South Carolina. The guy doing the hiring was a West Virginia graduate. The job was training director for a pumped storage facility to be built in the Virginia Mountains. At the end of the interview that went well, the interviewer told me that it was too dangerous for me to work the project, that I'd likely have an accident on the road between my housing and the construction site. I had driven most of the roads in that area of the Appalachians and mountain roads all over the West, and had encountered every kind of road and weather condition, including confronting lumber and coal trucks. I never had any trouble. He presumed a lot about my driving ability and my physical ability to do the job. I shook off my disappointment, knowing that I didn't want to work for people who doubted my ability based on my disability. I just told myself that they lost a damned good employee by not hiring me.

Finally, I landed an assistant professorship in the School of Business at Marshall University in the fall of 1974. Students had used up the entire rental housing in town, so I rented the manager's apartment in one of the dorms.

The first day of class, I had a section of Introduction to Business, taught in an auditorium from the stage. I was nervous about this because the class was small and I enjoyed the intimacy and security of a classroom with a chalkboard. It was about a block from my room to the auditorium. Halfway there, I was caught by a downpour and got soaked. I stopped in a restroom and combed my hair, but I couldn't do anything about my wet clothes. When it was time for class, I stepped out on the stage. A few scattered students were in the dark seats where I could barely see them. I wasn't sure how I would begin the class. Suddenly and unannounced, the department head came in.

Dr. Bob Alexander had been a pilot and career-counseling director before becoming a professor. He reminded me of "Smilin' Jack" from the cartoon series. He always landed on his feet. The rain had stopped and, although he carried an umbrella, he was dry and impeccable. He saw that I was in trouble and immediately took charge. From the right side of the stage he welcomed the students to the University and the School of Business, and spent the period introducing these new students to what they could expect. Then, he dismissed them early. I was relieved and grateful; he had saved the day. The next time we met, it was in a classroom, and I followed the prepared material.

I found a new apartment about three blocks from campus. The previous tenant had moved out after only one day. It took me longer to find out why. The apartment faced busy 3rd Avenue, and had no windows except on the street side, and these windows were heavily curtained to keep the street noise and lights out. So the place was dark, but nicely furnished with new vinyl furniture. Behind the apartment it was open for a half block to the Ohio River. It was obvious that old industrial buildings had been demolished as part of the city's redevelopment to create this open space. Anyway, there were many river rats in the garbage cans out back. Otherwise, the apartment was nice and ideally located for me to walk to work.

My social life was limited to department functions and a singles club. I spent a lot of time preparing lessons, correcting papers, and working on book outlines Paul sent me. He had been made chief author and editor of a textbook series. I was asked to review book outlines as part of the project. I submitted an outline myself, but it was not accepted. My nose ran the whole time I was in the apartment, but it would stop abruptly when I left. I thought it was colds or a sinus condition, but later, I learned that vinyl and some plastic building materials and glues could cause allergic reactions. Anyway, all the hours I spent working in the apartment were hampered by my allergic symptoms.

My 66 Olds Toronado was showing the signs of years of neglect. It had rust and dents and its transmission had developed a shifting problem after 153,000 miles. I wanted to buy a new small car like the recently introduced Volkswagen Rabbit, but when I tried it, I couldn't release the hand brake or shift it from park. Many of the cars I tried had recessed handles and controls for safety, making operation difficult or impossible. Finally, I found that the two-year old '73 Chevy Monte Carlo had controls that I could operate easily without modification. I bought one with 22,000 miles on it and had the seat belt warning disabled. The seat belts were the only thing I couldn't operate, so I pushed them into the seats and never used them. I missed the 6-way power seat and power windows on my Toronado, but I could still operate the manual ones on the Monte Carlo. I didn't miss the gas mileage and repair bills that haunted me with the bigger, more expensive car. I liked the grip and pull door handles. On the Toro I had to push the door button with the heel of my right hand, or the toe of my right shoe if I had something in my arms, while gripping the handle with my left hand. My father once complained when I used my toe to open the door on his car that way.

In the spring of 1975, Paul DeVore made me an offer I couldn't refuse. He had obtained a two-year Benedum Foundation grant to seed research activity in the study of technology. The opportunity to participate in research that would fundamentally change the way we perceive technology and prepare ourselves for dealing with it was overwhelming, so I resigned from my assistant professorship at Marshall. The faculty at Marshall had always complained of being "second" when it came to support from the state. I didn't like that second-class attitude, even if it was true that more money flowed to Morgantown. While I was beginning to become acquainted with Huntington, living there had been like being in a time warp. The city enjoyed being a bit of old Virginia protected from the wilds of Kentucky and industrialization of the North, preserving a culture that was about ten years behind the rest of the nation. After a few years, I would be accepted, or perhaps become a part of the genteel that ran the city. But, I wanted to be at the cutting edge, so I left.

My appointment at West Virginia started on July first, so I planned a trip back to California and a return to the wilds of Canada before I got back in the academic saddle. Tim and Tom were fifteen. I asked them if they wanted to take me back to the Boundary Waters wilderness. Their Scout Troop had an offer from businessmen to fund a week at the National Scout Ranch, Philmont, but they opted instead to go with me.

After turning in my grades in mid-May, I packed everything I owned in my car and headed for California. Aside from visiting Lenkurt and my old friends, the high point of my visit was attending the Stanford alumni conference. At one session, my former advisor was present, so I approached him. He said, "Oh Ron, it's so good to see you again without your wheelchair." It was obvious that he had forgotten me, or at least what the extent of my disability was. He'd never seen me in a wheelchair.

When I returned to Wisconsin my brothers had done their homework. They wrote the Ely, Minnesota Chamber of Commerce and picked an outfitter from the many brochures they received. The complete outfit, including canoe, tent, food, and camp gear cost $210 for seven days, or $10 per day for each, a real bargain vacation.

We launched the trip from our cottage in Northern Wisconsin. It was a five-hour drive to Ely. After picking up our gear, we drove another 28 miles to Moose Lake to begin our trip. We had plotted a 97-mile journey, following the same path I'd taken fifteen years before, only in the opposite direction. Tim and Tom were a year younger than I was on my trip and smaller. The first test was removing the canoe from the car. The two of them handled it, but I wasn't sure they could carry the canoe alone. I could carry a light pack, but the food pack was big and heavy and one of them would have to carry that.

The first day out we found Knife Lake Dorothy's place. A local legend, Dorothy had left a life as a nurse in Chicago, settled in this remote spot many years before, and did a little business with latter day Voyagers like us. From her place on, we left behind the put-put one lung motors of the local canoe traders and entered a world where occasional park plane engines and canoe paddles dipping in the water were the only unnatural sounds.

The first short portages showed how tough the trip would be. I wished that I could help, but my brothers had to do all the heavy work, and the canoe was nearly impossible. They wouldn't drink the water because there were small bugs in it, they wouldn't go back in the woods to gather firewood or go to the bathroom because of the mosquitoes, and they didn't want to fish. They did know how to clean pots and pans and wasted an hour each morning and evening getting them spotless. Since my last journey, some campgrounds were closed because of over use. But we welcomed the occasional lashed table or fire pit left by past travelers to these favored campsites. It started to rain, and rained five of the seven days. We passed a place where a tornado had cut a quarter mile wide swath through the forest, leaving a clear path of destruction, and a lot of new wildlife habitat.

The second day we turned north, following a creek. The forest in this area had experienced a fire recently, altering its normally pristine lush greenery to a more barren, rocky look. We passed two men who told us of losing a huge fish and then pressed on to Lily Pad Lake. We arrived in a rainstorm. I decided to camp on a small island to avoid bears. We couldn't get a fire started with the wet wood that we found. At one point Tim panicked, and shivering in the cold rain, blurted out something like, "What if we die here. Will they find us?" Finally, Tom found some dry moss under a stump and we had a hot meal cooking in fifteen minutes. So much for being stranded, cold and hungry in the wilderness where no one knows where to find you.

After we ate and set up camp, it quit raining. I tried a lure off the rock face we occupied while they were cleaning pots. Bringing a small daredevil up from the deep water off the rock we were on, I saw a fish follow. It looked like a northern pike, about 23 inches. I told Tim about the northern and he said I was lying—there were no fish—I was just trying to get him to fish. I was. Reluctantly, he made a cast into deep water. When he brought it up the sloping rock, a fish struck. Soon, we had three northerns swimming in water in the canoe. The first one was 23 inches, but they got bigger. We went out on the lake in the canoe. We caught fish every time we cast up against the rocky shoreline. All seven fish were over 27 inches, and the largest, 32 inches, pulled the canoe around before we got him in. We didn't lose a single fish, even though we didn't have a net. We threw them all back except the first three, making some good eating.

We didn't catch any more fish, but we trolled between stops and each stop we would test cast to see if we would have that luck again. The next night, we ate the fish and camped on a rocky spot by a river. I didn't tell the guys, but the next morning I found fresh bear droppings near our fire. I warned them about securing the food pack out of reach of bears. They had been hanging it about six feet off the ground. A large bear can reach eight feet with ease.

We arrived at our first portage that morning, about 300 yards through the woods. A party was hurriedly loading their canoe as we arrived. They didn't say anything other than, "Hello".

I was in the lead, followed by Tom with the canoe, and then Tim with the food pack. About 100 yards up the trail, I met a bear coming toward me. He stopped about fifteen feet away and we both stepped off the trail to the left. The rule is, *get off the trail*, when you meet a wild animal on its path. A threat of blocking a bear's path could cause a confrontation. The bear looked and I looked. I said, *"A bear, Tom, a bear."*

Tom would have none of it. I always led on portages and would announce anything interesting as we came upon it. He was struggling with all his might to keep the canoe steady, step by step, over roots and rocks and muddy spots, with mosquitoes buzzing around his sweating, straining head. It was like being in an aluminum cocoon of intense concentration, seeing how far he could go before propping the bow of the canoe against a tree, and releasing that awful weight from his shoulders. He was concentrating on carrying farther than Tim did, hopefully to the end of the portage, and wasn't interested in cheerful comments from his older brother, breaking his concentration.

*"Tom, a bear, put down the canoe...get the camera,"* I emphasized without being too loud. Tom dropped the canoe right behind me. I raised my arms, lunged forward, and yelled *"Huhhh!"* The bear bounded back into the brush, leapt up a tree in a single bound, all 400 pounds of him, and looked back at us, hanging on to the tree with one paw. He looked comfortable there, about ten feet off the ground, safe from my threat and able to see us well.

Tim came up behind and Tom looked in my pack for the camera. By the time we got the camera out, the bear had climbed down from his perch. We walked back in the brush to get pictures. Tom got a couple of pictures, but the bear wasn't posing. Back on the trail, I told Tim to bring the food pack with me. I grabbed my pack and we headed down the trail to the put in point. Once there, I grabbed a paddle to ward off the bear, and told Tim to go back for the rest of the gear.

I didn't see the bear again, that was okay with me. Tom had waited and got a picture of the bear lifting up our canoe, looking for food, I guess. Heading back for more gear, the bear began following him. When he caught up with a guy from the other party carrying a heavy pack, he yelled, "A bear! A bear is right behind us!"

The guy acknowledged, "I know, I know," in a resigned voice, stopped, turned, and confronted the bear face to face. The bear turned and ran. It seems they had been camping there and the bear had been bothering them all morning. They were clearly tired of it.

I waited for a long time for the guys to bring the packs and canoe. Finally they arrived, and I was glad to shove off to the safety of the water. We got into large lakes after that. We tried sailing with some success. But it rained and rained. It was hard to navigate the large lakes in the rain with my glasses perpetually wet, staring at a wet map and the coastline for the bay or inlet marking the next leg of our trip.

Sleeping bags got wet and we got soaked and cold, but at the end of each day we had a hot meal and slept warm and dry in our tent. The guys complained about my frequent stops to the bank to pee, but I couldn't kneel or stand in the canoe, and the cold, wet weather added to the stimulus of my morning coffee. They started drinking coffee, too. By the end of the trip they were seasoned Voyagers. Tim carried the canoe over the longest portage, a half-mile, without stopping to rest the last day. I wondered how long this paradise would last, with so many people wanting to experience it.

My parents' home Yellow River, Marshfield, WI and '73 Monte Carlo
taking Tim and Tom to a Boundary Waters for a canoe trip in June 1975

EdD at WVU's Program for the Study of Technology in January 1974

# 13

## Another New Role

On July 1st, I was back at West Virginia University. Besides me, we had three new faculty members. It was a heady time. My job as coordinator of research and assistant professor was to stimulate research funding. We wrote sixty-three proposals in the next three years and got four or five small ones funded. It was a stress-filled, seven-days-a-week job. But, with few interests other than the thrill of accomplishing a good proposal within the deadline, I thrived on it. I called it working hard, playing hard. When I finished the work on time in the best way I could, I enjoyed a party, a day in the mountains, or whatever life had to offer. And it offered a lot.

At first, I went back to a student efficiency apartment like in my doctoral study days. But soon, I wanted a home that would define who I was. I found a cottage on Cheat Lake, eight miles from campus that fit my need. So, I bought it. Located in Cheat Canyon Park, an exclusive development established in the 1920s when the Cheat Lake dam was being built, the cottage had been in the same family since it was built in 1928. The foundation and fireplace were made from rounded river rock, salvaged from the riverbed before the lake was flooded. The property included three small lots, bordered by the upper and lower loop road that split at my property and provided access to the other lots in the Park, and by flat stone walls that retained the steep, sloping hillsides.

The cottage came furnished with old appliances and the 1928 wedding furniture of the couple selling it. The park came with membership in an association of fourteen owners of homes and cottages, including mostly elderly but accepting members of a club that dated back to the horse and buggy days, and one genuine national hero, Herb Morrison. Herb was the radio pioneer who, while recording for WLS in Chicago the arrival of the Third Reich's jewel, the Hindenburg, beginning its second season of flights to Lakehurst, New Jersey, happened upon the tragedy that gave him lifelong fame as the first person to record his eyewitness to what unfolded before him. Cheat Lake came in an eerie blue green color caused by acid run off from many abandoned coalmines upstream. A stone monument proclaimed President George Washington's crossing of the river, just below the Park, in 1779.

I borrowed my neighbor's mower and discovered what I'd acquired. The three lots comprised three quarters of an acre of sloping grass lawn, shaded along the edges by tall trees. In order to mow the steepest parts, I had to tie a cord, in this case a spare extension cord, to the mower and lower it down the slope. I tried rope, but the rope was rough and gave me friction burns. The soft rubber and wire cord left many red marks on my arm, but no burns. One time on the steepest part, I lost my grip and the mower got loose and rolled rapidly down the slope toward the house of my neighbor, jumped the wall and ended up upside down, still running, in the road. Another time it ran over the cord, cutting it. When I took the cord to my neighbor's wife, asking her to tie it back together, she balked. She wasn't a technical person but she knew you couldn't repair a cut electrical cord by tying the ends together. I had to quit mowing until I could get someone to tie it. I also had to get someone to tie on my shoes whenever I mowed the lawn. My 73-year-old neighbor, Gwen Wiedebusch, was glad to accommodate me. She was pleased that I was eager to keep the grounds looking good.

It took several hours to mow my yard. In the spring of 1976, I bought my own mower and started mowing my neighbor's lawn too, about a half acre. The retired accountant that lived in the stone house below me was 93 and lived alone. Mr. Cuthbert was frail and unable to do any yard work. He had supported a young man and his family who would occasionally come and mow, but his property was clearly neglected. I made a deal with him: *you buy the gas and I'll mow.* He agreed and always came up with money when the gas can was empty.

Soon I was in his roses, clipper in hand, removing weeds that obscured these native beauties. This hardy variety bloomed profusely throughout the summer. I also took on the roses at the park entrance. They never looked better, but I got a rash, perhaps poison ivy.

I also got a more serious malady. Mowing the slope one hot June day, the grass was deep and wet from heavy rain. The electrical cord I was using dug deeply into my right arm above the elbow as I struggled to keep my footing on the upper gravel road pulling the mower up the slope on each pass. I went back to the house to get a cool drink. I reached into the refrigerator for a pitcher of iced tea I'd prepared and my wrist went limp, causing me to spill the pitcher. After I cleaned up the spill, I discovered that I couldn't pick up the pitcher because I couldn't lift my right hand at the wrist. This action I'd adapted as a way to use my useless hand with stiff fingers to grip glasses and handles. It was also the action required to operate my hand splint.

I went to a neurosurgeon at the Medical Center with my problem. He was incensed because I'd damaged my Ulna nerve—cut it off by the pressure of the cord on the nerve just under my skin. He calculated the distance from the nerve damage to the muscle, from just above to just below my elbow, and concluded that if the nerve had to regenerate a centimeter a month, the three inches or so the nerve would have to re-grow would take six to eight months.

The injury affected my writing the most, and I found myself dictating proposals and memos rather than being able to write them. Finally, I took two weeks vacation and returned to Wisconsin and the lake to mend. By the time I returned from vacation, about a month after the injury, my wrist action came back. I bought some plastic strapping and rigged a rope and strap arrangement that didn't cut into my arm and continued to mow without further injury to the nerve.

Gearing up for a role as a leader in the study of technology as it affects our culture, I became president of the West Virginia Chapter of the World Future Society. I also wanted to take an active role in the American Association for the Advancement of Science. It was here that I would meet Margaret Mead, Carl Sagan, and Peter Drucker, real people with imagination and nerve, forging new paths for society to emulate. I wanted to be like them. I wanted to make a contribution.

I also took in roomers. The first was an instructor from Southern Illinois University who spent a couple of months with me trying to formulate a doctoral program. Like many in the field of industrial arts education, he was good with his hands and undoubtedly a good teacher, but when it came to formulating his thoughts and ideas on paper, he was at a loss. He was in his forties, so there was a lot of pressure for him to get a doctorate. If he didn't complete soon, he would lose all chance to be promoted to assistant professor, and, perhaps, lose his college teaching job. He refused my help to get started, and left after a couple of months without gaining approval for a doctoral program.

The second guy stayed a semester to work on his dissertation. Iver Johnson was also in his forties and came down from Mankato State University to devote concentrated time to finishing his doctorate. He worked diligently and quietly and had finished his dissertation and defense by the end of his allotted time, requiring nothing from me except the quiet lodging of my cottage.

And then, there was Vitoon. Vitoon Upathamp arrived at the department in the fall of 1975, directly after completing his Master's Degree coursework at the University of Calgary. About 55, Vitoon was a high-ranking official in Thailand's Ministry of Education. He oversaw industrial and technical education for the country and was the author of a series of technical textbooks. Vitoon's English, being quickly picked up through reading and conversation, was flawed, to say the least. Seeing that he was having trouble understanding what to do, I stepped in to help him get registered for our doctoral program. We soon became friends and he stopped by my office often whenever he needed something explained. As the elder of the more than 100 Thai students on campus, he became their leader and mentor even though he was struggling with the American way of doing things. By the spring of 1976, he had completed his coursework and returned to Thailand. I didn't realize the trouble he was in until later.

The competitive nature of our doctoral program was not conducive to friendship building. There was camaraderie built with each new class, starting their assistantships each July 1, but that waned as one student gained advantage over another in this very serious quest for the pinnacle degree of a career. Some students, like I had, breezed through, while others took up to ten years of struggle to be called "doctor", only to find their job prospects limited.

As a professor without students who had this "cushy" job writing proposals, I did not form strong bonds with the young students coming through, affectionately called, "Young Turks." After Vitoon, the exceptions were the foreign students who came to me because I was open and not threatened by them, and not in their particular competitive circles.

Raj and Mahfooz joined us in July 1976. They became friends and a part of my opening up my thinking to the larger world.

Mohammed Mahfoozal Haque came from Karachi and a recently received Master's degree from Northern Illinois University. Originally from India, he had taught in East Pakistan before the separation. He was married and had six brothers who were medical doctors, scattered throughout the Middle East. He was short in stature, about five feet tall, but more mature and worldly than his fellow students. Mahfooz loved hunting, fishing, beekeeping, and gardening, all he undertook as soon as he had time. Mahfooz made friends easily, and was accepted by everyone in the program. Our age group and experience, and our mutual interest in fishing and hunting strengthened his relationship with me.

Aminur Rahman Chowdrury came from Dacca, Bangladesh and a recently received Master's degree from Texas A & M. In 1969, Raj's father had spirited him out of the city before the Pakistan Army came to seek out and kill all the young men. After pumping gas to put himself through Sam Houston State, Raj found his charm with Americans an asset as he first headed to Texas A & M, and then sought a doctorate at West Virginia.

I was working 80-hour weeks. I was up at 6 am and would get to the office from 7-8 am and work straight through, except for an occasional lunch on campus. I'd head home about 4:30 or so, spend an hour and a half cooking my evening meal, relaxing while I caught the TV news, and then work until 10 pm or so. Except for those long hours mowing the lawns, I worked weekends too.

The proposals we wrote had short deadlines, too short. I had to push to get support and ideas from the professors involved. Students and professors who wrote some of the ideas could not flesh them out with methodology, timetables, budgets, and other requirements. These details always fell on me to complete at the last minute. I became adept at getting approvals, even the university president's, at the last minute, and then make the four-hour drive to Washington, D.C. Then, I'd rush up elevators and down long halls to make the deadline.

We did sixty-three proposals in three years. Only seven were funded. These were simple, straightforward projects to provide services to people the federal government wanted. The grants supported a few students, but didn't bring in any real money. The grand, theoretical, multiyear plans we made were not well received. It would take a lot more political clout than we were able to muster to get the big agencies like the National Science Foundation in our corner.

I became a master at persuading people who were strangers to our cause to ally with us, at discerning if we had a chance of receiving funding from the quality of the proposal, at pulling together needed parts of a proposal, and at eluding the many Maryland Police, traffic conditions, and weather bent on thwarting timely delivery of our proposals.

All this pressure and concentrated work took its toll. On top of the physical challenges of my paralysis, the stress of the job was immense. My cure for stress was simple; I'd get in my car and explore. East of where I lived rose the Appalachians. On one-day outings I'd allow myself, I'd drive up into the Monongahela National Forest, visit Spruce Knob, highest point in the Eastern United States, or travel some of the unnamed dirt roads that snaked through little-known places of beauty and solitude like Alpine and Canaan Valley.

These trips were always pleasurable, especially if I found a good sandwich at some little roadside stop at noon. But, invariably, I'd find myself racing exhaustion, an empty gas tank, and nightfall as the curves became sharper and sharper before the long straightaway home. In fall, the colors were spectacular. In spring, vistas were clearer without foliage and there was always a chance of ice on the road. Always, the direction the road took was defined by a creek or river, like the ancient Indian trails that these roads had sprung from.

On holidays, I would work until the last minute, but have my car packed and immediately head for my cousins' in Ohio or more directly to Wisconsin via the Ohio and Indiana Turnpikes. The stress and tension would slide off my stiff neck and sore arms and shoulders as I left town and my attention turned to the long drive into the night. These trips were mostly uninteresting except for winter weather that always put an edge to the monotony. I was lucky. I never slid into the ditch or spent time stranded. I sometimes drove for hours on roads so slippery that I would arrive at my destination as tight as an over wound clock, my mind still straining to keep the car straight as it skated down the road with a mind of its own.

West Virginia roads were far different from the freeways and turnpikes and very dangerous. Coal trucks were common on some back roads and they would hog the road meeting you on curves and unnerve you as they ate up your tail as you tried to carefully climb a grade. When a powerful truck came too close to me from behind, I'd exit the road to the right at the next turn out and let him pass. It was hard to enjoy the scenery when a huge truck was breathing down your neck.

My Monte Carlo was rear wheel drive. I learned to use low gear to slow my descent on icy West Virginia roads. The drag on the rear wheels kept the car slowed and straight as I gingerly steered around curves overlooking steep inclines, often without guardrails. In the valleys, I would shift to high, accelerate, and then gently reduce throttle pressure and gradually slow until I reached the top of the next grade. Attempting to accelerate on the grade resulted in my tires spinning and loss of control. Although I never had to do it, one trick the locals knew was to "burn" your way up a hill. An eighteen-wheeler didn't make the hill by my cottage one day. I watched him through my kitchen window. He spun the tires on his tractor until they were hot enough to melt the ice down to the pavement, grab, and pull the whole rig forward a few feet. Doing this over and over, he managed to work his way up the hill, foot by foot, until he reached the top about two hours later. The technique is hard on tires, but it beat an expensive tow or being stranded on a deserted road in winter.

I always put snow tires on the car and kept a blanket in the back seat in winter. But I carried no boots, heavy parka, chains, or sand. I had this recurring dream of sliding off the road in a storm, being unable to open the doors in deep snow, and freezing to death before someone found me. The dream didn't stop me from driving alone in horrendous conditions, but it was on my mind. I thought of writing a short story about it, but never did. Stephen King did in "*Misery,*" but my thoughts never included a car crash, or a rescue by a diabolical killer. As a teenager, I could conquer winter, dig or push a car out, build a fire, or walk for miles in deep snow. As a paraplegic adult, driving alone at night on a deserted, icy road, I felt vulnerable to conditions of Nature I could not control. As terrible as the thought was, it never kept me from driving out into the cold night. I watched the weather reports. I drove the good roads. I avoided driving where I shouldn't. I was lucky. I needed to be fearless to continue my life; I did not have to be foolish.

In the fall, I would climb the hill above our Park, following ancient trails up to the cistern used as a water supply in the past. I would also follow the Greer road along the lake, under the new highway bridge, and then up the hill on the other side, cut off now from park property by the wide swath of Highway 48, to an ancient oak tree. From under that tree I'd view the valley below as if I were some Indian watching for game to move on the same spot two centuries earlier. I'd often slip and fall on the steep, sometimes muddy, trails, but I'd pick myself up, grab onto a small tree or vines, and pull myself up. The struggle to climb made making it to the top more exhilarating. One time, I slid down a steep slope and got caught up in old blackberry brambles. I was hung up so bad it took a long time to extricate myself from the brush and reach level footing. When I finally did, I was ready to climb back up the hill again. Just not in that spot.

I read that West Virginia had been cut over four times since Mountain Men first ventured into the hills. Pictures of barren hills surrounding a now state park about the turn of the century bore this out. My view of those hills was trees—the way it always was and should be. But, the view from the air was different. Strip mining, leaving acid-laden rivers and spoil fields in its wake, scarred much of the landscape. Then, on one spring flight by small plane we took to the South, the horizon was marred with as many as fifteen forest fires, all burning out of control. I worried about what we were doing to this beautiful land in the name of progress.

The mountain laurel blooming below the basement garage of my cottage in Cheat Canyon Park, WV. While painting the concrete basement wall from the top of a step ladder, I fell backward over the top of this laurel on my back on the steep slope below it, flipped, and landed on my feet on the drive below like a good circus act. Wish I had a YouTube of that 20 footer.
May 1977

Two friends at Cooper's Rock, Cheat Canyon, 3 miles from my cottage.

# 14

## Time to See the World

By the spring of 1976, Vitoon had completed his coursework, his program, and approval of his dissertation topic. He returned to Thailand. During the summer he wrote often. By the fall, he was back and I offered him a room in my house.

Vitoon had learned cooking from his Chinese roommate the year before. He would cook one evening, and I the next. It was an interesting change of pace and I enjoyed his new found culinary skill. The first thing he asked was for me to edit his Master's thesis from the university of Calgary. It was characteristic and ironic that he hadn't finished his master's degree, but was nearing the end of his doctoral program. The thesis was about 120 pages long and beautifully written, but Vitoon's command of English required rewriting almost every sentence. I had to continually ask what he meant by a particular phrase or sentence. In the end it was the best we both could make it, and it was approved.

Vitoon then concentrated on his dissertation. He hired an editor so I didn't have to help him so much. By December, he was finished and ready for his defense. To this day I don't know how he did it so fast, but he is a great educator and author, and capable of great concentration despite the odds of writing well in a strange language.

Early on, he asked me if I'd like to come to Thailand. By the end of his stay, I was ready to give it a try. I put together the Christmas holiday and two year's worth of vacations. Vitoon got cut-rate one-way tickets from New York to Bangkok by way of Pakistan International Airlines. Raj and

Mahfooz gave me the names, addresses, and phone numbers of relatives I was supposed to visit. We had to take a trip to Washington, D.C., to get visas. Vitoon was able to get the Thai consulate to get his visas. On my day in D.C., I managed to get a visa for Thailand, Iran, and Egypt, but had to wait for Bangladesh to send one to me. Fortunately, we didn't need visas for England, France, Germany, and Pakistan.

I bought a large soft side suitcase and a briefcase-sized second bag to carry on the planes. Then I went to an Army Surplus store and bought some heavy woven cloth adjustable straps with hooks. With the straps slung over my shoulder, I could carry both bags against my right hip. This proved to be a lifesaver. I packed light, but carefully, knowing that I would be in both winter and tropical conditions.

We drove to Roger and Lin's house in Philadelphia on December 20. Then on the 21st, Roger joined us and we drove to the docks in lower Manhattan to ship Vitoon's trunk, and then to Kennedy International to depart. Our departure was originally scheduled for 4 pm, but the plane was delayed several times until, at 2 am, we were instructed to carry our luggage to a gate on the other side of the terminal. This was the first test of my ability to carry my luggage long distances, swinging on my right hip as I took long strides with my stronger right leg. The long walk wore me out and I had to stop every hundred yards or so, but it worked. The metal feet on the large suitcase slid easily on terrazzo floors, making it easy for me to push it ahead of me as I waited in long lines. I could sit with the small case on my lap, open it up, take out my pen and hand splint, and use the bag's surface to support writing on forms that we were frequently required to fill out. Slung over my shoulder, that small bag contained everything I needed except a change of clothes.

We boarded the plane and took off—almost. The pilot shut down the plane's engines as we were about to reach liftoff speed and returned to the terminal. We got off the plane, waited until 3 am, and then got on again. This time we took off for real, bound for Paris.

It was the shortest day of the year. Soon after we left New York, the sun came up. The day was waning as we crossed Ireland and England. As we approached the runway in Paris, I was thinking of the prospect of three days in this city that Vitoon found alien and I'd heard that they wouldn't speak English to you. We didn't have a hotel, but it was early, only about 5 pm. Early enough to find something for the night. We were landing, I could see the runway lights on the side, and then the pilot gave full power, we pulled up, and flew back to England. PIA didn't give any explanation, just as they hadn't for our eleven-hour delay and aborted takeoff in New York. I began to wonder about the efficacy of buying cut-rate tickets from cut-rate airlines. Anyway, we were flying in an almost-new Boeing 747, so it wasn't the plane's fault.

We circled London for an eternity. The confinement of seventeen hours in the air and two days without sleep was taking its toll. We landed at Heathrow about 8 pm. We saw this as an opportunity to see London, and then head on to Paris in a day or two. I just got on the phone to Raj's sister when they announced that the plane was departing for Frankfort. We asked if they had taken our luggage off the plane and they said no. Given all the confusion, we decided to stay with our luggage and got back on the plane.

We arrived in Frankfort about 10 pm, tired and disoriented. We were negotiating with a cab driver for a $16 ride to a good hotel downtown, when an American who taught German and had been on the plane with us came to our aid. He told us to take the train into town with him for one Deutschmark, about 43 cents. Then, he helped us find a good hotel across from the main train station and a coffee shop where we could relax.

Frankfort was cold and damp. Our hotel room had little heat, so it took a long time under a feather comforter to get warm and a long time to get enough courage to hit the cold floor in bare feet to go to the bathroom down the hall. The wine was great, but the street food was all wieners and sauerkraut. I got tired of everything with vinegar on it until we discovered a good meal in our hotel dining room. Christmas Eve, we visited the Cathedral; full of fur-coated worshipers, and then took the trolley across the river to the old city. The crowds of young people riding with us disappeared into local nightspots and we decided to walk to the Budigen Beer Tower.

It was a long walk. When we got to the Tower, it was beautifully lit up, but closed. Vitoon announced that he was tired and cold and wanted to go back to the hotel. There were no trolleys. The holiday had rolled up the streets. They were now vacant as the cold night. We walked until Vitoon announced that he couldn't walk any more. I was cold too, but set out for a major street hoping to catch a cab while he sat on a bench. Finally, a cab came along and we got back to the hotel. Vitoon slept through the next day. I got us a warmer room by the elevator shaft.

Our last day in Germany, we took a train ride to Cologne along the Rhine. It was warm, sunny, and comfortable. The number of castles we passed, each one exacting a toll on river travelers in its prime, impressed me. There was snow at Bonn; the only snow we saw in Germany. The

Cathedral in Cologne was worth the trip, but the replacement windows after Allied bombing could not compare to the stained glass wonder of the originals that had survived five centuries.

We had another eight-hour delay leaving Frankfort and arrived in Cairo about 10:30 pm. Fully armed troops escorted our bus to the terminal. The Men's room was flooded an inch deep and a man sold toilet paper by the square at the door. An Italian woman screamed hysterically when the cashiers wouldn't change her lira for Egyptian pounds. I had a visa but Vitoon didn't. After they scoured his passport for any evidence of Israeli approvals, they granted him a tourist visa. We checked through customs easily while we watched luggage being mangled by the conveyer where it entered the building. A salesman appeared distressed as customs agents sifted through a huge pile of woman's undies on a large table. The vultures were at the door when we left.

At that time of night, the tourist bureau was closed. Over one hundred people were yelling, "Carry your bag?" "Cab to hotel?" and other entreaties, with no security in sight. At a booth with a makeshift sign announcing the "Hotel Viennese" a one-eyed woman assured us a good room. She motioned to a young boy who jumped the counter and grabbed my bags. It was hard to keep up with him through the mob to a waiting cab, but we made it without losing sight of our bags. We jounced for fifteen miles on bad roads through bombed-out ruins, past cars with badly aimed headlights, to the central city.

The hotel was 19th century and the desert dust of the Sahara had seeped in everywhere. We were too tired to sleep, so walked the deserted streets until 2 am to get oriented. We found some bodies, some sleeping, some perhaps dead, before returning to our room. All night long, the ancient toilet down the hall, one with an oak seat and a large, high porcelain tank, would noisily fill up with water, and then dump with a "whoosh!" so loud that it made it nearly impossible to sleep. By morning, Vitoon was ready to leave the country. He spent the morning checking with airline offices and even wanted at one point to take a JAL freighter to Singapore. He couldn't speak to anyone because his accent and the Arabic accent of the Egyptians were so different that I had to act as an interpreter, even though we were all speaking English. We discovered a Russian bookstore where we could buy good books in English for 15 or 20 cents each. Then, Vitoon discovered that he could bargain with Egyptian shopkeepers with dollars. He stuffed his suitcases with books and brass and finally decided that he could wait until our scheduled flight out.

We took a day trip to Memphis, the Stepped Pyramid, Great Pyramid, and Sphinx. That day, I learned that a "tip" and a "bribe" were the common fare of poor Egyptians, willing to do anything for the American dollar. Contrasts were everywhere. In one very poor looking village there was a huge pile of tomatoes by a building. Before I could ask what they were doing there, a brand new fire truck roared through, scattering villagers, its sirens and lights blaring. I doubt if there was a fire and the fire engine, like the pile of tomatoes, seemed out of place.

We stopped at an outdoor restaurant for lunch. I invited our driver and guide to join us. I bought a bottle of wine while the others enjoyed beer. The wine was red, heavy, and sweet. It went well with the "Italian" food. Our guide asked for the bottle, mentioning his many children. Memphis was a mess. The statue of Ramses II lay amid a pile of columns and statues that hadn't been cared for since the British left. At the Stepped Pyramid, our "guide" made a serious attempt to extract his pay, but we opted for giving the old man a cigarette. At least I got to see a tomb. Then we saw the Sphinx as it really was, crowded by vendor stalls and excavations, not sitting alone in the desert as it is often pictured. We declined a camel ride past the Great Pyramid. Sadat's home could be seen on a hill overlooking the pyramids of Giza.

That night in the hotel room I finished the bottle of wine, remembering that I'd promised to give it to our guide. The bottom of the bottle was lined with dead fruit flies. At least I didn't have to worry about catching a strange disease from the wine; it was strong enough to kill flies.

I spent two days in the museum. It was amazing to see the face of Seti II, five thousand years old, uncovered from his mummification and still recognizable. Ramses II, for all his vanity and wealth, could not duplicate the feat of his ancestor, and lies there as a pile of dust and cloth. The riches in art and in hieroglyphics are immense. I wanted to read all the translations, but there were too many. The glyphs, faithfully recreated by scribes for thousands of years, were as precise as if done by computer rather than individuals. Whatever happens to Egypt, I hope that the remnants of its ancient culture remain. A large Nubian exhibit was closed, but I could see its splendor beyond the cordons.

Our guide told us of perfume made from the famous Lotus blossom. Near the museum, he led us into a building that became a labyrinth of passages, until we came to a room like those in movies, filled with boxes and all kinds of wares. We were directed to cushions. Our host, an older man, served us tea and revealed the secret of Egyptian perfume. Unlike the

French, who use alcohol for their perfume, he explained, Egyptians used Lotus blossoms and water. To prove its worth, he had us sample the perfume, and then asked us how many cases we'd like to buy. The sample smelled like a weak version of the cologne I'd bought earlier in Cologne, and was probably watered-down French perfume. We declined as politely as we could, and left. Cairo was filled with traps like this, contrived over thousands of years to catch unwary travelers.

The streets both denied and reaffirmed the legacy of the pharaohs. The dogs that roamed the streets matched images from the glyphs, as did the carts and animals of the city's commerce. Unwashed since its last rain, the city was covered with dust of the ages, obscuring its coffee shop windows, and softening its crumbling streets. Millions roamed the streets, refugees from the last clash with Israel. Young men raced with and caught the rear windows of arriving buses, cheating death under the wheels for the pleasure of catching a hot, dusty, long ride with many others, crammed to the ceiling. At the hint of a traffic jam, dozens of police, ticket books in hand, would rush to the scene to mete out justice to the culprits.

I found a dirty little French restaurant that I liked but Vitoon didn't. Besides an all-inclusive dinner each evening, it provided the interesting image of a waiter shooing a rat out of the room while trying not to get the attention of the guests. It also gave me an opportunity to meet a tall, well-dressed Black man we had seen in the Russian bookstore. Since he and I were eating alone, I introduced myself and asked if he'd join me for dessert. He was the manager in Cairo for Somalia Airlines and pleasant company.

The view from the Cairo Tower was remarkable, giving us an unobstructed view of the Nile with its white-sailed boats as it cut through this sprawling city of exotic architecture. In the distance, near the ancient flood banks that rose to the high desert, several fires burned, I assume from garbage dumps. Up in the tower, the dust and noise of the streets were muted but clear, and the blue sky and river gave contrast to the sun-bleached white of the desert landscape.

I wrote a long letter to my mother, detailing our adventures in Egypt, but I didn't have a stamp to mail it. When we got to the airport about noon for our 4 pm flight, I looked for a place to mail it before I changed my money. Finally, a guy at one of the airline booths said that he'd mail it. I gave him an Egyptian pound to do it. He pocketed the money and never mailed the letter.

Again, PIA was experiencing problems. We heard that the flight from Frankfort had returned to England to fix a flap. Anyway, we waited on hard plastic chairs far into the night as the cold desert wind blew in through doors left open. I was chilled to the bone by the time we finally boarded the plane.

By noon the next day, we landed in the shimmering white sand of Dubai. I got off the plane just to experience the warmth of the sun while walking to the ultra modern white visitor center. While there, I tried to call Mahfooz's brother in Abu Dhabi, but couldn't figure out how to use the phone.

By 4 pm, we arrived in Karachi. The international terminal was being remodeled, so all 400 or so of us crowded into the domestic terminal and there was much confusion as passengers tried to make connection with continuing flights. Vitoon had talked of going on to Singapore, but now was concerned with getting a flight to Bangkok. I wanted him to stay with me, but he had little interest in staying in Pakistan.

I tried to find Mahfooz's uncle who was the Chief Customs inspector, but he wasn't there. I finally got him on the phone. He sounded excited, and said that he couldn't come and get me because they were preparing for someone to come from America. I had telegraphed from Cairo that I was coming, but had told him the wrong day. After I explained who I was, he came to get me. In the crowd I lost Vitoon, but hoped that he had caught a flight out.

I stayed in the home of Talha Siddique, Mahfooz's brother-in-law. About the same age, Talha and I soon found that we had a lot in common in spite of our heritages. There are some people you are just in tune with, and he was like that to me. It was as if we were twin brothers. From opposite sides of the globe and opposite cultures, we still understood each other perfectly.

Four sisters stayed in the house, including Mahfooz's wife Farkhunda. Each one spent a great deal of time cooking exotic dishes for me and would watch me carefully as I ate to see how I liked each one. Talha took me to lunches with his colleagues in the German pharmaceutical company he worked for and on tours of the city. One time, when taking me to see the villas of oil-rich Arabs, he stopped by the road and disappeared down a bank. He reappeared with a hand full of dried weeds, apologized, and explained that he was gathering a dry arrangement, the same thing that I'd done in my travels in the States. Later, when he bargained for me at the brass market, I had him buy a large brass vase. I paid for the vase and gave it to him for his arrangement.

Talha's friend was a manager for PIA. When I told him that we'd flown PIA and that I'd lost Vitoon at the airport, the friend agreed to help find him. The manager's staff called around and found that the Thai Consulate had picked Vitoon up and housed him in a motel near the airport. I visited Vitoon at the motel. He had scheduled a flight that day to arrive at 11 pm, one hour after curfew. He planned stay the night in the airport, and then head home at 7 am. I was expected to do the same on the same flight three days later.

One day several men, including Talha's young sons, Akif and Kashif, piled into Talha's VW Beetle, and we headed north for a day of adventure. North of Karachi, we crossed the Trans Asian Highway. If Vitoon and I had driven, we would have passed the same intersection on our way to Bombay.

We stopped at Banbhore, once on the Indus River, now left as an ancient ruin while the river runs its course kilometers away. The site was littered with potshards, but no whole pots could be found except in the small museum. The clay remains of pots were the only visible indication that this was once a thriving part of the ancient Indus River culture. While not as old or as rich as the people of the Nile, these people established the caravan routes between Egypt and China. In the parking lot we came across a mangy, perhaps rabid dog. In this country they were indifferent to dead and dying animals that, in their final hours, often headed for the sea looking for water, to die on the beaches. Scavenger eagles filled the air everywhere, and white-headed crows picked the bones that remained.

We drove north to a reservoir that Talha hadn't seen for sixteen years. At first he was disappointed that no vendors were selling fish. But we still had a picnic, watching exotic birds that migrated from Siberia, and he mused about the fish that used to be there. As we left, he asked a local villager where fish could be found. Suddenly, several men appeared from a canal with long stringers of fish.

Talha bought about sixty pounds of four different kinds of fish I'd never seen before. One resembled a crappie, another a carp, and another a cross between a catfish and an eel. The fish were loaded on the floor of the small back seat of the Bug, leaving no legroom for the two adults and two kids back there. Luckily, I was up front. On the way back we lost the brakes, but there were no grades and Talha's skillful use of the gears and emergency brake got us home safely. That night, we had a feast and I had to eat each kind of fish and give my opinion.

The next day, we went to observe the procession of mourners for the celebration of the 10th of Mahanran. This is a Shiite Moslem holiday mourning the massacre of the faithful. The participants, a million strong, carry coffins representing the fallen ones for two days through the city, ending with ceremonial burial in the sea. The mourners chant and beat their breasts in anguish as they pass. Some use knives, razor blades, or glass to cut their heads or chests, causing blood to cover their bodies. Others, through repeated breast-beating, raise huge blisters that turn into bloody open sores. Rival groups often clash with the mourners who are agitated and mesmerized by the marching, chanting, and self-flagellation. It was a sight I'll never forget and helped me understand the control the Shiites have over the people of Iran.

As planned, my plane landed in Bangkok at 11 pm. As I picked up my luggage and prepared to spend the night on a bench, I saw Vitoon motioning to me to follow him out a side door. He said that he'd borrowed an official-looking car and that his credentials could get us home. We drove about fifteen miles on the highway to the city without seeing another moving car or police.

I spent ten days in Thailand the first time. I wanted to see every wat, temple and Buddha. Vitoon would take me to a shrine, and then rest in the car while I climbed the steps and tried to decipher the intricate murals on the walls. The Thai have a good way to gild their statues of Buddha. The statues are originally made of concrete, stone, wood, or cast metal. Worshipers entering the temple to burn incense bring small squares of gold leaf to put on the Buddha. After many years, each Buddha becomes completely covered in gold leaf.

We traveled throughout the country. First we went to Sri Racha, Chol Buri, and Patayya southeast of Bangkok on the Gulf of Siam to see Vitoon's sister and the resorts that catered mostly to Europeans. The beaches were shaded by palms and beach squatters catered to every need as we watched incredible sunsets over the water. At a compound where a relative lived, a fence made of concrete piers and barbed wire fifteen feet high ran along the back. Behind the houses it was open, with a few trees in the distance. A short while later, a herd of a dozen elephants came up behind the houses, and I realized the need for the fence. One elephant had huge tusks that reached to the ground, and then curved up another six feet or so. At Sri Racha, there was a small island connected to the beach by a short bridge. The island jutted high up out of the sea. We visited the highest point, inhabited by a Buddhist Monastery with intricate walkways.

On the road, a bus had stopped so that children could taunt some monkeys. I was told they were dangerous. On the way back, we passed a young boy astride a huge water buffalo galloping down the highway shoulder toward us. I wished I'd had a movie camera to catch the scene.

In Bangkok, the Thai were busy filling in their famous canals. You could still go down to the river in the center of town and take a long-tailed taxi to your home if it was on a canal. Driven by 4 cylinder automobile engines and transmissions balanced on a pivoting support, with a long propeller shaft reaching rearward to the water, these 40 foot long, wooden taxis were driven fast and skillfully by their drivers. As I took the taxi to Samboon's house I marveled at how easily little old ladies jumped in and out of the boats on their way to and from market. I needed help. The ideal Thai home is half in the water and many bathe every day from the docks that line the banks. Unfortunately, many of the homes' bathrooms empty into the same water under the houses.

By this time, Thai food was starting to get to me. Vitoon declared that he was rich, so we ate out at sidewalk cafes far and wide. I loved the fresh fish, fried cucumber, and miniature corn. But the spices and mint in the meat made it hard to eat, sometimes. The heat was a factor too. Even with a Siberian cold front, the nighttime temperature rarely dropped below eighty-five. I had Kik's room upstairs and would lie awake for hours watching the small lizard that parked in the middle of the screen over my head until I finally went to sleep. It was supposed to be really miserable in the April-May rainy season, when it rained every day and the humidity is so high that wet things don't dry. I'm glad I missed that.

Thailand is a vast and varied country with several subcultures. We drove to the Ancient City, a replica of the country. On the east side of the park along the Mekong River is an eight story manmade mountain, representing a sacred site. Although a bit run down, the park was a tribute to the Thai resourcefulness and concern for preserving their culture.

Restaurants often had a theme. That day was no exception. At noon we ate at a floating one that featured thousands of ravenous fish that ate everything we didn't. That evening we went to a restaurant on a pier, a relic of the Vietnam War. A sign in English at the entrance proclaimed, "You can afford to eat here!" The featured attraction was the gulls that occupied the place like cats and dogs haunted the sidewalk cafes. On the way back to Bangkok about 9 pm, the Fiat 124 stopped on the road. Two young men on bicycles brought some gasoline in a bag, but that wasn't the problem. A policeman went and got four mechanics on two bicycles, but it was getting late. I was grateful for tall reeds by the road where I went to relieve myself several times while we waited. It was getting dark, and Vitoon worried about getting home before the ten o'clock curfew.

Samboon motioned to me and said to follow her. We caught a small Datsun pickup with seats on the sides of the bed that was used for public transportation. The locals stared at us, clearly uncomfortable riding with this white man and his Thai lady. After a couple of miles we came to a bus depot. There, we boarded a bus driven by a driver who viewed himself as a jet pilot, accompanied by a beautiful young stewardess who sent signals and kept on her feet in a kind of balancing dance as we careened through the streets. I was glad that we got on at a station, because I never would have made it on the streets. We would race other buses and cars, and then slam to a stop. The girl would grab an old lady and pull her on the bus and take the fare in the same motion, blow a whistle, and the driver would waltz up through the gears as the passenger struggled to get to a seat. At times we hit 70 to 80 miles per hour on city streets, and the whole bus would become airborne on the arched canal bridges. As we got deeper into the city, he slowed down. Perhaps he feared the police. Perhaps the other bus he was racing was no longer on the route. I was relieved.

We got off the bus at the end of the line and boar4ded another, larger truck for a few more miles to the center city. Then, Samboon hailed a cab that took us to her house. I spent the night sleeping on a mat on the wood floor of her sitting room, fighting mosquitoes because the room had no screens, only shutters. A smoke coil in the room didn't do much good. In the morning Vitoon was furious. While Samboon was saving me from the indignity of being caught out after curfew, he had the car running with a set of new ignition points fifteen minutes after we left on our wild survey of Bangkok public transportation.

I had bought a round trip ticket to Dacca for a four-day excursion and got back to Vitoon's just in time to go to the airport. Thai Airway's "Royal Orchid Service" began before departure with lavish food and drink from a traffic jam of stewards. After we had taken off, I started talking to the Japanese businessman seated next to me. He asked me if I'd seen the crash, and then went on to tell me that he'd seen a military plane crash at the airport as we left. I didn't see it, so it didn't bother me as I concentrated on what I'd find in one of the poorest countries in the world. He traveled the route often, and explained why the Hindus and Moslems took advantage of the lavish food and drink while they could before arriving at destinations where these luxuries are either illegal or unavailable. When the flight left Delhi on the return trip late in the day, supplies would be depleted.

When I arrived at Dacca on January 11, I sat down on a chair to complete some form I was given. When I looked up, the contents of my case that I was using to write on were strewn all over the floor. As I started to pick up all the brochures, receipts, and other papers from my journey, a man in an official-looking uniform appeared and helped me pick things up. He then whisked me to the head of lines through customs and immigration. He started to carry my bags out of the airport. I passed through a waiting throng, asking every man if he was Mr. Chowdhury. Finally, a man and woman stepped out of the crowd, greeted me, and we headed for a waiting car. The smile on the face of the man who had helped me disappeared, as he grimly followed us to the car. Rahman Chowdhury waived off my offer and tipped the man, hence the source of his disappointment.

Dacca was a small place compared to Bangkok. Life was slow and orderly and Rahman Chowdhury commanded much respect. He left his village in the North as a young man in disagreement with his father, the chief. He went to Calcutta and made his way on the streets. He joined the Royal Air Force during World War II. After twenty years he retired and set up three auto repair shops in Dacca. He brought his four younger brothers through college and into the business. After a brief retirement in the United States, he had returned to help the business rebuild because it had declined in his absence.

Dacca had few cars and broad streets. Cycle taxis were the primary transportation. They crowded the right side of streets as we passed. We stopped and Rahman got me a Coke, thinking that, as an American, I'd need a soda in my hand as we traveled through the city. His home was located in a compound behind a bazaar, and as we wound our way through the passage lined with small shops and stalls, I was amazed at the paucity of goods for sale. Food was not in evidence and I think the Chowdhurys killed several of their chickens for my visit. Rahman complained of a cat that had frightened his pigeons—another source of food.

Starvation could not be seen except for the slow pace of life, and the general thinness of the people. What I remember was the peace of the streets, with thousands going about their business without the roar of motors and diesel fumes. At night each cycle rickshaw carried a single kerosene lantern, hanging from the back to ward off collisions with cars. Passing hundreds of these taxis at night with their lanterns swaying with each rotation of the driver's feet, was a silent sight to behold, almost romantic, a sea of lights in perpetual motion, flowing along the thoroughfares and around the many squares and traffic circles.

Chowdhury was not impressed, either with the condition of the laboratories in the national university, or with the deteriorating condition of the old city, the lost legacy of British grand colonialism. While there were beggars, young and old in every city I'd visited, here, young emaciated women would approach cars with young babies, holding them out in the hope of a handout for food. Most men were so poor, barely able to feed themselves, that when they got a young girl pregnant, would reject her and the burden a baby would bring. Similarly, her family would throw her out because she got pregnant and threatened the existence of the family. Most women were held in such low esteem that they and their babies were outcasts, beggars in the streets.

For the rich like the Chowdhurys, it was a different story. Elaborate searches and lengthy and costly ceremonies insured that the marriage of young men and suitable wealthy young women would be successful. And, in fact, these arranged marriages seem to endure when the open, democratic marriages we Americans favor, so often fail. Raj was in America, where the temptation to marry the American way was great. So there was urgency in Rahman's purpose for taking me around Dacca,

First, I had to check in with Immigration within two days. It was only a formality, but perhaps to insure that my purpose was only to tour. The rooms in the building were large with little furniture. The one I needed to go into had several men in it and a few tables. When I approached the table with the official I was to see sitting behind it, a uniformed man who was sitting on the only chair there got up and offered it to me. As I nodded in appreciation for his generous gesture, I could see that his face and uniform insignia showed that he was a Chinese officer. Chowdhury explained later that the Chinese were building a road from China to Bangladesh through Tibet.

We went to visit the head of the country's power company. The office of the company was more like a very large home. I sat in the back of a huge office while Chowdhury conferred with the father of a potential bride. "She's ancient!" He muttered as we left.

That evening we went to a new part of town to the home of a movie producer. Movies are very popular with the people of the Subcontinent. While Lillie and the women conferred in back, we sat with the producer and his two college-student sons in the front room. The meeting was cordial, but when we left, Chowdhury was upset that the girl had hid herself away and he hadn't seen her.

The next day, we left the city for a tour. We stopped for a picnic at the national war memorial, recently finished to commemorate all the people who had lost their lives in the war with Pakistan. There were very few cars on the road. When we passed a bus stop, there appeared to be about three hundred people waiting. Buses were stuffed to the ceiling and young men would ride on the roof, fenders, and hood. Travel was torturous for the poor. I wondered how long that crowd would have to wait for a ride.

Everywhere, men were hand watering small crops of rice by receding water holes. The landscape was picked clean during this winter dry season, and everything was barren except for the many islands of woven jute houses, little villages that dotted the landscape on higher ground. When the monsoons come later in the spring, everything will flood except the islands. When cyclones roar up the shallow Bay of Bengal, these fragile houses wash away, only to be picked up and reconstructed again.

We drove to the edge of the "jungle", where tigers were reputed to roam, but here too woodcutters and the dryness of winter had decimated the vegetation. We returned to Dacca to one of the several channels of the Ganges that runs through the city. Everywhere on the channel there were boats in full, white sail. There were pull paths on both sides, but the wind enabled all traffic to sail on this day. Even with all this traffic, no motors were heard. It was an eerie and incredible sight rivaling the rickshaws at night. Chowdhury stopped at a warehouse by the river where he often bought fish, but was disappointed because it was closed. We drove home without fish.

When I got back to Bangkok, Vitoon picked me up in a different car—a rear engined Renault. We immediately headed out the next morning for his birthplace in the upcountry eighty miles northeast of the city, to visit his relatives. We drove through dry rice fields populated with grazing water buffalo. Vitoon said that in the rainy season the fields would flood and they would be full of fish.

About noon, we came to a village that was hidden in an island of trees amid a sea of rice fields. When we got out of the car, we were faced with a pack of about thirty small, viciously barking dogs that seemed to announce that they ate white intruders. Somehow, we eluded the dogs and arrived in Vitoon's uncle's office. The walls of the office were covered with pictures of his uncle's exploits as a major participant in helping the Allies rid the area of Japanese during World War II. At 76, he had a 350-acre farm and was the patriarch of the village. Recently, he had become the head of the whole region. He immediately announced that I had known Vitoon in another life—a great compliment.

About ten miles further, we arrived at Vitoon's village and visited Vitoon's 85-year-old mother and two of his sisters. The sisters' families shared the house. We brought canned goods and they gave us rice. As Vitoon chatted with his mother and a sister sitting on the wood floor, Samboon told me that she could not understand the dialect that Vitoon was speaking to the two beetle nut-chewing women. Life was very primitive here. Except for the electric wiring Vitoon's nephew had tacked to the poles that held up the building's roof, the house was ancient and traditional. Samboon was concerned about the open well where the got their water, next to the house. Sent to a Buddhist monastery as a child while his father was dying of Malaria, Vitoon was evidence of how far one can come in one generation.

Then, we went to a park in a waterfall area. It was obviously the off-season because few people were there. The paths leading up river were lined with abandoned refreshment stands for the throngs of summer. I was surprised by the amount of litter, but litter was one of the legacies of Thai involvement with Americans during the Vietnam War. In the evening we met his brother, a doctor, in a recreational club in a park at Nakorn Nayak.

Vitoon took me to see the Siamese Crocodiles. All ten thousand remaining of the species are said to be confined to one farm. Crocodile feeding is a spectacle not to be missed. But we got caught in one of Bangkok's infamous traffic jams, and had to return home without seeing the crocs.

The next day, Vitoon drove me to the Oriental Hotel early for a guided tour to the Ancient City. We left the hotel on the Empress of the Orient, a two hundred-passenger excursion boat that plied the Pra Cha River. Only about twenty passengers enjoyed all that space as we cruised up river past the city center, Royal Palace and Royal Barge, dining on a lavish buffet and enjoying the sights.

About eighty miles up river, we disembarked and took a bus to the Summer Palace and the Ancient City at Ayutthaya. The Summer Palace was the old vacation home for the King of Siam. Inside, furnishings from China represented the riches of Dynasties in ways modern China can't. The Ancient City thrived in the 1700s, but invasion by the Burmese in 1765 left it in ruin. Our guide warned us about hawkers, beggars, and thieves at the site.

As we tried to tour men who offered to sell us gems and ancient idols harassed us. On the bus as we started back, a school teacher from Australia discovered that the star sapphire she had hung around her neck was missing. She had recently bought it during her tour in India. To this day, I don't understand why she wore it. Perhaps she was afraid to leave it in the hotel. Some passengers wanted to go back and get the guy who stole it, but our guide suddenly seemed to have trouble with English.

That last weekend, we drove south to Hoa Inn, an old railroad hotel on the way to Malaysia. On the way to Hoa Inn, we stopped at some mystical mountains that jutted up sharply from the fertile plain like daggers. A Buddhist wat occupied the wooded area at the base of one of the mountains. There was a large door on the side of the mountain and we entered. Inside, the mountain was nearly hollow, creating a huge cavern and there was a large reclining Buddha in front of us. There was also a lot of bat dung and an eerie feeling in the place, filled with intricate passages and high up openings to the sky.

We came out and Vitoon told me that there was a sitting Buddha up on the mountain and pointed out a trail. As usual, he declined going with me, so I set out alone. The trail started with steps and was not too difficult except for a few steep places. It wound up the mountain until it reached the high point of a saddle between two mountains. Now high above the plain, I could see both ways for many miles. I kept thinking of monkeys and what I'd do to avoid an encounter if I ran into them. When I reached the mountain on the other side of the saddle, the trail entered a hole in this mountain. Far below, I could see a black sitting Buddha. I was looking down on its head like a bird flying over. The trail was too steep for me to enter the mountain, so I returned.

When we reached Hoa Inn, the grounds of the hotel featured trees carved in the shape of animals. We stayed in a beach bungalow near the hotel. It was Saturday, but when we stopped at a little beach restaurant in the center of the little town, the beach was deserted. January was the off-season. Squatters on the beach brought us everything we needed, including a large fish that they cooked for us for a small share.

In the morning, I wanted to get up and see the sunrise over the Gulf of Siam, just as I'd seen the sun set at Chol Buri two weeks before. It was foggy at dawn, and all I could hear was the shrieks of children and the roar of small outboards. Five buses with campers had pulled up before I got up, shattering my thought of a peaceful time watching the sun float up from a peaceful sea. It was too foggy anyway, and I could barely make out the kids making all the noise.

Again, we drove to more temples, shining from small mountains like images from a movie. I climbed steps to see them all. Vitoon and Samboon waited in the car each time as I explored, dutifully awaiting my return, giving me all the time I wanted. It was a strain to do all that climbing, but my curiosity could not be damped by exertion. I gritted my teeth and pushed on, always hoping to see something, learn something, I had not seen or known before. My thirst for knowledge of Buddhism was insatiable, but without a guide, it was purely visual.

Most temples were dirty and run down. But one was different. Almost new, it had a fountain, pools with fish, and beautifully crafted paintings in the temple. The paintings covered the usual ancient themes, but also depicted cars, houses, and clothes of modern living. From a distance that mountain was particularly striking, with many temples, chedis, and Buddha images rising from it.

On January twenty-third I flew alone to the Philippines. A fellow passenger, a young Pakistani named Akbhar, on the flight to Bangkok from Karachi had told me to visit him in Bagio City, but I only had four days, so settled for Manila. I stayed in a mid range hotel downtown. My room was on the ninth floor, but I awoke to the sound of roosters crowing each morning. The hotel was populated with weird but friendly people. Too friendly, I was suspicious of everyone.

The first day, I set up tours and tried to find Akbhar by taking a cab to the posh suburb he was staying in when in Manila. But I couldn't locate him. My cab driver filled me in on Ferdinand Marcos and the effect martial law had had on his business. He said that he liked Marcos. Before Marcos, he kept a gun on the seat beside him and used to point turns. Later, walking the streets, a young man approached me and walked with me for several blocks. He did not want money, only to tell me, an American, that he had just been released from prison. He had been a student. One day, Marcos's henchman came and threw him in prison. He wanted me to tell other Americans of the cruelty of the Marcos regime. I listened but felt helpless to help him. Two well-dressed middle-aged women in the street asking for a donation to some cause also approached me. I refused based on the rule I set for myself for the trip: not to contribute to the problem of beggars by encouraging them. I did find it rather odd that these women would do it.

Dusk found me at the romantic Fort Santiago. Lovers were everywhere, strolling. I thought about how my trip would have been with a female companion. My thoughts were shattered when the cannons were fired at 6 pm. It was a regular evening ritual, but my immediate response was to run for cover. Sadly rusting in an old gun port at the Fort, was General MacArthur's open parade car. It seemed doomed to fade with the memory of the War's impact on this modern city of young, beautiful people.

The second day, I took a tour to Pagsanjan Falls. I joined a group that took a van to a hotel on the Pagsanjan River. While we had brunch, the tour guides set up pairings for the dugout canoes. Since I was alone, I was asked to wait for a Japanese tour guide that would arrive later. All the others left and I was alone. Eventually, the young lady arrived and I waited again while she ate.

They had saved the best canoeists, the Rodrigeus brothers, as our paddlers, and we quickly began to catch up with the slower canoes. The scenery on the river was enhanced by palm plantations that ran from the river to the surrounding mountains with the regular pattern of a mowed lawn. Rounding a bend, we came upon a grass hut that looked authentic but was probably put there for tourists to see how life on the river had once been. Then, around another bend, we came upon what looked like an ancient temple. The brothers, who spoke English, Spanish, and Japanese, explained that the temple was built for a Marlon Brando movie and that it was going to be blown up. Later, I learned that it was the set for Francis Ford Coppula's "Apocalypse Now!" At the time I thought it looked too good, like it had been there a hundred years, to blow up.

My canoe mate was educated in Oregon, but didn't want to talk to me and didn't seem to be enjoying the tour. After a while, I quit trying to make conversation and enjoyed the scenery. The river entered a canyon so narrow that its foliage-laden sides closed in overhead. We were paddling upstream, but the brothers either poled us forward against the rushing water or jumped out on either side and lifted us up over rocks. Our momentum was hardly slowed as they carried us up over the rapids and forced us upstream against the current.

We reached the end of the canyon where the falls plummeted forty feet into a lagoon and caught up with the others. We had been instructed to wear swim clothes if we wanted to go under the falls, but most of us were unprepared. I stripped to my jeans and put my clothes and billfold aside in the canoe. A group of elderly Japanese, both men and women, stripped to long white underwear and giggling joined me, waiting to get on the bamboo raft, that when pulled along ropes, would take us up under the falls.

The Japanese got on the raft all at once. They screamed as it sank in frigid water to waist deep, and then came back up. I hung on in relief that we were still floating. The Japanese, cameras in hand, were clearly having a good time on their dangerous adventure. The young woman I was with sat on the bank and sulked. We floated out across the lagoon until we went directly under the falls. I was unprepared for the force of the water and nearly lost my glasses. The view from behind the falls was something the timid souls who didn't take the raft didn't get to see. The trip back down river was swift and anticlimactic.

That evening, I walked the streets again looking for food. There were Chinese, Italian, French—you name it—food in this cosmopolitan city, but I was looking for something different, Filipino. After about an hour of walking, I passed a restaurant filled with young people and music, open to the street. There was a group of about twenty young women standing in the middle of the floor. I entered and was escorted to a seat. A young lady from the group was assigned as my waitress. She steered me to a typically Filipino meal with the works at a reasonable price. The young patrons would take turns grabbing a microphone and singing or lip-synching to the music. My waitress stayed at my side until I finished; a level of service I'd never experienced before.

The next day, I rented a car and driver and went to the rim of a volcano named Tagaytay, the most active in the area. The view of the crater's lake included a "small but deadly volcano" on an island that had killed three tourists a few years earlier. After a huge buffet and native dancing, we returned. On the road, we passed piles of pineapple. Although I was full of good food, at my driver's insistence, we stopped for a dessert of a whole pineapple eaten from the stock like a juicy ice cream cone.

Before I left, I got traveler's checks. I struggled to sign about twenty checks with two hands without my hand splint because I knew that I would probably have to sign the checks without my splint on the trip. As I was leaving the Philippines, I needed cash. So I went to a cashier to cash a check. I signed the check in front of him. When I handed it to him he said that the signatures didn't match and he wouldn't cash it. I was upset and afraid to sign additional checks that he wouldn't cash, so I asked him what I should do. He said that maybe the cashiers on the domestic side would cash the check.

The international side of the airport was cordoned off from the domestic side, so I had to go through a maze of checkpoints to get there. Now, I was concerned that they wouldn't accept the signed check. But, there was no problem and the cashier cashed it without seeing me sign it or asking for any further verification. I still don't know why it happened, but I was glad to take the money and leave the country.

On the plane, the Filipino woman sitting next to me had carried on two large shopping bags. When I asked what she was taking back to California, she said it was fish. I didn't smell anything, so I didn't ask anything more. We stopped at Honolulu to go through Customs and Immigration. It was my only time in Hawaii, but I had no time or money to stay and tour. I'd much rather have gone to Easter Island than walk the sands of Waikiki.

When we got back on the plane, I noticed that my seatmate had only one bag. She said that Customs had taken the fish. I still wonder if they only took half the fish or if she had something else in the second bag.

At the airport in San Francisco, my friend, Jack Swanson, and his family met me. His three sons were all taking pictures with flash cameras. It was a bit embarrassing until he told me there was no film in their cameras.

There was a lot of snow in Philadelphia, and my car had been buried in front of Roger's house most of the time I was gone. I returned to West Virginia and dove into my work. But the trip and those exotic places remain on my mind and I'd like to return to see them again someday.

Except for Germany at Christmas, much of the trip was in the tropics, so we dug the Monte Carlo out and returned to West Virginia  Feb 1978

# 15

## Reality in Higher Education

The house was okay after five weeks of neglect except that in our rush to pack we had failed to put a piece of plywood used as a fireplace cover in place. We were burning papers in preparation for Vitoon's move and forgot to put the plywood back. There were bird droppings and damage to the old couch and chair I'd inherited with the house. I put the plywood back and forgot about it.

Later that week, when I went to light a fire, I removed the plywood and discovered a dead Screech Owl that had flown down the fireplace and hit the plywood. That ended the mystery of what was in my house. I took the dead owl to the wildlife department at the university.

Soon after I got back, a student in our department had arranged a trip to Guatemala to explore native weaving and other technology. I was eager to go but had no vacation time left. Because it was a study trip, I was still justified in going. About a week before we were to depart, major earthquakes rocked the country. Thousands died and communication was disrupted. The tour was canceled.

We had developed a method for turning ideas into proposals that was working, but we needed to get funding if our work was to continue. Dissatisfied with our progress, Paul wrote a memo to me criticizing my work and inability to attract funds. My strong suite was proposal preparation, not the politics that goes into landing the big grants. I did take some intense trips to Washington, cultivating contacts, but I knew it would take years before my track record or persistence would pay off for the innovative projects we were proposing. Our proposals meeting funding agency requirements often weren't very good because of the restrictions in the requirements. Our best ideas, while received with interest, often proved unfundable. These were the ideas that would take years to gain acceptance in the funding community. Most projects were funded for one year, and many of ours were long-term projects, spanning several years.

On July1st, I was told to continue working, but it would be month to month as long as funds would hold out. I was determined to stick it out and dug into my work as never before.

My younger brothers had graduated from high school. Tom chose to study computer science at the local extension of the University of Wisconsin. This meant he would stay home for the first two years. Tim wanted to get away from home, so I agreed to take him in as he entered chemical engineering at West Virginia. He arrived in a '69 Austin America that he'd picked up that summer. Although it had only 40,000 miles, he stopped every 100 miles to check the oil as he drove out East and worried constantly about the automatic transmission, said to self-destruct in Austins of that mileage.

Tim wanted to pay his own way, so we looked for work he could do and study full time too. Luckily, Lakeview Inn and Country Club was hiring bus boys. The Inn was directly across the Lake and the nighttime hours did not interfere with class. He got some of his food there and I had the evenings free to work, so the arrangement worked out well. My only regret is that by working and staying with me, he missed out on many of the activities of his freshman class. That was a time I cherished as a full time resident student myself.

A neighbor had two Americas, a '69 and '70 for sale. I suggested that Tim buy them for parts. The green one was easy to tow home, but the yellow one was up on a nearby mountain. I enlisted a friend with a powerful '70 Barracuda to go fetch it. The car was back in the woods off a mountain road. With a few brush scratches we dragged the car off the mountain. My basement had been added to the house after it was built. Because of the steep slope the house was on, the basement had a high ceiling. It was also quite large, broken up only by the chimney and gas furnace in the left center as you entered the large single garage door. Through this door, we were able to get his and my cars in side-by-side, the green America left through the door in front of the sink and washer/dryer, and the yellow one left behind the furnace. That left room to store the 'Cuda friend's motorcycle for the winter and an electric car a fellow faculty member stored when he had no room out of the weather at his house.

Tim took to the situation quite well. He started to pick up the groceries and wash the dishes, jobs that were onerous and difficult for me. He also started doing bodywork on the green America. Tim corresponded with a best friend from high school who had entered West Point, Shawn Heckel. School seemed to take a back seat to all these activities. He was out of my way.

About this time, Raj announced that he was getting married and showed us a picture of a girl his family had found in England. He had seen her once when she was 13. Now she was seventeen and the families had decided on their marriage. I was amused that his father had finally found someone, but wasn't sure that it was real because Raj had had a series of liaisons with women going back to Texas. His stories of the strange places he'd been always enraptured the ladies.

It was fall and I wanted to get away from the grind of work. I could drive up to Cooper's Rock State Park and see deer from the car most any evening. On my best trip, I saw six bucks in different locations from near the Rock to the Henry Clay Iron Furnace three miles down the mountain. I saw no does so it must have been the rut that brought the bucks out. They would probably be hard to spot in the hunting season, but that night the sight of a big rack silhouetted against the sky up the mountain where a electric high wire cut through dense trees set my heart racing.

Later, I took Tim up to the same spot and told him to take the trail from Rock City down to the Furnace. Although I had explored the wonders of Rock City many times and had hiked the quarter mile to the Furnace on the lower trail, my previous experience on the mountain and steepness of that trail had kept me from it. That evening I dropped Tim off, and then drove down to the Furnace parking lot. I didn't see any deer. After waiting what seemed like an hour, Tim finally appeared. He had run the entire downhill trail, kicking up deer left and right, and, an occasional turkey. He was afraid of losing the trail in the coming darkness and hadn't taken time to savor the experience. I longed to be able to go that way down the mountain again, he dashed it off as mere exercise.

In early November, I pried him away from his activities for a day trip to the Monongahela National Forest. We took Mahfooz along. It was an overcast day, muting the usually brilliant fall colors. Once in the Forest we traveled a dirt road that was fast and level through the trees. Approaching a small rise up ahead at about fifty miles an hour, I saw what appeared to be deer in the road. As we got closer it became a flock of hen turkeys. I expected them to fly away, but they didn't. Finally, when I realized they weren't moving, I hit the brakes and slid into them. Turkeys and feathers flew everywhere, as we slid to a stop. While the dust cleared and the turkeys scattered, Mahfooz and I turned to each other with the same thought: "Why didn't you hit one?" I don't know how I didn't. Later, a wild turkey hunter told me that hens usually weigh about nine pounds. I would have liked to take a couple of them to Roger and Lin's for Thanksgiving.

By 11 am we dropped Mahfooz off at a trout lake to fish on the way up to the top of Spruce Knob. As we climbed the mountain, a Ruffed Grouse flew out of the ditch. I accelerated and caught the bird with my bumper. I stopped, backed up, and told Tim to go get it and throw it in the trunk. We then drove up to a picnic area and ate lunch, sheltered from the cold wind that was blowing fiercely. We went to the top, but didn't leave the car because it was so cold.

When we got back to Mahfooz, he was nearly frozen and had to taken refuge from the wind in the rest room. He had no luck with fish either and was glad to get back in my warm car.

We stopped at Blackwater Falls. I waited at the top while Mahfooz and Tim descended the many wooden steps to the Falls. I had been there in the early seventies and didn't want to navigate the rain-wet steps in the growing darkness. When they returned, I asked Mahfooz to check the trunk for me. He opened it, looked in and said, "Hey, where'd you get the chicken!"

Mahfooz cleaned the grouse in my basement sink when we got back to my house and ate it later that night. I didn't even get a taste. I'd rather have had turkey, anyway.

At Thanksgiving, Tim and I took his car and drove to Roger and Lin's. As we indulged in turkey, we thought what it would have been like to be eating a couple of those wild hens. I'd heard that they're pretty tough. After a pleasant weekend, we returned Sunday rather early. Things went well until late in the day when his America started missing. There were many hills and it got so we hoped for the crests so that we'd gain momentum on the downhill side. Finally, it was snowing and getting dark and we were halfway up Cheat Mountain, five miles and the last obstacle from home, when the America began to buck and lurch and finally died.

It started to snow heavily. A yellow VW Beetle came along. The student, driving back to WVU from his holiday, offered us a ride. We were home in ten minutes. As the VW snaked up the hill, headed for town in four inches of new snow, I was glad he had come along. I didn't relish the thought of spending the night in the car on the mountain. The next day, I dropped Tim by his car and drove six miles further, looking for a place to turn around and a garage in the next little town where there might be a wrecker. When I got back he had the car running—fouled plugs.

At Christmas, we drove to Wisconsin in my car. There was no snow so it was smooth all the way. We took a classmate of Tim's with us and dropped him off literally at an overpass on the Tri-State Tollway in Chicago. He had to climb up the bank to the highway above. Once we got to Mom and Dad's, I relaxed and Tim partied, and then it was time to return. Halfway back, on the Indiana Turnpike, I developed a fever and was grateful that Tim could take over driving. My fever got more intense as night approached. Finally, near Pittsburgh, we stopped and I loaded up with liquids before he drove me on home. I spent one day in bed. If I'd been driving alone, I never would have made it home.

It was a rough winter, but Tim put knobbies on the front and we always got through. In January, we got eight inches of snow one weekend. My neighbor had a new Dodge 4 x 4 with a plow and enjoyed plowing out the roads in the Park. The following Thursday night, it snowed an additional 13 inches, leaving 21 inches on the ground. This was too much snow for the City of Morgantown, but not for my neighbor, who plowed out our neighborhood Friday morning. Morgantown had sold its only snowplow, so the City and university were paralyzed.

We learned that one of our students, Linda Wigington, had spent the night stranded at the house that served as my office. State Highway 73 out front was plowed, so Tim and I decided to go in to town and rescue her. We drove the entire eight miles in a single lane the plow had opened. There were no cars on the road because the high banks had closed all driveways. The highway went right past the house on university Avenue, so it was easy to pick Linda up. We brought her back to my house and called her husband in rural Pennsylvania to tell him that she was all right.

The next day, we drove her back to Campus, dug her car out of the snow, and she headed home.

Raj got married by telephone. He told the faculty and staff to join him at his house to witness. Mahfooz stood by to assist with the ceremony, held in London, and relayed via telephone. The ceremony was at 4 o'clock so he told us to be there at 8 pm. When we arrived, Raj apologized for inviting us at the wrong time. He had received a call just before noon and had to hurriedly call Mahfooz. He got mixed up in his excitement and none of us thought that London time would be four hours later than ours.

137

We had a good time anyway. At more than one point I worried that there were too many of us on the 2nd story balcony that doubled as an entrance to his flat, and that it would fail. It didn't and I spent a lot of time out there.

In February Raj's wife, Shammi, arrived in the States. Raj's car was old and he needed moral support, so I offered to drive him to Kennedy Airport to pick her up. It was a ten-hour drive, so we stopped at my brother Roger's both ways to break up the distance. I thought it would be good to introduce Shammi to American family life, and my sister-in-law and nieces agreed.

As we approached New York, Raj became more anxious. Raj was not sure who he had married. To make matters worse, the police stopped us on the New Jersey Turnpike. They asked Raj all the questions, so I believe they stopped what they thought were a Black and a White in a suspicious car. They waved us on when they found out who we were.

The plane from London was a 747 with over three hundred passengers. Raj asked anyone who looked to be Indian if they had seen a girl on the plane, but no one had. He paced up and down in the runway worrying more and more as the last passengers passed us. She was nowhere in sight. Finally, a few minutes after the last passenger had filed out, she emerged smiling and resplendent in a green leisure suit and scarlet blouse. She explained that she had stopped to check her make up after the long flight. Raj was relieved, but far from relaxed, as he faced marriage to this beautiful young woman he hardly knew.

It was a good thing I was along, because it took the edge off the getting-to-know-you process. When we stopped for a couple of hours at Roger's, we were all able to relax, and they both slept some the rest of the way home.

One of our students was a Presbyterian minister. Raj wanted an American wedding, so we decided to have it at my house. The same gang was invited and we all had a good time. It was one of the high points in my life.

As president of the West Virginia Chapter of the World Future Society and with my longtime interest in the space program, when an opportunity to attend the 20/20 Conference in Huntsville came up, I jumped at the chance. The conference celebrated twenty years of space exploration and offered a dialogue on where the next twenty years would take us in space exploration. The day before I was to leave, a blizzard was predicted. The university was closed. Winds reached 70 mph but we got little snow. I was worried that I couldn't go on the trip. By nightfall, the wind had not died down, and my flight at 7 am the next morning looked threatened.

After our evening meal, I entered the living room to find a screech owl flying from wall to wall. This was perhaps the mate to the one that died in the fireplace the year before. It had found my chimney to get out of the weather. The owl ended up on the curtain rod in the dining room. I called Tim out of the kitchen. As he approached the owl flew. It startled him so much he knocked the TV stand over. The TV was OK, but we still had to get the owl out. We got a broom and I pushed it up under the owl's feet. Instinctively, the owl clutched hold of it and the broom became a roost. As I raised the broom, I was amazed how little this ten-inch tall creature weighed. It was literally as light as a feather. I carried it gingerly toward the back door, the owl glaring at me, while Tim held the door open. When I held the owl out in the wind, it wouldn't fly. I had to turn the broom upside down before the owl finally released its grip and flew away.

A few minutes later, I heard a scratching sound coming from the living room. The owl was in the fireplace, trying to get through the plywood covering the opening like it did before. I took the plywood out and got the broom again. After I let the owl go again in that cold, fierce wind, I thought about putting it up for the night in the basement. I left the plywood off in case it came back again. The owl had scratched a triangular-shaped hole in the bottom and managed to squeeze through.

Soon after that, the power went off. We went to bed early as the temperature dropped and the wind howled. Lights were on across the lake, so in the worst case I would have Tim help me get my 93 year old neighbor, Mr. Cuthbert, and drive over to Lakeview Inn. As I lie awake, shivering even though all the blankets I had were on the bed, I forgot about the owl coming back and worried more about being able to catch my plane in the morning. I was relieved when the power was restored about 11 o'clock, but rested uneasily until morning.

The morning was clear and cold, and the wind was gone. My flight to Pittsburgh was on time. When I got to Pittsburgh, the airport was filled with travelers who had been stranded for two days. My flight out was delayed, and then rerouted through Nashville and Memphis. I finally arrived in Huntsville about ten o'clock. There was no transportation to the Conference or even to town so I called a cab and finally settled in my room very late, exhausted and disoriented.

The Conference was better than I expected. I met members of Werner Von Braun's team who had lashed Explorer to the top of a Redstone rocket and put us in space after the failure of Vanguard. I also got to see Baker, the Chimpanzee that was part of the pair of Chimps that preceded men in space travel. The high point of the weekend was the keynote address by Hugh Downs. Stripped of the restraints required by his television persona, Downs echoed my thoughts about the exhilarating opportunity for space exploration and travel, and the potential for intelligent life elsewhere in the universe.

Back in Morgantown, Tim became disillusioned with school and work and being away from his buddies from high school. At the end of the spring semester, he sold the green Austin America, junked the yellow one, and returned to Wisconsin. I was about to embark on another great adventure at the same time.

When I arrived back from my trip around the world, I was told of a travel-study tour to Guatemala two of my colleagues had put together, scheduled for the end of February. I didn't have any vacation, but planned to go anyway for the educational value of the trip, that would include exploring technologies used in the region. A week before we were scheduled to leave, a devastating earthquake struck, thousands died, and our trip was canceled.

A year had passed, and, although it was the rainy season, the tour was rescheduled for June. Our small group was to pick up another small group in Miami, and then continue on to Guatemala City. The flight from Pittsburgh to Miami was the same distance as the one from Miami, but the shift in climate, culture, and geography was much more dramatic.

The earthquakes of the previous year had been accompanied by increased volcanic activity. As we flew into Guatemala City, El Fuego (The Flame) was erupting, spewing smoke high into the stratosphere and lava down its sides. I was excited.

At the International Airport we rented a Toyota van that nicely carried the eleven of us and our luggage. Two elderly ladies, who had shared a seat row from Miami with me, lost their luggage and had to wait three days before it caught up with them. The tour leaders had promised lodging and board at a price we couldn't refuse, a dollar a day! We were to stay in the family compound of a friend in the village of San Antonio, nestled in a valley at the base of El Feugo. We were promised that the outdoor accommodations would be comfortable and that the food would be good. However, the friend couldn't be reached. Family members said she was in Miami, so we were on our own.

We drove out of Guatemala City on a long boulevard flanked by American companies into the mountains, sixty miles to Antigua. Antigua, destroyed at least four times by quakes, was the Capitol city until its unstable earth forced the government to the firmer ground of Guatemala City. Nestled in the mountains at 6000 feet at the base of the volcano, Agua (Water), Antigua was a small, but vibrant center for trade and artistry. Colorful hand-woven fabric was everywhere evident in this picturesque land.

We waited in the central square while the tourist bureau found us housing. The group was split three ways. I headed with about half the group to a German-owned resort, El Roserio, on the outskirts of town. On the way, at a corner, we could see lava flowing a third of the way down El Feugo. The next day, the lava flow was gone and we never saw any eruptions the rest of the trip. I shared a large room in a dormitory-like structure with two other guys for about five dollars apiece. The resort was on the edge of town. The view from the balcony was dense jungle, filled with a cacophony of sounds that rivaled rush hour traffic. Instead of large, dangerous, unseen animals, this din was created by many different kinds of birds, each with its own way to call out to others. In the morning, I stood on that balcony for a long time, taking in the sounds and watching huge ravens fly over like bombers with a mission into the forest.

The next morning, we left by van for a three-day trip to the interior. Each Indian group, most descendants of the Mayas, has its own way of weaving, clothing, and colors like the Scottish clans. We went to San Antonio first. The long mountain road into the village was lined with roadside vendors, each hawking their woven red cloth patterns. As expected, the friend was not there, so we continued on to Lake Atitlan.

We traveled over newly paved, earthquake-damaged roads, winding in and out of mountain passes to some of the most spectacular landscapes on the planet. The volcanic soil was very rich. In some regions, the mountainsides were terraced with rows of corn at several stages of maturity growing together. The plots were small and hand-tilled, broken occasionally with patches of blooming irises, cannas, other flowers, and groups of banana plants. The road leading to Lake Atitlan reached 12,000 feet, passing beautiful villas clinging to the mountainsides with breathtaking views of the water 4,000 feet below. We stopped in Panajachel, a lakeside resort and artist community, for the night.

A block from our hotel, after our evening meal, we came upon the strong odor of onions. Just around the corner, under the awning over a board walkway, a huge pile of onions lined the wall. A group of farmers, mostly women, was busy cutting them up, creating an eye-searing atmosphere. In the morning, when I returned to see the results of their work, the boardwalk was bare and there was no evidence of the activity of the night before.

I went to the post office to mail a postcard. It was a small building, maybe ten feet wide. There was a single counter with one postman behind it. Several people clamored for his attention with no regard for waiting in line or courtesy to their fellow customers. I finally got the postage I requested and left with a new respect for the US Postal Service.

Atitlan is a large, natural lake set at the base of three 13,000-foot volcanoes. It is on the continental divide and the Pan American Highway. The next morning we drove up the Highway toward Mexico. Our first stop was Monostonango. Located twelve miles off the Pan American Highway by dirt road, Monostonango offered the best wool blankets. On the road in, we saw beautiful orchids hanging from trees. It was against the law to take them, but we saw many for sale in the markets. There was a huge market, located in the center of town. We saw few Americans, and it was refreshing.

We returned to Atitlan for the night. The next day at noon we took the mail boat across the lake to Santiago, an Indian village of lava rock and thatch, with yet another, market. Although I saw pictures of huge bass, the fish in the market were only four to six inches, a sign of over fishing. The lake was majestic, nestled amid its three volcanoes, but rather barren.

In the market, little girls were selling bean necklaces. I thought my nieces might like them, so I bargained with a girl for two, down to 25 centavos. When I reached for my money, I had no change. The girl, about seven years old, was very disappointed. Later, I got some change and approached her again in the crowd. This time she was frightened, cried and tried to run from me, probably thinking I was playing a cruel trick. Somehow, I convinced her to stop and listen, confirmed the price, and gave her the money. Her face lit up in delight, having made the sale, and I left knowing that I'd not left her and her family thinking that I was a cruel American who tricked little girls.

Back in Antigua, I was tired of markets, so asked the local tourist bureau about climbing Agua. The man told me that Agua required a guide and that I shouldn't go because it was the rainy season. He recommended instead that I visit the Candeleria, a 400-foot hill on the outskirts of town, lined with candles, some kind of shrine. It was obvious that he didn't think me capable of the climb and he angered me when he thought I'd be interested in local religious superstition instead. I was determined to go.

I was now staying in a little "Holiday Inn," the Santa Lucia Guest House, built after the quake to house overflow tourists not booked in local resorts and hotels. It was nice and cheap. I paid a small boy the equivalent of $3.50 in quetzals in the furniture less lobby each day to stay there. Santa Lucia was ten blocks from the nearest restaurant, but near bus routes. The others in our party were in other locations, so I had to walk to see them. There was no telephone. Each night, I linked up with the two old ladies for dinner. Otherwise, I was on my own. As their unofficial guardian, I walked them back to the German resort. At night all the doors and entrances to the courtyards were boarded up, making the narrow walled streets quite barren. One night walking back it started to rain. I was walking quickly, head down, along the wall on the narrow sidewalk, when I ran into wrought iron window bars in my path that stuck out about six inches from the wall. I was knocked off my feet and my glasses went flying. But the lady with me helped me pick myself up from the wet pavement. My face was skinned but nothing was broken.

On a second trip, we headed for Chichicastanango further north up the Pan American highway. Chichi is a famous tourist site, noted for its display of the villagers' religion, a mix between Mayan and Roman Catholic rituals. The high point of my visit there was dinner at a new hotel, built after the quake, complete with marimba band and hummingbirds in the courtyard. I was tired of markets.

On the way back we stopped at IXMHE, a Mayan ruin in the high mountains. The site was small and not impressive, but I was having trouble walking on the steps of the ruins, so I didn't explore it fully. We stopped at a village of thirty thousand that was reduced to rubble and corrugated steel roofs after the quake took five thousand lives. The tile roofs were now corrugated galvanized steel panels because so many villagers died from falling tile. The place took on the tin shack look of so many slums instead of the picturesque look of adobe and red tile. The quake took the beauty and the spirit of the place. Villagers now wore polyester flowered shirts and carried plastic water pots instead of the native wool shirts and clay pots. This strange aberration was a direct result of US relief after the devastation and it was sad to see.

All the walking and light meals were doing me good. My pants were falling down, but I was walking stronger each day.

143

I caught up with George Maughan, our tour leader, and asked him if he and Gay would join me on my trek up the mountain the next day, Friday. I'd already decided to go to Tikal on Saturday and there were no more days left in the tour. George said that he had planned to go but the missing weaver friend had returned to San Antonio and everyone was invited for the day. No one wanted to go to Tikal with me either, so I borrowed plane fare of $90 and planned to do that alone, too.

That night I got back to my room about 10 pm. I was excited about my climb the next day so wanted to go right to sleep. My room was open to the interior of the guesthouse. Two young women and a man came in late and made noise talking and laughing. The noise kept me up a long time.

I left about 5 am, walking the streets that led out of town to the road to the village of Santa Maria de Jesus, on the route George had showed me to the dormant volcano, Agua. I expected to catch an early bus to the village, but there were none, so I walked and enjoyed the cool morning. There was no place to eat, but I passed a bakery on the way out of town, the sweet, irresistible aroma hit me as I passed the open door and beckoned me in. Amid an unbelievable array of breads, cakes, cookies, and snacks, all based on corn meal or flour, I bought two corn flour rolls for 15 centavos. I ate one as I walked, saving the other for lunch. I'd planned to travel light. The roll was the only thing I was carrying in my bag except my Antigua map.

After seeing no buses, I asked someone where they were. They told me the first bus wasn't until 8 am. I decided to keep walking until one came along. About two miles out of town a large open truck passed, filled with about fifty troops. I thought nothing of it because the Guatemala Army was everywhere, often setting up roadblocks to check for rebels or people traveling illegally through the country.

Finally, about five miles out, a bus came along and I got my ride to the village and the start of the trail. I was the only American among the few passengers. We were deposited in a large, empty, and treeless square that probably served as a soccer field and market on market days. Most villages held market days once or twice a week.

The locals evaporated and I was alone. I drank deeply from a public fountain and walked out of the village. The sun was already high and I decided to turn back if it got too tough going up. Each street heading up the mountain became a trail heavily traveled by people and cattle as they made their way either to fields or the forest each day. All the trails merged to a single road that snaked its way back and forth up the mountain. The main walking trail took a more direct route up, sometimes crossing, sometimes merging, with the road. The trail was a concave of hard packed mud and rather easy walking.

I was alone as I left the village and the lower fields for the tattered forest higher up. Many years of grazing and wood gathering had decimated the forest. It was an hour before I reached trees of any size. Most of the small trees showed scars from machetes.

I passed two boys with a burro. One said "Buenos dais" and held out his hand. He gave me a small, green apple. I was grateful and decided to save it for lunch.

Finally, I was on the road in tall trees. The road was badly rutted and steep. The air was getting thin and cool, but the sun was hot. I ate my roll and the tart, green apple. I wished I had some water, but in its place, the apple was refreshing. I passed a road crew. They looked like criminals and probably were. I joked to them about my red "Gringo" nose and was glad to leave them behind.

Up ahead, an Army truck had to jockey back and forth to make a sharp curve. It looked like the one I'd seen in the morning and probably was. It too, was filled with troops.

Soon, I reached the tree line and the landscape was mostly red cinders and eroded ravines. The view opened up and I could see Antigua at about 5000 feet below to the north, its white buildings forming a square surrounded by green jungle. To the east, I could see Santa Maria about 2500 feet below, and beyond that the expanse of coastal jungle leading to the Caribbean Sea. I passed a concrete block shelter and headed up the steep road toward the top.

I came upon three young people on the road. My legs were screaming in pain, so I had to stop every few feet to let them rest. But, I was not having trouble breathing. A young man was lying on his back and said that he was sick. Two girls were tending him. They said that they were students from the University of Iowa. I asked them if they had any water, but they had drunk all they had. Maybe that's why the guy was sick. I decided to head on up and they said that they would catch up.

It got tougher and tougher to walk, until I was taking only three steps before I had to rest. I was hot from exertion, but the cold wind tore at my exposed arms and face, cooling them from the burning sun. At the base of the final cinder cone to the top, two soldiers rested by a Jeep. I approached them and said "Agua?" asking for water, but the older one, who appeared to be an officer, shook his head and waved me away with his rifle. I skirted the cone to the left of their position, looking for a place to go up, and to find water. Tufts of moss and grass clung to the shifting steep slope of ash to the top. Some of these tufts were large enough to collect the daily rains and mist that accompanied the clouds constantly colliding with the mountain. Where they overhung eroded ash below, droplets of water were constantly falling, beginning their descent leading to mighty rivers far below. I looked around for cans or discarded cups that thoughtless tourists often leave in such places, but I found none. There was no way I could collect the drops. So, I sat below one of the largest tufts, lay back and opened my mouth. The cool, pure water dripped, not always from the same spot, into my mouth.

I stayed there resting for fifteen minutes or so until I got restless to be on my way. I got little water, maybe a mouthful, and decided that I would have had to stay all day to completely quench my thirst. Fast moving clouds obscured the top of the cone. After several attempts to climb upward on the shifting red ash, and sliding back down, I decided that I didn't have the strength or agility to climb into the crater. I passed the two resting soldiers and returned down the road.

Now, I saw the full expanse of how far I'd come. It seemed that I could see all the way to the Caribbean Sea, and I'm sure, the Pacific beyond El Feugo, if I was on the west slope. Below, Santa Maria de Jesus seemed so far away, but I new that steady downhill walking would bring me to it. After a short walk, I came upon the shelter, sitting below the road on a leveled foundation of ash to the left. A trough on its corrugated metal roof funneled water into a large barrel.

I trotted down the steep trail leading to the shelter and over to the barrel. It was uncovered. Heavy moss clung to the sides, but the water was crystal clear all the way to the mossy bottom. I stuck my face in and drank deep. It would be easy from here.

I started up the trail to the road. About halfway up, I lost my balance and fell backward on the cinders. I rolled, so, although I got a bit dirty, I didn't hurt myself. I got back up on unsteady legs, grateful that I wasn't hurt, and more respectful of the toll the day had taken on my body, and carefully worked my way up to the road.

The road and trail were easy going downhill, so I moved along at a good pace. About half way, it got dark and ominous, so I began to worry. I was on the trail and it was a concave of hard-packed mud, smooth and easy to walk on when dry, but possibly a slippery, muddy slide, when wet. I knew now why they warned me about the season. I rushed now, hoping to get as far as I could before it rained and I'd have to leave the trail for shelter.

The thunder rumbled but the danger passed and I reached the village. About half way to the square, I passed a store that sold pop. I entered a room filled with bottles in cases. Showing the clerk what I wanted, I pointed to a bottle of orange soda near the bottom of a stack of crates. To my surprise, she reached down, lifted the crates and retrieved the bottle I pointed to! I gave her the equivalent of five cents and walked out with a very dusty, but refreshing, reward for my climb.

While waiting for a bus in the square, the sky opened up. It was a short downpour, but I was glad to be under the awning, wondering about those kids still up on the mountain. I got back to my motel about 4:30 and joined the old ladies at the hotel that evening for dinner. They had enjoyed their lunch in San Antonio, but were tired of markets too and envious of my stories of the mountain.

Late that night, I caught up with the students from Iowa at the motel. They were the same ones who had kept me awake the night before. The guy had recovered from his sickness and made it to the top. They had gone to the right of the two soldiers and climbed the cone to an opening where they could enter the crater. The clouds were thick, but they could hear yelling. Then, the clouds lifted and the yelling was troops playing soccer in the bottom of the crater! Some of the troops were playing chess and generally having fun during their high altitude training. There was also a chapel built in the crater. Since I never saw it, I don't know how big it was. They said they didn't get rained on, so they were as lucky as I was.

The next morning, I caught a bus for Guatemala City about 8 am. Buses often raced for a fare and I was the prize of one of those scuffles. For about 65 cents, or a penny a mile, the bus took me to Guatemala City. I caught another bus for a short ride to the domestic airport. Our flight, at $90 with money I'd borrowed, via DC-6, took us directly to the coastal jungle site of Tikal.

The DC-6 was comfortable, with wide seats and big windows. When we reached Tikal, our pilot circled and banked the plane so that we could see the site. Set in a sea of trees, the ruins rose up above them in a geometric pattern that survived 600 years of jungle growth. Tikal was once a city of 30,000 people, covering 24 square miles. The University of Pennsylvania had worked ten years, removing centuries of growth from the structures, and had uncovered only a fourth of the complex.

We landed on a dirt runway. The dust flying and the jungle surrounding the vintage plane made it seem like I was in an old movie, landing in another time and place. We ate lunch at the Jungle Lodge, a rustic and outdoorsy hotel, where tourists could experience "roughing it" with outdoor showers in a hotel setting.

After lunch I joined a tour group led by a young expatriate from North Carolina everyone called "Jungle Jim". After touring the museum that sheltered the bones of a Mayan chieftain burdened in death with silver and jade from New Mexico, as well as exquisite art from the former inhabitants, we ventured out into the great plazas, palaces, and pyramids.

I joined the group climbing up on the Palace and saw a spider monkey in the tree canopy nearby. But I felt insecure, constantly worried about tripping on the uneven rocks or falling on the steep steps. And then, I watched as even old ladies grabbed hold of cables and climbed the Pyramid of the Jaguar and other monuments. I could only watch, content in the thought that the day before I had stood at 12,500 feet on a volcano I'd climbed alone.

On the flight back, the only evidence of the rainy season was the puffy clouds our pilot shirted on the way back over steamy jungle to the cool air of the mile high capital. I walked up the aisle and watched the pilot fly the plane through the open curtain to the cockpit.

Even losing a half hour when a cab driver took me to the center of the city rather than the highway to Antigua to catch a bus, I still got back in time to share my stories of the day with my lady friends at dinner. On the way back to Miami the next day, George told me that he had climbed Agua alone while I was at Tikal. Gay had allergies to the jungle vegetation and decided not to go. A week later, George gave me photos he'd taken on his climb; it was a nice memento to show family and friends of where I'd been.

About the first of the year, I had agreed to work on half salary because we had not received enough grant money to cover my salary for the rest of the fiscal year that ended June 30. It was hard because my pay hardly covered my house payment. But my savings from earlier and Tim's willingness to buy all the groceries carried me through. Before July 1st, I got word that my contract would not be continued, so I began a job search.

Dressed in my Sagan turtleneck, my leisure jacket, and platform shoes,
my resume photo gave the impression of a confident young professor.

# 16

# Heading South

I made many applications, but opportunities were slow in coming, so I focused on painting the house to make it more saleable. Originally, I enlisted Tim, but he wasn't interested, so I started painting myself and got the help of Mahfooz and another student I hired to do the trim and high places I couldn't reach. I surprised myself with how well I did the interior trim and doors, but the porch was a challenge. I had to use the stepladder to reach the white washed ceiling. The old whitewash was flaking off along with sawdust from dry rot. Reaching up, paint would run down my arm and onto the floor. Covered with paint, I'd have to stop painting often and wash down the green enamel floor. Mahfooz finally helped me finish the ceiling.

The house had white asbestos siding that didn't require painting. But the basement on the lake side beneath the porch formed a concrete block wall ten feet high. There was about two feet of level ground next to the wall, and then the yard dropped steeply down to a lower stone wall, three feet high. There wasn't enough room to set up the stepladder, so I was forced to lean it, closed, up against the wall. With a roller or large brush and paint pail in my hands, I had to work my way up to the second step from the top to reach the top of the block wall. Reaching up from there put strain on my back and legs trying to keep me balanced on the ladder as I struggled to paint with my chest held tight against the wall.

At the worst point, above a native laurel about four feet high that bloomed each spring, I lost the fine balance I'd tried to keep, and, paint pail and brush flying, fell backward off the wall, over the laurel and on my back, head down, onto the steep slope below. I slid down the slope, rolled, and came to my knees, unhurt. When I looked up, I'd fallen over twelve vertical feet. No one saw what happened. I gathered up my equipment, repositioned the ladder, and climbed back up with a new respect for my luck and that wall.

Rushing in to grab the phone with paint on my hands, I may have missed some job offers. I interviewed at Waynesburg College for a position doing coordination of grants and contracts. Although I had a cordial visit with the president, it was obvious he couldn't get enough funding to pay for the position.

More promising was a job as Training director for a pumped storage facility to be built in the Virginia Mountains by Daniel Construction Company. Daniel, and then the world's largest construction company, needed someone on site. A campus interview with a former WVU graduate went well, so I was invited to Greenville, SC, to company headquarters. As I reached the airport to return home, the old nemesis arose again. I was told that the job was "too dangerous"... not the work that I would do, but the drive on the mountain road to the site. This fellow Mountaineer seemed to have learned nothing of my ability to drive, or my ability to run a training program, only that somehow my disability made it impossible for me to do the job... at least in the eyes of someone already in the company.

I didn't press the issue. I didn't want to work for anyone who felt that I couldn't do any aspect of a job. The fact is that questions people continually asked about my ability to clean, cook, and drive, especially from family members who should have known what I could do, led me to understand the suspicion, deep down, that most people felt about the ability of a man with withered arms and hands to do the ordinary tasks of life, let alone the responsibilities of a leadership or supervisory position. A gimp, however experienced and educated, did not present the appearance corporate America wanted in its leaders.

An opportunity presented itself in August. I accepted an offer of an Associate Professorship in the Graduate School of Business at Atlanta University. Atlanta University was a private, predominantly Black institution founded in 1865. AU's degrees were all graduate degrees, supported by several small four-year colleges in the Atlanta University Center.

I continued my interest in research, but was met with some opposition from my colleagues, some of whom were suspicious of my credentials, especially my doctorate in education. I taught Public Policy and Private Enterprise. The university's director of grants and contracts met with me once, but was uninterested in sharing the limelight for any funds the university would receive, so he never followed-up on my offer to help.

A magnet for the Fortune 500 companies, the Graduate School of Business Administration attracted students from Black institutions all over the country and from several foreign countries. The students ranged from highly-motivated, intelligent individuals with excellent undergraduate preparation, to poorly-prepared leftovers from academically poor schools who hadn't gotten jobs. Many were seeking an MBA without any idea why they were studying for a degree except to get a job.

The course, Public Policy and Private Enterprise, was about ideas and how they affect business. I was challenged from the start because I was White and didn't have any experience running a business. I told them that, if they were interested in starting a business, and then graduate school wasn't for them. If they were interested in graduate study, and then corporate America might hire them, as long as they did well in school and showed promise in management or other disciplines.

The ideas presented in the course stirred controversy. My first semester the Dean, Augustus Sterne, called me into his office and showed me a hate letter a student had written anonymously accusing me of racism. He was clearly upset and seemed to believe that I was the cause of all the hate the student expressed. Although the letter clearly was from someone mentally disturbed and shouldn't have been given any credence, Sterne never trusted me again.

The course developed a response that gravitated to two poles. Students either loved me or hated me. Since I presented a wide range of ideas, students assumed that ones I believed in and either liked them or hated them. It was hard for most Blacks to accept the ideas embraced by corporate America when corporate America was not developed or run by Blacks. Young Black men particularly had trouble accepting their role in large organizations.

However, Black Africans did not have centuries of response to prejudice to deal with and Black American women accepted diverse opinions more readily than their male peers. The first semester was rough, but after that I began to enjoy the course and the students, and the diversity they brought to the learning table.

The second semester, I was given one section of Business Statistics. After a week, two thirds of my students dropped the course. Assistant Dean George Neffinger called me in and asked me what I was doing to cause the students to abandon ship. Since I hadn't graded anyone yet, I didn't know. Later, I found out that I was using the recommended text while the other instructor opted to use a popular crib book of example problems sold in bookstores. The students thought that since I was using a textbook, that my course would be harder.

I developed a set of transparencies illustrating the text concepts more clearly and copied them for the students. I told them to follow my notes and write notes on my notes. It worked. After that first semester, students took my section for what they could learn and they surprised me with their success. Of course, there were always those who didn't take the course until they were sure of an "easy" professor. I was never considered easy.

One student complained that he couldn't miss a class because he would miss too much. I wasn't strict about attendance. I was primarily concerned that the students covered the material and completed all assignments. One student who was in sales and traveled a lot, appeared in all my sections and missed a couple of classes, but he got an A because he worked with me to complete all the requirements and tests.

I continued my involvement in the World Future Society and my personal research as I sought to establish myself in the research community. In the fall of 1978, I attended a conference on the Future of Education at the Clear Lake campus of the University of Houston. It was an opportunity to see the Johnson Spacecraft Center, the site of my early dream career, but now only a tourist stop on my quest for a place in higher education.

The conference, held in a new, high tech campus all in one building, was predictable, but the thing that stayed with me was Houston. I arrived at Intercontinental Airport about 10 pm. A bus was waiting to take people to Clear Lake. It was hot and humid. After a long wait, the near empty bus drove off into the night on an endless freeway of run down, garish business places that lit up both sides of the freeway with their own form of eye pollution.

I decided that this was what unbridled business growth brought and preached it in my classes. I vowed never to live in a place like that. In the spring of 1979, I presented a paper on "Coping" at a conference at Middle Tennessee State University. I was convinced that I could establish myself as a business catalyst and critic and a viable contributor to the growing knowledge about business enterprise. National recognition was only a matter of time.

My colleagues viewed me with suspicion and doubt. Some doubted my motives as an atheist. Some doubted my doctorate in education and my background in engineering. Some doubted my lack of involvement in a personal business. And, no doubt, some doubted my ability because of my disability. My only ally was the man who hired me, George Neffinger, the assistant dean.

I shared my apartment for a while with Robert Henry, a former salesman who marketed himself as a marketing professor. We were not close because he was from the old school and disagreed with my ideas, approach to teaching, and concern for learning. He taught basic marketing by anecdotes from his experience in business. I taught ideas and problems from cases affecting business, especially emerging technologies like the increased use of computers. He lectured and gave multiple-choice tests. I illustrated concepts with visual aids (that he despised), led discussions, and tested through essay and short answer questions.

Bob Henry hopped from school to school, negotiating higher annual teaching contracts with each one, while his wife kempt a home base as a teacher in Westchester County, New York. He was milking the system for all he could get before retiring. I was trying to establish myself in my profession at one institution.

In January, I got an opportunity to test my resolve. I had an interview for a research associate position at an MIT think tank on technology and social change. I took a day off from my classes and headed for frozen Boston. It was cold, about 30° below zero, so I was confined to my motel room until just before my interview. To stay out of the cold, I had lunch at the cafeteria until my appointment. The dungeon-like cafeteria was midwinter dirty, busy, and dreary. Unlike other interviews, I ate alone. The interview in a converted brick laboratory building went well, but everything was dependent on funding. The best part of the trip was taking off, finally warm again, as the sunset glowed red behind the Boston skyline.

Dining room of the solar passive efficient home I built 1980-2001.

6055 Highview Drive. 8 miles from Atlanta on Bear Mountain. My retreat.

# 17

# A Dream of My Own

I was tired of moving. Trying to establish a home base of my own, I'd bought the land in Irvington and the cottage on Cheat Lake. I didn't want to spend my life in apartments and high rises like Bob Henry. I wanted a place where I could retreat and read and write, commune with nature, and develop a circle of lasting friends—and perhaps get married and have children.

My apartment was on the west side of Atlanta on Bear Mountain near Six Flags, three miles from the Chattahoochee River. It was only eight miles to work, but the area had undeveloped land and was more rural than suburban. My apartment balcony faced a wooded hillside. A wren raised a family in a fern I hung on the balcony. The woods were mixed conifers and deciduous trees and presented a constantly changing view with the seasons. It was especially beautiful in spring when the white dogwood blooms filled the space beneath the pines. Walks on the hillsides revealed wild azalea of many varieties and hue. I wanted a piece of this land.

I looked at houses and land in the area. Houses were cheap, but they tended to be basic three-bedroom ranch-style on flat lots carved out of the trees and hillsides. The newer homes and developments were more interesting, taking advantage of the hilly, wooded lay of the land to create houses angled on curving streets in a more relaxed, rural style. Many of these houses were contemporary, with great rooms, sunken areas and more interesting, open layouts. These houses, too, were often small, on small lots, and made from the cheapest of materials.

After looking at new homes in several developments, I found one with a layout I really liked, except I wanted to swap the kitchen and dining room around and add higher quality windows, roofing and other interior improvements. The model, built by Benchmark Homes, had unique, overhanging closets on the outside walls of the bedrooms, providing roof overhang for the windows, more insulation from the closet contents, and a tight configuration for bedroom access. Sliding doors on the master bedroom balcony and the dining room deck provided passive solar potential if the back of the house had southern exposure.

Benchmark said that they would work with me, either building on a lot in one of their developments, or on a lot I'd provide. I set about sketching alternate floor plans and elevations showing how I wanted the house to look. Many houses in the area were being sided with red cedar. While I liked the look of the new cedar, I was concerned with how it would age. I found out that cedar would require no painting or stain, would weather to a natural wood look, and probably last longer than any other covering. The contractor was also using galvanized gutters and downspouts that required no paint. A house that blended into the natural beauty of the Georgia woods seemed to be the right way to go.

I was concerned about energy and decided to use all that I'd learned to make the house as efficient as I could without installing experimental, unproved systems. I attended all the home shows and sought out as many energy-saving, maintenance-saving, and convenience-providing features as I could find. I chose triple pane casement windows with interior storm and screen panels for easy changing and cleaning from inside the house. These wood windows had anodized aluminum exterior trim to eliminate painting. I added a half-inch of Styrofoam to the walls to increase their insulation value to R-25. Styrofoam kernels in the attic raised the ceiling R-value to 35. I used fluorescent lights in the kitchen, bathrooms, and basement and plenty of 3-way switches so that I could easily turn off all the many decorative and exterior lights. I added an energy efficient fireplace that could be used to heat the house, and an electric heat pump for heating and cooling.

For convenience, the plan had the washer/dryer located at the bedrooms. The kitchen space was designed so that I could move heavy, slippery, or hot items around on the counters to avoid the spills and other small disasters my paralyzed hands often caused. The oven was placed at waist height for the same reason. All surfaces were smooth and seamless for easy cleaning, including the smooth top range built into the counter. A lazy Susan built under the counter corner became the center for easy access to cooking materials. An open counter and doors on both sides of the kitchen cabinets facing the dining room made it easy to set and clean the dining room table. I added outlets for a central vacuum system to be housed in the basement and outlets and coaxial wiring throughout the house for use by computers and cable TV systems in the future.

The bathrooms included washerless faucets, Corning fiberglass tub and shower enclosures, imitation marble seamless, easy-to-clean sink and counter tops, and tile floors. I added closet space in several areas and combined shelving and clothes racks in some for improved use. The basement contained two single car garages with a space between for storage. A lower level provided a space that I could plumb and wire for a small apartment

I sold my land in Irvington. I also sold my cottage and half my land on Cheat Lake. The other half of the land took longer to sell. Eventually, I sold that piece too, to a young man who wanted to build an energy-efficient chalet overlooking the lake.

I too, wanted lake property or view property. I looked at houses and land on four lakes. Each one turned out to be undesirable because the land was generally unsuitable for building. I was drawn to one development on a mountain with established older homes. The view of the Atlanta skyline to the east was spectacular, especially in the glow of the waning sun of evening. There was a spot on the road that opened to a view of Stone Mountain, lying like some giant beached whale in the green rolling hills twenty miles distant, ten beyond the outcropping of buildings marking Atlanta city center. This spot was equally as high as the famous landmark, on the opposite side of the city. An architect I knew, Frank LeGate, had built on this overlook. I checked on two lots left on that road. Both were too expensive and too steep to build on without resorting to pilings.

A few blocks east, there were houses and lots for sale along Highview Drive. At the end of the street, a drive curved off to the left. This driveway crossed the earthen dam for a small, three-acre lake, and then curved into the back of a large ranch-style house. Two lots remained on Highview just before the lake. After that, the strip of land between the lake and the street was too narrow to develop. The first lot was 100 foot wide and the second 150. Together, they were 268 feet deep to the creek bed below dividing the space between Highview and the next street east. I stood one autumn day on the slope under the trees overlooking the lake. It seemed like a wonderful place to build a house.

Horace Bolton owned a furniture store on the Bankhead Highway and the land I was interested in. He was developing the land, lot-by-lot, building small three bedroom houses, and then selling them. The builder, JT Green, was a local contractor who did most of the work himself with his son. Bolton said he'd build one of the models they were building or he'd sell me the land and I could build what I wanted. I showed JT my plans and he said that he could build the house on a cost plus basis. Having seen the quality of his work already on the street, I decided to buy the lots and go with him.

When we went to the bank for financing, I showed the banker my sketches and JT showed his estimates of the cost. It wasn't good enough. The bank wanted formal plans before loaning the money I needed, even though I had enough money to cover nearly half the cost. With the proper drawing tools, I was capable of drawing the plans, but I lacked the tools and the time to do it. I would have to hire an architect to get approval of the plans and I didn't want to pay an architect to assume or even dispute my ideas. Besides, most of the upgrades I requested added to the cost per square foot. Lenders were reluctant to put this kind of quality into a small house. I was trying to build a quality house of modest proportions that I could afford to live in. The dollars and cents guys would allow higher quality only in larger, more expensive to operate, houses. As a consequence, many of the larger houses I looked at in developments were cheaply built to provide a reasonable initial cost.

I was discouraged and started to look at newer houses that were on the market with mortgages I could assume. Invariably the site locations, layouts, or quality of these houses left me cold. After living in over twenty apartments and owning both an ideal building site and a cottage on a lake, I wasn't willing to buy a bit of standard suburbia as my American Dream.

I decided to go back to Benchmark. They agreed to build my house but they wanted me to do it their way. After a three-hour negotiating session, we agreed on what to include in the specifications. Kip Berry, a young University of Georgia graduate that I liked, agreed to manage the project. I would get a construction loan that Kip would draw on. The construction loan would convert to a conventional loan when the house was built.

When I pulled out from the curb leaving the meeting, I felt a bump and stopped. I was in such a daze after that grueling, intense meeting that I'd left my briefcase next to the car and driven over it. Although it was damaged slightly, its contents, including my handsplint, were okay.

Back at school, things were going okay too. Gradually, I was winning the confidence of the students, especially the international ones, and the ones who were better prepared and came to study. In business statistics, my classes were small, but my technique of providing handwritten notes of my examples was working and my students began to show real progress. My course in public policy and private enterprise was gaining a reputation as I worked out a way to present it. The debates I held on business issues near the end of the course were quite popular, but my required reading and course paper forced some students to switch their major to accounting, the only major that didn't have my course as a requirement. I never got to teach production management, my forte, but I was pleased with the progress I was making.

My acceptance by the faculty was mixed. Some accepted me socially and collegially, while others remained aloof and distant. I started a research committee and wrote a proposal for funding with Ted Rankin to investigate the causal factors involved in Black business failure. We were not funded. I tried to involve myself in the club and social activities of our students, and to attend all functions of the school. Since I wasn't married and didn't have a girlfriend, my social calendar was free to participate, and the students came to count on me as one they could count on for faculty support. I attended weddings of both faculty and students, and was on hand for graduations and seminars as well. One memorable event was a conference on establishing business in Africa, hosted by Billye Aaron. Henry Aaron, an executive with the Atlanta Braves and former home run king, stood by. During breaks in the program, autograph seekers, especially the faculty, rushed Hank. Finally, when all had finished their requests, I walked up to, as I said, "Shake the hand of the man who had given my dad so much pleasure as a Milwaukee Brave." I didn't get an autograph, though my father probably would have treasured it.

I developed a circle of friends among some of the faculty and staff, and some of my students. The MBA program had many single Black females seeking opportunities opening to them with an MBA. As a bachelor faculty member who "had rhythm." I was in demand at social events to dance with the young ladies. I enjoyed the music, the "I didn't know you could dance!" and the exercise my muscles got on these occasions to let loose and relax. It felt good to break down the stereotype of what a disabled White faculty member should be. To many of these young ladies, I provided a role model that would help them enter the mostly-White corporate world.

One time, a group of the brightest female students and a staff member who was an Atlanta U graduate invited me to a birthday lunch of quiche at a small house near campus. It was the kind of appreciation for teaching that I cherished, and a break with tradition that was refreshing.

To be sure, I worked hard. I kept long office hours counseling students and contacting people to participate in research or my classes. I required written assignments for most classes and typically took ninety papers home to correct about three times a week. After an early meal that I cooked myself, I'd dive into these papers and make notes on every one. The students weren't used to so much individual attention and either loved or hated my comments and notations. My grading, based on points given for every aspect of the course, properly weighted to be as fair as possible, raised a lot of controversy. But, after students discovered that my methods did not automatically lead to failing grades and were inherently fairer than the haphazard grading most professors used, the controversy died down. Long hours sitting at all this took its toll, so I took part in social events to get out and get some exercise. I took walks in the woods when I could, and planned to get out of town during major breaks in the school year.

I loved the Atlanta area and tried to take in all I could. In the summer of 1978 Roger visited from Philadelphia with his two daughters, Tracy and Kelley. One of the places we visited was Stone Mountain. I had been to the top on the tram from the visitor's center, but we decided to walk up from the west end on the trails. I found myself falling behind everyone but Tracy. Finally Roger had to help me up the steepest parts near the top. Remembering my climb of the volcano, I knew I wouldn't be climbing like this much longer.

The first year at Atlanta U, I'd developed a friendship with one of my first semester students, Danny Lewis. He was from Bombay and, while young, very mature and supportive of other students. His wife, Bina Khandwala, came from India the next summer. I helped them buy their first car and get an apartment. They helped me out in return.

I decided that it had been a long time since I'd had a good physical and wanted one done under the supervision of a neurologist or neurosurgeon. I was told that Emory Clinic was the best place in Atlanta, so I called them up and made an appointment. When I explained what had happened in 1971 at Marshfield and the Mayo Clinic, the surgeon, Dr. Alan S. Fleischer, explained that surgery and diagnostic techniques had improved considerably. He recommended that I enter the hospital and have a myelogram and CT scan to see if there was anything he could do surgically to stop my deterioration or correct the paralysis I already had. I scheduled my time in the hospital in late December after spending the 1979 Christmas with my family in Wisconsin.

I hadn't told any of my colleagues except Bob Henry about the checkup and he was with his family in New York, so except for Danny and Bina, I felt very alone entering the hospital.

Medical students conducted the myelogram with me lying face down on the CT table. The contrast fluid was injected by needle directly into my spinal column in the old injury area of my neck. After pushing through two inches of neck muscle, the needle had to go between two vertebrae and puncture the spinal sac. Novacaine deadened the place where they inserted the needle. They used a fluoroscope to guide them, but kept hitting bone as I strained to remain still, balancing on my chin. Finally, they injected the fluid and subjected me to thirty minutes of X-ray scans.

I had to sit in a partially reclining position on a hospital bed for two days until the fluid had dissolved and the danger of myelogram headache had subsided. I remember the experience as being cold, dark, and lonely. When I got out of the hospital, I went directly to Danny's and Bina cooked me a good meal. We checked my neck and found several holes where the students had restarted the needle after hitting bone. I had a sore neck for weeks after.

After all that, I was declared physically fit and Dr. Fleischer concluded that there was some atrophy and old scar tissue, but nothing he could do to reverse my paralysis. I decided not to let surgeons take me into unnecessary myelograms in the future.

I continued my involvement in the World Future Society by joining the Georgia State university Chapter, attending conferences, and writing articles. I was especially proud of my ideas in 'Beyond Coping," a presentation I made at a conference on Coping with the Future in Birmingham. There was a certain amount of concern raised by Alvin Toffler in his book, Future Shock, and it permeated the community of ideas. There was talk about a major shift in the way we live, our paradigm, and a certain amount of fear of the unknown. People were looking for ways to put up with what was happening, a way to cope.

It was all very negative. My theme, based on my experience with disability, other races and cultures, philosophy, and religion, was an optimism that stemmed from a belief that all the societal forces underway were positive and that the only negative thing about them is our tendency to hang onto old prejudices and beliefs to our detriment. In other words, "The enemy is us," in the words of Charlie Brown.

From the Book of Revelation onward, many people imagine a diabolical future that they believe will happen and they must guard against. I believe that I will die—we all do. In the meantime, it is worthwhile keep on living. A catastrophic injury at twenty is no reason to quit being who I was, only a condition to who I would become. After my presentation, Konrad Sadek, a management information system consultant from Canada who was born in Austria, approached me. He asked me to join him in his publishing efforts, so I signed on. We collaborated on several articles.

I continued to return to Wisconsin whenever I could, making the drive in two long days, stopping off at Behram and Gool's in Louisville at the halfway point. When I got to my parent's house in Marshfield I relaxed, forgot about school and enjoyed the holidays with my family. But, duty called, and I decided to attend the 1979 annual meeting of the American Association for the Advancement of Science in Houston. I would leave January 2 early in the morning, and register the evening of the 3rd. My car had been parked over a week in a neighbor's driveway, so my brother, Tim, had agreed to clean off the snow and ice and get it going for me in the morning. When Dad came home that evening, he told us that a front was coming through and the temperature was expected to reach 35 below zero. The battery was dead, so Dad and Tim got the car started and took it over to a garage where my Dad's company kept their trucks inside

At 6 am it was more than 30 below zero. Tim had the car in the driveway, running and warm from the heater. As cold as it was outside, it was strange to start out in a warm, toasty car. It was dark until I got to 173 south of Pittsville. The dawn was breaking in a fog of ice crystals that hung on the deserted landscape. I noticed that my headlights were dimming. Although it was still dark, I turned off the headlights, the radio, and the heater, anything that would draw electricity. It was about thirty miles of scrub brush nothing to Tomah and I didn't relish being stuck on a deserted highway without heat. In time, the car got colder and colder, and the steering seemed to stiffen up. There were no oncoming cars, and no way to signal one if we met. My mind wandered to my greatest fear—freezing to death in the middle of nowhere. At least I was on a road. Finally, with my hands freezing on the wheel, and my feet becoming numb, I reached the intersection with I-94 and there was a gas station. I pulled up to a service door and the attendant let me in. I was sure glad to get to a warm place.

My problem was a loose belt on the alternator. The belt was replaced in fifteen minutes and I was on my way. Later that morning, as I drove west on I-90 into southern Minnesota, the wind on the backside of the front blew an inch of new snow across my path in a dizzying pattern of drifting whiteness, obscuring the road, but not impeding my progress. On I-35 headed south, I stopped for gas. I decided not to get out of the warm car in the bitter wind. The woman who came out to pump gas was dressed in a heavy parka. I didn't envy her as she stood in the wind. I pulled off at Kansas City for an evening meal and discovered 18" of new snow. The wind had blown the interstate clear, so I hadn't noticed so much new snow by the road. I had planned on taking US 71 south into Arkansas, but decided against heading into the mountains. Instead, I drove west on the Kansas Turnpike and made Wichita that night. There was 10" of new snow piled up in the motel parking lot.

As I continued south the next morning, Oklahoma City was icebound. I-35 was clear except for occasional patches of ice on the road, and near Dallas many huge oaks had lost limbs from the weight of ice that covered everything. I encountered a disoriented goose in the left lane near Denton. Fortunately, I was in the right lane as I passed it. When I got to the raised highway around downtown Dallas, the sun was shining brightly, but a combination of four inches of water, sand and salt on partially melted ice created a slippery, groovy, milkshake of a roadway. I had to grip the wheel tightly and avoid being swamped by truck splash of light brown mess as I bounced and slid through heavy traffic. The ice lasted all the way to Huntsville, 70 miles from my destination.

While I wasn't delayed at all by the massive storm, my cousin Terry Wenzel and his wife visiting friends in Dubuque at the same time and tried to drive from there to Dayton the same time with his pickup camper pulling two snowmobiles on a trailer. He got stopped in heavy snow in Illinois and stranded for two days. Terry's snowmobiles were out of gas from use on their vacation. At least they had the camper.

I got to Houston by nightfall. I stayed in an overflow hotel nearby the first night. My cousin, Jackie Warmbold, convinced me to stay at their house the rest of the week 25 miles to the west in Bear Creek. The AAAS Conference was held in the venerable old Shamrock Hotel in the Medical Center and was memorable because I got to meet Peter Drucker and attend a session by my former professor from Stanford, Karl Pribhrim. Dr. Joshua Hill, a friend of mine from my WVU student days, was teaching at Texas

Southern University, and invited me to attend a holiday faculty conference and retreat there.

At lunch, I joined Josh, TSU's President Sawyer, and other administrators to lunch across the street at the student center. We all had to use the bathroom with Sawyer in the lead. The cold weather had frozen the pipe and a sign warned not to use the restroom. We all did. All that coffee gave us no choice.

The day before I left, I had some foul tasting chili for lunch at the hotel's little lunchroom. The next day, I was invited to Josh and Etta's house for Sunday lunch. Etta had prepared a huge spread of soul food for us. Josh got a call and said that he had to go to the university. I ate alone and finally had to leave before he got back.

After a week at the conference, I drove back to Atlanta, fighting diarrhea the whole way, and a new semester.

Home from Atlanta University for lunch in my breakfast nook.

# 18

# Forced Out

The dollar-a-year dean, Augustus Sterne, did not like to run the school, especially when it came to faculty matters. He decided to hire an executive dean to run things. The faculty was requested to attend an interview dinner at the exclusive Diamond Club. The interviewee, Dr. Roosevelt Thomas, a Harvard grad and business researcher, used the dinner to give a scathing indictment of Atlanta University and the Center schools. We were not allowed to ask questions and I never found out if he had any teaching experience. Thomas was hired for the job. I, along with other faculty members, was upset by the way he had been selected, but we had no say in the matter. Thomas and I never had any real communication, and whether it was my reputation, my EdD degree, my disability, or my degree from Stanford, he hated me without ever knowing me.

Perhaps Thomas was hired as a hatchet man. We were undergoing scrutiny by the American Association of Graduate Schools of Business, our accrediting agency, and he was put in charge of that effort. The AACSB had strict rules governing the makeup of faculty, especially limiting the percentage without doctorates or with doctorates that were not in business administration. At the same time, AACSB required more expertise in computer applications, but focused on those with computer science rather than the engineering experience I had. AU had hired MBAs in order to get courses taught and had hired me for the same reason. In the spring of 1980 one fourth of the faculty was cut, a combination of financial and accreditation action. I was among the four that were cut.

All the notice said was that my contract would not be renewed. No reason for my dismissal was given and my request for an explanation fell on deaf ears. It was a real blow, because I had finally established my course, was just becoming recognized for my research activities, and had built the new home to stay. I talked to the other faculty and got little sympathy. One, an endowed professor of some reputation, said that he had warned against hiring me in the first place. I filed a formal grievance and was granted a hearing. In the hearing, I again requested a reason for my dismissal. No response was given and none of the committee members, my faculty peers, came to my defense. This was devastating. It seemed that all of them had turned against me. George Neffinger, the assistant dean who had hired me, was the only one who stood by me. But there was nothing he could do.

Paa Kwesi Adams, a brilliant marketing student from Ghana who was a political leader among the students, came to me. He requested my permission to circulate a petition on my behalf. I told him that I couldn't endorse a petition, but I was happy for any support the students could give me. Paa Kwesi got the signatures of more than half of our MBA students and took it to the dean. Dean Sterne was angry and told Paa Kwesi that I had instigated and orchestrated the whole petition idea. I think that he was embarrassed to see how much support students gave me. He and Thomas had probably based their decision on that hate letter, listening to the rumors circulated by both faculty and students, and talking to disgruntled students who had encountered my tough class work and grading requirements and complained.

After all, I was an anomaly to the idea of a business school, and the faculty it attracted. I was White, but didn't act like a White was supposed to in a Black setting. I was an atheist in an institution established by the Presbyterian Church in a deeply religious and conservative community, both Black and White. Being atheist put my morality in question. I was disabled, but didn't act disabled. Trying to participate in activities that would seem to bring embarrassment to my able-bodied colleagues. I was interested in progressive (some would say liberal) ideas that would revolutionize business. But my colleagues were a community of teachers interested in maintaining the status quo. My innovative teaching and quantitative grading techniques were alien to the conservative, traditional practices of my peers. Finally, I was not interested in enriching myself through my own business activities, a practice that was commonplace in our faculty. Self-promoting eroded the quality of teaching by those who spent more time on their businesses than with their students.

I blamed the narrow provincialism of the AACSB as the primary reason for my demise as a business professor. But it was the leadership of the school that had used those requirements and the financial condition of the school to sweep me out the door. With the support of the students, I decided to sue to get my position back. One of those also let go, a Black MBA who taught marketing, had retained attorneys who were professors at Georgia Tech. I decided to use them, too.

The attorneys listened to my story and agreed to take my case. They also suggested that I had a good case against Dr. Salibi and the anesthesiologist in my 1963 surgery. When they checked, the statute of limitations had run out. AU obtained the most prestigious law firm in Atlanta, and both firms took depositions. My attorneys decided that my best case was to file in Federal Court for discrimination based on my disability. I disagreed, because, as I stated earlier, I believed that I was being discriminated against based on conditions in the school that violated my academic freedom and that my disability was a minor issue. They convinced me that the disability route was the best course of action. When they filed in Federal Court, the judge threw the case out. I wrote the judge requesting further review, but I received no response.

That last semester was bittersweet. I had finally gained the confidence of the students, my house was nearing completion, and I'd put together a panel for a World Symposium on Alternative Futures in July in Toronto. With the help of Danny and Bina and some other students, I moved into the new house in late March. Mom flew down from Wisconsin to help me get set up and shake the construction dust out, and I started inviting my friends over.

I held an open house in early April and invited faculty, students, and friends. The dogwoods were in full bloom, adding a special touch. It reached 104°, and my heat pump failed. Everyone took their coats off and enjoyed the event anyway. Roosevelt Thomas arrived, grinned a lot, and didn't say much. It was obvious he had underestimated my ability to undertake such a project. He and his wife, for their combined high salaries, didn't live as well.

I started sending out resumes and checking with my local contacts. It didn't appear that I had a future as a business professor, so I tried to put together all my experience as a strategic planner or business analyst. I also applied to universities seeking researchers in the study of technology or grants coordinators. But responses were slow in coming, especially with the summer coming. I had two courses for the first summer session and for that I was grateful.

With a big house and time on my hands I reached out to my sister who had three young sons. I called Judy up and asked her if Paulie, her oldest, 13, would like to come for the summer. Paul, Jr., as he liked to be called, was getting to be a problem to manage, so I thought a little time with his professor uncle would give him a different perspective. About half of this turned out to be true.

About this time Gloria came along. She had finished her MBA in accounting and was hoping to get a job with one of the Big Eight firms. She came to a dinner party I had for friends one night and stayed the summer. I was in the middle of my lawsuit and didn't want anyone knowing that a student, even though she never took my course and had graduated, was involved with me. She was agreeable to that and didn't tell her friends either. It was a bit awkward with Paulie coming, but she agreed to work with me. She was renting part of a house on the near West Side, and went back there for a few days when Paulie arrived.

I was late getting to the airport. As I entered the doors of the main terminal, my name was being called on the PA system. It was a long walk out to the outer terminal where the 13 year old's plane had landed. My legs carried me as fast as they could. I found Paul leaning up against the wall, worried that he'd come all this way with no one to meet him. It must have been a frightening experience, but he didn't admit it.

We rented a luggage cart so he could push his bag out to the car. We left the cool terminal into the warm night and a huge, empty parking lot. This was obviously all new to him. On the way back home, I announced that we were going to Florida the next day. He was ready to go without question; 13 year olds are like that.

The next morning, we headed for Florida. That evening, we stopped at a seafood place and I ordered him a platter. Paul had never eaten seafood, but enjoyed it all. Said he liked lobster the best. In Orlando, we stayed over night with an AU colleague, Philip Hicks. Phil was also let go when I was, but he didn't fight it. He had an industrial engineering consulting business going and had commuted to Atlanta. He included my resume in his group of resource people, but nothing ever came of it.

Paul loved Disney World. Right away, on his first ride, I thought I lost him on the racecars when he didn't reappear with the other cars coming around the track for the first time. After some time, he finally showed up. I was really getting worried. A girl driving in front of him had stalled her car and he couldn't get around her until the track operators intervened. I was happy and relieved that that was all it was.

I had my own scare. We heard a lot about Space Mountain and decided to try it. I expected it to be some sort of Disney special effects ride and was looking forward to experience a simulated space ride through a colorful galaxy. I was misled and near dead wrong. As we neared the loading point, signs warned those who were elderly or with heart conditions not to ride. My heart was fine, so I didn't worry. Nobody told me it was a roller coaster. They strapped me in, but not very tight.

After the first acceleration down a dark shoot and wrenching right turn in total darkness, I decided that this was not my idea of a space ride. But I was on my way and had no way out. With each turn centrifugal force pushed my arms outside of the narrow compartment. As I struggled to keep them in, I had visions of losing a hand or arm as it struck a support hurtling by in the dark. My glasses, affected by the same forces, began a march down my nose as they tried to fly off my face in the dark. I couldn't reach up to put them back in place. After an eternity of punishment, the car finally stopped and I got out with my glasses and arms intact. I vowed never to ride a roller coaster again. Paul thought this dark body assault was great, so I waited while he rode it again several times.

We drove south to Pompano Beach where my cousin, Terry Wenzel, had moored his thirty foot 1947 mahogany Chris Craft behind a suburban home. Although it was illegal, he and his wife, Rosalie, were living on the boat. The house's owners, living beyond their means, rented out two slips to Terry and another couple. The idea was to keep quiet so the neighbors wouldn't complain. We changed that. The house's owners had a 13-year-old daughter who could swim like a fish. Paul fell immediately in love and spent all his time in the pool or trying to sneak out alone with her.

Terry had hired two girls to refinish the mahogany decking on the Chris Craft. He had been restoring it. He warned me not to mess with them, because they were lesbians. One story was that the lady of the house, the big, loud-mouthed mother of Paul's new love, came into her kitchen one day when everyone was at work and the girls were working on the boat, and found the dyke trying to peer through the silvered, one-way glass that faced the entire side of the house overlooking the pool and channel. The owner, standing just inside the one-way glass, panicked and almost called the police, but the dyke went back to work and mom didn't get seduced or raped or anything else.

We enjoyed the leisure life by the pool while Terry and his wife worked at an electrical supply business. We had to retire at dark without lights to make it look like no one lived on the boat. Our cabin was in the forward hull, and so hot it was hard to sleep. Paul soon developed a sunburn that made sleeping even worse.

The lesbians had disconnected the lights on the boat's six-volt electrical system and apparently caused a short. The battery kept running down. Terry recharged the battery most of the day on Saturday, so that we could go fishing. Finally, we were able to leave about 3 o'clock. We followed the channel out to the Atlantic, and then motored out just far enough so that we could drift back over weed beds that were about a mile off shore.

Terry did just that, shutting off the power and letting the onshore wind blow us back. The chop was about 2 to 3 feet and it rocked the boat enough to make it hard for me to keep my feet. I couldn't get anchored anywhere and my stomach was wrenched from side to side until I started to feel seasick, an experience I'd never felt before. At least the fishing was good. I wished that I could take part. Using squid for bait, Rosalie and Terry caught a Red Snapper, three Bonito, and a 30-inch Barracuda in fifteen minutes. Watching helped keep my mind off my stomach.

Then, Terry tried to start the motor to head out for another pass, but the battery was dead. He radioed a Mayday until the radio went dead. As we drifted inexorably toward grounding on the beach, our concern began to grow. Soon, a large boat appeared, part of the Coast Guard Auxiliary. They came fast when the radio died thinking we were in serious trouble. They towed us back to Boca Rattan to a pier where we could recharge the battery. After a couple of hours we took the Intercoastal waterway back to Pompano. It was dark by that time. The water was smooth as glass as we cruised along past miles of million dollar homes lit up for the night. Paul got the thrill of taking the wheel part of the way.

The next day we picked up Terry's daughter, Tara, at the airport, spent some time on the beach at Fort Lauderdale, and bought some shrimp and lobster for a fish and seafood party that evening. In the middle of the fun, the police arrived. Terry told them we were all going home after the meal, so we had to cut the party off and go to bed quietly. We left the next morning. The neighbors kept complaining and Terry had to move the boat a couple of weeks later.

When we returned, I had to teach in the morning four days a week for the first summer session. Paul was a late riser so it worked out well. He didn't mind my cooking and helped with the dishes. Soon, he met Gloria and they got along okay. I thought he might like the local swimming pool, so I showed him the way on a map. A neighbor had let him use their grown son's bike so he could go alone. When I got back that day after class, Paul told me that after a long, hard ride through hills to get to the pool, they wouldn't let him swim in his cut-off jeans. He never went back to the pool.

Behram, Gool and their three sons arrived on a summer tour and spent a couple of days with us. We enjoyed a day at Six Flags over Georgia, but I avoided all the roller coasters. Danny, Bina, and Gloria joined us for a picnic and tour of Stone Mountain the next day. Again, we decided to climb the mountain from the west side. I made it to the top with Behram's help, but I knew it was the last time that I'd make such a climb.

When the summer session was over, Danny, Bina, Paul, and I headed for Toronto. I had arranged a panel of five presenters at the 2nd World Assembly of the World Future Society. We stopped in Morgantown and stayed with Mahfooz and Farkunda in their student apartment at WVU. To save money, we spent the week in a dormitory several blocks from the conference hotel. It was oppressively hot and there was no air conditioning and poor ventilation in the dorm, so we spent some sleepless nights. I enrolled Paul in a student program to keep him busy. He quickly fell in love with a 14 year old from Chicago and spent his afternoons running the streets. The Assembly afforded me the opportunity to meet some of the great thinkers from all over the world. One of the most interesting sessions was a debate between Timothy Leary and Herman Kahn. I was surprised at how lucid Leary was after having supposedly "fried his brain" on LSD years earlier. I had used Kahn's optimistic book to offset Robert Heilroner's pessimistic, **The Worldly Philosophers,** in my classes.

Our session on *"Metaperspectives for the Future"* was the high point in my intellectual career. Over 150 packed the room to hear our views of how the future would evolve. I knew I wanted to continue my research into the ideas I was forming. It was uncertain whether I would have a chance to continue, but I was determined to, even without the support of an academic institution. Without having written a successful book, it was hard being accepted by this group of intellectuals.

I returned to the reality that I had no job prospects in sight. I tried the private, government, and higher education sectors without much luck. I concentrated on my research and job applications. I had a first interview with the Tarkington Group, one of Fran Tarkington's various enterprises, but it was obvious that he wanted a young, sales-oriented image rather than an engineer-professor-gimp type. This group reminded me of the Young Republicans and a role model for the Yuppies who greedily ate up the eighties. I had an interview with a vice president of Georgia Power for a strategic planning position. I was being used to meet EEOC requirements. He went out of his way to inform me that he was grooming a smart young lady from the organization as his chief strategist. He even went so far as to introduce me to her. It was a bit humiliating that he seemed to value her experience over mine.

Someone told me to contact an Eric Ericsson, a hotshot consultant that I was told would be open to my ideas. I met him for dinner with a colleague of his. He said that he was in the business of business formation and he and his friend spent time testing my knowledge of aged wines rather than what I could do. My cynicism of consultant snake oil was increased after those encounters. The technical world of the Atlanta business community seemed to be tied up in Georgia Tech grads and professors, and high profile hype types with no substance. My search for honest, hard work with a chance for creativity was being dashed in this crazy world of one-upmanship, full of insecurity and immaturity. The good, honest, hard working success stories who offered to guest lecture in my classes faded when it came to helping me with a job. For some of them, self-made entrepreneurs without formal education, I may have been a threat. Most offered to consider my proposals for consulting work or to work part time, but nothing happened.

Onuma Onuma, a Nigerian student with an arrogance that allowed him to finish his MBA in Accounting in one year when two years were required, was having a party. His wealthy cousin, Eme Eme, was footing the bill for a bash that would be Onuma's sendoff into the international business world. The party was held at the clubhouse of an upscale Black apartment complex. I assumed that it would be an affair for AU faculty and students. I arrived there about 10 pm. Although there was a great disk jockey and free food, beer, and booze, very few people came. There were no other faculty members and only a few AU students. I tried to get comfortable with those that were there, but couldn't because they kept coming and going.

About midnight the streets arrived. I found myself surrounded by strangers from the night looking for the action and freebies from the party. I was the only White guy there. Black guys kept coming up to me and asking me offhand questions like, "Whatcha got?" It seems they assumed that I was a drug dealer. Why else would I be there? I played it straight and said who I was and why I was there, but more than one guy didn't believe my story. I left about 2 am. It was early for that crowd, but I wasn't sticking around to see what happened by morning. Onuma got a job with a prestigious London Bank. A year later he called me from London, and after that, from Houston, promising to involve me in some business deals he was putting together. I never heard from him again.

Solomon Ogado, a good student from Kenya, and Atlanta cab driver extraordinaire, was getting married. His love, Bella, a fellow Kenyan county-woman with an MFA in Library Science from AU, planned a formal wedding in a Northside Presbyterian Church. I asked Gloria if she wanted to go, but she declined, still unsure of being seen out with me.

The summer of 1980 was one of the hottest in history. This Saturday wedding day in August was no exception. I arrived at the church just barely on time for the 4 o'clock ceremony, but no one was there. Soon, others started arriving and I determined that I was at the right place, just early. The air conditioning was out and it was hot in the church. We waited and waited, and finally found out that the couple hadn't gotten a license or blood test until church members intervened that morning. The bride was the last to arrive and the ceremony started two hours late. Afterward, we sat through endless speeches at the church school while the champagne got warm and the goat got colder and tougher. The home of a Georgia State professor became the site of a late night reception. I danced in the hot garage to Zairian music until 3 am.

Gloria drifted back to her apartment. She got a dog to keep her company. Both of us looking for work was not good for either of us. Once into September, I gave up hope of an academic post that fall, and concentrated on the private sector. I started to use my credit cards to pay the house payment and living expenses and, although I had the credit, it was weird to be borrowing each month to live. I collected unemployment for a while, but it was only a fraction of my living expenses and it was over almost before it began.

One opportunity looked promising. I was told to contact a former Emory University professor who ran an environmental research consulting firm. I called him for an appointment and he agreed to meet me at noon the day after the 1980 Presidential Election. As a Georgian and engineer, and a believer in the decency of the man, I voted for Jimmy Carter. That night, I watched the returns and learned that the country, anxious about Carter's failure to get the hostages out of Iran and worried about his ability to improve the economy, had selected Ronald Reagan to speak for us on the world stage.

The next morning, running late, I stopped for fried chicken so that I wouldn't arrive at my interview on an empty stomach. When I got to the small, beautiful office building, set in the trees, I had to wait some time for the boss to get free. As I waited, I saw signed pictures of Jimmy Carter in a canoe, a pastime he was known to enjoy.

I remember little of the substance of the interview. He offered lunch. I declined and said that I'd take dessert. We got in his classic 250 SL Mercedes convertible and drove a short distance to an exclusive club. He was hurting. He was the other man in the canoe with Carter. Now that Carter was defeated, he saw that many of the consulting contracts that came his way would be lost as focus turned away from environmental issues. He saw in me a colleague, a kindred spirit, but he could offer no opportunity for me to join him. I never saw him again. I hope his business survived supply side, trickle down, economics.

I wanted to do research on the implications of technological changes leading to fundamental improvement in human intelligence. I received some support from local colleagues and tried to get the attention of national funding, namely the National Science Foundation. I was able to submit a proposal through one of NSF's established programs, but it fell on deaf ears. Without institutional support and little publication, I wasn't going to get anywhere. I decided to continue the work as best I could with my own resources until I could establish a track record that would attract the attention of funding sources. I knew that it took years to build a body of knowledge that the scientific community would respect. This topic was something that would shake the very core of our values, but appeared too controversial to get serious attention.

My idea was basically this. Human intelligence is thought to have evolved gradually through evolution of the species. This process has been traced backward perhaps two million years. If the theory of natural selection is correct, the process creates ever more intelligent, robust humans through survival and reproductive dominance of the species. Technology, a natural product of intelligent activity, changes everything. Technological tools have given those with poor survivability superior status, disrupting natural selection. For example, myopia, a genetic defect affecting vision, is epidemic in the Western, technological, world, largely due to success of eyeglasses in correcting this condition. In primitive, hunting and gathering societies, myopia is not prevalent.

The robust improvement of the individual and collective intelligence of primitive societies, if any still exist, probably continues, but the gene pool of most of the world's technological societies is filled with defects like myopia that modern medicine and cultural tools have given survival. It is doubtful all of our well-meaning intervention has improved our intelligence; the reverse is more likely the case.

This is all about to change.

My case is a case in point. I have a severe myopia with astigmatism that comes from my father's side of the family. While there is high likelihood that I will pass it on to my offspring, no one stands in the way of my having myopic children. While I don't consider myself particularly intelligent, my performance on tests of ability compared with others in school and my intuitive ability in wilderness environments often showed me to be far superior to my peers. This was astonishing to discover, because normally I'm quite average. It becomes immediately a controversial question if I should consider passing this innate intelligence on to my children. However, unless my IQ is so low it affects my ability to function at the most basic level in modern society, no one questions my right to have as many offspring as I wish, intelligent or not.

On the other hand, if, as Dr. Salibi alleged, I have a congenital defect in my cervical spine that leads to this progressive paralysis or, at least the propensity for injury to the spine, should I avoid children as Salibi suggested, or should I go ahead and have children like everyone else has suggested? While all experts, medical or not, seem to think it's my right to have children, many have expressed concern that somehow a paralyzed father, even one of superior intelligence, is less fit for raising children than a ordinary, healthy one. If I do have a defective gene that causes spinal defects, why wasn't my identical twin brother or other members of my family counseled against having offspring? Aside from myopia, our family seems to be relatively free of genetic defects. There is no evidence whether our family intelligence is increasing or decreasing with each generation.

Whether or not the human gene pool is diluted may be moot. The same technology that may have changed the course of human evolution for the worse is about to change it again. On several fronts scientists are about to change the course of human evolution, from eliminating genetic defects in unborn children to lengthening human life. These breakthroughs have the potential to fundamentally change individual and collective intelligence of humans. While governments spend time and money on social and political problems, little attention is directed to these scientific endeavors that have the potential for a revolutionary change in human evolution.

I wanted to be on the forefront of understanding where technology would take us. It didn't look like I'd get the chance. View of Atlanta three blocks from my home (below).

The sunken greatroom was large with a stone, energy-efficient fireplace that could heat the house and triple pane, screened wood windows

# 19

## Forced to Leave My Home

I finally got a call in December. The UW-Eau Claire needed someone to teach production and operations management for the spring semester. I stepped off the plane on December 20 and was greeted by 20° below zero and a strong wind in my face. I wasn't looking forward to working in Northern Wisconsin again in winter. The school had closed for the Christmas holiday so I didn't meet any faculty. Over dinner at the Holiday Inn I stayed in, the management department head told me that he was headed to Los Angeles to help run a company and that they needed someone to fill in for the spring semester. With no other prospects in sight, I agreed to help out.

Back in Atlanta, I had a lockable enclosure built in the basement and moved my furnishings, books, and papers into it. I decided that I would return to Atlanta if I could, and put the house up for rent for now. I packed my car with what I would need and drove north. The trip was memorable because I encountered snow when I turned north on I-65 at Nashville. I was making tracks on a deserted, unplowed highway all the way to Louisville. At times the snow was six to eight inches deep, but my car, weighed down with all my belongings, cut through the white landscape with ease. Still, I was exhausted when I reached the haven of Behram and Gool's house for the night.

The next morning, I left early and, after driving all morning, stopped for gas at Indianapolis. To my shock, I found that I'd lost my billfold. The owner of the station filled my tank on the promise that I'd return to pay him when I found my money. I drove three hours back to Louisville and found Gool at the technical school where she worked. She told me how to get in the house. My billfold was on the dresser where I'd left it. I was tired and not looking forward to retracing my steps on the long drive home, but grateful that my billfold was not lost. In late afternoon, I returned to the Good Samaritan at the station, paid him, and refueled again. There were no more bad roads, so I made it to my parent's house very late that night.

After Christmas, I drove to Eau Claire and easily found an apartment. It was quite new, but rather confining compared to my house. The owners had permanently wired the exhaust fans in the kitchen and bathroom "on". They said it was to remove excess humidity caused by the stucco drying and the excessive amount of insulation in the building. I was worried about the heavy doors in the halls to ward off the winter wind and the unprotected parking lot.

My cousin, Janice Becker, lived in town, and she and her children helped me move in. It was a nice day, hardly a hint of the winter underway. Another cousin, Duane Hull, was a college senior in accounting and had an apartment nearby. He had taken production and operations management the first semester, and I was glad that he wouldn't have to take my class.

The interim department head showed me my office and that was it. Faculty parking was a block away from the building, so I arranged to use the loading dock space by the entrance. The dean had left, too, and the Business School was rudderless, so there were no faculty or committee meetings. I befriended the young archeologist across the hall over coffee, but otherwise had coffee and lunch alone in the lunchroom.

My classes were strange. Used to the mix and controversy surrounding graduate students with high motivation and drive, I was suddenly confronted with a homogenous, under-achieving group of Northern Wisconsin young people of northern European origin. These business students had determined that my required course was something they had to endure rather than learn. There was one young lady of Native American background in one class who was a refreshing light in an otherwise dull, unenlightened bunch of young people who were apparently in college because it was, "The thing to do." There were bright students to be sure, but none that I can remember now. I sometimes longed to be teaching again at my Alma Mater, thirty miles away, where I would know some of the faculty and the students, however poor, would at least be more interesting.

There were some high points to my winter of discontent. There was a small faculty group on campus interested in the future. I presented my ideas to them one evening and was well received. I never met with them again. One day, I was eating my lunch in our lunchroom when I was asked to join two other faculty and a woman who was animatedly describing her life with gorillas. She was dressed in a work shirt, jeans, and boots and her long black hair, pulled back in a ponytail, was streaked with white. The others sat in rapt attention to her stories, while I tried to figure out what all the excitement was about. Later, I learned that she was Dian Fossey, on a fund-raising tour of colleges and universities, and had spoken earlier on the campus. A couple of years later, she was murdered by poachers at her mountain home. She was immortalized in the book and movie, ***Gorillas in the Mist***

My job search resulted in two interviews. I flew to California State University, Long Beach, for the first. From my motel balcony, I viewed a strange world of iron donkeys pumping oil amid expensive new condominiums as the sunset in the blood red air. The position, as campus-wide research director, paid little and required a faculty retreat to provide a viable living in the high cost of living environment of Southern California. I had lunch with the Dean of the School of Business and looked at some housing I couldn't afford. I didn't get an offer, but I did enjoy a brief respite on that sunny campus from the dark of the Wisconsin winter.

The second interview was more difficult. It was for department head of a communications department at Clarkson College in Potsdam, New York. I had to fly into Syracuse and then take the bus to Potsdam. I was coming down with a cold when I left and the two flights to Syracuse had dehydrated me to the point that I was miserable. I boarded a bus and spent the next four hours as the bus, driving in a snowstorm, headed in and out of several small towns. The department head, stepping down from his post for health reasons, met me and took me to a motel. I had taken the local bus instead of the express, and arrived much later than expected as a result. I was too sick and tired to do anything except go to bed. But, I still asked one favor of my host, to get me a bottle of orange juice. He stopped at a grocery store on the way. I forced myself to drink the entire quart and went to bed.

Whether it was adrenaline or that orange juice that beat the bug, I faced the next, bitter cold day with renewed enthusiasm. I attended several meetings and interviews, a dinner at a local nightclub, and, finally, a long meeting with the faculty. I was convinced that I'd impressed most of the faculty, but one young lady, perhaps considering herself a candidate for the post, was aloof, even hostile. Whatever the case, I never got a call back. I was somewhat relieved, because while I enjoyed the ambiance that private school with a great heritage offered, I wasn't sure I wanted to live so far north again and so far from an airport.

On the way back, at Detroit, air traffic thwarted our landing six miles out because of icy runways. After a couple of hours on the ground in Flint, I got back to Detroit. The short hop to Chicago turned into a two-hour nightmare of circling O'Hare Airport until traffic cleared. Arriving at the deserted terminal at 2 am, the airline gave me lodging in a nearby, dinghy motel. My secretary proctored my morning tests while I got back to Eau Claire about noon. My car was frozen in its parking space with a dead battery. I called Janice and she picked me up and got me to my afternoon classes.

It was a long, dark, lonely winter. Cooped up in the apartment, my nose ran constantly as I struggled with grading homework and continuing my job search. I believe the reason my nose ran was either formaldehyde or vinyl chloride out gassed from cheap plastic building materials. It was the same thing that happened in my Huntington apartment. Fortunately, the problem didn't affect my sleep. Sometimes in the late afternoons and weekends, I'd go for a walk, but the bleak landscape offered little to ease my depression. At least Joyce had rented my house to a couple, but that meant I couldn't go back until the lease was up in a year.

One day, the interim department head introduced me to a guy, fresh from his MBA, who would take over my course in the fall. I didn't protest, knowing that I wasn't comfortable in this cold place of homogeneous under achievers who weren't interested in research.

# 20

# You Can't Go Home Again

I had come to a hard point in my life. I could have gone back to Atlanta and rented an apartment until my money ran out, but that wasn't very attractive. Instead, I decided to move back in with my parents until I could get work. My mother understood my situation, but my dad was less sympathetic. I moved in, kept a low profile, and concentrated on my job search.

That summer, we spent several weekends at the lake. I found that I couldn't swim anymore, so I would lie on my stomach on an inner tube, and paddle around the lake. It was great to be so close to the water and the sky. The only drawbacks were strong winds that tended to blow me off course, occasional weeds and stumps that would tie me up in the shallows, and the hot sun, that would burn me mercilessly. I spent whole afternoons on the water without a care and even paddled out to the island and back.

In mid August we had our 20th high school reunion. It was easy for me to go, since I was right in town. This reunion was much more relaxed than the 10th, when everyone was showing off his or her success. This time, we had an abundance of rock 'n roll and Beatles hits and everyone let their hair down and had a good time. Well, not everyone. There were many divorces and some hopeful new marriages. Some careers, like mine, had gone sour and it showed on faces that once had the world by the tail. The Old Maids huddled at one end of the dance floor. In some kind of time warp, nothing had changed for them since high school. I had a hard time convincing people that I was unemployed. John Green refused to hear it, "Oh Ron, don't tell me that crap...."

The biggest surprise was a woman none of us seemed to know. She had attended a few months during our senior year, but no one remembered her. As a flirtatious divorced secretary from Milwaukee, she took the reunion by storm, and was voted the "most improved."

I danced with all the girls. One, Jan Genett, played the gay divorcee, also much improved. She was surprised to hear that I was in Marshfield and asked me to give her a call. I somehow made amends with Ruth Kohs, the friend who had gone to our Junior Prom with Roger, double dated with me later, and, as a nurse at St. Joseph when I was there during my failed surgery, failed to see me. I carried her in my mind all these years as an example of all the friends I lost when I became paralyzed. Now, with two daughters from a failed first marriage and as a widowed businesswoman from a successful second marriage, she was ready to talk to me. I dissolved my animosity and we agreed to get together.

The week following the reunion, I made a date with Jan and spent an evening with Ruth at her house. Marshfield is small and lives intertwine. Ruth and I had a long talk over a big bottle of wine in her unrestored, but perfect, Victorian mansion on Ash Street. Since her husband's untimely death from cancer, Ruth was having a hard time running the businesses and controlling her teenage daughters. When we talked of my upcoming date with Jan, she gave me a warning I'll never forget. She said that she and Jan had been in the same crowd for many years, but that Jan was a user, and she no longer considered her a close friend. I learned a long time ago not to judge people by what other people say, but what she said stayed with me like a signpost seen, but unheeded.

My mother had bowled with Ruth and was high on the idea that I was talking to her, but was lukewarm about Jan. On our first date, Jan wore a striking white summer outfit that made her look a lot younger than her forty years. We went to see a new James Bond film, *From Russia with Love*. Before the film, we stopped in an adjacent bar for a drink. There were some young punks there who made a big deal out of how Jan was dressed. She was overdressed for a movie date, but I felt defenseless with my paralyzed arms to defend her from this petty, small town outrage. We solved the problem by leaving.

Jan had married an ex Marine medic right out of high school. She worked to help him finish nursing school and raised their two children. Her husband was abusive, so she had to work many years to get a driver's license, a car and better jobs. For many years she worked in clothing sales, and finally, got to manage an upscale woman's clothing store. She finally had enough financial independence to divorce her husband three years earlier. A year after that, her mother died. Jan now had a new job selling outdoor advertising in Central Wisconsin. She loved traveling through the beautiful countryside to her appointments. Jan had a passion for antiques that she enhanced with an artistic flair for decoration. She wanted to start a business related to her artistic talents. Jan was a self-made woman and I liked what she'd made of herself. She was blind to my paralysis and seemed genuinely interested in my adventurous life and what I'd become.

Jan's daughter, Jill, was 16 and took charge of their apartment in a remodeled old house on North Central Avenue. Her son, Michael, was 19 and a junior in political science at the University of Wisconsin-Madison. Jan's family, the Thiels, were prominent in the business of early Marshfield and a building on Central Avenue bears the Thiel name. Her father, Wilfred Thiel, born in 1900, enlisted in the Army in 1916 and went to war in Europe. Later he got a medical degree and established a thriving medical practice working for companies like National Cash Register in Dayton, Ohio. Jan was born to wealth in 1942 and spent her early years in the care of her nanny. By 1950, her father was burned out and suffered a breakdown that caused him to lose his practice. He was declared incompetent, his money placed in trust funds, and he, his wife, and two daughters returned to his mother's house on Fourth Street in Marshfield.

When I arrived in Marshfield in the seventh grade, I knew Jan as a quiet, thin, almost anorexic, girl who lived across from our junior high school and stayed with a close circle of friends. In high school, I remember seeing her ride horses with friends and she was going steady with a guy named Lloyd Mueller. I assumed she would marry him.

Before her mother died, a family attorney got her father admitted to the Veterans Hospital in Tomah. I saw him there twice. Although he didn't identify with the other veterans, he seemed happy with his existence. He died at 93.

About that time, things started happening with my job search. I was invited to interview at the Marietta, GA, Lockheed plant. Reagan's policies had given rebirth to the plant that produced the C-130 Hercules, and an occasional C-5A. The plant was about fifteen minutes by back roads through Smyrna from my house. The job, in quality assurance, was to motivate the workers to produce zero defects. I was asked if I could motivate groups of workers and I honestly replied that motivation was an individual thing, requiring us to look at each worker's self image and what motivates them to do their best work. On the whole the interview didn't go well. It seemed they were looking for something I didn't have and overlooking my strong management and planning skills. Still, they made me an offer to train for zero defects and oversee a newsletter for workers stressing quality with a young assistant writer.

I had seen an ad in the Chronicle of Higher Education for a Director of Computing Services at Texas Southern University. The Vice President of Administrative Services offering the position was an old friend and fellow graduate of West Virginia's doctoral program, Joshua Hill. I wrote him a letter congratulating him on the Vice Presidency and enclosed my resume. He called me after he received my letter and asked me if I was interested in the position of directing the computer center. I told him that I didn't think I was qualified.

Josh told me that he needed an executive assistant and that he needed my help and a couple of years to "turn the school around." I told him that I had an offer from Lockheed and he offered me $1000 per year more than Lockheed was offering.

I told Jan about this and she suggested that I create a checklist comparing the advantages and disadvantages of each job. The comparison came out in favor of continuing to work in a university. I made the mistake of calling my contact at Lockheed and telling him that I had an offer for more pay at TSU. This angered him and he told me the offer was off. I guess he sensed that we were both uncomfortable with the situation and my attempt at bargaining was the straw that broke the deal's back.

This was a major turning point in my life. I wanted desperately to return to Atlanta and my house. But if it meant working as a low-level functionary in a company that epitomized the military-industrial complex, it would serve only to keep me employed and able to live where I wanted. While many professors at Texas A and M, Georgia Tech, and the like saw nothing wrong accepting lucrative research contracts to further their careers and line their pockets, I had come to the conclusion that I would not further the ends of war or environmental destruction in order to become wealthy. I saw this was also true of many businesses that took resources from the environment without restoring it. My hope was that working for a company like Lockheed, I could change it from within. I never got to test out my theory. By being forced to go to TSU, I closed the door on work in the private sector.

Before I headed south, I decided to invite Jan and her family to join our family at the lake. She came with enthusiasm and impressed my mother with her helpfulness around the cottage. It was the last time I drove the speedboat and Jan enjoyed our carefree weekend together. I rode back to Marshfield with her. She wanted to continue our growing relationship.

I loaded everything I had in the car and drove to Houston. I stayed with my cousin, Jackie Warmbold, and her family until I found a place to live. The commute to TSU took an hour and a half one way. The city was filled with unemployed from the north and others who had come to cash in on the mythical prosperity of the American oil patch. The threat of OPEC and oil shortages had caused a boom that seemed endless, but also created a crush of disenfranchised and immigrants in the city. After a few frustrating days trying to find suitable housing for my work, I finally decided to stay at Brompton Court, a rather expensive complex catering to professionals in transition and patients in the Medical Center.

It was hot, lonely, and confining in that apartment. I desperately longed for a view and connections to a city I didn't like. I spent a lot of time writing and calling Jan, and she sent me a cute, appropriate card almost every day. We planned to get together at Thanksgiving.

Deck off the dining room, a place I missed in Houston.

Surrounded by woods, the cedar siding blended with the green. 1980

# 21

## Another New Start

I liked my job. I shared adjoining desks with a woman my age in the personnel records room. But our room was spacious in this building that had been built in 1950 before air conditioning—now cut up into dirty little cubicles where the staff eked out a daily existence doing just enough to stay out of trouble. Armed with an edict from the United States Office of Civil Rights, a new president, a new layer of young professional managers, and a commitment from the State for more funds, we were going to change that. First, we had to overcome a long-standing attitude that, as a Black school, TSU wouldn't get any money to change anything, even if we planned it. What little extra money there was went to support the highest levels of the administration. Since these administrators controlled budgets, little trickled down to the working staff or facilities. A comparison of TSU with six "sister" institutions in the state showed major discrepancies that the state had to correct or face loss of federal funding.

An engineering study of our buildings, by Page Southerland Page Engineers showed that they were in serious need of repairs. Some buildings had been under funded initially, leading to construction that was inferior from the start and needed to be replaced. Some, while well built, were suffering from inadequate maintenance. And, finally, some of the buildings had aged to the point where they needed renovation.

We were optimistic that we could change things, but had a problem getting the staff to believe anything we tried to plan. The day I arrived, Josh introduced me to Don Hall, a newly-appointed safety manager. We joked about Hill, Hull, and Hall being confused as we got to work. One week later, there was a lot of commotion in the office. I learned that Hall, a minister in a small Black church, as well as a university employee, had been indicted for rape. My office mate, Gloria Metoyer, was incensed because she had known and trusted Hall since he was a student. Gloria later confided in me that she thought I was a spy sent from Austin. Nothing was quite as it seemed and rumor was more powerful than the truth.

A White man in a Black-dominated environment is always suspect. While some of the staff were open, helpful, and friendly from the beginning, there were many who viewed me with suspicion and distrust. While I won some over with my performance and helpfulness, some never came to fully trust me. My disability opened some doors, but it also kept me from supervisory roles. Blacks, particularly those who gravitate to Black-dominated workplaces, dislike being supervised by Whites. Josh considered my style of supervision too lax, and this too led me to staff, rather than line, management. If I tried to use any strict rules with subordinates I was immediately labeled as "trying to take over", and worse. I got much more cooperation from well-educated peers than from the rank and file.

I had developed a work hard, play hard, philosophy of work. I was no-nonsense, concerned, and kept a tight schedule every day. There were few existing paperwork guidelines and procedures in place. I literally had to start from scratch on every problem, and I worked hard to establish a record that others could understand and follow. But, when we got together to celebrate a holiday or other event, I'd join right in. It seemed to surprise people to discover this carefree side of my personality.

Hurricane Alan blew in and gave us a scare, but nothing came of it. I sat in the heat of my apartment and wrote poems for Jan. I did get down to the pool on weekends, but no longer felt like swimming. I remembered the beautiful swimming pools in California. Houston's were more like wading pools. I wasn't encouraged to get wet or dive in.

I did meet a beautiful young lady who was recuperating from a broken neck at TIRR. She was unfortunate to be at the tragic tea dance on July 17, 1981at the Hyatt Regency in Kansas City and under the walkway when it fell and killed 114. She was fortunate to only have broken her neck when so many died. Her brother and an attorney sister were there to encourage her. But, it was obvious that, although she had survived the disaster and corrective surgery had restored most of her function, she was depressed. I was doubly concerned when she openly shared joints of marijuana with her siblings. But I didn't intervene or attempt to tell her my story. At that point she would only be reminded of what she'd lost.

Depression runs with spinal cord injury, and it runs deep. When you are young everything is physical, including friendships. A young engineer who worked for Singer-Friden in the Stanford Industrial Park and belonged to the Stanford Bachelor's Club with me, ended up recuperating at the Stanford Medical Center after surgery to remove a spinal tumor. Urged by the president of the Club, I went to see him. A beautiful young woman was with him, tending to his every need. He had nothing positive to say, and my presence didn't encourage him. A couple of months later, he was at a yard party the Bachelor's Club held. Everyone was out in the yard dancing, but he spent the whole time in the kitchen moping and complaining to two women.

A young woman at Redwood Acres was athletic to the point of obsession. Although her body didn't show it, she had had polio and seemed injured by it. She would come by the pool where I often lounged, talking of tennis, golf, or other activities she was constantly going off to engage in. She avoided me, and after a brief romance of about a week, announced that she was marrying another newcomer to the apartment complex. It seemed to me she was trying to live her life at full speed ahead, afraid that paralysis would catch her again and lay her low.

Somebody, I can't remember whom, in Atlanta told me about a 14 year old injured in a beach accident and could use some encouragement. He dove into shallow water at the beach in Savannah and in an instant, broke his neck. I visited him in the hospital. Although my injury was similar, he couldn't identify with me, and, I suppose, wondered why I was there. He seemed relieved when someone came to give him his therapy and he didn't have to talk to me anymore.

Then, Jan flew down for Thanksgiving and things changed. After a hectic, hurried weekend, memorable only for a sunset ride on the Bolivar Ferry, we decided to get married.

I had looked at new apartments and condos near work, and even put a down payment on a condo on Holly Hall. Jan liked the condo, but living with a stepdaughter who was approved by the management and a dog that was not approved by the management was a dilemma not resolved. Fortunately, Brompton Court approved of both temporarily. Very few apartments did.

On December 20th, I left my car parked in a shopping center on Main across from the Shamrock Hotel, took the shuttle bus to the airport, and flew into a new phase of my life.

Janet Genett Thiel and Ronald W. Hull were married on Dec 26, 1981

# 22

# Trying Marriage for a While

We married in a side room of the Presbyterian Church where I spent my teen years and Jan had recently become a member. My family was so large that I elected to invite only aunts and uncles, my brothers and sister, and their families. Jan's family was small, so she invited friends. It snowed 8 inches that December 26th, 1981, and I was pleased to see that all my elderly relatives made it in spite of the weather.

I sensed trouble had begun in our marriage when Jill rushed up crying after our vows to hug her mother and prevent the guests from welcoming us to our new life together. It was the first of many episodes where she expected her mother to choose between her marriage and the wishes of her child. Strong-willed as I was, I couldn't come between Jan and her daughter. In these situations, Jan always rallied to Jill's side and I let her do it. I thought that if she loved me she would stay by me no matter what her children thought or said.

We took a three-day honeymoon in Northern Wisconsin. It snowed the entire time, but not enough to make driving hazardous. The trip was a winter wonderland of green trees in Christmas white. Her warm Toyota replaced an open sleigh. Every turn was a picture postcard of farms, hills, and valleys filtered through a dusting of new snow still drifting in the air. Without reservations, we got a room at the Old Rittenhouse Inn in Bayfield. The room was drafty and the bath was in the hall, but the good food, fireplace and Victorian splendor made for an ideal honeymoon retreat. I'll never forget how the Apostle Islands rose out of Lake Superior like white mushrooms of sparkling snow and frost against the deep blue of sky and water.

As we enjoyed New Years Eve at a club back in Marshfield with high school friends, I realized how much she was leaving. At the same time, I felt that she could bring back a lot that I'd lost. I returned alone to Houston the next day.

By the end of January, Jan, Jill, and Toby, Jan's Lhasa Apso, arrived at the apartment. After frantically looking for a house to rent where there would be a good school for Jill, we found a condominium to rent in Sharpstown. Soon, Jan's furniture arrived, and it crowded the small condo until we got a storage space for the excess.

Jan got a job as manager of a Cargo furniture store in Westwood Mall. Her experience paid off and soon the store was selling more than any other in Houston. She won an all-expense paid trip to San Antonio. We hadn't been married six months, and already we had a second honeymoon.

Our flight was delayed that November morning because of fog. We finally got there by noon, rented a car, and drove to our hotel, the Hyatt. I was fighting off a cold but wanted to enjoy everything, so I joined her on the Riverwalk. Where before, unathletic Jan had been content to take long, slow, walks with me, now she walked out ahead, leaving me behind. Suffering from the effects of my cold, and falling behind in the crowd, I felt that although Jan seemed impervious to my paralysis, she couldn't empathize with it either and help me when it really counted.

We returned to the hotel, ate dinner to the tap of Flamenco dancers at El Mansion, and enjoyed a quiet evening on an overlook in the Hyatt. Like so many other times, a good night's rest and breakfast in bed rejuvenated me. Although Jan still walked out in front, I was able to keep up. We decided to stay later that Sunday and took a romantic ride on a horse-drawn carriage through the Prince William district before we caught the last flight home.

Jan had a great need to return "home"—Wisconsin. In the winter, I indulged that need by helping pay for flights to Milwaukee and Chicago. My family and her friends helped her get around on those occasional trips. Except for a quick car trip to Atlanta during spring break in 1982, I waited for my vacation in the summer to travel by car. Jan's Toyota Corolla didn't have power steering, required by my license, but because it had rear wheel drive and light steering, I was able to drive it easily.

In May 1982, we had a fund-raiser for beautification of the campus. We decided on a Los Vegas style theme of gambling for chips that was popular at the time. We scheduled it for the eve of Mother's Day. The mistake affected attendance as did the aversion some people had for gambling. But those who came had a good time. The evening was not entirely enjoyable for me because I was drinking gin and tonics and the bathroom was a long way from the main cafeteria floor. I was wearing a light-colored suit and a couple of times I didn't make it to the bathroom on time. I sat out part of the evening drying off outside so that I wouldn't be embarrassed.

The next morning, I awoke to a nagging, dull pain in my groin. I told Jan that I thought it was a hernia. A friend of mine had said that Kelsey-Seybold was a good clinic, so I went there on Monday. Dr. Jackson, a general surgeon, confirmed that I did have a hernia and that it should be surgically corrected. I decided to schedule it for the next Thursday. I asked for local anesthetic because my experience with general anesthetic in 1963 had been so devastating. I went to Josh and told him that I'd have to miss a little work. He was distraught, thinking wrongly that I'd be out for months. He seemed always to be expecting the worst case to happen.

The surgery was interesting. I felt some pain, but it was blunted by the sedatives they gave me. Although I couldn't see what Dr. Jackson was doing, I could feel him cutting and stitching in a remote sort of way, like when I'd touch hot pans in the kitchen and know I was burning but not feel any pain. They wheeled me directly to my room where Jan was waiting. Almost immediately I was up with help from Jan and the nurses to begin many trips to the bathroom. Jan was fantastic, hovering over me and catering to my every need. In the evening, she brought popcorn and gin and tonic in a Thermos bottle. We had a party.

I returned home on Saturday. Monday, I spent part of the day by the pool, but it felt strange, so I returned to work the next day.

I recovered quickly and we took an important trip north in late May of 1982 to celebrate my parent's fortieth wedding anniversary and Dad's pending retirement at 62 in the fall. I'd planted the idea of the party at my wedding and Jan and I carried out the details long distance via phone and letters. We didn't surprise them because it was too difficult. We had a picnic for family in the afternoon and a party at the VFW club that night. The high point of that occasion was that Tim met Kris, his future wife, as she passed through the park with a friend who knew Tom. They stopped to talk to Tom. That night, Kris came up to me at the VFW Club and told me that her mother had been my personal secretary the summer I spent in Marshfield. I remembered Kris as a teenager in the house.

We looked hard for a more permanent place to live. Jill was a big concern, because Jan wanted her to go to a good public school. Jill abhorred the bus ride to Sharpstown High School in the district our condo was in. The schools and cost of living close in forced us out to new developments that promised dream homes at high interest rates. The frenetic activity of thousands of newcomers to the city was forcing home prices to escalate a thousand dollars a month, putting pressure on us and a lot of others to buy. With Jan's promotion to district manager, her child support, and my anticipated raise in the fall of 82, we were able to swing a tract home in Keegan's Glen, a new development of three thousand residents set on land amid older developments. Jill would go to a new high school opening in the Alief School District.

The move was traumatic. We rented a trailer and hired two guys from my work to help out and do the heavy lifting. We had to make several trips. After I dropped and bent a prized antique pewter lamp, Jan ordered me not to carry any more of her things in. It hurt me not to help. Instead, I stood at the door and directed each box or piece to its appropriate room—she later thanked me for that.

Later, we almost got to blows over the reassembly of an oak church pew my parents had given us. My father and brother-in-law had broken the glued-on ends free so that we could transport it to Houston on top of the car. It fit nicely in a niche in our new kitchen. Jan had to get the heavy oak ends on the back, seat, and brace together at the same time. Without clamps, it was hard to pull all the pieces together for re-gluing. We decided to use long screws. Still, it was difficult to keep everything in line. Jan struggled and struggled while I watched, guided, and encouraged her, unable to help her finish the job. She got angry and quit working a couple of times, but finally she succeeded in getting the pew together and it looked great in that spot. After that, Jan often remarked that she, "...wished she had a man around the house." I wasn't concerned about my manhood. It did bother me that I couldn't do simple little household repairs without help.

Jan had collected many fine antiques and pine furniture dating back to the 18th century. She liked "country" and set about to decorate the house suitable for Better Homes and Gardens. She allowed me an upstairs bedroom, bathroom and closet space, but the rest of the house was hers. I approved. The only inconvenience was avoiding all the clutter of cute things that filled the house and delighted visitors. It didn't bother me as long as I didn't have to clean house around it all. Jan was very resourceful—most of the artwork was her own creation. So, our round formal dining room table was an old wooden wire reel covered with paisley cloth she sewed to disguise it.

The yard was another matter. I wanted to plant plants that would be perennial and help me maintain our small lot. Jan wanted flowers. I spent a lot of time digging flowerbeds. Houston soil has a clay base that becomes as hard as brick when it is dry. I remember the shock that would go through my arms and shoulders when I'd break the surface with my tined spade. I had to move dirt with small pails because that's all I could handle. We planted three additional trees and many shrubs. It took me three to four hours to dig the hole for each tree, and then Jan helped me plant it.

The first year our flowers were beautiful. Jan was good at planting but not too interested in maintaining. I started getting interested in flowers, bought a pruning book, and started spending many weekend hours nurturing our plants. The summer heat and humidity in Houston can be oppressive, but I enjoyed the outdoor work. Sometimes, I labored well into the evening. It was refreshing to be physically involved after long hours in an air-conditioned office or fighting city traffic. Like the time I spent alone in the woods or on the open highway, it was a time to forget my worries.

My limitations did bother me though, and I couldn't climb into my trees and prune them right. I struggled to fill a barrel with stones and dirt so that we could plant it with beautiful arrangements just outside our window. Jan volunteered to operate our new weed eater, but when she didn't have time do the work, I figured out how to use it just like I learned how to use other tools. The fact that my hands didn't work made things harder, but not impossible. I dug weeds out with a trowel or my spade rather than pulling them. I used small pots to move dirt because I couldn't pick up handfuls. I never pushed dirt down hard around plants but they still thrived. Seeds were the hardest to handle, because they were so small and easy to spill.

Jan helped me with planting so that the seeds would be even and at the right depth. Bags of soil, mulch, and fertilizer were also hard for me to handle and open. I learned to lift 50 lb bags out of my car trunk with my teeth, gripping them in a bear hug once I got them high enough. I opened bags with pokes from my spade, a tear with my teeth, or jabs with a big knife, whatever would get them open. Like dirt, I had to spread mulch by shoveling it into a small pail, and then carrying it to the site. Sometimes, Jan would carry the bags and spread them, making it easier. I didn't worry about the strain this work put on my body; in fact, I relished it. My only regret was that so few people saw the results of my work. Roses I planted in the sun thrived, and I took those to work where the secretaries appreciated them.

Jan was made district manager for Cargo, a furniture company based in Fort Worth and a subsidiary of Tandy Corporation. Her territory included all the stores in Austin, San Antonio, and Houston. She traveled often, always opening, refurbishing, or closing a store. Her schedule suited mine. We shared in the cooking and cleaning. And I was always there to feed Toby and water the plants. Jill, now at Elsik High School, lived her own life mostly in her own room. She rarely ate with us, but occasionally cooked, cleaned dishes and cared for Toby. I was not allowed to handle Jan's stoneware because it had a tendency to slip from my hands and break. She allowed me to put the cooking pans and utensils where I could get at them to cook and she often enjoyed my cooking after returning from a long day at the stores or a road trip. The kitchen was a friendly, cooperative place for us, and we talked and ate there freely.

Jan did not understand my need to study and work on finances every evening, after that I liked to watch a good movie on TV. She would have enjoyed it more if we had gone out to dinner often and cultivated a circle of evening friends. The bills and finances were entirely mine, and Jan bought all the groceries. She never asked for anything for Jill. Instead, she covered her expenses with the child support she received, her pay, and the money Jill earned working as a sales clerk after school and during the summer. I insisted that Jan have her own credit card and checking account. We didn't have enough to engage in Jan's real passion—buying fine antiques. But we had enough to travel modestly and buy the things we needed to furnish the house the way Jan liked.

# 23

# Turning TSU Around

At work, things went from strange to worse. The president's plan was to close the street that ran through campus, build peripheral parking lots, and both restore buildings that had fallen to disrepair and provide a wide range of expanded new facilities—all that expected from the civil rights report. We got the first money for the purchase of land, renovation of some buildings and our thermal plant, and a new health and physical education building. We began aggressively buying property to make way for a Master Plan that would change this ethnocentric, small, inner-city school into a large, multicultural institution capable of meeting the needs of young people into the Twenty-First Century. But, there were immediate problems.

Before I arrived, armed robbers had taken $80,000 from our cashiers at registration. Burglary on campus was rampant, often perpetrated by employees, while our police officers were often accused of inappropriate or illegal behavior. I was given the task of responding to a Governor's Commission review of the police department. Morale was low and leadership was inadequate. Turnover had reached nearly eighty percent per year and was blamed on defections for opportunities in other area police forces. After hiring consultants, changing police chiefs several times, securing buildings with motion detectors and other devices, and improving staff training, we eliminated most of the burglary. Automobile theft was harder, but fencing parking lots and providing more on lot security reduced that. The problem of misuse of budget funds by managers was exacerbated by condoned increase in drug use by professionals. Several managers were found to be using university property or funds for their own purposes. These discoveries were always a source of great concern and embarrassment.

The university was in a high crime area, and we had our share of rapes, muggings, assaults, and even murders. While each incident was traumatic, and sometimes our police were ineffective in preventing or solving a crime, the police could not be blamed for crimes that were going to happen, regardless of police presence.

The buildings were dirty and in a state of disrepair. Our maintenance workers worked out of metal buildings with dirt floors behind the old gym. Although concentration on our grounds crew had resulted in regular cutting of the grass and garbage pickup, junk from inadequate campus maintenance spilled out on the grounds and into every unused cavity of our buildings.

I was asked to follow up on a Workers' Compensation inspection of our buildings. The inspection had found many safety problems caused by unsafe management of laboratory chemicals, unsafe use of materials and tools by our custodial and maintenance staffs, and unsafe conditions cause by poor maintenance of buildings. I received opposition to requests to start correcting the problems, but eventually wrote the plan that created a safety division, safety committees, and set us on a course that eventually corrected the problems.

A committee was established in the Governor's Office to provide disabled persons better access to State Institutions. I was asked to develop a plan for access to facilities, degree programs, employment, and services at the university. We created a committee and provided a plan to the State. The Texas Rehabilitation Commission had limited referrals of its clients to TSU because of barriers in our buildings, especially housing. We set out to correct that by including access modifications in our renovations, primarily parking spaces, curb cuts, ramps, door improvements, elevator, and bathroom modifications.

We were going to close Wheeler Street through campus and create a pedestrian mall. We wanted to establish areas of beauty to help promote a sense of campus and tranquility that would encourage the learning process. A committee of community people was established to get ideas and promote the process. The committee decided to have a dinner to raise money. I suggested that we get Alex Haley as a keynote speaker. The committee chairperson wanted Miss America to appear. At the time Vanessa Williams was Miss America. Miss America's schedule is booked two years in advance so it was impossible to get Ms. Williams to appear. Fortunately, Suzette Charles, the first runner-up, was available, and we booked her to sing two songs. I was asked to get Mr. Haley to come.

I called Playboy Enterprises because I knew he was one of their staff writers. They put me in touch with his agency. He was on a cargo ship trying to finish a book about his hometown, Henning, Tennessee. We were able to book him after he returned from his self-imposed exile at sea—the only time he could write after the tremendous success of Roots.

When the day of the dinner arrived, I was assigned to greet Ms. Charles. There was a news conference in the downtown hotel, followed by an impromptu lunch for Ms. Charles and the university president's wife. I was asked to join them. The organizer had ordered the lunch without planning it. The hotel manager demanded payment for the lunch from me. Fortunately, I was able to call the office and arrange payment to avoid embarrassment.

That evening, Jan arrived early, and we helped open the dining hall. Alex arrived relaxed with some Black Muslim friends. Josh said Alex enjoyed stopping at Frenchy's Fried Chicken on the way from the airport. I asked to take his jacket, and he allowed me to take it to the cloakroom. Ms. Charles arrived nervous, concerned about the location of the campus and the attention of the crowd. I offered to take her fur coat, but she refused, taking it with her to the dining hall rather than trust me with it.

Jan and I were honored to sit at the head table, between the two stars, and I was asked to say a few words. Suzette's songs were exceptional, and Alex warmed everyone's hearts when he spoke of the role Black universities had played in the education of youth who would not otherwise have the opportunity. The high point of the evening came when Suzette was signing a picture of both stars together, already signed by Alex. I came over to ask her something, and she handed one to me. The photographer was upset that I got one, but there was nothing he could do.

He planned to sell them all.

The evening ended on a sour note. Suzette's chaperone asked me to pay her for the evening. Being unfamiliar with show business, I refused, saying that we would send a check when the university fiscal office cleared the paperwork. The chaperone became irate and the next day called the president's office and told them that I'd been rude by not providing immediate payment. There was no problem for Alex, we simply sent a check to his agency, but I remained uneasy until a check was sent to Suzette's family. Apparently it is common for fundraisers to refuse to pay entertainers, especially if they don't raise enough money to cover expenses. The common practice was to pay entertainers in cash immediately after their performances. I was familiar with the slow, but sure, way the State of Texas paid its bills, but unaware of the ethics of show business. After her father called, Susette was paid. I hope she doesn't still hold it against me.

On our honeymoon at the Old Rittenhouse Inn, we dined on Lake Superior lake trout and enjoyed a room in the Bayfield Wsconsin winter wonderland. This was the style of life Jan wanted to live.

# 24

# The End of a Brief Romance

Our marriage began to unravel. Jan's friends, Bob and Karen Rasmussen, came from Wisconsin, and we decided to go to San Antonio for something to do. Jill was to stay home and watch the house and Toby. Before we left, Jill came down with a sore throat that she said was strep throat. I didn't know how serious strep throat was and insisted that Jill would be okay alone at home. This launched an emotional tirade about how insensitive I was and how much danger Jill would be in if we left her. Finally, after much discussion, we decided to go under the gloom of guilt about leaving Jill alone with Toby.

We took old highway 90 and Jan drove her car. It was a cold, windy, dreary day. Jan apparently got warm from the argument and with all of us in the car, turned on the air conditioning. She insisted on using the heat setting so that the cold air came out at our feet. Before long my legs were very cold and I had to stop to urinate. There weren't any places to stop and she refused to switch the air to the top vents where I could direct the cold air away from me. I got agitated but could do nothing. Finally a rest area appeared ahead. There were no restrooms, but I went behind a tree and relieved myself. When I came back to the car, I asked to sit in the back with Bob. Karen agreed to sit up front. While I was still getting in, Jan drove forward, running the car's rear wheel up on my right ankle. I yelled, "Stop!" and she did, allowing the car to roll back. I was unhurt, but Jan's anger never allowed her to say, "I'm sorry," or even acknowledge that she could have caused me serious injury.

We called Jill when we got to San Antonio. She was okay. I made the best of things and enjoyed the company of her friends the rest of our time there. Bob drove us back on the freeway. Jan didn't trust me to drive.

In the spring, we decided to spend a weekend in Corpus Christi. Jan wanted to take Jill and Toby along. Spring wild flowers were in bloom and we enjoyed the trip down, stopping occasionally to look at the flowers by the road and let Toby run. We got a late start, so it was getting dark by the time we got to Corpus. We checked a couple of motels and found that they wouldn't take Toby. Finally, we were at the beach and all the hotels were very expensive. After driving back and forth along the beach and over a high bridge that, in Jill's words, "Makes me sick..." We took a motel unit with a view of the Bay. In the morning it was cold and foggy and the beach was deserted, so we left. We explored Corpus's beautiful homes and North Padre Island, and then stopped on the beach at Mustang Island. Heading out in Sunday traffic, we were caught in a line waiting to take the ferry at Aransas Pass. The ferry is usually a pleasure because dolphins can be seen playing during the crossing.

Two couples were in the convertible ahead of us. The driver reached over and emptied his ashtray in the road. I said, "Did you see that! I'm going to tell him he can't do that."

I got out of the car with both Jan and Jill yelling at me to stop, and walked up to him. I told him that it was against the law to litter and that it was guys like him who left the beaches a mess. He said, "I go to the beach all the time," as if that gave him some kind of right to litter.

I said, "That's your problem." And returned to the car.

Jan and Jill were livid. "Do you want to get us killed?" They didn't talk to me after that, and we drove home in silence. Somehow I had, in their eyes, gone from being this knight in shining armor, this brainy guy who had overcome serious injury to conquer the academic world, to being a jerk that always did and said the wrong thing and put them in discomfort and danger. I was only doing what I'd always done, telling someone what I thought when they were being thoughtless. I knew the next time that guy went to empty an ash tray on the street he'd think of me, get angry, and maybe, stop doing a stupid thing. Jan and Jill couldn't understand that. They only saw me provoking a fight. I never provoked a fight in my life. I'd provoked a few thoughts, but never a fight.

Some would say that I deserved it, but I never was in a fight because I was paralyzed. I'd say it's because I knew when to walk away. The bullies of this world love to pick on the weak, and would have loved to fight me because I would be so easy. I never gave them a reason or a chance. Knowledge is power, and doing the right thing is power, it disarms the bad guys when you catch them at their game.

Our next trip, July of 1983, was eventful and got off to a bad start. I had bought an overhead car carrier for the Toyota that increased its carrying capacity and freed the back seat for Jill and Toby. With our neighbors' help, we got it installed the night before our trip. Just before we left, I went out to the garage and tried to lift a suitcase up over my head into the carrier. I slipped and fell to the floor on my right elbow. My right shoulder was torn as badly as my left had been on the ice in December 1964.

Jan told me not to load anything else. I was in pain but knew that going to the hospital would only delay our trip. Instead, I took an aspirin and decided to head out anyway. I could still drive with my left arm. The only comfortable place for my injured arm was cradling it at ninety degrees across my lap. Driving would keep my mind off the pain and give Jan a rest from all the trip preparation and a hard work week.

We left about 10 am. It was already dark when we reached Little Rock. We stopped several places, but without reservations, couldn't find a motel room. Finally, about midnight, after much bickering and no motel in sight, I told them to go to sleep while I drove on through. Jan offered to drive, but after about an hour, she couldn't stay awake, and I took over again.

At Memphis, before reaching the Mississippi River, I turned north on Interstate 55. Up ahead, I crossed the river to take I-57 to Chicago. I crossed too soon, taking I-155 and finding myself on an unfamiliar military highway in northwestern Tennessee. Jan and Jill were asleep, so I couldn't check the map. Finally, I reached US 51 and drove north on it, knowing that it would take us to Wisconsin.

At dawn, I stopped at a McDonald's and felt refreshed from the food and rest. Jan and Jill were still sleepy, so I continued to drive through little towns and occasional showers. Suddenly, as we came over a little rise, the next valley was a lake! The downpours had caused a small stream to leave its banks and cover the road for a half-mile ahead. We were late and off course; now, I feared we'd have to be delayed some more.

I pulled up to a truck with a flashing yellow light. A man came out and told me that I could make it across if I stayed to the left. The road was like a dam, overflowing with water. As we eased across with the water reaching the bottom of our doors, I was grateful that we were so loaded, keeping us from being swept off the road. When we reached the bridge, it was high and dry, but then, another two hundred yards of water faced us. We got through easily, and saw no other flooding.

By mid-morning, after crossing the Ohio River at Cairo, we were stopped dead on I-57 for a half hour. Apparently some guy had crossed the median and flipped his car. He was killed, but no other cars were involved. The ambulance had left when we finally reached the accident scene.

By evening, we reached Mike's apartment in Madison. We showered and, although I hadn't slept, I felt refreshed enough to drive on. Jan insisted that Mike drive. Near Baraboo, Jan had Mike pull over to the side for a brief thunderstorm. We finally made it to the lake about 11 pm, after a snowy owl had startled Mike like a ghost when it flew up from the middle of the road on a 22-mile lonely stretch of gravel. In spite of my arm, I slept well that night.

The rest of our vacation, Jan had to accompany me to the bathroom because I couldn't use two hands to operate my zipper. The pain in my shoulder came and went, mostly when I tried to straighten the arm. I endured by keeping the arm cradled and still, and with an occasional aspirin. By the end of our vacation, I was able to use the arm normally again. It was a good thing, because Jan was tired of having to help me.

We spent a honeymoon night at the Old Rittenhouse Inn 12//28/81

# 25

# New Responsibilities at Work

The political seas at TSU were stormy, so one day Josh called me in and made me director of land. He said it was for my job security; Vice presidents were subject to being fired and their assistants with them. Since I couldn't "retreat" into teaching like he could because I didn't have a faculty appointment, he gave me a functional position useful to the university.

The university had been quietly buying over three hundred properties in the vicinity of campus to provide sites for proposed buildings and parking lots. Some of the owners left after selling and the university leased the houses, some were simply vacated, and some owners, mostly elderly, stayed in their houses rent-free until the university needed the property. The area was mostly poor, Black, and there are many rental houses, duplexes, and small apartment buildings. During the early 80s, mental institutions were releasing mildly disturbed people and giving them a bus ticket to cities like Houston. Some of these people, as well as the usual winos, drug addicts, and the unemployed, found their way into the vacated houses and apartments.

The vacant houses could be dangerous. But, over months of visiting the properties, I rarely faced a dangerous situation. The people were friendly and as concerned about vandalism and stripping as I was. Squatters were often difficult to dislodge, especially after we had encouraged them to stay in our apartment houses to discourage stripping. Strippers would take aluminum windows, copper wire, fixtures and furnishings, lumber, and even brick, if they could get some money for it. The squatters did a lot of the stripping. In some cases, we had to use court proceedings to evict squatters. In others, a nudge of the building by a demolition bulldozer sent the vagrants scurrying with their belongings in hand. In one case, after several months with no rent, we had to evict a young welfare mother with three children. Her sometime boyfriend had threatened to kill some of the elderly residents on the street. She sat on her belongings with her children and read from her bible. A fellow staff member felt sorry for her and moved her to an apartment house we owned for student housing. Even with help that was brought in she continued not paying her minimal rent and was eventually moved to public housing.

The hardest were the elderly. These people owned their own homes and had often planned to spend the rest of their lives in the only house they'd ever owned. Some were sick and had no help from relatives or friends. Leaving was a heart-wrenching process, tearing them away from the only neighborhood they'd ever known. Even though the university paid generously for the properties, often it wasn't enough for the owner to replace the home. Although I didn't track it, I believe that the trauma of dislocation caused the death of some of these longtime residents.

"Red" is a good example. Willie Jones was 82 and lived in a ramshackle house on a little back street with his mentally-retarded daughter and a grandson. He and his buddies often worked on cars in his small front yard under a large Crepe Myrtle. Red claimed that he was the first to convince his neighbors to sell their houses to the university. One by one, over a period of four years, houses were sold, vacated, and torn down.

Red never signed the papers to sell his place though, claiming a small discrepancy in the paperwork for the $11,500 the university had settled with him. Finally, his home was the only one left. Our contracted realtor found him a couple of houses, but Red turned them down. I saw one that was quite nice, but Red said it was in a bad neighborhood. Finally, the lady next to him had moved out and I sold him her house for $50. He bought a lot in Sunnyside near one of his daughters' house and moved the building to that site. A colleague and I visited him in the new location and found the house totally unfinished on the inside, without wiring or plumbing. We promised to find help to help him get it finished, but never got back. I feel guilty that we couldn't do more for this man who had to give up his lifetime home so that we could build a parking lot.

I was responsible for demolition. I tried to save as many large trees as possible; but sometimes, the roots of saved trees were damaged, and they died anyway. This was especially true of the native Loblolly Pine. I was proud of an area along the southern border of campus that was not developed and became a park. In other areas all the trees I saved were bulldozed out to make all concrete parking lots. We saved the Crepe Myrtle that marked Red's place. It's the only reminder that the sea of concrete called Parking Lot E was once a thriving neighborhood.

I was also given the facilities inventory. The FI was an accounting of all buildings and rooms on campus, including coding them for academic use and measuring them for square footage.

While tripping and stumbling around demolition sites was often difficult, measuring and coding rooms for the FI was particularly onerous. It was impossible to use a tape measure without help, and difficult to use a clipboard and carry a rolling measuring stick from room to room. The record keeping was relatively easy and the information we obtained was essential for calculating formulas that provided budgets for university maintenance. Students were not as much help as I'd hoped. Some had difficulty measuring and some with coding. Most had difficulty completing work without close supervision. Often, I had to redo work done by students for me.

I was also given responsibility for energy conservation. Initially this consisted of identifying and recording consumption in all of our utility accounts. Working with the city water department, we identified 63 unused accounts from properties the university had acquired. By closing these accounts, we eliminated underground leaks that had existed for years. We eliminated campus natural gas lines that were dangerous and subject to constant maintenance, and facilitated the acquisition of natural gas from Texas land at virtually no cost. I discovered double billing on our main electricity account that resulted in an $80,000 refund.

# 26

# Our House Comes Apart

Jan started experiencing personnel problems with her stores and frustration that she was away from home a lot. We talked and, although I knew it would mean less pay, I told her that it would be all right to quit Cargo and start a business or work at whatever she wanted. She got a job at Hofer Furniture, but quit in a couple of days because she didn't like a homosexual on the staff. Mr. Hofer apparently gave Jan a job the guy wanted and he made it hard for her to work there. She started working for Lord and Taylor in the Galleria, selling cosmetics. After a month, she joined Marshall Field's, looking for a better job, but returned to Lord and Taylor after a week. She was clearly dissatisfied with her situation, but I could do nothing to help her except to encourage her. Later, I heard that she said I made her quit Cargo. I recall encouraging her to stick it out with them. Maybe she felt she had to quit because of my situation and me. Maybe she was just looking for someone to blame for her bad decision.

Jan decided to sell Mary Kay cosmetics. I encouraged her and helped her out with the initial expenses. She was enthusiastic at first and developed several contacts. But, before long, her enthusiasm cooled. The Mary Kay business had a loss the first year and I don't know how she did after that. At some point, she quit giving me her paychecks. We had established separate bank accounts because I wanted her to be financially independent. She bought all the groceries and things for the house. I paid the mortgages and all the bills. She had child support money from her ex husband for Jill and Jill worked, so I was never asked to pay anything for Jill. Neither of us spent a lot on ourselves. She wanted to go to Wisconsin more than we could afford, but I paid for the airfare because I wanted her to be happy.

When I complained that I had to borrow money to pay our bills, Jan asked me to sell the house. When I asked where we would live, she didn't know. I knew that we could only sell the house at a loss, and renting a smaller apartment would cost us more. I started a nationwide job search, focusing most of my effort on landing something in Atlanta. After applying for over one hundred positions in the Chronicle of Higher Education and sending my resume to and contacting a hundred more companies in the Atlanta area, I got no interviews. It was hard to explain that I couldn't replace my job easily, when Jan could land another job in a week. With all my experience and education, it was hard to break into equivalent work.

It was depressing. Before this I had a plan for my career. Even though I'd received some setbacks, I had overcome my paralysis to reach a certain level of success. I couldn't leave my house and job without a plan, without something to fall back on. In retirement, I'd planned to return to the house in Georgia. All we had to do was stick it out until my retirement fund grew to the point where it could sustain us. Jan didn't want that. She wanted out. She wanted to return to Wisconsin. I couldn't return to Wisconsin. Those few short months I spent there in the spring of 1981 told me that I could no longer take the cold winters. At an impasse, we sought counseling and Jan planned a divorce.

I found a counseling service that we would have to pay. Jan rejected that. Even though we hadn't gone to church, I found a church counselor who would take us. First, he talked to us separately. Then, he had one session with both of us. He wanted Jill to join us, but she wouldn't come. Jan didn't go again either. I returned alone. The minister said that Jan was suffering from several losses in her life: her father's breakdown, her mother's death, her son's absence going to college, her divorce, and the potential of losing me. He said that she needed counseling and he wasn't sure just what she wanted or needed. I got more depressed. I saw him two more times alone. He told me that he could do nothing for us without Jan's participation.

Jill graduated from high school and drove for college without any savings. She chose UW-Milwaukee and entered as a resident student because her father lived in Milwaukee. With Jill gone, Jan moved out. She stayed with friends a few weeks, and then shared an apartment with a young girl she worked with. She left me with Toby, the house, and the bills. It bothered me that she didn't leave me an address or phone number. But, I didn't try to find her. She returned most Sundays, did my laundry, cooked me an evening meal, and groomed Toby. We didn't argue. I just accepted what she had to do.

When she had saved enough money, she announced that she was moving to Wisconsin and she wanted me to get a divorce. She said that she'd seen a lawyer and he told her to go to our bank account, take all the money, and close it. She said she couldn't do that, so she walked out. She told me that I could have the house; all she wanted was to take her things and leave.

Finally, it was time for her to leave. I hired a couple of guys from work and Mike flew down to drive the rental truck back. I went to work that morning as Jan and Mike started packing. He shook his head as I passed by, as though he disapproved of what was happening. Like me, he could do nothing to stop it. When I returned home from work the house was empty. It finally sank in. I was alone. Jan told me later that a few hours out of Houston she got sick, stopped by the road, and just shook from all the tension and exhaustion. It wasn't like that for me. It was just an emptiness... an emptiness as empty as the house.

Jan left me my desk and desk chair, my TV, and the sofa bed from Cargo that we bought on sale. I couldn't operate the sofa bed, so I bought a mattress and slept on the floor until I could afford a bed. It was four years before I had any furniture.

I hired an attorney that had worked for the university but was now in private practice. He filed a simple, uncontested divorce. Jan signed the papers through her attorney in Milwaukee and wasn't present in court. When I received the decree, I discovered a serious mistake in the wording. It was a typographical error, but required two court appearances to correct. I also learned that the house wasn't included. My attorney, unwilling to change the decree, and her attorney, thinking that Jan could gain if I sold the house, refused to change that.

# 27

# Buried in Work and Debt

I was one of the first to move into our new general services building. I was assigned a large office with a window. A couple of days after I moved in, workmen appeared to move me across the hall. I complained, but nothing was done about it. Two years later, the guy who had me moved was locked out of what would have been my office and banished to a waiting to be renovated, empty building. But I never moved back. When our new furniture arrived, I got a secretarial desk instead of an executive desk like the other directors. I heard later that the architectural director had forgotten to order a desk for himself, so he took mine. I did get a covered parking space, farther down from the architectural director, but out of the large puddle that formed under his car after each rain. Sweet justice.

High interest rates and the economic downturn that hit Houston in 1985 devastated my neighborhood. Except for the two families who lived across from me, all the houses on my street were either abandoned or put up for sale. With few options, I gritted my teeth and continued to use creative financing to pay my bills. I focused on growing flowers and bringing work home to soothe my pain. I didn't go out. I didn't spend money on myself except to buy clothes for work. And, I didn't travel except to the lake each summer.

Jan had put my socks on each morning. She hated it when I got up at six and woke her up at seven thirty to help me put my socks on. When she left, I tried new approaches like sewing elastic on socks at great expense only to find that it didn't work. Eventually, I developed a technique that amounted to a struggle on the bedroom floor as I alternately rubbed, pulled, and stretched my socks on. It kept taking longer and longer, but I just kept getting up earlier.

My legs got stiff easily and I started to drag my left shoe, wearing the sole out quickly. We had an HMO called Maxicare at Kelsey-Seybold Clinic. I went there for help in 1986. I was referred to a neurologist, Dr. Antonio Arana. Dr. Arana was concerned with the deterioration we perceived. After a number of tests and a review of my medical records, he concluded that aging caused my condition and he could only give me assistance. I was given a series of exercises to increase strength and flexibility. He then fitted me with a plastic ankle brace to keep my left foot from dropping. The first day I tried it, it broke off just above my shoe heel as I started down a flight of stairs. The sudden break was quite a scare, almost throwing me off balance. A cold chill ran down my back as I balanced on the thought of falling down the stairs, but somehow, I stood there quavering a moment, and then recovered. Later, Arana prescribed a heavier brace that eventually became indispensable. Still, it took me a long time to start wearing it because I was not used to walking without my foot dropping. Having my foot locked at a ninety-degree angle required a different way of walking. The awkwardness caused more tripping until I learned how to move my foot with my ankle locked in place.

My problems with physical strain, loneliness, and money spilled over into my work. I became irritable and impatient with my fellow workers and students. The dulling routine of work and my home life left me isolated. I wanted someone to care, to empathize with my situation. Most people considered what was happening to me my own fault and gave me advice like, "Why don't you buy a new car?" When I couldn't even qualify for a loan. "Why don't you go to church (and meet a girl)?" When I am an atheist. "Why don't you join the YMCA?" When going there would mean dressing in a locker room and getting home about 8 pm. Going to public events became difficult. Navigating parking lots and hotels was hard. I was always hoping that a restroom was nearby. It was difficult to stand alone. A drink that I enjoyed at these events became difficult to hold, and sometimes spilled as I was bumped into others or tried to pick it up from a table. Invariably, these events had "finger food." If I ate at all, I had to find a table, usually far from the conversation. I made an effort to meet and talk to people. Often, I was still left alone in a room full of people, all of them in animated conversation except me.

# 28

# A Way Out of Depression

I had to do something different, something to get away from the rut I was in. I tried taking drives, but driving in Houston took me to more traffic and urban clutter than I cared to see. Finally, about a half hour drive from my home, I found Brazos Bend State Park. The Park was just what I needed. It consists of several small curved lakes formed by the Brazos riverbed when floods changed the wandering river's course, the river, a couple of miles of road linking the lakes, and a few thousand acres of abandoned Texas farmland. All of this land and lakes was gradually returning to wilderness. There were many trails. I was drawn to them and the adventure they promised.

I became familiar with friendly armadillos that seemed to like to dig for food along the trails. One always appeared under a streetlight, searching for food the light brought, as I left the park each night. I enjoyed the alligators, either sunning themselves like old tires by the water's edge or pushing v-shaped waves with their snouts as they glided silently across weedless stretches of calm water. Herons and ibises glided serenely along the trees near the water's edge or walked, hesitantly along the reeds, intently looking for a morsel to spear with their sharp beaks. Cormorants, ducks, and coots noisily foraged the water's edges or sat silently in their roosts, enjoying the sun.

Overhead, buzzards wound their dizzying search patterns on afternoon thermals, flying as though they were always coasting to a landing, but never reaching the ground. Eagles, ospreys and hawks swooped in and out of view from high perches, sometimes screaming their hunting cry, sometimes silently descending on their prey with only a shadow or wing whistle for warning. Sometimes, the brush was alive with the bursting flights of small birds, always in a hurry, as they darted in and out of the shadows. More often, the brush was silent in a way that soothed my troubled mind.

I choose the paths less traveled, the ones that headed for the river or for a secluded lake where I could sense the stillness and warmth of the waning day. Watching dust and insects rising in the angling light, waiting for a bird or animal to wend its way to me. Oblivious of my presence, the little dramas of daily life, feeding and resting, were carried out. I savored these moments, knowing that I was only an observer in this world. Still, I longed to be a part of it. Something ancient stirred in me. I knew how Thoreau and the Indian felt. Life in the natural world is so wondrous and precious. Why do we want to destroy it, bulldoze it down, and build artificial boxes filled with artificial technological things to amuse and comfort us? Watching squirrels, rabbits, and black birds sharing the food rich ground under spreading live oaks in the evening should teach us something about peacefully coexisting with our fellow creatures. Life in nature is harsh, and death comes swiftly. But there is peace and comfort too. Sharing is better than fighting or fearing.

On weekends, I would wake early and spend the morning cleaning the remains of a week at work. Some places I couldn't reach to clean, like the deep recesses of cabinets. After hours on my knees, my legs would hurt, but I usually managed to clean the floors. Other days, I would be in the yard early, digging out weeds, mowing, edging, or trimming shrubs. I managed to handle my old electric weedeater all right, but occasionally, I would slip, and the cord would slice my bare ankles like a hot knife. With my altered feeling, it was a searing pain that I would ignore, like the strain in my shoulders as I fought to hold the powerhead high and steady as it cut its path through St. Augustine grass grown wild.

I'd spend hours on my knees in my flowerbeds tilling and weeding my impatiens, geraniums, begonias, periwinkles, salvia, and pinks. But not without discovering an occasional fire ant bite unfelt in the heat of my work or the panic of a swarm of fire ants as I beat and struggled to rid myself of their firebrand savage bites. When bags of fertilizer, mulch, and insecticide got too heavy to lift to my arms with my teeth, or carry on wobbling legs to the back of the house. I often found them falling or spilling, me with it, before I got to my destination. Then, I'd open the side of the bag with the sharp tines of my spade and shovel the contents into small pails that I'd carry to their destination.

I enjoyed trimming my shrubs with a two-handed shears. Standing up and pruning was a lot easier than working on my knees in the beds. It was hot work, and sometimes hard to reach where I had to cut off new growth. It was also hard to hold the shears stable at arms length. Many times my sweating hands would lose their grip and the shears would fall to my feet. It never struck my feet, but often, blades open, it fell to the ground and stuck, like a well-aimed knife into a log. Every time that happened, I thought of the awful wound the five pound tool could inflict if it stuck one of my feet. But I shook the thought off, readjusted my grip on the handle, and continued clipping.

Twice, maybe more, while reaching far back into a shrub to reach a branch, I fell onto the shrub. Caught in the broken branches, sharp edges digging into my skin, with my feet off the ground and my arms twisted and tangled, I lay alone in the back yard wondering how I could extract myself from this painful predicament. Somehow I managed, after minutes of struggle, to work myself into a position where I could get to my knees, and then push myself up, grabbing whatever solid support I could.

After these hot, dirty, bruising sessions in the yard, I'd enjoy a shower to wash the grime off, and then head upstairs to my study and face the bills and correspondence that had piled up all week. By three or four o'clock, I'd stop what I was doing and head for the park. Through the rice fields on the way, the road was straight and clear, punctuated with sharp turns every mile or so. I would let out the V8 under the Monte's hood on the long straight-aways, sometimes exceeding 100 mph, and then ease off for the curves, avoiding the brakes, letting the engine and centrifugal force slow the car to the point where, emerging from a curve, I'd accelerate once more. With the warmth of the afternoon in my face, I enjoyed these wild, free drives almost as much as my arrival at the destination that I was hurrying to reach. All the pain of yard work, the loneliness of an empty house, and the burden of money worries were shed. I was free.

I'd park where I thought I'd come out at dark and head away from the noise and civilization of the picnic areas. Around the corner, down the path, beckoned a world as timeless as the continent. In mid summer, it was hot. On late Sunday afternoons, the public areas were almost deserted. Still, I hurried to leave the cries of children behind, walking as fast as my faltering legs would take me through the darkening forest trails to the openings where the deer came out to feed and play. Sometimes, there would be mosquitoes, and I would walk fast to avoid them. These mosquitoes were nothing like the hoard that would rise at dusk over Wisconsin lakes, or the giant black ones with stings like hypodermic needles that attacked me as soon as I climbed over the dunes from the windy beach to pee; they were a minor annoyance that I could walk out of the shade and away from.

My favorite spot on evenings when there was little time was by a small lake at a point where a bridge now crosses to an observatory on a small rise. Ironically, the first disabled access trail in the park. Deer moved along the lake at that time of day, and often I could hear them coming to me along the brushy water's edge long before I'd see them. Nervous and cautious, sensing me but not seeing me as they made their way, these deer walked familiar paths. Twice, close to where the observatory now stands, a big buck appeared, his large rack of antlers in velvet, less than ten feet away. We stared at each other, and then he was gone.

On an overgrown road leading to a clearing where the deer came out to graze in the remaining sun, I heard a loud screaming sound. I froze in my tracks and stared at the tall grass and brush, moving as the noisy intruder passed through. I did not see what I think was a bobcat, screaming at I don't know what, perhaps a squirrel or rabbit it was pursuing, perhaps a female in heat? The sound sent a shiver down my spine. But I was not afraid, only curious to see what made the unseen sound.

When I had more time, I'd head for the river about a half-mile from the nearest road. The initial woods here opened into long fields and pecan groves, once farmed but now left alone, except for occasional cutting and burning by the park service. Old road and fencerows were still clear, and some vehicle tracks could be seen, even though vehicle traffic was prohibited. Here, the deer moved more quickly as I came upon them. Bucks were more common, but more wary than the does, as they stayed back, close to the brush and snorted their disapproval of my scent in their territory.

The old roads had low spots where rainwater formed puddles. Some of these were pig wallows for ferrule pigs that lived along the river. One evening, rounding a bend, I saw a large sow with piglets in the road a couple of hundred yards ahead. As she faded into the brush, I moved ahead, more curious than fearful. When I got there she was gone. That area contained several wallows, and areas completely dug up by pigs looking for roots. I always walked with trepidation, not wanting to come between a protective sow and her young, or in the path of a rampaging boar. Still, my curiosity was greater than my fear, even though I couldn't run or climb a tree. Wild creatures had always given me respect, even deference. I trusted that thought over stories of wild, rampaging beasts attacking any unsuspecting person who entered their territory. I still respected the small potential for danger.

One gloomy Sunday, hurrying back along the field road that bordered the brushy area where I saw the most evidence of pig activity, I saw several dark shapes cross from the deep field grass to the brush on the left, about one hundred feet ahead. When I got to where they had crossed I saw about fifteen javelina rapidly disappearing into the brush. They weren't the pigs I'd hoped to see, and I only got a glimpse, but aside from three times from the car along the road, these were the first I'd seen in the wild.

A couple of weeks later, going the same way in about the same spot, I passed a couple. We said hellos and continued. I rarely saw other people on these trails. Suddenly, on my right, the deep field grass was moving and I caught the profile of a five foot long monster, tail and long, dark brown hair flying, huffing and puffing and squealing, heading for the brush behind me. I turned toward the commotion, but it was moving about thirty miles an hour and quickly crossed into the brush between the couple and me. I yelled at them, now turned toward me, "Did you see that?" And they said, Yeah!" We said nothing more and the scene was again silent. I had a lot to think about as I returned to the car and back to that place again. I don't know if it was a sow or a boar, or why it decided to charge for the cover of brush like that. Perhaps it felt trapped or angry that we were in its territory, I don't know. I only know that I was glad not to be in its path.

Sometimes, near dark, I'd wait by one lake behind which was a slough that was the rookery for area blackbirds. In waves of undulating black, thousands of birds would fly in from the surrounding countryside for the night. It was fascinating to see so many birds in one place, especially when they'd flair up from some dispute or scare. It looked like someone waving huge, but almost transparent, black flags in the distance. But I'm sure local farmers wished this sanctuary didn't exist.

One evening, I took a new route along an old road that seemed to lead away and eventually out of the park. Standing on the trail looking for deer, I felt a burning sensation on my ankle. Looking down, I was standing on a fire ant mound with dozens of ants swarming on my shoe. I stepped aside, stomped my foot, and eventually had to kick off my shoe. It was hard to get my shoe back on, but eventually I did. I continued on my way, wary of ant mounds after that. I passed a large cage, presumably used to capture animals, and onward along a shallow lake, hoping to see more deer ahead.

It grew dusk, and then dark, and the lake came alive with the sound of tree frogs and booming alligators. A fog rose up and the landscape became surreal. Searching for the sight of deer in the growing gloom became like looking for ghosts. An owl hooted. I made my way down the trail toward the car.

One time I took the river trail after it had rained earlier that week. I had to skirt some flooded and muddy stretches of trail going in, and several bad areas of mud near the pig wallows, but I was doing okay. Coming back along a familiar field, the trail was flooded with one to two inches of water. I gingerly walked the high ground along the old road, often in water, until my feet were wet. After a half mile of this, I decided to take a wooded trail to the left out of the water. The trail wound up and down, working its way through the trees. It became muddy. I started up a rise, started to slip, and slid back down, putting my hand out, I went down on one knee. As I forced myself back up to my feet, my legs started to shake. I was afraid that I'd fall and be unable to get back up. It was getting dark, and unlikely anyone would come along. It seemed that slippery mud was everywhere as I worked my way back to the field. Now, I was afraid of falling on the wet grass, no longer muddy but still slippery, and covered with water getting deeper as I went. There was no place to stop and rest, only more and more water. Finally, near the car and dark, I reached a ditch and mud hole that was impassable. I had to stumble through tall grass and brush to reach the road. I was glad to have made it.

Twice, late in the fall, on warm days, I found a kind of paradise. Far down the road past the pig wallows, perhaps beyond the park, a group of deer lounged in a large field close to woods. There were bucks in the group, standing off from the does. Afraid to upset them, I moved no closer, but watched them from a distance for a long time. A week or so later I returned to that place a little earlier in the day. This time there were more deer, about thirty, in the field, and six bucks with large racks. The does and yearling fawns grazed in small groups, and the bucks circled and sometimes locked horns in tentative combat. A farm road bisected the field on the right side and disappeared in the distance toward the river to the north. I inched my way down this road, one step at a time, until I reached the deer. They seemed not to pay any attention to me as groups grazed and frolicked closer, than farther, away.

Ahead, an older-looking, nine-point buck was on the right near a tree. A bigger, younger-looking buck with eight points separated from a group of bucks on my left and headed toward the older buck directly across my path. I continued walking slowly forward. Finally, I saw what was drawing the bucks; a doe was lying under a tree. The older buck was apparently guarding her. They were now on my right, the older buck about ten feet away, raising, and then lowering his head, paying no attention to me. The young buck was working his way toward me on the left, apparently coming over to challenge the older buck for the doe. I was in the middle on the road, between them. I began to worry that one would charge and take his aggression out on me. Instead, they seemed focused on each other, ignoring me. Eventually, the younger buck moved off, returning to the group of bucks. I continued down the road and it seemed to continue forever along the river as the landscape opened up to a treeless area beyond. I turned back. The old buck and doe were gone, but deer still played on my right, a primeval paradise with no predator but man.

Those evenings at the park were precious. I considered them exercise for the body and mind. Sometimes, racing darkness that might cause me to lose my way returning, I exerted myself too much. I remember reaching the car exhausted, my legs trembling, barely able to open my car door—never locked. Then, collapsing on the seat, glad to be sitting after so long on my feet. And then, driving slowly out of the park, watching the sunset colors, and for deer in the headlights, savoring the effortless glide of my car through this peaceful, silent place. Once on the road, I would again open it up, watching the bugs flare in the beams of my lights as I powered down long straight-a-ways and churned my tires round well defined curves. Overtaking the unsuspecting traveler with a flash of lights followed by my taillights disappearing into infinity, I passed with impunity. Only once, rounding a curve, did I face the profile of a doe I hoped to see earlier, cross in front of my careening car, only to disappear in time to allow me to recover and blast down the next straight. I'd arrive home tired but relaxed, grab a bite to eat, and plunk down in front of a good movie on TV. I slept well those nights.

Photo by Theodore Scott. I've seen 30 deer playing at Brazos Bend

Flickr photo. I may have seen this old guy nearby at the fishing pier.

# 29

# My Economic Struggle

By 1986, the economic downturn had reached its peak, and up and down my street the homes were still vacant. The increasing rate mortgage that the home builder had bought down to get us to buy in the first place had backfired, and the combination of 15% and more interest rates, low home value, and jobs and business lost, led to a wholesale abandonment. Many people left, and the S & Ls foreclosed, only to be stuck with properties they couldn't lease or sell. Those that could, took their losses and moved into better houses at lower cost. Interest rates began to drop, and I tried to refinance a couple of times, only to find the economic rules wouldn't let me. The fact is that with both Jan's and my income we could barely qualify for the house. Alone, there was no way I could qualify for the loan I was paying on every month.

At some point, after failing to refinance with my mortgage company and others, I told them that I was borrowing over $200 a month to stay where I was and would probably have to declare bankruptcy or walk away from my house. Finally, they heard me and called me in and agreed to "adjust" my loan interest to 10% per year. There was only one obstacle. Jan's name was still on the deed. I called her and she agreed to sign the paperwork. Her attorney balked at first, but I called back and explained the situation, and he finally allowed her to sign the house over to me.

Apartments were cheap everywhere, but with my condition deteriorating, I no longer wanted to carry groceries in the cold and the rain from my car parked out in some lot, a long way and downstairs from my car. The AIDS epidemic had hit the Montrose Area close to my work and there were many "cute" apartments available in what had been a high rent area. I didn't even look. I was not up to the physical difficulty and disappointment of looking at crummy apartments. And I could end up with a homosexual landlord or neighbors that I didn't particularly want. Areas were changing and deteriorating so fast it would be easy to rent in a high crime or dangerous area without knowing it. I didn't have the strength to become an apartment nomad like so many. The good apartments were expensive and had little to offer when compared to my house. I dreaded long walks from parking lots over uneven walkways, steps, and stairs, struggling to carry groceries, and fumbling with keys. The thought of doing my laundry in a room downstairs was also unsavory. At one time, I thought nothing of it. Now apartment living seemed like a sentence to physical inconvenience and lonely living.

Condos were affordable, especially around the Medical Center. Unfortunately, the prevailing floor plans had the bathroom upstairs. The only flats I found were in apartment complexes converted to condos that were as undesirable as apartments, without the flexibility of moving on if the place deteriorated.

I started looking at high rises. Most of these were either too expensive or old, with dingy and dark parking garages, elevators, and hallways, and the flats usually needed remodeling. One, called The Spires, was new and attractive, and in the Medical Center near my work. A one bedroom flat was about $80-90 thousand, depending on its location. Even if I was able to sell my house and get some money out of my Atlanta house to cover the loss and swing a loan, the monthly maintenance fee of $400 pushed me out of that opportunity too. I gave up.

I decided that I'd stick it out as long as I could at TSU and my house and go to Atlanta when I retired. But, that dream was beginning to fade too. I began readjusting my life at the house. Now, I wasn't just knuckling down in my depression and disappointment. To come out ahead in the end, I was starting a change in my lifestyle that was irreversible and dramatic. The war was on. Either I was going to defeat what was happening to me or it was going the defeat me.

# 30

# Work, Not Just a Job

At work, things were going well and badly at the same time. Josh reminded me that I was not a politician. He was and sought every opportunity to get recognition by inventing activity and getting people involved. We started to get funds to do many things, and I was asked to help carry them out. I represented the university in many meetings but was always careful to include him so that I wouldn't be viewed as having more political power than he. Serving at the will of the president, and beholden to the Board of Regents, Josh was subject to calls at all hours for anything from personnel problems to crimes that occurred on campus. I loved representing him and the university, and helping to solve the difficult problems we faced, but I didn't have to accept the consequences like he did. I loved the power and excitement of working on these tough problems, but I often said that I didn't want to be vice president because of the demands it would place on my physical and emotional condition. I'm sure that doing the job would not have been as bad as I perceived it, but I never had the opportunity to find out.

A study of TSU and Prairie View, the other university created in Texas to provide higher education for Blacks, compared with six "sister" four-year institutions with comparable student populations and programs, found that the university was deficient in several areas, especially facilities. The Civil Rights Commission had mandated that Texas could no longer maintain these institutions as separate but equal without upgrading facilities. In the early 1980s, Texas accomplished this by increasing our operating budget and appropriating funds for building and renovation projects on a project-by-project basis. Each project had to be proposed and argued in the political arena of the State Legislature. This approach enabled people like me to be hired to improve the operating staff, but funding for facilities was still inadequate and slow in coming. The first half of the decade we received over $60 million for specific renovation, addition, and new building projects. These funds were limited to the specified projects and sometimes inadequate once the real costs were determined through architectural cost estimation. The economic downturn helped by lowering the cost of construction, but we were faced with the business failure of some of our contractors and subcontractors, delaying and increasing the cost of some of the projects.

By the mid-eighties, Texas passed the Higher Education Assistance Fund (HEAF). HEAF was designed to give the schools facilities funds directly through a formula and each school more discretion on how the funds were spent. All activity would have to be approved by a statewide Coordinating Board. TSU and Prairie View received a supplement to the formula amount to correct the long-standing deficiency caused by inadequate funding in the past. Over time, the supplement was supposed to remedy the inequities identified by the Civil Rights Commission.

TSU received about $6.9 million per year for five years beginning in 1986. Following the lead of other institutions, TSU offered a $26 million bond issue to fund projects, to be paid from the annual HEAF appropriations. Board members, all political appointees, saw this tremendous pool of money as an opportunity and forced the hiring of project management firms to assist the university with the process of carrying out the projects. We were overworked with all the projects underway, but we would have rather had good staff help rather than these highly paid consultants who seemed more concerned about negotiating their fees rather than doing the best thing for the university.

In 1983, the university got a 3% HUD loan for converting local apartments into student housing. The original loan application called for purchasing and renovating two small complexes on the university's perimeter. Both complexes were in disrepair and half abandoned. Private investors bought and renovated one of the complexes, while Hurricane Alicia and subsequent vandalism destroyed the other. Alicia caused a lot of damage to our buildings as well. After we agreed to insure all of our buildings operated by student use fees, FEMA reimbursed us for all our repairs. In our haste to get the buildings back in shape, our crafts people did not keep good records. I spent a lot of time recovering estimates of what it cost us to make the repairs. It was always frustrating to get good information, but eventually we put together a report of damages that was acceptable to FEMA.

When HUD offered to give us the loan, the people who had submitted the original application resubmitted the application using a larger, 180-unit complex as the vehicle for the project. The complex was capable of housing 690 students @ two to a bedroom. The resubmitted application agreed to house 484 students (the original amount in two complexes) and requested the maximum loan of $3.5 million. When we got the loan, I was given primary responsibility for spearheading the project.

Rosewood Apartments had 140 tenants when we started negotiating its purchase. After a year of negotiations, we bought the complex for $1.8 million. That left $1.7 million minus expenses for renovation of the complex. We were shocked when we found that federal regulations not only required expensive institutional renovation specifications and union wages, but payments for relocation of displaced tenants. We retained the resident manager to help us maintain the project during the transition. Fortunately, the City had a relocation program funded by a HUD grant that provided up to $3000 for relocation or home purchase down payment for each tenant family. Things were going well, but Josh got worried and hired a woman to handle the relocation. She was to report to me.

After a year of work, the architect came up with a viable design that met the federal specs, including a water-source heating and cooling system that was innovative and very efficient and reliable. The only problem was that the cost estimate to renovate, about $3 million, was twice what we had left to complete the project.

We bid the project anyway, hoping to get an idea of the real costs, and no contractor placed a bid, fearful they would show their hand, even though several contractors were desperately positioning to get the job. Contractors told us that they couldn't do the job with union wages.

We called HUD in. They agreed to remove the union wage requirement, but required us to stick to the 484-student requirement, providing enough revenue to repay the loan. I had prepared four options: one of these appealed to the president. It involved using general State funds to buy back the land already bought with the federal money, freeing $700,000 to go back to the renovation. Instead, the university refused to put any matching funds into the project, a normal requirement, and decided to cut the project program, hoping to meet the budget.

Following the federal edict, we bid the project in two stages, the first to renovate enough apartments to house the required students, and the second to complete the entire complex. Three firms bid. The lowest bidder was within $200,000 of the funds we had in our budget to complete the required stage. I prepared a list of items to negotiate with the contractor that I thought would keep them in line with our budget. I thought it was do-able. Then Josh told me that our attorney had ruled that we had to re-bid the project. I was devastated. We were so close but denied the opportunity.

Josh decided to cut the project into four stages, using renovated units to fund renovation of additional ones. At the urging of the contractors, he required us to substitute cheaper materials used by local contractors. We cut the porches and patios, the primary architectural feature. We cut out all energy-saving systems, some security, insulation, improved fixtures, and roofing. We cut everything that made the project worthwhile. Then we bid it again.

The first stage made our budget and the Board approved the project. But the first stage did not have the required number of students under the loan, and HUD would not allow us to begin. The project stalled and would come back to haunt us.

The facilities inventory required measuring and coding all of our rooms, about 3,000 in 44 buildings. The initial inventory had been done by students from Texas A & M in 1976. My job was to keep it current. Data from the inventory was used to generate our physical plant budgets, so its accuracy was important. I measured and coded many rooms myself, but always thought that students could do the work. Work-study students didn't seem to have the diligence to stick to the tedious work, so I was assigned an assistant. He was the son of a faculty member and a community activist and was hired as a favor because he was out of work. I was led to believe he had a degree but later learned that he'd dropped out of college. He was bright, but not self-disciplined enough for this work. He wasted my time for over a year, and then quit. Little productive work was done. I was glad to be rid of him.

I measured and coded one of the largest buildings alone. It was very tiring and difficult as I struggled with carrying a wheeled measuring device and clipboard, trying to find a place to sit down in each room to record my measurements and make notes.

The Governor's Office sent several teams of engineers to audit the campus for energy conservation. Since I was collecting data on our utility consumption, they often consulted with me. Finally, an engineering firm was sent to provide technical assistance in determining if buildings would qualify for grant money available from the Department of Energy. After two years, the university received grants of $650,000 to complete energy-saving measures in about half of our buildings. The university had to match the grant dollar for dollar, and follow federal requirements, to use the grant money.

Several large companies were interested in doing the work and recommended that we provide an energy management system and measures for the entire campus. They all offered complete financing for some share of the savings, estimated to be over $500,000 per year. I saw no value in having these companies make a profit after the project was paid for and recommended that we pay outright for the project with the grant and construction funds. Our maintenance and plant operating people agreed, so we decided to use HEAF money to supplement the grant money and do the entire campus. A preliminary request for proposal was offered by one of the companies and we decided to modify and use that. As a precaution, I suggested that we hire an engineering firm to do oversight work to insure that the company that proposed the work would meet the government requirements and provide sound measures for the campus. We hired a firm to provide this oversight before we sent out our request.

In spite of my efforts to insure that proposers submit detailed cost information on what they proposed to do, the proposals we received were missing some key information. I headed a five-person committee to review the proposals. I selected the proposal that best met the university's requirements for energy conservation and the federal requirements, the one from Viron. The four others, unsure of the quality and commitment of the company I selected, chose a hundred-year-old company with an energy management system that had become a standard for the industry, Johnson Controls. We negotiated for some time with JCI and finally came to an agreement on what was to be done

The facilities inventory got behind. I couldn't go out and measure, and work-study students just weren't doing the job. An engineering consulting firm owned by Lydia Jones, a licensed civil engineer, had been hired to assist the architectural department with projects, and they assigned me a half-time assistant from the firm, Marsha Wilson. At the same time, computing services gave us three new Macintosh computers and one laser printer. Marsha told me that she had sold Macs, and immediately started using the one we had in our workroom. She also put on her hard hat and began going out in the field, creating spreadsheets of information on the computer that I'd previously done by hand.

Meetings were filled with smokers and liquor flowed in those days.

Josh and I at a Christmas Party, one of the ways we celebrated.

# 31

# Trouble at Work

My depression over the divorce, my finances, and my failing physical ability had made me argumentative and critical, partly because when things went wrong at work, I wasn't able to garner support, and partly because Josh had a way of assigning people to me rather than allowing me to hire them. He also assigned the same tasks to others that made us compete rather than cooperate. This strategy often came up with better results, but the competition created a lot of animosity, especially with someone as competitive and result-driven as I am. The word was that I couldn't get along with anyone. Josh was good at pointing it out in public meetings where it was especially demeaning. The fact was that I got tired of trying to accomplish what I had to do without cooperation or support. The shoddy work that I often received from others was depressing as well.

Managers and staff often put appearances over performance. Some worked hard but not smart—laboring over work they should have dispatched easily. Some talked a lot, but rarely came up with real improvements. Most were more concerned with what they had rather than what they did. Some even made a fine art of doing nothing at all. I was always the first to offer information or support to further the progress of the university. When my enthusiasm and energy was not reciprocated, it made me angry.

But Marsha had no ax to grind except her own. She had been competing with Lydia since they were childhood friends together in Gary,

Indiana. She was most like a precocious child, over eager and often off by a mile. She overpowered most people with her aggressiveness. I heard that she was assigned to me because everyone knew we wouldn't get along. Knowing that, Marsha outdid herself, she bent over backward to please me, and with the help of the computers, we were soon making real progress on the facilities inventory. When we had coded or recorded a space, we sent the information to the Texas Higher Education Coordinating Board for entry into their database. Sometimes, we called officials and staff members for clarification. Things were going quite well. Mostly coding and data entry into the Coordinating Board's database.

Marsha was a single mother struggling to make ends meet with the half-time assignment with me and a teaching job in TSU's weekend college. When she lost her teaching job in a dispute with the director, she tried to market her skills as a consultant. Part of her pitch was that she worked with me and with the Coordinating Board, the politically appointed governing body that oversees Texas higher education. We only sent required building information to THECB with no other involvement.

Before Christmas, Marsha caught pneumonia and was out for a couple of weeks. She apparently got desperate at the thought of being sick and trying to make it and made an appointment with the President of the university, Robert Terry. Marsha knew that Lydia had gained her contract with the university through political influence, so she went to him, sick and desperate, stating things that were exaggerated or untrue to prove that she could do some consulting work. At a reception, President Terry approached me and spoke briefly. He indicated his concern about Marsha, telling me that he'd share with me what she had said. He never did.

Sometime after Christmas, Marsha came to me and resigned, stating that she couldn't make a living working half time. About this time, one evening when I was working late, Josh came and stood in my office door and asked me, "What have you been telling the Coordinating Board?"

My response was matter-of-fact, that we had been sending facility inventory information and discussing proper coding, and that all information we sent had been approved by him. I didn't know it then, or even connect the two, but something Marsha said or did in her desperation led to political upheaval within the university and gave Josh a reason to distrust me in a way that would undermine our working relationship after that. Josh never trusted me again and became quite paranoid about threats to his position. He was right to be, but not from me.

# 32

# A New Friend

When Marsha resigned, I was assigned Jeanie, Lydia's firm's half-time secretary. I was disappointed because Jeanie didn't possess the skills Marsha had. But Jeanie assured me that she knew how to use a computer and could help with the inventory. In spite of my rebuke, Jeanie liked me, and soon we were working together and sharing a growing friendship.

Like all members of the firm, Jeanie had her own business. She had pulled together family and friends into a loosely organized dance and entertainment troupe that put on shows wherever she could book them. An excellent dancer and trained model, Jeanie had a style and figure that belied her age. She asked me what I did with my weekends. I said that I spent them relaxing at home and working on my yard and flowers. She said that I ought to get out more and invited me to Saturday practice of her dance troupe at a neighborhood club.

It was a long drive to where Jeanie lived, but that Saturday afternoon I was there to watch them practice. The troupe had a nice high kick routine to classic music, a routine based on Michael Jackson's Thriller, and a fashion show. All of her six grown children, three of them men, and three of them girls, participated, along with some cousins, neighborhood friends, and grand children. Jeanie was in her element, and it was obvious she enjoyed being with her family doing what she liked best. When the session was over, I offered to take some of the kids in my car. Her son, Cedric, directed me to her house a short distance away. When they got out Jeanie seemed upset. I drove home. It would take a while to learn why she didn't want me to know where she lived.

Like most of us, Jeanie had gone through some trauma, and it colored who she was. She was open and very friendly, but seemed reluctant to let me know who she really was. Slowly, she unraveled her story and included me in. Her great uncle was the Archbishop of the Texas AME church and was instrumental in founding Texas Southern University. Her mother was college-educated, a graduate of a Paul Quinn College in her native Waco. In 1947 when TSU started, Jeanie's mother worked as a secretary. At some point after Jeanie, her third child was born, she divorced Jeanie's father and moved to San Francisco. Jeanie's father remarried. Jeanie grew up living at various times in Houston, Waco, and San Francisco. She married quite young and had six children in quick succession. Her husband was abusive, so she separated from him after their sixth child, Subrena, was born.

In 1970, a year after Brena was born, Jeanie was working in the trauma unit at Ben Taub Hospital, one of two jobs she had to make ends meet, when her husband, a car accident victim, came in. He was comatose with extensive injuries. After a few days, Jeanie had to give permission to turn off life support, and he died. She used her insurance money to assume a VA loan on a small, two-bedroom house. Over the years, she often worked two jobs and raised her children as best she could. She closed off the garage and made another bedroom. When I arrived on the scene, her grown children, their children, friends and relatives were coming and going. As big as her heart was, she needed to escape the pressure and daily little dramas that continually affected her loved ones.

When they closed a medical center where she worked, Jeanie lost her job. She took a modeling course and decided to harness her kid's love of music and dance. She and her son were runners-up in an audition for Dance Fever, but that was as far as she got. She took the half-time job with Lydia so she could have time to pursue promotion of her business.

Seeing that I was interested, and hoping that I could help back her, she asked me to join her at local clubs where she was promoting her troupe. These were mostly Black-owned places, but the patrons were always cordial to me. Jeanie loved to dance, often with guys twenty years her junior, and with me. She and I clicked, and even though I was never sure where my left leg would go, her pirouettes and spins kept attention off my stumbles and we often got applause for our solos on the floor.

When she was out by herself or with girlfriends, men often surrounded her. But she always left alone and was careful not to let anyone follow her home. With me it was different. She was comfortable with me, and started asking me over on weekends. She cooked and the family came in and out to eat and play card games. When things really got rough, she'd hop in her car and drive forty miles down the old Almeda Road to the beach. I was privileged to ride with her there a couple of times.

There was some talk about us at work, but we were coy and eventually everyone learned that it was none of their business. Her nephew was getting married in Richmond, California. On impulse, she wanted us to go. Jack Swanson met us at the airport and loaned us Lois's Cadillac for the weekend. We were tired and everything we did went by very fast, but I met Jeanie's mother and her sister.

After that, we took several short weekend trips together: to McAllen to visit my parents and experience shopping in Mexico; to Atlanta to experience the beauty of spring and to see my house; to Phoenix to visit Tom and Kathy and see the wonders of Jerome and Sedona and check on Jeanie's relatives in Prescott; and to Waco to visit Jeanie's uncle and check out an all school reunion of the high school both she and her mother attended, now long demolished.

Whether by plane or car we had fun traveling, especially driving along with the windows down and the radio up. It was getting very hard for me to pack my bags and handle everything on a trip. Jeanie was the ideal traveling companion. She loved to travel light and to share the driving, free ice, pickles, and deep-fried pig skins. I rarely got out and walked more than a few feet now. But Jeanie was always there, my helper and friend, willing to walk at my pace and help me up the inevitable stair. Flights were more difficult because Jeanie had a penchant for being late. With our houses being far apart and long distance from the two Houston airports, we were often the last ones to board our plane, an experience that added to my bladder stress, muscle strain, and unstable stomach. It was always a pleasure settling into my seat and shedding layers of tension as the plane accelerated toward takeoff knowing that we'd cheated the clock one more time.

# 33

# Falling Out of Life

Jeanie came along at the time when I began to struggle just to get to work. Even after Jan left I was still able to put my socks on, but doing it involved extraordinary exertion that lasted up to fifteen minutes. I spent six dollars having elastic loops sewed to a pair of socks, but couldn't get my toes in the openings with the loops on.

Trying a highly modified method that kept changing, I still managed to do what was needed to get my socks on. I started by sitting on the edge of my bed, pulling up one foot at a time, Yoga-fashion to my lap, and then forcing a sock onto my foot by pushing, rubbing and pulling with my hands, fingernails, and teeth, if necessary. Then, I tried things like starting the sock on my toes, and then rubbing my foot against the carpet to force it into place. Positioning the heel at the start was most important, because the sock would turn around my foot as I worked hard to get it on. The heel had to end up in the right place or I'd go to work with a painful lump in my shoe where the extra material of the sock heel ended up. Eventually, I had to fall to the floor and contort my body to reach my sock tops and pull them on with only the strength of my permanently-curled left index finger. This exercise left my finger sore and my legs exhausted to the point that it was sometimes difficult to get back up on the bed.

I started wearing slip-on shoes when I was paralyzed and they served me well. My feet were good and most of my shoes were easy to slip into and wore well. The increasing drop in my left foot and the gradual loss of my high runner's arches led to fitting problems and uneven wear. Bob

239

Henry had given me one of those long shoehorns with an eagle handle. I carried it with me unused until I discovered one day that it really helped me wiggle into my shoes. At some point the eagle handle broke off, but that only made the tool easier to put in a suitcase, it was still easy to use.

The ankle brace Dr. Arana had prescribed fit inside my shoe and acted like a shoehorn, making it easy to force my left foot, that had lost all of its muscle tone, into my shoe. The brace took up shoe space and caused pressure and circulation loss, but the foot only hurt when I didn't use it. After a while, the brace didn't bother me anymore. It was like an extension of my ankle. Like my hand splint before, it was comfortable and familiar on and off.

Walking, however, wasn't easy. I had to start watching my step for hidden obstacles. One morning, as I rushed to leave the house, loaded with my briefcase and mail to put in the mailbox, my foot caught on the aluminum threshold and I spun to the wooden deck, catching the corner of my glasses. As I lay there recovering from the fall, I felt warm blood running down my neck into my shirt and sport coat. One lens had popped out with force and made a nice incision along my eyebrow. Fortunately, the gushing blood stopped. The lens was lost. I never found where it flew. I soaked my shirt in cold water before washing it—I was getting good at removing bloodstains. The cleaners couldn't do much for my coat, so its liner stayed stained and it never was the same. I got taped like a prizefighter at the Clinic on my way to work to close the cut. My muscle aches and pains went away in a few days. I had to buy another pair of glasses because they were once again obsolete, and couldn't be fixed.

I bought two pair. The first pair was elegant and light, made of carbon filament and quite flexible. The second pair was heavier but had spring hinges at the bows. If there were no safety or break proof glasses available, I was determined to get the safest ones I could find. I knew I'd fall again. I just didn't know when or how hard. I wouldn't have to wait long.

Dr. Arana was genuinely interested in helping me. He suggested an expensive new procedure called an MRI, for magnetic resonance imaging, to look at my spine and see what was happening. Although Jeanie joined me for reassurance, I liked MRI because it was unobtrusive. All I had to do was lie quietly in a narrow white chamber, listening to music and looking at butterflies painted right above my face while the magnets clicked and buzzed and created a color, three-dimensional image of my neck and spine. Finally, perhaps, I would find out what was wrong. Although the pictures were beautiful, Wilkinson and Arana together came to the conclusion that my problem was caused by aging and I would have to continue to manage it myself.

Dr. Arana referred me to a Dr. Mancini, a rehabilitation physician, at the Rosewood Clinic. I saw him once. After reviewing my voluminous file, Mancini said that he would set up a program of treatment that would help me deal with the changes happening to me. I told him about an upcoming change in my insurance, and he agreed to hold off until my status was clear.

In the fall of 1987, TSU abandoned Maxicare and carried a new insurance plan by Sanus. I was pleased with the promise of the plan and took the Plus option that supposedly gave more flexibility in choosing who would provide my care. Kelsey-Seybold Clinic was supposed to be included in the program, but not immediately. So, reluctantly, leaving K-S's familiar physicians behind, I chose the Baylor Family Practice Clinic, hoping that they would understand and continue the course of care I was on.

I liked the Baylor Clinic's location and that it was easy to park in back and get into for service, but that's where my favor ended. After discussion with the staff, I chose a physician who was supposed to be brilliant. He was most willing to meet with me and treat infections or minor ailments. I was experiencing reflux caused by a gradual loss of nerve control of the valve on my esophagus. He told me to raise the head of my bed to prevent acid from flowing out of my stomach while I slept. He would not refer me to anyone about my falling, muscle pain in my legs, or other indications that I was soon going to lose my ability to walk. I cajoled, threatened, and harassed, but in the end, he only told me that I had very good insurance. I had to go out on my own. The question was to who and where. I wasn't getting any good advice. It was obvious I needed help.

Late one night, soon after Jeanie and I met, I fell in her drive. We had been out to a club and closed it. I followed Jeanie home and parked at her curb. She didn't want to disturb her kids and grandkids asleep in the house, so I joined her in her car in her driveway as we talked and listened to music. Finally, sleepy and tired, I got out and headed for my car. Her concrete driveway was old, broken, and uneven from tree roots. I turned to wave and fell in the same motion. I remember how hard the concrete felt as it jarred my hip and the side of my face as my glasses flew off into the darkness. It was like being hit by a car. At first, Jeanie laughed, thinking it was a joke, until I caught my wind, crawled to my knees, and started to look for my missing shoe and glasses. I couldn't get up. Jeanie helped me to my feet; found my glasses; put on my shoe; and helped me to my car. I just sat in the car, numb from what had happened for a while. Finally, I started it and drove home.

I used a story that I had slipped and fallen while starting to go up stairs to explain the cuts and scrapes on the side of my face from the concrete and my scratched glasses to the curious at work the next day. I was stoic about my scraped shin, bruised hip, sore shoulder and jaw. I was getting used to pain. It was something I just lived with.

I started to worry about my shoes. My walking had become so labored that when Dr. Wilkinson observed me going down a hall he'd asked me if I was eating enough. He said that I was engaging in a major workout just to get around. My shoes were wearing out at a tremendous rate as my gait and foot dragging scraped them on every surface. I could almost feel rough concrete tearing leather as I struggled along. I tried buying half soles and heels, and even new pairs I bought cheap in Mexico; but my soles were always worn, frayed, and in danger of catching the slightest of obstacles.

I started driving to meetings across campus. My hands reached out for every rail, post or wall as I struggled to carry my briefcase to every event. The heavy case, carrying my papers, lunch, and hand splint, served as an anchor to my stronger right side as I crab-walked my weaker left side across open spaces. Open spaces became great gulfs as I collected my thoughts for the concentrated push across the void to the safety of the other side. Rooms large and small became difficult, especially if they contained people moving about, worn or uneven carpet, and expansion joints. I walked with gritted teeth and determination, and with enough force to make progress. I couldn't present a good demeanor as I struggled to get to where I was going. People admonished me to "Be careful," or "Take it easier," but they would not stand still and wait for me to work my way across an open room to greet them. It was frustrating to set out to talk to someone, only to have them walk away before I could reach them.

The gap between my covered parking space at work and the building grew and grew, especially when it was windy, rained, or when it was hot and I was tired. Hot pavement radiated its heat up through my body, making its presence felt—it was hot, hard, and rough, and waiting to hit me. One morning it was warming up to what was going to be a hot day when I arrived late. I pulled out my briefcase, slung the strap over my shoulder, and worked my way around my car, heading for the corner of the building, swinging my case in stride with my walk. While I was distracted or merely concentrating on my objective, my right toe caught on a piece of redwood expansion joint that was sticking up slightly above the slab. My case, with its own momentum, swung around in front of me and its base landed solidly on the pavement just as my knees hit the top of the case. The case stopped dead, but my body continued forward as I struggled to regain my balance. I didn't, and I fell forward, pivoting on my knees over the briefcase. Arms flailing to the side, I saw the concrete come up fast, and felt the loud "crack" of my forehead smashing into the pavement.

I never lost consciousness. I struggled to regain my knees over my case and wondered what had happened to my forehead and glasses. Blood was dripping on the hot concrete. Milton Williams, our locksmith, happened along and helped me up. I told him that I probably should go to the Health Center. He agreed and ran to get one of our utility trucks to take me over there. He also found a cloth that I held to my head to stop the bleeding. At the Health Center, Nurse Helen Johnson sprang into action and cleaned and bandaged my wound. She said that I needed stitches.

I went back to the office and called Baylor Family Practice. A young doctor worked for over a half hour to close the wound, so vigorously that at one point blood hit the wall. I went back to work with a 'Z" stitched dead center above my eyebrows. I was pleased that he was able to find enough unpulverized skin to close the wound. It healed without a noticeable scar. My glasses suffered only a scraped frame.

Jeanie provided entertainment for our Christmas party for many years.

Jeanie's family, Subrena, Phayla, a troupe member, join Jeanie in dance.

# 34

# Unsafe at Home

Home, where I'd carefully placed things so that I wouldn't trip and I could reach the walls or other handholds, wasn't safe either. My office was upstairs and it became a source of worry. One morning while I was still married to Jan, I come to the top of the stairs to go down and my briefcase strap broke. The briefcase then slid smoothly down the carpeted stair edges, accelerating until it hit the floor with tremendous force and flipped over. Jan ran out from the kitchen, fearing that I'd fallen downstairs, only to find me safe, but a bit shaken. That incident and the one where my ankle brace broke made me doubly cautious each time I started down those stairs. There was a good rail on the left, but none on the right.

Carrying my evening meals upstairs became precarious. There were many spills that cost me hours of carpet cleaning, but I never fell or lost a meal. It was easier to salvage what I could from the carpet, sit down and relax and eat it while it was still warm, than start over. I didn't worry about contaminated food. But anticipating the dreaded cleaning ahead hampered my relaxation. Sometimes I just went ahead and cleaned up first, returning to my cold meal tired and late.

Bare feet and water on my kitchen floor were a bad mix. After falling flat on my back (my head didn't hit) and sliding into painful splits I was incapable of attaining, I learned to respect any spill or water that got on the floor when I cleaned. Still, tripping was my biggest problem as I fell over my desk, the kitchen island, tables, chairs, or anything else in my way. When I couldn't find anything to grab onto or fall on, it was worse. One time, I missed the island in the kitchen and did a layout head butt of the drywall next to my pantry. I wasn't wearing glasses and the wall board broke, absorbing the blow, so I got only a small head cut and a sore neck instead of a skull fracture, broken neck, or both. The same thing happened upstairs as I rounded my desk to relax on my couch. I remember tripping on the carpet, trying to regain my balance, and flying headlong into the wall. A neat, four-inch in diameter, depression matching the curvature of my forehead was left under the window to the lower level.

I remember someone said that you lose a year of life for every minute you are knocked out. I was lucky to have remained alert and conscious through all of those blows. But I was more worried about my neck. I could make my hands and feet go numb by merely rolling my head forward or back. The same numbness, tingling, and sharp nerve pain I sustained whenever I tried to read a book sitting in a chair or propped on a pillow face down in bed. Through the normal range of motion, my strong neck muscles controlled motion within a safe range of those telling sensations. But when I fell, those limits were exceeded, often resulting in total paralysis of my limbs for a moment, followed by burning and tingling in my hands and feet. I became worried that my next fall could be my last.

# 35

# Getting Help

I had known about TIRR, The Institute for Rehabilitation and Research, for some time. After I heard that TIRR was doing a study of post-polio syndrome, a condition similar to the one I was experiencing, I signed up. I was turned down because I was never known to have polio, but decided to go to TIRR for treatment anyway, even though Sanus would pay only 70% of my bills.

I went to see Dr. Rebecca Clearman, a well-known rehabilitation physician who specialized in spinal cord injury. When I told her my story, she looked worried. She said that I'd been very unlucky to have this happen to me. She said that something was going on that she didn't understand, but that she was going to get to the bottom of it. When she saw me walk she became very worried, asked me if I had any help, and suggested that I get a wheelchair to reduce wear and tear, and the potential of falling.

Clearman introduced me to Dr. Jeffrey Jackson, a crack neurodiagnostitian and enlisted Dr. Nuriama, a neurologist, for a week-long hospital stay to try to diagnose what was wrong. I had another MRI at the hospital, and then CAT scans, EMGs, kidney x-rays, bladder flow tests and other tests to try to diagnose the causes of my decline. All the tests proved inconclusive. Dr. Jackson had thought it might be diabetes, but all those tests were negative.

Dr. Clearman suggested a week-long stay at the TIRR hospital, but I declined. I wasn't interested in sitting long hours in a hospital waiting for advice and training that I could get easily from consultations and out patient visits. Dr. Jackson had an idea she suggested I try, steroid therapy.

Prednisolone, a Cortisone derivative, is dangerous stuff. Besides obvious facial and stomach swelling, it can cause damage to liver, kidneys, and other organs. It is addictive, and withdrawal must be slow and gentle to avoid serious side effects. Still, the drug had been known to reverse paralysis because of its ability to reduce congestion in the spinal column caused by injury or disease. I agreed to try the treatment and was put on a 200 mg dose a day program.

I took the twenty little bitter pills with my evening meal. I also had to take Zantac, a stomach acid blocker, twice a day to counter the excess acid generated by the Predisolone. Zantac had its own nasty little effects such as causing forgetfulness and falls. These effects bothered me more than the steroid.

My sinuses and ears cleared up immediately and food tasted better than I had remembered it; even from the days I deprived myself in the name of wrestling. I started wanting extra helpings. Evening snacks became a ritual obsession. There was a rather warm glow, elevated body temperature, and euphoria that came with the drug, but it couldn't blunt the pain of my legs rewinding every night and the struggle I was having at work.

Jeanie and I took a weekend and traveled to see my cousin, Dennis, and his family in El Paso. On the way back, we stopped to see Carlsbad Caverns. Tom had told me that they had wheelchairs. When we asked to rent one, the manager told us that they didn't have any to rent, and we couldn't use the one they had, because it was for emergencies. We took the elevator 22 floors down to the main cavern. Even with my jacket, it was cold and my legs, already tired from the trip, tightened. Jeanie went to explore the cave while I waited on a cold, stone bench.

After a while, I got bored and started to move around the room. Eventually, I was working my way along the trail. The trail was smooth and quite wide, but it was wet and sloped gradually as it started to follow the cave around the bend out of sight of any cave features. I wanted to see some. Unable to touch the cave wall for support, I reached a point where the trail was too steep to navigate, so I decided to work my way back, trying to avoid being knocked down by unsuspecting tourists hurrying by. After struggling for some time, I lost my balance, and landed on an elbow on the wet floor. Passersby pulled me up, but cold, tense, and wet, I spent the remaining time talking to spelunkers. These cave explorers gave up their vacations to restore the cave from past abuses caused before it became a national park.

I went out and bought a portable wheelchair. Put it in the car for use when I'd need it.

After my hospitalization to diagnose my deterioration, Josh changed his attitude a bit toward my needs. I saw a TV ad about a scooter that gave old folks more freedom, so I checked into it. After a demonstration on campus with our transportation supervisor, Bob Shepherd, we decided to buy two Sierra models. Originally, I planned to have one be available to students or staff who were injured to use temporarily. Instead, the spare was put in storage—always ready to replace the other one if it failed.

The Sierra, a three-wheeler, was good outdoors, and compact enough to navigate elevators, restrooms and small offices. It had bicycle-type steering and the throttle attached to the small handlebar, making it hard for me to push the throttle all the way down and maintain a straight line as I bounced over rough surfaces on campus. Although my paralyzed hands didn't get in the way, straight-arming the heel of my right hand into the throttle for any distance brought enough pain to my right shoulder to cause me to stop every 20 yards or so to relax my right arm.

I saw Dr. Jackson at three-month intervals. At first he was sure that the steroids were helping me, but I was only feeling the effects without any change in the gradual decline of muscle use I was experiencing. He kept saying that I was stronger and had more movement. At home, I found no improvement, my decline continued unabated.

Dr. Clearman, in an attempt to take advantage of the steroids, a treatment she was not too keen about, enrolled me in "Strength Unlimited" at TIRR. Strength Unlimited was designed to give para and quadriplegics, and other physically-disabled people, an opportunity to work out on equipment designed to build muscle flexibility and strength for specific muscles. Most of this equipment was used in physical therapy and normally unavailable except by therapy appointments. The theory was that disabled people need physical activity to overcome the debilitating effects of long hours of sitting and lying without movement. After therapy hours, therapists and volunteers made the equipment available to participants. Each participant was given a specific set of exercises. I started with leg lifts on the mat, and followed that with work on a hand-bicycle and a device that forced leg movement with my feet strapped in.

Clearman, recognizing my difficulty walking, had told me to park on the outpatient clinic side of TIRR. Construction was underway when I started coming to SU three days a week after work. The lot, marked exclusively for the disabled, was designated for doctors and TIRR vehicles. It was difficult to walk to the PT room where SU was, but almost impossible from the other side where the patient parking lot was. Transportation people told me to park on the other side, and even offered to park my car for me. But, it was the end of the day, so the lot was mostly empty, and I was only there about a half hour, so I wasn't bothering anybody.

The sessions were going okay. I left work a little early and got home a little late. I started to make friends with a volunteer, a biochemist who was there most afternoons. I didn't interact much with the other participants. I also didn't notice any physical improvement except that I was more tired than usual. I started getting nasty stickers stating that my car would be towed. They were stuck to my driver's side window and I couldn't roll it down. I had to get a guy at my gas station to razor blade them off. I called the director of TIRR, but she was adamant that the lot could not be used, even temporarily, by me. I reminded her of the ADA, allowing for reasonable accommodation. She turned the matter over to her attorney, a quadriplegic in an electric wheelchair.

One night, I came out to find my car being towed. They would not unhook my car, and drove off. I was staggering by that time, but managed to get back in the building where I called Jeanie. Jeanie came and took me near downtown to my car, located on a dirt lot that was very hard for me to walk in. The manager of the impound lot was upset that I'd been towed and only charged me $10 to pay the driver. It started raining as I drove home. I was grateful that the rain had held out; that Jeanie had come through for me again; and that the impound lot had freed my car. I got home at 9:30 pm, exhausted and hungry.

I called Clearman to ask her help. She called me back late in her day, obviously overworked and angry after talking to the TIRR director about my indiscretion. Blaming everything on the steroids, she ordered me to stop going to SU, and said she was going to have Jackson take me off the Prednisolone. I told her that she didn't know me, that it was normal for me to take the hard road. We were two rocks in a hard place.

Jackson gradually took me off the Prednisolone. At one point I had a flu or something that affected me, I can't remember what it was exactly, so I called Jackson about it. After I described to him what was happening, he ordered me to go back to the full 200 mg course. I regretted that complaint, because it prolonged my use of steroids another six months.

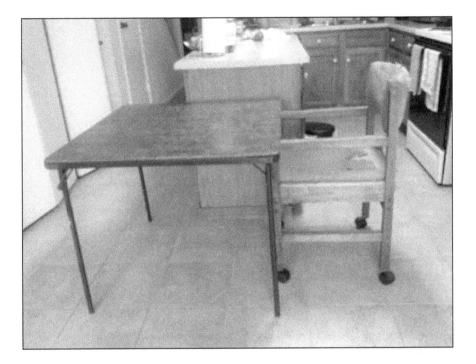

    While I could still stand to work in the kitchen, I scooted around the house in my wheeled office chair to prevent falls that came more often than I liked. I set up the card table at the end of the kitchen counter so that, after preparing my food by sliding pans back and forth and across the chasm between counter and range while preparing my plate of food, I could slide the plate to the card table and could sit down to eat.

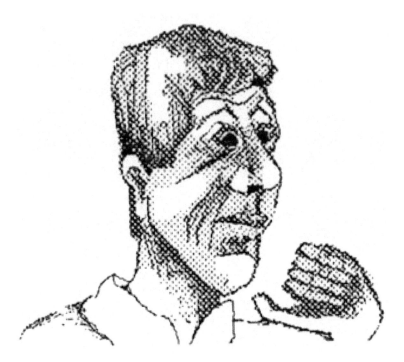

Samantha Griswald, a brilliant architectural student from the University of Houston who served as my energy intern one summer from a progressive Texas A & M funded program, drew my caricature during our staff meeting. She got the stress lines in my face right and my left hand contracture. Not so sure about those beady eyes. After graduation, Sam joined our architectural staff for a while before joining a large project management firm.

# 36

## Getaways with a Little Help from My Friend

My declining health made getting away all the more important. I regularly planned trips that would allow me to get my mind off work and the routine I was stuck in. In the fall of 1988, I planned an epic journey east for two weeks. Jeanie was willing, but said that she could only take a week. It could be done—so we did. After our usual late start, we made Atlanta the second day. After a quick check of my house and a night with friends Duane and Anne, we drove for the coast through Columbia, SC. We arrived late and exhausted.

The next morning, as we drove out down the highway from our motel, I heard something slide off the roof. It was my address book; the one Jeanie had given me for Christmas. I saw it fly off the car in the rear view mirror to be run over by an eighteen-wheeler following close behind. I pulled to the shoulder, backed up, and Jeanie retrieved the book. It was heavily gravel-marked and the three metal rings were crushed. My addresses were still readable. I used the book several years after that.

About noon, we met Barry DuVall, a friend and former colleague from WVU in North Carolina. He took us to his home in a small country development by the river. Then he helped me into a small boat in a pond nearby and took us for a boat ride in a channel to the main river. It was one of those idyllic Indian Summer afternoons, when sun, sky, and land merge in a harmony that is so peaceful that it soothes the soul. We glided down that fall leaf-draped channel as if in a movie, oblivious of time. Barry said that if there were time he would take us out on the main river in his big powerboat. I was glad we took the slow boat to nowhere.

That night, we had dinner in an inn that was reputed to be a hangout for Blue Beard, the pirate. The next morning we headed up the coast to Norfolk, and then on to Old Williamsburg and Richmond. Near the foothills of the Appalachians we came upon a tanker truck by the side of the road with a tire on fire. The fire had already spread up the hillside in the dry grass. It seemed only moments until the freeway would close, but we got by. I watched in the mirror for more smoke but didn't see any. Hopefully, the fire was quickly put out and the truck was saved.

It was late in the day when we got to Staunton. We stopped at a Farmer's Coop to get gas. I asked the attendant how the road was over the mountains to Elkins. He advised me to take I 85 down to Bluefield, and then head north to Charleston. We didn't have another day to take that route, so I drove due west into the waning light. A few miles out the paved highway gave way to a dirt road that snaked its way upward through steep switchbacks. I had to keep the power on to make the steep turns, but Jeanie begged me to go slower. Above 6,000 feet the road got a bit icy. I hoped we wouldn't hit snow. Finally, long after Jeanie had closed her eyes in feigned sleep, we crested the top and entered West Virginia. The road was now paved but terribly steep. I put it in low gear and started down. When my momentum got too great, I used the brakes, but it was obvious that there was something wrong because they shuddered under hard braking. Finally, we reached the high valley and we drove in comfort and darkness to Elkins where a new motel and hot meal awaited us. I wondered if the brakes would hold out the rest of the trip.

The next morning we awoke to a white world of frost. Jeanie thought it was snow. By noon, we reached WVU at Morgantown, met with former colleagues in the Technology Education Office, and had lunch with Paul DeVore. That afternoon, we headed out to my Cheat Canyon cottage. Now clad in gray vinyl siding and sporting a new deck and kitchen entrance, it was ready to go another 50 years. We stopped to see Herb Morrison, but learned from his wife Mary Ann that he had been in a nursing home for a week, suffering from the affects of diabetes. He died within three months. It was sad to have missed seeing him, but knowing him and his kindness was enough. The chalet on the back half of the property I sold to Kennedy looked good but I heard that he was transferred and had to sell it.

On the way back to town, we had a long talk with Esther Caddell, confined by her weight and disabilities, but not by her imagination and love for children. Jeanie really enjoyed the talk we had with her. We stopped for a hot dinner and headed for Dayton. I hoped that the brakes would hold out.

It was late when we got to Dayton. My cousin, Debbie Goessel, and kids greeted us warmly. We plunked down on the couch. Bill arrived and we listened to their plans to expand and remodel their house. Debbie brought us martinis and I enjoyed mine until it was past midnight. We decided to call it a night. I tried to get up, but couldn't. With Bill on one side and Jeanie on the other, lifting my weight, I was able to struggle into the bedroom. Whether it was exhaustion or the drink or a prelude to losing my legs, it was disconcerting not to be able to get up and walk.

The next morning, we were on our way. After a brief overnight at Behram's in Louisville, it was downhill through Memphis and Little Rock to home. Jeanie did most of the driving and enjoyed it. As hard as the trip had been, she enjoyed the adventure of the open road.

Two days after we returned home, five blocks from home on my way back from work, I turned a corner, heard a noise, and my brakes made a loud scraping sound. I took the Monte Carlo to the shop the next morning. My right front brake pad had fallen off. That was why the brakes had shuddered in the mountains. I was grateful that they'd waited until we got home to fail completely.

I was now defining my life by these trips, these carefree flights from the dreary struggle my life had become. I hoped that I could keep going and exploring. I knew it would end someday, but I wanted to put off the inevitable as long as I could.

Early in September, my nephew, Paul, got married. He was marrying a girl from Elgin, IL, so we could see Roger at the same time. Jeanie and I flew to Chicago, rented a car, and drove for Tim's place in Madison. We ran into a prolonged thunderstorm near the Wisconsin border, with wind and rain so strong Jeanie couldn't continue driving. I didn't want to stay under that overpass all night, so we switched places without getting out, quite a trick in that Mustang, and I drove on.

We visited Tim's family in Madison, and then Judy in Marshfield, and then went to the lake for the Labor Day weekend. We enjoyed boat rides and the peaceful afternoons by the lake, and we went to the last water ski show of the season at Minocqua. It was a cool, but wonderful, way to end the summer. Still, Jeanie felt out of place, always uneasy in strange surroundings, unsure how people felt about her, a Black woman in a White world.

I took her down State Highway 29 to meet my relatives. After a day of stops, she was tired and confused, and just wanted to relax. We stopped at the family cemetery and tried to find my grandparents' graves. I couldn't walk far in the grass, so Jeanie looked through the whole section. We couldn't find them. Later, my Uncle Ed told me that they were right where I thought, but that shrubs planted over the flush stones had covered them up, making them hard to find.

We drove back down to Roger's, stayed over night, and attended the wedding. Roger introduced us to his girlfriend, Sue. Kelley and Tracy were there, too, looking beautiful. There were some Blacks at the wedding so Jeanie felt more comfortable. Dancing on the concrete floor of the garage was hard for me but we enjoyed it. Everyone, including Mom, was surprised to see me dancing. After the wedding, the family gathered at a Pizza place by the Fox River. To top off the evening, Roger invited us to join Sue and him at a club that featured live music.

When we got to the club, Roger refused to drop me at the door. Instead, he looked for and found an outlying parking spot. Roger and Sue headed on into the club. With Jeanie's help, I struggled over holes and rocks in the unpaved parking area to make it to the door. The club was crowded, so it was hard to work my way over to where they were. There was no place to sit except some high stools. A man got off his stool and offered it to me. In the din of the crowd, I refused. Sue and Roger took it as an insult. I tried to explain that a high stool was dangerous and uncomfortable because I was afraid of losing my balance and falling off. It created a scene I didn't want. I was too tired to stand and there was no place to sit. Jeanie held me up while Roger and Sue simmered in anger over my rebuff of the man's kindness.

The band played any request. Jeanie requested "Lady in Red." So many people wanted to dance to it that we had a hard time getting on the dance floor. It was our only dance. I was glad to get to the car so I could sit down. The next morning, we left for Platteville to see Mahfooz and his family. I was tired and sick and we had to make several restroom and roadside stops, but we got there about noon and had a pleasant lunch Farkunda made at their house. Then we drove back to Madison. It was too early for fall color, but the crops were at their peak and a drive through this part of glacially carved Wisconsin was spectacular. When we got to Spring Green, I suggested that we stop at The House on the Rock. I had stopped there in 1966, and again about 1975. The brainchild of an engineer with an artist's eye, the House was a blend of nature, architecture, and art like no other. By now the place had become a major tourist stop and I didn't recognize the private cliff house that the owner had left to curious, paying visitors.

I told Jeanie to go on in and I'd wait outside. I stayed around the visitors' center and watched a film about the owner and the house. After about two hours, Jeanie returned. I missed the opportunity to go and see whatever I wanted. At least I could still go there.

We returned to Madison and had dinner at Tim's. Jeanie wanted to get back to Chicago so we left after the meal. I wanted to stay in Elgin for a short drive to O'Hare the next day. She insisted that we find a hotel near the airport. Jeanie was driving, so we passed all the exits and were soon in Chicago. I didn't know of any hotels near O'Hare, so tried to follow signs by the expressway. Soon, we were ten miles from the airport and still hadn't located anything. Finally, we found a sleazy, high-priced place and crashed for the night.

We slept late, and took a lot of time getting ready. Our flight was about noon. It took a while to find the airport and drop the car. By the time we got to our gate, the plane was leaving. We negotiated with the airline, and they gave us a 4 o'clock flight.

We spent some time in a little restaurant. I remember falling off my metal lounge chair, causing a commotion but not hurting myself. If Roger had been there he would have known why I avoided that stool in the dance club. As we waited, I heard that there was an incident at the airport. An airplane's landing gear had collapsed. While no one was hurt, traffic at the airport was disrupted.

We left the restaurant and waited at our gate. From time to time, I asked Jeanie to check our flight. I was too tired to leave my seat. It got late, so I asked her to check again. She said that our gate had been switched to the other side of the airport. All of the other passengers had long gone. It was less than five minutes to flight time. I didn't know how we would make it. They called for a wheelchair. I started yelling. I didn't want to miss another flight.

Just then, Mahfooz and Mahboob came along and saw me yelling. They had dropped Mahfooz's sister off for a flight to San Francisco and were going home. Mahfooz had heard me upset like that before when he slid over a safety island while I was trying to teach him to drive, but he was clearly upset by my anger at Jeanie.

Before I could explain, my wheelchair arrived and we had to hurry. Jeanie went on ahead to hold the plane if she could, while a small, middle-aged woman pushed me as fast as she could. It took a long time and my helper was breathless when we got to the gate. We rushed to our seats, only to wait nearly an hour for the plane to take off. Jeanie and I hardly talked. It took me a long time to call Mahfooz and try to explain why I had exploded.

He reassured me that he understood, but I still doubt it. My penchant for being on time and Jeanie's for being late was wearing on our relationship. We enjoyed so much together, but the contradictions kept getting in the way.

I wanted another "grand tour" while I could still do it. Since we'd done the East, I put together the West for the following fall. The plan was to go north to Waco, to visit Jeanie's Uncle, and then head north and west through Colorado and Nevada to Reno for gambling and to her relatives and my friends in the Bay Area. From there we would turn south to LA, and then east through Phoenix and home.

October was a good time to go except for early storms in the Rockies, so I planned to use I-40 along old Route 66 as an alternate route to California. But there was no plan for what happened.

On Tuesday, October 17, 1989, five days before we planned to leave, the Loma Prieta earthquake hit the Bay Area. Jeanie was already aware of it that night when I called her. She was worried about her mother and sister. It was hard to get through, but when she did, she found out that they were okay. But she wasn't okay. In Jeanie's mind, the quake had canceled our trip. In my mind, it presented a minor inconvenience. A struggle followed. We spent hours on the phone as I tried to convince her that her mother and sister would welcome her, but she was convinced that there was great danger and her loved ones could not entertain us and get their houses back together. I called Jack, and he said "come on down"—they had sustained no serious damage in Redwood City. On Saturday morning, the day we were to leave, I talked to Jeanie by telephone until 11 am, until it was obvious that she wouldn't go, not even if I waited a week. It was hard to leave without her help, but I knew I'd be miserable staying home, so I packed my bag and left.

By 4 pm I reached her Uncle's in Waco. The house was quiet and empty, and when I waited a while, no one came around. So I left. Emotionally exhausted, I pushed on to Wichita Falls. I was so tired; I don't even remember where I stayed.

Interstate 40 was interesting, sprinkled with reminders of Route 66, gateway to California, described by Nick so many years before as, "A continuous strip of gas stations and taco stands." Route 66, a road I'd vowed I'd never take because it was too hot and too touristy, became my route. My chance to leave that road came up about noon, just after I'd entered New Mexico from Texas. At a point where the road intersected the one north to Colorado Springs, I stopped at a McDonald's that seemed to have no level ground to park on. A busload of some sports team from Texas A&M was there, having come down from Colorado. They talked of snow. I didn't relish going over 11,000 foot passes with snow in the air. Given the weather reports of snowstorms in the mountains, I decided to take the southern route.

I got gas at a teepee from Indians, and saw some of the charm of the romantic '50s roadway, but New Mexico was a disappointment. In valley after valley, the hillsides were littered with debris that had been dragged in by desert rats for a century, leaving the once pristine desert cluttered with junk that would never rot, rust, or go away. Lush vegetation covers much of West Virginia's sins, but New Mexico's remain in the sun for all to see. All the cars, buses, and trucks that couldn't navigate 66's hills and heat and mechanic shysters ended up here, America's armpit.

By evening, things got better. The junk gave way to broad vistas of natural landscape, especially into Arizona. I raced darkness to Flagstaff amid a sky show of mystic proportions. Pink dominated, but the shades of pink that evening had to be attributed to dust in the air from the recent earthquake or some other spiritual force.

It was late, construction and full motels hampered my stop, but finally I settled in that cold Flagstaff night. I called Tom and kidding told him to rescue me. Then I told him I'd see him in six days. The next morning, there was light snow and heavy fog as I drove west into California. At Kingman, I stopped for breakfast at MacDonald's. They were expanding; while I ate in the new part in front, I had to walk past the old one to some outdoor restrooms out back. It was so far. I thought I was going to trip and never make it.

I stopped next door to get gas. Two fiftyish couples were gassing up their identical red and white Porsche Speedsters. I knew I was close to California. When I got to Mojave, the Space Shuttle had just arrived at Edwards. I drove to the entrance, but they weren't receiving visitors until the next day. After that, it was Joshua Trees and wind turbines until I got to Barstow. I stopped to get gas on the main drag between LA and Vegas. It was a zoo of activity with strange characters headed both ways.

Then, I crossed over a pass into the Central Valley, watching tiers of trains winding around hillsides far below, and then up 99. I got worried about my oil and got a quart put in past Fresno, just before dark. It started to rain heavily. I was glad I hadn't taken the northern route. Donner Pass was closed by heavy snow in the Sierras. If I made it there, over the Colorado mountains, I would have been held up at Reno.

I arrived in Oakdale about 8 pm. My great aunt's daughter, Virginia, still lived in the same house in the center of town I visited often in the sixties. Now it was unfamiliar and I had to ask directions. Her daughter, an unmarried bridal consultant with a territory as big as the West, arrived from San Francisco, and we talked about an hour.

I called Jack Swanson. He said the coast was clear, so I drove on in. After getting lost on the Nimitz Freeway and asking directions, I was crossing the San Mateo Bridge at 11 pm. At that time of night, those that were struggling daily to get to and from work in San Francisco with the Bay Bridge down had gone home, making it easier to cross. About half way across, I was passed by a car doing over a 100; either he was afraid of being on the bridge when another earthquake struck, or the turmoil of the past week had wrecked his sense of reality. Maybe he had a death wish. Maybe he was late getting to the Airport. Maybe he just wanted to speed. I'll never know.

Jack welcomed me in his usual, open way. Their house sustained no damage. Once, when I was talking to Jeanie's Mom on the phone, she said, "Did you feel that." I told her that I hadn't felt the 4.2 aftershock that just occurred. Jack's dog did, and jumped up from his sleep on the living room couch to whimper and cower.

Like me, Jack was taking steroids. He developed severe arthritis just after retiring and went through some bad periods until he found the right medication. His bones were so brittle he told me he'd fractured his spine in seven places just trying to mow the lawn.

One night, Terry Holmes and Hank Zuschlag, guys that had worked with us at Lenkurt, came over. Then, the last day, we had lunch with Bill Hemminghaus, our former boss and mentor. Bill was retired, but still consulting. He had a bad back too, having been blown out of his ship off Sicily on WWII when it hit a mine. A young communications officer in the German Navy, he spent hours in the water hanging on to floating debris and getting strafed by Allied planes.

I left Redwood City, relaxed, and drove south to LA. A woman in a red Acura Legend Coupe passed me—fast—over 90 mph. Five miles down the road, the California Highway Patrol had pulled her over. Five miles further, and she passed me again with abandon. It made me long for the day I'd plied these roads with the same abandon. Still, I wondered what money or power allowed her to travel like I couldn't. An hour south of San Jose, my radio started to squeal. I turned the radio down but the loud squeal still split the air inside my car. An exit came up, so I took it. I pulled into a corner gas station. The right front wheel bearing was completely gone. The wheel almost fell off. After being towed to two shops, a tire shop finally agreed to rebuild my front wheel. I lost about three hours. I called my Aunt Alta and told her that I'd be very late getting to LA.

Pismo Beach was beautiful, but after that California became too crowded. There was no romance at Santa Barbara during rush hour. Los Angeles was no better. Everyone seemed desperate to get home. Maybe they were all a little edgy after the big quake to the north.

I got to Aunt Alta's late, had some heated-up chicken, and went to bed in her room, decorated with her crocheting. The next day, I went to see my cousin Sara. Ron, her husband, had just returned from a Colorado deer hunting trip. Sara was teaching her three children at home, unwilling to send them to public schools. Their house was small and old, struggling to get remodeled—the price of housing in California. The air was October orange, a combination of heat, gasoline fumes, and ozone, trapped between the mountains and the sea.

That evening I met Konrad Sadak at his dry cleaning business, just as he closed down for the night. We had dinner across the street and talked of our articles and getting back to writing again. We never did. I left late and spent the night in Mineral Wells. The water tasted terrible. By noon the next day, I was at Tom's in Phoenix.

It was time for cars. Tom took me for a ride in the Austin Healey Sprite he was restoring. It reminded me of the time Nick and I had crossed the country in his. I drove Tom's 733i BMW. It appeared a bit sluggish until Tom told me the emergency brake was on. He cleaned my car inside and out and discovered that I was down four quarts of oil—just short of engine failure. Luck was riding with me again.

I headed for home. At Tucson I stopped for a rest room, parking on the side of a gas station. I passed a guy who stared menacingly at me, as I entered the restroom. He headed for a station wagon with a woman in it parked on the side by the fence under some trees. Inside, I remembered watching America's Most Wanted at the motel in Mineral Wells. A man and woman from Phoenix wanted for child molestation were supposed to be traveling in a yellow station wagon. When I came out they were gone. Two weeks later the couple was found dead, a murder-suicide in a campground near Flagstaff in the yellow station wagon.

Later, in New Mexico, I was admiring the desert and the Fuji Film Blimp flying overhead, when I heard a tire blow. All I could do was open the trunk and wait. A van pulled up in front and a large Mexican family piled out. While the young men changed my tire the old man told me they were from Corpus Christi and stopped to help a fellow Texan. When I offered money, he refused. Fifteen minutes later, I was on my way, waving to my fellow Texans as I passed them.

I spent the night in Fort Stockton. As I approached San Antonio in the Hill Country my oil light came on. I stopped for oil, a practice that would become a ritual in the next year. It was Halloween and I-10 in San Antonio was under construction. As I passed a big cement truck the door opened and a man in a wig and housedress waved. Hardly anything passed me as I raced into Houston. Near Katy an old flatbed truck did, its engine revving to what must have been beyond the red line. I gained going away as the truck headed for the next exit. Then, I saw dust or smoke under the cab as the flywheel or engine blew. It was coasting off the exit as I passed. I hope the driver was okay. When I got to the toll booth at the Sam Houston Tollway, I held up the plastic bag that carried my toll money and most of my receipts from the road. The attendant was put off, thinking that I was holding her up. After my explanation, she took the bag and retrieved my toll money. I was home. My legs and car had not failed me. It was an empty achievement, for my adventures were once again alone. Jeanie would have loved it.

# 37

## A Struggle to Keep Things Together

After that trip, the guys at the Mobil station became my friends. I got gas about every four days, and had them add a quart of oil. It was also a convenient time to run into the bathroom. My morning coffee caused me to stop at gas stations I'd picked out for their convenience on my way to work. The trend in Houston was toward locking restrooms to keep vagrants out. I sought those by the road with the door open. They weren't new, clean, or nice, but they became a necessity.

The Summer of 1990 came quickly, and I wanted to visit the family at the lake for the Fourth of July. Again, I asked Jeanie to go with me, but she didn't have the vacation time and didn't want to go. I wasn't prepared to go alone any more, but I had no choice—either go alone or not go at all. I decided to go alone one more time.

The first day out, I asked for a quart of oil the first stop. Then, near Denton, I was navigating heavy Saturday traffic, when a state trooper pulled me over along with another car. As I idled by the side of the road, the oil light kept coming on, so I shut the engine off. The trooper came up, announced that I had a sharp-looking car, and warned me not to weave in and out of traffic. I pulled off the freeway and got oil. I arrived exhausted to a small town off the Kansas Tollway. The motel I stopped at had a busy restaurant out front, so they agreed to bring some food to my room. I crawled in and crashed.

Sunday morning, in road construction coming into Kansas City, the oil light came on. My engine began to clatter loudly. It was two miles before I found an exit. I was in a panic because this exit didn't have signs for any gas stations. I turned down a promising street into one of the poorer sections of town until I finally pulled up to a fortified convenience store/station. Thankfully, a guy there, putting some fluid in his power steering, grabbed the oil I bought through the barred window and put three or four quarts of oil in my engine, and I was rolling again. My mind was clouded by thoughts that I could have locked up the engine right there. I had the oil checked every gas stop after that. I stopped at a McDonald's just south of Minneapolis and remember going into the rest room to take my steroids and almost lost the whole container of pills into the toilet. I had to force myself to be calm and take it easy. Driving a thousand miles on the Interstate was easy. Walking into restaurants and motels required planning and great effort just to keep from panicking or falling.

Cutting across Wisconsin as night fell on US 8, I ran into road construction again, further slowing my progress. At Rice Lake, I stopped for gas and oil, and marveled at how adept a girl, who seemed about 14, was at checking my oil. I pulled out of there and drove straight into a dead end in town about five miles down the road. Looking for signs coming back for what seemed forever, I finally got back to the station where that girl worked and noticed that US 8 had turned right while I, looking for gas, had thought it continued straight ahead.

My car was missing and sputtering, but I drove on through vaguely familiar territory made strange by fog, darkness, and fatigue. At one point a Corvette, traveling slowly, passed. There was a time when a car like that meant a driving challenge. Instead, I sputtered and bucked along, hoping not to look too embarrassing as the Corvette driver passed me. Finally, I pulled up to the familiar lights of the cottage about 10:30 pm. Everyone came out, but I just sat there, too tired to even get out of the car. Fortunately, there I had help.

Paul changed my plugs and the engine smoothed out. After a pleasant stay at the lake, I curtailed my usual visits to relatives and headed toward home. I spent one day talking to relatives on Highway 29 and stopped that night in a motel in Eau Claire. Before starting out the next morning, I stopped at a discount center and bought a case of heavy weight oil at the checkout counter in front. A young woman went back and got the oil, brought it to my car and put it in the trunk. I really admired these young ladies taking on physical work with ease.

I went to Menomonie to drop in on my 25th reunion. I'd asked Roger earlier if he'd planned to go, but he wasn't interested. Driving into town on

29, I passed Harold Halfin, walking. Hal had been with me in the doctoral program at West Virginia University. I circled the block and pulled up in a driveway as he walked up. We talked for an hour. Then, I drove over to the reunion site. I had to walk up a long ramp, but once inside the building, I was close to the reunion headquarters. In early afternoon, there were few people there, but I did get to talk to an old friend of Roger's and was sorry that he wasn't there to see her. Finally, I tired of standing there, said my good-byes, and went back to the comfort of the car and the road.

The trip home was more cautious. I ran without air conditioning and stopped every hundred miles to refill my cold drink, get gas if necessary, go to the bathroom, and add a quart of oil. At every stop, I relied on the kindness of strangers to put oil in my crankcase. I stopped the night at Fort Smith. Somehow, I managed to traverse torturous route 281 coming into town. It was on this stretch of challenging road that I realized that I could no longer control the wheel and brakes well enough to safely drive these roads. In the morning, I called the desk for help with my shoes and socks. I left my long shoehorn there with the guy who helped me. I discovered the loss later, but there was no way to get it back.

My car was limping again when I got back. I took it in to Ben's shop and they changed five spark plugs. It was time to overhaul the engine again. This time I did it right. I took it to a major rebuilder and the job was done in two days with a lifetime warranty.

# 38

## Retrieving the Past

The summer was leaving and I began to worry about my papers and furniture in the basement of my Atlanta house. These things had been in the basement ten years. I still had little furniture and didn't know if I'd ever get to review the papers there, thrown in boxes in my hurry to move out back in 1980.

I thought about renting a truck and going. I checked with moving companies and they were outrageous; and I didn't trust them after the two times I'd used them before. The best deal I could find was to rent a U-Haul trailer in Atlanta and pull it myself. I made a reservation for the Labor Day weekend. I knew I needed the largest trailer, a sixteen-footer. U-Haul assured me that one would be available.

Once again, I asked Jeanie to go along. She was a good driver and knew the route well. She protested, saying that she thought it was unsafe and she didn't want to be responsible for taking care of my car, the trailer, and me. No, she just couldn't do it. I was committed, stuck on the idea that I was going to do it—had to get my stuff back, somehow.

I asked if Jeanie's sons could help unload. She said that they would, so I made plans to call them when I got back. I called Joyce McGuork, my manager in Atlanta, to have her get me some guys to load the trailer. She said that I needn't bother, that her family would help me out, even on a holiday. So it was set—all except my anxiety about setting out alone one more time.

My Monte was running great. The rebuilt engine had good torque and wasn't using any oil or water. As directed, I changed the oil at 500 miles, and then again at a thousand. Now it was time to go. I was unsure about pulling a load with the engine barely broken in. I had to change the oil again in another thousand miles. Atlanta was 776 miles away; the next change would have to be in Atlanta.

The first day, Friday, was easy, especially since I didn't have to stop and check the oil. At Slidell, Louisiana, just before turning north on I-57, I hit heavy rain. My window, only cracked a bit, was hard to roll up at 70 mph. The rain on the windshield was blinding and I had to slow, but I soon left it behind and slept peacefully that night in Meridian.

The next morning, I stopped at a McDonald's for breakfast on I-20 on the way to Birmingham. A guy was there with a big truck, towing his car behind. He was moving to Maryland, I think. He said it was going well and that the truck was easy to drive. His story assured me that I could complete my upcoming mission, but I knew there was no way I could handle a rig like his without help. Hell, I probably couldn't even climb into the truck!

By noon Saturday, I reached the west side of Atlanta. I got a motel room along Fulton Industrial, and called Joyce. I was going to get the trailer, rest, and start in the morning. But she said that we should just wait until that evening, say four o'clock, when it was cooler, and then get it over with. I drove over to the U-Haul outlet nearby. The guys there didn't know anything about my trailer, but checked an outlet on the east side and sent me over there.

I had to drive about 25 miles to get to the place I was directed to. On the road over there I looked for a place to get the oil changed, but couldn't find one among the shops and self service stations. The U-Haul Center didn't have a trailer either, so while they located one, I drove up the road to get lunch and my oil changed. Across from the place I ate, there was a service station. A sign said that they were closed for the holiday weekend. I drove back without finding a place and got the hitch put on.

A trailer was located about ten miles away, so I drove over there to pick it up. Again, I looked for service stations up and down the road, but found none. Time was running out, so I went over to the U-Haul Center and hooked the trailer up, knowing that I wasn't going to get the oil changed until I got back to Houston.

The drive across town gave me a chance to feel out the trailer. "Do Not Exceed 45 MPH" appeared large on the front of the trailer in my rearview mirror. I knew I'd have to ignore that to get home on time. The trailer followed amazingly well behind my car and the mirrors gave me a good view of the trailer and the road behind. It seemed heavy unloaded and I wasn't sure about the electric brakes that caused it to pull, lurch, and jerk on my back bumper when I stopped. The trick was to stop smoothly.

I headed straight for the house, arriving about 4 o'clock. It was hot and I was very tired, so I turned the car around in a cul-de-sac and pulled up on the side of the street just beyond my mailbox. I rolled down the windows and waited about an hour. Then Joyce, her husband, two sons, and a son's girlfriend arrived.

They decided not to try to back the trailer down my drive. Instead, they backed their pickup down, loaded it, and then drove it back up to the trailer. I was too tired to even attempt to walk down the drive to the house, so they got me a chair and I sat and watched them struggle with the weight of the boxes and dust of a decade in the basement. Mr. McGuork planned the packing, putting the papers and books to the front and providing a cushion on all sides with the mattresses. I threw out the old full-sized bed and mattress, and they took my old overstuffed chair and two metal lawn chairs home, but every thing else fit very well.

In a couple of hours the trailer was loaded and the door padlocked shut. I walked around front and discovered the weight had pulled my bumper down about two inches. That worried me a lot. And it worried me more when Joyce said her sister had pulled a bumper off while going down the road. I pulled ahead a few yards, got out, and took a look. Everything was still in place but the bumper was still pulled down. The front of the car pointed upward and the back almost dragged on the ground. John had seen to it that I had the 60% front, 40% rear required weight distribution in the trailer. But that 60% in the front was way over the recommended load. I vowed to take it easy and put as little pressure on the bumper as I could.

Even with all that weight, my rebuilt engine pulled the trailer easily, and after the first two hills on the way out to the Bankhead Highway, I quit holding my breath and eased the trailer up and down the hilly landscape to my motel. My fatigue overcame my uneasiness, and I slept well that night.

The next morning I drove south on I-85. After a few miles at 55 mph, I grew more confident and speeded up to 65 or so. The car steered easily with the weight on the rear wheels lifting the front end, but I seemed to have good control. Incredibly, acceleration seemed barely affected, and the whole rig worked up through the gears as if all that weight wasn't even there. Before long though, I realized that I was getting only about six miles per gallon. It seemed as though I could watch the needle move toward empty. As I approached Mobile near mid-day, I had to drive five miles down a side road fearing that I was going to run out of gas. Finally, I came upon a rural station and paid a kid to pump me some gas. I stopped at McDonald's for lunch and tied up the drive thru window getting something to eat. I pulled over to the side and ate in the car. Some cars not going through the drive thru had trouble getting by me.

It was a great feeling, that drive with the window down, the heavy weight of half of my belongings and professional life riding smoothly behind. I had beat the odds and got my own stuff back. Anyone riding with me could see that it wasn't foolhardy or dangerous. But there was a sense of trepidation that I couldn't back up or turn around, lock or unlock the trailer, open the trailer door, walk very far from the car, or little else for that matter.

Later, heading west on I-10 into the sun, I ran bumper-to-bumper with heavy traffic, easily passing semis and keeping up with cars full of Labor Day travelers. Near Gulfport, I stopped for gas, to cool off with a drink, and rest my eyes. The station was a madhouse of activity, and I was glad to get back on the road. Just when the heat and dust and sun were getting to me, I found a new shopping center with a nice restaurant. I staggered in, too tired to eat, and had a salad while resting my eyes. When I came out, three pastel-colored hot rods graced the parking lot. I would have loved to talk to the owners, but didn't know who they were even though I ate with them.

Back on the road, the sun finally and mercifully set. I decided to stop on the west side of Baton Rogue for the night.

A motel with a familiar name appeared on the right. The entry to the lobby was hard to approach, but I drove as close as I could. When I got out, a large gob of gum, very flexible in the heat, smeared my carpet and covered my shoe. I couldn't reach down and remove it, so I just put up with it, trying not to smear the gum, acquired back at the Gulfport gas stop, any further.

The lobby was empty except for a guy complaining about two drifters who, after asking for beer and cigarettes, were starting to bother him. A sign said, "No refunds 15 minutes after checking in." I was too tired to be concerned and paid for a room. I was directed to the side of the building so I got back into my car and drove around to a small parking area on that side and pulled the car and trailer around, aimed toward the way out. The place appeared deserted except for the guy I'd seen in the lobby, standing in his open doorway.

I met the woman from the lobby and entered the room next to that guy. The building appeared okay from the outside—newly remodeled. Inside, the remodeling seemed to be only half finished, and the shower had a lot of paint on it. There was no TV and when I went to make a call, no phone. I didn't like this situation at all. I grabbed my bag and started back out. The two drifters, whom I hadn't seen before, were just beyond my car, lounging by a dumpster behind a gas station.

I approached my car behind it, hoping that they wouldn't see me. I came around to the driver's side, put my bag down, and started to shake as I struggled with the key to open the car door, not daring to look over my shoulder to where the men were. Finally, I got the door open, shoved my bag inside, and got in. As I turned to close the door the men were still at the dumpster, to my great relief. I pulled around front, struggled with the mess on my shoe, entered the lobby and asked for a refund. More than a half-hour had passed. My refund was granted without complaint. I suggested they call the police.

Across the freeway, I found a well-lit Motel 6 with a disabled unit next to the office. I had to drive all the way around the place to park, but soon was settling down to "Batman" on TV. The next morning went well except for a quick stop under electric brakes in Baytown and getting around a jackknifed eighteen-wheeler as I approached downtown Houston. I got home about 1 pm and backed the trailer into my garage. I was proud of that. I checked the bumper; except for being pulled down out of place, it was okay.

I called Jeanie. She asked her sons, but they said they couldn't help me. First, I began to worry, and then, I called a former graduate student assistant of mine, Columbus Anyanwu. Columbus was now studying law. He said he would get a friend and help me out. They came about 7 pm. It was still hot, over 90 degrees. Columbus and his friend got everything in, in about an hour and a half. I was amazed as he ran upstairs with box after box of heavy journals and papers. His friend quit in the heat, but he finished the job. Columbus told me he planned to return to his studies, but returned home to a shower and bed instead. My job was ahead, sorting through the accumulated papers, books, and journals that now filled my upstairs guest bedroom.

After four years in a barren house, it was good to have furniture again. The odd collection of semi antiques from West Virginia was very dirty, and some of it was broken, but by hiring cleaning help and enlisting my parents when they came through in October, I was able to make it serviceable again.

Furniture, books and papers stored in Atlanta basement for 10 years.

# 39

## Another Diagnosis

The steroids had not worked and I continued my decline. I walked everywhere with one hand reaching for or touching a wall. After that terrible fall in the parking lot, I parked close to the entrance and walked in along the front of the building with one hand on the wall. My walls at home became marked with greasy fingerprints as I made my way through my painful routine each day. Each night that ordeal would end as I went to bed, only to find myself kicking the foot board all night as my legs wound down from the tension of the previous day's activity. Only near morning, when my legs were completely relaxed, did I get some good rest. Then, the alarm would go off, and I'd begin the struggle all over again.

I turned the house cleaning over to cleaning ladies and the yard over to lawn care services. Meanwhile, my house got dirtier and my flowers were replaced with bare dirt as workmen raked away all my ground cover, leaving my yard as barren as Houston. No amount of money could get these people to care for and clean my house and yard as I had. So-called "handy men" were the worst. They overcharged for shoddy work and always claimed they could solve all my problems—for a price—usually a high one.

I went to Dr. Clearman again, determined to find out what was happening to me. She decided to have me see a neurosurgeon. The surgeon, Dr. Baskins, wanted to do another myelogram because the MRIs had not shown what was going on in my spinal column. As much as I hated the idea of a fourth myelogram, I agreed to go ahead with another few days in the hospital.

The myelogram went well, less difficult than the others, but my overnight in the old neurosurgery ward with older nurses was torturous, and I readied myself for the verdict. If surgery was the option, I was faced with months of recovery and perhaps even more paralysis. Jeanie prepared herself to come to my house to care for me. Dr. Clearman had my bladder capacity and flow checked. I knew I had had problems with urgency to urinate since becoming paralyzed, but this was new to me. She said that she was concerned about my kidneys. The reason I urinated so much was that my bladder wasn't emptying completely. Urine could back up into my kidneys and damage them. X-rays of my kidneys showed them to be healthy, and she decided to do nothing to treat the problem then.

I went to Dr. Baskin's office. He showed me x-rays from the myelogram of my neck that were shocking. My cervical spine was no longer straight, but took on an S-shape with the vertebrae crushed together, showing many stress fractures. I thought of the many times I picked up fifty pound bags with my teeth, and my many falls, each one jarring my neck and bringing numbness and shooting pains to my toes and fingertips. Could I have stopped some of the damage? I don't know. All I know is that I lived my life expecting occasional strain on my neck bones and muscles, and avoided falls as best I could. Unfortunately, many accidents had happened.

The cross sections of my spinal cord from the fourth to the sixth cervical vertebrae told another story. "Your cord is floating free," Baskins said. He had feared a fluid-filled sac or sarcoma that often occurs in the middle of an injured spinal cord, putting pressure on the surrounding neurons. The dangerous treatment for this condition is to insert a needle into the cord to drain off the fluid. Sometimes a "shunt" is left in to drain the fluid off. There was evidence in the form of scar tissue that a sarcoma may have once existed, but what remained of the cord was a new moon-shaped thread. It was like looking at the end of the fingernail on my little finger.

Dr. Baskins summoned his nurse and said, "Look! It's only two millimeters across!" Two millimeters from cutting all messages from my brain to my body. Two, maybe only one from death. I didn't know why I was standing there, feeling normal, or as normal as I could remember, rather than lying comatose, my life supported only by machines.

There was nothing further surgery could do. The cord was floating freely and not touching anything. The few neurons I had left below C4 were doing all the work; sustaining what function I still had left. The earlier diagnosis was correct: aging caused the decline. We begin with 20 billion single neurons in our brains, connected to several thousand spinal neurons, some as long as three feet. During our lifetime many of these neurons die and are never replaced. In a normal long life, there are still enough left functioning to operate the body. The loss of neurons is generally not a factor in senility or frailty; disease and the breakdown of tissues and bones lead to these inevitable outcomes.

However, I was left with so few functioning neurons below my injury that each lost neuron from aging and perhaps from trauma caused by my falls was having a noticeable effect. Short of some agent to regenerate or regrow neurons, or some way of transplanting neurons, the thread I had left, diminishing at an undetermined rate, was all I had left.

I could expect all of my bodily functions served by my cord above C4 to keep on functioning for the rest of my normal life. But I could expect all muscle control below my chest and vital bodily functions like bowel and bladder control to disappear. I could expect eventual kidney failure, loss of stomach function, and diaphragm operation. Poor circulation, shallow breathing, and loss of blood chemistry control could make me susceptible to urinary tract infections, pneumonia and many other diseases.

At that point I resolved to do what I could to make myself comfortable and maintain my lifestyle as best I could against the onslaught to come. To do that, I needed help.

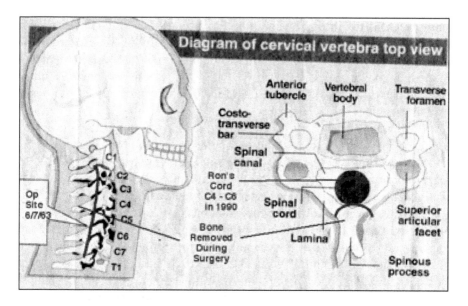

During the 1963 surgery, much of the supportive and protective spinous process was removed making Ron's neck weak and susceptible. 1990 study found very little spinal cord left C4 – C6.

# 40

# Help Can Be Hired

I remembered that Dr. Clearman had admonished me to get some help and had given me the phone number of the Texas Rehabilitation Commission. I was familiar with TRC through a counselor I knew who regularly sent students to TSU. I had good memories of the help the fledgling rehabilitation program in Wisconsin had given me to finish college. I called for an appointment with the counselor for TRC at TIRR. When I came for the appointment, I was told that the counselor was in the hospital. A month went by while I was shunted back to TIRR after being temporarily assigned to a counselor I never met.

When I finally got an appointment, the counselor, Kassandra Humphress, was a pleasant surprise. Vivacious and engaging, she promised to help me lay out a program that would help me overcome the transition from a totally independent working lifestyle to one that was dependent on others for support. She said that TRC could help me pay for an electric wheelchair and lift, supplementing what my insurance would cover, help me get started with six month's support for home health care, and pay for modifications to my home needed to help me go to and return from work. Similar assistance was available for modification of a van, if I needed one.

The plan was a joint effort, with TRC's contributions shared by modifications made at work, my insurance, and me. At work, I had already obtained the two Sierras and was allowed to take a computer home. A supplier of locks for the campus changed the door handles on several doors I used regularly in the building. A new concrete ramp was poured to the door off the breezeway where I was allowed to park my car, out of the weather and close to where I parked the Sierra over night.

I went to TIRR and got prescriptions from Dr. Clearman. She sent me to physical therapy to be measured for a lift, and to occupational therapy to be measured for the wheelchair, a home evaluation, assistive equipment and a driving evaluation. The wheelchair was to be built to accommodate self transferring at first, and then provide comfort and support needed as I got more confined to it. After reviewing many assistive aids, I bought some doorknob extenders, but nothing else seemed to be of help.

My driving evaluation was the most difficult. After a cursory workup in the clinic, we took a hand-controlled car out to a parking lot. The late model, front drive, Buick had very stiff steering and the hand controls kept getting in the way of my feet. I couldn't steer the thing, and operating the brake wasn't much easier. If it weren't for the unoccupied parking lot, I couldn't have driven at all. I asked to show the evaluator, Chad Strowmatt, how I drove my car, but he declined. He advised me to quit driving.

There was another option, METROLift. METROLift provided "curb to curb" transportation to the metropolitan area at a federally-subsidized cost of about a dollar a trip. But there were two problems: service only extended to Wilcrest Road, two miles from my home, and worse, they didn't stop at restrooms. I might have been able to ferry to Wilcrest daily on my way to work, even with all the extra time it would take, but I never knew when I'd have to stop and empty my bladder. Until things changed, I'd have to continue driving.

Getting help was another matter. Aside from a couple of guys at work who lived many miles from my home, I had no friends in Houston. My family, a thousand miles away most of the time and unsure of how to help me, was of little help. My reclusive life-style, forced by my condition, hadn't allowed me to establish strong ties with neighbors. Besides, neighborhood relationships are usually based on kids, common interests, or co-helping. I offered none of those and got nothing more than a friendly wave. Aside from Jeanie, no one was close. And she lived 24 miles away.

Still, I was happy with my limited, but free, lifestyle. Many people were worried about my being alone. I wasn't. I enjoyed working, reading, cooking, and on occasion, cleaning. Proud of what I could do without help. I was worried about having someone there, taking away what was mine. My experience with handymen, housecleaners, and yard mowers was that they were expensive, often did poor quality work, and were more trouble than they were worth. I didn't want some nurse coming into my home, forcing her idea of a healthy lifestyle on me, and have to pay her a high wage to do it. On the other hand, hiring minimum-wage workers opened my home to people who may have little understanding of the life of a professional educator and researcher. In the worst case, I might hire criminals who would steal from me.

I sought help from TIRR. A social worker in an electric wheelchair offered me a "how to" book on hiring personal attendants.

I didn't realize that I would be starting a business and have to withhold Social Security taxes. Selection required an application form and references. Checklists of the work to be performed were also recommended. Using my computer, I created the documents.

The first checklist was for maintaining my yard and plants. I originally did it to try to get bids on gardening. But the local yard maintenance firms, used to lowest cost cutting and edging rather than maintaining flowers and a variety of plants, refused to bid. Although they all claimed to be able to take care of all aspects of my yard, they wouldn't bid on it. Still, the list was useful as I taught attendants to take care of what the professionals refused to.

The second checklist I made was a grocery list. I never used a list to shop, but as shopping got tougher for me, I gradually came to a routine of shopping once every two weeks on a Friday night after work. The single cart would get heavy, about eighty pounds, and very difficult to push near the end, so I planned my course so as not to back track. If I did forget something while shopping, I'd leave the cart and go back to get it. If I forgot to get something or ran short, I'd do without until my next trip.

Gradually, over a period of three or four years, I started to use store staff and other shoppers to reach items I couldn't. The cart provided support like a walker, and a convenient place to rest, but as time went on, the whole process of shopping became more taxing. I gave up runs to the store for a few items, fresh fruit and vegetables, except after my shopping nights, and miscellaneous shopping in general. Trips to stores had always been an annoying waste of time, but now they were becoming an ordeal, where I had to plan every move from parking the car, to how I would pay, to how I'd get the package open when I got home.

I'd get home with the groceries late, have to haul them all into the kitchen, and then put them on the shelves. Meat had to be broken down and frozen, and vegetables had to be cut and prepared for storage and eating. I'd often end up eating at 10 pm, leaving dry goods and other imperishables on the counter for the next morning. After sleeping late from the long, hard week, Saturday mornings were reserved for laundry, cleaning up from the previous week's meals and putting away all the things that had collected.

After instructing the baggers to make lighter, more manageable loads, and opting for plastic bags to make carrying the heavy items easier, I finally had to enlist the help of the store. After some run-ins with less empathetic managers, I found one who'd help me. He agreed to let one of the baggers, usually a high school or college student, ride home with me and bring in my groceries. They loved to help me out and get a break from their routine. They invariably liked Jazz and he would calmly ride in their laps as I took them back to the store, only to have him turn on them and attack the window viciously as they closed the door to leave.

This help worked for about a year. Finally, it just got too hard to push a full cart, and the manager agreed to shop for me. I left several copies of my list with him. Then, on days when I needed groceries, I'd call him up, we'd go over the list, and he'd bring the groceries. When he broke the bad news that he was being transferred to another store, I'd already hired my first attendant.

Mom and Dad came through on their trip south in October and spent a couple of days helping me with all the furniture and papers I'd brought from Atlanta. Dad did a good job cleaning, fixing, and arranging the furniture. Mom and I tackled the boxes and papers upstairs. We got through the boxes of pots and pans and miscellaneous household items, but only began to start on the papers. I didn't know when I'd get to them.

By Christmas, 1991, I wanted to visit my parents in McAllen. Jeanie wanted Christmas at home, but agreed to go with me starting December 26. Then, about the 18th, the rains came. It was cold and rainy for several days. All Texas rivers west of Houston began to rise. By the 26th flooding had reached 100 year levels. It rained all day, and I talked to Jeanie several times. She was afraid of "*the flood,*" and wasn't going the leave her warm, dry home. So, one more time, I pulled myself together and left on the morning of the 27th, alone.

President Bush was surveying the flood damage by helicopter that day, heading down US 59 a little ahead of me, on his way to his usual Christmastime retreat at Beeville. It was gray, but not raining. I crossed several bridges where the water was out of its banks, spreading across the land. The San Antonio River was over the road in Victoria but I bypassed that. I stopped in Beeville for gas and made some crack to the clerk about Bush, like he was going Quayle hunting, but it didn't register. The struggle in and out of that store was all I could do. It was sunny and warm when I got to the Valley. We had a relaxed and pleasant time together and I made it back without incident—my last trip alone.

But not my last trip. I got an offer for a cruise. It was a come-on deal to view a time share high rise but had three days in the Bahamas thrown in. Jeanie was eager to go as long as we weren't driving, so I set it up for late January. Jeanie was late getting to my house, so she drove us to the airport, sometimes hitting 85 mph. She dropped me with an attendant and my wheelchair, and then parked the car. We arrived in Miami late and took a cab to our hotel in Ft. Lauderdale.

The next day, we endured the sales pitch at the high rise and then returned to our room. The next morning, we left early for the docks and the day cruise to Freeport, Grand Bahama Island. The cruise boat was small, with an elevator that I had to stand up in to use. There were narrow and obstructed areas in restaurants and passages. Still, Jeanie was able to push me around, and fold the chair and hold me when we had to navigate narrow spots. We ate, gambled, watched shows, and enjoyed ourselves. I didn't get seasick and managed to get in and out of the bathrooms walking on my own when I needed to—very scary as the ship rolled in the waves.

We arrived in Freeport late midday and disembarked through a hole in the side of the vessel. Four porters carried me down a flight of stairs to exit this hole. After a lengthy wait while Jeanie had to take my papers upstairs in the hanger-like immigration and customs building, a fleet of family luxury cars awaited our arrival. These entrepreneurs paid for their stateside-acquired used behemoths and made a living ferrying shipboard passengers to local hotels. It was cold, too cold for a tropical island. Our driver explained that they were having a cold wave—after all, we were only 90 miles from the mainland, and cold waves from Canada came down every few days this time of year.

The cabana-style resort we stayed at had a steep ramp leading to the lobby area about four feet above the drive. It took a strong man to push me up when we arrived. Concrete walks led to all the cabanas. After we rested, we decided to go out gambling at the Princess Hotel Casino. We dressed warmly for the chilly night. Jeanie pushed me rapidly through the empty lobby to the front where we'd find a cab. She pushed me to the top of the ramp without slowing, until sensing disaster, I yelled, stuck out my feet, and reached for the brakes. Fortunately, she stopped at the brink. I had visions of accelerating down that ramp, ripping the handles from Jeanie's grip as she fell forward, crossing the drive in a flash, and then catapulting across the flower bed when my chair's front wheels stopped dead against a four inch curb. It was a vision from some Jerry Lewis movie I'd seen. Only instead of laughs, I could only think of uncontrolled terror, injury, and pain.

There was no rail, but with Jeanie's help, I got up out of the wheelchair and made it safely down the stairs, step by step, into the cab, and off to the casino. Inside, the Princess could have been Vegas or Reno. After a night of trying to win, the house took our money and we returned to the resort in the wee hours.

A shuttle boat took patrons to another resort and the Hay Market in town. We decided not to try to take the shuttle because it looked like I'd have to be carried onto the boat. Instead, we took a cab. Most the market was easy to access, and the decking around the dock area made that easy to get around too. It was cool, and we had our jackets on, soaking up all the sun we could.

We decided to take the glass-bottomed boat. A ramp from the waterfront deck led to the long dock to the boats. We navigated that okay. The boat was large, "The Largest Glass-Bottom Boat in the World," and it was easy to lift me onto it. I climbed the stairs to the second level for the trip out to sea. When we got to the reefs, I climbed back down and was able to watch the divers swim among the coral and feed the fish. A hungry forty-pound grouper that loved to be hand fed and appeared to be a regular on the show, and stingrays lying outlined in the sand were the high point of our tour. It was disturbing to see how the coral was being damaged by polluted water.

There were few people on the boat. We did meet two couples from New England who were drinking their way through the attractions the island offered. They were helpful and friendly but a bit too raucous for me. Jeanie joined them for beers. When we got to the dock, the guys helped me out of the boat, but not without worry that they'd drop me. The drunks then proceeded on their way while Jeanie pushed me toward the ramp leading up to the deck. She started up the ramp okay, but about half way up, ran out of steam. I could feel us slow down, come to a stop about six inches from the top of the ramp, and then slowly slide backward as she tried to control the weight of the chair pushing her. We yelled at a guy passing above, and he came over and grabbed the chair, pulling while Jeanie pushed me up. We made it okay. We thanked him and he left. While we were catching our breath, one of the drunks came over, sympathetic as could be, but unable to help when we needed him. Jeanie again thought it was funny, but I, for one, didn't relish the idea of the dip in the cold Atlantic we'd narrowly missed.

That night, we went to a smaller casino, enjoyed the show, and dinner. This house too, took our money. The show featured look like, sound like, imitators of big name stars. I wondered what it must be like to spend your life in some two-bit tourist attraction, pretending to be somebody else. It seemed like a pretty dreary life to me. But then, I knew nothing of their lives, just like those who stared at Jeanie pushing me in the chair knew nothing of ours. By early the next afternoon, we were headed back. The cruise back was anticlimactic. We were old hands now.

When we got back to the hotel, I called my cousin, Terry Wenzel. The next day he drove over from Naples, gave us a tour of the Gold Coast and treated us to a fresh fish dinner at a restaurant on the dock where he once captained party boats fishing out of Boca Rattan. He suggested the dolphin. I balked until he assured me it was a fish—and a tasty one at that. On the way over to the docks, Terry got a taste of my disability when he half carried, half walked, me into a convenience store restroom.

# 41

# A Day in the Life of

By now, my routine had become numbingly difficult as I struggled with changes in my body by accommodating changes in what and how I did things. A typical day would begin at 5 am with my radio alarm going off. Grabbing the bed to push myself up, and walls for support, I'd head for the thermostat in the hall to set it up or down, depending on the season, and then go through the bathroom to the shower. I'd get a towel and prop it up by its natural stiffness against the outside wall of the tub and the wall. My tub is recessed, so it was easy to step down into it with my right foot and good right leg. Hanging onto the wall, I'd then drag my left foot in, being careful to keep my balance. For many years, a rubber bath mat had made the difference between standing relatively safely and slipping to a terrible fall on the steel tub or against the cold, hard tile walls. Fortunately, I never fell there, but cleaning the tub had become an ordeal. After spraying the walls and tub with a strong, spray-on tile cleaner, I would get on my knees and scrub with a small sponge, my legs aching and my knees stinging from the chemicals. I worked as quickly as I could, trying not to fall or breathe too much of the strong concoction. When I would slip, it became very difficult to get back up on my knees.

For many years, I had used shampoo to wash with because bar soap was too slippery to hold and I also had a hard time hanging onto a liquid soap bottle when it was wet. I used tube concentrate shampoo until it became too difficult to screw and unscrew the cap with my teeth and hands and squeeze the right amount out without dropping it. I started using a plastic bottle with a snap cap that I opened with my teeth and closed with my chin. The hard part was getting the tube or bottle back to the window shelf without dropping it. If it did fall, I'd have to push it with my right foot up the sloped back wall of the tub to where it would slide up on the flat four inch wide lip of the tub. I could then bend down enough to grab the bottle between the heels of my hands and pick it up, being careful not to fall as I struggled to keep my balance and hold the bottle at the same time.

I would wipe the shampoo from my hand to my still dry hair, removing as much as I could. Then I would reach down and pull the washerless faucet on. I had to change the faucet twice because it became too hard to pull. Once the water was flowing full force, it was easy to adjust the temperature. My shower valve was low, on the end of the spigot, and had no cap since the original mismatched one the contractor had glued on had come off. Fortunately, the pin was threaded, and that, coupled with the force of the water, made it easy to lift with sideways and upward pressure from my left index finger. The move required only a slight bending of my knees, and was easier than pulling the large plastic faucet knob out.

I would wash my hair first, and then taking the lather from my hair, wash the rest of my body. Except on cold mornings, when the tile walls of the enclosure were like ice, this was the most refreshing part of my day. The heat and pressure of the water massaged and removed the stiffness sleep had left in my body.

My ritual was to grab an old towel I hung at the end of the tub towel rack and wipe down the shower enclosure. It kept the enclosure clean and dry, reducing mildew and the need for cleaning. It was relatively easy to do; only I could no longer bend down and get the tub. Getting the towel back on the bar was also getting difficult, and I resorted to using its wet weight to flip the end over the bar I could no longer reach.

Sliding the shower curtain back from the unstable side of my tub, I'd then reach down for my towel propped in the corner. Toweling off in the tub to avoid getting any water on the floor, I'd leave a lot to air dry that I couldn't reach. Then I'd step up to the floor, grab the wall, and drag my left shin painfully up over the edge of the tub. Grabbing the small door opening that separated the toilet and tub from the rest of the bathroom, I'd hand walk my way to the main towel rack, hang the towel, and then proceed, hand over hand into the kitchen. Ugly smudges along the walls and woodwork bore testament to these daily forays. I was ashamed of the way my house had begun to look.

In the kitchen, I headed to a little red TV in the corner of the card table I used for eating. I had to go around in back and push a smooth round pin conveying dc power into a hole in the back of the little 9" set, picking it up to do so, to turn it on. After the plastic end on the on/off switch came off and was lost by the cleaning lady, I could no longer push it back and forth. With difficulty, I could still select channel ranges, rotate a knob to focus on a channel, and push a slide for volume. This was an improvement from a previous 9 " set, with volume and on/off knobs that turned so hard that I resorted to leaving the set on a constant high volume so I could hear it outside the house and plugging the dc connector into the back rather than attempting to try to turn it on.

After all this effort, I had the morning news. I was always interested in what was going on in the world, but now weather and traffic reports held my attention more. I planned not to drive in flooding rain in the morning, but that never happened except two weeks after Alicia in 1983, when I waited until 11 am to cross flooded Keegan's Bayou on my way to work. Most traffic situations didn't affect my driving to work, but I wanted to know them anyway.

Making coffee was difficult, but one pot lasted several days in the refrigerator. After my coffee maker quit, I started using a simple funnel and filter system. It began by filling the teakettle under the faucet, a job made difficult by the spring-loaded whistling cap. I'd push the cap open on the counter, hold it open with my left hand, shove it into the end of the spigot, and force the kettle up into the spigot to keep it open with a push from my right hand. The pot's growing weight as the water flowed in would just about force my right hand down into the sink as it filled to overflow. Jerking the kettle to my right to the counter, I'd slide it over to the rear burner. I rarely had to open a can of coffee, but if I did, I'd go to the pantry and grab a three-pound can. Holding it by pressure of my right hand against my left arm, I had to be careful not to let it slip. In addition to the immediate danger to my bare toes and my plastic floor, it was no longer possible for me to bend down and pick up the heavy, rolling can from the floor, except by bringing a chair to the spot, sitting on the chair, the reaching down for the can.

My old can opener worked well for large cans like this, but it required pushing a lever down hard while holding the base of the can up toward the blade. If the top was not cut off completely, I'd hit it with the heel of my right hand. Somehow my hand wouldn't get cut and this worked well except with cans of liquid that would splatter all over the counter. Sometimes I resorted to a table knife to pry the top up to where I could get a hold on it, and then work it back and forth until the metal fatigued and broke free. I always worried about cutting my fingers or hands, but except for superficial wounds that didn't bleed, I didn't.

To save the coffee flavor, I would pour coffee from the three-pound can to a one-pound one, and then put both in the refrigerator. This usually resulted in spilling some. Initially, I measured coffee into the filter with a small scoop, but, with practice, I just poured it from the small can. If I got too much, I'd pour some back from the filter paper.

The water in the teapot usually boiled over just after the whistle went off, and I'd drag it off the burner to stop that. Then I'd drag the pot over to the sink, too heavy to lift. I put the coffee pot and filter in the drying rack in the sink, down to avoid spills. Grasping the button in the heel of my left hand, and lifting with the stiff fingers of my right hand, I'd carefully hoist the boiling water to the edge of the filter and tip it, allowing a small stream of water to fill the filter. As the teapot emptied, it would get lighter, until the point where I could hold it with my left hand alone, ever fearful of my wrist giving out and spilling boiling water. Sometimes I'd bring the pot back to rest while the water drained slowly through the filter. Then, come back to wash down the sides of the filter and fill it again. Usually, there was too much water, so I'd grab the top of the filter and move it to a saucepan. On days when I'd heat up coffee, the same saucepan served well. The hardest part was pouring the coffee into a plastic coffee cup with the handle clamped between my hands quickly enough to avoid burns as the boiling coffee heat radiated to the aluminum handle and my hands. I often spilled coffee on the counter, but in many years of making coffee this way, sometimes dropping a full teapot into the sink, boiling water flying, I never scalded myself.

Except for cereal for variety, my staple breakfast was 2 eggs, two slices of toast, and one slice of bacon. Getting bacon out of some of the innovative shrink wrappings was often a challenge, but I managed by stabbing an edge with a sharp steak knife, and then sawing my way down the side with the serrated edge of the blade. Some plastics cut like butter, while others were tough and required a lot of sawing with both hands while I held down one corner with an elbow. I even had to cut zip-lock packages because I couldn't open or seal the seals. Using a table knife, I'd separate one strip of bacon and put it in a Teflon fry pan. The pan was becoming a problem because the pan storage under my oven was so low. I'd have to bend my knees and reach down, hanging onto the island counter with one hand while I stuck my other hand into the storage handle and pulled it out, struggling to keep my balance. Then I had to reach down, again bending my knees, and in one motion grab the pan handle with my left hand and sweep it up to the top of the range before my hand grip gave out, or, I caught the front of the pan with my right hand, making it easier to balance and lift.

Sometimes, the pan would fall back, clattering into other pans. This was scary and tiring—I didn't want to fall down.

I put the bacon in to fry, using a fork to turn it. Operating the front range controls was easy, even though they required "push in and turn" for child safety. Instead of grasping the control bar between the thumb and forefinger, I forced it into the space between my index and middle fingers, and then pushed hard against the control and turned my wrist right or left to the setting I wanted.

Eggs were always risky. I carried them one at a time from the refrigerator egg tray in the door. Jazz loved it when I dropped one, but I rarely did. After years of practice, I'd developed a way of cracking an egg on the edge of the fry pan, and then opening it with both hands. My left thumb had a way of breaking through into the yokes. Some egg white would run down the side of the pan, but most yokes ended up intact in the hot bacon grease. With a plastic spatula, I could easily turn the eggs and cook them quickly.

While my eggs were frying, I'd toast two slices of bread. After years of spreading soft margarine with a table knife, I now used a liquid variety that I squeezed between my chin and chest.

Moving my plate and coffee cup to the counter, I ate standing up. It was easier to cut the egg and eat standing up. I'd wait until evening to sit down. I used to eat at the folding table, but it got too difficult to cross to it carrying a plate. And hot coffee would spill or burn my hands through the cup as I carefully inched my way to the table. Dirty dishes were now piled at the sink. While at one time, most of my single life, I hand washed dishes after every meal, now I waited until I ran out of dishes or until Saturday to load the dishwasher. I worried about roaches, but somehow escaped them. I did have ants, and couldn't seem to get rid of them as they came for bits of food to carry off. Using the counter as a slide, I'd move the coffee to the refrigerator, where I'd have to risk carrying it to the top shelf.

With the dishes pushed to the sink, and water run on them to carry the larger pieces to the disposer, I'd return to the bedroom, careful, as I rounded the stair, to get a good grip with the inside of my wrist on the stair rail.

Often, I made unscheduled trips to the bathroom to urinate or worse. My bowel control had become so bad that a sudden urge would send me careening for the bathroom in a race to see what would get there first, the bowel movement or me. Sometimes, I wouldn't make it. Cleaning up was very difficult, especially since I could no longer bend down. First, I'd have to secure the dog outside, and then make several trips for cleaning supplies, and then spend whatever time required cleaning up on my knees with plastic pails and chairs to hold my supplies. Then, I'd have to shower again to clean myself up.

Back in the bathroom, I'd pour some pre-shave from a plastic, flip top bottle into my right hand, and then wipe it on my face. Dropping this bottle into the sink was less stressful than the earlier glass bottles that, though they rarely broke from the short fall, threatened to spill all their contents as I chased them around the slippery sink. Flipping the top with my teeth tasted bad, but easier to handle than the plastic screw caps found on the glass bottles. My old two-headed Norelco razor, battered from many drops into the sink, still shaved me pretty well, once I got the switch on.

After my left thumb could no longer operate the button, I'd learned how to push the flip top release button up against the faucet nozzle to open it, ending the struggle with my failing fingers. Now, I just banged the razor up against the side of the sink rather than try to brush whiskers out with the little brush held in the failing grip of my left fingers. It never got fully clean, but kept on giving me a good shave.

Laying my electric toothbrush on a folded towel, with two hands I could still apply toothpaste to it. My electric toothbrush had served me well, brushing vigorously with only pressure to operate it, since Roger and Lin got me one in the early 1980s. Still, a dentist in 1990 told me to floss and use a toothbrush I couldn't operate. I did the best I could, but my gums had started to bleed, and tarter started to build up on my teeth between dental cleaning. I worried that I'd lose my teeth if I couldn't get them cleaner.

Heading for my bedside, the hard part of my morning would begin. My shorts, always easy to get on before, now became difficult to get over my feet. Still, by sitting on the edge of the bed, putting them on the floor, and then slipping my feet through the leg holes, and then falling back on the bed, and raising and bending my legs, I'd reach up and try to get my hands inside the waistband to pull them on. Often my right foot would slip through easily, but my sluggish left foot wouldn't go through the leg hole, and the shorts would catch on my foot and snap back. Often, I had to try several times to get them on. Sometimes, I thought about giving up and not going into work at this point, but I kept trying until the shorts were on.

My socks were the next challenge. Sitting on edge of the bed, first I'd lift my left foot to the top of my right knee, struggling to keep it from sliding back off my knee to the floor. There was no good way to prepare the sock to put it on. Believe me, I'd tried everything—including sewing elastic handles on at great expense—only to find they didn't work. Sticking my thumbs in the hole, I'd spread the opening as much as possible, and pull the sock over my toes, and then reaching in again, try to pull it on as much as possible, hopefully over the heel. Most times the sock would not go over the heel, but wad up at the heel's base. Then I'd put my left foot down and raise my right.

My right foot would come up and stay up easier. But, because the foot was not atrophied like the left one, it was harder to slip the sock on. Now the fun began. I slid off the bed to the floor. If the sock wasn't already over the heel on my right foot, in a sitting position, I'd pull the foot up to me by the shin, and then hook my left index finger under the wad of sock where my inside ankle bone protruded. Straightening my leg, my finger would pull the wad of sock over my heel. Rubbing the side of my foot hard against the carpet, I'd force the sock to slide further up my foot, rotating it as it worked its way up. Then, I'd roll on my left side, pull my leg up again, and try to hook the top of the sock from the back of my ankle with the same index finger. If I got a hold of it, I'd wiggle and rub the carpet and pull with the single finger until the sock was all the way up and my finger was sore. Then I'd start with the left sock, rolling on my right side, pulling my foot up by grabbing my shin, and hooking the sock with my sore left index finger. This sock came on the same way, by repeatedly hooking it and rubbing it against the carpet. The rubbing forced the sock around my foot, and I never knew where the heel would come out. Jazz usually took this opportunity to play with me, so he tended to aggravate the difficulty of rolling around on the floor, trying to get into position.

My left index finger and legs aching, I'd pull myself up to my knees facing the bed. Then bringing my right knee up to put my foot in position, I'd push down on the bed rail with the heel of my right hand, elbow locked, until I was up on my left knee and the momentum carried me up to my right leg. Once standing with my left hand on the foot rail of the bed, I'd turn around and sit down. Then, I'd reach down to both sock tops, straightening them as best I could, and rubbing my foot against the carpet again if I needed to push them on further or straighten them.

My pants were like my shorts, except they were usually easier because I could hook a belt loop with my right thumb, making it easier to pull them up. Sitting on the bed, I'd work my feet into the leg holes. Then, I'd rock back on the bed, raise my feet with bent knees above me, hook the belt loop with my thumb, straighten my legs and slide into the pant legs. Often, my feet would hang up going in, and I'd be stopped in mid thrust. This was very frustrating, like being short-sheeted, because I used all my momentum and strength and found it difficult to stop. My arms would be pulled and my legs would transmit that pain of being unable to fully flex. Relaxing was now required and often the hardest part. Jazz would jump on me as I rolled back, helping to make it more difficult. Sometimes, it would take several tries to get my legs in. As I lay back on the bed, meditating and letting the pain drain from my legs, the urgency to get going was still on the back of my mind.

Once my pants reached my thighs, it was easy to stand up briefly to pull them up with my hands, palms open inside, pressing out a pulling up at the same time, even if I was standing on a cuff. Then, I'd slip my shirt, already positioned next to me on my bed, over my head, and then stand up, again hooking the belt loop with right or left thumb. Then, I'd waddle over to the door opening, holding my pants up, reposition my shirt, lean my left hip and shoulder against the door frame, hook both front belt loops with my thumbs, push my waist band together until the pants hook was in position, and release.

Then I'd head back to the bed with my left shoe and brace. Sitting down on the bed and pulling my left pant leg up over the knee, I'd position the brace in the shoe and place it standing between my legs. Then I'd lift my left leg, push my foot down into the shoe, and, using the brace as a shoe horn, stand up and force my foot into the shoe. Sometimes it would take several tries, putting my whole weight on the leg, to push my foot all the way in. Standing on the foot when it was only part way in was always painful, but it was pain I had to stand to get going every day. Then I'd sit down on the bed again and pull the Velcro band on the splint through its D-ring and pull it back as tight as I could on my calf.

Heading back to the closet doorway, I'd position my right shoe in the center. Bracing myself against the left door frame, I'd reach down with my right hand to get the long-handled shoe horn I kept propped against the inside door frame. Standing next to the shoe, I'd position the end of the shoe horn at the back of the heel, lift my right leg, and step in, pulling up on the shoe horn to keep it vertical and from being forced back, crushing the heel of the shoe. This usually required a lot of wiggling, pushing, and pulling up on the horn until my heel slipped in. Sometimes it required several tries.

Heading back into the bathroom, I'd comb my hair and insert my wallet, a two-handed maneuver that required holding the pocket open with my right hand while balancing the corner of my billfold over the opening, and then pushing and wiggling it until it slid into place. Using a button hook given to me years before by the Easter Seal Society, I'd run it through the second button hole on my shirt and hook the button, pulling it into place. Hooking and releasing the button was becoming more difficult, and sometimes I struggled with it, especially when shirt button holes were new, or frayed with fine strands of thread getting caught in the hook.

One last chance to urinate before I left. Leaning hard against the wall by the toilet, with my left elbow against the wall and my left thumb in the front belt loop, pushing hard. At the same time I'd jamb my right thumb into the right front belt loop and force both belt loops together, sucking in my gut, until the pant hook came clear.

In the morning, my pants were unzipped, but if they weren't, I'd pull outward hard with both thumbs on the belt loops until the zipper lock would pop out and the zipper would go to the bottom. Letting my pants drop to my knees, I'd hook my shorts band with both thumbs at the hip and force my shorts down. Often, while doing this, I'd be fighting an extreme urge to urinate, brought on by muscle spasms, and have to stop and relax or hurry to avoid an accident. I'd used this method since first going out in public in 1964, but it always bothered me to have to find an empty stall. Sometimes there were no doors on the stalls or no stalls at all, so I'd have to wait until no one was around or hide myself as best I could. Other men frowned on me dropping my pants. I often had to wait for a stall to get free.

I always urinated standing up like any man, only now my balance was so bad I had to hold onto the wall, sometimes straining to reach behind the toilet and stay standing, and lean forward to go.

At least here at home I could relax a bit, resting my forehead against the overhead cabinet directly over my toilet.

Reaching down quickly to retain my balance, sticking both hands inside my short waistband, I'd spread the band and pull the shorts up. Regaining my balance, I'd use the same motion to get my pants, making sure my shirt was in place. Then I'd stick my thumbs in the belt loops, lean left hard into the wall, and hook my pants. I'd had all my zippers sewn off about a half inch from the bottom to keep the handle from being hidden and caught in the folds of fabric.

For many years, I'd struggled with first only the meager grip between my left thumb and forefinger to pull zippers, and then a combination of left forefinger and right thumb. By 1986, even that approach was failing when I discovered that I could cut a couple of teeth from the end of a large comb and the end could hook the little hole that is in the end of every stamped-metal or plastic zipper handle. Forcing the zipper lock open like I did tended to damage the top zipper teeth, making it hard to pull the zipper up past the damaged teeth. Pulling the comb with both hands solved that. Now, my biggest problem was keeping my balance as I fished for the small hole in the zipper handle.

As I headed for the kitchen, I'd turn the air conditioning up to 90 (or down to 50 in winter) for the day, and then go back into the kitchen. Going to the sliding glass door in the back, I'd roll the rod I kept in the door out with my right foot. Pushing the door open was hard because the door never rolled smoothly. Still, by leaning against the door and grabbing the handle in my left hand and pushing against the edge of the frame with my right, I was still able to push it open.

Reaching down to get the hose out back on the deck had become very difficult, so I often left it propped on an old whiskey barrel where I once grew flowers but now showed ballast rock and broken, rotting staves. A toad had taken up residence in it a couple of years before and totally destroyed the last of the flowers planted in it. With the nozzle in my right hand, I'd reach down and turn on the faucet with my left. Then I'd quickly walk around the deck and water what few flowers had reseeded or were planted by my grass cutters. Mostly, I surveyed the decayed remains of what had once been a well cared for flower garden.

Returning the hose to its perch, and reentering the door, I'd push it back, throw the lock, roll the security rod back into place, rush into the bathroom and urinate again. If I hadn't done it before, I'd go to the dresser, select a tie, and take it to the kitchen. Going to the stair, I'd work my way up by placing hands on both rails, and leading each step with my right foot, and then dragging up my left, now stiffened by the brace. Halfway to the top, the left rail stopped where the wall came down. At this point, I'd lean my left shoulder into the wall and push on, keeping up the rhythm and pace to keep my balance until I reached the top. Many times I teetered there, on the brink of falling, but whenever I did, it was onto the landing, not down the stairs.

I'd go behind the desk, load my handsplint, computer disks, papers, and anything else I'd need for the day into my waiting briefcase, close it up, put the sling over my right shoulder, and pull it off my desk. Heading down the stairs, I'd hug the left rail, the weight of the briefcase giving assurance that my stronger right foot would not slip on the carpet. A swinging momentum with each step would get me to the bottom.

Heading for the kitchen, I'd swing the briefcase up onto the center island, open it up, and load my lunch and tie. Then I'd head for the door. Putting my briefcase down by the door, I'd close Jazz's doggy door, and then he'd follow me out. When it was hot and dry, I'd drag a hose from the front of the garage to water the plants in front. When it got dry enough to affect the lawn, I'd bring it out earlier and let the water run, flooding the beds. Water always stood under the front deck because the builder dug a depression there that collected water. I didn't worry about mosquitoes because of all the fertilizers and insecticides and that the area dried up quickly during the heat of summer.

One more time, I would head back to the bathroom to urinate. The twenty-mile ride into work had become a fight to get to a restroom before I had an accident. Fueled by gas caused by a poorly functioning bowel, liquid stored from the night before, muscle spasms, and tension caused by my inability to move quickly and handle my clothes, my mornings consisted of periods of extreme anxiety as I tried to get to where I could void, followed by periods of relative calm after I had voided, sometimes only a small amount, followed by periods of contemplation of when and where I would have to stop again. On the worst mornings, I would work my way to the bathroom as many as ten times. Finally, it would be time to go.

I no longer locked the front door, trusting Jazz and the front gate to keep intruders out. It was now a struggle to lock the deadbolt with a key, and I needed the door open that night if I rushed in with a full bladder. Closing the back garage door on Jazz, leaving him to roam the yard, I'd swing my briefcase to its familiar spot behind the front driver's seat.

I was thankful for the electric garage door opener I bought in 1991. Before that I enjoyed the push it took to force the door open—my "stretching exercise"—except when it rained against the door and it soaked up water and became heavy as the world while I struggled like Prometheus to raise it high enough for a new grip to the shoulder high point where the weak spring would finally take over the job of raising the leaden door the rest of the way overhead.

Starting the car and backing out was easy, as was reaching up with my right hand to push the large control button with the heel of my hand. The hard part was heading down the road or back into the garage to "go" one more time before I left. I kept a plastic pail by the water heater for watering plants, and started using it for those emergencies rather than go back inside.

My route to work passed a service station on the right just before I reached the freeway. There was a service area containing a men's room on the side away from the pumps. In the past it had sometimes been locked and the door was sprung so heavily that I had to wait for someone to let me out when I couldn't force it open enough to get my foot, and then my arm, behind the door to open it. This restroom was also dark and dingy and was often dirty. At least it had a good heater in cold weather, something most restrooms didn't. Now it had been remodeled and brightened up a bit. The door spring was less aggressive, and a good, curved handle installed so I could open and close the door.

If I had to stop, this was it. I'd pull in through the pumps and swing around facing outward to bring my car's side as close to the door as I could. If there were other cars I'd park so I could use them or the building to get to the door. Most days, I'd pull up to just beyond the door, pull my car door handle with the help of a leather thong I'd tied on the handle so I could pull it open with my left fist clenched and pushed through the loop with my wrist. The door, forced out by my shoulder and elbow would open all the way, almost hitting the building. If I had to stop the door from hitting something, I'd control the speed the door opened with the loop of rawhide still around my wrist. Steadying myself in the car door frame, and walking along the open door, I could get up over the curb and into the restroom door. I no longer worried about my car or the keys still left in the ignition with the door left open. Fools and drunks, and even the disabled, are protected from evil at times like these. No one ever bothered me because I left my car and briefcase vulnerable to the world.

Inside, the routine was the same as I described at home, except finding a clean corner to open my pants was impossible—I just did the best I could.

Depending on the traffic and the weather—cold and wet days were the worst—I headed onto the freeway, planning my next stop. During the four years US 59 was being reconstructed, I found a station along the frontage road with old fashioned restrooms on the side. I could see the open doors ahead assuring me that they weren't in use. Here, I'd pull up like before. Sometimes street people who frequented the area would sneak in from the back, and I'd have to use the ladies' room. The men's room wouldn't lock and the light didn't work, so I'd leave the door open a bit. When a car parked next to the rooms, I'd pull up behind, and then work my way along a tire rack and the building to the doors.

By contrast, a new station had installed a disabled restroom at the rear outside of its food store. It was always locked, so I'd have to hail an attendant to get it opened. The disabled parking space next to the restroom had wheel stops that made it impossible to park close if I backed in, and hard to get over the curb to the wall, so I always asked someone for help. The room itself was large and bright, too large. Across that cavernous smooth tile floor to the toilet with no high handholds was treacherous, but opening my pants was near impossible. One time, forced to open my pants at the back wall, I inched my way forward with my pants at my knees, nearly falling in the process over the toilet. My legs strained and I urinated on myself as I struggled to regain my balance, thoughts of cold, hard tile and porcelain as my landing place kept me upright. With nothing to hang on to, urinating was difficult too. I avoided that room unless I absolutely had to stop, and asked others to unhook my pants before opening the door for me as I went in the room after that scary incident.

I'd try to drive all the way in without stopping, a trip that took forty to fifty minutes, depending on traffic. I had ways of avoiding traffic problems, escape routes, but, sometimes I'd get caught by an accident or stalled car, and the pressure would build to get to the safety of the building. Rarely, did I get close to campus without a tremendous urge to urinate that gave me flashes of heat in my body, difficulty breathing, stomach cramps, and lower back pain. Braking, accelerating, and turning became difficult as I worked my way down the last streets to my parking space. Sometimes, I'd wet myself a little as I'd grit my teeth against the urges running through me, all the time trying to relax. With all the concentration it took from my driving, it's a wonder that I didn't get in an accident. Long years of driving the same route and conditions, and, a little luck, saved me from that.

When I got to my parking space in the breezeway under the building, sometimes other vehicles blocked my way. I'd wait, as patiently as I could, until workers passing by would move them. I always parked the Sierra next to the wall and drove my car up next to it. Opening the door until it touched the basket in front of the scooter, I'd pull myself out, reach behind the seat and hook the strap on my briefcase. Then pull the briefcase out with the strap and swing it to the back of the scooter. I'd loop the strap around the seat back and position the briefcase, that didn't fit but rode okay, on one end. Then I'd lift the armrest, turn, and fall back on the comfortable seat. Grabbing under my knees, I'd pull my feet to the platform.

The small key to the scooter had been fastened to a 4 inch long piece of clear acrylic plastic shaped like a banana with a 3 inch loop of stiff wire through a hole on the end opposite the key. It was made for me by Kirk in our carpentry shop and fit nicely in my shirt pocket. The loop of wire made it easy to pick up from the floor or wherever it fell and pull it out of the keyhole. The scooter had a small dashboard about sock top high. Hooking the key handle by the wire in my shirt pocket, I'd grip the curve of the handle in the palm of my right hand and reach down to insert the key. Before I got the handle, I was forced to leave the key in the dash. Many times, I found that others had used the scooter, even though I lifted the simple throttle rod out of its hole to discourage meddlers. The scooter was left outside, parked with other university vehicles; some of those were also electric, but somewhat protected from street traffic. Still, one time the batteries were stolen and quickly replaced by the ones from the spare scooter.

Inserting the key wasn't easy. Gripped in a wrist-raised inner hand hold, right arm extended, I'd shakily point the key into the little slot now damaged by many such insertions. The urgency to urinate made this action difficult, and often I'd ask for others to help me with my briefcase and the key to speed things along. The key had to go all the way in to work, and those who stuck it in half way and turned it with the leverage of the handle caused the key to bend to the point where it wouldn't enter or turn on easily. Once in, the key had to be turned to the left before it would go to the right with a lot of wiggling. Once on, lights would go from red to yellow to green very quickly to enable me to drive the scooter. Unless someone tampered with it, the speed control was set at a medium fast setting for rushing to the bathroom. If it was off, I'd reach down with my right hand and turn it by clamping the knob between the inside of my right index and middle fingers. It was easy to reset the speed but I had to stop to do it and that took time.

Pushing on the reverse lever, I'd back up toward the door to the shops. Most days, it was open or someone would come by and open it. I could open the heavy door by driving up the ramp until the front tire touched the right door, reach up and hook the left door handle with my permanently-curved left fingers, and then pull the door open part way while releasing my right hand on the lever, letting the front of the scooter roll back into the door, holding it open. If the scooter rolled back too far before the electric brake engaged, the door would slip out of my hand and past the front wheel and shut. Sometimes I'd have to try several times to get the right position. If the scooter stopped or I got my right hand back on the lever, I'd stick my left hand inside the door and push out with my wrist until the door opened more. At the same time, I'd push the handle bar to the left with my right hand then quickly reach and push the throttle lever forward, forcing the nose of the scooter into the opening I'd created. One more push on the door with my left hand to get it to clear of the left rear fender and I'd bounce up over the threshold and down the hall.

My scooter had two small horizontal wheels on the front on either side to open doors. With these wheels up against a door I could easily push open the outer, and then the inner doors to the shop men's room. This I would do with great speed, sometimes banging the doors against their stops. Once inside, I'd drive around to the stalls, being careful about my position in front of the door I would enter. Experience had taught me not to use the large disabled stall. Although properly constructed with all the right stuff, this stall, like that cavernous bathroom was too big, without close, reachable walls for support and the door opened the wrong way, making it hard to close.

Pushing the handle bar out of the way, I'd push my feet out and stand up in the door opening. Getting inside and past the door, and then closing it with my left shoulder as my hand reached for the slide to push it in. When I got the door shut there was always relief. The walls were my friends. They closed in on me and supported me. In that corner, fighting waves of urges to urinate, I'd have to bend down and squeeze in to release my pants. Then, bend down again as I pushed down my shorts. Then, I would lunge forward, grabbing the concrete wall behind the toilet, my shins screaming in pain against the edge of the toilet bowl, my body rigid to keep from slipping and falling, and release. The toilet seat, mercifully, would be up. If not, at this point, I'd learned not to reach down for the seat. Instead, I'd let the urine flow as it would, hopefully through the open hole. Most times it didn't. The seat, the floor, my shoes, and pants were often game for errant urine that fell where it would as I struggled to empty safely. I knew the custodians hated the messes I left, but I didn't know what to say to them. When I couldn't get my shorts down, I found that I could go right through the thin cotton material, and I sometimes did. It left a small wet spot, but, after an hour or so it would dry, and it was more comfortable than wet pants that were the outcome of not taking this shortcut to relief.

And relief it was. Collecting myself, I'd climb on the scooter and head for the privacy doors. Positioning my scooter just right, I could pull the inner door open with my left hand as I backed up, swinging the front of the scooter into it to hold it open. Then I'd drive along side the outer door, grab the handle, and pull it open about six inches until it hit the scooter, and then I'd stick my arm outside and hold the door open against me while I watched the busy hall. When someone would come along, I'd hail him or her and ask them to help me get out.

But, let me back up and tell you my worst day. No, it wasn't the time I got the front of my light gray pants wet and had to wait an hour for them to dry—that was embarrassing and happened several times. It was a horrendous accident. By the time I finally made it into that final restroom and reached for that concrete block wall, I sometimes hit my head on the wall, and my legs would spasm with the release of the tension built up trying to keep from going earlier. On this particular day, I lunged forward too far, my feet slid back on the floor, and I lost my grip on the wall.

I fell fast and hard onto the open-ended toilet seat! It jammed hard around my ears, wrenching my neck as it stopped my fall. When I gained my senses, I was balancing my outstretched spine on my toes and my vice-clamped jaw, straining against the pain and consequences of losing my footing altogether and strangling or breaking my neck as the weight of my body tried to pull me to the floor over the rim of the toilet.

Realizing that help would not come in time, and if it did, they couldn't get in the locked stall easily, I had to do something before my straining, spasming muscles gave out and I'd go down. Pushing thoughts from my mind of how they would find me, somehow, I summoned the strength to pull my right leg up along side the toilet, pushed down hard on the top of the toilet valve with my right hand, and willed my body upward until my head came out of the toilet seat and I fell to the right against the stall wall. The strength was gone from my quavering legs, but the relief I felt was immense—until I discovered that I hadn't urinated and still had to tend to that. I pulled myself up from between the toilet and stall wall and managed, thankful to be alive one more time.

My scooter pushed doors open easily, and the elevator controls in the front elevator were well placed, so I headed upstairs to my office easily. Mildred, who occupied the first office, had taken it upon herself to open my door every day. Jeanie was still my secretary about half the time, but Josh had moved her across the hall to his office suite to act as receptionist-secretary. I had to rely on a series of graduate assistants and summer interns from the State Energy Conservation office to get my work done. In emergencies, Shirley, who occupied the office next door, would help me out. I had been in a coffee club for years. Now, I could no longer work my way back down the hall with a shaky Styrofoam cup, spilling a bit on the way, and had to rely on my students or other employees to get my morning coffee.

Paper handling, always a problem, had become a serious one. I could no longer manage extensive files without parts of them being misplaced or lost. Jeanie was never efficient at maintaining my files. Paperwork piled up in my out basket and got misplaced on my desk. A central filing system I advocated got installed, but no one was assigned to staff it, so it was useless to me on a day-to-day basis.

That's where my computer came in. Starting in 1985 when we got the first Macintoshes, I stored all my work on my computer. Josh didn't like computers, but put me in charge of purchasing them. Then, after experiencing failure of my first hard drive discovering computer viruses, I built a network of computers and printers with file sharing and other versatility that was the envy of other departments. I got a $5000 plotter, $3500 color printer and accompanying $3000 scanner that enabled us to produce color presentations and graphics for publications. The network soon reached the entire building, and a file server enabled everyone to share and back up files. I had upgraded my Macintosh II to a IIfx, and then the fastest computer made, and equipped it with a Voice Navigator II that, when it worked, made operating the computer easier and faster as it responded to over 500 trained voice commands.

It wasn't easy. All the managers with some control over their budgets requested computers to meet their needs without too much regard for the needs of others, leading to a lot of purchases for redundant or incompatible equipment and software. This caused the president to form a committee to limit purchases to those that were planned and contributed to the purposes of the university. The idea was to provide high level personal computing to all.

These technologies caused a dramatic change in the way I conducted my work. In 1982, I wrote everything out in a characteristic lettering style used by engineers and architects and then had secretaries type it. Once a secretary got used to my writing and formatting style, they did quite well. But most work, especially that using tables or other graphics, took a lot of drafts and rewrites. With my computer, I rarely wrote anything out by hand, relying on dictation to Jeanie for memos and my own ability to write, type, and compose spreadsheets, graphs, and other visual material into any document I created. Where before, I spent a lot of time with the staff gathering and putting together information to present, now I spent a lot of time on the computer gathering information I already had in place to construct highly accurate and visual presentations of my work. It was lonelier but more fulfilling when, unencumbered by others' expectations, I achieved more than what was expected on a regular basis. And on time. No more last minute late nights working to a deadline.

My desk was a mess, but my working world was well organized at my splint-braced thumb nail just behind my desk. People out in the university began to respect me for my prompt, fully-developed responses to their requests. I still disliked those frequent surveys and other requests from outside, but the data I was developing made it easier to respond. It was still hard to get people with information I needed to give it up, and my inability to go to people easily and ask for information complicated things, but I met all survey deadlines even if it meant sending a response with some data missing.

Physically, work was more complicated. I parked my scooter against the wall by my desk. Hooking my briefcase with my right hand by the sling, I'd lift it out of its resting place and swing it up to the table behind my desk, next to my computer. I'd then open it and leave it open while I took out computer disks and papers I was bringing back to the office. My swivel chair was now a real friend, enabling me to scoot to my briefcase, the end of my desk, the telephone, or any other place within the confines of the space behind my desk. Even with this arrangement, I frequently spilled coffee that was kept on a cup heater next to my phone, and couldn't easily get at papers on the back of my desk or in files or desk drawers.

My frequent trips to the restroom just down the hall from my office were complicated by my inability to walk well and my urgency to pee. It wasn't uncommon for me to interrupt a meeting I was having in my office with someone or a telephone call to head out for that room down the hall. The routine was the same as downstairs except for the long, difficult walk, and the use of a larger, disabled stall. The difficulty I had standing in this space occasionally caused me to end up on the floor. In every case someone would come in, get the door open, and get me up.

Meetings on campus became difficult. I'd have to leave at least fifteen minutes early to get to where I was going, navigating curb cuts and sidewalks, elevators and doors, often with help from passing students and staff, I'd locate near a door if I could. Some rooms had a lot of chairs, making it difficult to maneuver. If I could, I'd park the scooter, swing my briefcase to a table, and use a chair. Often, I was forced to stay in the scooter, making it difficult to handle papers and impossible to write. I got very good at taking mental notes. Most meetings were fifteen percent protocol, eighty percent unnecessary discussion, and five percent salient information. The salient stuff I stored in my head. Meeting people became very awkward as I struggled to exchange business cards. Names and meeting times were hardest to keep in focus, and I was often embarrassed meeting people a second time without remembering their name. They always remembered me. I stood out like a sore thumb.

In the past, I initiated many meetings related to my work. Now, more and more, I just attended. Walking together to and from meetings, always a way to renew acquaintance with campus colleagues, became a lonely process as I had to abandon routes others took to get back to my office. Head down and pushing hard on the throttle as I tried to steer and bounce along, I didn't present the image of someone casually strolling the campus—rather someone determined to get where he was going. It was a long way from the days I walked campuses a respected professor, smiling and speaking to everyone I met.

Some of my best teaching had been by example, teaching my students and graduate assistants by having them watch me do something like measure a room and code it. That was getting harder to do and I was often frustrated with the ability of my assistants to just go out and get good information. Not knowing the best techniques, they were often slow and inaccurate. I spent a lot of time on the computer showing them what I needed. I developed a management plan with devices designed to improve workflow and efficiency. It was some of the best work I'd ever done. I turned it in, but it fell on deaf ears. I never got any response from foot-dragging superiors. Only Josh encouraged me and advocated for my ideas. And he distrusted my loyalty.

I took my lunch to a lunchroom adjacent to my office. After the steroids, food from the local fast food places didn't appeal and besides, someone had to go and get it for me. I found it very difficult to go out to eat anymore. Not only did someone have to push me in and out in my portable wheelchair, usually I experienced some stomach upset and had to ask to be rushed to the bathroom. Over the years, different people from time to time shared their lunch with me in the lunchroom. Lunch partners came and went, but they could always count on me to be there.

After I ate, there was always the danger of a sudden bowel movement. Accidents were infrequent, but they caused me stress and concern when they happened. Several times after lunch, I had to ask the custodians to put plastic on my car seat so that I could head home early and clean up.

Normally, I would leave for home about 5:30 pm. I'd load my briefcase with my disks and any work or reading I was taking home, swing it to its place behind the scooter seat, and then head out. My office door was always locked, so I'd just close it behind me. I'd leave the outer door for others to lock. Before, I always locked it if I was the last to leave the suite.

When I got downstairs, someone at the Police Dispatch station would open the two doors leading to the back hall. After that, I could push open the back door and pull up along side my car. An eight-inch loop of rawhide around my car door handle made it easy to open the door now that the fingers of my left hand failed to do it anymore. Swinging my briefcase to its spot behind my seat, I'd slip in behind the wheel and position my body and legs for the drive home.

Before starting the engine, I'd set the windows where I wanted them and turn on the lights, if needed, so these things wouldn't have to be done in route.

Going home was different from the morning trek in. I didn't feel the need to urinate often, except when it was cold or rained. Still, it was twenty miles to go and I avoided anything that would slow me up. I had just endured four years of reconstruction of the Southwest Freeway. They did the job in record time, keeping three lanes open all the time. Many people abandoned the freeway during construction, making traffic move better than I expected. Still, the narrow lanes, rough old sections, and detours called for a diligence in driving that I could handle mentally, but worried about physically. Gradually these bad spots in the road gave way to smooth, wide new pavement, making my way easier and easier as my ability to drive failed.

I gave up signaling lane changes to keep my left hand on the wheel and using the power of the Monte to slip smoothly into an opening first. I picked my route carefully, gradually working my way to the fastest side of the freeway, learned from years of experience with this road others feared to tread. I knew every escape route, every shortcut, and every trick that would get me down the road and past every obstacle the evening rush hour would throw at me.

I used the mass of my car to gradually tuck my way into an opening behind another car, even if it was moving more slowly than I liked. Sudden slowing and speeding up, the province of most rush hour drivers, gave way to a smoothness in acceleration and braking that enabled me the go with the flow rather than beat it or buck it. I left plenty of room between the next car and me, a space that was constantly filled by enterprising drivers with ABS and air bags that somehow gave them invincibility even when driving stupidly too close.

Cutting through a neighborhood that despised interlopers like me, I made it home usually about six o'clock. The electric garage door really had become handy, especially if I had to go to the bathroom. I still had to get the mail, so I'd leave the garage door open, swing the briefcase up to the top of the trunk, and open it up. I'd then work my way out to the mailbox, empty its contents, and then pick up any flyers, paper, or newspapers I could reach. Getting back to the car, I'd dump whatever I'd collected into my bag or the garbage bin. Then head on into the house. First, I'd close the garage door, and then let Jazz into the garage. Sometimes, I'd let him run outside for a while. Jazz especially liked to chase teenage girls because they'd run and scream, slamming gate doors in his face or jumping up on available cars.

He chased anything that moved, yipping ferociously with his black fur flying, and kids ran in all directions when he came out. He'd tire of chasing in a few minutes and come on in. I never could convince the kids that he was friendly. One day when he was out, a kid opened a gate down the street and three medium-sized dogs came out. They met Jazz in the middle of the street and surrounded him, and then attacked him twice. The biggest dog grabbed him by his shoulders and threw him, and his screams told me he was hurt. Dazed, he limped past the drive, trying to get away. I, like all the kids, stood there in horror, unable to act. None of them seemed to hear my pleas for them to step in and help. Just up from the drive the dogs caught him again. I was afraid they'd kill him. One of the bigger boys, who called the biggest dog by name, finally stepped in and grabbed his dog by the collar. That broke up the fight, and Jazz, hearing my voice, ran to me and into the garage, collapsing in fright and fatigue against the garage wall near the door. I closed the garage door and let him onto the deck where he had the first of many seizures, screaming and twisting in pain.

When I opened the front door, he ran to my bedroom where he holed up, first in the closet, and then under my dresser, shaking in fear. I got him some water and food. He drank a little, and would eat only if I put it right in front of him. He lay there for two days refusing to eat or drink any more. I didn't see any blood, but was afraid of internal injuries. So called the vet.

They encouraged me to bring him in, but there was no way I could pick him up and carry him to the car. Then, he climbed the stairs to my study, and somehow leaped to my side on the couch.

I petted him gently, but couldn't move him or he'd scream in pain. Then he started having seizures when I stroked him and I couldn't even do that. He stayed on the couch for four days and didn't eat or drink. Finally I got him off the couch by getting him on my lap, and then sliding to the floor. Still, he'd jump back up if I got on the couch. After several days upstairs, I was worried that he'd make messes. He never did. When he tried to go downstairs himself, he'd jump back in pain from the first step. In the morning he'd stand at the top of the stairs, wanting to but unable to come down for the day. Finally, one morning before I left for work, I sat at the top of the stairs with him, worked him up onto my lap, and slid down the stairs on my butt with him riding free. Soon, he'd go back up there, and I had to do the slide two more times before he would painfully come down on his own.

It took him two weeks to recover fully. The next time I opened the garage door, he rushed out as though he didn't remember what happened the last time.

Most days Jazz jumped all over me. I'd open the back garage door and he'd burst through, ending his lonely day guarding the house. The French door off the deck between was unlocked, a chance I had to take since struggling with the key made it difficult to enter the house when I had to get to the bathroom in a hurry. I deposited my briefcase by the stair and head into the bedroom where I'd pull off my fake tie, hang it up, and then sit on the bed to remove my leg splint and work my socks off by first stepping on a bit of loose stocking, and then pulling back with my other foot to pull my socks off, alternating first one foot, and then the other, until both socks worked off.

Then I'd head for the kitchen. One channel had national news at 6 pm. I wanted the news for company while I made supper. First I'd sit down on the chair and grab the 8 inch TV and set the controls to the station, and then I'd turn it around and push in the plug—a repeat of my morning ritual. Once the news was on, I'd turn to cooking a meal.

Except on shopping days, all my meat was frozen in plastic in the amount I would need for a meal. If it was frozen to another piece by accident, I'd give it a Karate chop on the counter with my right hand. Having no feeling on that side of my hand helped, and one or two blows separated the pieces nicely. On nights I first cooked fresh chops or chicken, or had fresh hamburger, I'd separate the portion I was cooking that night by putting it directly in the pan, and then, using a long cooking fork with a hooked handle for grabbing handles, I'd pick up one piece of meat at a time and drop or slide it into bread bags or other plastic, separating each piece, and then folding it into packages to put in the freezer. Hamburger would be cut into small cubes with my spatula, slid into a bag, and then pounded into a flat, if not round, shape for frying.

I never thawed meat. Just cooked it from scratch, either by frying or baking. I didn't freeze hot dishes I prepared, just divided them up into old butter containers in one meal portions, and put them in the refrigerator. After Jan took the microwave, I hadn't replaced it and heated everything in my fry pan with a little water.

On nights I fried meat, I'd cut up a small potato or pour out a single portion of rice in salted water, and boil it while I fried the meat. If I made a hot dish, handling large pots with boiling water was a problem. With a two-handed grip, I got good at sliding hot pans to the sink on the counter without picking them up. More than once I spilled macaroni trying to pour it in boiling water into a colander, jumping back as water, macaroni, and pot flew around in front of me. Losing my dinner was one thing, severe burns was another. I'd rather suffer the former, and often did to avoid the latter.

I'd load my plate from the counter or island, moving it from side to side in one move to avoid spills. Preparing food became an orchestrated set of moves with my supplies and utensils strategically placed to limit movement. Bottles wet with condensation and large cans became difficult to move. Parts of the refrigerator and cabinets, those I'd always bent easily down to reach, became a challenge to my balance as I reached down and grabbed whatever it was I was reaching for with two hands, pulled back and straightened up, juggling my balance and the item I'd grabbed to the counter top. Heavy cans were a danger to my bare toes and vinyl flooring. Bottles spread glass that more than once cut my feet long after I thought I'd cleaned it up and splattered valuable contents in ways that were hard for me to clean up.

Two years earlier, I made the trip upstairs with my full plate, sliding my left arm along the left rail for stability, and then my left shoulder as the rail gave way to wall near the top. Often teetering on the brink of falling backward as I reached the top, somehow willing my stressed back and leg muscles to carry me up, one step at a time, until I reached the safety of the top. I never fell, but I dropped my plate several times. After I rescued what

I could of my meal from the stair carpet, it usually had to wait and get cold while I cleaned the carpet. Like earlier, when I was able to microwave plates before Jan took the microwave to Wisconsin, it was also a race against burns that raised blisters on the edges of my hands as the heat of my food conducted through the plastic plate into my unfeeling, but firm grip on a plate of hot, potential disaster.

Inevitably, I was forced to eat downstairs, watching my 8" television, before heading up to my study for the evening. Now, even the precarious four feet from the island to the card table was too much, and I had to move the table adjacent to the island, enabling it to serve as a station for moving items in and out of the refrigerator and the pantry. Everything was moved from surface to surface without my having to take any unsteady steps or reach too high or too low. I was completely dependent on plastic grocery bags to carry and move things in the pantry, refrigerator, and throughout the house. One bag was always on the island; ready to accept any garbage I threw in it. Not one to stand on ceremony, I accepted the presence of the ugly bags everywhere. It was what I had to do.

Since starting with tetracycline for zits in 85 and multivitamins in 87, I took my pills at the island before eating. When I took steroids, I took up to twenty three pills at a time. While I could open child-proof containers like my vitamins came in, getting them out of the plastic skin wrap package with the point of my steak knife proved a lot harder. I used smaller plastic vials with pop-tops for daily administration. I pulled the tops off with my teeth and poured the pills on the counter. Sometimes they would spill or roll off the counter. Then I'd have to try to pick them up or keep Jazz from tasting them. To get something safely from the floor, I was reduced to using a chair, sitting on it and stooping down to get whatever it was had dropped to the floor.

I washed the pills down with whatever was handy—in the evening it was Rhine wine. Wine glasses, with their hourglass shape, were easy to handle. Still, I tipped over some and broke them, or they ended up broke in the dishwasher. I started getting two liter bottles with a handle because they were easy for me to carry. Still, a full bottle was too much for me to pour a glass every evening, so I decanted half of a new bottle into an old one. Then I could swing it onto its side on a shelf in the refrigerator. I liked my wine cold, but there came a time when swinging the bottle out of the frig hooked on my left thumb and cradled in two hands also became dangerous. The cold, wet bottle was just too slippery. Instead, I learned to drink my wine warm, and left it on the counter where the glass felt warm and stuck to my skin as I hooked the handle with my left thumb and cradled the back of the bottle in my right arm like a baby to pour it gently into the glass.

I'd sit down to eat, relaxing for the first time since I left work, watching whatever was on the little TV at the time, sipping my wine. Finishing as quickly as I could, trying to get done eating before the 8 o'clock movie, I'd get up, lift my dishes to the island, empty any bones or other garbage into the waiting bag, and then slide everything to the sink for a quick rinse. I dragged any pans to the sink and ran hot water into them. I'd rinse the plates and cups in hot water, but left utensils the way they were. When forks and knives got into the bottom of my sink, they were hard to pick up so I left them on the plates.

Earlier, when I was still able, I had rinsed and put all dishes into the dish washer, and then washed and toweled all counters to a shine before going upstairs. Now, I just put them on the counter, leaving it full of dishes for three or four days until my meager store of unbroken plastic cups and dishes ran out. It took me over a half hour to load the dishwasher and clean the counters, so I postponed it as long as I could—I wasn't adverse to picking out the cleanest plate, rinsing and wiping it off, and using it again for dinner. I didn't like what I'd become—the slob who messes things up and seems comfortable not cleaning up. Roaches weren't a problem, thanks to the new roach baits that effectively kept them from multiplying. Ants, however, began to invade my countertops regularly to raid the leftovers on my plates. Once my supply of Hot Shot in squirt bottles ran out—the ones I'd used to zap errant Japanese Water Beetles on the ceiling by holding the bottle tightly in my left hand and pushing the depressor down by placing the heel of my right hand on it and pushing down hard on my hand with my chin. This method had been effective even if I tended to miss my target, spray a fine mist of insecticide on my face, and wet the edge of my hand closest to the spray.

But, like most good things, they quit selling the squirt bottles, probably because they were a health hazard or too effective, and I had to resort to aerosols that sprayed a mist only a few inches, were hard to aim and push, and sprayed back a lot in my face. Wetting the counter where my food went with insecticide was not my idea of a healthful place to prepare food, but I had to leave the poison there to keep the ants from coming back.

Turning the light out on the ugly mess, I'd head for the stairs and my briefcase. Swinging the briefcase with its strap to my shoulder, I'd climb the stairs, its weight reassuring the grip of my good right foot on each tread as I pushed my left shoulder up the rail and then the wall as I passed that spot where the rail gave way to wall and my balance depended on moving forward to the safety of the landing. Once upstairs I'd head to the back of the desk and swing the briefcase up, flat. Then I'd go to the TV and turn it on and the head back downstairs.

Using the big orange plastic glasses I bought in 1966 to take out to the pool, I'd mix a drink of booze and whatever juice I was currently drinking. Although the plastic was soft and easy to carry before condensation wet its sides, I sometimes had other things in my hands and resorted to gripping the lip of the glass in my teeth. This worked, but as I approached that unsteady spot at the top of the stairs, I often spilled a little, splashing it on my cheeks, my shirt, and leaving a lot of tracks on the carpet. Back upstairs, I'd open the briefcase and sort my mail and the daily papers I brought from work. I'd read what I could, but by now it was nearly 8 pm and I'd find myself putting away mail or work for the weekend. I might pay a bill or update something on the computer, but then a movie would come on and I'd quit.

I had to go to the TV to tune it, but I'd picked one with touch buttons so it was easy to switch channels when I got there. I didn't get the $15 remote when I bought it fourteen years earlier because, "I need(ed) the exercise." Now I often had to put up with, "Why don't you get a remote." Actually, it was still easy to tune the TV, just harder to kneel down and check all the channels.

Finally, I could plunk down on my sofa bed. But, before I did, I'd get a snack and put my drink on the arm of the sofa bed. I always wanted a neat, clean appearance, so I kept my snacks in the kitchen pantry. Now, to avoid trips downstairs, I had them all on the desk. It made quite a mess and was tempting for Jazz. I kept the chair tightly against the desk so he couldn't jump to it. But he was resourceful and took every opportunity when I was lax, gorging himself on any bag he could get to the floor and open. He cringed when I said, "Naughty! Naughty!" but learned only that he could get away with it. I made it a point not to treat him while I ate. He accepted that and stuck to his dog food, daily milkbone and vitamins. I wanted him to stay healthy and not pester visitors for food. This changed when all the others came into my home.

I love popcorn. I'd make a batch during a commercial, put it in a big wooden bowl Jan left me, and rush upstairs. When I got paralyzed, picking up items one at a time became tedious, and picking up handfuls became impossible. So I used a light plastic bowl to scoop up the ration I wanted. Then I'd nibble on it like a pig at the trough. No one faulted me for it. The trip upstairs relegated putting the popcorn in a plastic grocery bag. And, I couldn't eat it all in one sitting.

The popcorn and drink would last past the movie into the news. I was rested and mellow now, and would often give Jeanie a call. Her phone was like Grand Central Station, but we managed to talk amid the constant interruptions. Then, I'd pick up whatever I could and go downstairs to bed.

Sending Jazz out in the evening was hard because some times he didn't want to come back in. A friend of mine at work made a doggie door and that solved that problem. My friend used cabinet hinges with strong springs in them for blocking the door, saying that no dog could open it. Jazz promptly learned how to. So Art put another door on the outside. Jazz, just as easily, opened both doors using his wiry seven-pound body to exert fifty pounds or more with his nose. We had to put a latch on the outside door to keep him outdoors during the day.

My Monk's bunk, now raised at the head 6"on bricks to forestall reflux, was both haven and Hell. In the summer I set the air conditioning to about 80 degrees. In the fall and spring I had the most trouble maintaining my temperature and had to adjust my covers according to the situation. It had become almost impossible to manage opening and closing windows, so there were few times when I left them open. And sometimes when it rained in because I couldn't get the windows shut in time or slept through the rain.

When I first went to bed, I'd get comfortable. Then, at some point I'd get the urge to pee and have to get up. I longed for the days I'd sleep until dawn, and there were days I did, but I averaged getting up five or six times a night. A neurogenic bladder, fueled by natural valve spasms, can't wait. I'd swing my legs out of the bed, sometimes taking the covers with them, struggle to get up, push off the end of the bed and reach for the walls. Navigating two small doors that supported me well in my struggle to get to the toilet on time, I lurched my way in, and went. I rarely missed on these nightly excursions, but by now it was too taxing and dangerous if I fell. I put a folding chair by my bed and put a two-gallon plastic pail on it. All that was required was peeing sitting by the bed, shortening the time and the strain getting back to sleep. Rarely, I'd have to get up in the night to empty the bucket, but most of the time that could wait until morning. I started carrying a bucket in my car, but I had to stand up to remove my pants, so I rarely used it.

Some time into my nightly sleep, usually around midnight, the strain I put my legs through during the day released in the form of leg spasms. I would wake up kicking the footboard or straining in a prolonged stretch

311

against the footboard with one or both feet. At times these spasms were relaxing like any stretch, but at other times they were very painful as my muscles contracted in a knot we used to call a "Charley Horse." Spasms became inseparable from my dreams. I often dreamed of straining to do something but not being able finish because the strain got too much. Waking didn't solve the problem. Changing position sometimes did.

I'd have to push myself up with my elbows, slide my butt back five or six inches, and lie back down. All the kicking usually moved my covers up, exposing my feet and bunching them up around my neck. Trying to get them back down with my feet was often futile, and I'd get tangled up to the point I had to get up and remake the bed, sometimes four or five times a night. From the time I was first paralyzed I couldn't stand having the covers tucked under the mattress at the end of the bed. It pulled my feet down when I slept on my back. I remember pulling into motels dead tired only to have to struggle to pull sheets, blankets and sometimes heavy bedspreads out from the ends of king-sized beds. Leaving covers free meant they were constantly displaced, every time I moved. My hands were no help and without triceps often ended up resting on my collarbone. To force errant hands down, I'd have to roll to the right or left to use my biceps to force them down. Any movement would cause my arms to contract and work them back up. If I slept with my hands up, they would often go numb and my knuckles would dig into my collarbone.

A fetal position was the most comfortable, but inevitably in my spasms I would roll to my back and my legs would straighten and start kicking. A sheet was the hardest to keep on, and it tangled easily too. Often I needed one, because the air conditioning was too cold, and I'd have to get up and put it back on.

When cold fronts came through or when I was sick, I had a hard time keeping warm. I used the furnace, my wool blanket from Guatemala and a comforter. Sometimes all three were needed as I shivered through the night. The blanket and comforter were heavier and less likely to move. But, if I got too warm I'd have to push them to the side. Too often, they got away and slid off the bed. Then I'd have to go around the bed, get down on my knees, and push them back up.

Then it was 5 am again, and I'd start over. Losing all that sleep and all the exertion took its toll. My pant size was growing faster than I could take them out; my shoes never got polished and wore on the uppers as well as the soles. I constantly faced the fatal fall through a window or headlong into a wall. Grease and dirt marked the walls I clung to getting around. I never cleaned any more, and pushed more and more to the weekend. I was tired and irritable. Some people at work started to take an interest in me and often joined me for lunch in the snack room. I tried to keep up with current events and invented lame jokes to keep my spirits up. Something had to change.

Telling jokes at a Christmas party. I didn't look like I could barely walk.

# 42

# Weekend Nightmare

On weekends my routine was different, more relaxed, but sometimes, harder. I would sleep in, but only until 8 or so because there was too much to do and I started to hurt if I lay too long. Every other week the kitchen bore the mess of cooking and breaking down groceries, a task that sometimes took me until 10 pm on Friday nights. I would make breakfast, eat it at the counter, move all the leftovers on plates into the garbage, and load the dishwasher. Vegetable cuttings were put in the garbage or down the disposer. Once the dishes were in the dishwasher, I'd reach down and get a big box of detergent in a plastic grocery bag and raise it to the counter. The big boxes were heavy, but easier to get hold of. Opening the spout, I'd tip the box over the counter and rain the powder onto the dispensers in the door, no longer able to cradle the box firmly in my arms and bend down to pour.

Letting the dishwasher do the heavy work, I'd wet a sponge, add soap to it and attack the stove, sink, and counters. I'd have to be careful to keep soapy water off the floor because one morning I was toweling off the counter and found myself flat on my back on the wet floor. Remarkably, I didn't hit my head, or even hurt myself, but I was that close to knocking myself unconscious, or worse.

Another incident was more telling. The night before I'd knocked my wine glass off the table, breaking it and spilling the wine. I got another glass and left the mess until the next morning, a Saturday. After picking up the big pieces and sweeping the rest into a dustpan, the dried wine and fine pieces of glass remained. I used a wet, soapy sponge to gently wipe up the glass, and then rinse the glass off into the disposer. I got all the glass and most of the wine, and then returned with a clean sponge to finish the job. I carefully got down on my hands and knees, the only way I was going to reach the entire spot. I thought my knees were on dry floor, but they weren't. Reaching out with my right hand, my left hand precariously on the wet floor, both knees suddenly slid outward and my body fell back and down. I came down easy to the wet floor from my chin to my stomach, because my legs, folded frog-fashion, reluctantly spread outward, were giving me excruciating pain as my groin muscles lost a battle to hold back my weight

The pain did not subside as I lay there, face up, straining on my chin. My arms could move on the wet floor, but they could do nothing. Working my head to the side, I freed my chin, only to have my right cheek resting on the wet floor. It was about 10 o'clock on a Saturday morning. As I lay there struggling against the pain in my groin and the wet floor, I thought about when I could expect help. It would be Monday morning when Jeanie or someone else would start calling because I hadn't shown up for work. It would be noon before their unanswered calls would prompt them to send a TSU police officer out to check on me. I could last until then, but it would be very hard. Thinking about it now, at some point the floor would have dried up, making it at least sticky enough so that I could push myself up on my elbows, in spite of my leg and groin pain. But I didn't think of it then. Only that there was no way out of this predicament I was in. Only pain and misery and struggle lay ahead.

And struggle I did. Flailing out with my arms, I reached my knees and every inch of that very wet floor. The wet was annoying but at least it wasn't cold. My legs were a problem. They were pulled so tight by the weight of my body that the circulation was cut off. Still, the pain continued. Finally, after what seemed like an hour, I managed to reach a chair at arms reach in front of me, and pull it in. The chair wasn't much help; it just moved around in front of my face. It had no better purchase on the wet floor than I did. Eventually, I was able to get my left arm over a chair rung and pull up. Twisting back to the left, I raised my right hip enough to free my right leg. As it snapped straight out behind me, releasing the tension on my groin muscle, I felt tremendous relief. Rolling to the right, my left leg did the same. I lay flat on my stomach for a while, relaxing, and then rolled off the wet spot and worked myself to the island where I could get up, first to my elbows, and then my hands, and then my knees.

After cleaning up the kitchen as best I could, I'd head upstairs. The week's mail had piled up, and I found myself stacking journals without ever reading them. There were always articles I wanted to share when I did read, a habit I acquired in graduate school, but cutting them out, copying, and distributing them became very difficult. Bills were the worst, and once a month I spent several laborious hours writing checks to pay them. Some times, I lost bills or overdrew my account and I had to pay the penalty.

Usually, it would take most of the afternoon to catch up on my mail. I used to write a lot of letters in the evening. Now, I made phone calls, more to my family and less to friends, rather than take the time and strain to write. If I did write now, it was on the weekends. A movie or car race or other sports event provided background. When I finally got free from my own work, I'd work on a database program for work. Taking the manuals home, I spent about two years teaching myself Double Helix, a relational database program. With that knowledge, I spent time developing and improving data collections. It was productive and rewarding work, and much easier to do than research. When evening came, I'd head downstairs and make supper. Two hours later, I'd be back upstairs for the evening.

On Sunday mornings, I'd water and feed my plants. I spilled water where I shouldn't and some of the plants needed repotting, but there was nothing I could do about it. Each time I carried plants in and out to avoid freezing I dropped some. My outdoor plants were down to those that I brought in or the purslane that reseeded itself each year. A toad got in my barrel on the deck, destroyed the alyssum, and then the begonias, and finally, the barrel itself, that began to fall apart before my eyes.

I buried myself in movies and my databases. Pursuing research and Columbia Pacific students, excursions to the park, my flowers, and travel, had all given way to the grim daily struggle to meet my basic needs. By the end of the weekend, laying low and withdrawing into myself, I was rested, but then the week began and I faced going to work again.

# 43

# A Trip to the Emergency Room

In late April 1992, my parents visited before heading north back to Wisconsin. I had a head cold, but my cleaning lady came by just before they came so I was relaxed. They came on Friday night. We all slept in and after a leisurely breakfast decided to visit my cousin Denise and see her new baby. I did my usual Saturday work upstairs while Mom worked in the kitchen and Dad read papers in the living room. I got finished just before we planned to go.

I came downstairs empty-handed, watching Dad sitting on the couch with his back to me, reading. I planned to turn the corner behind him at the bottom of the stair, check my hair in the bathroom, and pick up my jacket in the hall closet. I didn't make it.

My left foot twisted on the second to last step. My left hand couldn't hold me as I pitched forward to the carpet below. There was a blank spot where I don't remember hitting. Instead, I came to my senses lying face down on the carpet, blood running from my nose. Still dazed, I called out to my folks that I was hurt, and they came to my rescue. Dad grabbed onto my arm to help pull me up. Jazz was all over him, growling and trying to protect me. I got to my knees, blood still dripping on the carpet, and went into the bathroom. I leaned over the sink, washing my face with cold water until the bleeding stopped. My sinuses, swollen from the fall and blood emitted a dull, steady ache. My face didn't swell up and the headache didn't get any worse, but I felt a need to go to a hospital to be safe in case I had internal brain bleeding.

Mom cleaned the blood from the carpet. When she was done, I asked them to drive me to emergency at Southwest Memorial Hospital. We got there about 1 pm. For safety, Dad wheeled me into the hospital in my wheelchair. Then, there was the agonizing wait. My head throbbed and, at times, became almost unbearable. My legs ached from sitting, but I couldn't lie down. Finally, about 7 pm, they took me in. After X-rays and another wait, they took a CT scan of my head. They told me I had a fracture of my left eye orbit, gave me some pain pills and sent me home. It was 11 pm. I don't remember what or if we ate. On Sunday, Denise and Rick brought the baby over so my parents could see him. The next day, Mom and Dad drove north and I went to work with two black eyes.

I went to an eye specialist. The fracture caused no lasting damage. I went back to Clearman. She increased my dose of baclofen and resubmitted the order for my electric wheelchair to my insurance. When I told her that I was having so much trouble at home and that I was afraid that I'd have to go to a hospital or nursing home if I got worse, she told me again to contact TRC and get some help. I went to see a TRC counselor. He was in the hospital. After being directed to the wrong counselor, I was sent back to TIRR where a new counselor was assigned.

My scooter at work 1991.

# 44

## The End of Independence

Kassandra Humphress was vivacious, engaging, and all business. In the crowded little office, with no secretary, she couldn't find my file, but promised me the world anyway. She quickly whipped up a plan. TRC would provide six months of attendant care, a driving evaluation and vehicle modifications, the electric wheelchair and lift, and home ramps to get me to work. TSU would provide my scooters, a computer at home for work, a van for transportation, and modifications at work. I would pursue all these accommodations, pay for attendant care, and any home modifications beyond the ramps. She was serious and reckless. I didn't believe her. But, I was in love, so what did it matter?

Everything was true. I was afraid of the idea of attendants, but not as afraid as I was of being hospitalized and made to conform. Still, attendants would be in my house and my business. If I hired a thief or bum, how could I keep them from stealing from me or abusing me? I didn't know, and what I didn't know bothered me.

I had to take a first step, so I put an ad in the paper—just for part-time help in the morning and evening. "Spinal injured male needs part time help, mornings and eves." I placed the ad in a local Southwest Houston paper that was delivered free each Thursday. Each time the ad appeared, I got a few calls. After discussing in more detail what I needed, the caller decided whether they'd meet for an interview and fill out my application.

I had to drive to the apartment of one woman who had no transportation. She lived ten miles away. An unemployed nurse came by my office—she would have had to drive an hour to get to my house from hers. An elderly man came by and said that he was a retired executive and tired of volunteering. He wanted to do some real work. When I tried to call him back, his wife gave me the impression that he was just a crazy old coot. One rough-looking girl who said that she'd worked for vets from Nam told me about one guy she'd worked for who was robbed and abandoned by his attendants. One man had been laid off from a factory job and needed work to support his family. A teenager said that he took care of his mother and wanted extra work while still in high school. A Pakistani woman who had taken care of an India Airlines pilot injured in a crash only wanted to be paid in cash and would take the bus from downtown. When she left our interview she gave me a crushing hug and offered to work for free rather than take my checks. A woman who had turned her home into a boarding house for the disabled and wanted me to move to her "beautiful" house where we could sit around and watch television. And, a couple of applicants never finished an interview because they were deathly afraid of Jazz, who accommodated by barking loudly and jumping all over them.

Fortunately, my one page application form that required references and my interview seemed to weed out the unqualified and uninterested. I interviewed a promising young lady who looked just like a young David Cassidy and sported a tattoo of a cross on her hand. She was leaving the care of a young woman who was spinal injured and didn't need help any more. She was the most experienced and interesting, but I hesitated to hire her. It took me a month to get started.

They Tran (Jacqueline or Jackie to her American friends), with a voice as sweet as honey, called. She was a Vietnamese refugee who had come seventeen years before but spoke English better than most Americans. She explained that she was doing customer relations at a bank but was a, "poor divorcee," needing more work to, "Pay her house payment."

"Hi neighbor," she said as she came through the door. She was dressed in executive clothes from her work at the bank, sizing my house and me up more than attending to the business at hand. She started filling out the application, but seemed more interested in me than in working for me. She had legal training and played the piano. When I asked her if she could cook for me, she started with, "Yes, Vietnamese or American, whatever you want," and ended with, "I could make some egg roll and bring it over for you sometime." When I told her I really needed help with keeping the place clean, she said, "I think I know where you can get a Mexican lady...." In my room, she sat on the bed as she, first asked for, and then listened to, my story. After talking about my situation for some time, I looked up and she was crying. We hugged and she left. It was more like a date than a job interview. She gave encouragement but no real help.

She was a whirlwind of nervous energy, this Maria del Carmen Lopez from Ecuador. The eldest of three "Maria dels" from a wealthy family, she had come to the U.S. to practice medicine. "I'm a plastic surgeon, but I want this work because it's only part time and I'm studying to pass the test for family practice. My husband has clinics in Ecuador, but I'm worried about what's happening in my country, so I want to come here and work and have my two kids, Paulo and 'Estephanie' (Maria Stephanie) go to school here." Bleach blond, good looking, and dressed formally in a rather short skirt, she chased me down the hall to my room. When I asked her whether she minded cooking and cleaning, she said, looking around my neglected living room, "I can do that, I'll clean and do your garden (lawn) if you want. I can cook you Ecuadorian food or hamburgers, whatever you want." I liked her attitude, but I wasn't sure I believed everything she said. But I was already in love with this sexy lady and I knew I was going to give her a chance to prove what she said. Her references were local: the retired seamstress in whose house she was staying, with a Spanish name, but an upper Midwest manner and character, and two prestigious teaching gynecologists from the UT-Medical Center who had worked with her on charitable forays to Ecuador and were sponsoring her move to the United States.

He called me at my office and made an appointment to interview with me there. Dana Anthony Yip was one of those rare individuals who was open to the world and could do anything. He wanted medically-related working experience, not money. He was looking for something interesting to do during his summer before his last year at Rice, studying biology and art history and bound for medical school. Dana was born in Ottawa. His father came from Hong Kong to Canada to study, and became a petroleum engineer. His mother was also Chinese, but had grown up in Bangkok. After growing up in Alberta and learning how to ski in the Canadian Rockies, Dana came to Houston to sail in the Gulf and became valedictorian at Spring High School. He had an apartment at Rice, but was watching his parent's home during the summer while they were on a job in Saudi Arabia. After working with Dr. Denton Cooley and his heart transplant team during his freshman summer where he held a beating heart in his hands and helped give birth to a baby, Dana had his sights set on becoming a surgeon. I knew I could use him. I just didn't know how.

A month went by and things got worse. I had plans to spend the 4th of July in Wisconsin and had to do something about that. Maria called frequently and I kept putting her off. Finally, I called the girl with the tattoo that looked like David Cassidy. Her former employer, a paralyzed young woman I never met, told me that she'd, "Gone back to her Mom's in Chicago."

I called Maria and told her that we'd start off slowly and she agreed. I started her out coming mornings and evenings. I needed ramps, to move my office from upstairs, and had a mountain of boxes and paperwork filling the spare bedroom that had to be dealt with before I couldn't go upstairs anymore. So, I called in Dana for that.

Following my book on attendant care, I made out checklists of everything that had to be done each morning and evening. But the checklists were dispensed with quickly as I showed Maria what I needed done. We went to the store together once. After that, with my list, she got my groceries every two weeks. From the very beginning we worked well together. It was easy to trust her with everything. I made arrangements for my trip. She would take me to and from the airport.

I called on Dana to move my office down from the upstairs bedroom to my master bedroom downstairs. He managed to move it alone, mess and all, and reconnect my computer, telephone, and everything else I needed. I had to rearrange my bedroom a bit, but everything fit quite well. I knew I was going to miss looking out the window, watching the seasons pass in the field under the high voltage power line right-of-way behind the house. The little dramas of cats stalking, spring flowers spreading and changing, birds passing through, kids and dogs, and even the occasional mowing that started the grass growing again. It was always warmer upstairs, and I knew I'd miss that and the comfortable couch to relax in. I wouldn't miss the climb upstairs or the fear of falling down them. It was one of the things I had to let go of, one less strain on my day. Changing my routine would become a habit.

Actually, with the help of attendants, it was great to discover that I was freed of the worry over getting daily things done. Maria got me packed and got my wheelchair and me to the airport on time. Jazz would be well-taken care of at home. What few flowers I had left would be watered.

My parents met me in Minneapolis. I rode comfortably in the passenger seat of their van as we drove the 80 miles to their cottage. The family arrived, and it was crowded. People were sleeping everywhere. Mom assigned me the couch in the dining area. I had a bad night sleeping on the couch, slid off, and ended up on the floor, tangled in my cover, until morning.

Dad made me a bed on the floor. It was okay except I had nothing to grab hold of and great difficulty getting up to go to the bathroom at night. We had fireworks and other festivities at the cottage, but I didn't come and go to town with the others. I did get to go on a couple of boat rides, and saw a mother loon with two babies close up, but mostly I just sat in my wheelchair and tried to keep the flies and mosquitoes from biting me. It was cold and rainy, so we stayed in a lot and played cards. By the end of the big weekend my feet were swelling from inactivity. I blamed the swelling on fly bites. Mom knew what it was, edema, caused by blood and other fluids being trapped in my legs, ankles, and feet from poor circulation.

Then my back gave out. Someone had pulled too hard or the wrong way when I got up from my bed on the floor, and pain and violent spasms greeted me every time I tried to get up from my wheelchair. Since I was unable to travel around the state visiting friends and relatives like I usually did, I had planned to stay the week at the cottage, enjoying the peace and playing board and card games with Mom. But Dad came to me and said that he couldn't help me after the others left, that I'd have to leave, to go home where, "He has everything set up for him at home...and help now too." My father, who was always out helping others build something—even built a tower for ospreys to land on—had trouble helping me. Frustrated when I didn't think like him or live up to his expectations, he distanced himself, claiming that I was too hard to please, too demanding. He didn't want to have me around. I would be a "burden" to their active, outdoor lifestyle. It was my fault for always wanting to be included. Now, when our active family got together, Ron's disability got in the way. It was easier to exclude me than figure out ways to count me in. I was hurt. It's hard to lose control of what you do with your life. Tracy, my niece, helped me shave and Roger helped me shower with the help of a folding chair. I agreed to cut my vacation short.

I was the last one off the plane. I could hear Maria's excited voice as I was pushed to the top of the ramp that led to the concourse. "He's in a wheelchair! Where is he? Check and see if he is on the plane." I was relieved. She had her two kids and her sister, Veronica, with her. They had gotten a bit lost and were late getting to the gate, after everyone had left the plane except me. Maria was excited and a bit scared.

I reached home with relief. Still, I was confined to my director's chair except for painful excursions to the bathroom and bed. Maria helped all she could while I worked on neglected homework and let my back mend. I could just squeeze my chair through the narrow door opening to my bathroom and the narrow aisle between the range and island. As I struggled to brush my teeth and fix my meals from the awkward position the chair offered, occasionally struggling upward to precarious standing position to reach the hardest things, I wondered what it would be like to be confined to the chair and not be able to reach a faucet or the freezer. Pushing myself from the bedroom to the kitchen and back with my feet was a strain and slow, but it was less painful and safer than trying to walk.

Dana and I got together and discussed options for making the ramps. I decided we could do them with masonite. After that he got all the materials, planned the ramps with me, and built them. We didn't have a heavy electric wheelchair to test them out on, just guessed at what would work. My deck in the back of the kitchen was the hardest. It was about six inches higher than the floor, and the raised sliding glass door tracks about three inches from the deck made an unstable base for a ramp. I still could walk over and open the sliding door with great effort. Dana built a light-weight ramp that fit over the track and butted up perfectly and securely to the deck. I had him put ropes on it so that I could pull it into place.

I used the rope on one side to put the ramp in place a couple of times. Later, with my electric chair, I found that I merely had to push or pull the ramp up to the window before opening it, against the track, and, backing over the 4 inch gap quickly, my big rear wheels would easily bridge the gap and my smaller, trailing front wheels would jump it. Once, while fooling around, I tried going across forward and the front wheels fell into the gap. Luckily, I was still able to get up out of the chair and lift up the front wheels as I powered the chair back up on the deck.

I was worried about the ramp in the garage because we had to provide a landing to allow me to open and close the door, and then a ramp to the garage floor. The landing had to be big enough to allow me to get out of the way of the door's swing, but small enough to keep my car from hitting it. In practice, although the ramp seemed precarious at times, there was enough room to turn around, operate the door, light switch, and garage door opener, and navigate the ramp. After falling off the ramp several times at various places, it proved sturdy and stable enough to give me good service without danger of tipping over. A bonus was that my parents' small van was able to park straddling the ramp—enabling my two car garage to still function as one. The other car had to back out to let me use the ramp though.

One weekend afternoon, Maria rode with me out to Stephen F. Austin State Park for a picnic. As usual, Jazz enjoyed exploring, but didn't find anything as interesting as the armadillo that Toby found when Jan and I were there Memorial Day, 1983. Maria pushed me in my portable chair to the picnic tables where we ate lunch. On the way back to the car, a front wheel fell off. Luckily, after searching a few minutes, Maria found the nut that came off, and we returned home.

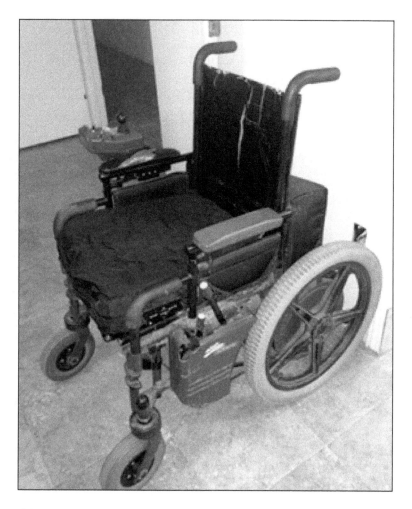

My custom made 1992 Invacare Action Arrow after 20 years of use.

# 45

## Living with Assistance

Texas Southern University was prospering in spite of the economic downturn in the city and state. The secret of our improved facilities was out, and new and returning students were coming to us hoping to improve their ability to find work in tough times. Enrollment exceeded 10,000, research monies poured in, and many new initiatives got underway. In 1990, we started a $2.8 million renovation of Hannah Hall, our main administration building, built in 1950. The Mickey Leland Center for Hunger and World Peace was established and a building was planned. The big concern was deferred maintenance, and we developed plans to reduce this $8 million backlog by 15% each year through the end of the decade. The School of Education, in cooperation with the Houston Independent School District, planned the development of a model elementary school. With the help of local organizations, the university planted over 500 trees and launched several campus beatification projects. We had plans to purchase more land and to continue to cooperate with the improvement of the neighborhood.

Earlier, I had direct involvement in these activities, from meeting the people involved, to planning and presenting options, to doing the required paperwork. Now, I supplied information and reviewed what was happening, and gave encouragement, but I couldn't "get out there" and get involved like before. I was named to the Disability Access committee, but not asked to lead it. Gradually, others took on work that I'd always done. It was the beginning of an insidious loss of faith in my ability that was unwarranted.

I worked with the Governor's Energy Office (GEO) to implement our energy conservation plan. LoanSTAR, a revolving loan fund from monies obtained from a lawsuit settlement from Exxon overcharges made during the seventy's oil crisis, was established to help state agencies fund energy conservation improvements. When I first told Josh about the fund, he was not interested, saying that he didn't want the university obligated for any more loans. But, gradually, he warmed to the idea, and eventually became an advocate. The GEO hired an engineering audit firm and the campus was reviewed for opportunities. Like our earlier project, our plant operations director saw the project as a way to correct some ill-conceived central plant design and maintenance problems. We applied for a $3.5 million loan. When installed, the improvements would save $650,000 per year. With that much money involved, everyone wanted a piece of the action.

I got our computer network installed in March 1992. I had the whole building connected through our existing telephone wiring to 72 places so that 35 computer users could print on any of six printers by simply selecting them on their screens. I also installed a file server that enabled more than one computer to use the same files. The file servers were a big help on shared projects like budgeting, data files, publishing, and planning. I got a new operating system for our computers that enabled our computers to "talk" to one another for complete file sharing, that is, making it possible for me to look at and use documents on Jeanie's computer and vice versa— Timbuktu. I installed a 19k modem on my computer at home, and was able to communicate with other computers through telephone lines while working at home.

I got a voice-activated control system for my office computer, Voice Navigator II. The microphone and software enabled me to dictate words and run the computer and most applications by voice commands. The commands were preprogrammed to do certain functions such as "delete" a selected drawing or word on the screen. I then trained the function by recording "delete" in my voice three to eight times. The problem was that to select the item to delete, I still had to point the mouse to it somehow to select it, and a command like "file it" often was mistaken for "delete." At least, I could say, "undo" to get back something I mistakenly deleted. When trained to a large vocabulary, this device had demonstrated to take dictation at 75 wpm. It saved me a lot of time and use of the mouse, but once in a while I had to repeat to get it to respond (not unlike Jazz or a small child).

This was getting close to the artificial intelligence I'd studied years before. Computer hardware and software was getting fast and complex, fast enough to mimic human function and complex enough to introduce mistakes like humans make.

All this was very good, but I had two problems. Some of the network often quit working, so some computers didn't have access to printing. My student technician wasn't able to determine what was wrong, so I had to contract with a computer company to fix the problems and teach him how to keep them fixed. My second problem was keeping up with the changes in software and hardware to enable our staff to best use what we had. All this stuff worked very well and was very reliable, but just getting information out to the fifty busy people who used it was a difficult task. I never seemed to have enough time to write a users manual or hold training sessions, so I did most training one-on-one in passing. At least every piece of equipment we had purchased since 1985 was still operating, but I had to upgrade and repair continually to keep everything current.

I used my Lark Sierra everywhere at work and I could drive it across campus at 4.5 mph when the weather was good. I parked my car in the breezeway next to the Lark and didn't have to walk any distances except in the restrooms. The Lark had a 22 mile range on each charge and I didn't have to charge it more than once a week.

By June 1992, I couldn't turn my head without ominous "cracking" of bones and tendons in my neck. The thought of what was happening caused me to greatly limit my head movements and the use of my teeth to do things. About the same time, I had to put leather bootlaces on my car door handles to open them. With Kassandra's encouragement and TRC's money, I drove to TIRR to take a test drive of a modified car. The front-drive Buick LeSabre was designed for paraplegics so the hand controls got in the way. My hands and arms were too weak to operate the hand controls. Chad Strowmatt, the vocational therapist evaluator, didn't test me on their zero-pressure steering van. He wouldn't hear of modifying my car's steering to zero-pressure. Zero-pressure steering cost about $850 installed on vans. I was not interested in buying a van just then. The economics, no matter how I looked at it, didn't justify getting rid of my old car and buying a new van. After the test, I was advised to stop driving.

I was trying to get METROLift to come out to my house and take me to and from work (twenty miles each way). METROLift was a branch of the Metropolitan Transit Authority (Metro) that provided door-to-door transport for disabled citizens. At that time, METROLift only came out to the Sam Houston Tollway, about 3 miles from my home. Since I paid city taxes and my home and work were in the City of Houston, I felt that I deserved service. I threatened ADA and called city council members, but got no help. The city ADA coordinator said he would work on it.

I began to depend heavily on Maria. Dana was there, and very helpful, but only occasionally did he help with a meal. It was Maria who changed my daily struggle to something more manageable—an assisted life.

I no longer set the clock for 5 am. Instead, the summer sun streaming through my window would stir that internal clock we all have and I would look at the clock on my Sony and see what time it really was. I'd swing out of the bed, stand up using my stronger right leg and straight-arm the heel of my right hand against the sturdy wood of my bed's foot board for support. It might take several tries to get up. The momentum of rocking forward helped me flex my muscles and prepare my legs to take the weight. Once up, I'd have to check my forward momentum and regain my balance. If my balance was off, I'd sit back down rather than take the chance of falling. Circling the end of the bed, my right arm locked and pivoting on my right hand, I'd reach for the wall with my left arm, hoping my legs would hold as I worked my way through the door into the bathroom. I'd reach for my pills, remove the cap and spill one onto the counter while my knees sometimes banged the cabinet doors when my legs quavered and spasmed. I'd run a glass of water and reach down with my tongue and pick up the pill. Struggling as I described before, I'd take a shower, and then work my way back. I usually got back into bed by 6:20, still wet, but clean and warm and ready to relax. Getting a pair of shorts from my bureau, I'd struggle and strain to get them over my feet and on, that made finally pulling up under the sheet all the more relaxing.

On weekends, it was easy to go back to sleep, but about 6:30 I'd hear the front gate slam and Jazz would come to life and run out barking. His barks would become more high-pitched as he jumped back and forth through his door and the dining room entry door first opened, and then closed. "Dr. Hull! Good morning! I'm here!" she'd shout, and then hurry into my room.

On the few occasions when Maria came early and caught me in the shower or not yet in bed, I'd shout, "Hold it, I'm not ready!" And she would discreetly head into the kitchen to work on breakfast and my lunch until I called her.

Maria was always cheerful in spite of the pressure her family situation put on her. Sometimes, she rode a bike, but often she arrived by car in a rush talking of some family crisis. She wore either tight-fitting sports clothes or green operating room coveralls. In the sports outfits she was sexy but dressed for hard, dirty work. In the greens she seemed more relaxed and detached. In either case, her family problem of the day notwithstanding, she was very professional, like having my own doctor with an excellent beside manner at minimum wage—only in America.

Except for my shoes, dressing was a snap. First Maria would grab the pail on the chair by my bed and take it to the bathroom. Sometimes, it was quite full. I no longer trusted myself to carry and empty the heavy load. The smell of urine never became a problem, but I had to be careful not to spill it. Then Maria would get my clothes; first, putting on my socks, and then my pants over my feet to my knees. Then I'd swing my feet out and sit up. She'd help me on with my shirt, and then grab my pants and pull them up as I stood with her help. When my shirt was tucked in properly, she'd hook the catch and zip me up. All quite simple and easy, not at all what I went through without her.

Working my way over to the doorway of my closet, and grabbing both sides of the opening for support, I'd lift my right foot and she'd position my shoe under it. Dropping my toes into the shoe, wiggling right and left and bearing down, she'd hold my long shoehorn in place until my foot would slide into the shoe. Then, I'd step backward two steps and sit back down on the bed. With my splint in my left shoe and in hand, Maria would sit down beside me on my left side, place the shoe on the floor alongside my left foot, and then help me lift my pant leg to my left knee and position my toes downward into the shoe opening. She'd then help me stand up and force my foot into the shoe. Once done, she'd pull the Velcro strap tight and pull my pant leg back down. We'd head for the kitchen.

Maria would make me a sandwich for lunch and make me eggs or cereal for breakfast. It was great to sit down and enjoy breakfast instead of standing and eating while I made it. Then I'd return to the bathroom where I'd shave and brush my teeth. Before long, Maria started shaving me with my electric razor to save time. It was luxurious to sit in my director's chair in the morning sunlight and be shaved by a beautiful woman. The relaxation helped with my bladder problem, but not entirely. Soon, Maria was not only carrying out my briefcase, but also helping me with my pants and a bucket in the garage, my last chance for relief before I set out for the long drive to work.

After I left, Maria would clean up, vacuum, and sometimes, mow the lawn. It was good to have someone so dependable and versatile. In the beginning, I did without her help in the evening, but when she did, Maria either heated up something I'd already made or made something that I helped make with her. My biggest worry was that I'd fall and be where I couldn't call her. I could still undress myself and make my bed, but it was getting very difficult and I constantly worried about falling.

By October, I could no longer get up if I fell, so I quit picking up things that I dropped. It was just too dangerous to risk losing my balance. It was becoming very hard to pick up and carry anything. To use the phone, handle mail, write checks, eat food, and open mail became so difficult, I gave up more and more to my help. I could still get up out of a chair and walk as long as I could hang onto something. But I could see the day coming when I would not be able to get out of bed alone.

Now that I was downstairs, I worried about all the stuff from Atlanta, my papers and journals. Maybe I'd have someone live upstairs. I had to take the time and make the effort to go through everything and put it where it belonged. Mom offered to help out in April, but, even though we spent a day, we only got to a few of the most important boxes. All the rest waited. On weekends, I'd alternate with Maria and Dana, poring over dusty papers, journals and books, trying to reorganize and restore the most important. Since I was unable to conduct my earlier research or spend time with my journals, I decided to donate my journals to a library. So we packed each journal in order in boxes and labeled them, and I kept a tally of each one by volume and issue. My papers were in disarray after so many years of neglect, and I threw a lot out and tried to pack the rest in a way that they would be preserved. I was amazed when I saw all the bags of trash we threw out. It was slow and dirty work, taking many hot afternoons over a period of months. Dana hung all my paintings and drawings that had been stored away when I left Atlanta, and I discovered many household items I had forgotten I had. Finally, I struggled down the stairs for the last time, confident that I knew what was still up there, and where it was.

# 46

# The Car Accident

In early October, Maria, her daughter, and I were running some Saturday errands when I decided to go get some winter flowers to plant after we saw that my usual haircut place was full. We were talking as I approached the left turn to the frontage road under the 59 overpass. Both middle and left lanes turned left. I usually turned from the middle lane. As I crossed the frontage road on a green light at about 30 mph I noticed the left turn lane turning yellow. The light ahead of me was still green. I looked in my rear view mirror and saw a car close behind me. Knowing that the car behind could not stop if I did, I decided to go ahead and make the turn. The left turn signal turned red just as I got to the intersection. There were three facing lanes to the frontage road. The car in the first row saw me coming and stayed put. The car waiting in the third lane stayed too. But, a car, apparently moving and anticipating the green light in the middle lane, came bursting out between the other two cars. I didn't see the car until it was right in front of us. There was no time to hit the brake. As the left front of my Monte hit the white 323 Mazda in the left front corner, my head pushed hard into the visor above my windshield.

It happened in a second but seems now to have happened in slow motion. I could see the windshield of the other car explode and fall inward as the driver, his passenger, and a passenger in the back all flew up in their seats and then came back down. I turned to see if Maria was all right. She said she was, and so was Stephanie. I sat there for a moment, disgusted with myself. I tried my door, but it would not open. The three guys started to get out of their car. They all were shaking off the shock and the one in the back seat was rubbing his stomach where it apparently had been wrenched. The front seat passenger had a small cut on his head that bled a little onto his white T-shirt. My car was still running. I shut it off. Maria told me she was going to talk to the guys, who appeared to be Mexican. I could see her talking animatedly with them but could not hear what she was saying.

We caused a huge traffic jam. A wrecker arrived and the police were called. Maria came back and told me that she had been speaking to them in Spanish. She told everyone in earshot that I was in a wheelchair and couldn't come out and talk to people. She told me that the driver had just bought the car and he and his buddies had just eaten a big meal before the accident. They were shaken up but unhurt except for hurting stomachs. A State Trooper arrived. An ambulance and medics arrived. They thought I was injured, but I reassured them that the only thing wrong was my blood pressure as I tried to deal with what had happened. The other guys refused treatment too. We got some Tylenol for Stephanie who had a headache.

I was cited for running a red light. It was the first accident that I ever had that was my fault. I started the car, the hood was pushed up, but it drove okay. The wrecker towed the other car away. We drove over to the nursery and bought some flowers. On the way back we saw the guys we hit walking. I stopped and we asked them if they wanted a ride somewhere. They refused. I didn't blame them for that.

I should have been happy that we were unhurt, but I wasn't. I worried about damaging the car. I worried about being the cause of the accident, even though my disability played no part in what happened. I worried about my insurance. The only thing I could think to do was to try to fix the car.

With the help of our body man at work, I started to search for parts. He sent me John Foreman to help as my agent. When I asked, John admitted that he was George Foreman's cousin—a real nice guy. John located a front end clip, and I dropped the car off at a shop and took vacation time to have it repaired. Then, when the junk dealer was lifting the front clip down from a high shelf, it fell and broke. The dealer wanted the same price for what was left that he had before the damage, so John had to refuse and left it. I took another week's vacation. Then, he got a front end. I got over to see it before they put it on, and found out that it was a '74. I had to take the car back and go back to work until John found the right parts. I didn't want to ruin a classic car by having it have a mismatched front end.

Finally, several weeks later, John located all the parts except the left headlight assembly from a car he found in a field on the south side. Finally, he located the assembly and the car was fixed and painted by Christmas. The hood was kinked and didn't fit right. Weathered paint and small dents were not removed from the replacement fender. The bright metal and plastic parts were dull and weathered, not like mine had been. But the Monte still ran great and became a classic in January 1993.

I was severely depressed. A bad case of raw, itchy, flaky skin developed on my face. It was diagnosed as seborrhea. It would reoccur every time I faced the stresses of everyday living after that.

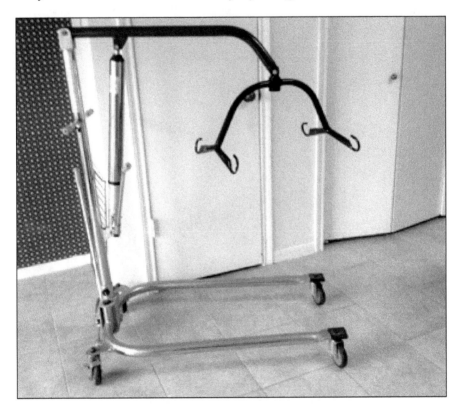

My Hoyer lift. Used only when I fell to the floor—rarely

Pool Hoyer lift installed by Dana used or showers from 1995

# 47

## New Help Arrives

Dana had to cut back his help when he started back at Rice that fall, so I had to hire another attendant. I placed an ad and got the usual responses. I got a call from a shy woman. We agreed to meet.

Xuam Vu arrived with her sister, but her sister did not come in. Xuam had just finished the requirement to be a medical assistant and was looking for work. She was single and 39, and had been in the country six years. She picked up the application materials and left. Convinced that she could do the work, I called Xuam to have her start one evening. The first evening she was to start, I waited an hour, and then gave her a call. She said that she couldn't get a ride, but promised to start coming a couple of days later.

The second night she was supposed to come, she was about a half hour late. I'd had a small accident in the bathroom, so I had her follow me into the bathroom and clean it up. It was a terrible way to start work, but part of what helping me was about. I started to ask her to help me with something else when, suddenly, she said that she'd only come by to talk and not to work.

I asked her what was going on, and she explained. She said she hated it in the United States and wanted to go back to Vietnam. She found my ad and wanted to work for me but her brother had told her that my work wasn't enough hours and had obtained a full time job in a Vietnamese clinic on the north side of town for her. She had argued and pleaded, but no one would drive her over to my house. Xuam thought she could learn English more quickly working with me. I could see she was upset, but I could do nothing about it but wish her well. I told her that I was available to talk to her any time she wanted, but we never saw each other again.

Then, I got a call from a young man, speaking broken English, "I have a sister. She work at home sewing. She like to work for you." He said that they lived on the next street in the same block. That was nice, but I worried about whether or not this "sister" spoke English or could speak for herself.

As usual, I left the garage door open so the interviewees could let themselves in. Jazz usually told me when someone was there. I'd call out to whoever rang the bell, and asked them to come through the back door of the garage. Because people often didn't show up, I went about my business as usual, and closed the garage door again after an hour or so. This night was no different. I finished eating. It was getting dark. No one came. I went out and closed the garage door.

The next morning, when I was about to enter my car, I saw a note left on my trunk. It said, "We were sorry we missed you. Please call us at...Quoc Nguyen," and left a phone number. I called the number from work. As a part of my screening, I rarely wrote down the numbers of people who called. Although I may have missed good people by not calling them back, I felt that part of a person's dependability was their ability to follow directions and call me if they needed more information. In the beginning, I wasted a lot of energy calling back people who were polite by giving me their number, but did not have enough interest in the work to pursue the application process further. This was different. I got Quoc on the phone and we arranged to meet again the next evening.

This time, I was ready when they came to my door, a timid young man and his more timid sister. They sat on either side of me at my table as I went over what was required. Quoc did all the talking, occasionally asking his sister questions in Vietnamese. He seemed not too interested in my requirements, as though his sister was fully capable of doing what I needed. Rather, he seemed concerned about her hours and how much I would pay and when. They did not seem to understand my need for references, but instinctually, I knew that they were very trustworthy, and just as frightened as I was of being used or cheated. I had never dealt with an agent before. I was trying to find out what *she* thought.

I tried to explain about my need for references, but it, like my application, seemed to be ignored in favor of negotiating when she would start. She would start the next day and her brother would accompany her to help her understand my English.

Hoai Huong Nguyen, "*Beh*" (the nickname they chose for me), was 35 and arrived in the US from Vietnam in May 1992, with five brothers and her father. She lived in her sixth brother's home about a block away, so she could walk over. Her only sister lived nearby with her family and the two oldest brothers and their families remained in Vietnam. She was a seamstress and the family had had a tailoring business in Saigon. Her father was a French and history teacher and worked for a Senator before the Communists took over in 1975.

The first night Beh came to help, Camthu, her brother's wife, accompanied her. Camthu translated and helped Beh get started with her work. Beh remained quiet but seemed to be catching on to what I needed. It was pleasant to have Camthu around. Two helpers for the price of one wasn't bad. After that, Quoc came with his sister. He seemed overly curious, monopolized my TV, and didn't let me communicate with his sister. Finally, I'd had enough of him taking my time and getting in the way of my nightly routine. I told him rather impolitely that I could communicate with Beh quite nicely without his help. He got the point and never accompanied her again.

Beh and I had our problems. I found myself telling her to locate things by, "Up, no, higher, no, to the right, down." An experienced cook, she caught on to my tastes quickly. But labels threw her sometimes and she got the wrong thing trying to read them. She was totally unfamiliar with household cleaning supplies and my papers, so it was a struggle sometimes to get what I needed even if it was right near me on the shelf.

The hardest part was eating. Beh would bring my food, and then disappear, supposedly back in the kitchen to clean up. But I would catch her watching, at the edge of the room, to see if I liked the food. She told me that she had learned English in high school, before the Communists came, but had not used it much. She and her father had spent six months working on their English before they came. She wanted me to talk to her and to correct her pronunciation. I agreed, and we spent a few minutes on the computer each evening before she left working on words. She hated my time sheets, and did them reluctantly. She was having some trouble cashing my checks and would rather have been paid in cash, but she didn't say anything. She decided to limit the time she charged me to the time she spent helping me with supper, not the time we spent together working on words.

Beh had been working at home doing contract sewing. As hard as it was for her to communicate with me, she considered helping me a "vacation" from her boring day of sewing and preparing food for her family. My cooking interested her, because it didn't require long hours in the kitchen like many of the Vietnamese specialties did.

Very curious, but not in the intrusive way her brother Quoc was, Beh wanted to know everything about me. She tired quickly of the computer and started exploring my magazines and TV interests. After about two weeks working with me, we were looking through a magazine together like she liked to do, asking me questions as she went. She stopped at an ad showing two people kissing. I asked her if she liked that. She said, "Yes." and smiled at me.

I said, "Would you like a kiss?"

And she said, "Yes."

Beh had had only one romantic relationship, with a married man, when she was in her twenties. She grew up with her eight brothers as one of them, taking care of the younger ones. Her sister, ten years older, had married at seventeen, to a Vietnamese pilot, but Beh's father considered her sister a "bad" girl. Beh went to a Catholic high school, and was isolated from men there. Then, with the fall of Saigon, when she was seventeen, everything changed. Her father burned all his papers and went into hiding to prevent being sent to reeducation camp by the Communists. Her mother started selling black market prescription drugs in the street to support the family. Her brothers were sent to the country to avoid being taken into the Army. Beh joined them and they homesteaded a patch of forest. With her mother's help instructing them what to do, they grew sweet potatoes and raised chickens. They were very successful and Beh got fat. They helped many others less fortunate.

Beh's sister and her family escaped by boat and ended up in Chicago. Beh and her brother, Paul, tried several times to escape, following first the way of their sister, the sea. Failing that, once abandoned on a desert island and landing in jail several times, Paul finally left on his own and made it to Thailand, and eventually, California. Beh and her two best friends from school remained single and dreamed of leaving the country and a better life. A husband and family would have to wait until then. Beh's mother, struggling to support the family with her dangerous occupation, often was arrested and put in jail. She suffered from high blood pressure and eventually had a stroke. Bedridden, Beh had to care for her for four years until she died.

Beh's friends got out: one to Austria, and the other to Australia. Beh took a tour of Cambodia, hoping to get to Thailand. Caught by the Viet

Cong, she tricked them and escaped, but had to return to Saigon. Finally, in 1992, Paul and Camthu managed to sponsor her along with her brothers and father.

On opposite sides of the world from her best friends, unsure of her English and working at home while her brothers scrambled and saved to go to school, Beh could have become lonely and isolated like Xuan Vu. Instead, she fell in love with me.

Beh was very happy working with me every evening, learning English and spending time with me. Then she went home to Camthu's house for the night. She got me ready to go to bed, but I was on my own until Maria came in the morning. It was getting hard to keep the covers on in bed on cold nights. Beh folded them carefully so that it was easy to get under them and keep warm. Soon, she got a job sewing at a Bridal shop. Her brothers took her to work each morning, and I started to pick her up on my way home from work each evening.

Maria agreed to accompany me to visit my parents in McAllen at Thanksgiving, but we had to take Stephanie and Paulo along. The trip went well. Dad cautioned against going to Mexico, so we didn't. The test came on the way back when we were stopped 60 miles from the border at the checkpoint in Falfurrias. We weren't prepared, so Maria had to go into the trunk to get her passports. Her multiple-entry visa presented no problems. I don't know what would have happened if it had.

At Christmas, it was Beh's turn to accompany me. This was a totally new experience for her. She marveled at the huge fields of crops, orange groves, and lemons in my parents' yard. Going to Mexico was out of the question. Having the bucket in the car became a necessity.

With Mom in front of a giant bougainvillea at McAllen Motor Park

With Beh on Musser Flowage. Phillips, Wisconsin 1993

# 48

## A Danger to My Kidneys and Other Problems

D r. Clearman referred me to an urologist who worked with spinal injured people at TIRR. She said that she was still worried about my kidneys and wanted them checked again. I wasn't sure what my frequent and urgent urination had to do with my kidneys, but I trusted her experience. I had a bladder flow test and kidney x-rays again. The urologist, Dr. Delbert Rudy, recommended that I increase my dose of baclofen to reduce spasms and have my kidneys checked every six months. The concern was that spasming bladder muscles were preventing me from completely emptying my bladder, and, in the worst case, could cause urine to back up into my kidneys, causing damage, and eventually, kidney failure. The increased dose of baclofen made urination less urgent, but it made my knees wobbly and less able to carry my weight when I stood.

I had become very frustrated at work because everyone was so busy that they couldn't "drop everything" to help me when I needed help. I like things neat, organized, and in good order, but when you depend on the kindness of others, your office becomes a "mess" as people inadvertently leave papers, pencils, paper clips and other things in your workspace and you can't move them to where they should be. You also spend a lot of time waiting for people to help you with turning things on and off, moving things into better position, retrieving documents you need, and so on. I had a very good, helpful, and conscientious graduate assistant from Belize, Lydia Valentine, who made it bearable, but when she wasn't there, I often had to yell, "Is anyone out there?" when I needed help. Directing by voice is very hard, too.

Beh quit the bridal shop in January 1993, and started doing alterations at J & J Tailors. It was easier to pick her up there because it was just off the freeway on the way home. While I worried about having car trouble, problems with traffic, or leaving work too late, we never missed each other. Sometimes, I had to come early. On those days, I'd park near the front of the shop and hail a passerby and ask them to go in the shop and ask for her. The shop closed at 6 pm, but was usually still open when I arrived most days around 6:05. On days Beh left work early, she'd call and tell me she had a ride with one of her brothers or she'd wait at a shop in the back where other employees made clothes.

I could no longer get out of the car or get to a phone, so I worried about the time we wouldn't connect, but it didn't happen. Beh's employer, an aging entrepreneur who said that he'd "started over" six times, was amused when I'd call, and once or twice came out to the car. He was interested in poetry, and, when Beh told him that I wrote some, he asked my advice on some Vietnamese poetry he was translating to English. Some of the poems he shared with me were rich in the ancient Chinese tradition and French influence of the colonial past. Others, written by prisoners of the Communists, were as sparse and brittle as the lives the authors were forced to lead, so devoid of nourishment and human contact that their expression was limited to the black and white of their meager writing instruments.

For my assistance in editing his translations, he had some of my poems published in a local paper, and gave me black lacquer and Mother of Pearl depictions of the four Vietnamese arts.

On those evenings going home, I offered to teach Beh to drive. We stopped a couple of times at a local school parking lot to begin. She immediately had trouble reaching the gas and brake pedals. We solved that by using my electric wheelchair cushion to get her three inches closer to the pedals. Her unfamiliarity with English terms and car driving made it difficult to verbally instruct her. We got around the parking lot without hitting anything, but she was not able to control the car or understand how to control it. Before long, she declined my offers to stop and said that she'd learn from her brothers. I had experienced the quality of driving her brothers' exhibited, and wasn't sure she should learn their bad habits, but at least they could teach her in Vietnamese.

After Mom and Dad visited for a couple of days in April before heading for an early start on Mom's hip replacement, I got a little restless, so Beh and Jazz and I went out for a couple of day excursions. First, we went to the beach. Jazz got to meet some friendly horses on the way and enjoyed running and running some more on the beach that was nearly deserted. Beh and I made creative use of the bucket. My portable wheelchair worked okay on the hard sand. Then, a week later, we drove up to Brenham to catch the Bluebonnets in bloom. We stopped by a beautiful blue field on a dirt road off the highway for lunch. Jazz explored as far as he could up and down the road. He ventured to a nearby house, and then came running back with three dogs in pursuit. He was glad to get back in the car. I was glad he avoided a fight.

Dana graduated from Rice University in the spring of 1993, with degrees in Biology and Art History. He hoped to enter medical school in the fall. I helped him out with a letter of reference. He and his father helped me by installing a wall mount for a new TV and VCR I bought.

With the two spring trips completed, I decided to drive to Wisconsin for my summer vacation. Knowing my limitations, I decided to take two weeks and stop a lot. Maria was tied up with her children, her parents who were visiting, and an upcoming medical exam. Beh could not get off work and was worried about not being able to drive. We finally agreed to take one week. This meant that I had to cut the trip short. I thought of buying a round trip ticket to O'Hare, and, after the first week with Beh, having Maria fly up to meet us at the airport. Then have Beh fly back while Maria would continue on to Indiana and Ohio for the second week with me. But Maria couldn't go.

Beh and I were going to leave the second week in July. Her father had a mild heart attack so we had to cancel. It was the peak of the 1993 Midwest flood so I thought it might be a good omen. It was hot and dry in Houston, and finally in mid-August, Beh felt comfortable enough to leave her father in the care of her brothers.

It was a hard, hot trip. Beh was wonderful and enjoyed every minute. We had some communication problems, but she learned a lot about road travel. Before the trip, I made sure the car was in top condition and that the air conditioning was working well. We started off early on Saturday morning. After a little rain leaving Houston, everything was going well until we reached Huntsville and the air conditioning *quit*. We stopped at Corsicana during the noon rush and couldn't find any place that would look at the problem, so we gave up and rolled the windows down.

We cruised through Dallas and Denton as the day heated up. I put a shirt over my bare legs to fend off the afternoon sun that angled through the driver's side window. I drove on, straight north, hoping to make Wichita by nightfall, the hot wind blowing through the car and the sun reflecting off car windows. By Ardmore, OK, at 4 pm, the temperature read 102° and inside the car it was probably 120°! Beads of sweat formed on my forehead, stinging my eyes and making my glasses uncomfortable. My back started to stick to the seat. Even with frequent sips of ice water from Beh's cup, by 5 pm I had to stop because I feared heat stroke or heat exhaustion was setting in.

Just as I was feeling my worst, we came to the site of the famous Cherokee Strip land rush. I saw a Best Western dead ahead and turned up the ramp. I tried to lift my right foot from the gas to the brake and it wouldn't budge. I yelled for help and Beh grabbed my right leg under the knee and pushed it to the brake. I forced my leg into action with a thrust of my hip as we rushed up the ramp toward the stop sign. Finally, I got the car stopped a bit abruptly and sighed a sigh of relief. Beh lifted my leg again to the gas pedal and I eased across the road to a spot at an angle in front of the motel office so I wouldn't have to back or turn the wheel when we left.

With my instructions, Beh went in and got a room. It was her first time, ever, getting a room. She had to come out to get my license number and other information, but she got the job done. We had to drive around the back, some distance, to the room. I knew I had to get in as soon as possible, so Beh got the wheelchair out of the trunk while I got out of the car. I swung my legs out, and leaned forward to get into position to stand up. My sweaty wrist slipped on the steering wheel and I tumbled out of the car to the hot asphalt on my face. As I watched blood pouring out in front of me, I thought the trip had ended. Then, two men with heavy German accents appeared above me, turned me over, and lifted me to the wheelchair. The bleeding was only my nose and it stopped when I got up.

The motel room was cold, maybe 65°, but I didn't notice until I got chilled about three hours later. Beh went to the front to get some food. She was gone a long time because she didn't know how to use the buffet and ordered instead from the menu. When she left, she had left the key on the dresser and closed the door, locking it. When she got back, she couldn't get in. She had to head back to the office. I got up from the wheelchair and worked my way over to the door. When I got there and released the lock, she was back with a spare key! We ate in the room. I almost couldn't eat, but forced myself.

I had a heat rash and didn't sleep until past midnight, but by morning I rebounded and was ready to continue. By Des Moines at noon the next day we crossed the Raccoon River with water at its banks on I-35. The freeway showed evidence of being flooded earlier. It was 82° and I was comfortable with the flood and the heat. We sipped liquids constantly and stopped often for me to stretch my legs.

Monday morning was cool, cloudy, and windy and we were in Wisconsin. Listening to the radio and watching the green hills heading east on I-94, Beh said that she was in a "movie." We stopped in Menomonie to visit my great aunt, Billy Richardson. She had been in a nursing home with a broken hip several years and had declined a lot since I last saw her. She said she had decided not to return to her home. Driving east on Highway 29, we encountered road construction and heavy crosswinds that made it difficult for me to drive. I had pull over at one point to let trucks pass. I didn't want to alarm Beh, so I didn't tell her. It was strange not being able to drive in a crosswind any more.

Then, we stopped to see my great uncle, Roy Hull. He was recovering from his fourth bout with pneumonia since marrying Julie in 1982. At 97 he was my oldest living relative. As I sat in his wheelchair, facing him in his recliner, he stared at me and marveled at how I had come to see him in my condition. He told my father later that I was a "Miracle Man." Earlier, Roy had showed Dad a cane that had been Nelson Hull's, Roy's grandfather, and my great, great grandfather, a blacksmith in Wisconsin who served in the Civil War. I never saw the cane. Uncle Roy quit eating sometime after I left and entered a nursing home. He also refused to be fed intravenously and died in early November at 98. I don't know who has the cane. My Aunt Billy died in the nursing home the next year. I was always drawn to my older relatives. Their lives were so rich with experience. I never passed up an opportunity to visit, if only for an hour or so, and kept coming back.

That day, we also visited my uncle, Don Marshall, and stayed the night with my aunt, Phyllis Wenzel. Don showed us his newly remodeled farmhouse and told us how he was using the old barn well for a water source heat pump to heat the house instead of the wood-burning furnace that he had fed by hand for over 70 years. Staying with Aunt Phyllis did not make up for missing a big party for her 75th birthday the following Sunday. She was surprised by her family and friends, and honored for her many years as an elementary teacher. If only I had reversed our trip's course I could have seen my cousins and attended a wedding. It had become hard to plan any trip. For many years, I just got in the car and drove out of town, stopping wherever and whenever I liked. Now, even the best-laid plans often went awry.

We only spent two days at the lake, but they were warm and calm and very pleasant. On Thursday, we went to Marshfield to visit my sister, Judy, before she went to work. We stayed in the yard because I couldn't get in the house. Paul and Andy were there too so we visited while Beh took pictures of the goat. We spent the night at Tim's new house. The next morning Tim gave us a tour of Madison in his Jaguar XKE 2+2. Beh really enjoyed that. Tim fixed my air conditioning with a simple fuse, but that gave out by Rockford, Il, so we were without air conditioning on the way back too. We met my niece, Tracy, in a motel in Champaign and had a pleasant, short visit. I was glad to stop there because a constant crosswind had made it difficult for me to drive all morning.

We saw some flooding twenty miles before we reached the Mississippi, but at the river it was obvious that the massive flooding had subsided. We blew a tire near Memphis. When it blew I was in the right lane and easily pulled the car to a stop out of traffic. Beh said something to the effect that we were going to, *"Die now!"* I told her to calm down, go to the back of the car and take out the wheelchair. She propped the chair against the back of the car and tied a white towel to it. In five minutes, a young man in a pickup pulled up. He asked what was wrong and I told him I sure could use a tire change. He agreed to help and started changing the tire. A county truck with flashing yellow lights pulled up, but when the older man saw what was happening, he pulled out and waved as he left.

The spare was low, so we had to drive to the other side of the freeway to get air. The ramshackle sheds we pulled up to proclaimed that they fixed flats in hand-painted signs on boards. These guys, with their rotten teeth, looked right out of "Deliverance," so I elected to add air at $2.00 rather than trust my tire to them. While we were there, Beh got some peaches at a roadside stand and we returned home without a spare.

When we got to Texarkana that evening, we stopped early because I was tired and the low sun was in my eyes. I couldn't drive anymore. When Beh went in to register, the manager confiscated my credit card because there had been a burglary in my house and Maria had reported my spare card stolen. Jazz may have scared the burglars off, but they got my new unused VCR, both remote controls, and a clock-radio. And maybe, two credit cards that I stopped payment on—all worth only about $350—so I was lucky. Lucky to have another credit card, too, because with it we were allowed to stay there that night.

I couldn't rely on luck anymore. I had to teach Beh to drive. Her schedule and mine left little opportunity for lessons.

## 49

## A Big Change at Work

Texas Southern University still had good enrollment, but the campus experienced turmoil when some members of our "Ocean of Soul" band stole electronics from a store while they were on tour in Japan. President Harris ended the Band's existence, he "Banished the Band," but later resigned himself over the controversy that resulted. There were allegations about the Bandleader's actions, and he was fired. It was easy to say that Harris resigned over the Band controversy, but others said that he resigned over disagreement with the Board of Regents about reorganization of the university.

Following the lead of business, and recognizing that the State general fund could not continue to grow like it had for two decades after the decline of the oil industry, the Texas State Legislature began steps that were designed to make the colleges and universities run more efficiently. State Comptroller John Sharp declared that millions could be saved through privatization, downsizing, and elimination of duplicate programs. Consultants were dispatched to TSU and other agencies to see where costs could be cut. Massive infusions of money had been made to TSU in the 1980s to meet the requirements of the Office of Civil Rights to offset inequities. Now the State was forcing cutbacks in the 1990s that would erase the progress made.

Bond money that had been used to pay temporary employees to renovate facilities was rapidly being used up, and budget reallocation and reorganization forced cutting back people for the first time in a decade. The first to go was my boss, Joshua Hill, who was sent back to the classroom in January 1993. This created a void of leadership and communication that permeated the area. A consultant was brought in to reorganize our area. Sharon Murphy happened to be a former top student of mine from the MBA program at Atlanta University. The reorganization she recommended eliminated three directorships and fourteen jobs. Many other jobs were lost across campus.

My responsibilities were assumed under three directorships that remained. I was told to report temporarily to the architectural director. I had continued some of my work, but others did some. It was the first time in my working career where I hadn't participated in planning, budgeting, and policy-making, and it was very disconcerting. At one point Jeanie was told to take my land and facilities inventory responsibilities to another area until they found out that she didn't want to and couldn't do it without me. There was a lot of intrigue and political maneuvering going on that I wasn't a part of. People were usurping my responsibilities and ignoring me to the point where I felt that someone was trying to get me angry enough to do something rash or quit. Other directors seemed to be experiencing similar difficulties. Being ignored was depressing, but it didn't make much of a case for a grievance.

When I confronted the temporary acting vice president, he assured me that all the measures being taken were only temporary, that I had a place in the institution, but he left to assume the role of internal auditor without making any change except isolate me further from management. Discouraged and upset, I met with the senior vice president, Howard Turnley, the man responsible for Hill's demise and all the changes. He too, assured me that the measures taken were temporary and necessary, and that I would assume an appropriate position, perhaps in institutional research as the provost, Dr. Layron Clarkson, had earlier suggested. Later a new director of institutional research was hired. I was not considered in the selection. It was obvious the administration didn't know what to do with me. My disability made it difficult to fire me. My increasing disability somehow also made them think I was less capable. Their refusal to give me good supporting help reinforced their thinking that I would be incapable of leading the area. I no longer met with or was included in high circles. I could no longer get involved in discussions of, "What to do with Ron." It was easier to bury me in the organization and frustrate me in the hope that I would quit.

On September1st, 1993, a new president, Joann Horton, was named. She immediately had trouble being accepted by the faculty because they wanted someone with good university credentials and she came from the Community College System of Iowa. At the same time, our former architectural director, Lloyd A. Hart, returned to assume Josh's old job as an assistant vice president, a position I applied to be promoted to. My application was acknowledged, but I was not interviewed, or, to my knowledge, considered for the job.

I met with Lloyd the day after he returned to TSU. He too, assured me that he was happy I was working with him and that things would go better. Still, he insisted that I continue to report to the architectural director Mashid Ahmadi. Shi Shi, as she liked to be called, had a more dominant personality than I, and disagreed with me from the first time she came on campus and imposed her immaturity and insecurity on everything we were attempting to do. Shi surrounded herself with women he promoted without credentials and men who were recessive. She even snatched my summer energy intern, a brilliant young architect, by offering her a position on her staff for more money, something Josh had done repeatedly to my displeasure, still glad to see my chosen people get ahead.

Shi Shi was confrontational to the extreme, insisted on having things done her way, and I was only one of many who had problems working with her. Cut off, I stonewalled. I buried myself in my work and refused to become one of her troops. Already, she was at odds with the assistant vice president, and I didn't want to buy into that. Later, I was assigned to report to the operations manager, a position created to meet the needs of a politically opportunistic TSU grad. She was easier to work with, but it was the same situation, being asked to work under the directorship of people who lacked experience with and knowledge of leadership. It is hard to work for those you don't respect.

I would have loved to quit. But that was not in the cards. My job searches in 1983 and 1985 in Atlanta told me that the same problems in perception I faced at TSU would haunt me as I tried to convince others that I still had the drive to help their operations. My only option would be to start a business or consult. Both would require time and capital to get started, and both would be more difficult because it would be harder to get out and meet those I'd work with. There was a lot I could do with my writing and systems development ability. The hardest part would be beating the pavement with my ideas. It would take time and money. I was willing to take a year or two developing what I'd do, but with my debt and no liquid savings, I couldn't quit until I could support myself without working. That would take a while—until my retirement income could support my attendant care and me. Besides, there is no greater calling than helping a university struggle to keep up with the needs of its students in a rapidly changing world.

I continued to work under these trying conditions. My pay remained the same while some who caught the eye of the new president were promoted. Those that were fired left in disbelief—many had done good work but were disliked because they were not political—just doing what they were assigned. Several filed lawsuits and won damages. It appeared that the cost cutters were leaving me alone because I was disabled. There had been some overtures about providing me with a van, etc., but they seemed unwilling to give me a leadership role.

I talked to Kassandra about my limbo situation and she told me to contact the EEOC. I decided not to do that because TSU hadn't reduced my salary or fired me. There were some subtle efforts to change my title, and I heard rumors that people didn't believe my degrees. I think they were trying to get me to quit, but were afraid of the repercussions of a suit based on reverse discrimination or disability. With my responsibilities stripped, I became all but invisible— trundling to and from work doing my job as I perceived it, but no longer responsible for a slice of the action.I used the time to mend fences. I had to work out how I was going to pay attendants after TRC stopped its assistance in six months. I had paid up front, so when the reimbursement checks came in I stretched the payments out about nine months. I worked hard to teach myself about relational databases. I worked with my student to complete years of neglect on our facilities inventory. I presided over conserving our computer resources as areas of our building were reassigned, people left jobs, and requests for group software and equipment were curtailed, and individuals purchased their own resources. The "personal" aspect of personal computers made it more difficult to give everyone a slice of our capability. Instead, individuals bought resources for themselves without consideration for the information needs of others. The result was that working together often proved difficult, and we ended up with less capability overall to benefit the needs of a few.

I managed to get a computer users' manual written. It needed revision the day it was issued. I moved some of our computers to ethernet, speeding data transfer. I added a 525 Mbyte drive to our file server. New computers and equipment were proliferating, and the prices were dropping. But our seven-year-old computers were still running, so I elected to upgrade them because I could do that, but I couldn't buy new computers for everyone on our limited budget.

My Voice Navigator enabled me to run menu-driven software with my voice by merely speaking commands. I trained the Navigator to accept about 500 commands and it was wonderful not to have to strain to use the mouse. It sped my work and provided a way for me to continue to use computers after I would lose the use of my arms and hands. Software provided by a company out of Canada, Madenta, (since defunct or bought out) enabled dictation and would predict words as I would begin to spell them out. Full dictation and voice control appeared to be just around the corner.

I duplicated the State's facilities inventory program on Helix Express and loaded our data into it. I also developed working systems for vacation/leaves and events. These were fine systems, easy-to-use and time-saving, but the people I developed them for failed to take the short time to learn them and I lacked management support to get them in use.

The $3.5 million loan for energy conservation we were granted was delayed to the point that it was cancelled. We should have gone ahead with the measures, because it just made good dollars and sense. But once again, management, through inexperience and ignorance, failed to understand the LoanSTAR program and saw it as a cash cow to finance the renovation of the malaise caused by poor funding and management of the maintenance of our facilities, instead of what it was. I got a good start on a lighting package with my summer intern from the Governor's Energy Office, but that had to be put on hold until I could get leadership that would support me and get it funded.

I focused on the facilities inventory. My graduate assistant and I finally made real progress toward an accurate and updated inventory. We scanned all the floor plans we had and I updated them and numbered every room. The floor plans became an integral part of the inventory. I lost my student computer technician because of funding, but gained a work-study freshman who seemed to be picking up the work well.

In July 1993, while I was eating lunch alone, a familiar stranger dropped by. I recognized him right away. He said, "Hi Dr. Hull, do you know who I am? Raj Chowdhury." Raj explained that he had been doing an accreditation review at the University of Houston and decided to stop by and see me. He and Shammi hadn't kept in touch. When his father and mother died, Raj's sister wrote me. That's when I learned that Raj was the head of the management program at North Carolina A and T. On August

1st, Raj joined the University as our new dean of the School of Technology. Raj confessed that he had been interviewing when he stopped by to see me. It disturbed me when he told me the Board of Regents interviewed him and that he hadn't told me earlier. It also was ironic that Josh was now working for him as associate dean. He and Shammi and two children, Immane and Omer, settled into a new home in Missouri City. I tried to establish closer contact, but they complained of no time. It was too difficult to pursue the matter. We only made contact over work-related matters after that.

With Beh in my unkempt office. Gov. Ann Richard's award for my statewide used energy conservation plan hangs on the wall. 1993

# 50

# New Ways to Extend My Reach

The Texas Rehabilitation Commission paid for a retest of my driving with a van in October 1993. I drove to the test at TIRR. My new wheelchair was there, so we used it to get measurements. After a brief interview, the evaluator, Chad Strowmatt, put me in a van with zero-pressure steering. I could drive the system, but it seemed awkward, especially on curves.

The prescription called for a Ford Econoline van with a 6" dropped floor and a raised roof. I would enter the van through a side lift and park my electric wheelchair behind a 6-way power seat. In the beginning, I'd transfer to the seat and move it into driving position. Later, the seat could be removed and I'd drive from the wheelchair. Gas and brake pedals would be standard, but close together and the same height. Steering would be a flat plate about 5" in diameter with holes in it positioned horizontally above my right knee. My right hand would fit between two pins and grip a knob on a cradle that dropped into one of the holes. I would steer by rotating the disk, leaving my left hand free to operate other controls from a panel positioned within easy reach. In time, the foot pedals could be removed and I would drive from the wheelchair. The basic van cost about $20,000. Modifications could run another $5,000-$15,000. Hopefully TSU would come through with the van and modifications, because I couldn't. Although I had a van earlier I never drove that Cruz Hinojosa used, Lloyd turned me down flat, stating lack of budget money. I was told that METROLift would serve my area starting January 1st, 1994, but indications were that it wouldn't be much help getting me to work... too slow and unreliable. So, I hoped for a miracle and kept driving.

My Hoyer lift arrived in September 1993, but I didn't have to use it. First, I parked it in the garage until it got in the way, and then I moved it to the kitchen. It became obvious that I would need another one for the bathroom because this one was too heavy for Beh to dismantle and move. When Dad came in October, he removed the mast and boom and checked to see if it would fit in the bathroom. It did, so I decided to try to get another lift for there.

My electric wheelchair arrived in early November. I had fun learning how to drive it without tearing up my house. It was more maneuverable than my scooter, but still prone to hitting walls. The power of catching the wheels on obstacles could do a lot of damage. At first, I parked it in the kitchen with my lift, but I knew I'd soon be using it. I needed to open up the entry to my bathroom from my bedroom so that I could move in and out easily, so I had that work done in early October. The project was expensive and I was unhappy with the painting, but at least I could get the wheelchair into the bathroom. I bought folding mirror doors to fill the four-foot opening. They looked great from the room side, but, because they were built for closets, looked unfinished from inside the bathroom. I put Dana on the problem, but he didn't have time to finish it. The doors opened wide but still got in the way of the wheelchair's movements. I soon caught an edge with the wheel and cracked a mirror. Dana came and took the doors down and put them in my closet. At least all the ramps were all working well under the weight of the heavy chair.

I started to experience real problems with my bladder the spring of 1993. I would drive to work not knowing if I'd make it or not. I came to depend upon my proven pit stops, even stopping was no guarantee that I'd make it to work without experiencing the flush of high blood pressure from autonomic dysreflexia as I struggled to maintain control of my car and my bladder. There was no relief until I balanced stiffly over a toilet bowl, draining what was left, often after frequent small involuntary releases that left me wet and embarrassed.

Maria's response was simple. *"Why do you wear underwear?"* She questioned. The time had come to quit fighting with my underwear as I struggled so many times to go. Still, even the convenience of no underwear couldn't overcome my physical struggle to control my body the way I'd always done since becoming paralyzed. I started to have trouble in the office, cutting off telephone conversations and meetings to rush to the bathroom. I learned to leave as inconspicuously as possible, but it still hurt when I couldn't finish a meeting or conversation without taking a break. My coworkers learned to expect it, but I often waited until it was too late. Small accidents were common. Occasionally I wet my pants so badly that I had to wait in the bathroom for them to dry out.

At Dr. Clearman's suggestion, I increased my Baclofen dosage slightly and made some other adjustments that allowed me to be more comfortable at work. I had an IVP in September 1993, showing no kidney damage. I also signed up for a study of urinary infection as a control. I was grateful to have avoided an internal catheter and the urinary infections that could accompany that.

I gradually gave up little things, one at a time. Walking and standing had become so difficult that I did them only to transfer from chair to bed, or to my car. I quit walking to the kitchen for breakfast and out to my car in late summer, 1993. I quit combing my hair about the same time. I still showered and shampooed myself, but it was becoming dangerous and difficult. Beh occasionally shampooed my hair to get it really clean. Dressing had become very difficult, so Beh started modifying some of my clothes to help out. The modifications consisted mainly of letting my pants waist out. The good food Maria and Beh were feeding me was putting weight on my stomach, making it hard to struggle with my clothes. I didn't change the clothes that had always worked for me; Beh just remade them to fit my changing needs.

I fell out of bed in August 1993, reaching for my TV remote. It didn't hurt because I relaxed and sort of slid the eighteen inches or so to the floor. I tried several times to get back into bed, but couldn't, so I waited two and a half hours for Maria to come. Lying on the carpeted floor wasn't bad; in fact it was quite relaxing. But, thoughts did creep into my head that I'd have to go to the bathroom, or worse, that she wouldn't come. Helpless as I was, I couldn't call her, so I just lay there and waited, relaxed, and tried not to think bad thoughts. Before long, Maria arrived and was surprised to find me lying on the floor by the bed rather than in my usual chair. She had a sore back, so we had a hard time getting me up. In order to help, I'd have to get to my knees, and then with her steadying, try to force myself up to my feet with my right leg. The pressure of my weight on my leg muscles caused excruciating pain, and there was no way she could lift my dead weight. Finally, after several tries, I got my feet under me, and with her help, I was up.

In November, I fell transferring from the chair to my bed. I didn't want to lie on the floor all night, so I forced myself up onto the bed without help. It was sheer will and momentum. I don't know how I did it, but I did. It was the last time I ever got up by myself again. I spared myself the agony of a night on the cold floor with no way to go to the bathroom or call anyone. Jazz was no help at times like this. He either thought it was time to play or attacked whoever came to help.

I had to give up doing some work and household things in the evening, because by the time I was through eating, it was too late. It took most of Saturday morning to review the week's mail and respond, even with help from the computer. The hardest part was sitting long hours at home on weekends and holidays. I experienced a lot of muscle spasms, tingling, numbness, and itching. It was often hard to sit or lie comfortably, and my feet became swollen from inactivity. All the inactivity and good eating had added four inches to my waist. Beh made me a traditional Thanksgiving Dinner in1993, her first. No one in her family ate turkey so I had a lot of turkey sandwiches at work and turkey for my evening meal until nearly Christmas. Turkey is low fat, but when you eat a whole turkey and all the trimmings by yourself, you can't help gaining weight. Beh was such a good cook, everything she made tasted fabulous. She kept adding a little more to my portions. I hated to leave food on my plate to throw away. I started accusing her of killing me with kindness. It was against her nature, but she tried to limit the amount of food she put before me.

By September 1993, I decided to quit doing catch-up work on databases on weekends and concentrate on a book. The book was to be about my experience going from an active, athletic life to one managing a spinal cord injury. I wanted to write it so that those who did not have this kind of injury could better understand what happens, and to help others with injuries like mine understand what's happening to them. I should have called it "In the Nick of Time" because it seems like every time I thought I was going to have to give up and become a "cripple" to fit the stereotype, I'd think of a simple solution (like using my comb to operate my zipper) or something came along (TRC, attendants) that gave me the initiative to keep on living the way I always had... with a little help from my friends.

# 51

# Working Things Out at Work

My plans were to work at TSU as long as I could. It would mean attendants at work and maybe fewer days in the office. People hadn't yet learned to "come to me" too well, so it was important that I was there to meet with people and confer. Then, I hoped to transition into a "working" retirement helping others with my computer, analytical, and writing skills. If my book was successful, I would do more writing. By the time I had to make my home my office, I hoped to be fully automated and connected. Macintosh had some new "AV" (voice-activated, motion picture) computers out. But I was waiting for new inexpensive processors to come out before starting to build a voice-operated environmental control system. The transition would not be easy. It was now costing me $8,000 per year for attendants. That would grow as I needed more help. Although I may have been able to retain my health insurance or have the new national insurance that the President and Hiliary were promoting, Social Security and my retirement would not cover my current living and medical expenses. Hopefully, when I retired, I would get enough work to pay for everything on my own.

Jazz started losing hair in August 1993, and acquired a bad case of fleas. He apparently had a flea allergy. The vet prescribed a change in food, and a brief course of prednisolone, the same steroid I took. I tried to get my helpers to get rid of the fleas in the yard, on the carpet, and Jazz, but they didn't fully succeed. Two winters without a hard freeze had caused the flea population to explode.

With my help, Beh gradually took up driving and enjoyed being seen in my Monte Carlo, "the airplane," as her brothers called it. She would drive me to her work, and then I'd drive on to mine. In the evening, I'd drive to Beh's work, and she'd drive us home. In August of 1994, Beh joined Expert Cleaners as a seamstress for four stores. She had to be to work early, so her brothers drove her there in the morning. I continued picking her up on my way home at night. Beh started community college that fall with an English class and enjoyed it. We'd get home and Beh'd quickly heat up some food and get me ready for the evening, and then head off to school.

Maria had to go back to Ecuador in the fall of 1994. She had to enroll her kids in school and didn't know when she'd be back.Beh was capable of taking care of almost everything and willing to help, but I was afraid that she would get too tired and we needed someone to back her up if she got sick or needed to leave for any reason. So, I put an ad in the paper again.

Maria Luisita Mago, "Malu" as she liked to be called, was friendly and engaging. She was a college graduate in home economics and a divorced mother of seven. She had come from the Philippines in January 1994, because her children were here with her ex husband. From a wealthy family, she had led a good life until her divorce. A pianist and singer, she once had an opportunity to play a piano that Imelda Marcos had put in her summer palace for Van Cliburn. She worked in California until May, when she came to Houston to be close to her children. She started working for me in October. Malu loved to clean, so my house started to shine after many years of neglect.

Malu lived with a Filipino woman whose American husband had had a stroke and was paralyzed. As part of her rent, Malu helped take care of the man. She couldn't drive, so she walked the three miles from her home every morning. This soon became a problem in mid Winter, when it was cold and dark at 6 am and she had to walk along Kirkwood without sidewalks. Many times she arrived late, or called Beh when she couldn't get a ride. It bothered Beh that she seemed so undependable, but I knew better. Malu had servants in her younger years. Now, at fifty, she was reduced to doing menial work for menial wages. She couldn't afford an apartment or a car on what she made. Beh never had to walk that far in the cold and dark, or pay for a cab that took all the money she made working just to get there.

Malu also cleaned houses and helped take care of another stroke victim on weekends, but it was not enough. She had a falling out with her landlady and moved into a nearby apartment with two of her children. I was relieved, because it stopped the dreaded long walk to my house. But the move put more financial strain on her. She got a night job at a nursing home. Sometimes, she had trouble getting home from the nursing home in the morning, so I got up late at times, lying awake until she would come and help me up. Finally she had to leave in October 1995, when she took a job working all week at a nursing home.

Neither Beh nor Maria, nor Malu could get free to go with me at Thanksgiving or Christmas, in 1994, so I stayed at home. It was strange. I had always used my vacations and holidays to go somewhere. Now I was totally dependant on others—others who had little desire to go where I wanted, and sometimes, couldn't even go. While I still drove every day, I could no longer trust myself to drive alone anywhere except to work. It wasn't until after Christmas that I enjoyed a couple of days with my parents in McAllen. I drove, but had Beh take the wheel part of the way. At first she had trouble holding her lane, and I worried about the wisdom of letting her drive as we wandered to the shoulder and across the mid line and slowed for curves and inclines or overpasses. Gradually, she gained skill and confidence, while I crossed my fingers and hoped we wouldn't encounter a dangerous situation she couldn't handle. By the time we were cruising the last thirty palm-lined miles into the valley, she had gained confidence enough to drive us on in.

We couldn't go to Mexico because of her single entry visa, but Mom and Dad took us to visit a border wildlife refuge where there were trails my wheelchair could navigate. Dad pushed me on the trail. We didn't see much, only some snakes and one Chukaluka, but it was good to get out again. Since we couldn't go to Mexico, on Sunday I scheduled a side trip to an area that had some African animals in a mile-square compound, a reservoir, and farmland. Beh drove and I navigated. There were a variety of roads, including dirt ones with plenty of potholes for Beh to try out her new skills. By the time we got back to my parents' place, we were both tired and upset. But, it was experience with driving she needed, and experience she got. The next day, she was again ready to drive us home. She began enjoying it so much she kept asking if she could pass another truck. The process of passing excited her and she would speed up. Soon she would be going 85 mph and I had to keep asking her to slow down.

I managed to put up with my bladder spasms until the spring. For many years, I had planned my life and work around the restroom and that was sufficient, but things were getting worse. Beh was emptying me halfway to work, but the times I didn't make it to the restroom at work were increasing. I routinely had to leave meetings—sometimes while I was conferring with people in my office. I found that even while I worked alone in the office, I rushed off sometimes, using the Sierra to speed my way, only to find that I couldn't make it. I fell in the bathroom several times, trying to control muscle spasms and my haste. Something had to change. I called Dr. Rudy's nurse several times, but she didn't give me much encouragement.

Finally, in March, I got an appointment. Dr. Rudy recommended that I start wearing an external catheter. The catheter fit like a condom and connected by tubing to a plastic bag hung on the inside of my leg. Malu and Beh had no trouble learning how to put it on, but it was some time before we came to a combination that worked well.

The 700 ml bag needed to be emptied once during the workday, usually around 11 am. I enlisted Jeanie and Lydia, my grad assistant, to help me with that. The catheter and bag was far from ideal, but solved most of my problem with frequent and urgent urination. It was a big relief on the road, but the plumbing failed quite often causing embarrassment and inconvenience. After about four hours, the bag would fill, and I'd gradually develop a panic trying to find someone to empty it. The university nurse told me that overfilling the bag could cause urinary infection, but my experience was that the system merely failed and leaked all over me. After experimenting with both plastic and latex catheters of various sizes, and the way we mounted the bag and connected the tubes, we figured out how to stop leaks. I still had the problem of trying to find someone to empty the bag. I didn't know so many adults were urine phobic until I asked good friends to help me out and they respectfully declined.

# 52

# Relinquishing the Reins

Again, I was really getting tired of being trapped in the house, so, in early May, before it got too hot, we flew to Tom's for a weekend in Phoenix. We took my car to Intercontinental Airport, parked in the long-term lot, and took a special disabled bus to the terminal. It was a lot easier flying with Beh than alone. She helped with my every need. Tom met us at the airport and had a full agenda planned. On Saturday, he loaded me in his car and we left at noon for the Apache Trail and Roosevelt Dam. The dam was being raised about 50 feet, covering the old dam road with water. That was a shame, because the old road, narrowly perched on the crest of the old dam, was the same one that Teddy Roosevelt had crossed visiting his namesake near the turn of the century, and Tom and I had enjoyed driving across a few years earlier. On Sunday, we headed out early for Jerome, Oak Creek Canyon, and Sedona. At the canyon, Beh experienced her first snow and Indians selling handmade jewelry. From there, we drove to the Grand Canyon. On the way, we stopped in the San Francisco Mountains so that Beh could throw some snowballs. I had a good view of the Canyon from behind the rail, but couldn't enjoy the trails. The light was right, so the views were spectacular. Beh became an eager trail explorer and enjoyed playing with the squirrels that begged along the way. We hoped to see Monument Valley, but ran out of daylight and returned to Phoenix.

The next day, we went to the newly enlarged Lake Pleasant near Tom's house. Then, we drove up a dry riverbed to a hot springs and hotel, reputed to be a hangout for JFK in the 40s when recuperating from his back injury. I couldn't figure out how he traveled 35 miles from Phoenix on bone-jarring roads in those days if his back was so bad. Maybe it was to meet secretly with lady friends. I don't see how they could help his back, either.

Beh was enjoying travel and felt more confident because she could drive. So, we decided to go to the lake over the 4th of July 1994.

We left early on a Saturday morning. I drove until north of Texarkana, where the road started to curve and get hilly. Soon, it hit me how much driving ability I'd lost when the first G-forces made it hard to control the car. I didn't tempt fate, just pulled over, and gratefully gave Beh the wheel. It was cloudy and cool through Texas, but by the time we reached the Arkansas mountains on 71 in mid-afternoon, the heat was overpowering the car's air conditioning and we rolled down the windows. Beh was concentrating on her driving, so she didn't notice the signs warning us of one of the state's most dangerous stretches of road in the mountains just outside of Fort Smith. She just drove on. I couldn't help admire how well she handled the steep slopes and hairpin curves, especially since it was now physically impossible for me to drive them. Hot, tired and windblown, we reached Joplin before dark. We drove to a nearby cafeteria and got take-out food, the easiest way to get in and eat out.

The next day, Beh drove and made it all the way to Eau Claire, arriving before dark. Beh picked up some Chinese at Jimmy Woo's, and we got a motel for the night. My cousin, Duane Hull, came over and showed us pictures of their new house. We didn't get to see it, but we saw how it was built. It was strange not being able to go over there ourselves, but we were too tired and even the thought of getting in and out of the car again made me sick. More and more, I had to experience things vicariously, through pictures or video. Still, I longed to be able to do the real thing.

The next morning, we stopped at my cousin, Janice Becker's, home. It was warm, sunny morning, and there was a big step into the kitchen from the garage, so I stayed in the car and we talked in the front yard. At least I'd seen the inside of her house many times before.

We drove on to Thorp, and had lunch with my Aunt Marian and Uncle Ed. I got out and got into the wheelchair. Ed helped Beh get me into the house. They had spent some time in Saigon in 1958-60. Ed was an Air Force advisor. They showed Beh pictures of Vietnamese friends. After a brief stop at Dan and Pat Hull's, we drove to Uncle Don Marshall's farm. Keith, Don's son, and his daughter Kendra were also there, so we had a good visit in the yard. I hadn't noticed my uncle's hands before, but from wheelchair height you see things differently. He had huge hands, toughened by eighty years of farming, yet they were gentle and caring, having brought many animals to life and nurtured the land.

From there, we went to Withee and had supper with Aunt Phyllis Wenzel. We stayed over until the next day, enjoying lunch with her, but the prospect of staying, forcing her out of her bed again, and struggling in the bathroom was too much, so we decided to head on to the lake before dark.

Rural Wisconsin in summer is so calm and unhurried. We took county roads north and east with hardly a car, in the calm of evening with the scent of new-mown clover in the air. Then things changed.

As we approached the outskirts of Medford, I began to experience a familiar but unsettling feeling—the urge to go to the bathroom. In the country it was easy: find a deserted area, pull off the road, find a tree or bush to hide behind, and go. But I could no longer do that, and the urgency I felt now gave us little time to search for a place to pull off. I saw a restaurant coming up on the right and asked Beh urgently to pull off there. The parking area was gravel, and there were a lot of cars near the entrance of the place. I knew there wasn't enough time to park, get out the wheelchair, transfer, work our way in, find the bathroom, wait if we had to, and then transfer to the toilet.

I told Beh to drive around behind the restaurant. There was a collection of small buildings and old cars, and enough structure to hide us from the busy activity out front. Across the field behind were a few isolated houses, but they were over 100 yards away and we saw no one moving. We carried a small plastic bedpan in the back seat and it was time to use it. Beh came around to the passenger side and brought the bedpan. I put my feet down, stood up in the door opening, and she helped me lower my pants. Somehow, she got the pan under me and I went immediately. With tissue paper and water we carried, she was able to clean the pan and me. With great relief, we drove into Medford. What we did was drastic, difficult, and offensive to anyone who may have seen us, but the alternative would have been far more disagreeable, and embarrassing once we got to the lake.

For those out there who say, "Hold it, you're an adult." "I've had that happen to me and I...." "You need to wear a diaper." or "You shouldn't go out if that's going to happen." I say that I'd thought of and tried all that. Unless you have nerve damage that affects your ability to voluntarily control bowel and bladder function, and the inability to walk, it's impossible to imagine the countless times I'd tried with all my conscious ability to act "normal" when I was taking drastic action to prevent an embarrassing accident. In earlier years, the tension and heavy, rich meals of taking a date to dinner often initiated episodes like the one I just described. At best, I excused myself and ran off to the bathroom. At worst, I excused myself and went home to clean up. Since these things happened infrequently, I tried not to let them interfere with normal living. For the most part they didn't. Most people didn't know I had a problem. Those close to me knew it was annoying, but that I managed it well.

We spent three days at the lake. Tom had his kids there, teaching them how to water ski. Tim came by with his kids and we enjoyed a great home fireworks show. Judy and Paul joined us for the Fourth. The boat rides we took were the most enjoyable. I had to be lifted into the boat and Beh had to hold onto me in the bow to keep me from sliding off the smooth fiberglass seat, but the wind and sun, trees and water, were worth the effort.

Beh enjoyed riding the moped until she lost her grip in soft sand with Tim on the back, fell, and cracked her front tooth cap. In spite of the danger, I sat there by the garage in my wheelchair wishing it were I riding down the road. From experience, I could still vividly imagine the feeling she had when the moped at speed hit the sand, rapidly slowing the front wheel as the rest of the bike and Tim's weight continued forward, twisting the wheel and wrenching the handlebars from her hands, pitching her and the bike to the ground. I can imagine the impact of her face hitting the hard gravel and sand, and her stunned dismay for it having happened.

A neighbor, Willie Nussburger, had won $1,000,000 in the Wisconsin lottery, but still was his same old self, eager to give us his annual complimentary ride around the lake in his pontoon boat. On the boat, sitting on the wheelchair, I had another bowel accident. I had Dad rush me off the boat, and Beh pushed me back to the cottage to clean up. We tried to be discreet, but everyone knew what had happened.

We drove south and had an outdoor lunch with my great aunt Nona Replogle and her son Albert, and his wife, Jackie, at the old homestead that Carl built in Waupaca. The rich food again got to me. We struggled to get into the house and to the old bathroom, only to find that I couldn't go. When we got back outside, the urge came again. This time there was no time to make it up the stairs back into the house. We got a pail and I went there in the garage while the others waited outside. The pain I felt this time was extreme, and I agonized for a half hour until it was over. The episode left me exhausted and ruined our lunch. At least everyone understood. But, I began to doubt if I could travel again and if we could get home without further trouble.

Then we drove over to Neenah, just in time to give my Aunt Eleanor Hull a ride home from her work at Burger King. After a brief visit in the garage out of the sun and wind, where I again stayed in the car, we drove for Tim's for the night. After surveying the new deck and hot tub, Beh, Mike, and Jenny got to take a ride in the TR 6 while I watched from the front porch. Again, I could imagine driving, shifting up through the gears, the wind brushing the back of my head, the tightness of the wheel in my hand, as I carved out the turns, feeling every change in the texture of the road. There wasn't room for me to ride, but I went along in my mind. The reins still in my hands.

We left Tim's for Chicago and arrived at noon. We had some slow traffic going in and it was very hot. You could cook your lunch on the car hood, watching the tall buildings crawl by. Heading out on the Skyway we stopped at a McDonald's at a toll station and ate in the car. Stopping like this was getting to be a habit. With the bucket, I didn't have to go in to pee, and the effort to go in and relax was greater than staying in the car and relaxing. Still, it was uncomfortable and sometimes hot to stay in the car. I insisted that Beh open both doors to let the breeze flow through. Sometimes, I'd swing my legs out to the side. The big problem was the stiffness and spasms my legs would endure during long rides. Shifting foot position usually helped, but was difficult to do while moving on the road.

Then, we headed out onto the Indiana Tollway into a vicious storm. It was Beh's first time driving in blinding rain and wind, and we had to pull off the road several times because we couldn't see. At times, it was hard to see the edge of the road as eighteen-wheelers roared by at speeds that belied the conditions. I worried that Beh would slow or stop at the wrong time, and one of these behemoths would overrun us. Stopped by the roadside idling, I asked Beh how much gas we had left. We were both surprised to find we had none. Service plazas can be 30 miles apart on the tollway, so I was worried. Fortunately, we saw a sign "1 mile" to the next plaza shortly after getting underway again. When we got to the plaza it seemed as though the World had arrived just ahead of us. Most of the cars and trucks fighting the rain on the tollway had opted to stop there rather than continue on. We had a hard time getting through traffic to the pumps. Back out on the road, we came upon an eighteen wheeler on its side in the median and several cars off in the muddy ditches. Beh had passed her first bad weather driving test, and I was proud of her.

When we got to Roger's, it had stopped raining. After he pushed me around his big block in my wheelchair, Sue arrived from work and we took a ride on the St. Joseph River in their pontoon boat. The evening was peaceful and cool, a fitting end to a hot and violent day. Ducks and geese lined the banks; reclaiming waterways the early settlers' guns had forced them to leave.

The next morning, we headed for New Albany in the southern tip of Indiana. I drove until we got to Indianapolis. By that time, I was so tired and tense that I could drive no further. It was good that Beh could take over. We stopped to see old friends, Behram and Gool Randelia, and their three sons. Everyone was at home, so I got to talk to them. The road in was narrow and crowned and it bothered Beh. Although I had many times before, I couldn't go upstairs for the night, so after dinner, Behram escorted us to a local motel for the night.

From there, we drove to Nashville, Memphis, Little Rock, and home. Except for a couple of close scrapes with eighteen-wheelers and the storm, it was a safe, smooth trip. The Monte didn't use any oil or water, Beh emerged a seasoned driver as well as capable of wheeling me in and out of motels and meeting my changing needs.

Maria came back to work for me mornings the summer of 1994. Then, she started an assistantship at the UT-Houston Medical Center in the fall, but still planned to help me out with my yard. Dana lost his opportunity to go to medical school but entered dental school at UT-San Antonio in the fall of 1994.

Finding it too much to take care of, Mom and Dad sold the lake home in Phillips in October 1994. I tried to rally support from my brothers to buy it, but Mom and Dad wouldn't hear of it. Tim and Tom joined me in an interest in keeping the place, but none of us were financially able at the time. Roger wasn't interested, and we knew Judy was in no position to help out. So, the family gathering place was lost. The fact that I found it so difficult to get there didn't eliminate my need to hang onto that little piece of Wisconsin paradise—cold weather, mosquitoes, and all. While they were showing it, a freak rainstorm in September caused a flood that reached the house and put water knee deep in the boathouse. After they sold the place and headed south, in late October, a storm came through and brought down all of the big trees around the cottage. A large Aspen in front of the cottage that had survived the downburst of 1977, fell on the roof and damaged it.

Mom and Dad bought a new mobile home in Marshfield and planned to set it up next to my Aunt Phyllis in Withee the next spring.

# 53

# Facing Reality

My bowels had become so unpredictable that I called Dr. Clearman when I returned from vacation. She started me on a bowel program. I started using a suppository every other night before going to bed. That reduced the constipation that caused my accidents. Still, I occasionally had accidents if I ate the wrong food or had a stomach virus or flu. I couldn't come up with a system that left me entirely without worry, especially on trips. But things became a lot better than they were. I never tried diapers, but thought about using them every time I was in trouble.

In August 1994, I started wearing medical support hose to prevent my legs and feet from swelling during the day. I had first noticed swelling while on vacation at the lake in 1991. At that time, I blamed the swelling on deer flies that stung my ankles with abandon because I couldn't feel them tearing hunks of flesh from me. Actually, the swelling was caused by my lethargy after my long trip, sitting around all day in fixed chairs playing games, watching the lake, and watching TV. As long as I used the office chairs all day and pushed myself around, and got up occasionally, my legs wouldn't collect blood and fluid, and swell up. But when I stopped using the office chairs and just sat still, swelling was inevitable.

The hose were quite comfortable, kept my feet warm, and helped limit the pain I experienced at night as the swelling subsided while my feet were up. Roger sent me a book from Simplicity with many ideas for wheelchair clothing, but we never used it. I expected that we would be experimenting with special clothing that Beh would sew. That never happened.

Texas Southern university was still experiencing good enrollment, but the campus had been depressed since reorganization and downsizing had made it difficult to function at an acceptable level. Joann Horton had lost the support of the faculty with her appointments of poorly-qualified people to administrative posts and by demoting some key people who had served well. Her brashness and arrogance raised eyebrows among the most jaded of us.

We acquired some bond money to do renovation, but lacked a clear master plan to guide us. I continued to work under these trying conditions and those in the lead left me alone, but I kept looking over my shoulder to see if the axe man was after me. The word was that I was invaluable because of all I knew. I didn't buy it. The decisions made in the years since downsizing began in 1990 haunted us and flew in the face of reason.

The result of all this was that a lot of initiatives were slowed or stopped in layers of approval and indecision. The $3.5 million LoanSTAR Program had been delayed and delayed, lost, and then renewed again while we wasted time deciding how to do it. Performance contracting was favored. This approach meant we would hire some outside firm to install all the energy-saving measures, put in people to maintain them for ten years, and have them guarantee some positive cash flow based on the savings created by the measures. I recommended that we simply hire engineers to design the projects, and then contract to have them installed, but I was outvoted. There just wasn't enough money in the savings to pay for the additional repairs and improvements some people wanted, and cover the outside company's profit, and maintenance. The problem was that when we'd saved in the past, the State rewarded us by giving us less money in our utility budget. The favored approach would keep our overall costs high and insure that our budget money wouldn't be lost—great logic. The performance contractor would take our savings as profit, and the taxpayers would pay the bill.

I moved eleven of our computers to ethernet, speeding data transfer. We bought some software that resided in our file server and linked the ethernet network to the LocalTalk network. I got a few very fast accelerators for our SEs based on one slower one that worked well. When the new accelerators started causing serious crashing problems, I called the company and found that it had gone out of business. I heard that when they knew they were going out of business, they substituted inferior chips in their products. I never had that happen before, and it caused a lot of grief. I also bought accelerators and memory upgrades for our Mac IIs. When I got them, I found out that I couldn't get an adapter to fit them to the IIs. I had to return those items but still hoped to upgrade the computers. It was especially frustrating because I had to rely on students and untrained staff to accomplish the upgrades. If I could have done them myself, I could have salvaged some of the accelerators. The rate of computer speed changes had increased to the point that upgrading old computers had become marginal when compared with buying newer, lower cost, faster ones.

My Voice Navigator started to cause my computer to crash too. I ended up returning it to the company that sold it to us. We had bought some AV (audio-visual) PowerMacs with built-in microphones and stereo speakers. These computers could be voice-activated with software. They also were fully MS/DOS and Windows compatible with software, making them very versatile. The bad news was that I didn't take one of these computers and the people that got them were not interested in voice operation. It took two years to get them to even listen to CDs in the background while they worked. Voice activation would have to wait.

I could now send the State's facilities inventory direct from my database to Austin. My link to the Internet wasn't established yet, but my system made the inventory easy to keep and update. I created some detailed reports for our work order system that made it easy to evaluate our maintenance process in a number of ways. I moved our record of utilities from spreadsheets to a database that insured more accurate input. I also developed systems for supplies inventory to help with maintaining inventory records and a construction record to keep track of construction contracts and payments.

I also prepared color transparencies for Josh Hill's management course. He wanted me to teach a class, but it was at night and was a logistical problem to pull off without a lot of help.

A sophomore student on work study, Nakia Lewis, learned to fix our computers and did quite well. After a summer without student help, he returned in the fall of 1994. My graduate assistant, Lydia Valentine, got her MBA in the spring and returned to Belize. Finally, in mid-October 1994, Cynthia Breedlove, an MBA candidate with chemistry and chemical engineering degrees, and seven years working with Corning Glass in New York, started as my new assistant. All summer, I had to go to the nursing station to get my urine bag emptied, but with Cynthia and Nakia in place, they took turns helping me in my office.

I used my Lark Sierra every day that I drove. I started using METROLift in September 1994, and, after some brief experimentation using my portable chair, I started taking my electric wheelchair to work on those days rather than ride the Sierra. METROLift cost a dollar for each one-way trip, but that was one of its few advantages. Van arrivals varied from 45 minutes early to an hour late. I had to rush breakfast and skip shaving to head for work early only to find myself sitting out in the cold night in the parking lot at 6:30 pm waiting for my ride home. Scheduling hours were limited and I could only schedule the day before. Phone lines were often tied up, requiring frequent callbacks to reach the schedulers. Sometimes, trips I wanted to schedule were not available. Although attendants could ride free, I couldn't take Beh with me half way to work and pick her up on the way back. My time to or from work ranged from 30 minutes on the freeway HOV (high occupancy vehicle) lane when I was the only rider to over two hours when we picked up and delivered two other wheelchair riders. I averaged over three hours on the road every day I rode METROLift.

The drivers were very helpful and most were friendly. Although I sometimes got the same drivers or riders, it was mostly different people every day. I transferred to a side-mounted seat when I could. The rides were bumpy and long, putting a lot of strain on my neck and torso as I stretched to see where we were going. The heated coach was nice when we were not loading or unloading in the wind. The air conditioning could be brutal when it was set too cold by the driver.

In October 1994, I took the morning off and drove Malu and Jazz out to Brazos Bend State Park. It was closed because of contaminated water caused by a flood a month earlier. I was upset because it had been so long since I'd been there. I asked to use the parking and service area near the entrance and they said it was okay. We parked under a tree and let Jazz run. A Park Ranger came by and told me that he'd let me in anyway to test their new ADA trail. It turned out to be the trail that I often took on my many visits in the past. They gave us a rope in lieu of a leash for my "gater food." Jazz enjoyed running alongside and getting tangled in the chair.

The new trail was wide, well paved, and marked with Braille. It cut across a small lake with a new bridge to a place I used to wait for deer to follow the shore in the waning light of day. From there it ascended the bank along the old trail around the lake to a place I twice encountered a buck with a huge rack at close range. Beyond had been an open area of wildness where once I'd heard the screams of a bobcat were now tamed with a gleaming white high tech-looking observatory. It was strange to think that hundreds of city star, comet, and eclipse gazers crowded to this spot some nights not knowing that I had considered it my secret hideaway to watch wildlife in solitude.

When we returned to the parking area, we tied Jazz outside the visitor's center. Inside, we found loose on the floor (in a pan) 20 or so of his favorite prey—lizards! Actually, baby alligators from an abandoned nest. If we'd let Jazz in it would have been hard to keep him away from them. There would have been mayhem to deal with. In October 1994, I negotiated with METROLift to get a subscription. I could only get one if I left for work late, after 8 am, and used the service three days a week. With that, I started driving to work only two days a week, letting METROLift take me the other three. To avoid the hassle, I went on a subscription schedule for Monday, Wednesday, and Friday.

The Monte still ran great and had become a way for Beh and I to get our shopping done. Beh got used to putting gas in the guzzler and I began to rely on her to do it. The gas gauge started acting up. Several trips to the shop failed to fix it. One evening, I asked Beh to get gas and she did. She didn't tell me that she paid cash and only had $5. The next day, we followed our usual routine. Coming home about a quarter to six, I got off the freeway at the West Loop, and started down Bissonett toward where Beh worked. The car faltered, and then quit, as I reached the stop light at First Street in Bellaire. I suspected that I was out of gas. I was in the left lane, so I opened my door part way and swung my feet out. From there, I waved the traffic that backed up behind past me into the left turn lane. There was a steady stream of rush hour cars. Some stopped and asked if I needed help. I told all of them that I couldn't walk and asked them to call AAA, my towing service. After about fifteen minutes, a tow truck pulled up behind me. Apparently, he didn't know how to get me into his cab, so he called for another tow truck. After another fifteen minutes, the other truck came and the first one left. This time, there were three guys. A Bellaire cop came along and asked them to get my car off Bissonett. The guys hand pushed my car to the right to a quiet spot on First Street.

By now, I knew that Beh would be concerned or panicked because I never was this late. I told the cop about the situation and he agreed to go and get Beh. The three tow truck guys appeared to be waiting for help. There was no way five of us could fit in the cab of that tow truck. I was willing to stay in the car with Beh and ride up on the flat bed, but that was probably against safety regulations. I again suggested that they try getting some gasoline. They left to get some.

The policeman and Beh arrived. She said that she knew I hadn't been in an accident and hurt because when she saw the cop come in the shop she knew I had told him how to find her. I thanked him for his help, he left, and we waited. Finally, the guys came back with some gas and got the car started without much trouble. We filled up at a nearby station and headed home. Beh always made sure there was enough gas in the car after that.

Finally, driving home for the Holidays on December 22, I decided to call it quits. Even with power steering, turning the wheel had become too difficult. Moving my foot from the gas to the brake was just too slow. On January 2, I started taking METROLift five days a week. The transition was relatively smooth. My struggle to drive was over. My struggle to get where I wanted, when I wanted, had begun. My car was Beh's now. She liked it and treated it well.

Jazz enjoying Quintana Beach near Freeport, Texas

# 54

# Keeping Healthy

I didn't get a flu shot in 1994 and got the flu twice. Beh had to tend me continuously during the first bout because it is so hard for me to keep warm and get enough fluids. She held a cup to my mouth often, and I drank all I could. The hard part was sleeping and keeping warm when I had to urinate every ten minutes during the peak of fever. We used the bucket and she would have to remove the heavy covers only to get a teaspoon of urine. I would get cold immediately. Beh would then tuck me in and try to curl up to sleep on the floor. Ten minutes later, I'd be warm, but begging her to get up and tend to me again. We went through that routine many times in two nights and it left us both exhausted. Fortunately, the second flu was acute and lasted only a few hours. I made sure I got a flu shot after that.

I had an EMG in February 1994, and an IVP in August that still showed no kidney damage. But I was told that eventually, probably within a year, I would have to have an urostomy to route urine from my bladder out through my abdominal wall. This surgery would eliminate backup and possible kidney failure, but would require wearing a permanent bag. Because my own intestine would used for the tube, I was told recovery would take about six weeks. I was not looking forward to the cost and agony of that.

I still could transfer from my bed to my electric wheelchair and from there to my wheeled office chair. But it was getting so hard to scoot around in the office chair that I gave that up in August 1994. I knew that once I started using the electric chair, I'd never get out of it again. I missed the comfort and maneuverability of my office chairs. I could still get into the shower and take one by myself but I waited a year for a floor-mounted lift that would swing me to the toilet and shower.

Three times in the morning, I fell going back to bed. I just lay on the carpeted floor until Beh came to rescue me. One time, I lay half under the bed with my legs sticking out. When Beh came in, she screamed when she saw my legs. I assured her that I was okay, just lying there until she came to get me up. I worried about that happening at night or when it was very cold, but I was still able to scoot along on my back to reach a comforter we kept in the closet. Otherwise, I was very careful about transferring to avoid falling. I never fell in the tub. The thought of me lying there bleeding from a bad fall, or in excruciating pain with my legs contorted under me, or with the water running and me unable to reach to turn it off, crossed my mind often all those times I showered alone. But it never happened.

Roger and I helping Grandma Orpha Hull with her chickens.
That fiberboard chicken coop was our first high jumping off point.

# 55

## The Chasm of Time and Distance

Sometime in 1994, I realized that I had finally lost touch. Everyone was an easy phone call away, but few of us would take the time to call anymore. After all those years of building bridges and friendships, I could no longer leap continents and retie knots that had unraveled with age. There was a lot of talk of the Internet, the super highway of communication, and I planned to get on it when I had a good vehicle. Still, it wasn't the same as being there and doing things with those you wanted to be with. My electric chair got me around, but the experience was still too confining, and I was bursting to travel the less trod path again. When I struggled with the kitchen, the yard, and the day-to-day, I crawled into myself and pulled in the walls. But once in a while, I pulled myself up and did something extraordinary. No matter how bad my routine got, I could still change it. In the chair, that changed.

My helpers took a lot of the worry away, but they defined my life in numbing routine. It was easier to do for rather than do with. There was something inherently difficult in helping someone do for him or herself. It was easier to do it for them. Since people felt obligated to do for you—open doors, get food, and so on, there was a lot less opportunity to do with—meet, travel, play, and so on. My friends and family seemed obligated to see me briefly on rare occasions. But they didn't seem to want to do things with me anymore.

I still did things with people at the office, but the perception of what I did there also changed dramatically. No one offered to make sure that I got to key social events, and if I did, few people socialized with me. I was no longer invited to power meetings or put in charge of major initiatives. It wasn't lonely when helpers were there, busily working on the daily routine, but it was lonely "out there" in public with most people trying to avoid the pain of being with me.

METROLift was an exception. Once I broke through the protective shell some disabled people live in for their own sanity, we would talk freely, establish kinship over remedies and complaints and form a community.

I logged many hours and miles in METROlift vans from 1995 to 1998.

# 56

# A New Way to Bathe

Finally, it came time to quit trying to get into the tub every morning to shower. After a long struggle with insurance to get the right lift, the one my dad and I had envisioned two years earlier when he took my other lift and balanced it on the floor to check clearances, it finally came to pass. A second Hoyer lift was delivered in February 1995. Of course, the company that sold it wouldn't install it. Originally, I wanted to drill a hole the same size as the brass mounting socket, about 3.25 inches in diameter into the concrete floor, and then force or epoxy the socket into the hole. But the instructions called for a larger hole with the socket mounted in poured concrete. I got a company to come in and drill a 6-inch in diameter hole in the corner by the tub. The drilling took an hour and left a neat hole about eighteen inches deep that promptly filled with water. After trying several other approaches to installing the lift, Dana came through and helped me out in April, when he was on spring break from his second year of dental school at UT-San Antonio. Dana mixed concrete and placed the brass socket precisely where the lift could swing 180° without hitting anything. He was upset because the center pole wasn't vertical, but leaned toward the toilet a bit. Fortunately, the post was positioned perfectly for all the clearances needed. Dana should have been proud.

As soon the concrete hardened, we began using the lift. I could still stand to transfer to the toilet. Once there, Beh would "hook me up" by surrounding me with a mesh sling that she would attach by loops to four corners of a tubular steel cradle that could swivel 360° at the end of a boom.

Once attached, she'd lift me by pumping a hydraulic jack until I was dangling like a fetal-positioned bird in a nest above the toilet. Pushing on the boom, Beh was able to spin me around and push me into the shower enclosure. With a flexible showerhead my father had installed, she could then give me a complete shower with little difficulty. The device could lower me into the tub if necessary, but we never did. I could no longer stand the pain my spastic legs would give me if I tried to sit in the bottom of the hard tub. Even the thought of it is painful as I imagine my legs thrashing against the hard sides and end. Not that being thrust up in the sling was comfortable, with the stitched edges cutting into my legs just above and behind the knee, and my knees so close to my chin that it was hard to move my arms, that either hang out with the stitching cutting into my upper arms, or jammed up against my chest. Sometimes, the sling would not be not positioned right, and my back, normally pushed hard against the fabric, would slide inexorably toward the hole that was the bottom. My legs, hooked by my knees, would not slide, so I would eventually fall all the way through and hit the back of my head on whatever was below. When that happened, Beh would quickly lower me to whatever was safe, toilet or wheelchair, under me and reposition the sling so that friction and gravity would hold me in place again.

Although the space was very tight and we had trouble with the mast binding in the socket, it was a relief not to have to worry about getting in and out of the shower and standing to take one.

Malu left in November 1994, when she took a job working all week at a nursing home. Beh took over the morning tasks Malu had done, and we did quite well. But I worried about her getting sick. We needed someone to help Beh out and back her up. After Malu left, I tried several times to hire someone who would only work weekday evenings. Four promising helpers fell by the wayside for one reason or another without ever starting work. In February 1995, I placed the ad one more time.

Jean Ouellette lived near Beh with her husband, Bruce. She wasn't working any other job and didn't mind the short hours. Bruce was soon helping with my lawn, too. From the start, Jean was very helpful and conscientious. Two weeks after Jean started working, I met Denise Crandon for the second time on METROLift. Denise was an active young woman with muscular dystrophy. When she complained that she couldn't get anyone to help her in the evening after work, I suggested that maybe Jean could help. I got Denise's phone number, and soon Jean was helping both of us, and she also started helping an elderly couple during the day.

In late January 1995, Beh took some time off and she drove me to McAllen. I could still work my way up the three steps to the entrance of my parents' mobile home, but I didn't think I could come back again. Inside it was just too confining. I was forced to sit in my portable wheelchair and navigating the bathroom was very difficult. Beh was there to help me every step of the way, and Dad helped too, but I could see the day when even together, we couldn't do it. We went to a wildlife refuge. Dad pushed me on a trail that was constructed to be accessible. After a quiet stay, we returned.

Tom surprised us in February, stopping on his way back to Phoenix after a trip to see Mom and Dad. I managed to get tickets to see Mary Chapin Carpenter and the Mavericks at the Houston Rodeo. Tom enjoyed pushing me through the crowds, the rodeo events, and people watching. The Astrodome was well equipped for wheelchairs, but I got very tired staying in one place so long. My portable chair was convenient, but sitting in it any length of time was becoming a problem. No matter how I adjusted my weight, the pain in my legs wouldn't go away. Only transferring to my electric chair, an upright, padded chair, or a bed, relieved the pain. I tried not to complain about it though, that was the only way I could get out without METROLift.

Mom and Dad came through in April, on their way north. But heading north to follow them was not on my mind. I was worried about the status of my Atlanta house. With the Olympics coming to Atlanta, and my need to improve my financial situation, I thought that I might sell it. I talked Beh into taking me there for Easter.

Beh enjoyed the first day's drive, especially the long bridge over the bayous in Louisiana. Our experience with travel was to take it easy, so we stopped early in Meridian, MS.

The dogwoods were past their prime but we started seeing them in the mountains near Birmingham. We got to Atlanta early Friday afternoon. Beh wanted to go directly to a motel, but I persuaded her to drive by the house first. The congested hilly roads were difficult for her, but we got to the house okay. We took the back road over to a motel I remembered. First, we encountered a bridge that was closed for repairs, and we had to detour. Then, I had her turn the wrong way, and as we worked our way back, she drove through a stop sign in front of a big truck. Fortunately, the truck driver was alert and stopped, but Beh was shaken, almost unable to drive any further. When we got to the motel, the clerk told us they hadn't cleaned the rooms yet. We crossed to the other side of the freeway and found a room. Beh got our things and me in the room and collapsed on the bed. I called friends and found no one home except Duane Hunter. He and his wife were planning to head for their son's home for the weekend, but he decided to delay their trip to spend some time with me. I told him that Beh was exhausted. He said, "Don't worry, I'll come and get you."

Duane picked us up about 4 pm. First, he took us quickly across town to their home near Stone Mountain. It was a French Provincial style with a circular drive in front, presenting a low, two-story appearance. The huge lot fell away two levels to patios, gardens and a large pool. A verandah stretched across the main floor from the formal dining room to the huge master bedroom. Several large azaleas were still in bloom in the back of the house.

Five minutes from his house, Duane took us for a quick trip into Stone Mountain State Park. The tram to the top closed at 5 pm, or I may have tested its disabled access. Instead, I waited in the car while Beh got pictures of the carving of the Confederacy on the mountain. Duane took a route cross-town through beautiful neighborhoods to his office. I asked Beh to take a lot of pictures of the beautiful flowers and sights, but she was so tired she mostly slept while we talked and drove.

The next morning, we met Joyce McGuork, my longtime realtor-property manager, at the house early. I couldn't go inside, so sat in the car and talked to my tenant while Beh and Joyce explored inside. The outside had weathered well and looked good. While I had to replace a lot of cedar siding to keep ahead of birds, squirrels, bees, and rot, it was nice not to have to worry about painting it or maintaining a lawn. I had thought about selling the house or trying to rent it out during the Olympics, but that didn't work out. As beautiful and secluded as the place was, the neighborhood had become less desirable and property values were low.

We said goodbye to my tenet and Joyce and drove south on I-85. By early afternoon we stopped at Calloway Gardens. Just when I thought we were too late to see any spring color, we came around a bend near the road out and saw a brilliant display of azaleas across a small lake. It was the very last of the spectacular colors that usually fill the whole area, and we still got to see it. When we arrived at our motel in Baton Rouge, Beh marveled at the sweet flower growing on the fence—wild honeysuckle. That's what I always enjoyed about traveling, the little surprises along the way. Later, she told me about a man who followed her back to the room when she got us ice at that motel. Fortunately, there were no surprises of that kind.

After that, I rarely left the house except to go to work. Beh's job was just too demanding and her schedule too busy to go anywhere. I missed seeing spring wildflowers. I missed going to the beach. I missed going to the park. I especially missed going to Wisconsin.

Finally I engineered a way out—I bought tickets to Miss Saigon. One night in early August, Beh, her brother Quoc, and a friend, Thu, both polio survivors, and I took my car downtown to Jones Hall for a big night out. The disabled seats were very good, center stage and close in. The play, known for its special effects, was spectacular, especially the helicopter that descends to take the last troops out of the Embassy compound. Beh asked me if it was real. I found the story though, a bit weak, maybe all the singing and dancing and exotic stage sets took away from the story.

Jean told me that Denise wanted to take a trip. Denise worked as an office assistant for a firm specializing in assisting the disabled get mobility. She had a year-old Ford Econoline van with a lowered floor equipped with a lift and special controls so she could drive it from her wheelchair. Her parents also had a van that they used to carry her and her sister in their chairs. Denise and Jean planned to take a trip in Texas. When I heard about their plans, I offered to help pay expenses if Beh and I could tag along. I guess it was too much when I suggested that we go to Yellowstone. When Denise tried to get vacation and Beh tried to get off work, both failed. I then suggested a shorter trip in Texas—Corpus Christi, San Antonio, and Austin—a day in each. That too, fell through. I thought that having help would give me more freedom. Instead, it brought in a lot of expectations and insecurities from others that I was unprepared to deal with. So many times in the past when others couldn't go, I just went alone. Now, I couldn't go at all.

Finally, Jean and Denise offered to take us to the Sam Houston Race Park in late August. We went on a hot Sunday. I was impressed with Denise's van. She confessed that it was the farthest she had driven with it. Denise handled the van well. It had a lift that swung around so that you entered and exited alongside the van, a very stable and convenient way that took very little space. We enjoyed losing money and watching the horses from the air-conditioned stands (mostly quarter horses in that heat). After that, we went to Pappasito's, a Mexican restaurant.

One Sunday in early October, I suggested that we have a picnic at Brazos Bend State Park. We took Jazz. At first, he refused to take a leash, so we took him without one. We stopped at a picnic spot, and Denise and I managed to drive our electric chairs to a fishing dock. I took a chance on steep dirt path to the dock, and Denise followed. The dock came complete with an alligator in the water below who ate any fish anyone caught and would throw to him. While we ate lunch, Jazz ran free. Then park rangers came by on bikes, ordering us to leash him. We got him in the van, but he refused to be tied, snapping at anyone who tried to approach him. Finally, while we drove over to the visitor center, Jean snuck up on him and hooked him while she petted him in her lap. He was docile after that.

We tied Jazz outside while we went into the visitor center. There were no baby alligators this time. When we came out, we tried to tie Jazz to my chair and he immediately got tangled, but he didn't get excited when several people worked to free him. We tried out the new disabled trail. It was smooth and new, so I coursed ahead, waiting every so often to let the others catch up. At the observatory, I easily climbed the long ramp to the top. On the way down, two deer came through the opening below. I called out, but the others couldn't see them.

We got back to the trail that skirted the little lake. As I passed the spot where I'd often encountered an armadillo years before, I wondered if paving the trail and building the observatory had altered the charm of this place. I'm sure all the traffic did. Now there was a new wooden dock leading out into the lake. The only problem was a 4-inch gap between the pavement and the first board of the dock. I bridged it by backing onto the dock with my big rear wheels. I turned 180° and headed out to the middle of the lake on the dock. There was little water, just a few feet surrounded by marsh grass. Still, it was a view I hadn't seen before, with or without the chair. It was hot, and Denise couldn't make it onto the dock, so I returned. On the small dam that created the lake, a few ducks were perched in a willow tree overhanging the water. A great blue heron stood nearby. It seemed strange to see web-footed ducks in trees. Across the dam, the trail led back to the entrance. Before we got there, another new wood bridge appeared. Only this time the gap between pavement and bridge was over a foot. I was getting hot and Jean had been struggling to keep up with us. I sized up the situation, and decided to leave the path and cross a shallow ditch some fifty feet to the road. It was rough, but the grass was short, and the ground was dry and hard, so I made headway. Denise followed. Both Beh and Jean said that they didn't want to go back to the park. In that kind of weather, most of the miles of trails were accessible—if I could only get someone to go with me.

# 57

## More Changes at Work

Texas Southern University still had good enrollment, but the depression of continual reorganization and downsizing made it difficult to function at an acceptable level. We lost another 14 jobs September 1st, 1995, and the campus grounds and buildings were beginning to show the effects of neglect. Joann Horton vowed to stay until her contract was up in August 1996, but she resigned October 1, 1995 instead, joined by two Board members who had supported her. James Douglas, longtime law school dean, was made interim president. The resignation of our assistant vice president caused another organizational shift that pushed me one more notch down in the organizational ladder. One plan had them "outsourcing" what I did by fall, 1996.

My new superiors brought me back into decision-making more and seemed to be seeing the need to use what I knew. After a poorly-executed attempt at performance contracting our energy conservation effort, the $3.5 million LoanSTAR Program had been canceled pending a new audit. I was put on a new committee working with the U of Houston on a joint performance contract that would span ten years and could involve as much as $20 million in retrofits. That too, fell through when the State Energy Conservation Office rejected performance contracting with LoanSTAR money and the local electrical utility was suspected of conflict of interest when they sought to be the performance contractor. In the meantime, we were still losing a lot of money waiting on lighting modifications we could have had done five years earlier.

The moves and changes seemed bent on destroying our computer network, but I had managed to keep everyone working with the help of our telephone technicians. We got a few more PowerMacs, and I managed to get a 6150 WorkGroup Server. Then I found that my interconnecting software would have to be upgraded to continue joint operation of Ethernet/LocalTalk, so I had to keep the old SE 30 server working until I could buy the upgraded software. My plans to fix and upgrade the old SEs and put them in the shop areas didn't materialize either because we couldn't seem to get the old computers working well after installing the bad accelerators.

I got an upgrade of Helix Express that ran native on the PowerMacs and installed it without a hitch. I set up a response database for financial aid questions, but they never used it. I extended our leave database to accommodate time card records and changed it to use a new form. Auditors had mandated that maintenance use the system I developed to record the cost of maintenance work done.

I prepared color transparencies for Josh Hill's management course in the fall. He got me to teach a class, but it was at night and logistically difficult. I had to reschedule METROLift to pick me up at 8 pm, ride my wheelchair over to the Technology building, and get someone to get me some food to go with my evening pill. Though tiring, the first class went well, so he invited me to do it again in the spring. This time it rained, so I had the custodians take my chair over to the building in a truck while Jeanie took me by car. I was coming down with the flu, so the class that night was long and difficult. I got so hot and my throat got so dry I could barely speak. Sipping a cold drink as I spoke helped me finish the two-hour ordeal. The students, interested in what I had to show them, were very patient with me. Finally, I made it. In the fall of 1996, I prepared two chapters for Hill's Ergonomics class and taught one. This time it was hot and I was dry, but it went well. I enjoyed teaching again, but it took so long to do the preparations that I knew that it would be very hard, perhaps impossible, to teach full time again. The idea of correcting eighty or ninety assignments a day was daunting, and preparing exams and correcting them was equally so. Still, I would probably take it on if given the chance.

Nakia Lewis continued working on computers for me the 1995-96 academic year and got very good at drafting requisitions. Cynthia Breedlove had a summer internship at Los Alamos in the summer of 1995, and was back working with me until she got her MBA.

I retired my Lark scooters and rearranged my office slightly to accommodate my wheelchair. The wheelchair was easier to get around with, so it was somewhat easier to get to meetings. I rode METROLift every workday. I missed the flexibility of taking my car, but I learned to relax and let the driver's schedule determine when I got to work or home. I arrived at work as late as 11 am and as early as 8:30 am. One summer morning I was the first of seven to get on and the last to get off.

My *"METROLift ride from Hell"* occurred in January 1995, before I hired Jean and Beh was working alone and going to school. Beh made me spaghetti and waited until 7:15 pm before heading for her 7:30 community college class. It was a misty, rainy night. My driver picked me up after 6 pm because traffic was bad. We had to go to the north side of town to pick up Dorothy, a lady with MS I came to know quite well. We got caught by a train and arrived at the elementary school where Dorothy volunteered very late. To make up time, our driver asked us if we minded if she picked up her next rider on the east side of downtown before taking us home. We said, "Okay."

She turned north leaving the school, and it was several minutes until we learned she was going the wrong way. After that, she took a city street past downtown to the east side rather than the much faster freeway. Then she got lost. After driving around railroad arms that were stuck down and asking dispatch for directions several times, we arrived at an east side Multipurpose center for our next pickup. Dorothy had to be let off to go the bathroom. At that point, I suggested that we get on the freeway and head straight home. She did. I arrived home at 8:50 after dropping off Dorothy to find that Jazz had used my chair to leap to my desk and sample my spaghetti. He apparently didn't like it as well as other snacks he often got this way. The meal was slightly disturbed and stone cold. I was so tired and hungry I pulled up and ate it anyway.

The regular drivers got to know me well and most worked with me. I'd transfer to a side seat, but it was getting to be very difficult. Metro got new vans starting in November 1995. These new vans were designed to be ADA compliant, but lost some advantages in the end. They were six inches higher, making them better in high water, but more prone to tipping over and lowered visibility for the passengers. The raised tie-down tracks were gone, but the new tie-downs were harder to secure. The seats were plusher and softer, but they tore more easily and the seat belts jammed easily. The ride was stiffer, so stiff that I wondered if the designers knew anything of pressure fractures and other bone and nerve problems some of us had.

Eventually, I tried using a city bus to go to and from the University of Houston and the Medical Center. It went well and would as long as the weather was good. From home, I could take 65 on Bissonett to downtown, or pick up the Express 262 at the Westwood Park and Ride and take the HOV (high occupancy vehicle) lane to downtown, and then pick up 42 to TSU. The only problem, other than 2 transfers, was that it appeared that 42, 65, and 262 did not have lifts, making it impossible for me to ride. Still, I started using city buses for going to appointments in the Medical Center. Route 68 turned out to be the best one, and it went all the way to the Sam Houston Tollway, connecting with 65 along Bissonett near Westwood Mall and home.

The Monte became Beh's primary means of transportation.

Beh quit working for Expert Cleaners the first of the year, 1996, to go to community college full time. After getting remedial courses out of the way, she planned to take a short technical course, maybe radiography.

I got a flu shot in November 1994, and got the flu once in April 1995. I recovered quickly but had trouble coughing and even breathing at one point. My doctor had me get chest X-rays in May and September. I then saw a pulmonary specialist because of a dark spot on one lung. I was worried that loss of my diaphragm muscle and ability to sit up or turn in bed would lead to a susceptibility to pneumonia. When I saw the specialist, he took another X-ray and said that I had had a virus that built up fluid between my lung and the chest wall. It was now scar tissue, but he wanted me to get another X-ray in May 1996, to see if it healed properly.

It took a long time to learn how to set up my catheter and bag properly, and to make sure I emptied it before it was full, but finally, I began to go months without a leak or failure. We experimented with plastic catheters of medium and large sizes, but, although they were comfortable, didn't seal well, and, in spite of various adhesives, would give out when gas or urine pressure built up. We settled for large latex ones, easy to apply, with adhesive that held even when the catheter would blow up like a balloon when my bag got overfull. My helpers, Beh, Maria, and Malu, and various nurses got used to the idea of rolling the catheter down over my penis, and then squeezing it to enlarge it and heat the seal.

With the catheter on, I could relax, and urinate at any time. I never got used to the feel of hot urine flowing along the tube my leg, and I often had to look down to see if my pants were wet. That rarely happened, and, when it did, I knew almost instantly. By drinking more water at night, I actually was able to go all day sometimes without emptying the bag. When my students weren't there, I still had trouble finding someone to empty it, but someone always came through for me, even strangers. My bowel program worked well too, but I would experience problems if I ate the wrong things because of my allergy to milk products and the sensitivity a dysfunctional bowel has.

I could still transfer with help from my bed to my electric wheelchair, but after that flu, I quit transferring to my office chairs at home and work. I had to move furniture a bit both places, and except for reduced reach it worked out. I actually became more mobile because I could quickly go where I wanted without transferring to my electric chair first. I missed the comfort and maneuverability of my office chairs, and the lack of exercise caused by not using my feet to push myself around. As a result, I had more edema. By mid-summer I would lie awake from midnight to 3 am with pain caused by the fluid leaving my legs and feet. We reduced the problem by stretching and range of motion exercises before bed and lowering my bed back to level. The bowel program solved most of the reflux problems I was having. Reflux was the reason why I was told to raise the head of my bed six inches in the first place. Putting my body back to level brought the daily swelling down sooner.

When I first started using the electric wheelchair daily, I removed my right footrest to give my right leg greater freedom and rode around like that all day. But eventually, I had to put the footrest back on and use it when I could no longer lift up my right leg to travel. I still released and swung away both footrests when at my desk because having my legs in one position for long periods of time became very painful. Moving my legs up and down helped alleviate the pain, but I wasn't going to be able to do it forever, so a higher dose of baclofen (anti spasm), or valium or even stronger drugs could have been in my future. In the meantime, I grimaced and bore it, and shifted my weight and feet as best I could.

I was now in the chair from about 6:30 am to 11 pm each day. Sometimes, I just couldn't stand it any more and wanted to get up and walk away, or at least, lie down for a while when I wasn't feeling well. In bed, I could no longer turn on my side, sit up, or swing my legs over the side. If I couldn't sleep because of a problem or muscle spasms, I couldn't get up and walk around, watch TV, or read. Instead, I had to wake Beh up to turn me, rearrange my bed covers, or comfort me. If I waited, all these things passed. Sometimes it was unbearably frustrating to be that patient, especially if I had an itch and couldn't scratch it.

My chair was great. After a year it required some adjustment and some plastic and rubber parts got broken or lost, but otherwise it was very reliable. I charged the chair at night about every fourth day. My gel-cell batteries had lasted over two years, longer than anyone I knew, and longer than those on my scooters. The chair had two drives, and two speeds in each. I used only one drive because the other was too jerky. The low speed was good for maneuvering in tight places, but too slow for hallways. The high speed was too fast for hallways, about 7 mph, but too slow when I wanted to head across campus or avoid a car in the parking lot or crossing a street. Hard rubber wheels in the front made for a rough ride and traveling on grass could be dangerous, especially in the vicinity of doggy do. People always accused me of speeding, but it was nice to get around quickly after all those years of struggling to walk.

Finally, I got lucky. It was almost like winning the lottery. After a year of looking at tile falling off the wall to my shower enclosure, I decided to bite the bullet and pay the estimated $1,000 to get it fixed. Before I did, I decided to call my insurance company. The agent toured my house with Jean, and then determined that it was water-driven rain damage that wet the tile from within the wall. He came to my office and gave me a sizable check. When I told him that I had had trouble finding a good contractor, he suggested one. After the contractor reviewed the damage, the estimate grew. The contractor ended up repairing roof leaks, window leaks, and damaged walls and ceilings, repainting the entire interior, replacing the carpet, tile and kitchen flooring, as well as putting up two ceiling fans that I bought, and some improvements for me like lowering my thermostat and fixing my ramps. After two weeks and $8,800 in repairs, my house was better than when it was new. And insurance paid for it all.

The new paint and carpet renewed my resolve to keep my house in good order. Jazz, perhaps upset by the change in his familiar environment, began to mark the carpet and kitchen floor. Jean came through with a spray that caused him to quit a particular spot, but we practically had to spray the entire house. To my frustration, she claimed that she couldn't clean the spots. Finally, in April 1996, before my parents came, I called a carpet cleaning service. Fleas less bothered jazz, but he began to shed his winter coat in May, leaving swatches of fine, black hair everywhere. Jean started helping Denise in the morning and spending more time helping an elderly couple. Several small things piled up and they bothered me. I asked her to come in early on Memorial Day and help me clear them up.

When Jean arrived she had already been to Denise's. She looked hot and tired. When she sat down on the bed to go over a folder that I needed to organize, I began to complain about Jazz's hair all over the carpet, and told her it was easier to pick up the small swatches than wait until Thursday and have it clog up the brushes on the vacuum cleaner. She reached down and picked up a patch of hair, and then she threw it down to the floor again and said, "I quit." She stood up, threw the folder on the bed, and left.

Beh and I both tried to call her later, but she wouldn't talk to us. Her husband told Beh that he was worried about her health. Jean tried hard to please, too hard. But she didn't always use good judgment. She was always doing something for me without my asking for it. She brought me cake. My allergy to milk, aversion to sweets, and battle with middle-age fat left me with no other choice but to eat it sparingly, like I didn't like it. She bought me "bargain" pork chops at twice the price I paid in the store. But it was my inattention to her concerns that probably sealed the deal. I remember a few days earlier, when she complained that it was too hot in the kitchen. The air conditioning had been on for a half hour. In my usual rush to get in and get my evening tasks done so I could relax, I pooh-poohed her problem, ignoring her plea for a fan. I should have taken time to talk to her about it. She was a good, dependable helper. We never talked again. When we met again years later, she was disabled with back problems.

In October 1996, a Manatee from either Florida or the Yucatan wandered into our polluted ship channel. "Hugh," as the locals started to call him, enjoyed the attention and the generous salad bar provided for him until it was determined that it was too dangerous for him to stay in such treacherous waters provided by modern progressive business. Hugh Manatee, (humanity), was trapped, netted by those who set out to help him from himself. It was learned that she, not he, was perfectly okay after her ordeal. Asked what she was going to do after such a great adventure as this, surviving in the wrong habitat, she replied, "I am going to Sea World!" And so she did (In San Antonio). But was humanity the better for it? Later, when she was healthy again, she was returned to her native Florida waters.

# 56

## Finding Comfort in the Change Zone

It appears the more one lives by a routine, the quicker time passes. My routine reached a boring repetitiveness. Anything non-routine sort of snuck up on me. I found myself continually bushwhacked by holidays and birthdays, meetings and appointments. Years rolled by in an ever more dulling and lulling cycle. I really had to force myself to remember things that didn't come up every day. Routine provided comfort and security. Routine was comforting and soothing. But routine was killing my spirit, my desire, and my chance to do something great. More and more, I had to force myself to go down that less-traveled path again.

After a struggle with arthritis, Dad had his left knee replaced in August 1996. Unexpectedly, he had a lot of pain that slowed his recovery. His right hip was also involved, so he had that replaced in March 1997. It was strange to see him struggling with physical problems; Dad had always been so strong. On the other hand, not many could say that their father had reached 75 and was still relatively healthy. I thought he would approach 100 like Uncle Roy Hull.

Jazz developed a habit of jumping on the METROLift van every night to give me a kiss, to the startled delight of drivers and passengers, and then he guarded me as I tried to leave. One evening in September 1996, after I got through interviewing a potential attendant, Beh and I escorted her out of the house. Jazz escaped and was exploring across the street, when he started back without looking. I saw a black car pass in front, and he was gone. Beh gasped, but a minute later he appeared in the garage. Beh said a red car had slowed down and Jazz emerged between its wheels. He had a little cut by his eye and a sore hind leg, but that was all. One night, a few days later, he came out to the van, and then started exploring the yard. A big black dog, one that had chased him before, appeared. He caught Jazz in my front yard, and started biting him. Beh cried out and waved her hands wildly from the drive, and I, helpless in my chair in the van, yelled to her to go kick the attacker. Finally, she went in the garage and got a broom. Before she got back, the big dog backed off and Jazz staggered to the gate, and then into the garage and house. The first night, he couldn't lie down, and his belly was badly bruised, but in a week he was back to his frisky self. I talked to the young owner of the big black lab cross breed, and I didn't see that dog on the street again after that.

Maria continued to keep in touch, sending me sample medicines for my skin and asking how I was doing. Her son, Paulo, at 16, took the SAT as a fluke and scored so high that many colleges, including Harvard and Stanford, courted him. Maria became and expert in a new hair removal technique that landed her TV spots locally and presentations at conferences nationally.

Beh quit all other work except occasional clothes alteration and baby-sitting to take care of me full time and go to community college in January 1996. With Beh's heavy schedule, we couldn't get to Mom and Dad's for either Thanksgiving or Christmas, 1995. In March, Beh drove me to McAllen. We still couldn't go to Mexico because of Beh's immigration status, but we had a good time at Pepe's on the Rio Grande River eating TexMex and listening to polkas from an aging Winter Texan band, instead. We also enjoyed a sing along, joke along, form of local talent show at the hall. Dad, Mom, and Beh all had to work together to get my wheelchair and me up the steps into the house, but they managed it.

After that, I rarely left the house except to go to work. Beh's school was just too demanding and her schedule too busy to go anywhere. In April, I did talk her into a day viewing spring wild flowers. It was so dry, and we were late in the season, so we didn't see many flowers through Bellville and Brenham. Heading east out of Brenham to the Old Navasota Road, we started to see blue fields. We reached an area where the bluebonnets were at their peak, vistas from road to horizon ready to paint. We stopped at a cattle guard with cattle grazing nearby and I thought it would be a good place for Jazz to run. He took one look and a sniff, and refused to leave the car. Those "doggies" were just too big for him to deal with.

Our one big adventure came when I noticed that I was not listed to go on the management retreat at work, a thing that happened more frequently as I was perceived to be more disabled—"ready for retirement." Charles, the interim assistant vice president and my supervisor, noticed it too, and before long, in spite of some protests, I was scheduled to join the financial administration at the Flying L. The Flying L dude ranch was located in the Texas Hill Country, 40 miles west of San Antonio in Bandura. Just getting there presented some problems. I planned to take both of my wheelchairs, so that I could participate more freely. All of us were to meet at TSU at 6:00 am the morning we were to leave. I checked on renting a van for Beh to drive. There were two places to rent accessible vans in Houston. Both were very expensive and were far from my house. No vans were available for the retreat dates, even though I called a month early. METROLift did not start early enough in the morning to get us there on time. Our TSU bus driver offered to pick me up at my house, on our way west, like I often did on business trips to Austin, but the committee made no exceptions, so we had to hire a cab, ParaCab, to get me to TSU by 6:00 am.

Beh and I got to TSU on time. My wheelchairs were stowed down under in the bus luggage compartment. Four guys, each with an arm and a leg, carried me to the door. They couldn't get their arms past the doors, so I called for Diane, our custodial supervisor, who was already in the bus, and the guys handed me to her. Diane dragged me in as best she could, and got me to the front seat. Once there, Beh and I rode comfortably.

After a four-hour ride, we arrived at ranch heaven, complete with a golf course. Guys carried me up stairs in my electric chair for our meetings. We enjoyed watching rodeo activities at the corral, a fabulous shish kabob meal by the creek picnic area, a hayride through fields of deer and cattle, and a party in an outdoor dance hall. Everyone got a picture of me wheelchair dancing with two of the ladies. The drive from our villa to the clubhouse was lined with flowers that attracted dozens of hummingbirds. We enjoyed ourselves, and the guys finally figured out how to get me in and out of vehicles by a two-man carry.

In the Fall of 1996, Texas Southern University experienced a dramatic drop in enrollment. The lost students were a direct response to the discovery that TSU was mismanaging federal funds in financial aid. When financial aid was tightened up in the spring, many students who had been getting too much aid, or shouldn't have been getting aid at all, were turned away. Since perhaps 80% of our students had been on financial aid, the result was predictable. The Downtown campus of the University of

Houston experienced gains that matched our loss. The result was severe cut backs that hit our area very badly. The directors' salaries were larger and first to go. We lost our directors of safety, operations maintenance, and plant maintenance, and then, in October, architectural services. I was the only director left. Anyone close to retirement was cut, and half of the custodians. We got a contract to dispose of waste, sold our garbage trucks, and reassigned our waste collectors. We bid a contract to maintain the thermal plants, heating and cooling, and controls, but couldn't pay for it. We awarded a contract for some custodial services and a contract to do all architectural and construction services. Finally, they let the senior vice president of administration, Howard Turnley, the guy responsible for the downsizing and outsourcing, go. He wasn't missed.

The area became like a morgue. The halls and rooms were bare of activity and the few remaining crafts people kept their noses to the grindstone, hoping against hope that the next move would not be to outsource all maintenance to some service company. Charles, an honest, hard working man, was patching holes in the dike and uncovering considerable funds mismanagement, but remained powerless to maintain the area the way it should have been.

The $3.5 million in LoanSTAR program funds TSU was promised were canceled pending a new audit. The committee working with the University of Houston on a joint performance contract was abandoned. After a consultant played with the project for a while, and then abandoned it, I again requested permission to proceed. I received no approval. The architectural services company we hired was given the job. They were again looking at performance contracting. In the meantime, we lost five years of energy savings because of ignorance, inaction, and ineptness.

I managed to keep our computer network working with the help of occasional technicians. We added a Quarterdeck email system that worked very well, but it got little use. We got some memory upgrades but not enough for me or some other folks who needed to do multitasking. With enough RAM, we could all get SoftWindows 3.0 and run all the Windows 95 applications on our Macs. I thought that adding RAM to our 6150 WorkGroup Server would enable QD mail, file servers, and our internet router (joined our LocalTalk network to our Ethernet network), all on the same machine. But, it slowed down our printing so much I had to put the router back on its old workhorse, the SE 30, with the older, non Power PC, software. All features then ran well, except transferring large files and running remote applications on the LocalTalk machines.

I was the last to get a PowerMac. In August 1996, I got a 7500/16MB with 1.2 GB Drive, 4XCD, and 20-inch monitor. The monitor was great, but the projection was set half the size of older monitors, so it took some getting used to everything being so small. I could get two full pages side by side on the screen and see a lot more of spreadsheets and drawings. The screen was so big; I routinely swapped windows from three applications by pointing to them on the screen—very convenient and efficient. The computer was a bit of a turkey, crashing with Helix and giving me a lot of false "out of memory" messages, but upgrading Helix and the operating System to 7.5.3, was some help. Still, many of the major problems I had in the past with incompatibilities and damaged disks, seemed to have improved.

The operations maintenance database I established was used more and more to track work orders, worker and craft performance, and cost. It proved that using our own workers, especially if we charged back the work to departments, cost less than contracting the work out. I entered all of our land data into a database and upgraded the facilities inventory database to help us calculate future budgets.

I again prepared color transparencies for Josh Hill's ergonomics class and taught a class in the spring semester 1996. It seemed that each time I prepared for teaching a chapter, it took longer. I am fond of graphics in my presentations, and I was running out of clip art. Creating and coloring my own artwork was very time-consuming. It seemed almost a waste to spend all that time on a presentation; coloring and perfecting the slides, knowing it would only be seen once by ten students. Crude workbooks, mere outlines, are sold to thousands of students. My work, far richer in content, has been free and in limited edition. The two-hour evening sessions were hard on my voice, my throat would dry up as I struggled for breath and expression, but I still enjoyed the opportunity to work with students again.

Nakia Lewis couldn't qualify for work study, so he had to quit working for me in the summer. Cynthia Breedlove graduated with an MBA in December. She continued working with me and on teacher certification until she started teaching math to high school hard cases in the fall of 1966. I requested another graduate assistant from the School of Business and they awarded it to Farid Ghouri, a 46-year-old retiree from the Pakistani Navy studying for his MBA and EdD. His son and daughter were also enrolled at TSU. We immediately began to make a real dent in obtaining data for the facilities inventory.

METROLift's new vans, while bigger, carried fewer wheelchairs. My schedule, especially in the morning, had become more predictable, and I usually arrived at work before 9:30 am. My evening ride was less stable, but I enjoyed a series of good drivers and the company of John Pruitt, an East Texan who was paralyzed in a car accident in 1979. John was director of the woman's shelter for the Star of Hope Mission and married to the City Attorney of Missouri City. He was more severely disabled than I, but had two small children, a dog, a cat, a faithful attendant of fifteen years, and a nice home. He had a van and got out to things like AstroWorld, Dallas Cowboy games in Dallas, and rallies with Bob Dole. Dr. Ken Krajewski, originally from Rock Island, IL, had been riding with us, too. Ken was a psychiatrist who had developed spinal atrophy and quit walking about 1992. His twelve year old stepson, Andrew, had leukemia and rode with us sometimes. In February 1997, Andrew's white blood cell count got too low, and he died. Ken had a rough period, but came back to join us after a few months. Andrew's mother hospitalized herself with severe depression for a few months. I was regularly using city buses to go to and from the Medical Center. Waiting up to an hour in the hot sun could be difficult, but the convenience and regularity of the buses was easier than trying to schedule METROLift rides.

The Monte Carlo started to show rust under the vinyl top. I took it to a couple of shops and they either refused to do it, estimated too much, or insisted on a total restoration at an unspecified cost. Finally, I found a friendly shop manager who liked old cars. He lied. The car languished in the shop for two months while he promised and promised. Finally, he was fired and I got the car back. The bodywork and paint came out okay, but several small things hadn't been finished. The new manager took the car for a week to do the things I listed. Later, I discovered he didn't do half of them. I checked back, thinking of suing the place, and it was out of business. Anyway, the rust was stopped for a while, and the car ran and looked great. Beh's experience with her brother's cars, Toyotas, Hondas, etc., convinced her that she liked the more reliable "Plane" better.

# 57

## Life on the Down Escalator

My condition continued its steady digression. The big loss in 1996 was my abdominal muscles. Sitting up in bed without help became impossible. I had to brace my arms to keep upright on the METROLift side seat. When I'd slip or get surprised by a sudden start or stop, I'd fall to the seat or against the person next to me, and then struggle to get up. I had to struggle to keep sitting up straight in my wheelchair. It became very hard to steady myself to write, eat, or use the computer mouse. If I had to reach for something, I'd fall that direction, causing pain in my lower back until I could push or pull myself back upright. Eventually, I would have to be tied in the chair like John, further reducing my range of motion. I cut back on food all I could, but my stomach continued to spread. I got fitted for an abdominal binder, but it gave me little support. The binder left deep marks in my skin, and Beh abandoned putting it on me. The binder's main function was to push everything up into my diaphragm so that it would work better and I could breathe more deeply. The opposite occurred. My breathing was restricted.

After three years, I finally got a referral to a rehabilitation specialist. Dr. Clearman had resigned to go on to other work somewhere else, so she referred me to Dr. Kenneth Parsons. Parsons was concerned that my vital (lung) capacity had dropped one third in three years, and ordered the binder, physical therapy, and a sleep study. We got some stretching exercises that greatly reduced night pain in my legs and reversed a contracture that was forming in my immobile left leg. I'd lived well with the contracture in my left hand all my paralyzed life. But the idea of my left leg and foot curled up under me seemed intolerable. The stretching appeared to be preventing that from happening. With the help of the doctor and physical therapists, I tried to get permission to use my insurance for additional equipment like a therapeutic bed, shower seat, and toilet support bars.

I had an all night sleep study in September 1996. It showed that I had sleep apnea. In the study, I stopped breathing several times in two hours, and for three minutes one time. The condition was not life-threatening, but it lowered blood oxygen, put some strain on my heart, and disrupted needed deep sleep. The cure, forcing air into my nose at up to nine atmospheres with a ventilator, appeared worse than the disease. I rarely breathed through my nose because my sinuses were so bad. If I must use a ventilator, I'd ask them to do something about my sinuses. A friend of mine found that she couldn't wear the ventilator, so she had an operation to open up her air passages. That approach had worked for her. I haven't heard the diagnosis yet, but my daily life wasn't affected too much by my loss of sleep, and, until it is, I probably won't need the ventilator.

I could still transfer with help from my bed to my electric wheelchair, but I didn't know how much longer. Duane Henson, our elevator repairman, had started to help me if I needed to go to the bathroom at work. I'd call dispatch, they'd radio him, and he would come to my rescue. Fortunately, I didn't need his help often.

My Invacare wheelchair continued to serve me well. My gel-cell batteries had survived over three years. Others were getting newer chairs with smaller rear wheels, but it looked like I'd have this chair a long time. The guys at the Flying L broke the left leg rest carrying it up and down stairs. Fortunately, they were able to weld it back together. I wheeled myself a few blocks to a friend's machine shop on Bissonett to get minor repairs. He refused to charge me for his work.

The Texas Rehabilitation Commission (TRC) had started contracts with firms that provide home care for disabled people who work. When Jean quit, I called Denise for back up for Beh because I knew she used a service for her attendants. Denise told me to call Americare, her service, and I did. I found out that Americare provided up to 35 hours of care a week on a sliding scale, depending on how much you earned. At first, I thought that I didn't qualify, but, after being interviewed, it was arranged for me to get the full 35 hours a week for $75. All I had to do was divert some income into my retirement—a very good deal. Beh signed up with Americare, and they paid her.

Ingrid Francis started working in late November 1996, to replace Jean. Ingrid and her husband, who was a construction worker, came from the New York, New Jersey area where they lived 15 years after immigrating from Guyana. Ingrid was calm and relaxed. Even though she was working three jobs to help her family, she was dependable and helpful, always willing to work more if I needed it.

In January 1997, Beh got a student job helping me at TSU and started going to school with me. When Beh quit going to night school and joined me at TSU, we decided that we didn't need Ingrid's help in the evening. I had to tell her that I didn't need her any more. It was hard. I knew how much Ingrid needed the little money she made working for me. I got her work through Americare, and I felt good about that. My only worry was that there was no backup for Beh. I would have to rely on Americare if Beh couldn't be here to help me.

Payments for a modified van could be used to lower my net income for my Americare subsidy, and TRC paid for modifications and evaluations. I got information on the Electro Magnetic Controls' (EMC) Digimatic joystick control system and arranged a third driving evaluation in August 1966. When Chad Strowmatt, the evaluator, came, he started setting up the same way he did in 1993. He said the joystick type of control wasn't approved by TRC yet. I told him I wanted to try it first, so we stopped the evaluation. I contacted Dr. Roger Koppa at the Texas Transportation Institute about using the joystick, but he wasn't encouraging. He said the system had some stability problems and wouldn't pass their tests, required for TRC approval. Through the Adaptive Driving Alliance, I found adapters who routinely installed the system as close as Louisiana. But there was no getting around TRC's rule in Texas.

There were three good vehicle adapters in Houston. All the carmakers gave rebates for adapting new vehicles. Roger and Tom visited companies that made lowered floor minivans for adapting. I just had to figure out how to get and drive one. It was a big step I wasn't financially prepared to take.

I didn't want to borrow money to buy a new van. I would have settled for a used van, but TRC wouldn't approve of that.

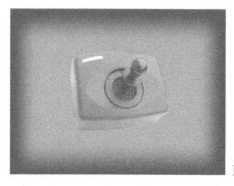

EMC Driving Joystick

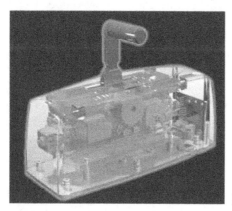

EMC Gas//Brake Unit

EMC Steering Unit

# 58

# Getting Connected

I first went online in 1972 with two modem connected IBM Selectric typewriter terminals in Allen Hall at WVU connected to the mainframe at the Computer Center by telephone using the word processor WYLBUR. The next year we got two Hazeltyne CRT terminals, a big improvement. About 1987, my telephone company offered a free little terminal for a year with several features like banking with wire transfers and social networking with two groups, America Online and Compuserve. There was a bulletin board where people could buy and sell goods and services, like eBay. After the trial was over, I dutifully evaluated the system, but never was offered to buy or lease it. While I had an Ethernet network and email at TSU in 1989, we weren't connected. Finally, I made a modem connection about 1991. Navigating the fledgling Internet at that time was quite difficult, but I did get to Duke Library and the University of Minnesota where lots of academic papers could be downloaded free—a boon for researchers.

Beginning with a modem I'd brought from work about 1992, when I got my first loaner Mac SE to do work at home, I'd been doing my banking on the computer for several years. Then, I bought one of the new, less expensive and faster 33.6 kb modems. It was a good buy. My banking continued normally, and faxing was easy with the software provided.

As I'd threatened for several years, I finally invested in an Internet connection in April 1997. It changed my life. I began writing much more. Letters that had become so difficult to hand write and send, were now easy emails. I began to keep in touch regularly with Tom, Tim, Judy, and Tracy. With the help of Southwestern Bell, my Internet provider, and a meager knowledge of html, the obtuse text language of web pages, I created my own web page. I began posting a poem a week to it. The good part of this commitment was that it forced me to write. The bad part was that I had to come up with a poem, even when I could think of nothing to write that week. I found myself writing poems about "nothing" and "not having an idea."

Information was now at my fingertips—a big time saver. I started downloading software useful to my work and me. My TV listings and stock market reports now came easily from the Net, along with maps for trips or how to find a place downtown. I found changed phone numbers of friends and their email addresses. I treated myself to a photo quality color printer for Christmas. So, for the first time, I was able to print documents at home that I'd had to take to work before to print.

My younger brother, Tom, like me, was drawn to high places. After he moved to Phoenix in 1980 directly from college, he began climbing peaks around the city. Before long, he had climbed nearly every peak in Arizona. By the 1990s, he got interested in the explanations for mystical places and climbed to Machu Pichu in the high Andes in 1996.

In the spring of 1997 he spent ten days hiking out of Katmandu in the shadow of Mount Everest. The high point of his hike was when he met and was filmed with Peter Hillary. Peter, the son of Everest's conqueror, Sir Edmund Hillary, climbed Everest seven times. Tom never reached the Everest base camp, but he and a Shurpa summited a nearby peak with a magnificent view of the final summit to Everest.

Tom married for a second time on December 21 1997 to Sonya, an engineer he met at work. Beh couldn't go, so Maria graciously offered to help out. Since I was confined to my portable wheelchair, it wasn't an easy trip for me. I was cold for much of the outdoor wedding and reception, but the warmth I felt being able to join my family for the occasion overcame it. Maria, resourceful and energetic, made it all possible.

Tom and Sonya honeymooned by hiking the Alps the next spring. Sonya ruptured her appendix on the hike, but managed to finish the hike and return to Phoenix for surgery.

It's hard to say where I would have climbed. Arriving on a mountaintop by helicopter is not the same as walking up, breathing in the sights and smells in the clear mountain air. It's all in the journey, not the destination. I had little desire for days of routine at sea, overcoming nature's hardships at the poles, in the deserts, or under the sea. I always wanted to see natural life up close. Sometimes, from on high, you can see more.

Jazz met with an evil fate on June 21, 1997. It was Saturday, and Beh had gone to Lake Charles gambling with her father. About 4 pm he wanted to go out front and check his territory, and I foolishly opened the garage door and let him out. He came back for a moment, and I closed the door, but he was quick and went back out before it closed. I opened it again and waited for him. I heard a growl and a shriek from Jazz to the right, not far away, but I couldn't see what was happening. The lab came into view and disappeared. Jazz staggered in and I closed the door.

It was the same black labrador mix that mauled him about a year earlier. I hadn't seen that dog out since I told the owner to control him. Jazz took a week that time to recover from his internal injuries, but he didn't bleed. This time he came inside and bled all over the house, trying to find a way to get comfortable, suffering seizures. I couldn't call Beh or anyone. I just had to wait.

Jazz stopped bleeding and I got him to go outside where there was water. I wanted him to stay out there. A short while later he was back inside. Going through his doggie door had reopened his wounds, and he lay on the bathroom floor in front of me a moment, leaving a pool of blood when he left to wander again.

At 6:00 pm a storm came up, knocking out power. I couldn't find Jazz anymore in the dark, so I thought he was dead in the closet. At 9:30 pm Beh arrived, and he came out to greet her. I was relieved. The power came back on. We gave him a little water. When I went to bed about midnight, Jazz came out and threw up by the bed, but there was no blood and it seemed like he was going to make it, lying down and sleeping.

Sometime during the night he moved around again, maybe tried to go in and out through the doggie door, and started bleeding again. There was more blood in the bathroom. In the morning, Beh found him dead in the closet. Beh shrieked at the sight and was inconsolable.

We went to the home of the owner of Max, the other dog. He said he was sorry, but claimed it was another dog that looks just like Max. But he came over, carried Jazz out and dug a hole for us. We buried Jazz in the front yard where he ran free and safe behind the fence. I missed him greatly. Jazz was my good little buddy for seven years. At least he didn't die in diseased old age. I felt bad though, that I couldn't get him to a vet to stop his bleeding and save his life. I'll never know. I heard about a dog ambulance service later. It made me feel guilty for not knowing.

After working with me and struggling to pass the TAAS test at TSU, Beh took the summer of 1997 off her work and school at TSU. In August, she started a dry cleaning and alterations business with a friend, Vi, right around the corner from my house. Their customer base grew rapidly and they were in the black, but they had heavy competition with very low prices, so didn't make much money. Beh did all the alterations and started making ties and scarves.

# 59

# Road Experiments

Using the Monte Carlo, Beh did all our shopping. She even drove the car the 300 yards or so to her shop, something I didn't like, but she insisted on, saying that dogs or worse'd attack her. Malu had walked and Maria had biked miles to my house. Still Beh deserved the convenience. When we drove to McAllen, she was the one who helped me into and out of the car, drove the whole way, and then pushed me in my portable chair when we got there. I waited, sometimes months, for her to take me somewhere. Beh hated pushing me around in that chair. I hated being confined to it without being able to move around by myself.

Beh cooked regularly for her brothers and father at their house and did everything for me. Some thought Beh was a saint. She wasn't. It was very difficult for her, alone, at times. Beh's free time was very limited. But she was very dedicated to helping me, no matter what, and I'm very grateful for that.

By April 1997, I was tired of the work/home routine, so we rented a Dodge Caravan with a lowered floor and wheelchair tie-downs so I could take my electric chair and Beh drove us to San Antonio. Our first stop was the Natural Bridge Caverns. I could get into the main building, and view a videotape of the caverns, but I couldn't get past the 52-step entry into the cave. We decided not to go to the Caverns and stopped at a nearby wildlife ranch instead.

At the ranch, Beh really enjoyed driving among the wild animals and taking pictures. Wild flowers were at their peak, so it was beautiful everywhere we drove. We then visited Beh's uncle. With a PhD from Columbia University, he was teaching philosophy at both Trinity and UT-San Antonio, and had just finished the semester. We parked on the street next to the Alamo, and I was able get around the grounds quite well. I could wheelchair to the Hyatt on the River Walk. Beh and her uncle followed the steps to the fountain gardens. I had to watch them from street level, and then take the elevator down at the Hyatt. It was great wheeling around the River Walk. I remember struggling to walk those same paths. Now it was easy, except I couldn't cross to the other side of the river. It didn't miss the treacherous crossings I'd made on foot.

The next morning we drove to Sea World. It was very easy for me to get around there. Beh really enjoyed the performing Beluga and Killer Whales, and loved photographing the fish in the Shark House. Four killer whales dutifully posed by the window after their show so that Beh could get her picture taken with them. Although it was difficult at times, we proved that we could travel with an accessible van without too much trouble. The wildflowers were spectacular.

My former private secretary, Dessiray Bell, now an attorney, offered to take me to Lake Charles, Louisiana, gambling. Beh and Dessiray's ex-husband ended up going along. We had a good time and I held up fairly well, even though I was in my portable chair so long. A couple of weeks later, Jeanie took me. When Jeanie's free hotel room fell through, I finally got one at 4 am. After two hours snoozing, fully clothed on the bed, we resumed gambling until late morning. I didn't win anything on either trip, but it proved that I could still get out and endure long periods of sitting without moving.

After that, I really wanted to get away, and set up a week's vacation in mid August. I wanted to go back to Yellowstone. I hadn't been there since 1971. When the time came, Beh was unable to leave her business and Dessiray had just put her sons in school, so we took a short trip to Corpus Christi instead. I rented a Ford Econoline 150. Dessiray made the trip a lot easier, sharing the work with Beh. She was also very enthusiastic about all we did. We ran up and down the sea wall, and out on docks. The first day we visited the Texas State Aquarium and the aircraft carrier, Lexington. I could only view the main deck, but it was very interesting.

After checking into the most expensive hotel, only to find that I couldn't get into the bathroom, we ate in a floating restaurant and took an evening cruise in the Bay. The next morning, we visited the museum and replicas of the Santa Maria and Nina. These ships were built in 1992 and sailed from Spain to celebrate Columbus's 500th discovery of America anniversary. The museum had artifacts from the recently discovered ship of LaSalle, the French explorer shipwrecked off Matagorda Island.

I became very familiar with city buses, often taking free rides to the Medical Center from work. Some buses still didn't have lifts, and sometimes the lifts wouldn't work or work well, but when the weather was good, it was a great way to get out. One day trip Beh and I took was to the museum from work. We got to see the Romanov dynasty jewels, on tour from Russia. It's one of the advantages of living in a big city.

With Dessiray at the Aquarium in Corpus Christi August 1997.

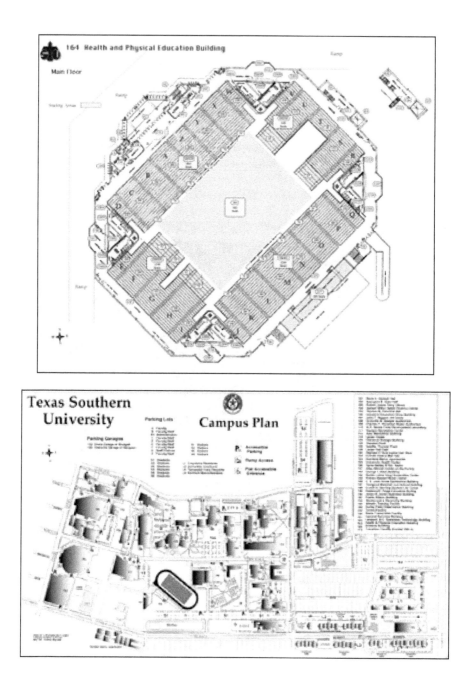

# 60

## Subtle Changes: Time Moves On

It was another light winter, with only a few mild freezes. Beh's peach tree showed great promise, and then dropped all of its fruit early. She planted azaleas out front, but they all died by the end of the summer. Her cucumbers by the deck did quite well though, and we enjoyed many.

Texas Southern University continued to decline and raise controversy. I was the only director left in our area. It appeared that there would be no effort to change that. A lawsuit by our former architectural director, Shi Shi Ahmadi, forced changes in the Board, but continued Board meddling seemed to compound, rather than solve, our problems. Our whole computer services area was outsourced. The private firm managing our planning and construction work came under question. The faculty and staff had little confidence in President Douglas, shoehorned in by the Board after the debacle caused by Horton. Douglas seemed to be spending most of his time keeping up appearances rather than providing strong leadership.

I served on committees to select a master planning firm and a performance contractor for energy conservation. A firm that promised fund-raising as part of the master plan was selected. We hadn't had a master plan since 1988, so one was sorely needed. I finally gave in to letting our construction contractor lead the selection of a performance contractor. The committee selected a good firm from several that could do the job. The firms that were rejected objected to the process and further delayed much needed installation of energy and cost-saving measures.

My function had become so limited that I couldn't plan any changes in our computing resources. Fiber optic cable had finally reached our building, but I was not allowed to manage its installation nor was I informed how we would link up. My computer crashed daily and my databases were slow. My solution was to upgrade to a faster version of Helix, install Mac System 8.0, and upgrade three computers with the new 750 processor and fast Ethernet. My requests were all denied. JT Glover, our moneyman, was exercising his power. He would do more damage.

My big accomplishment with the utility database was to come up with a way to project utility budget needs. This had been a complex task that required that I first enter all bill data, and then create a large spreadsheet. It often took two weeks after a request to complete and correct the numbers. Using the database, I just had to repost annual data, which took a few minutes, and the projection became automatic. I added a leak affidavit utility that returned $10,000 in wastewater charges, and an evaporation credit record that brought back $40,000 in 1997. Farid did the hard part, reading muddy, flooded meters in inclement weather.

I did some consulting for Josh Hill and signed up with MacTemps. MacTemps was a national company providing consultants to help businesses with their Mac computing. The work was ideal for me, but I got no assignments because I was employed and unable to go to clients' sites without METROLift. My plan was to use some of my free and vacation time to build rapport with local businesses so that I could continue to work after I officially retired.

# 61

## METROLift: My Way to Travel

I rode METROLift every day now. My METROLift schedule, especially in the morning, became even more predictable. Every other morning, I rode regularly with a woman on dialysis. Willie, my morning driver, was so predictable that I could rely on him. Willie had many years experience, was unflappable with some of our eccentric riders, and we enjoyed each other's company.

I found some seats on the new vans that have rivets or something that could be felt through the seat padding. These rivets were quite painful, once I began to feel them. I reported the problem to METROLift. A small wound, inflicted on someone whose body either could not feel it, or, in the case of the retarded, who could not report it, could become infected and life threatening.

My evening ride also became more stable. I rode most nights with John (Bob) Pruett and Ken Krajewski. We joked and gave our drivers a rough time. Bob would doze and Ken would call his wife on his cell phone. It all helped make the waiting and ride go faster. We always dropped off in the same order. I was always last to get home. Taking me first on the HOV lane would have been faster for all of us. That never happened. I was out voted.

The Monte finally got fixed when Beh discovered that the body shop manager that had made so many promises to me was back working at the Murphy Road Body Shop. I confronted him, and he said the new owner agreed to honor all the things unfinished last year. After a month and a half of more aggravation, he finally got everything done. They cleaned and lubricated my seat belts rather than replacing them. More and more, my Monte's original parts were better than anything anyone could find.

415

My condition continued its steady digression. No big losses, but it was getting so hard to stand up that transferring that way might have to end. I was taught how to use a sliding board, but Beh didn't want to use one. It was getting harder for her to put my bathing sling on well. Sometimes, when it's wasn't right, I'd slip through the hole. This was very dangerous because I would end up hanging by my legs and could hit my head if I fell through. It was also harder for me to get myself back far enough in my wheelchair seat

Dr. Kenneth Parsons saw me every six months. My annual check of my bladder and kidneys showed that everything was still okay, and I hoped to go many years before I needed surgery. I never got a written diagnosis or any treatment for my sleep apnea, so I decided to just live with it, knowing what it was. Sometimes, I woke up clearly gasping for breath.

My electric chair became my life. There was no transferring to wheeled chars any more. My gel-cell batteries seemed to last indefinitely. A wrecker driver helped me add air to a low tire one day. He apparently put too much pressure in it. The next morning, about 6 am when we were sleeping, a tube blew. Beh awoke thinking she was shot! It was Saturday, and my chair wouldn't move. I called Ben, my friend who has fixed my Monte all those years, and he agreed to help. It was a 20-inch bicycle tire, so a local bicycle shop had tubes. Ben got one. When he tried to pump the new tube up, it blew. He went out to get two more. Finally, it was fixed. Once again, I wheeled myself a few blocks to my friend Miguel's machine shop on Bissonett to get minor repairs to my footrests. They were easily damaged going through doorways. The pins would bend or break, and Miguel would fix them.

Americare reevaluated my service in June 1997, and determined that I would have to pay a co-pay of $750/month. They told me that attendant pay would go from $5.25 per hour to $6.00 on September 1. Then, in July, I got a letter stating that they were cutting weekly hours allowed from 35 to 25. I, along with many others, wrote the TRC and protested. The State responded by agreeing to continue 35 hours service a week. When September came, attendant pay was only raised 5 cents to $5.30. I'd already raised Beh's rate and was determined to stick with it.

It bothered me that attendant care was relegated to minimum wage. By limiting care to 35 hours a week, attendants wouldn't receive benefits. Beh worked hard to keep me working so that I could have health insurance, Worker's Compensation, and retirement. If she worked a lifetime for me under Americare, she would have none of these. It wasn't fair to attendants and it wasn't fair to the disabled who needed their care. As for Beh, I had long since included her in my will. TSU allowed her on my healthcare plan. I set up IRA and supplemental brokerage accounts for her so she would have more than Social Security in retirement.

At the controls of my high tech 1998 Windstar with
$70,000 in modifications.

An outing with my '98 Windstar. 95,000 miles 1998-2006

Permobile Corpus wheelchair required for driving 1997-2005

## 62

## Behind the Wheel Again

Americare auditors explained that payments for a modified van could be used to lower income, and TRC would pay for modifications and evaluations, so I finally decided to get a van and let Americare help pay for it. I arranged a fourth evaluation in September 1997, and drove Chad Strowmatt's old evaluation van forty miles in all kinds of traffic. Still, I wasn't comfortable going over 45 mph. The setup would consist of a 6-inch wheel placed horizontally over my right knee. A cradle and pin in a hole on the outer rim of the wheel would allow me to steer with my right hand. On the left, over my knee, would be a t-stick. I'd push it forward to accelerate, and pull it back to brake with my left hand. My left elbow would operate lights, signals and wipers. Once fully braked, my left elbow would also operate the transmission and all other functions of the van.

The evaluation was positive. The "*catch*" was that I must have *purchased* a van before TRC would *consider* paying for modifications. I had set the wheels in motion and took the next step. Using the Internet and my AAA membership, I bought a dark green 1998 Ford Windstar GL in Tempe, AZ, at $100 over invoice in late October 1997. I bought the van there because it would go to Vantage Mobility, International (VMI) in Phoenix to be modified.

The TRC counselor who originally set up the process disappeared, and I was faced with a poker-faced disbelieving Francis DrePaul. "Are you sure you want to drive?" He questioned.

419

I explained that I had driven unmodified vehicles for 40 years and would not have bought a new van I couldn't afford if I wasn't committed. DrePaul was finally convinced by my sincerity, and completed the needed paperwork.

The van modifications, costing $17,000, were to be done by Vantage Mobility, International on an assembly line in Phoenix, Arizona, and consisted of lowering the floor 10 inches, removing the front seats, raising them on rolling platforms, and providing slots to lock the seats in place, mounting a fold-down ramp in the right side sliding door, an airbag kneel-down suspension for lowering and raising the rear of the van, and a keyless electric entry system placed in the right rear taillight. The work was completed in late January 1998. The van was then shipped to Independence Vans in Houston.

Independence Vans was about twenty minutes from my house off I-10. The van, once there, was fitted with my controls, costing another $30,000. The controls were by Electro-Mechanical Controls, Inc. (EMC) of Baton Rouge, Louisiana, and all digital. Signals from the devices operated all the normal equipment by servos. The steering, brakes and every other control remained in place, and could be operated normally by disengaging the EMC system.

Driving the van was rather complicated. First, I'd strap myself securely in my driving position using a Velcro belt permanently attached to my chair. I'd enter the van using a remote switch on my left armrest that automatically opened the side door, kneeled the van, and lowered the ramp. Then, I'd drive my electric wheelchair into a v-shaped clamp called an EZ Lock that secured the chair electrically. I'd start the engine from a panel of buttons at my right elbow, and then raise the ramp and close the door from the remote on my chair's left armrest again.

I'd set other controls I'd need like turning on lights at my left on another panel on the door. My steering, mounted on a six-inch disk over my right knee, must be "engaged" twice and reset by buttons twice to activate the back up steering system. The electronic gas/brake control, mounted on my right, operated by pushing it forward for throttle and pulling it back to brake. My hands slide into tri-pin cradles to hold them steady and insure positive control. Once I'd engaged the brake, I'd shift to a gear on the panel to my right, slip my right hand onto my steering tri-pin, and proceed. Driving was fairly normal, except I'd have to use both hands continually. I'd signal by tilting my left hand right or left to initiate. The turn signals were automatically turned off by shifting after a turn or by initiating again. A large button on my headrest operated light dimming, horn, and wipers, by holding the button with my head, and then releasing it after one "beep" (dimming), two "beeps" (horn), or three "beeps" (wipers). The headrest button worked very well except I'd have to repeat three beeps several times to go through the various wiper speeds and get the wipers to stop.

I had forty hours of training in the evaluation van. Chad Strowmatt drove to my house one morning in February 1998, and my training began. Chad's van had dual controls so that he could maintain control when I couldn't. I expected that it would be more tiring to drive this way, and I would have to practice to feel comfortable in all driving conditions and situations. I also expected my many years of driving experience would help me with that. It proved to be more tiring than I thought. The constant vigilance this type of driving required, with the van constantly on the verge of veering off course, was draining.

At first, we took it slow, driving on side streets in my neighborhood until my controls were adjusted right and I felt comfortable and confident to face traffic. Then, we'd set out on a long trek through busy city streets. I was glad to stop when we'd finally get to work after twenty miles of battling bumps, stoplights, and traffic on Bissonett or Braeswood. The freeway was downright scary. While I could cruise fairly well at forty on the city streets, accelerating to sixty to keep up with freeway traffic had me on the edge, worried if I could maintain control at that speed.

Independence Vans got my van from VMI in January 1998. Progress was slow as I visited several times for fitting the controls and mounting a pin to my new wheelchair, an expensive Permobil with a function to elevate the seat and tilt. I used the tilt to obtain an optimal driving position. I rarely used the elevated seat function. A young man worked solely on my van. He was fired (twice) and an experienced tech, Troy Hamilton finished the van in September, nine months after that baby was started. I was exhausted and my nerves were frazzled the day I drove the van home from the shop. The next morning I tackled the freeway and rush hour without incident on my way to work and the disabled parking space by our building.

Then, I had to take the DPS test, pay my car payments and insurance, and maintain the van. It would not prove easy, but driving again gave me a bit more freedom. If I couldn't drive, Beh could wheel a seat into the driver's side and drive either my rig or turn it off and normally. I could tie down by her side in the front, and may even be able to lie down on the back seat. I prepared for the worst.

As of about 2005, all Houston METRO buses were accessible and free to ride with a disabled Freedom Pass along with the extremely smooth, fast and beautiful, light rail connection, making it easy to get around town.

# 63

## Becoming an Author and Computer Geek

I finished the first draft of this autobiography in August 1997. After six years of writing, it ended up being 480 pages. I contacted about fifteen publishers via the Internet. One publisher told me that I'd need a literary agent. That may be so. Vantage Press would publish it for $10-20,000. Commonwealth of Alberta showed interest in September, but I heard nothing after that. I contacted One Step Ahead, a newspaper for the disability community, but then their publisher, a quad, died. It seems he had used his accident settlement money to support the paper. Without his financial support, One Step Ahead died too.

I put excerpts on my web page. The book needed extensive editing. It lay dormant on my computer until I could get to it again.

By 1998, the Internet had become my indispensable servant. It also enslaved me. Mom joined the rest of us with a free Juno email account, and my niece, Kelley, and her dad and my brother, Roger, the last to come aboard, rounded out our family's new way of communicating. When they were laid off from work in the winter of 1998, my nephews, Matt and Andy, developed their own web pages.

In August 1998, Beh sold her dry cleaning and alterations business to her partner, Vi. She moved her alterations business to my house while looking for a shop of her own. She closed on a beautiful little shop on Westheimer in February 1999. This shop put her in touch with millionaire customers, so I expected it to flourish once they learned of her sewing skills.

Beh and I visited Mom and Dad in McAllen after Christmas, 1998 before my van arrived. Beh drove. It was such a great feeling to ride in the Monte Carlo again. In the spring, we went to the museum again by METROLift. We got some great pictures in the sculpture garden. Then Beh bought my camera and sent it to her older brother in Vietnam with the pictures in it. His kid opened the camera and exposed the film. I've lost too many pictures like that. Then, there were great pictures that were never taken because I could no longer take them myself.

We had another light winter into 1998, with only a few mild freezes. Beh's peach tree again showed great promise, but its fruit dried up in one of the greatest droughts in Texas history. She replanted azaleas out front, but they all died of thirst by the end of the summer. A geranium she kept blooming for two years shriveled along with her impatiens. My old peach tree died. Only her Chinese lucky plants and an impatien that came up in the asparagus fern made it through. Most of Texas's crops were ruined. We got rain and floods in September. I watched it all happen from my window and through the windows of moving METROLift vans.

Texas Southern University continued to decline and raise controversy. Early in 1998, the State Comptroller's Office sent seventeen people to help us get our financial act together. They stayed on the financial side, so I never saw them. State auditors also went through with a fine tooth comb. They never asked me about the records I kept. The Governor declared that if TSU didn't meet audit requirements, we'd be merged with another institution. The auditor's report was published in August and required many changes. Fall enrollment was only about 6700, a low that hadn't been seen since the '60s. Budget cutbacks followed.

Charles Carter, my boss, was asked to transfer to the University Comptroller job. They hired Harold Johnson in February 1988, from University of Houston-Clear Lake to take over the helm of Facilities Planning and Operations. I immediately set up a spare computer for him on our network so that he could see what we were doing. It had an annoying password setup installed by its previous owner. I should have disabled that feature. Harold didn't like Macs, and said so. He ordered a top of the line PC for himself and began replacing our Macs with PCs, dismantling the network.

Harold seemed uninterested in what I did or had done and assumed I was a computer geek who would do his bidding. He reminded me that he started out in computer science and told me that we were going to convert to an NT network. My task was to convert everything I was doing to NT and create an Internet presence for FPO. I tried to get NT training, attending two-week long courses in June and August, but didn't get an NT computer until late August. It wasn't connected to our new network or the Internet until I made a special request in the spring of 1999. Others had working connections months earlier. The moneyman, JT Glover, our purchaser, told me that he wouldn't support any more Mac improvements. Glover's technician, Charles gradually moved into my computer workroom. Without student help, I lost control of the scanner and color printer there. My paper files, in a room behind the workroom, became inaccessible. Everything I had was on my computers and back up drives.

Johnson developed a new organization in June 1998, splitting my responsibilities and giving about half of them to others. I tried to help transfer these functions to the people designated, but no one would take them, so I continued doing them all. Finally, in September, Harold demoted me to an assistant director spot under his pick for director of the physical plant. Jim Anderson was hired in July and was an okay guy, but seemed very uncomfortable directing me. My job description was rewritten and my job was posted. I was asked to reapply for the lesser job under the threat of losing it altogether. I was not the only one. It was the way Johnson forced his will onto the organization. Most of us resisted his effort's to "Do it the way we did at Clear Lake," and threatening approach. There was nothing wrong with the way we were doing things. It just wasn't Harold's way.

My graduate assistant, Farid Ghori, graduated with his MBA in June and went to work for Charles Carter in the Comptroller's Office. The School of Business appointed Gina Orebe, an MPA candidate from Nigeria, to take Farid's place. She was learning the job very well, and helping me out a lot. But, when it came time for her to register in the fall, foot-dragging by everyone involved caused her to decide to quit TSU and enroll in the University of Houston. Harold Johnson would not let me replace her, citing budget cuts. It was the first time I'd been without employees or graduate assistants since 1985. Supposedly for budget reasons, Charles and Farid were let go in August. Both filed grievances, followed by lawsuits.

I began the stages of filing a grievance myself. Under the ADA, disabled persons are not supposed to be demoted. Most people think that as long as my salary wasn't reduced, I wasn't being demoted. However, loss of title, responsibilities, or status was also considered a demotion. By reapplying for a lesser job, I would not lose any pay, but those who have been required to reapply for positions with greater responsibilities would eventually get higher pay. The worst part was being left out of decision-making. I was no longer asked to attend important meetings and help run projects and programs. I was only supposed to provide data on command from my superiors—very military.

Our interim human resource director wasn't much help, so I threatened go to the EEOC or a private attorney if due process didn't work out. Our former architectural director, Shi Shi Ahmadi, settled for a sizable sum. Our carpentry supervisor, Arturo Saldana, did the same and kept his job. It seemed that TSU would rather pay lawsuits than run the university right. Most of us in the traces just shook our heads, kept them down and kept working. It's sad when a higher education institution gets so subjected to greed, power, cronyism, and nepotism that it can no longer function.

I was again asked to serve on the Steering Committee for TSU's self study, leading to re-accreditation every ten years by the Southern Association of Colleges and Universities in 2000. In 1988-90, I led committees and wrote part of the report. This time my role was considerably limited to attending meetings. A color flow chart of the process I created was never used. Harold was incensed when he heard that I was on the committee—thought that he deserved my spot.

Johnson liked my work order system. I had hoped to put it on the Internet with Frontier Scripts, but since I didn't have an Internet connection, that wasn't possible. My Macintosh network was still working, and working well considering we had no upgrades for three years. I did get to install PowerSecretary on my Mac 6500. It enabled me to dictate text and run most programs. It was okay for straight text, but I had to disable it to edit, or do database, spreadsheet, or graphic work. I ordered an Orbit trackball and IBM's Naturally Speaking for my NT machine. There was no substitute for a good mouse. The two-button Windows mouse was very hard for me to use, so I was trying to come up with something as productive as my Mac mouse.

The 266 Mhz DTK computer I got came with Windows NT, Internet Explorer, Microsoft Office 97, and a photo editor. I could convert our Word and Excel files easily. Photos were also easy, but I was not sure about all the multilevel drawings I did in MacDraw Pro. Until I could get it, I would miss the versatility of PhotoShop. I scanned and colored an 8.5 x 14 campus plan and ran it off on my color printer for the police to distribute to visitors. All of my floor plans were in the same, multilevel format. I would need software to continue to edit and improve them.

Helix had no plans to go to Windows, so my database programs would have to be converted to SQL, Oracle, or some other database used with

Windows. I easily corrected any year 2000 problems I created by subtracting 1900 from the year to get two digit years. It took only two hours to convert our facilities inventory (FI) emulation to match the State's Y2K record format. I updated the FI on my Helix database, dumped the formatted data to a floppy disk, took it home, and then uploaded it to the Coordinating Board's server in Austin. I used a great little free program from the Net, Fetch, to send and receive files to any server I had access to. Our old Microtek MSF-300ZS scanner did a remarkable job of capturing photos and drawings in high resolution. The scanner was not Windows compatible, and, when I tried to connect it to my 6500 PowerMac, it wouldn't work. It worked well with the Mac IIfx it was connected to. I moved the scans through the network or compressed files on floppy disks. In two years or so, I should have been able to make the transition. In the meantime, the changes were traumatic, time-consuming and unproductive.

## REQUEST FOR LEAK ADJUSTMENT

ACCOUNT NUMBER: 550193001-08
SERVICE ADDRESS: 3501 Wheeler
Houston, Texas 77004
DAY TIME PHONE NO: 713 313-7777

A City of Houston ordinance allows for a employ assess credit because of loss of water through an "excusable defect" in the customer's water line. An excusable defect is due to a rupture or leakage caused by weather, settlement, corrosion, wear or accident. Credit may be given for one-half of the rate charged to usage in excess of the average. This adjustment is limited to a maximum of three (3) consecutive months and must be requested within six open (6) months of the repair. **Visible leak such as faucet and hose leaks are ineligible.**

I, __Ronald W. Hull__ nd the responsible party for the account at the above service address.
(Give in full legal name and/or business license)

I am familiar with all the facts stated in this document and they are true and correct. Making false statements on this government record is subject to criminal prosecution under Chapter 37 of the Texas Penal Code. I certify that this application and attached documents contain no false statements.

I am asking the City of Houston to reduce the water bill for this account, to the extent allowed by city ordinance because of the leak beginning on (date) __5/1/96__ and repaired on (date) __8/26/96__ . During this period, the following additional water appliances (washer, a dishwasher, spa, etc.) were installed at the service address. State "NONE" if none were added: __None__ The water lost from this leak was not used by anyone.

> *IN ORDER TO PROCESS YOUR APPLICATION QUICKLY AND EFFICIENTLY, PLEASE READ THE FOLLOWING CAREFULLY AND GIVE A COMPLETE AND CLEAR DESCRIPTION OF THE REPAIRS.*

Type of leak on customer's side of meter: _____ ▼

Description of repair: __See attached Work Order Report__

Attached documentation of repair date, address, type of repair, and cost. Acceptable documents include plumber statements/Bill or credit for parks business with in-house maintenance may submit a statement signed by two (2) employees who witnessed the repair.

In all cases, the City returns right to make field verifications' before approving leak adjustments.

You will be notified by mail when your request is approved or denied.

*Signature of person requesting a leak adjustment:* _Ronald W. Hull_

*Print Name:* __Ronald W. Hull__         *Date:* __1/8/97__

**COMPLETE FORM AND RETURN TO:**   *UTILITY CUSTOMER SERVICE*
P.O. Box 4863
Houston, Texas 77210

**One of many forms automatically generated by my Facilities database. I could emulate most forms, making paperwork well organized and simpler to do.**

# 64

## Perils of an Active Life

When I stopped riding METROLift in September 1998, I immediately missed the company of my drivers, Willie, in the morning, and Jo, in the afternoon. Most of all, I missed riding with Bob Pruett and Ken Krajewski. I stopped by to see each of them after I started driving, and they were both impressed with my van's set up. Ken would get one if he could. Bob had a full size van, but probably would never drive unless the operating systems improved more or researchers came up with a way to reverse his paralysis, more severe than mine.

Beh drove the Monte every day. She also threatened to get a newer car, but finances got in the way of that. To improve my financial picture, I started renting the empty room upstairs. In addition to help with expenses, it provided a tax break and an extra someone in the house to help us out. My renters didn't work out too well. The first guy left when he couldn't hold a job and pay his rent. Beh saw him later, and he appeared to have gotten his act together. The second guy was no problem, but he reconciled with his wife and went back to live with her. My third tenant got behind on her rent and didn't help me as she promised. I had to tell her to leave. Parking was a problem, but we managed.

My decline slowed because while I rode in the chair there were fewer stresses to my spine. Dr. Parsons saw me every six months. My annual check of my bladder and kidneys showed that everything was okay, and I hoped to stave off surgery for many years. Dr. Rudy, my urologist, was surprised that my condition remained so stable. In March 1998, I got a C-PAP (positive air pressure) ventilator and mask for my sleep apnea. It seemed to help with blood circulation and discomfort in my legs, but it dried out my throat and the effort to keep my mouth shut kept me awake. Eventually, the mask got so irritating on my face that I quit wearing it. I got about the same amount of sleep with or without it.

Duane Henson became a reliable helper at work, helping me go to the bathroom, fixing my wheelchair, and even helping me with computer moves. He got fed up with the demands our new management gave him, and quit in late August 1998, to pursue his carpet cleaning business. He came by to replace my ramping in the garage that had deteriorated by getting wet. When Gina left, I started going over to the nursing station every day in another building to get my urine bag emptied. The two nurses liked me, and came over to help me if the weather was bad.

I spent about twenty hours with Chad Stromatt of Drivers Rehab Services in February and March 1988 in his old Ford 150 Econoline Van learning to drive my rig. During that process, Chad determined that it would be best to get a new wheelchair since mine was approaching five years and showing signs of structural fatigue. I was fitted for a Permobil chair. Made in Sweden, this $16,000 wheelchair was fully adjustable and could elevate me to standing height and tilt back 45 degrees to relieve pressure from sitting. It had gear driven front drive and dual rear dolly wheels. The Permobil was much heavier and a real tank compared to my Invacare sports car. When it arrived in May, we found that its height, about an inch and a half higher, was a big problem. Also, the leg rests didn't swing away. Great Bear, the provider, found that the standard cushion wouldn't work, and gave me a thinner J-Cushion, filled with form fitting silly putty, in its place. It took two months of modifications and fittings before I could use the chair, and it was still not comfortable to sit in for a long time.

The van was having its own problems. There were problems with the controls and shorts in the wiring. Finally, in June, I got to drive it for the first time. Signals from the EMC controls operated all the normal automotive equipment by servos. The factory-installed steering, brakes and other controls remained in place, and could be operated by disengaging the EMC system. Before I could drive, I had to pull a Grandmar belt, fastened to my wheelchair and covered with Velcro, tight across my chest to hold me upright and in place in my chair. The belt greatly restricted my reach, but was necessary to keep me stable while driving.

I entered the van by using a remote on my chair arm that allows me to automatically open the side door, kneel the van by letting air out of its air suspension, and lower the ramp. I then drive my electric chair into a v-clamp in the EZ Lock system bolted to the floor. The EZ-Lock locks onto a heavy post under my chair that positions and secures it for driving. I have to lift the lap and chest safety belts over my knees to get in. Then, I'd push a button to electrically swing my headrest in place.

The headrest had large blue button on its right side. If I held the button in with my head for one beep, and then released it, I'd dim the lights. Two beeps, and the horn would honk. Three beeps and the wipers operated. The head button was easy to operate at any time or driving conditions.

I started the engine using a sequence on the control panel at my right elbow. Using the remote on the left armrest of the chair, I'd raise the ramp, and close the door. An air pump would raise the van and kept the suspension level while underway. I'd engage the steering by moving it to engage and release a backup system every time I started the van. Then, I'd set the lights, a/c, or anything else I'd need before getting underway. When I pulled the hand gas/brake back with my left hand, I could shift to a gear on the right panel by pushing its button and then proceed. I'd drop my right hand into a tri-pin to steer and move my left hand forward to increase throttle. I'd signal by leaning the gas/brake tri-pin to the left or right. Driving was fairly normal, except I'd have to use both hands continually. It was a bit like driving a video game or flying an airplane without foot pedals, except I couldn't crash and start over.

The control unit on my new wheelchair went out. Chad had to push me into place for our training drives until a new unit came in. One day in mid July, I asked him to help me get the license plates for the van. Locked in place to drive, I decided to stay in the van with the a/c on because it was so hard to push me around. It took Chad over two and a half hours waiting in lines. The van's engine stayed cool, but I nearly cooked as the sun beat in on me. I had to be sure that I'd never get stuck in the van in hot weather without a/c and the windows up—a real possibility without electrical power.

After several delays for parts and repairs, I was finally able to take my DPS driving test in July 1998. The a/c acted up again, but I was able to go ahead with only the rear air on. I lost points for speeding, but passed the test. There were more delays and repairs to both the chair and the van.

Finally, on September 4, two evaluators from Texas A & M went over everything and the Texas Rehabilitation Commission paid for the van and chair and released them to me. I was ready to leave at 3 pm, but problems with the EZ Lock and lap belt kept me there until five. I drove the van home alone, exhausted, for the first time. All that waiting in the heat with my muscles spasming and cramping had finally paid off.

Driving to work in heavy traffic was scary, especially when my head button and wiper control went out. I had to turn the wipers and headlights on if it looked like rain before I left for two weeks until parts came in. Four or five times, when I didn't get the transmission shifted fully into Park, the ramp wouldn't work and the engine wouldn't start. I'd get frustrated trying everything I knew, and then finally figure it out.

One evening when the van wouldn't start and my batteries appeared to be low, I decided to take the bus home at 5:20 pm. I caught the wrong 68 bus and had to transfer half way home. That worked out okay, but I had to transfer to 65 about three miles from home. The first 65 bus was inaccessible, but a supervisor on board assured me that the next one would be. Four inaccessible buses later, I was exhausted and cold. I crossed a busy street and called METROLift. They got me home at 8:30. Beh was frantic.

One day, when I was stranded in the street for an hour and nothing was working, I asked a guy helping me to push the van. When he did, it went into Park and everything started working. That problem was fixed, and, if it happened again, I knew what to do. The trick was remembering.

It took a long time to get comfortable in heavy traffic. The steering would bind and I'd over correct. My braking response was so slow that I couldn't drive over 60, even though everyone around me was going 65. Changing lanes to the right was hard. But I was getting better with the mirrors and the right signal. After driving three weeks, I started to develop a pressure sore. It was like sitting on a marble. I suffered excruciating pain most of the way home until I could unbuckle in my driveway and relieve the pressure. Searching for an answer, I tried a Stimulite cushion I'd had for three years but didn't use because it had cut off circulation to my legs in my Invacare chair. The Stimulite cushion not only cleared up the problem, but it healed the sore while I sat on it in two days. I tried to get another cushion for a back up, but my insurance wouldn't pay for it.

# 65

# Turning 2000

The new millennium, actually the year 2000, was fast approaching. While I didn't see the Y2K problem as apocalyptic, I expected minor glitches that would be annoying, like my VCR clock that I hadn't reset since a power outage over six months earlier. All of these little equipment resets were hard to keep up with. My helpers were not as technically competent as I'd liked, but they would help me if they could.

With the Internet, my communication with my immediate family jumped tenfold. By January 1, 2000, I had four email addresses. I hung onto my first primary ISP for a long time, but finally let go. The transition to new computers and ISPs gets more difficult as I invested in more software and documents while developing my Internet web pages.

Beh got a computer in May 1999. It had a 17-inch monitor and a good scanner. The printer wasn't very good, but it was serviceable. She didn't have any time to use it, but I got her a cheap Internet connection with Everyone's Internet for ten bucks a month. Since Southwestern Bell had been nickeling me to death, I transferred our pages to ev1.com, too.

Roger and Sue couldn't get to Aspen in April 1999, for their annual ski outing, so they went to Lake Louise, Alberta, instead. He was skiing on ice, with a light covering of snow, when he fell and went numb from the neck down. Roger was flown to emergency in a helicopter. When everything started moving again, he went home. Then, he suffered through most of the summer with tingling hands and weakness. Kelley, Roger's daughter, lined him up with a neurosurgeon in Cleveland. An MRI showed that he had an injured spine, similar to mine. The operation lasted four hours. He had disk repair at C2 and his vertebrae fused C3-5. He recovered quite well, but didn't regain full strength in his hands for some time. It was amazing how close his injury was to mine. Our mother wrote, wishing that I'd had had his surgery in 1963. So did I.

Tim and Tom took their kids and went the Canadian Boundary Waters in June 1999. They wanted to retrace the route Tim, Tom, and I took in 1975, but weren't allowed to. In order to maintain its wilderness status, the Canadian government strictly controlled access to the area. The memories of those two trips I took there flooded back. I wished that I could go again.

After Beh bought an alteration and dry cleaning shop on Westheimer in February 1999, I had to wait for her to close at 7 pm and then take at least 15 minute to drive home. I usually arrived home from work around 5:30, sometimes distressed from a need to go to the bathroom. Waiting for her only added to my distress.

I tried to hire some help to meet me in the evening. After three tries, we gave up. Amiesha, a former TSU cheerleader, was wonderful for a week. Then she disappeared. She reappeared one day in August, asking for my reference for nursing school. Her grandmother had suffered a stroke, and she had to leave suddenly to take care of her. Then, I hired May, from the Philippines. May was a problem from the start, so I let her go. Then, she hung out with Beh until Beh refused to put up with her. May borrowed money from Beh that she didn't pay back.

Finally, I hired Gilda. Gilda was from Brazil and married to an American petroleum engineer. She cleaned my house beautifully until she got another job with hours that overlapped mine and had to quit. I stopped trying to hire someone. Beh and I both learned to wait and depend only on us.

We worked on my bowel program to ease that problem.

Beh's former partner, Vi, the one who bought her out, was robbed and beaten in that shop in October 1999. She then lost the shop because she was afraid to go back there to work. I often wonder if Beh would have been targeted if she had stayed at that shop. I told her to be careful, especially when leaving her shop with money, but there is only so much she could do.

Beh and I visited Mom and Dad in McAllen at Christmas, 1998. It was my first trip in the van and Beh's first time to drive it. We had to enlist the help of strangers at gas stations to swap the front seat. Vantage Mobility showed a picture of a woman wheeling the seat around, but it took a strong man to horse it into place. It was warm our whole stay. My father gave up the reins and I loved driving us around, especially when we had dinner at Pepe's on the Rio Grande—Ah freedom!

Then, on New Year's Day, 1999, we took a weekend run to San Antonio that tested my fledgling driving skills. Maria was going to go with us, but when heavy rains were predicted, she backed out. It rained as we left Houston, and it turned colder, but the weather didn't slow us down.

We stopped at Market Square and the Riverwalk, and got to see Everest on IMAX. It was so real I felt like I was on the mountain. We visited Beh's uncle and revisited Natural Bridge Cavern. An employee saw me waiting in the cool morning for Beh and took me to a back entrance. I was able to enter a great room and see wonderful formations from my wheelchair. It was tough driving Beh's cousin out to the suburbs late at night, but after I drove all the way home, I knew I could travel again.

And travel we did. I planned a trip to Yellowstone, and after attempting to get Dessiray and Beh's brothers to go with us, it came down to the two of us.

We left Saturday morning, 7/31/99, with only a week to make the trip. Beh had started preparing early, and had everything ready. Still, it took a long time to pack and get going. I was anxious and tired before we left. I drove Highway 6 through College Station to Waco. Then took I-35 through Ft. Worth to US 287 (287goes all the way to Yellowstone) and Wichita Falls. By that time, fighting traffic, the wind, and the sun in my eyes, I let Beh take over and get us to Amarillo.

Knowing we had a long way to go, I began to doubt if we could make it. The next morning we left late again and faced construction delays, and then rain in Eastern Colorado. After I started driving in midday the battery warning light came on in heavy rain. Beh took over driving again, worried that I'd have trouble driving if we lost power to my controls. Then, the ABS warning light came on as the rain stopped. The brakes seemed to be all right. I decided not to go to the Rocky Mountain National Park because there was rain in the mountains above Denver. Beh braked hard in Denver construction to avoid a car coming in from the right. My portable chair and all our stuff came off the rear seat and hit the back of our seats—nothing damaged. Frontier Days in Cheyenne forced us into a Holiday Inn in Ft. Collins. The expensive disabled room was a converted standard room, mostly inaccessible.

Monday morning, I called Trey Morris at Mobility Plus about the warning lights. He told me all he could at a distance. The warning lights disappeared when we started up. Beh complained about her first mountain driving to Laramie. I worried about the real mountains ahead, but said nothing. I spotted antelope, but Beh didn't see them. She started handling the mountains well and wouldn't give up the wheel. We crossed Wyoming very quickly. She loved Dubois with its new wood rustic, tourist town look. I'd never heard of Dubois, but it was obvious that thousands were flocking there. Finally, I spotted a herd of antelope running uphill. Beh got only a glimpse. Late in the afternoon, we entered a valley with marvelous scenery and the Tetons in the background. At the gate to Grand Teton Park, my Lifetime Pass appeared to be left at home. It turned out to be in my wallet all along. I had to fake it, and they let us in free.

Then, a buck came down the mountain on my right, *fast*, landing on the road and losing his footing, before I could warn Beh. She braked hard, and he got up and bounded down the hill to Jackson Lake, 30 feet away. Beh wanted to stop, but I urged her on, grateful that we just missed him. The Yellowstone fires had bared a steep canyon going in. Beh, afraid, didn't look. I was on the bent rail steep side, oozy from fatigue and glad I wasn't driving.

We stayed at Grant Village that night. Grant Village on Lake Yellowstone was beautiful, new, and very accessible. We wheelchaired down to the Lake House for a pasta buffet. We watched cutthroat trout pick hatching larvae off the water, and then relaxed in our room for the outdoor amphitheater show at 9:30. The trails were totally dark as we drove out into the cool evening. Beh was scared, but I enjoyed the solitude. I finally heard a loudspeaker as we arrived just as the slide show was ending—I had wondered why they held it so late! We had changed time zones or I read the flyer wrong. A flashlight shined ahead of us on the way back. I don't know who was holding it. I preferred the dark, cool, moonless night.

The next morning I drove easily over Craig Pass (8262 ft) through burned out forest from the fires of 1988. Old Faithful was erupting when we entered the valley. We then waited a long time in the hot sun for Old Faithful to do it again. At the Lodge, Beh thought that she had lost her credit card and heavy worry set in about that.

My worry faded and my enthusiasm grew as I wheelchaired the entire Midway Geyser Basin with its amazing colored pools. Beh took many pictures. At the Norris Geyser Basin, I got rained on and had trouble coming up a steep gravel trail, filled with Chinese tourists. They offered to push, but I made it alone when they cleared the path. We stopped and Beh climbed rock at the Obsidian Cliff. We stopped for elk at Gardner River and Beh got close pictures—she was so excited!

At Mammoth Hot Springs, a herd of elk lounged on the shimmering white flats like they have for thousands of years without burning their feet. Then, it was rough road and high passes to Tower Falls. In 1966, I pulled up to a bear there. There were miles of beautiful habitat, but we didn't see any animals. I got out at Tower Falls, but didn't get to the falls. By the time we got to Canyon Village it was getting dark and I was exhausted.

At Canyon, we stayed in a brand new building with expensive rooms, no phones, and poor disability design. We had to drive to the Lodge to eat.

The next morning, Beh got great cloudy pictures of the brink of Yellowstone Falls. I was strapped in and couldn't get out. I made her stop for deer, and she got some close pictures. Then, along the Yellowstone River, we came upon small herds of buffalo. We didn't get to see any bear, moose, or sheep, but Beh enjoyed every animal she did see. In spite of the rain, the Tetons were majestic, and Beh got pictures.

Jackson was crowded with summer tourists and bikers. We couldn't stop to see the elk horns in the square because of heavy traffic and no parking.

After driving the high pass over the shoulder of the Tetons from Jackson, we entered Idaho. Here, the high wheat fields were marvelous, and Beh wanted to stop for potatoes. I took over driving and drove us south on I-15 to Provo. With the mountains on my left and the Great Salt Lake on my right, it was a race to get there before dark. After miles of narrow construction lanes in Salt Lake City, my right hand was spasming to the point that it was coming out of my steering tri-pin. Beh pushed it back in place. We only relaxed in our motel room. A cafeteria wouldn't let Beh take food out. I incorrectly ordered our meal at a fast food drive through. Beh was tired and angry. We decided to stop earlier the rest of the trip.

By morning, we were feeling a lot better. I drove out over Soldier Pass to Green River on I-70. In the high desert, I had trouble keeping my speed up. Beh took it for fatigue again, and insisted on driving. We stopped at Arches National Park. We wasted a lot of time looking for arches we couldn't see from the road. Finally, we saw several arches, but I couldn't get out because it was raining. There wasn't time to go to all the sights in the area. We drove on, only stopping briefly at the entrance to Mesa Verde National Park, and then to Durango for the night.

I had made the mistake of not getting a reservation. The Budget Inn had only one three bed, non-disabled room. The Comfort Inn called several other motels—no rooms. I had visions of driving to Santa Fe in the night, Beh in hysterics. Back at the Budget Inn, we took the large room and it was very comfortable. We wheelchaired down to a KFC and brought back chicken in a light rain. The dome light was on in the van. Nothing we did would turn it off. Beh worried about a dead battery in the morning. I knew the emergency battery would start us.

The next day, I wanted to make Santa Fe by noon. I directed Beh onto a wrong turn off US 84 at Chama. Before we knew it, we were climbing along a tourist steam train track to a 10,250-foot pass. It was the closest we got to Rocky Mountain National Park—beautiful. On open range, we came upon an Angus steer in the road and had to drive around him. At Antonio, three huge round mountains rose from the high desert like green backed turtles. It gave reason to call New Mexico the *land of enchantment.*

After being caught in a mile of very slow road construction and heavy traffic, Beh didn't want to stop in Santa Fe. She didn't like the adobe buildings. We stopped on I-40 to buy gifts and I began driving. I started out well, but on grades the van would slow, even with me pushing full throttle. I would pick up speed on a downgrade, only to lose it on the next upgrade. It ended with me going 40 in the shoulder with the flashers on, 18-wheelers roaring by. I could stop and start out okay, only to slow when I tried to hold speed. Beh started driving again. We couldn't shut the flashers off with the engine running.

At Clovis, New Mexico, we stopped for the night. I took a look at the map. We could make it home the next day. Beh wanted to honor the anniversary of her mother's death with her family on August 8th. Flashers going and people flashing us back, we drove home on great roads through small towns like Brownwood, Texas.

We saw three dead deer in the hill country and ran into hellish Saturday afternoon traffic going into Austin. We stopped in Hempstead and bought the biggest, sweetest watermelon I'd had in years. The 290 bypass had ruined business for the farmers' market. They were selling out.

I took the van to Mobility Plus Monday morning. The gas/brake problem was a badly frayed steel cable. It was replaced Thursday, and the van became much easier to accelerate. That problem had been there a long time. The gas filler vent tube had to be disconnected and drained because overfilling had filled it with gasoline, making it hard to fill the tank. The electric gremlins disappeared just like they appeared. Beh caught up quickly with her work at the shop, and I returned to work as usual. The memories will last a lifetime.

With Beh at her brother's house in Pearland, TX 1999

With the Monte Carlo in the garage, the Windstar got the driveway.

## 66

## More Trouble at Work

We had another light winter without a freeze. Beh's peach tree grew wildly, but didn't produce any fruit. She had to prune it into shape. My peach tree finally died. I just watched it fall apart. It still served as a roost for birds. My flowerbeds were wilder than ever. Beh was so busy I didn't think I'd ever get anything planted in them again.

Texas Southern University managed to clear reports by the Texas State Comptroller and the State Auditor's Office. However, President James Douglas had to step down, along with his vice presidents, except for Harold Johnson. Pricilla Slade, who had been Dean of the School of Business, replaced Douglas. Slade had secured funding from the Jesse H. Jones Foundation to build a building to replace Allen Hall, suffering flood damage and deterioration. She began running the university like a business, relying on outside consultants and outsourcing. In October 1999, her interim status was dropped after a search failed to provide a challenger.

Charles Carter's lawsuit continued. It was some of his reporting that brought the auditors in. Most of the bad guys were now gone, but Carter wasn't reinstated. The problem was the Board of Regents. As long as the Board was politically appointed and allowed to bring their favorites in and run the university from the Board Room, our problems would continue.

My problems magnified. When Harold said that he was buying The Maintenance Authority (TMA) in the fall of 1998, to replace the work order system I had in place. I didn't stand in the way. I saw it as a way to bring our supplies, keying, construction, and deferred maintenance tracking into a unified system, something I always advocated and tried to put together. TMA operated on both Macs and Windows NT, so all I would have to do was download data from Helix, and upload it into Omis, the database driver for TMA. We bought TMA in February 1999. We were trained in April. When I inquired about when we were going to install it, I was told that we were waiting for more NT computers. We got the computers, but no TMA. Rumor had it that they didn't buy a multi-user version or the server it required in place. When they found out what it would cost, and that they'd have to give me a lead role to get it working, they backed out. I fixed some Y2K problems I had put in my system and kept upgrading it. Helix got new life in February 1999, when The Chip Merchant bought it. I became a Beta tester, and got free updates. Helix had plans to go cross platform, so I hoped to be able to move my systems to NT.

I was told to transfer the land and facilities inventories to JT Glover. When I tried to teach the woman JT hired to do the facilities inventory, she almost quit over having to review the files I carefully kept on each building. She was made Jeanie's supervisor, which infuriated Jeanie. Without help, I was unable to continue the updates I'd planned.

Then, in May, without consulting me, Harold hired Harry Montgomery, former director of campus planning for the Texas Higher Education Coordinating Board (THECB), as a consultant to *correct* the inventory. For some strange reason, it was all about measurement, a small part of the inventorying process. I guess a guy in a wheelchair couldn't measure correctly. The numbers had to be off. Harry immediately got my floor plans and room listings and set to work. Harold and JT had several staff members go with him. I never received that level of support. Harry's changes to my room entries were minor, and he only finished about a third of the buildings before he quit. He told me (and Harold), "Ron's got a good system. It isn't broke; no need to fix it." A former student continued the work for a while until he was ordered to stop. I recorded all the changes and electronically transferred them to the Coordinating Board's database in Austin.

In August, I learned that Page Southerland Page, an engineering firm, had been hired to outsource the inventory for $100,000. I was told that they were going to "*fix*" the inventory. The problem rested with the university's dismal classroom and laboratory utilization rates. When our enrollment dropped and we added many new classrooms and labs with President Slade's new business building, our rates became dead last among all Texas universities. They blamed me for coding the inventory wrong. They couldn't see that it wasn't in the coding. Nobody asked me.

After I was unable to replace Gina, JT had moved a lot of new computer equipment and his technician into my workroom. Then, he changed the lock. I had to ask to have the room unlocked to get to my files and my computer scanning system. Over the Christmas holiday, all of my office furniture had to be moved out to have the entire suite re-carpeted. The student that was assigned to help me did a good job, but he never got all my papers back in my office or my computers and file server back working after.

Nothing was connected to the new university network. Finally, I rearranged my office so that all the computers were together, behind me, and I could get them reconnected. My PowerSecretary dictation system wasn't working on my Mac. When I tried to fix it, the software was missing. I missed struggling with it and the control it gave me of my computer and dictation.

I was told to develop the area's web pages. I continued to use my Mac because I didn't have the software on my NT to do the graphics. I had no scanner or color printer with it. I developed an outline for the web pages and was told to pursue them. When I went to scan some graphics, my Mac scanner had been removed to the warehouse. It really upset me. I had to go retrieve it myself. I never got the scanner back, but I did get the backup fileserver drive attached to it, with many of our historic documents, dating back fifteen years, that were on it. After that, any scanning I did was on my scanner at home. I got some digital camera shots and some graphics from the Internet, and developed 13 pages. I sent them out for review, but no one responded except Jim Anderson. I shared them with Donald Dement, the new TSU webmaster. He liked them and put them up. The sad part about it was that I got no feedback about them from anyone else. You could see the pages by going to www.tsu.edu, and then Administration, and then Facilities Planning and Operations. Those pages were removed later in upgrades and no longer exist.

I no longer had any responsibility for land. However, Jeanie had to check with me often to get land information from our files. I'd had to print my land data every time they needed land information. No one seemed to be able to keep good records.

I was never asked to review the Viron contract of 1999, our energy performance contractor, or their work. I was lined up to take a course at Texas A&M to verify and evaluate the contract's savings, but that was stopped. Then, the Coordinating Board rejected the performance contract. The university was required to change the work to a design/build contract. Contracts were granted to review the work that was already done and to evaluate the savings. There were no funds to pay Viron for the work already completed. The university stalled and Viron sued. It was Harold Johnson's downfall. He was on his way out.

My energy management certifications were up for renewal, but I had trouble verifying that I'd been involved in energy management work. I still maintained energy consumption tracking and provided budget projections for utilities. The evaporation credit program I oversaw saved us $100,000 in fiscal year1998. The Energy Engineering Association didn't seem to care, as long as I paid the renewal fees. I would have rather been actively involved in conservation measures again.

When I got my van, I paid for and requested an administrative parking space. I was told to park in our visitors' disabled spaces. When I objected, I was told to park to a stop in the lot marked, "handicapped." I had no one to help me in my office. I relied on whoever dropped in or I could summon to help me. Several people volunteered and came to my aid regularly, but I had no official help.

Diann Massingill, a custodian, started helping me in late 1998. She expressed a desire to travel, so we took her with us to my parents' place in McAllen. After that, she came a few nights to spell Beh for free. It was the first uninterrupted sleep Beh had gotten in several years. My interrupted sleep continued. If I didn't thrive on it, I survived on it.

I saw our new human resource director, Princess Gardner, twice about my situation. She was retired from AT&T, and was appalled to hear what was happening, but seemed powerless to do anything about it. Unable to wait any longer, I requested a meeting with President Slade. I was told to write my concerns to the university ombudsperson. Dr. Alma Alexander was an old friend and a cancer survivor. I thought she would help. I was sure some of my problems stemmed from the president herself, but I wanted to lay out my concerns to Alexander, and then tell Slade to do the right thing, or I'd go to the EEOC. I never got that opportunity.

One of my biggest problems remaining was how to transfer my multilevel MacDraw drawings to the NT computers. The solution was simple, PowerPoint. Although I lost the layers, PowerPoint transferred all the objects, so I didn't have to redraw anything to paste it into AutoCad—a big relief. I continued to maintain and update the campus plan. I put a copy on TSU's website. Everyone liked it.

# 67

# Maintaining Health, Home and Wheels

W e rented the room upstairs to a college student with a rich father in Cairo. He wasn't any help and used our phones and computers like they were his. Then, he went to Pakistan, came back, and stopped paying rent. Beh then found this wonderful Vietnamese spinster, Hwa, to solve all our problems. Hwa was asked to watch the house for us while we went to Yellowstone. While we were gone, she drove the college student out and took his room. Helpful at first, Hwa wanted to run the house like it was her own. Hwa paid the rent on time. When Hwa couldn't get what she wanted, she moved out. I was okay with that.

My primary care physician, Dr. Marilyn Rice at the Kelsey-Seybold Clinic, retired in April 1999. I had a hard time replacing her. I was assigned a doctor. When I got there they had switched me to a Pakistani who seemed little interested in me and a nurse that said she couldn't help me transfer. I complained. Dr. Nicholas Solomos stepped in and proved a young, energetic and able replacement. Dr. Parsons reviewed my condition every six months at TIRR. Dr. Del Terzo, my new urologist, was pleasant and helpful. I had to have a series of "pain in the butt" sessions with outpatient surgery. That's all I'll say about that (hemorrhoids removed). Sitting all the time and muscle spasms made my life miserable at times. But I just waited it out until I could get help to change position and relieve the pressure. In August 1999, I had a second sleep study to get nose pillows for my C-PAP (positive air pressure) ventilator. We never used them.

I made a ritual of wheeling over to the Student Health Center every day around noon in good weather to empty my urine bag. When one of the nurses quit it was a bit difficult for a while, but people came forward. Five people volunteered to empty my bag and two guys helped me go to the bathroom. As I lost my abdominal muscles, my stability continued to decline. I started keeping my swing-away lateral supports in place all the time on my Permobil chair to keep me from falling to either side while typing. With the help of the tilt, I could still reach down and pick things up from the floor.

Handwriting became very difficult, as I grew unstable at the waist. I didn't realize how much the abs play in writing and holding things steady. I wrote with the computer whenever I could. I could still hit keys fast and accurately with the thumb on my splinted hand. Reaching for some keys threw me up against a lateral support and off kilter until I could straighten up again.

By December 1999, my Ford Windstar GL had 18,000 miles on it in a year and three months of driving. Except for the trip to Yellowstone, most of it was to and from work. I had many minor problems with the van, ranging from electrical glitches to safety issues. It took a year to get back into the left lane. At first, I tried to blend with traffic in the slow lanes. I let everyone pass me and didn't try to keep up. Position became everything in my life, and position of the controls was critical to my driving. It took a long time to get the controls positioned and working right.

Independence Vans, now called Mobility Plus, worked with me every step of the way, repairing every problem I had. They replaced the computers for the steering and electric gas/brake, several wiring harnesses, the gas/brake cable, air suspension pump, and numerous switches and actuators. Thirty trips for repairs and adjustments in the first year.

Aside from my daily concern with just driving, I had my share of scares. Soon after I got the van, while approaching my freeway exit at 60 mph, my right hand came out of the steering tri-pin. I slowed the van while it gradually veered to the right, until I could get my hand back in the tri-pin enough to gain control. I found that spasms in my right hand would lift my fingers out. We fixed that with a washer on top of the main pin on the tri-pin in August 1999. We also put a leveler on my gas/brake tri-pin to keep it from tilting back when I stopped. Sometimes my hand would nearly come out while I braked at an intersection.

One day in the spring, I heard my gas/brake alarm "chirping" as I left work. The alarm became constant well before I began to exit the freeway

15 miles later. The van stalled uphill just before the exit ramp. All my power was dead—not enough even to run the engine. I nearly panicked because it was hot and the power windows wouldn't open. When I pulled my red emergency battery lever to engage the rear backup battery, everything worked. I could start the engine with it, but had to let go of the lever to drive. When I did… everything on the panel began to flicker, and the engine ran badly, sputtered, and then died. I started the engine three times and drove on until it died completely off the freeway about 3 miles from home.

I hailed some people walking with a cell phone who called AAA for me. A Houston police officer arrived. It was about two miles to home, so I offered to wheel with my chair. The officer wouldn't allow it. I rode home in the van on top of the flatbed AAA tow truck with a nervous police escort. My battery isolator between the main and backup batteries had shorted out.

One day in June, I was driving home in the center lane of five lanes of new freeway at 60 mph. A Civic came from my right, skidding, and violently hit the back of a Suburban directly in front of me. Both cars spun rapidly like tops, spewing black tire smoke, the Civic spun to the wall on the left, and the Suburban to the wall on the right. I slowed to 5 mph, my heart in my throat, and continued, unscathed, along with two other cars alongside me on either side across two sets of spiral black skid marks and the heavy smell of burned rubber in the air. Luckily, no other cars were involved.

The van got good mileage. In August, I was low on gas, so I picked a station near home to stop at on my way home. The warning light came on half way at the Loop. Eight miles further on, in the left lane, I felt the van buck. I crossed three lanes of traffic and picked a spot where an on ramp came on and stalled there. I wanted to call AAA, but a young man crossed three lanes of fast traffic four times to get me gas. After that experience, I stopped at any station at the first sign of being low on gas. I got strangers to pump my gas. The new credit card pumps made it easy for them. Some people even helped me go through car washes.

The first week in December 1999, started with my steering faulting out four times Monday morning. It went into backup with the alarm on. I had to stop the van and turn off the ignition and steering to reboot it. It hadn't happened before. After that it began to fault often. The steering computer had to be replaced and the mountings had melted.

One day, I had just entered the freeway and got up to speed when I saw a small car spin out behind me in my rear view mirror. Further up the road, I stalled in the left lane when I stopped for traffic. I must've had some bad gasoline because the van never stalled before. I couldn't get it started. A wrecker pulled up, and the driver said he'd have to tow me off the freeway because it was rush hour. I had trouble getting the van in neutral because the bright sunlight made it hard to see the panel lights. The tow truck driver got out and shut down the freeway and then towed me off in the van. At a gas station, my ramp wouldn't work. After the tow truck driver called AAA and METROLift, and another wrecker driver tried to help, he called Mobility Plus. I heard Cliff, the technician say, "Was it in park?" It suddenly dawned on me. I was so embarrassed when I put the van in park and could operate the ramp and start the engine again. For that mistake of mine, the poor wrecker driver had to get me down off the freeway and wasn't paid.

My 1998 Windstar in the high country of Wyoming. August 1999

Elipical Pool with burned trees on far slope. Yellowstone Aug 1999

Elk on both sides of the river.    Beh at Yellowstone Falls

A buffalo herd in Yellowstone. August 1999

My first small novel, completed in January, 2000

## 68

## Getting Published

Beh prepared for any Y2K problems by getting us two weeks of canned and dry foods and some water. I was not worried that we'd lose power, but I'd had my own vexing little Y2K problems at work. Early on, I subtracted 1900 from the year in my Helix databases to get a nice, 2-digit year to display. When we went to Fiscal Year 2000 on September 1, 1999, I had a devil of a time finding and correcting all the errors I'd created. It's amazing how much work it was to correct them.

My plan was to move my retirement assets (mostly stock) to safer ground in August, and then move them back after the 2000 new year. I didn't do it. By mid October, I regretted not doing it. By December, I was money ahead again. I didn't think the economy would be affected by Y2K problems and I was right. Still, it took billions to correct the problems that existed.

We were overdue for a big freeze, a big hurricane, or a big flood. Beh had not seen one yet. The food and water she stored for Y2K would come in handy for that eventuality. I was grateful for the warm winters we were having. In the van, I could go everywhere with just a sport coat or sweater. I had to think I could control my environment, or it would control me.

In early January 2000, I finished my first novel, **The Kaleidoscope Effect.** It was a long time in coming. I started writing my first book in 1970. It was true tales of meeting hitchhikers on the road. I never finished it. In October 1999, I put aside this autobiography and, took an old idea I developed in 1973, and, in three months, published **The Kaleidoscope Effect** on the Internet. I self published and posted the novel to Booklocker.com according to their guidelines in 1999. Angela Adair was very helpful and the novel ebook sold well at first, but after a year, sales dropped off. Booklocker could no longer carry the book.

When I corresponded with Toby Endem, starting his own print on demand (POD) firm, **Kaleidoscope** was picked up, edited, reviewed, and promoted by Bookbooters.com. In January, 2001, it became available as a paperback from Amazon, Barnes and Noble, Borders, and others. **Kaleidoscope** was one of eight books considered for 2000 eBook of the Year Award by Bookbooters on March 1, 2001.

I finished the first draft of this autobiography, **Hanging by a Thread**, in 1998, after six years of one finger typing on weekends and evenings. This presentation is the culmination of that work. Since 1997, I'd published a poem a week on my website. I may publish a book of poems from that effort, but haven't yet.

Beh bought a 2000 Corolla VE in February 2000. She looked briefly at used cars, and then settled on something that would be economical, reliable, and practical. The Monte was relegated to the garage. Beh took it for "exercise" every so often.

I got word of the annual THECB Facilities Conference early. It was being held in March at the George Bush Library at Texas A&M. Given the climate at the office, I didn't dare ask to go. I knew I could drive there and back on my own, if necessary. So, I hatched a plan. I decided to take a day's vacation and pay the fee myself, freeing me from obligation to the university. Elaine Sobotik was planning the conference at the Coordinating Board and bought into my idea. To my surprise, Beh decided to take a day off from her shop to go with me. Two days before the conference, I received an "order" to attend an all day "mandatory" training session on "managing change." The timing was exquisitely painful. My vacation request was denied. I decided to go anyway.

It was a warm and sunny day with a strong north wind. We arrived as the conference was opening. Harold, Danette, and JT all showed varying degrees of surprise when they saw me. I avoided them. I enjoyed the information provided in the sessions. Beh was bored. My efforts to get her to go to visit the Bush Library failed. At noon, we enjoyed a pleasant lunch together, and then toured the grounds. A stroll around a large pond got me thinking of where to retire.

The gusty winds nearly blew my van off the road going home, but we arrived earlier than we usually got off work. The real storm occurred the next morning when Harold ordered Jim to issue me a written reprimand. It was a futile gesture from an ineffective manager. It hurt him more than me. He knew he couldn't push me around after that. We rarely saw each other or talked. When we did, it was strictly business.

Suddenly, in May, Beh wanted to go see the wild flowers. I drove the familiar roads, but it had been too dry or it was too late to see many flowers. I felt like driving further, so we went to Somerville Dam and took back roads back to Brenham. I used the drive to look for possible retirement locations. Some areas close to Brenham looked very good. Beh loved the German sausage in Brenham.

As usual, I had to force my vacation. I originally planned to spend ten days going to Wisconsin and back again to look up old friends and relatives and show them my renewed ability to travel by driving myself. Diann was eager to go along, so I saw it as an opportunity to give Beh a break. Beh, fearing that I couldn't do the trip without her, asked us to move our travel plans up to the week of July 4. With less than a week to plan, I got on the phone and Internet, and everything came together quite well.

"The *(Two) Grand Tour*," as I dubbed it for its cost, was hectic, but relatively smooth, given the logistics involved. There was too little time at most stops, but I did get back in touch with many I haven't seen in a long time. Even with reservations at motels, it was sometimes difficult to get in for the night. The hard part was missing people I really wanted to see.

The first day, July 1, 2000, I drove 550 miles. Except for a period of bowel distress when Beh and Diann were sleeping, it went well. My cousin, Danila (Hull) Ousley had reserved a room for us in the Jameson Inn in Grenada, Mississippi. It was the best room of our trip.

The next day, we got lost finding my Uncle Bruce Hull in rural Kentucky. My Internet directions led us to Decker Lane. But we couldn't find his address on Decker Lane. A man we asked didn't even know who Bruce Hull was. After two trips five miles down the highway to a gas stop and a failed cell phone call, we found Decker Road about two miles from Decker Lane, and my Uncle and his family.

After missing my friend Behram Randelia (They were vacationing in China) in Indianapolis and my cousin in Dayton, we arrived at Roger's for the 4th. We used a folding table to get into the house and off the deck. Getting on and off the pontoon boat proved tricky because my chair was so heavy. We had a pleasant, warm evening ride on the river that was the highlight of the entire trip.

After watching the 4th flotilla, where my brother's boat joined 50 others on the St. Joseph River in Elkhart, we toured the campuses of Notre Dame and St. Mary's. Notre Dame was like most large campuses—well-planned and rather bland. St. Mary's was special. The trees and quiet walkways were an invitation to pause and think. I wish I could have spent some time there just meditating and enjoying the scenery.

The next day, in Chicago, we stopped in The Loop to meet my friend and former brilliant student from Ghana, Paa Kwesi Adams, at the Quality Inn. Later, we had a brief visit with Mahfooz and Farkhunda Haque at her alteration business, the Cotton Club, in DeKalb.

At my brother Tim's house that night, an old door helped get me into the house. We had to stay in a motel though, because his bathrooms were impossible to reach upstairs. The next morning, we stopped at old friends, Roger and Pat Smith, toured their yard, and then on to Jackie and Albert Replogle. Albere Repaul, the Iceman in my novel, **The Kaleidoscope Effect** was a name I borrowed from Albert. The Replogle family has been traced back the Alsace-Loraine region.

That night, we met some of my family at a motel in Marshfield. It was strange, but necessary. My sister, Judy and her husband, Paul, were joined by their sons, and my niece and nephew, Tom's kids. There just wasn't time or access to go to their houses.

The only place we stayed over was at my parents' mobile home in Withee the next night. Then, I used my portable chair and had to be lifted and pushed by Beh and Diann.

The next day, I visited more aunts and uncles and cousins and we were in Minneapolis and on our way home. The long drives were difficult, but I could have driven the whole 3,500 miles myself. The only incident we had was when a driver in a small car fell asleep and drifted from the right lane across in front of Beh, and then lost control momentarily in the median. He recovered and returned safely to the freeway. He had his wife and a small daughter with him. I was glad that he didn't get our van or roll over in the median and hurt his family.

Roger readies his pontoon boat to take us out on the St. Joseph River.

Diann before her first pontoon ride. Elkhart, IN, July 2000

Diane at Roger and Sue's home in Elkhart Indiana. July 2000

With Mom, Dad, and Beh at their mobile home in Withee. July 2000.

# 69

# A Turnaround at Work

The auditors finally gave the university a clean bill of health, but not before the henchmen who bought Charles Carter down were, themselves, dismissed. President Slade hired a young friend as her fiscal chief. Paulette Frederich was a bit idealistic and tried to change things. She resigned within a year.

Former President Bush keynoted President Slade's inauguration. I parked my wheelchair in the front row. A thin lady in a rich brocade outfit excused herself as she passed me by. It was Jennifer Holliday of "Dream Girls" fame. She sang beautifully for the occasion. Slade demanded that the charter for TSU be upheld: "(TSU) ... be a university of the first class, equivalent to the one (U of Texas) in Austin." The "be equivalent" would mean $200 million to create medical and engineering schools, among other things. It was a bold measure; but, with George W. Bush looming as the next president, and she leading the Lt. Governor, Rick Perry's transition to the office of governor, she could not lose.

Charles Carter's lawsuit forced other changes. Longstanding abuses in fiscal areas and facilities contracts were uncovered and the abusers were dealt with. It became a question of who would fall next. The Board may have been forced to stop meddling. But the faculty was decimated. Several professors had died recently. They were not being replaced. People enticed to fill long open positions resigned after a few months, unable to deal with the lack of support and internal politics. Some tenured professors were forced to resign. Dr. Slade and the auditors were all accountants. Accounting ruled over scholarship.

My problems continued. The Maintenance Authority (TMA) replaced my work order system on July 1st, 2000. Although I requested access to the data several times, my reporting of work order data, spanning a decade, was ended. It was not that the data couldn't be acquired, it's that they didn't want me to obtain the data—to be involved. From the dispatchers to our workers, the complaint was that they didn't like the new system. It was faster, and, in some ways both more comprehensive and simpler. Yet, it was rigid and unable to be revised, too. Where I had changed aspects of the system in days, all changes now had to be requested formally from TMA. If accepted, they wouldn't be incorporated in the next update. We had to buy updates. We couldn't do the reports I'd generated. We hadn't bought the report generator.

As a Beta tester for Helix, I received free updates. Helix Technologies launched RADE (rapid application development) 5.0 in September for about $300. With RADE came the ability to operate their client/server system over the Internet—just what Harold had wanted me to do. TMA had an Internet package. That package cost $5,000. Helix had plans to go cross platform too, so I hoped to be able to move my system to NT. But it was already too late. The university committed to TMA, and hired and trained people for it. Where two people had operated my work order system, it required about six people at the dispatch station to run the TMA, and custom reports like I had done, were almost impossible to get if they weren't part of the templates provided by TMA.

Page Southerland Page finally completed their reentry of the facilities inventory in February 2000. PSP used Archibus, a drawing-based database program, to remeasure all rooms on campus. With Elaine Sobotik's help, I downloaded PSP's inventory and loaded it into mine, creating parallel reports. My analysis found seven things wrong with PSP's approach. Not only had they violated the rules of measurement set forth in the Coordinating Board's Manual, but also they failed to code properly, upsetting a balance between state funded and auxiliary funded activity we'd worked a decade to create. As usual, my detailed memo to herald about the problems was unheeded. PSP was to update their work in September. Since I was no longer involved, I don't know if they did. Others would be asked to update when renovations or programs change the room inventory on campus. I was still being asked for my building information.

I still did all my work on my Mac. The mouse and dictation aids I requested for my Win NT machine never came. The software on the NT computer did not compete with my old Mac applications. Finally, the vagaries of Windows NT and its double button mouse made it very unproductive. I tried to install Macintosh emulator software on my NT, but I had to stop when computing services wouldn't set up my CD drive to accept my Mac OS CD. I updated to Mac OS 8.1 using the Internet, but my superiors refused to pay for any updates or enhancements of Macs.

I continued to maintain and update the campus plan. I got a 32" x 50" copy printed at Kinko's to put on outdoor campus display cases to guide students. The display cases were taken down, but our overworked carpenters never got them put back up.

After I developed the area's web pages, the webmaster, Dr. Donald Dement, liked my campus plan and featured it prominently on TSU's home page. Interested parties could print it with a single click. In the spring of 2000 Dement was promoted and left with his corporation, SCT, we'd outsourced computing services to. Our project management firm was building two new buildings, so I updated my campus plan to accommodate the buildings and rooms. I also updated a campus locator map. When I tried to email the two maps to everyone on campus, I was told not to do it—put them on our website instead. To my shock, the TSU home page had changed. Not only didn't it open well, but also the link to the campus plan was removed. I contacted the new webmaster, Kevin Collins, and he promised to change things. The last time I checked, the old map was still buried in the facilities area pages I had done.

Viron, our energy services contractor, came to me in the spring to obtain our utility bills. They had been very optimistic about the savings they would obtain. The data I provided showed otherwise; it appeared that they "owed" us for guaranteed savings. CCRD Partners, a consulting firm, was hired to oversee Viron's calculations. They came up with widely divergent results. I never saw the details. TSU had not paid Viron for the work they had done. The impasse reached the point of a lawsuit.

The grievance memo I filed with the university Ombudsperson was never returned. When I started to file a complaint with the EEOC, I was told to hold back; that big changes were coming. Slade hired a consultant, Phillip Encino, from Berkeley and KPMG to evaluate our entire organization. Encino was working closely with our human resources director, Princess Gardner, when tragedy struck in May. Princess took an evening ride on a horse carriage in downtown Houston with her husband.

The horse spooked and bolted, throwing the driver. When the carriage crashed, Princess broke her pelvis, left wrist and elbow, and received brain damage. She was in intensive care for four weeks. She had a stroke during surgery on her elbow. I visited her three times in the hospital. She recovered, but never returned to work. I heard later that she filed a lawsuit against the university.

Harold had his own tragedies. He came home one August night to find his eighteen year old son had committed suicide, a victim of drugs. Within two weeks, a cousin, as close as a brother to him, also died.

Encino and a planning committee ran things. Gray Padfield, a project management consultant, was brought in to run projects for the university. The middle managers feared for their jobs. Some heads rolled. Encino told me early on that he wanted to "pick my brain." We never talked, but I leaked him information through emails and he requested some additional information.

While serving on the Steering Committee for TSU's self study, I attended the opening session with the visiting committee in May. I sat next to President Slade at the head of the table. She seemed pleased to have me by her side. I still wasn't able to speak with her. No committee assignments came my way since that last opening session.

On December 1, 2000, Encino's work was done. Harold went on extended disability leave. JT Glover was temporarily assigned to replace him. JT immediately asked me to help with land matters. I was asked to attend staff meetings. Things had turned around, but I still had little to do except make JT look good.

# 70

# Dangerous Equipment

After Hwa left, we left the room vacant a few months. Then took in Janda Zardee, a Liberian student. Except for her youthful lifestyle, she paid the rent, too.

Dr. Kenneth Parsons, my rehabilitation specialist, told me in July 2000, that he only needed to see me once a year because the wheelchair had stabilized my condition and it wasn't deteriorating as rapidly as before when I was walking and putting so much stress on my spine. In June, I tested my nose pillows for my C-PAP (positive air pressure) ventilator. They made my mouth so dry that I had to get a humidifier. I never use them again.

It had become routine to go to the Student Health Center every day around noon to empty my urine bag. A new nurse, Pam Taylor, was hired in the spring of 2000. Pam was a big help. I rarely needed help in the office anymore. If I did, Diann would step in and do it.

My Ford Windstar GL had 31,000 miles on it after two years and three months of driving. I continued to have problems, ranging from electrical glitches to safety issues, but the worst seemed to have been dealt with. There was little that could happen that I hadn't already experienced. I'd had the van to Mobility Plus over forty times under warranty. By spring 2000, I finally got back to driving the way I used to—with a hefty dose of restraint—because response times were slower with my system. I developed a *"feel of the road"* that was soft and fluid, but gave me good feedback on my driving.

Mobility Plus worked with me every step of the way, repairing every problem I had. When they replaced the steering system in the spring, my electrical problems with the EMC controls faded away. My latest problems were with the Vantage kneeling and locking systems, still under warranty until September 2001.

One day in July, my suspension wouldn't pump up. By the time I got to Ben's shop to add air, the suspension was already pumped up. I continued on Bissonett to work. At Beltway 8, traffic had stopped for a red light. With two cars ahead of me in the right lane, I eased into the empty center lane coming up on the traffic light. A Corolla I'd seen in my rear view mirror ran into me, her mirror gouging out a dent below my mirror. The woman was very nervous, insisting on a police report. When no police came, I went to the Westside station that evening. They didn't look at my van; just told me it was an insurance matter. Mobility Plus fixed the damage for $800. My insurance paid for it.

On September 11, 2000, I left work at noon because I had an appointment at the Wheelchair Shop. At 1 pm, Matt, the technician, took my Permobil joystick control apart and cleaned it, reset the computer program, and generally tuned it up. The chair had been stopping and jerking momentarily, probably due to dirt in the control contacts, but the problem always went away.

When I left, I noticed that the joystick swing-away was harder to operate. Matt fiddled with the wires that were in the way and binding it— freeing it up a bit. The joystick control box still stuck out too much. When I got to Mobility Plus to fix my ramp gearbox and motor (balking), I carelessly backed out of the E-Z Lock and my joystick got wedged between the back of the passenger seat and its arm rest, wheels spinning. I managed to turn it off and get my ramp open, but I couldn't release the seat back to get it out of the way. A lady waiting there came over to look at my van. She moved the seat forward and released the seat back for me, it popped forward, and I was free. My wheelchair joystick and controls still worked okay. I vowed to myself to be more careful.

After my van was fixed, I decided to surprise Beh at her shop. When I got there, the guys had turned my E-Z Lock off in the shop, so I couldn't get out! I honked and honked until Didi, Beh's friend, came out of the nail shop. She went to get Beh, who was lying down inside with a headache. Little Teresa, the nail shop owner's daughter, came out and turned my E-Z Lock on so I could get out.

When I got home, I must have gotten careless again, because my joystick immediately jammed into the same spot on the passenger seat armrest! Only harder this time. The chair was trying to turn left into the door and there was no way to reach the button as it churned away. I reached for the tilt switch, twisted down under the armrest, and it caught and started to tilt the chair forward, pushing the lift switch into the bottom of the armrest, causing the chair to elevate!

As the chair rose, tilted forward, and struggled to turn left, my head rose to the roof and put pressure on my neck. My thoughts were of my neck breaking from the pressure. I watched helplessly as the control box turned into the seat fabric until there was a loud *snap!* The control box broke off, and everything stopped running. I could just reach my van controls, so I turned on the ignition and ran the van windows down.

A little boy came along and agreed to help. I ran my ramp down and asked if he could reach the tilt control, still jammed into the seat. He tilted me back and the control box fell to the floor, surprising us both! We fished it up by the cable. I lowered myself down with the control box on my lap. I could drive the chair, but everything was 90 degrees out of kilter, making driving difficult. The kid left, and I had to ask a passing woman to reach my garage door button. Janda was home. She tried to help me transfer to the other chair. I fell to the floor, and we had to use the Hoyer lift to get me up.

Beh lashed my control back on. I went back to the Wheelchair Shop the next morning. One small mounting bolt had broken off. Matt had it back together and working properly in less than an hour. My car seat was okay. I didn't know an inch would make such a difference.

On November 15, 2000, while I was eating my lunch, I decided to tell our new safety director, OG Gray, in the office next to mine, about a safety issue I had spotted. I had my right leg rest swung out and my foot down. This was my usual working position because my right leg was more comfortable that way. While I usually put my foot up on the rest to travel anywhere, I often left it down to go out into the hall briefly, sliding on my shoe.

As I squeaked through the doorway to my office, I ran over my foot with OG watching. There was a loud cracking sound. I felt no pain so I thought my footrest had caught the door and snapped back. He said, "Can I help?" There was nothing OG could do, my foot was behind the right front wheel and my leg was hurting and pulling me off the 469 lb chair, so I backed up over my foot again to get free. My foot was twisted off strangely to the right, and I couldn't lift it up. OG re-positioned my footrest and pulled my foot up on it. My shoe had my tire tread embossed on it.

I went directly to an emergency room. A television station was there, filming their operation. There was a lot of laughter and activity, but they were very slow to get to me. Three x-rays of my foot showed no breaks. The doctor told me that she had looked at the x-rays for a half-hour. I had a burning sensation on the top of my foot, but no abrasions or bruises showing through my support hose. I got cold waiting there for the doctor and started experiencing stomach muscle spasms and shivering. It was good to be back in my warm van going home.

Beh put me to bed at 7:30 after I ate. It was a challenge since I couldn't stand on that leg. The stomach spasms started up again, and I developed a fever that lasted past midnight. By morning I was comfortable, but my leg really ached when I moved it. My twisted knee was a problem. I developed large bruises on my shin and ankle that were sensitive to touch.

Beh got the Hoyer lift down from upstairs to transfer me. I stayed home through the weekend. Going to work was not a problem—sleeping was. My left leg, more inactive during the day, developed sympathetic pain that reached all the way to my lower back. I agonized through two weeks of nights, unable to find a comfortable sleeping position. I increased my spasm medicine and took painkillers. Nothing helped until I started to move my legs again. When Beh would move them to ease the pain, she'd tell me that my ankle was broken. From the x-rays, there was no way that it was. In the wee hours, I'd kick my legs until they were tired and I could fall off to sleep.

I was okay during the day, but the pain kept up most nights until Beh couldn't stand to help me anymore. After one painful, sleepless night, I decided to see Parsons to see if I could get some sleeping pills and night nursing help for Beh. I called his nurse, Madeline. She called back after work, Friday, 12/1/00, and said I could see him Monday afternoon. The constant pressure on my right heel had caused a pressure sore that Beh told me about.

Got to TIRR at 2:30, Monday, 12/4/00. Earlier, I'd gone to work, only to have to drive back 25 miles to Beh's shop to get closing papers for my Atlanta house notarized and Fed Exed back for a next day closing. Drove 30 miles back to find TIRR was unprepared for me because Madeline wasn't there. Luckily, I got in on an old insurance referral. The intern who first examined me declared that my right leg was *broken!* Both the tibia and fibula were "*twist*" broken cleanly about six inches above the ankle. The pressure sore had created a hole in my heel.

Dr. Parsons wanted to send me over to St. Luke's Hospital to have stabilizing pins surgically installed. When he called Kelsey-Seybold, the orthopedist told him to have me come in the following morning for a cast. Parsons was worried that a cast would cause pressure sores.

I took Beh with me to Kelsey-Seybold Tuesday morning, 12/5/00. I didn't have an appointment, but Dr. Parson's orders were clear. A short time later, we were looking at a foot shot of mine taken 11/15/00 that showed a fracture on my tibia from an angle 6 inches above the ankle. Dr. Duetsch discussed a cast (change it often), a shell cast (open it up often), and a boot. We settled on the boot. Beh was glad I drove her home and she didn't have to get lost trying to find her way driving herself. I then drove back to the Medical Center and Precision Brace.

The orthotist got out an off-the-shelf medium boot and put it on. The boat was steel-framed from open toe to just below the knee. All Velcro, so Beh could easily take it off to inspect my skin for pressure sores and bathe me. I could still stretch my legs and wiggle my toes. I was told it was an easy break to heal, and would, once stabilized, in about six weeks. Some movement would stimulate healing and the breaks should heal stronger than the original bone. I was very happy to hear that.

I went back to work at 11:30. Fellow workers were astounded to see the iron man back in the traces of TSU. My leg and foot felt better right away. My sympathetic pain was gone, and I began to sleep better, because the boot protected my heel and kept it from rubbing so that it could heal. But spasms, my legs' way of shaking off stiffness, became a problem. The forced inactivity of the boot increased spasms that often jerked at my legs without warning, fortunately, with little pain. The boot was light, but I could not lift it with my weakened leg. The spasms caused my leg to creep up to my chest. I had Beh tie my ankle to the foot of my bed so that it would stay straight and not creep up. Spasms then felt like they were pulling my leg out of the boot. Beh said my toes didn't move, but I worried that the breaks wouldn't heal. Dr. Deutsch looked at them on December 21, and then again on January 5th. Both breaks were healing, but would take longer, another six weeks. At least by then my leg was back to nearly normal. The boot was light, and my leg stopped creeping up when I slept.

The downturn in the technology sector during 2000 first slowed, and then reversed, the growth of my retirement funds, but I had confidence that the sector would return to solid growth once the dot.coms were sorted out. I compared the situation to the automobile industry at the turn of the last century. The Hupmobile and Pierce Arrow are gone, but investments in Ford, Cadillac, or Oldsmobile were still paying off (except Oldsmobile, after a century, it was gone, too).

I finally sold my Atlanta House on December 5, 2000. My depreciation had run out and it was time to abandon the idea of returning to the place in retirement. I invested the profit from the sale after hefty taxes, so we hopefully would have choices of what and where to build or buy when I retired.

Pam, who emptied my urine bag daily at the Health Center. Dec 2001

# 71

## The Promise and Despair of the New Millennium

As the year 2000 dawned, we were invited to Beh's sister, Tammy's house for the new year celebration. The headlights on my van weren't working, but the flashers produced enough light from the large front running lights to illuminate the street ahead, so I took a chance and we drove the 10 miles or so, mostly on residential streets, to her house. We arrived about 11 pm to enjoy food cooked by Beh's nephew, a chef, and watch the $1500 spent on fireworks in the street in front of the house by a another nephew who had a successful business. The fireworks show went on for more than an hour and was quite spectacular. Quite a way to bring in the new year and millennium. Although the police were out in force, we didn't run into any coming or going, and I didn't have to explain why I was driving with just my flashers on and a glass of wine under my belt. The local constable came around to watch the fireworks—legal in Fort Bend County.

I learned that PowerSecretary, my rather expensive dictation system at work, had been sold to IBM and repackaged as IBM's ViaVoice Pro. While I had two dictation systems before, ViaVoice was very good at picking up my natural voice, and capable of keeping up with me as fast as I could speak. It took some time to train the vocabulary to understand my voice, but recognition and my voice file got better the more I used the program. I used ViaVoice to write the last few chapters of **Alone?** I found that I was twice as fast using ViaVoice as typing and my spelling vastly improved.

Unfortunately, the process inserted wrong words in some cases that I didn't catch and came back to haunt me later.

Dad's trouble started in April 2001 when he got a sinus infection that many of us contracted here in South Texas. The infection didn't go away and he developed a cough. By midsummer, dad was diagnosed with a form of leukemia that they don't treat, just watch. The leukemia lowered his immune system enough so that he developed shingles. The shingles were very painful and the medicine dad was given didn't work well. Finally, in late August, he was diagnosed with pneumonia and sleep apnea and the doctor had to change his medicine for shingles. Dad had a reaction to that medicine that put him in a deep sleep, so he had to go back to the original narcotics he was on. All the time, dad was losing weight and lethargic. Mom had to do most of the driving, but dad insisted on coming back down to McAllen in October from Wisconsin. He gradually recovered after that, and started riding bicycle again and tried bowling. I was as surprised as he was to see that the strong, almost invincible, father that I knew had lost so much weight and became weak. Even too weak to play his beloved golf.

When my broken leg took so long to heal, it became very difficult for Beh to help me every night. She got tired from lack of sleep and overwork. I hired Daisey Ashley to help out two nights a week. Daisey had her own cleaning service and took care of her husband when he was severely disabled by lupus before he died. Daisey was a big help and gave Beh more than a few good nights' rest each week.

Traveling became a problem. My broken leg prevented trips until it healed in April 2000, and Beh's shop prevented her from getting away. I tried to find someone who could travel independently with me, but was unable to. It became much harder for me to stand and transfer. Daisey took a long time to get the knack of transferring me properly. She never really did.

Beh and I still got to make our annual trip to see the wild flowers near Brenham in April. Using the Internet as a guide, I misread the signs and we arrived too early for the bluebonnets. Usually we were too late and they were all bloomed out. We did stop in Brenham to get some good German sausage. It was a warm, pleasant day, so all was not lost. Beh didn't have time to take care of all the flowers and plants that she would like to at my house. But she bought them in season and tried to keep flowers blooming through the brutal summer heat.

The trip I regretted not taking was to my fortieth high school reunion. Roger went in my place, but he didn't take a camera, so he only sent me green-tinted, blurry ones from Doug Boucher. The reunion was a short, casual, evening affair. Roger said that there were a lot of old, retired classmates he couldn't recognize. I couldn't even find Jan in the balding, paunchy, white-haired crowd. Maybe it was a good thing that I didn't go.

In May, I was surprised to learn that my good friend and former colleague-boss, Dr. Joshua Hill, Sr., had died in Bush Intercontinental Airport trying to pick up his luggage. His death was caused by a lung aneurysm returning from a research trip to Nigeria. Josh was 57 and left his wife and four grown children. Josh's was a big funeral. I saw many friends that had retired or left TSU since Josh's tenure as vice-president. Congresswoman Sheila Jackson Lee said that she would read a resolution before Congress placing Josh and his good deeds in the Congressional Record. Josh left at the high point of his career leading the School of Technology's research effort as associate dean. Many missed him, including me, for the way he had touched our lives.

Within a month, Dr. Alma Alexander, a longtime friend and university ombudsperson, died from a long battle with breast cancer. As I looked around the university, I found that fewer and fewer of my long time allies and colleagues remained. Charles Carter's lawsuit reached the phase where his case went to federal court. He was hopeful of a settlement. Charles was someone who I could count on at work. Still, like so many, he was forced to leave by doing the right thing and going against the political establishment.

President Slade adjusted her TSU organization in ways that didn't help me. She selected JT Glover as the new assistant vice president for maintenance and operations. She then made Bruce Wilson senior vice president and placed Glover under him. Our new architectural director was promoted to vice president and removed from the area. I still reported to the director of the physical plant, Jim Anderson. I got trickle-down requests from JT or Jim. I was told to channel all requests through them, so little or nothing from me got to the president. Any effort I made to innovate or improve procedures or policy resulted in a reprimand. Jim told me that it wasn't him. Told me that his job was also on the line. We both had to adjust to the paranoid policies of the henchmen, JT Glover. Glover was quite good at spreadsheets and he probably modified mine to look like his. His approach was quite Machiavellian.

A new safety director, Oscar G. Ray, was hired. All I knew was that he was supposed to have worked for OSHA and was a former pro football player. OG immediately hired two staff members and a secretary. There was no money for a graduate assistant, half time, for me. Ray moved into my suite. He placed one of his hires in my workroom that had previously been taken over by JT's computer technician. Within a month, Ray had to fire the secretary and one of the safety technicians he had hired. It seems OG hadn't considered credentials, and, in the case of the secretary, how she would fit into his organization. Ray's crew got very busy. However, new things seemed to keep coming up that they hadn't handled before or even considered. I advised OG about a few things at first. He tended to ignore my advice. When those problems came back to haunt him later, I think he resented it. Ray got very busy talking to contractors and installing fire and security systems. I wondered why he had so much help and funds while there didn't seem to be any money or help for my work and me. Later, I learned that there was a special phone in the president's office. When that phone rang, certain individuals, mostly from Washington DC, were given key positions in the university and budgets to do their work as well as bring their people in without the usual human resources processes. These golden appointments rarely lasted very long because they were so politically motivated and alien to the university purpose of educating young people. However, the appointments lined the pockets of those involved.

The university received $300 million based on an appeal to the EEOC from the Civil Rights Commission. The Commission determined that the university had been under funded by the state for many years and, therefore, needed the funds to reach parity with sister institutions. Ironically, back in 1982, a study by the Legislative Budgeting Board had concluded the same thing, awarding TSU and Prairie View A&M substantially more in annual allocations from the Higher Education Assistance Fund (HEAF). Sister institutions were not happy with the allocation. And, apparently, neither was TSU. Hence, the request for more reparations, spearheaded by former president Douglas and provost Bobby Wilson.

With the civil rights money, President Slade enhanced any area of the university she saw fit; like remodeling the presidential suite to make it look more like one of a corporation's. I saw some of the trickle-down money. After several years of requests, I finally got a new, used Gateway PC, a larger monitor, and an Epson printer. It was a hand-me-down, but quite usable. Others got more powerful and functional computers with specialized software like AutoCAD and OmniPage. Software I could use, but was not allowed to. My aging 7500 PowerPC Mac was still more productive and its 20 inch CRT screen was unmatched by the new 17 inch flat monitor on the PC. Since the new Epson Color Stylus 880 printer would not print on the Mac, I brought my Epson Color Stylus 660 from home and connected it to the Mac at work—giving me two printers. To be productive, I did my work on the Mac, and then would email most of it to the Gateway Windows98 machine for backup and storage. The setup was a bit awkward, but I could print from both computers in color and still operate my Helix databases. The Mac sorely needed upgrading. I hoped that that would be in the works as my Helix database collections continued to prove their worth. That didn't happen right away.

In June 2001, we were surprised when tropical storm Allison came and wouldn't leave. I warned everyone at work on Thursday when I saw a large mass of showers coming off the Gulf on the Internet radar. We got most of the rain on my west side of town, and the feeders to the Southwest freeway were severely flooded, but I made it home safely that night. On Friday, it cleared up a bit, but I elected not to go to work. I didn't want to flood my van with its 5 inches of ground clearance. The storm continued, but it turned out to be rather nice day. On Saturday night, Allison worked her way back south, dumped 30 inches of rain, and flooded the entire east end of downtown and the Medical Center. TSU suffered damage in only eight buildings—in ill-conceived basements with inadequate sump pumps that couldn't run when the electricity was out. The new construction on the Southwest Freeway near Greenway Plaza, well below grade with pumps, was completely flooded. I passed that way every day to and from work. I took vacation the next week to work on my book while the university conducted repairs, but had to venture out to a doctor appointment on Tuesday. Although I saw evidence of flooding, with many cars being dried out, the Kelsey Seybold clinic was operating and when I swung by TSU, everything looked fine from the street. TSU lost far fewer trees and limbs in Allison than it did in Alicia. There was also much less wind damage to windows and roofs.

When I got back to work, Jim asked me to come up with measurements for all the basement rooms that had been damaged by water. The PSP facilities inventory couldn't provide that information, but my old Helix facilities inventory could. I produced spreadsheets for all the damaged buildings that were submitted to FEMA. The FEMA representative was so impressed with my spreadsheets that he came by to see me in my office and praise them. All the bosses tried to hide my work or take credit for it. They began to see the value of my Helix databases but wouldn't admit it directly.

Jim had given me a copy of RS Means CostWorks. With the square footage figures that I had, I was able to cost out all of the projects accurately.

We hired two young carpenters. One of them was good at building out spaces. We had done small renovations before Allison. After Allison, we did some of the restoration work that wasn't done under contract. Jim decided to create a suite of offices for the physical plant because we were spread out in several suites. OG immediately eyed my office as a way to expand his territory. As time went on, it seemed he couldn't wait for the new suite to be completed to get me out. There were several delays in getting the new space built, but, by November, the new area was completed enough so that I could move. OG wanted the space in my old storage room to increase the size of his office. I asked to be involved when the old files were removed so that I could decide what needed to be kept and what needed to be thrown out. The day came quickly, and OG and his two men swiftly boxed everything and had it hauled out. It would have been easy for me to make determinations from the way I had organized the paperwork on the shelves. But OG ignored my request. What they did made it very difficult to open the boxes and review everything again. I was very angry about what happened and told Jim and JT what I thought of it. It was very obvious OG wasn't thinking of the university or me, only about how OG could increase his empire by increasing his square footage and the size of his office. The way that the administration determined their value to the institution—the size of their office—not their contribution to higher learning.

I moved into my new office on September 11th. The very same day as the attacks on the World Trade Center. I heard about it happening on the radio on the way into work and immediately thought of terrorism. After I got to work, I got so busy with the move I didn't get any news about what happened until I returned home that evening. My new office was not as long as the old one, but it was wider. Jim made sure it was the same square footage. I was able to sandwich my two computer tables and filing cabinets along one wall, giving me a bit more room to maneuver around my desk in my wheelchair than the old office. The hallway was narrow, too narrow to meet ADA standards, but, for the most part, I navigated it without scarring the walls too much. I had to push my feet into the closet at the end of the hallway in order to, just barely, push the buttons on my digital lock with my knuckles.

I kept reviewing all utility bills and made budget projections. From time to time, information from my land inventory was requested, so I tried to keep that up by gathering bits and pieces as I discovered them from purchases and sales that the university made. I got most of my information about land from Jeanie. JT hired a new business manager, Deborah Torry, a girlfriend of his, and Jeanie was asked to give up all the work she was doing on land. Jeanie was upset after working so hard so many years to become knowledgeable in real estate. I wasn't sure I would be able to keep up the land inventory unless Deborah cooperated fully with me. I was called into a meeting with the City regarding the railroad property that runs through TSU. Later, I was questioned about my involvement. It became clear that they didn't want me involved in planning, negotiating, or any other land discussions. I was *persona non grata*. I was getting used to it. Not happy... just getting used to being left out.

After my work on the Allison information, I repeatedly pointed out in writing that the Page Southerland Page facilities inventory was two years out of date and inadequate in several ways. TSU continued to have the lowest utilization of classrooms and labs for all Texas institutions. With all of the new facilities we were supposed to build to meet the requirements of the civil rights award, president Slade had a difficult time arguing for the facilities when we were not fully using a classrooms and laboratories we already had. Enrollment was the culprit and improving, but not enough to keep up with the addition of new facilities. The culprit had to be the facilities inventory—meaning *me*.

The Coordinating Board for Texas Higher Education suggested that they were going to audit the facilities inventory. This frightened the powers to be into allowing me to continue my work with the FI. When I requested help, they offered a graduate assistant with no place for that assistant to do his or her work in our crowded little suite. I needed to be close to the assistant so that the work would proceed and they would learn quickly. The graduate school did not cooperate with a tuition free opportunity, but the School of Business was willing to appoint another graduate assistant like they had always done before. Since I no longer participated in meetings and decision-making, I felt that the graduate student would not benefit from just doing menial inventory work. I suggested that if we hired a part-time assistant or understudy that I could train to continue my work after retirement, it would be better. That option was flatly denied. Any graduate assistant of mine would have no office and would also not be involved in meetings, decision-making, and other activities associated with graduate level learning. It was very disappointing when they disregarded my best advice. Anyway, I was faced with the huge task, maybe three to four months of full-time work, to get our facilities inventory back in shape.

After several attempts, I was finally allowed to send everyone on campus a copy, via Internet, of the campus plan and locator map that I developed. I continued to make changes as the campus changed, and the police finally started using the map to give to new arrivals on campus. Other, more primitive maps and obsolete maps from master plan reports became more expensive to reproduce and less informative. My map was more accurate and less expensive to print... and was infinitely easier to update.

My attempts to reverse my demotion from director to assistant director in 1998 continued to be stymied. After Princess Gardner was injured and could no longer return to work, a young lady she hired, Lesleigh Brown, became compliance manager. Lesleigh worked hard to correct many inequities among the faculty and staff. I contacted her in May, and she asked me to detail my grievance and why I had not received redress. She put me off into the summer, at one point stating that she had, " ... too many sexual discrimination cases." Lesleigh was transferred to the general counsel's office, primarily to fend off lawsuits rather than advocate for the staff and faculty. Finally, she quit in August 2001, in disgust. A new human resources director, Kefus Falls, was hired in September. I called him about my case, but he put me off because he was so busy, and didn't call me back.

With all the new money from the civil rights settlement, there were many opportunities for misuse. Carter's lawsuit and state audits began to uncover those misuses in time. I didn't know if I was ever going to get redress, but it appeared that the university needed my expertise and were willing to put up with me to get it.

Helix developed an Internet version of their Mac server that I could have made great use of for our operations. But the powers to be stayed committed to The Maintenance Authority, regardless of its inflexibility. TMA was so limited that I wasn't even able to get data dumps for spreadsheets. Like the PSP facilities inventory, TMA proved less flexible and versatile than my system in Helix. Helixtech planned to have a Windows version of their database available within a year. I didn't think it would be as easy to work with as the Mac version, but I hoped that I would be able to do my work on the Mac, and then convert it to Windows like so many programs. Hopefully, some of the trickle-down money could be used to beef up my Mac. If not, perhaps they would allow me to buy the Windows version of Helix so that my databases could continue after I'd left the university. It would be easy to teach someone to use the databases, and a shame if their powerful functionality was scrapped. Out with the old and in with the new isn't always the best thing to do.

TSU's IT services people were a revolving door, but service gradually improved with new technicians all the time from our contracted service. I stopped working on web pages and made suggestions for updating them. Without good information, it was very difficult to create good web pages. TSU placed enrollment management on the web and it was a very good move. Online enrollment was one of the reasons for TSU's enrollment gains.

Janda Zardee decided to get an apartment on her own in August 2001 and moved out. We quickly filled the room with Corale Thompson, a physical therapy graduate student at UT and an avid bicyclist. Corale was also avid about cleaning—Beh liked that. He liked to work in food services and soon was bringing home food samples and condiments to share—and I expect, *sell*. Beh found some quarters missing in a decorative bowl on my desk and she suspected that Corale was the one that took the money. Corale turned out to be quite a pilferer. That's why he couldn't seem to hold a job or keep an apartment. The physical therapy study story was just a lie, a story. We asked him to leave and he went peacefully. Before Corale left, he had acquired two new racing bicycles. I suspect they were stolen. Without any proof that Corale even stole the quarters, I couldn't turn him in.

By 2001, my 1998 Ford Windstar was approaching 40,000 miles. My warranties ran out, so every time I took the van in for an electrical repair or a minor adjustment, it began to cost me big bucks. In the spring, workers at Mobility Plus left a dash panel too loose. Twice, as I accelerated from a stoplight and backed off, the throttle foot feed caught under the panel and the van continued to accelerate. Fortunately, the brakes were strong enough to slow me down in both cases. Tightening the panel up out of the way solved the problem, but it was scary when it happened, nonetheless.

I replaced the tires on both my wheelchairs and renovated the old Invacare one. I was still running on the original batteries for both chairs—eight years for the old set. I used the old chair every day at home and charged batteries about every four days. The tube tires on my 1998 Permobil wore out fast. Thank goodness my health insurance covered my wheelchair repairs. Unfortunately, my healthcare insurance did not cover repairs to my van.

I was grateful for no new medical surprises. I got a sinus infection in April 2001 that wouldn't go away. I went to an ENT. She gave me an antibiotic and told me that it wasn't worth surgery on my chronic sinusitis condition. The infection affected my left ear, eye, and a tooth directly below the sinus cavity. I asked for and got a battery of allergy tests in case it was an allergy causing all the irritation. After the tests, the doctor explained that I wasn't allergic to any of the common known irritants. However, I seemed to have a "sensitivity" to perfume, milk, and other things in my environment. The stress caused by my paralysis apparently affects my immune system and the sensitivity of my nerves, creating all the allergy-like symptoms. Exercise, cleaning, and massage helped reduce the stress and relieve the symptoms.

In February 2001, I finally bought my own computer and took the old Mac I borrowed for my work at home back to TSU. I was glad to have gotten rid of dependence on work equipment for home computing. There was always the thought that using the computer for personal use would jeopardize my justification for bringing a computer home; always suspect by those who couldn't. More than once I was asked to provide the paperwork proving that I had legitimately removed the computer from campus. I bought a 500 MHz DVD iMac for both home and work use at home. I had to buy an Epson Color stylus 777 printer because my old printer would not connect. This worked out well because I was able to take the old printer to work. With OS 9.1 installed, I found that everything worked great on the new iMac except the Microsoft Office I had brought from work, and the Faxcilitate fax program I obtained with my old Supra modem. The iMac came loaded with a fax program, but I was never able to make it work. I missed the Faxcilitate one, because it worked incredibly well, faxing from all my applications with ease. Updating computer hardware and software often caused problems that made the process difficult, especially since I could not physically install components and sometimes even handle software provided on computer DVDs.

I was happy that the upgraded Quicken program provided with the iMac worked seamlessly with my old banking files. I called my educational sources and was able to acquire Microsoft Office 2001 for the Mac for $199. Using that new MS Word with its grammar checking capabilities, my writing improved 100%. With all this and compression tools like Stuffit from Aladdin Systems, I was able to seamlessly transfer files between my two computers at work and my two computers at home. External drives helped with backup and file transfer—a necessity.

My iMac came with movie editing capability and played crystal clear DVDs. I bought a Canon digital video camera to both take movies and still pictures at the same time. The only problems I had were finding someone to use the camera and time to edit the movies and storage space for the ones we took. I bought an Iomegma zip drive with 100 MB removable disks to solve my storage problem. The zip drive had a feature that had it backing up my hard drive daily. This feature was a great relief knowing that if something zapped my hard drive, I would be able to recover all my files and applications easily.

My web page suffered from a bit of inattention. It was just too much work to continue to add to all of its links. However, I managed to continue to write a poem a week and post it on my website. In the beginning it was difficult to come up with new poem topics, and I sometimes repeated myself, but all in all, posting poetry was a good experience in writing discipline. People seemed to like my poems and I surprised myself with how well some of them turned out. I was especially motivated by the World Trade Center disaster. I had a counter that told me that I was getting 6 to 8 searches for poems coming my website way each day. As a result, I intended to put together a book of poems someday.

In the spring 2001, I learned that my book, **The Kaleidoscope Effect**, was one of 10 finalists in the Bookbooters eBook of the year 2000-2001. In July, I learned that I missed the award by only a few points. My editor, Toby Endem, explained in great detail how one of the eight editor-judges had done me in. Bookbooters had shifted its focus to nonfiction and Toby was interested in my autobiography, so I spent three months revising and updating this tome that I originally I finished in 1998, typing with one finger for six years. I submitted that draft in April 2001. **Hanging by a Thread** probably wasn't good enough to be included among Bookbooters offerings—that draft was never published or returned. Or at least, Toby never got back to me, which he was want to do—a whiz at multitasking, he promised too much and delivered too little.

Along with the demise of so many dot.coms, the ebook trade took a dive in 2001. Some of the companies I was affiliated with either went out of business or dropped **Kaleidoscope**. Fortunately, Bookbooters remained in a strong financial position and continued to support my work. Through a third-party, Bookbooters was able to offer paperbacks on demand (POD). The paperbacks were quite good and inexpensive to produce and buy. In August, when sales of **Kaleidoscope** and all ebooks had dropped to almost nothing, Toby went against the industry and dropped prices for ebooks. **The Kaleidoscope Effect** sold for $1.50.

By midsummer, with 2000 manuscripts to review, Bookbooters stopped accepting new fiction. I got worried, because I was in the middle of the mirror to **Kaleidoscope** called, **Alone?** When I finished in October, to raves by my only fan, my sister Judy, I was worried that I wouldn't get it published. Fortunately, because I was an established author with Bookbooters, Toby wrote that he would fast track my new book to publication. I'm glad I started out when I did, because it became much harder to get started with so many publishing companies going out of business and the ones still in business backlogged with manuscripts. Everybody and his brother became an author in the cyber world.

**Alone?** assumed that there are no extraterrestrials coming to save us from acts of terrorism, war or nature. It was an epic journey of humankind from Neolithic woman to immortal space traveler. Because of the vastness of the story, I left much out. I was criticized for that. However, I tried to fill in some of the characters from **Kaleidoscope** that were not well developed in that book. The sexual nature of some of the passages could be offensive to some, but I was only portraying either the way things were or the way I expected them to become. In sex, as with all things, with human progress comes more diversity.

The weakness in the technology sector that brought down the stock market greatly affected my retirement savings. I kept thinking that the market would turn around quickly and it never seemed to. Then, there were other challenges, like over $25,000 in taxes for selling my home in Atlanta. It seemed that at every turn there was a new financial challenge to be dealt with and overcome. My 3% raise in October 2001, my first in years, did little to stop the bleeding. The $74 I made selling books did not cover one third of the cost of selling them. Only then, after so many years of struggle since my divorce, was I beginning to see the light at the end of the financial tunnel. I projected that I would have to work at least a year longer than 65 to be able to live like I wanted to in retirement. An option was to declare myself working disabled and not retire. That way I would get full Social Security and hold off my retirement until I was ready. Becoming a full-time starving author was an option I seriously considered. When I approached Social Security with my idea, they told me that I had to quit working in order to be declared, "disabled." Somehow, the good Congress had passed laws that required, according to common misconception, that disabled people didn't work, and therefore, were eligible for Social Security. The flipside of this was that if you had gainful employment according to Social Security, you were not disabled. Thus it was, "all or nothing." Not a very pleasant prospect. I chose to do nothing and continued to work full-time without any real benefits from being technically disabled except from the state of Texas. The supplement helping to pay my attendants and the funding of my van modifications allowed me to continue to work and maintain some type of normalcy against great odds.

I thought a lot about what happened on September 11, 2001. It seemed that in the 21st century, the idea of war would became obsolete. In a way, war was. The new threat was terror. Terror can only be overcome by tolerance and understanding, *not by waging traditional war against it*. While I mourn for the 5000 Manhattans whose lives were cut off senselessly and suddenly by an unknown enemy (at the time), they were but a drop in the bucket of the millions worldwide who die each year because of injustices we don't know about or seek to act upon. It's a bit smug of Americans to be so patriotic when we let our money and a few young men and women do our fighting for us. It's another thing to have to fight just to live every day in the land we grew up in like so many have to do every day. People who are alienated and disaffected become terrorists—it's as simple as that.

It was a horrible way to begin a new millennium. To think that whole groups of people are so disheartened by their prospects for the future that they would resort to terrorism to fulfill their distorted needs. There may be those that say it's a signal of a coming Armageddon. I just say that it's the result of continuing ignorance and misunderstanding that has kept our world in war. Hopefully, we will find a way to resolve our differences and end war soon. We can start by treating terroristic individuals as criminals and dealing with them in that manner, rather than blaming whole groups of people considered our enemies by association and not by character; and seriously starting to understand groups of people we misunderstand.

With Jim Anderson, physicist and my superior, trying to improve campus facilities.

# 72

# Movie Making and Losing Computer Files

I came to sad realization by 2002. The open-ended retirement I'd planned would have to be postponed, perhaps for several years, much more than I originally thought. The dot.com collapse started it all. I knew that the stock market and tech stocks were overrated and inflated. I knew that many of the highflying schemes for making money on the Internet wouldn't work. But I was caught up in the thought that technology and population growth drives our economy, and this technology would grow and improve indefinitely. After all, weren't the Baby Boomers putting their retirement money in 401ks? While others panicked and took their money out—I could have done that—I kept my money in and waited for the return of the market. I was wrong.

The terror of 9/11, the threat of war, and the excesses of corporate leadership and many putting what little savings they had under their mattresses or into living for today, greatly reduced the value of those savings. Everyone was driving bigger SUVs and pickup trucks each year. With money sitting in banks instead of being invested, people were buying bigger houses they couldn't afford on lower, but variable, interest rates provided by quick buck mortgage scam artists. I could have warned others about that, having gone through it during the early 1980s. No one was buying my books anymore. The novelty and luster of ebooks had worn off and paperbacks never sold. I don't know how many got their copy of my ebooks by hacking, but I suspect quite a few. And, I suspect there may be foreign-language copies of my books that I will never see a royalty for.

Beh 's computer got infected with the W32. Magistr virus and it corrupted my ViaVoice Pro. Since I was using that computer to dictate all my work, it was a major setback. When I tried to reinstall ViaVoice Pro, the cd drive wouldn't install it. At work, I had to get an upgrade to release 10 when my computer was upgraded to Win 2000 Pro. That installation went well, but I still was having trouble installing it on Beh's computer. Viruses were becoming a major problem and I spent many hours trying to correct problems caused by viruses with Windows 98. I also spent considerable time trying to get Beh to use the computer productively. I kept dragging that horse to water, but she wouldn't drink.

After several years going to 24 Hour Fitness, Beh was looking and feeling better. Still, she looked forward to the best body and facial plastic surgery that money could buy. In addition to having Daisey help her at night, Beh got help at the shop in the morning hours from 7 am to 10 am, so that she could get morning chores done and go to the gym. Since Daisey worked out so well, I decided to hire another helper for weekday evenings and two nights. Rosie Yarbough applied, but was deeply troubled. She begged me for the job. Rosie was staying with her sister after spending nine years in prison for selling marijuana to support her three children. Her children were split up, the two boys with her twin sister in Tennessee and her daughter with the sister in Houston. I reluctantly allowed Rosie to start work on a trial basis. Rosie was very grateful and did a good job for a few months until she found that working for me was too hot (I kept the temperature at 78° in summer). She found a job working for a laundry in a nursing home and quit. However, she invited Daisey and me to her wedding with the father of her three children, a chef, and got all three children back living with her in a new home with a new car. We kept in touch and I'm so glad that she came through prison and joined society again. Rosie is just one example of how unfair the war on marijuana has been and how the Texas justice system destroys lives for nonviolent crimes. I began to favor the decriminalization of marijuana and fairer sentencing for crimes.

After a bout with pneumonia, dad gradually recovered throughout the summer of 2002 and fought off the effects of shingles. By the fall, he put on more weight and returned to league bowling in McAllen. Beh and I spent the weekend after Thanksgiving there. Mom filled me up with all that good food I was trying to avoid. Sitting in a wheelchair without exercise was putting weight on me I didn't want. My brother, Roger, had his hip replaced in November 2002. He blamed his golf swing, but the arthritis probably was the result of his spinal injury during skiing. Every check that I had showed no arthritis in my joints. The hip replacement got Roger back out on the golf course without pain.

We made our annual trip to see the wild flowers. There weren't many, but Beh got to try out my new Canon MiniDV movie camera. She took still photos of bluebonnets and other scenes. While okay for the Internet, the photos weren't high enough resolution for printing. We stopped in Brenham to get some good German sausage again. This stop was getting to be a habit. It was a warm pleasant day, so all was not lost. Beh was expecting to get her green card, promised by the Clinton Administration many years before. Without a green card, Beh couldn't leave the country. I wanted so much to take her on a cruise. In April, with favorable fares out of Galveston, we decided that I'd go without her and gave Beh her first weeklong vacation from me in ten years. I took Daisey and Diann with me on a seven-day jaunt around the Caribbean. We sailed on the Royal Caribbean's Rhapsody of the Seas with 2000 others. Surprisingly, the ship wasn't crowded. It took us a while to get oriented, but once we did it was relaxing and easy.

We left Galveston on April 28th. Right away, the girls didn't get along, but the weather was perfect the whole trip. The first stop was Key West. Our inexperience hampered us, but we were able to walk to the first attraction, Mel Fisher's Sunken Treasure Museum. While Daisey and I took the disabled ramp, Diann went around to the front and located an employee. That employee led us into the museum, but Diann didn't follow. Daisey paid for all of us, but Diann wasn't there. After we started to go into the museum, about to catch a movie about the finding of the ship, we heard a commotion. The front desk would not let Diann in because the theater was full and she hadn't paid for a ticket. We finally persuaded the cashier to let Diann in, and we toured the rest of the museum, missing the movie. After that, we walked by the Eisenhower Key West White House and then to a busy street with a lot of bars and saw a woman draped in boa constrictors. Daisey would have none of that! Made us walk on the other side of the street. Diann got tired of walking, and sat on a bench while we toured a statue park of notable Key West figures. I decided we would go to the waterfront and catch a drink, but Diann refused to go with us. At the waterfront, we got a drink and watched a guy juggle while walking a low wire. There was also a guy with trained birds but I don't recall his act. We watched a beautiful sunset before leaving for the ship. Back on board,

Diann told us that she had seen the woman painted white that pretended to be a statue.

Except for its pristine white beaches, Grand Cayman Island was a bit of a tourist trap. The ship anchored offshore, just off the deep that plunges more than a mile down just off the island. We then took the ship's tenders (lifeboats) to a crowded small dock area accommodating the tenders from four cruise ships at once. We booked a trip to see Hell and the Turtle Farm. Along the way, our driver stopped at the governor's mansion, now a park. 7 mile Beach was pristine white coral and very beautiful. Hell was a geological formation of what looked like lava rock with a tourist gift shop—not much to look at. The Turtle Farm was more interesting and our driver guide pushed me in my portable wheelchair as we observed several large tanks with various size turtles that you could reach out and touch. I asked our driver if hurricanes ever came through. He said, "No, we never get any hurricanes here." I took his word for it. About 15 minutes after we left the tour van back near the dock, my butt started to hurt. In their hurry to get me from the van, the driver and his helpers had neglected to put my seat cushion under me! We rushed back to the place where we were dropped off, but the van was not there. Back on board, we called the tour service, and asked for the cushion back, but it was never returned before we left that evening. Fortunately, I had an identical cushion on my electric wheelchair, so all was not lost.

Cozumel was more inviting, but it was very hot there. The tours were either physical, touristy or shopping, so I decided that we would freelance. Leaving the dock, we hailed a cab and asked for a ride around the island. I sat in the front seat, and Diann took video from the back seat. The trip was rather uneventful because the island does not have much geography. But when we got to the South side where strong winds whipped huge waves crashing into the shoreline, the girls got excited. Daisey lost her straw hat into strong wind but our driver caught it. By the time we got back to town it was hot, even with the air-conditioning in the cab. We had the driver take us to a Mexican restaurant for dinner and mariachi music. Back on board, I was people watching by the swimming pool. I saw an elegant black woman at the bar, alone, I thought about approaching her, but decided against it. Instead, wheelchairing right by her without saying a word, only nodding, on my way to the other side of the pool. That evening, the Fifth Dimension treated us to a show. To my surprise, the woman I had seen at the bar alone was Florence LaRue, the lead singer! I had to chalk that up as another missed opportunity among many in my life.

We made some friends and enjoyed the luxury and hospitality of the ship. It was a chance to try out my Canon. While my camera women did not always hold the camera steady, I made a 53-minute digital movie of our adventures. My only regret was that Beh couldn't be with us.

In July, we decided to take a weekday trip to Moody Gardens. Our friend and former tenant, Janda Zardee, joined us. It was a beautiful day and everything was uncrowded, so we got to take in the whole place by late afternoon. Beh took some wonderful video of the rain forest and aquarium. As we walked from the aquarium to the IMAX theater, Beh accidentally left the camera on and the left dangling from a loop that she had tied it to her purse. That made an interesting video. On the way home, we stopped at the Kemah Boardwalk for a meal on the waterfront and a live band in the square afterward. A young black singer did a great job with Train's, "Drops of Jupiter." A beautiful end to a relaxing day.

In August, TSU's President Slade put on a picnic at an Eastex ranch and campground. Even though it rained heavily most of the day, we had a good time. Beh got to ride the train and see many alligators. In October, I drove to Austin for a workshop on emerging energy technologies. Rosie joined me at 5 am. We got back about 7:30 pm. It was a long and tiring day but I was glad to be back traveling for the University again.

2002 marked the death of several people I knew at work and close relatives of those I work with. It made it clear to me that retirement planning doesn't matter if you die on the job. Otherwise healthy people can die suddenly, too. Roger's hip replacement was a sure sign we were aging and wearing out. I still planned for the long haul. Trying to stay healthy and active as long as I could.

Charles Carter's lawsuit continued on another year. Charles remained realistic that it would take a long time to settle. In the meantime, he became the accountant for A-Rocket Transfer, a moving company that did business with TSU. After eight months of delay by the new human resources director, Keffas Falls, I refilled my complaint in May 2002 with Keisha David, the replacement compliance officer for Lesleigh Brown. My complaint was tabled. The problem remained that the compliance officer worked for the general counsel, not human resources. The position was designed to fend off lawsuits, not help employees. The delay was a stall. The only way I could get action was to go outside the university.

President Slade dealt with her organization harshly. Probably in an effort to meet the political desires of the Board and the powers that be in Washington DC. Contracts with outsourced computing services and construction project management, the brainchild of Howard Turnley carried out by Harold Johnson, were dropped suddenly. Viron sued TSU for its mishandling of their performance contract and failure to pay. Fortunately, I couldn't be blamed for that one because I was not allowed to work with Viron. Unfortunately, if I had been allowed to work with Viron and keep good records, the university probably would not have defaulted on their part of the contract. The telecommunications director and vice president for architectural services were fired. It was a surprise to learn that the architectural VP replacement was Bill Beckham, the former director of campus planning for the Texas Higher Education Coordinating Board. Bill was an older man, looking to retire near his brother in Katy. Hiring Beckham was clearly a political move to get the THECB off TSU's back. From Beckham's experience, I was hopeful that he would assist me in my work on the facilities inventory. That never happened. Bill Beckham was primarily out for himself and found it rather hard to lend a helping hand to anyone else.

The campus web page was outsourced to be upgraded. When I was asked to update our pages, I found that architectural services had used our link for their pages, dropping ours altogether. I was upset that they would do that without notifying us, but I was able to reinstate our pages with the outsource company. I had trouble getting good pictures to put on the pages from our areas. Jim got a good digital camera to record the needed repairs and the completed repair, as well as provide good pictures for publicity. It was just a matter of obtaining good pictures. The hardest part was getting someone to take them. It was at times like this that I wished I could still take pictures, or at least have someone working for me who could.

A salary adjustment study was to be funded with the EEOC money. Sharon Murphy, one of my former students at Atlanta University, and her consulting firm, was hired to do the study. Unfortunately, the study was conducted on job descriptions, not qualifications. Over the years, many of my responsibilities had been stripped from my job description. Others rewrote it. Still, I had a one-on-one interview to describe what I did. Salary adjustments were promised, retroactive to September 1, 2001. The study was to be concluded by August 31. In July, the president held meetings with the staff and promised that the study would be concluded by November 17, but only retroactive to September 1, 2002. We were to expect the adjustments in the January check. Some said it would never happen. And it didn't happen—except for some privileged unknown executives. I think the fear of lawsuits delayed the release of the study results. In the end, Slade and her mentors on the board got their way. The university continued to suffer low salaries.

As a result of the mishandling of the facilities inventory, TSU's classroom and class laboratory utilization reports showed TSU with lowest utilization rates in the state for several years. The low rates were one of the reasons the facilities inventory was taken from me and outsourced for $200,000 in 1998 to Page Southerland Page Engineers. Eventually, my FI proved to be more accurate than the PSP one. The PSP inventory was severely out of date when I finally convinced the people involved that utilization had more to do with course registration levels than the fixed room inventory. Classrooms and laboratories changed much less often than other space, like offices. JT and the powers to be let me carry out a plan to correct the inventory and gave it back to me. There was a lot of hard work without much assistance, but I got the inventory back up to date and, working with a staff member from enrollment services, David Chu, eliminated most of the coding that led to low utilization. The next utilization report in February 2003 put us back in the middle of Texas state universities, where we should have been all along with the cooperation of the administration allowing sharing of information.

After some inquiries and with the permission of Jim Anderson and help from Robert Alaniz, assigned to assist me with the facility inventory, during the summer 2002, I was finally able to retrieve my old files that were taken out of my storage room and dumped in the unused automotive shop paint booth by OG Ray. There were items that dated back to my teaching days and research papers I wanted to save. Intellectual property that did not belong to the university. For some time those files occupied a corner of my office in boxes because there was no way that I could go through them without assistance. I could no longer handle paperwork at all except on computers Barbara Allen, our secretary, helped for a while until the dust and mildew got to her. Diann offered to help, but couldn't get free from her custodial work. I asked for Jeanie, but she was moved downstairs to work with custodial services and couldn't get free to help either. My biggest frustration became handling paperwork—*period*. Without my computers, I would have been buried in unfiled paper and unable to do my work. As it was, paperwork collected on my desk until it became an eyesore. It took a lot of persuasion to get someone to help me clean my desk off. So many had messy desks, it seemed to be normal. It wasn't normal for me. A messy desk made me look like a poor organizer—I never was, but it was hard to prove that from the way my desk looked. One of my pet peeves were people who came into my office and then left, leaving things like papers, books, pens, and other articles that I couldn't reach... to return to them or trash them. The trash just collected. An eyesore and a mess.

The area that I could command in front of me on my desk amounted to a small space for eating my lunch from a plastic grocery store bag that always sat on my desk and looked ugly and out of place. I would read or review papers, proposals and books there. Items that I could no longer markup or sign, but still get a view of and then use the computer to convey my opinion of the things that I read. I scanned my signature and put that on my computer documents. Any other documents I had to sign required both hands and came out rather shaky and unnatural . All of these things contributed to others' impression that I was not as productive as I had been during my earlier years on campus. The very worst thing was not having dependable help. I relied almost entirely on volunteers who could only help me momentarily before going about their regular jobs. It seemed like a conspiracy to get me to quit. *It was a conspiracy to get me to quit.* I refused to let them make me retire too early by continuing to be highly productive and responsive to any request.

I still reviewed all utility bills and made budget projections. From time to time, information from my land inventory was requested. It was very difficult to keep the land information up. After Jeanie was removed from work with land, I received little information. We were buying land, but I was no longer in the loop. The general counsel's office had some records that were virtually inaccessible. I began to doubt if I would be able to continue to update the land inventory at all. JT Glover and his business manager, Deborah Torry, kept that information close. It would be his undoing.

My copy of the campus plan was the one that people used. I updated the plan several times in 2002. Enrollment management wanted me to provide a "*You are here*" version for new students. The drawing was blown up to a full 4' by 7' size for student viewing and placed on the walls of the enrollment center in Bell Hall. Unfortunately, that size revealed the flaws in the old scans of Johnny McDonald's drawings, scanned in 8.5 x 11 sections and then pieced together. An AutoCAD version needed to be redrawn. But, no one had done an AutoCAD drawing yet. Several attempts to outsource the campus plan failed to materialize. I didn't have AutoCAD on my computer and no training on using AutoCAD. I did everything with

MacDraw Pro and Photoshop. These were both very powerful tools, but not on the par with a drafting tool like AutoCAD.

Helixtech sold the name, *Helix,* to RealPlayer and garnered enough money to upgrade to rapid application development environment—RADE 5.1. I participated in the beta testing and gained developer status. The next step was to take advantage of the Unix-based OS 10.2 for the Mac. Once Helix crossed over into the Windows world, I could rest assured that my database would have a life after I retired. There was no guarantee that it would.

Tenants came to my room upstairs and tenants left. The next three men didn't stay very long; their circumstances changed, and they moved on. I had a window unit installed because I needed to have it warm downstairs, making it too hot upstairs. The window unit made the rental room more comfortable. Musical parking and telephone use continued to be problems. It was like having a family.

My 1998 Ford Windstar reached 50,000 miles. I got a new set of Michelin X1s at 48,000 miles. The best tires out there, X1s gave excellent traction and handling, especially on wet roads. The rough Houston streets took their toll and I had to replace the sealed ball joints, front brakes, and a crushed fuel filter, placed directly under the front of the lower floor pan where any road obstruction would hit it. The plastic ground effect side panels below the doors got beat up. Fortunately, they were inexpensive to replace. The electronic gas and brake unit was replaced in an EMC recall. After that, I had to take the van to Mobility Plus many times for problems with the automatic door and ramp; it never got fixed once and for all. A battery in the Monte Carlo led to a new alternator after someone reversed the battery cables. Repairs on the van continued to grow and little problems never seemed to go away.

I was still running the original gel cell batteries for both electric wheelchairs—nine years for the Invacare and five for the Permobil. My backpack got threadbare, but I didn't replace it. In the spring of 2002, I broke my hand splint. I had dropped the splint in my van and backed over it with my 500 pound wheelchair. I had also bent the split so many times and then bent it back into shape, causing the stainless to fatigue and become weak where it was bent. After having the splint bent back in shape so many times, the splint finally just came apart. There had been trouble with fit from a repair the year before. It was hard to grasp things like my pen and calluses formed on my fingers from the ill fitting rings. I decided to have a new splint built.

Ric at City Brace called in Tony Medina for the job—the only guy in town who did that kind of work. Tony had worked for TIRR and had an award-winning design. First, Tony fixed my old splint so that it worked quite well, and then he built me a new one. The new one, Tony's design, was hard to put on and failed to do what the old one did. Tony then modified the new one to be more like my old one, but it still wouldn't allow me to type, pick up my coffee cup, and operate my computer mouses. I asked Tony to come by my office so that I could show him the two splints in action, but he never did. In August, I accidentally backed over my workbag with the old splint in it, crushing it again and breaking it in pieces. When I called Ric, he told me to come over. Tony was nowhere to be found; so Ric, in two sessions lasting about seven hours, got the old splint back together once again. The splint still needed a little fine-tuning—it always did—but was still doing its job after 38 years.

A sprained and swollen left ankle, likely caused during transferring, put me back in the boot for a couple of months in the spring of 2002. My bowel control continued to deteriorate, but, through good management and my help, I did better than in previous years. The big surprise came when I had my annual bladder flow test. Something during the rather normal, not painful, test improved my bladder function immensely. Much later, I learned that a bladder infection may have been restricting my output and the flow test, with its saline solution, may have cleared out the bladder infection.

Every year I became more affected by temperature changes and sometimes had trouble getting warm when I went to sleep at night. I continued to lose function and it was getting harder and harder to transfer. Someday, I wasn't sure how long, I predicted that I wouldn't be able to stand up to transfer. Acorda Therapeutics was working on five initiatives to cure spinal cord injury. I signed up for Phase III trial of a drug called fampridine that was designed to enhance nerve signals through plaque built up at the spinal injury site. Hopefully, the drug could reverse some of my deterioration. Dr. Parsons was testing the drug in Houston. I wasn't allowed to participate because of the nature of my injury (hemorrhaging), but once the drug was approved, it may help me. Stem cell research was already showing promise and I constantly looked for news on that front.

My iMac 40 GB drive was a wonderful workhorse for me. My only regret was not waiting until 2002 to get DVD-RW capability available on the new models. I was happy just writing books until I learned how easy it was to make movies with my Canon ZR-30 and iMovie. The Canon worked in many light conditions and had excellent stereo sound. Editing was very straightforward and uncomplicated. There were two problems: Each frame was sized and compressed to optimize digital movie making. Stills and pictures, while good, were nowhere the quality of a mega pixel digital still camera shot. The thousands of frames in a digital movie take up gigabytes of hard drive space and quickly use it up. To make space for new work, I had to put my edited movies back on miniDV tape and trash the movie work files on the computer. I simply ran out of drive space very quickly.

While working on movies, I discovered that my hard drive wasn't working properly. With my Iomega Zip Drive for back up, I wasn't worried. The Zip drive backed up all my files automatically on 100 MB disks as I made file changes. However, while editing movies, my 10 disks were quickly used up, so I made the mistake of not buying new Zip drive disks and began writing over my first disks again. The final diagnosis from Apple was that my hard drive was bad. The drive had to be replaced. Electrical power problems damaged it. I bought a CD-RW drive to get a second back up, but, by that time, many files wouldn't copy from the damaged hard drive. Then, to my dismay, huge movie clips had been *written over* my primary drive backup on the Zip disks. All of my recent computer activity, supposedly saved, *was gone.*

After saving all I could, I erased the drive and tried to reinitialize it, but I couldn't. I ended up getting a new 40 GB drive for $87 in two days. The cost included saving my files—*damn!* It took me two weeks to retrieve my files from my zip disks, computers from work, back up CDs, Beh's computer, and my Internet server space. I recovered all my personal, financial, and old stuff, and everything on the Internet server. But I lost all of my email and email addresses and a ton of funny stories and pictures I'd saved to put up on the Net. It's a tough lesson I never really learned very well. When my Zip Drive quit backing up automatically, it took a while for me to start backing up files again. At least I had all the original sources I used to put my new drive back together again. It seems like everybody that I talked to with a PC had lost everything more than once when their Windows computers locked up. I only lost a complete drive without backup once at work. I was pretty good at "*saving*" files from other peoples' Macintoshes at work by using some tools I had like Disk Doctor.

I finally broke down and bought Norton SystemWorks. The tool found about 400 copies of an old virus and fixed them. SystemWorks updated automatically and an occasional use of Disk Doctor kept the new drive running fresh and clean. SystemWorks cleaned up my three drives at work, too. One drive was about 12 years old at the time and only 500 MB, but it still did a great backup job there. I had no qualms about buying tools and equipment for home use and taking them to work to improve my equipment there. For the most part, my superiors were very slow to give me the tools I needed to keep current, productive, and innovative. Time and time again, I found that something that I suggested turned up in the bosses' offices on their computers with little or no use by them. For those social climbers, it was all about appearances, not productivity. They were continually buying things they didn't really need or use, just to keep up with the Joneses. What a waste of good resources and limited funding.

The CD-RW drive worked well on Beh's computer, so I made a CD of her stuff for backup. In September 2002, ViaVoice on her computer got corrupted and quit. After that we had a lot of annoying problems— programs that wouldn't quit. I tried to reinstall ViaVoice, but couldn't. We got Norton for the PC on special. I found W32. Magistr had infected her computer badly. Norton Antivirus found 480 copies and fixed them. Magi was a "Trojan" that disguised itself as something else, so even though I followed every procedure to a T, I couldn't remove the worm. Finally, I used her system disk to go back to a 2001 configuration. That seemed to have done the trick. I reinstalled ViaVoice and was able to continue dictating my novels.

Bank of America dropped their support of my Quicken-based computer banking and went to Internet banking. Initially, when Bank of America bought my previous bank, North Carolina National Bank, in order for me to continue banking with a Macintosh, I had to close my Texas account and open an account in Florida. That was when I started using Quicken over the old UNIX-based funds transfer system I had used since I first got a modem at home. While the online version had its advantages, I still kept my Quicken books parallel to plan and track my finances and assets. I discovered that Quicken TurboTax online did a great job with my complex taxes. My Excel spreadsheet version still worked, too, but not having to copy numbers over to the 1040 forms and having the final form mistake-free was a big advantage. It was very hard to keep up with tax law changes with an Excel spreadsheet.

My rhythm of writing a poem a week and posting it never changed. I had over 500 pages up and growing. To further complicate my life, I created a poem index and put each poem on its own page with an illustration accompanying the poem. I joined AuthorsDen.com and posted the poem there, too. It was interesting to see the reviews I got. I started writing more provocative and controversial subjects to see what response I would get from other authors. Most of those responses were positive. My website was getting about ten unique hits a day, mostly from search engines. Total hits averaged around thirty hits a day and growing. Search engines came to my "Funny and Inspiring" link often. I just didn't have time to update that link anymore. There were copyright issues with posting other peoples stuff. Lost so much with my hard drive, too.

Bookbooters nearly went under. Before that, Toby invested everything in updating the site's software. I submitted **Alone?** In October 2001. It got lost. Toby got a draft manuscript in December and read it over the holidays but did nothing with it. Meanwhile, the relaunch of the Bookbooters site was delayed and so was **Alone?** I was promised February, and then April, and then the book went into limbo. Angela Hoy had approved **Alone?** for BookLocker.com in December, but I wanted to give Bookbooters the shot. The relaunch didn't happen until April. The new Bookbooters site looked good, but contained all the old promotion, unchanged for months. Toby and his wife were wading through 2000 manuscripts and rejecting 95% of them. **Alone?** was on the schedule for June, but it never appeared. Finally, in August 2002, I laid my concern out to Toby and he responded. The ebook came out in August, and with some prodding, the paperback in October. I had top billing under "Featured Authors," above Stephen King, until that page was updated. In October, Toby announced in a long email that Bookbooters had turned the corner and promised to do much more for the few of us original authors in the future, including getting our books in bookstores. Those promises were empty. Toby was jousting with windmills. So many other websites were going out of business. So was Toby and Bookbooters.

Both of my books received good comments from those who read them. Toby told me that the ebook of **Alone?** "Was selling like hotcakes at W.H. Smith.UK" in October 2002. Max DeVore of the *Conroe Courier* would have reviewed the books sometime after the first of the year, but he declined after he read them in airports on a holiday trip. Max said that he didn't want to give me a "lukewarm" review. He liked horror and mystery and wanted to give favorable reviews. DeVore gave me some good advice and wished me luck. I discovered the primary reason for his concern much later. The books had been poorly edited.

I started writing **Tor, Last of the Thals** after **Alone?** was finished. It was an unsatisfactory start; one I think I can improve when I go back to that book again some day. And then, I had a dream one night in June 2002. My dream was that terrorists had dropped an atomic bomb on Washington, DC. Thinking about how we would, and should, respond, led me to start writing **War's End—The End of Terrorism in the 21st Century**. Like my first two novels, **War's End** was ambitious and far-reaching. I wasn't sure that I would be able to pull it off. Like my other books, **Wars End** contains little violence and action. Violence and action sells, but I have trouble justifying using violence in my work just to increase my sales. Sex is much better than violence. However, while sex can boost readership, it can also make the book off limits for younger readers. Extreme violence doesn't have that problem for some reason. It's an upside down world.

As for the future, I saw war. I saw energy shortages and higher prices. I saw more terror. Still, Texas A & M hired a man to coach their football team for about two million dollars a year. I waited to see what great contribution to society his students would make—maybe bring back the bonfire? It became the fashion to rip off ridiculously rich music stars by downloading their music for free from the Internet on sites like Napster. Piracy didn't just hurt the rich. It stifles creativity and limits entry into the arts. The next crisis may well be the disparate wealth between those that have and those who have not. I could see that coming, too.

Clonaid jumped out in front with their announcement that they had cloned a human being. The announcement proved that technology will forge ahead regardless of what people think of it. Whether or not IT, Ginger, or Segway, would revolutionize the way we travel remained unknown. The fact that giant SUVs were dinosaurs was lost on most people, clamoring to buy one. The gap between the richest and poorest was visibly widening. Terrorism grows from these disaffected people in insidious ways from frontal attacks like suicide bombings to backdoor attacks like identity theft and scams that made up one third of the Nigerian economy. AIDs was being controlled in the U.S. while it ran rampant across much of the impoverished world. And the sleeping giant, China, lay out there waiting to take over the world.

Jazz, getting a little gray on the snout, but not slowing down.

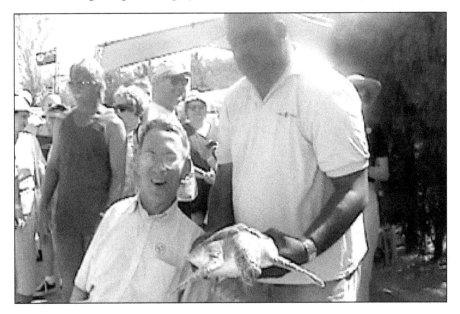

Ron pets a turtle at the Turtle Farm, Grand Cayman Island April 2002

Daisey on 7 Mile Beach, Grand Caymaan Island April 2002

Diann at the Turtle Farm, Grand Cayman Island April 2002

# 73

# A Solution to War and to the University's Problems

The year 2003 opened more opportunities and threw a few roadblocks my way. The stock market turned around and so did my retirement. It still looked like I would be working until 65 or 66 in order to get full Social Security. I got a fantastic array microphone at work. It was a freeing experience to dictate without an annoying headset and cord. I got Beh a new computer with Windows XP for Christmas and installed ViaVoice release 8 allowing me to dictate much faster. That computer, located in a quiet area in the dining room, was where I began writing my books with my voice.

Dad had pneumonia again in the spring of 2003 and a persistent cough. By midsummer, though, he was gaining weight and back on the golf course. Both mom and dad looked very good when they came through for a brief visit in October. Dad's doctor in McAllen gave him a nebulizer to help him with his breathing. They looked at a new assisted living complex in Marshfield before they came down... always moving. They were thinking about the time when they could no longer make the trip back and forth between Wisconsin and Texas. To help with their long tripping, they bought a 2003 Ford Windstar.

My twin brother , Roger, got a new high tech hip after his old hip wore out. He returned to golf better than ever. Roger said that it was his golf swing that put wear and tear on his hip joint. I don't have any evidence of joint arthritis and believe that it was his spinal cord injury, combined with severe injury to the tendons in his knee, repaired by surgery years before, that brought about the deterioration of his hip. My younger brother Tim, got an infection in his foot that traveled to his heart valve and damaged it. After surgery to replace the damaged valve with a valve from a pig, Tim recovered and was able to resume an active life.

Daisey got a five night a week job taking care of an old woman and quit shortly after Rosie did. After sifting through many applicants, I selected Janice Earles, a young Jamaican woman, to help us out. After two months, Janice quit because her five year-old son had came back from Jamaica and she had to take care of him. I called Daisey. The old woman she quit to take care of had died within two weeks of Daisey's employment with her. Daisey was glad to have her old job back with me.

Beh and I traveled to McAllen just before Christmas 2002 and got some beautiful evening film of the decorative lights in the park. In February, Reliant Solutions gave us free tickets to see Julio Iglesias at the new Reliant Stadium during the Houston Rodeo. I took Beh and Daisey. I got lost from them in the carnival crowd after the show. I waited near the car after cruising up and down the whole carnival midway a couple of times, and finally, they appeared. Soon after, in March, Roger and Sue arrived for a visit. We took them to Space Center Houston and to Kemah for sightseeing and dinner. I had never parallel parked the van with my high tech equipment before. I slid into that spot in one try. Old skills never die. By nightfall it got cool, and Beh had to buy me a sweatshirt to keep warm. The afternoon had been very hot.

Instead of our usual spring trip to see the wild flowers, Beh and I drove to Lake Conroe and looked at some of the neighborhoods. I thought that I would buy a lot there and build a home that would fit our needs when we retired. It would be close enough to the city for my medical needs and Beh could still get back to the Vietnamese neighborhood in southwest Houston once in awhile. After thinking about it, the area was already crowded and I-45 was just too congested for the trip into Houston.

I planned all summer for a fall trip to California through Arizona. It looked like I would need two weeks. In the end, I couldn't find help to go with me that long. Diann saved up vacation in the hope that she would be able to go with me the following spring.

Beh and I settled for a four-day trip to Arkansas when the leaves changed. We took Daisey and stayed two days in Hot Springs. I had planned to drive to Eureka Springs, but our first day trip proved too slow, so after seeing the beautiful, scenic Petit Jean State Park and a wonderful automobile museum, we returned to Hot Springs. The next morning, as we left the hotel, I was going down a concrete ramp in the parking garage at full speed when my wheelchair suddenly stopped. I could see my feet sliding off the footrests as I pitched forward and began to fly in a swan dive. I landed with a grating crunch on my right eyeglass lens, my knees and my breastbone, sliding over the ridges in the concrete ramp meant to prevent slipping.

A man working in the garage ran over, and with Daisey, picked me up while Beh maneuvered the wheelchair under me. I had two little skins on each knee, a scrape on my forehead and nose, and a sore neck; otherwise, I was okay. I could still see past the scrape on my eyeglasses, so we packed the van, and I drove us off. We visited Garvan Gardens that morning. The trails were poorly marked, so I ended up leading us on a trail by the lake that was not wheelchair accessible. I got bogged down in the sand a few times but made it okay. Coming back up the steep hill on crushed rock, my wheels spun, but made it back up there okay, too. My PerMobil had weight, traction, and tremendous power, great off-road capabilities.

My health remained quite good and I didn't get sick in 2003. During my annual bladder test, the nurse who put me back in my chair, pinched my butt with the strap of the lift. The bruise was painful and bothered me. Checking my cushion, I discovered that it was falling apart and starting to cause a pressure sore on the side opposite the bruise. I quickly bought a new Stimulite cushion. Since the new cushion wasn't broken in, the sores continued to get worse until I took a few afternoons off to lie in bed and take the pressure off. That worked, but we still had to watch the sores to keep them from returning.

I decided to became more militant. I was tired of being singled out for my disability and discriminated against. I was contacted by the Houston Independent Living Center (HCIL) to help their cause. Texas, like many other states, suffered a deficit in 2003 and had to cut the budget. Programs for the elderly, children, and the disabled were on the chopping block. HCIL was all about getting disabled people out of nursing homes and state schools and into their own homes in neighborhoods using state and federal funding at lower cost, rather than being warehoused and secluded from society in state schools and nursing homes. What HCIL was doing made a lot of sense to me because, but for good fortune and hard work, I might have been in a nursing home.

My state representative, Talmadge Heflin, was chairman of the Texas House Appropriations Committee, leading the charge to consolidate and cut services. In addition to writing letters, I led a march to Mr. Heflin's office

March 14, 2003 and drove to Austin with Tony Koosis, HILC program director, and Rosie, and testified before the committee. I also supported a City of Houston resolution and attended a candlelight vigil. Heflin assured me, in a handwritten note, "Essential services will not be cut." Throughout the summer it looked like that would not be the case. But finally, by the end of the summer, funds were found to cover, at least the first year of the biennium, the services needed. I also attended and commented on the reorganization of the Texas Department of Health and Human Services, a conference call on the MiCASSA bill before Congress to increase in-home services over institutional ones, and the passage of a Houston city ordinance providing "visitability" in new housing for disabled residents.

We wrote our congressman to see if he could help Beh get a green card, but he wasn't much help. With the help of a lawyer, Beh hoped to get that done soon so we could go on a cruise. Beh's business was slow, so she explored other business opportunities. She didn't find anything suitable.

My persistence finally paid off. In April 2003, I was granted an ADA hearing for my demotion in 1998. Although there were old friends on the committee, there were no disabled persons or anyone other than African-Americans. Two of the committee were quite hostile toward me, notably a Dr. Henry North, a professor of education who seemed to see nothing wrong with my being in the demoted position—like I should be with my lot because I was doing so well in spite of the obvious oppression. When I received the results of the hearing, I was told that I did not supply enough evidence. I requested an appeal and time to gather evidence. I found a discussion in a Board of Regents meeting where I was described [but not named] as the person who caused our classroom and laboratory utilization rate to be so low and that I had been, "Removed from that responsibility [scapegoat]." Harold Johnson's response when he was asked by a board member what he was going to do about the problem. Since I had proof that the facilities inventory did not determine utilization that should have been enough evidence of discrimination. It wasn't.

I had already regained responsibility for the facilities inventory and proposed a plan for increasing our utilization rate. Working closely with David Chu in enrollment management, we projected figures that would bring our utilization rate up to where it should be. In the meantime, another hearing committee was formed and I had an opportunity to submit the evidence I found. This committee, while it still appeared to not have any disabled persons on it, was a better balance of our faculty and staff. It was also more friendly and empathetic. Jim Anderson, my superior, attended to represent the administration because JT Glover, the assistant vice-president, was called to an emergency board meeting. Jim was most helpful and said that he could not comment on my demotion because he had not been hired yet when it happened. Jim had been forced to reprimand me and deny me assistance at risk of his own job.

The emergency board meeting announced the naming of three new board members and a new chairman. Rumor was that they cleaned house. Later, my hearing committee called JT Glover back separately to answer my claims. I wasn't present to defend myself. I received a letter from the second committee that I had not provided enough evidence once again. When I called the committee chair, she told me that Glover told them that I had received a salary adjustment in the recent salary adjustment survey. He also told them that he had provided me with all necessary computer upgrades. Both were lies. My salary record showed no increase and Glover repeatedly denied my requests to upgrade my Macintosh and software so that I could provide him reports in a timely way. The age and type of my work Macintosh clearly proved that no upgrades were made. The Gateway PC that I received was a hand-me-down, out of date and underpowered. I had requested to make the upgrades at my own expense to improve my database performance. Glover was a very convincing liar. He never put his denials in writing. However, I believed I had him on this one and couldn't wait to get him on the witness stand. The committee was wrong to have JT go before them without me present to challenge his lies.

In the meantime, with all the board shenanigans going on, President Priscilla Slade put on a good face and promoted the positive aspects of her administration by *spending money*. Slade had former president George Bush in commercials advertising TSU and declaring how our enrollment had risen significantly. The fact is, although enrollment rose significantly in the short run, it was just slightly higher than 1993, when Howard Turnley began downsizing and outsourcing the entire facilities area. Constant renovation did not improve the quality of our campus buildings. Poor construction review and management resulted in serious, costly problems emerging from a replacement health center, recreation center, and an addition to the pharmacy building. The purchase of land and an apartment complex for student housing resulted in cost overruns and overly expensive housing for our students. TSU had to make it mandatory for freshmen students to live in those new, but overpriced, apartments. Otherwise, no one would have paid the exorbitant rents that were charged to pay back all the "missing money" in the projects.

The $300 million TSU got from the Office of Civil Rights resulted in the building surge and the salary adjustment survey. The university administration soon received salaries comparable to corporate equivalents like the former Enron leadership, while custodians, competing with illegal aliens in the City of Houston, received almost nothing. TSU had problems with NCAA violations, the selling of grades, the mishandling of federal financial aid funds, the comingling of education and general funds with auxiliary funds, and admitting criminals as students. There were many sexual harassment complaints, and complaints like mine. Only pretty girls and handsome guys were allowed to rise high in Slade's organization. The disabled were catered to and given lip service, but not given equal rights and responsibility.

Several lawsuits from fired employees were under way. The former police chief, Cordell Lindsey, won his case against the university for being fired improperly when he uncovered theft by an employee handling event money. Any person managing events was always under suspicion because of the amount of cash involved. Tiffany, the young woman discovered stealing, had been placed in the position by her uncle, a TSU board member.

While Lindsey was a favorite of president Slade, he had to go when a board member was threatened to be exposed. Lindsey's girlfriend, Eva Pickens, the longtime university media director, was also let go, probably because she had information beneficial to Lindsey's case. A couple of year's later, Lindsey's lawyer set up a sting and recorded Tiffany taking a cash bribe. The administration was paid well to keep their mouths shut and paint a rosy picture, but the faculty and staff could see through the hype. Loyalty was rewarded over honesty and productivity. Everything was rosy as long as everyone played the game with the board and the president, but things were starting to come apart. Like Enron, the problems began to get too great for rosy pictures to handle.

In the meantime, we partied. Beh couldn't go, so I took myself to the president's summer picnic. It was stifling hot and we had to wait until 5:30 p.m. to find out who won the grand prize of *anywhere USA* plane tickets. A lavish catered Thanksgiving party was offered every year for the faculty and staff. Beh and I also went to Slade's lavish Christmas party at the Hilton America next to the expanded George R. Brown convention center. Only the people Dr. Slade invited were allowed to come to these off-campus parties. In spite of my obvious disapproval of some of the practices of the administration, Slade seemed to find me interesting enough to put me on her party list. She even asked me to dance. While I could do a semblance of a wheelchair dance for her enjoyment, I declined because of my growing case against the entire administration. At that party, I was given the cold shoulder by several of the higher-ups when I tried to engage them in conversation. I wondered who paid for the lavish parties? We used to all chip in for the annual Christmas party in our area. Everything was potluck. The staff or contractors donated the liquor. For the past few years, JT Glover paid for the area party with university funds. There was no alcohol allowed, but it was available on the side. There were many catered Christmas parties and no one paid for any of them. Quentin Wiggins, Slade's CFO and right-hand man, held his lavish Christmas party off campus for everyone in the entire division. Slade gave me a gift every year—a TSU colored Christmas tree ornament. The parties and gifts were misguided compensation for the way that faculty and staff were being treated. I could have told her that it was a tactic that wouldn't work.

Toby Endem, my publisher, became very ill in January 2003. As a result, in July, his wife, Lee, suspended operation of their publishing business. Bookbooters still sold our books, but wouldn't accept or process any new submissions. My meager sales of ebooks increased, but not by much. No one, except me, was buying paperbacks. By November, Lee announced that Toby was getting better and should be back by the first of the year 2004. In the meantime, I completed Chapter 17 of War's End. I expected the book to run about thirty chapters and to finish some time in the summer of 2004.

My involvement in Author's Den (AD) increased. I posted a poem a week both there and on my site. AD started a poetry contest, too. I never won. I posted some poems on poetry.com. They published several of my poems. *Honeysuckle Rain* was given an Editors' Choice Award, and I wrote *The Great Passing* for a book of two hundred of the "Best Poets of 2003." And then, I found out that poetry.com was a sham, eager to take poets' money and give constant praise, regardless of whatever crap one was writing. I'm not saying that all Internet sites and contests are fake. But a good number of them are and it takes some insight to find the ones that are legit. I'm glad to say that I never sent any money to poetry.com.

After twenty years, the paper composite siding on my house had deteriorated to the point where it was sagging and crumbling everywhere. While the fiberboard material may have originally been better than wood, it had been improperly installed and sealed, causing water to get behind and gradually destroy it. After much effort, I found out that a company named

Champion made the siding. Champion went out of business in 1984 and sold their plant to Masonite. While Masonite maintained the warranties, they had left the country for Canada and sold warranty responsibility to International Paper. I took pictures, filled out a form, and sent them to International Paper. Even after twenty years, I was fully compensated for the cost of the initial siding, $785, but not for the labor to install it.

I got bids ranging from $9,000 to $26,000 to replace all the siding with Hardiplank. I chose the second lowest bidder because he was an old friend of mine and promised to bring my home's exterior back to its original condition. Ebenezer Onyanwou and his crew started in January when weather conditions weren't favorable. First, they chose the wrong siding and covered half of one side of the house with it before I caught them. Second, Ebenezer tried to use old broken or substitute pine for the rough sawn cedar trim. Third, lack of right materials and rain delayed them for two months while they destroyed my shrubs around the house. Ebenezer had Sherman Williams mix a special batch of paint for the trim that was the wrong color. I had to go back and pick a stock color that was closer to the original.

The workmen broke my water line, causing my toilets to get jammed up with sediment, resulting in large water bills for three months until I got the toilets fixed. And then, in April, when I turned on the air conditioning, the workmen had run a nail through my coolant piping between my compressor and condenser. Even with a new furnace that I had installed in August 2002, the house was cold all winter. Finally, my a/c installer found a large plenum in the attic that was disconnected. The house was warmer after that. In June and July, we were under an invasion of large roaches that apparently had stayed in the walls and came out when the new siding sealed them in. In spite of all that, the house looked better than it did when it was new. The new exterior was suggesting that the interior be upgraded as well.

Vicky Harris and I lead a march to Talmadge Heflin's Office 3/14/03

Michael Thomas of ADAPT. Vicky 2007, Michael 2008, Tony 2011

I drove Tony Koosis to Austin to protest budget cuts by Heflin 3/30/03

Tony ready to speak. All of these friends died too young [dates above]

# 74

## Trips and Equipment Troubles

Another year, another novel. The tragedy of 9/11 got me thinking. I had started a novel related to my first and second that I called **Tor, Last of the Thals**, but the idea of an even greater tragedy kept nagging at me until I wrote the first chapter. What I thought of was *the unthinkable*. A terrorist attack on our government using a nuclear weapon. And the villains weren't the usual suspects. I found myself writing chapter after chapter quite quickly, drawing on some things that I knew about the Middle East from my friends from there, and some things that I didn't know about, like basic training, that I got from my nephew who had gone through basic recently, Matt Woltmann.

The purpose of the book, **War's End**, was to show a *kinder, gentler* way to end terrorism. Not the way we were pursuing it by attacking whole nations in an attempt to weed out terrorists in the process. Lacking action and unrealistic violence by super characters, **War's End** got some good reviews but didn't sell like the rest of my books. As long as there are vast differences in the quality of life for people on earth, and greedy, corrupt people running things, there' will be a need for force. Hopefully, a better way to root terrorists out like the novel suggests, will be found.

While ViaVoice was a fine voice recognition system, I struggled with its idiosyncrasies and had to do a lot of keyboard editing with Microsoft Word to get **War's End** out. To replace ViaVoice, I ordered Dragon NaturallySpeaking, Release 8—supposedly much better and more accurate.

I hoped so, because I needed something to write with and my typing was getting worse as I lost abdominal control.

With no contact with Toby Endem and Bookbooters.com, I looked for another way to publish. Fortunately, my first publisher, Booklocker.com, was still in business. After heavy communication with Angela Hoy, the owner/editor, I edited, proofed, formatted the text, and designed the cover of **War's End**. The print on demand (POD) paperback became available in mid January 2005. I was excited about this book because it was so timely and because it was a good story. Sales, however did not verify that.

Mom and dad spent their last winter in McAllen. Beh already missed picking oranges and lemons whenever we got down there. They planned to sell both mobile homes and move into an apartment in Marshfield by fall 2005. I knew we would miss their annual visits coming and going each fall and spring. Dad had lung surgery in August 2004 to remove lung scar tissue and infection. The surgery allowed him to eat and breathe better and enabled him to go back to bowling once again.

My twin brother, Roger, started out as a industrial engineer after college doing time and motion studies in three companies until he became a member of a consulting firm for a holding company and worked in efficiency studies in over 100 companies. After a brief period as vice president for manufacturing for a small company, Roger decided he was through being a member of a firm and started his own consulting firm in the Chicago area. After Roger married Sue and moved to Elkhart, Indiana in 1990, he found it difficult to commute to Chicago to maintain his consulting business in the greater Chicago area. Eventually, he gave that up and hired on as a manufacturing engineer with local Elkhart and nearby Michigan companies, all the while looking forward to an early retirement.

For his 16th birthday, I gave my nephew, Michael Hull, my '73 Monte Carlo in April 2004. Michael and some friends started a garage band with Michael playing the drums. With a classic car to drive, Michael became a big man on his high school campus.

Tom and his wife, Sonya, were released from Lucent in August and June 2004. Both continued to work there because the projects that were outsourced to Brazil still needed their help. Finally, Lucent pulled the project from Brazil and Tom took it to China. In the meantime, they got heavily involved in selling Xango, a health drink derived from mangosteen. Tom also investigated Whey-Cool, a startup company out of Chicago that had its first retail store in Marshfield, Wisconsin. With whey, Whey-Cool made ice-cream like products, cakes, cookies and candy. Tom hired on without pay to develop the California, Nevada, and Arizona territories. The company never really got off the ground, so Tom returned to managing software development for a firm doing avionic software with some of his former colleagues at Lucent.

Beh's days were filled with her alteration and dry cleaning shop. The economy and competition hurt her business. She spent long hours of painful sewing with little profit. During New Year 2004, Beh accompanied her sister to Las Vegas. She brought back a love of Circ du Soleil and a nasty flu that I caught.

In February 2004, Reliant Solutions gave us free tickets to see John Mayer at the new Reliant Stadium. I took Beh and Daisey. The young kids loved him, but I found that he ran his lyrics together in a way that was very hard to understand. I'd grown to like his songwriting style better since . Beh wanted to see Enrique Iglesias, so we went to see him, too. Enrique was very good. During Reliant Field Day, I got close to the Texans by visiting their locker room and their practice field with a couple of the players. Also got to meet some of the cheerleaders and had my picture taken with them.

In April 2004, Tom told us about a Xango demonstration on the North Side. After we participated in the Xango demonstration at a motel, we came out to find my van was parked in with a car on my ramp side. With the help of the motel manager, we pushed my van out, but Beh had to start it while standing outside so we could turn the front wheels. When she went to put the transmission into park from neutral, she stopped at reverse and the car started backward. She then pushed on the gas instead of the brake. The van accelerated backwards with Beh in the open door running backward with it. The van then hit a parked car with great force and knocked that car over the curb, up against the motel building. Beh was knocked to the ground by the sudden stop of the impact, and amazingly, bruised but otherwise unhurt. I thought she was going to be *killed!* My van had a badly damaged rear door, but was still drivable after all that. A policeman came by and took a report. The other car was reported as stolen. It turned out that it was a rental car that someone in the motel was driving. The car had been stolen before and then returned, causing the confusion about whether it was stolen or not. The repair consisted of replacing the rear door on my Windstar van.

Beh's sister offered Beh her 1992 SC 400 Lexus. The car had 108,000 miles and was in excellent condition. Beh still drove her 2000 Toyota Corolla every day, but had the Lexus to drive on weekends. Beh kept that Lexus for a couple of years and then sold it to her sister-in-law. I thought she should have kept it because that car would have eventually been worth a lot of money.

A guy robbed Beh in her shop with a knife . Beh was angrier than shaken by it. After he left the shop and started across the parking lot, she chased after him, along with the owner of the restaurant next door. The guy threatened her again with the knife and crossed the busy intersection of Westheimer and Great Falls. The restaurant owner followed at some distance, and saw the robber get into a vehicle with another guy at the Wal-Mart parking lot. The restaurant owner took down the license number of the thieves' car. Beh filed a police report and those guys were caught, but she didn't recover the small amount of cash they took.

Instead of our usual annual spring trip to see the wild flowers near Brenham, Beh and I drove to Lake Houston and looked at some of the neighborhoods. I thought that I would buy a lot there and build a home that would fit our needs when we retired. Lake Houston was closer than Lake Conroe and close enough to the city for my medical needs. Beh could still get back to the Vietnamese neighborhood in southwest Houston once in awhile.

In April 2004, I was finally able to take my long delayed California trip. I originally planned two weeks, but Beh couldn't go, and Diann had only a week's vacation. I drove hard the first two days and reached Tom's home in Phoenix by midday on the second day. After a wonderful, relaxing stay there, Diann and I drove to Lake Havasu City where an old friend, Lois Nottingham, Jack Swanson's widow, who lived with her second husband after Jack's death, Clyde. With some tickets that Lois gave us, Diann and I took the ferry across the lake to a California casino. So, I got to California after all, if even only for a brief time while we gambled before taking the ferry back to Arizona in the heat of the night.

The next day we drove to the Grand Canyon and found both the canyon and the weather beautiful. We stayed in a luxurious room that was fully accessible for wheelchairs. The next day, it turned cold and windy. I drove through dust storms through Monument Valley and on into Colorado. The only sightseeing we did was from the warm comfort of the van. At one point driving through Indian country, we had a local radio station on playing native flute music. With the dust swirling up all around and the flute music in the background, the video we took was surreal. It was so cold at Mesa Verdi that there were snow flurries and I didn't want to get out of the van. We hadn't eaten, so we ducked into the cafeteria for a bite. Diann couldn't decide on sharing some buffalo steak with me, so I ordered chili.

Soon after eating, I had to go to the restroom. It was times like this that someone like Diann was indispensable.

The weather got worse when we got back to the van. Before descending that steep winding road, I put the van in low gear and was glad that I did. As we slowly descended the long steep mountain road, I saw my first tornado ever, ripping up the canyon floor below. I told Diann to get a video of it. Diann tried to get the camera working, but finally said that the battery was dead. We missed the tornado, but she was able to get the camcorder working soon after and we got some film of the storm going down the mountain. There was snow at Durango. We stopped briefly there, but we didn't stop at Santa Fe and the drive home was long and uneventful after that.

I had a few episodes of bronchitis in the spring of 2004 from that bug that Beh got in Las Vegas. In February, while being fitted for a new wheelchair, a mapping of pressure on my bottom showed that I was getting too much pressure from my new Stimulite cushion. A Roho air cushion was recommended and my pressure sores began to heal as soon as I got one. The Roho made sitting very unstable because I was sitting up on air columns encased in rubber. For the first time, I had to use my seat belt and watch my balance more. After Christopher Reeve died from having infection from pressure sores reach his heart, I decided to do everything I could to prevent sores from forming. With my annual flu shot, I went a long time without getting the flu.

I started doing more travel for the university. They seemed to be bending over backwards to accommodate me in that regard after my challenge. In the summer 2004, I had to get training for the land inventory I still maintained with the Texas general land office. Beh accompanied me to Austin for the one-hour session on how to log into the inventory on the Internet. It certainly wasn't necessary for me to go all the way to Austin for that, but JT had gone earlier and I guess he decided he didn't want to do Internet entry even though it was only once a year. In September, the annual Congress of the Association of Energy Engineers moved from Atlanta to Austin. Once again, Beh joined me for a most pleasurable three days of talks, dinners, and ceremonies in the huge Austin Convention Center. Our hotel was right on Interstate 35 at Town Lake. Beh enjoyed walking by the lake every day. One morning, we saw two swans from our window. Beh videotaped them and I later wrote a poem about what we saw. The high point of our stay was watching a million Mexican Freetail bats leave from under the Congress Street Bridge on their nightly forage for insects.

Toby Endem recovered from his illness, but Bookbooters.com was not the same. There were very few updates on the site and I was unable to contact Toby or his wife. I sold very few books in 2004. For a long time I received no report or any royalties. Finally, through Content Reserve, I learned that I did have royalties coming and Bookbooters posted them to my PayPal account.

I continued to post a poem a week on my site and then provide a link on Author's Den. Most of the authors there were looking for praise or encouragement, not constructive criticism. There were a few who were very serious about their work and I enjoyed communicating with them. My works were very well read there. In 2004 I had over twenty-five thousand hits of my works recorded at the site. A bookstore was planned. AuthorsDen.com was continually improving and providing new services for authors. I obtained a lifetime membership.

In 1981, Beh's brother, Paul, and sister, Tammy, had already escaped to the United States. Beh's family signed up to immigrate, sponsored by Paul and his wife, Camthu. In 1992, the family was allowed to come, and Beh's father immediately received his permanent residency, or green card. Beh and five of her brothers signed up and spent money several times with local Vietnamese lawyers to get their permanent residency, too, but were always denied. There were so many Vietnamese in Houston, it took an inordinately long time for their hearings to came up. Beh finally got her hearing in November 2004. Just before Christmas, she got her green card.

After my two hearings the previous year both proved negative, in February 2004, I took the next step and met with Bruce Wilson, TSU's senior vice president for administration. After he listened to what I had to say, Bruce told me that he could do nothing about the past, but he could and would do something about the future. Wilson never wrote me any confirmation of what he said and wasn't specific about what he'd do. I waited and waited for something to happen, but nothing ever did. When I called Keefus Falls about the situation in June 2004, Keefus said that Bruce was going to reorganize (supposedly in my favor). That never happened either. On September 1st, everyone was to get a merit increase. The increase didn't come until the December 1st paycheck. Mine was just average. I had heard that Bruce was worried about losing his job under the new Board of Regents. When I called Keefus about my concern, he was still stalling, saying that he was going to talk to Bruce. I decided to go to

President Slade. If she was unresponsive, I would contact the Office of Civil Rights and the EEOC.

TSU's general counsel and others were fired. Before that, Dr. Joseph Jones, longtime dean of the graduate school and coordinator of the 10 year accreditation process with the Southern Association of Universities and Colleges, was fired for mismanagement of a grant he received to promote awareness of the dangers of tobacco. When the renovations for the law school building and student life center went way over budget and were poorly monitored, Bill Beckham was fired. Another information technology director, who I barely got to know, was also fired. There were probably others. President Slade regularly cleaned house to make sure no ill will surfaced about the university. Unfortunately, lawsuits were on the rise. Many of the people fired were scapegoats for mismanagement by her favorite henchmen.

There was good news. In the summer of 2004, Tavis Smiley, a PBS anchor and graduate of Indiana University, gave $1 million to the university to establish a School of Communication Science. He also pledged to gave the university $1 million a year for the next ten years. TSU's enrollment increased another two thousand.. Fuelled by the poor economy, heavy advertising, and new apartments that were very expensive and relied on taking the students' financial aid, the campus came alive with activity. Admissions standards became so lax that the number of criminals in the student body increased dramatically. A young freshmen coed was accidentally killed in a campus apartment parking lot in a gun battle between two non-student drug dealing groups. Campus life after dark became dangerous, requiring more patrol officers and escorts.

I got a request to recall the steering unit on my van. The recall was free, but the requested "routine maintenance" on the steering amounted to $2,500. I was also experiencing problems with the EZ-Lock, the automatic ramp and door, my driver's side window, and my seat belt. I called TRC, now called DARS (Department of Assistance Rehabilitation Services) for assistance. I was told that they only allowed for a one-time vehicle modification in a lifetime. However, my counselor then told me that if I got a new van, they would replace my system entirely. I couldn't afford a new van, but asked DARS to help with the repairs. They agreed.

Unfortunately, the paperwork provided by Mobility Plus didn't include all the repairs I requested. A second and third request had to be written before work began in July. When the van was finished, several things, including the seat belt modification, were not done. I decided to wait until I got my new wheelchair before replacing the EZ-Lock.

After I complained about pressure sores and the comfort of my Permobil wheelchair, Dr. Parsons scheduled me to be fitted for new one. Mary Dunn, an occupational therapist and rehab specialist, took on the task in February 2004 of providing me with the best replacement possible. At first we talked about a standing wheelchair and she ordered one. Since the new Permobil chair had to be built in Sweden, it took a very long time. When I went to Austin with Beh, the Permobil representative brought me a standing chair to try out. The standing mechanism made the chair 2 inches higher than my current chair. When we tried it in the van, my head hit the ceiling, and the controls ran into my driving controls—an impossible situation. I decided that I couldn't get a standing chair.

Mary ordered a reclining chair instead. The chair required a headrest for me to recline, but the headrest had to be moved out of the way for my van headrest with a head button control to move into place while driving. In midsummer, I got a picture of the $2,000 device. It was a big ugly box on the back of the wheelchair. I began to worry.

The new wheelchair arrived in early December. By that time, I was fed up with trying to operate my van ramp and door; having been in several times to have it adjusted. I was told that I should get a new van, and that I should have the motor, clutches, pulleys and other parts of the ramp mechanism replaced. I told them that I couldn't afford a new van, and they needed to replace those parts and come up with a new way for me operate the ramp and door.

The first fitting with my new chair lasted two hours. The rocker switch box providing four functions wouldn't work, even with toggle extensions. The box was moved to the back of the chair for my helpers to use. My new control had flat buttons for on/off, function, lights, signal lights, flashers, and horn. The function button allowed me to change the speed of the chair and to operate the four functions from the joystick. The only problem was that I had a hard time reaching and pushing the function button. A 5¢ solution was to place little jelly buttons over the flat buttons to make it possible for me to push them with the side of my hand. Unfortunately, setting the speed of the chair and operating functions this way, while easy, was still quite time consuming. I never got used to that.

In the meantime, my *check engine* light came on. I was scheduled to have the van and the chair in the shop, so I took it in to have the EZ-Lock put on and the chair fitted. Trey, co-owner of Mobility Plus with his mother, came up with solutions to two of my problems. Trey said we could remove the seat belt that was hitting my knees and put one on my chair that would reach all the way to the EZ-Lock frame. He also said that we could tie my remote for operating the ramp and door to a toggle switch on my chair that would be easier to operate. Unfortunately, Trey hadn't included both of these modifications in his proposals, so it required a new proposal once again to DARS. I drove out in my new wheelchair without those modifications being finished.

The van computer said that the engine light problem was my torque converter. I drove two more days to work, but on Monday, December 19 2004, the van stalled several times backing out of my driveway and I had it towed to a transmission shop. The van was towed back on December 24th after a $2,900 overall—a nice Christmas present. I still had much work to do on the chair and van until everything would be working smoothly again at 75,000 miles and growing.

Houston Lighting and Power invited me twice to tour Reliant Stadium and Texans locker room and inflatable practice field. March 2004

In my office. My cup heater and lunch within reach and my computer a swivel away. My books and papers mostly out of reach.

In September 2004, I joined the World Congress of the Energy Engineering Association in Austin. Beh and I got to see the freetail bats leave the Congress St bridge at sunset.

# 75

## More Van Repairs and a New Van

The year 2005 was more hectic than ever, but also, in some ways, more relaxing. The most remarkable thing was, while I was traveling and doing more things with the van, it never failed me, even though it was continually in the shop and getting things large and small fixed. In the summer of 2004 the Department of Assistive Services spent over $6,000 repairing my van. From September of 2004 to December 2005, I spent a total of just over $10,000 on van repairs. Everything was fixed and the van ran well at 88,000 miles. I could buy a new, 2006, used, lowered-floor van with about 10,000 miles on it for $15,000. So, I was contemplating getting a new van.

After 23 years, mom and dad decided that it was too difficult to move back and forth between Wisconsin and McAllen each year. They found an apartment in Marshfield and decided to sell both of their mobile homes in McAllen and Withee. They rushed north in March because they had a buyer for the Withee home. That deal fell through, but they were able to sell the McAllen home in April. In June they moved to their new apartment in Marshfield.

In July, dad developed an irregular heartbeat. To correct it, he received a pig valve and bypass in August. He already had a metal valve for many years. I talked to him on the phone after his operation and he was recovering quickly and feeling much stronger because the pig valve and bypass were working so well. During recovery, dad picked up an infection in the ICU and caught pneumonia. They had to put him on life support with breathing and feeding tubes. His only kidney (dad had only one kidney from birth) failed and he was near death. After three months of gradual recovery, dad was sent to a nursing hospital near Milwaukee in West Allis. That made it difficult for mom, the family and his friends to see him because it was so far from their homes. After a short stay at that hospital, dad caught another infection and died November 26, 2005. He was 85 years old. The outpouring from friends and family at his funeral in Owen showed that he was much loved. I couldn't make the funeral, but I saw him in October and that was enough for him to know that I cared enough to drive all that way from Texas just to see him.

For the umpteenth time, Roger lost his job in a cutback at Manchester Tank, a job that he thought he would be able to retire in. The Chinese had dumped a large quantity of steel cylinders on the market at a cost that Manchester couldn't compete with. Sue joined Prime Office Supply with an increase in pay over her local office sales job, but had to work out of the Merriville, IN office, 60 miles away. And then Staples acquired Prime and things got much better for Sue and her loyal customers to resume business in the Elkhart area.

My younger brother, Tom, bought some land adjacent to a State Forest about two and half hours north of Phoenix and planned to build a log chalet on it within the next two years. Although he never told me, it looked to be a retirement home.

Tim and Marla took the big step and got married October 15 in the Rotunda of the Wisconsin State Capitol. After a long drive, Beh and I were able to attend the wedding and reception on Lake Mendota. That was how we were able to see my father one last time during that same trip.

After a 13-year wait, Beh was eligible for citizenship in five years. She bought her brother's old house just like mine on the next street down. Her father and brother, Bao, stayed there. They sold the old family house after Beh's brother Quoc moved to Dallas with his new wife. Beh's brother Bao went back to Vietnam during the summer of 2005 to marry a young woman there. She was eligible to come to live with him in five years.

Daisey accompanied me to Dr. Slade's 2005 Christmas party at the Post Oak Grill. I did some wheelchair dancing with some strangers, local newspaper reporters and had a good time. Daisey met Dr. Slade, and told me that her cousin, a rich entrepreneur, had met with Slade when they both were staying at the Waldorf-Astoria in New York City during some high-level meeting there. I also heard that Barbara Bush invited Dr. Slade to Kennebunkport, Maine.

I completed **War's End** just before Christmas 2004. Since I did all the editing myself, **War's End** contained some errors. However, I got a good review from my good friend and fellow author, Leland Waldrip. My books sold better in 2005 but still nowhere near a point where I could quit my job and write full-time.

My poetry began to draw attention. The English Department at TSU asked me to read at the annual Poetry Day and their Christmas party. My poem, *Mesa Verde*, was selected by the Educational Testing Service to be part of a workbook going out to 400,000 students across the country. Some of my best work was *From Little Acorns Grow* and *A Hellava Way to Die*. *A Buffalo Soldier's Saga* and *A Flight of Whimsy* were most read on Author's Den. I submitted my short story, *A Hellava Way to Die,* to Playboy. The manuscript didn't come back. I also completed my first children's story, *Brian Bushytail and the Urban Forest*.

With Beh's green card, we were able to take a 7 day Caribbean cruise on February 13, 2005 with mom and dad to Key West, Grand Cayman Island, and Cozumel, knowing that it would be mom and dad's last year in McAllen.

I offered to take my second wheelchair because I knew that both mom and dad would have difficulty walking long distances. They refused. They drove up from McAllen a day early and we crammed all of our stuff into my van to drive to Galveston. We boarded the Rhapsody of the Seas. Mom and dad soon discovered that even getting around on a ship that large was difficult. An early dinner was mandatory and we were assigned a late one. After some discussion, we were seated at a large table with the family of Roland Martin, a syndicated columnist and broadcaster for CNN. Roland kept the dinner conversation lively while his beautiful wife, Rev. Jacquie Hood Martin, and both of their parents, were more subdued. Mom enjoyed the varied menus, while dad enjoyed New York strip steak every evening.

At Key West, I told my parents that they could enjoy the evening with us on the pier with all the street acts there. Beh and I took in the Mel Fisher Museum (again, for me) featuring the sunken treasures of the Spanish Galleon, Atocha and had a good time videotaping some of the street acts, but mom and dad stayed on the ship. When we got to Cayman Islands, I booked a trip to Stingray City. It was the first day that the Cayman Islands was open to tourism after Hurricane Ivan had devastated the place several months before. I remember what my guide had said on my last trip there: "We never get any hurricanes here in the Cayman islands." After a ship's tender boat ride to Georgetown, a van took us to the far end of Grand

Cayman Island where we boarded a power boat that took us off shore a few miles to the shallow area called Stingray City. There were about 100 boats in a circle around the area with many people in the water, only waist chest deep. I couldn't go in the water, but Beh donned a life preserver and jumped in with her clothes because she didn't have a swimsuit. Before long, Beh was with the rest of the people from our boat, feeding and petting the stingrays that came from everywhere to join in the fun and food. Beh returned very wet with a big smile on her face, still saying, "I don't know how to swim."

When we got to Cozumel, I had planned for us to go to the mainland to Xcaret to view the ruins, underground river and ecological theme park. I told my parents they could enjoy the shops just off the pier, but once again, they decided not to leave the ship. Our tour left early. I brought my portable wheelchair in case it was needed on the trip. The guide told us that the park was not accessible and I couldn't go. I insisted that Beh go, and told her to catch up with the group that had already left. Beh took off after them, and I decided that I would still do something, since I was familiar with Cozumel from before. I decided to go to the National Park that was only a couple of miles from the pier. After some wrangling, I was able to get a wheelchair van to take me to the park. The van was not lowered, so I spent the drive over to the park with my head bent downward to avoid banging it on the roof. Fortunately, the road was smooth. Immediately, I discovered that the park was also the location for getting up close and personal with dolphins. I watched the excitement of people feeding dolphins and riding them for a while. A guy came over with a macaw on his arm and asked me if I wanted, "*A kiss.*"

I was game for anything and didn't hesitate to say, "Okay." I was quite surprised when the guy tilted his arm forward so that the macaw could reach forward, open its mouth and rough tongue kiss me *on the mouth!* I wouldn't have believed it if it hadn't happened to me! I didn't get sick, so the bird must not have been carrying any avian flu. After that, I wandered around the park, filled with replicas of artifacts from all over Mexico. In a cornstalk hut with a Mayan lady making tamales, I watched little birds come and go through ample cracks in the hut while she served me tamales made over an open fire. I promptly got my EZ-Lock pin caught in cracks on the rock walkways, twice, and was rescued by passersby who heard me calling for help.

When I arrived at the museum and shop, I decided to go in even though there was soft sand by the entrance. I powered on in okay. When I left, I took a different route, and got stuck in the sand. Museum employees came out to help me and pushed me out of the sand and back on the trail again. While I waited at the entrance for my van, the manager of the national park came over and gave me a cold drink. I was hungry and thirsty and had been out in the sun all day, developing quite a sunburn. Finally, the wheelchair van came again, and I returned to the ship.

When I got back, I wheelchaired all around the ship, but couldn't find anybody. I didn't expect that Beh would be back, but I did expect to find my folks. Finally, I came upon dad in the main lobby where he had been most days just to watch people go by and see what was happening there. Mom came a little later and Beh was close behind. I was surprised to see her and asked her how the trip to Xcaret was. Beh told me that she didn't go. She said she followed the guide to the ferry going to Playa Del Carmen and got on. On the way, she was talking to someone about shopping and left the ferry with them instead of the tour group. After shopping a bit, she had returned. I got a little upset with her not going on the tour and suddenly, I felt very high and my stomach didn't feel very well.

We rushed to our stateroom. While Beh was transferring me to the toilet, I fell to the floor. She got help and I eventually got restored to my old self. That was the closest I'd come to heat exhaustion in my life. After that, I would make sure that I was adequately hydrated on any hot day and stay out of the sun as much as I could.

I asked about selling my books on the ship. At first, they said I had to sell them at the gift shop. And then, the events manager told me I could sell them in the library. The five or six people who came in the library that first morning were interested in my book, but weren't buying. I needed more traffic and the events manager approved, so I moved up to the pool deck near the Windjammer cafe. I sold books to about 15 happy customers. Book signing was very hard for me because it was so hard for me to keep stable and write my signature. Later in the week, I gave a lecture on how to set up a personal web site. There were about 15 very interested people there and I enjoyed the time with them very much. Beh and I eventually learned how to keep in touch after separating on such a large boat. She would wander off, but always know where she could find me after.

The high point of selling books was when a guy came by, and, after looking at my books on the table, said, "I know about that *kaleidoscope effect*,. I heard about it on the radio." I questioned him further and found out that he had heard about the term some 25 years before in Toronto where I led a panel and talked about the kaleidoscope effect at the World

Congress of the World Future Society in 1981. It's a small world. He bought the book. I gladly signed it.

I got my third new wheelchair in January 2006, a PerMobil Chairman 2 like my second chair, but with more functionality... and more cost. The sticker said $35,000, but my insurance got it for a mere $30 grand! A DARS supplement covered the co-pay, making it free for me, like all my wheelchairs—obsolete every five years. I could raise my feet, lower my seat back, tilt the chair back and generally, assume a lying down position. It was faster, 7 mph, than the old one and sprung so that it gave me a better ride. My van had to get a new EZ-Lock, repositioned, to accept the new chair. The headrest on the chair tilted down out of the way so that I could swing the headrest on the van into position for use. Mobility Plus mounted two toggle switches for me to operate my remote van door opener and the seat elevator on the chair. Both switches had to be moved several times because I kept hitting them with my elbows. Eventually, the elevator switch was removed but a door lock switch was added for locking and unlocking my van. Beh and Daisey did not like the new chair because it was 2 inches higher than the old one and so much harder for me to get in and out of and into position for driving. With the Roho air cushion seat that I got the year before, the new chair was more comfortable for long periods of driving, although I could not move my legs as much as I did before, something I regretted.

Once the new wheelchair was mated to my van, my troubles began. The combination of the bouncy ride of the van, plus the bounce of the suspension on my wheelchair, plus the bounce of the air cushion, made driving quite difficult. Not only did my driving become very jerky, sometimes my hands would *jump* right out of the controls! Fortunately, this only happened at slow speeds so that I could brake and regain control. After months of toying with the problem, it appeared that the airbags on the van were inflated too high, creating the rough ride and causing all the other problems. When I had the wheelchair set right and the van was working well, I could drive over eight hours straight without discomfort. Actually, driving was much more pleasant for me than sitting still. Driving kept my circulation flowing as I continually moved my arms, was massaged by road vibration, and kept my mind involved keeping the vehicle powered and on the right track on the road. With my zero pressure controls, I never dozed while driving that van. Full attention was required at all times.

In July 2005, I took my first long-distance trip in the new wheelchair with Beh and Janda to visit Beh's brother, Quoc, in his new house in

Arlington, Texas. I was only briefly in Quoc's new house before we went out to eat in a Vietnamese restaurant. Otherwise it was a rather uneventful trip. Janda and I did manage to get to the Farmer's market in Dallas the morning before we left for home. I never saw so much produce in my life. After driving up there and back, I didn't much care for taking I-45 to Dallas. Too much traffic and speeders.

We all watched in horror as one hurricane after another began to build to the south. When Katrina hit New Orleans many of those forced out came to Houston and Houston opened its arms to them. Many ended up staying in Texas permanently. I was moved to write two poems, *Ole Lady Down* and *Big Easy*; a song, *Katrina*; and a poem and short story titled, *A Hellava Way to Die*. Finally, it was our turn. Rita showed promise to be worse than Katrina. It was right for all those in low-lying areas to be able to evacuate and escape the wrath of the storm. It was wrong for so many, including my and Beh's relatives, to panic when the exact direction and strength of the storm was unknown. After having hurricane Alicia's eye go directly over my house in 1983, a category 3 storm that left a lot of damage in Houston, my plan was to stay put and only take the best route out if I had to. We had a lot of water stored and four cars with full tanks of gas. If everyone hadn't panicked like they did, a lot of suffering could have been avoided. As the storm built in our area we had a hurricane party with champagne at 9:30 pm and went to bed. If it had been much worse, we probably would have done the very same thing. I hope the people of Houston learned the lesson that it was not good to rush off like lemmings into the storm and heavy traffic without gasoline. I felt sorry for those that really had to evacuate because they ran into all the traffic of those that didn't. Much human turmoil and cost, including unnecessary death, was the result.

In September, I once again attended the World Energy Congress in Austin. Because hurricane Katrina evacuees were housed in the Convention Center, the Congress moved to the Renaissance Hotel on the north side. Fortunately, I was able to get a room there. Beh could not leave her shop, so Janda Zardee accompanied me. When we got back to Houston, we ran into heavy traffic, so I took an alternate route to Janda's apartment on city streets. While we were waiting to make a turn, a rear air bag broke like a tire blowing out. Fortunately, it was a short drive to her apartment and on home. The van rode rock bottom like a buckboard without air in those bags. I had the van towed to Mobility Plus by AAA. I was only allowed four or five free tows a year and exceeded that the following spring. I got a record of my free tows and discovered one at the Renaissance for the conference—

a dead battery start. I couldn't remember having trouble starting the van while there, but a towing service from Round Rock had charged me. I called AAA but they ignored my complaint. I suspected it was a hotel employee that had my information, so I complained to the hotel management. I don't know if the culprit was ever determined. I was upset when AAA seemed disinterested in investigating.

In early October, I attended the Facilities Conference for state universities and colleges in Dallas. Diann Massingill accompanied me because, once again, Beh had to tend the shop. While there, I didn't have to drive because the conference provided a van like mine to take Diann and me to the various events. We got to enjoy a wonderful, warm evening at the Texas State Fair. It brought back memories of many fairs attended in my youth. Big Tex lived up to his reputation and the sights and smells were wonderful. The next day, it turned cold, but we still enjoyed an evening inside in the Aquarium of the Dallas Zoo. I hoped to see my old nemesis, Harold Johnson, at the conference, but he didn't attend. Harold had hired Bill Beckham to do the facilities inventory at Texas Women's University. Bill had lost his Houston home, divorced his wife, and wasn't too happy when we saw him at the hotel.

My health remained quite good, although there were subtle changes that led me to believe that I was still losing spinal neurons to aging. When I saw Dr. Parsons, my rehabilitation physician, in January, I complained of an aching left arm and tightness in my chest (that morning). Parsons called it a, "Wake-up call," and asked for me to be checked out by a cardiologist. Parsons also wanted me to have a colonoscopy because I hadn't had one for over five years. When I had the colonoscopy in August, Beh had to accompany me because they said they were going to put me under sedation. When I told them about my cardiac arrest during my spinal surgery in 1963, they backed off and told me they wouldn't give me any anesthetic. I breezed through the procedure with very little pain—just a little discomfort. Everyone, especially Beh, was amazed that I could do that without anesthetic. The proctologists gave me a clean bill of colon health for another five years.

In August, I had my annual bladder check. Over the years this procedure changed from being conducted by a single nurse to being conducted by the doctor, his nurse, and an x-ray technician. The cost of all my medical procedures skyrocketed, while my insurance only paid 80%, where before it paid 90%. I told Dr. Hairston, the urologist, that, from there on out, I would only have my bladder checked every other year—he agreed. Finally, in early November, I went in for an electrocardiogram and heart scan. To test my heart, they gave it a chemical "stress" with x-rays and the full CT scan. What I got back were meager results that said that my heart was "normal." That was a welcome relief. For the high cost, more information would've been better. Much later, I learned that my left arm always gave me pain in the morning if I slept with it bent and above my shoulder, a natural place for it to end up after it spasmed. If I woke with my arms straight down by my hips, there was no pain.

Growing concern about the West Nile Virus and a possible pandemic from Avian Flu made me very conscious of preventive medicine. I was always one of the first to get my flu shot every year. I remained active with the Christopher Reeve Paralysis Association and, whenever I could, promoted stem cell research. Perhaps, in five to ten years, stem cells would be used to grow replacement spinal neurons. Until then, Beh and I were making sure that I stayed as healthy as I could for that inevitable day when a cure comes along.

At TSU things changed but remained the same. In January 2005, Bruce Wilson, the senior vice president for administration, and JT Glover, assistant vice president for facilities, were fired. Apparently, they received a kickback from a real estate deal. People were upset about Bruce, but almost no one mourned the passing of JT. Quentin Wiggins, the senior vice president for finance and CFO, assumed Bruce's organization and Gray Padfield was placed in the spot formerly held by JT. Gray had been operating as a consultant on six-month contracts until the major, $200 million, push for construction was completed. With Padfield's help, I met with Wiggins and Padfield in February and told them about my demotion. They told me they were going to reorganize and that I should sit tight and everything would be all right. Same old stall tactic.

Some things changed for the better? Jim Anderson was removed from his responsibilities as physical plant director and given the role as executive director of facilities planning—a rather hollow undertaking; no personnel action forms was ever filed. Robert Alaniz and I were to report to Jim, his only remaining organization. While this spot gave Jim much higher visibility with the administration, direct contact with the Higher Education Coordinating Board and the Board of Regents, I still was not invited to Quentin Wiggins's staff meetings. I was expected to provide all the information I had before and more, without any additional help other than Robert. Robert could be highly unreliable; the reason he had been rejected by architectural services. He was a hand-me-down to me. And not a very good one when working on any job he didn't like.

Our merit increases were cut in September 2005, so I decided to meet with President Pricilla Slade. She had Wiggins with her when we met. It became obvious that she didn't know anything of my background or my capability. Probably judging me by my disability and little else. She seemed quite defensive while Quentin appeared very nervous. She didn't do anything about my request to be given more responsibility and visibility and to be reinstated from my demotion, so it was time to act. My friend and former supervisor, Charles Carter, reached an undisclosed, but satisfactory, settlement with the university over his wrongful firing suit in 1998. In April, the Federal Court of Appeals in Louisiana ruled that states like Texas did not have sovereign immunity from the federal ADA laws and allowed a long standing lawsuit against Texas Tech University for discrimination against women and people with disabilities to be tried. In addition, TSU did not meet its obligation to the Office of Civil Rights for the $300 million in reparations received in 2001.

With Jim Anderson as my supervisor, my working environment got much better. I continued to update my database collections in Helix and they became ever more useful and powerful. I served, for a while, as a Helix 6 beta tester until my equipment, both at work and at home, became inadequate. With Helix 6, we would be able to run a Helix server operating with Mac OS X. Shortly after Helix 6 was released, Helix Technologies expected to release a client for Windows. When that happened, I expected to be able to gave the client to any person who would need to access my databases from anywhere on campus. If all went well, this would happen within a year. Once everyone saw the value of using my databases and that we were able to enter data from remote sources, even off-campus, my many years of work would have paid off. Even with Jim's support, any discussion of a client—server set up seemed to fall on deaf ears; although that was exactly what we were buying from expensive, rigid sources like TMA.

Through my affiliation with our writers' group on campus, NuRoots, I was called upon more and more to read my poetry and submit my writing to anthologies. The English Department adopted me and I felt quite honored that they appreciated my hard work. Although I did detect a little jealousy on the part of some faculty who had aspirations but had never completed a novel.

By 2005, I was dictating with Dragon NaturallySpeaking 8. It was better than IBM ViaVoice 7 in several ways. However, DNS 8 was my fourth voice dictation system and still not perfect. I was dictating my book chapters faster, but finding less time to do it. And even with an 80 GB drive on my iMac, I was running out of space to store digital home movies. Fortunately, I acquired a 180 GB backup drive that worked quite well. In order to be able to write DVDs and have more space for our movies, I bought a 200 GB eMachine with a 64-bit Athlon processor that improved both computing, DVD writing, and dictation. A also got a wireless mouse and keyboard. Couldn't wait to use a mouse without the wire tangling and slowing me down. Unfortunately, without a cord, the mouse would easily escape my hand and fall to the floor. In practice, the new computer nearly doubled my speed of dictation by removing delays in making corrections.

The tsunami in Indonesia and the devastating hurricanes on the coastal United States showed me that we live on a constantly changing planet with a fragile layer of life on it. It was time that people recognized the dangers and began to live where the chances were better. The seacoast is so tempting, but it is very dangerous. It was also time to end war. Each year that the war in Iraq dragged on, we were faced with ever more difficult decisions about what to do. No one tolerates an occupying army, and, as much as I supported our troops in their effort to bring democracy to Iraq, I thought it was time to divide the territory into regions that could be governed by Kurdish, Sunni, and Shia interests. All three new countries would be Moslem and, hopefully, democracies.

As predicted by futurists 30 years before, India and China were quickly leapfrogging from Third World to First World status by competing well on the world stage. What this means for the use of fossil fuels and global warming was still unclear. However, the United States economy was already being heavily affected. Will the United States remain an economic superpower in the 21st century? Will we be able to provide for our growing population of retirees? Will we be able to offset the effects of global warming and the increased cost for energy? I didn't know. In my books and articles, I was laying down plans that young people of today could use to solve the problems of tomorrow. Some people, even members of my family, disagreed. Only time would tell.

Beh and I in formal picture taken on our Caribbean Cruise Feb 2005

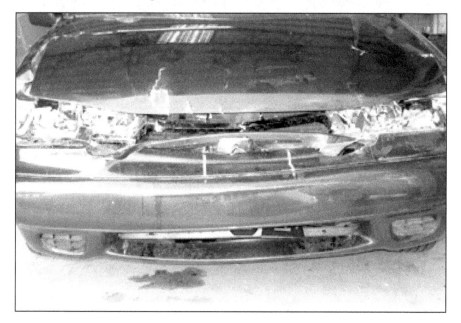

Damage to the 1998 Windstar, still driving, was minor, but expensive.

# 76

## My Brakes Go Out and a Shake Up at Work

The year 2006 was a sea change for us. People finally realized that throwing our brave young soldiers into the meat grinder that the Iraqi war had became was a wrong approach for fighting terrorism in the 21st century. There were no big countries out there that we needed to defend ourselves from. There were bad people that good police could take care of. People also finally realized that the rich getting richer at the expense of hard-working people and using illegal workers to support our economy was wrong. Arrogant cronyism didn't have the shine it used to. Old habits were still hard to dislodge though.

I told people that I won the lottery. *Actually*, in the summer of 2005, I signed up for long-term care insurance that waved pre-existing conditions the first time it was offered by the university. Texas A&M had acquired the insurance earlier and it spread to all Texas funded higher education institutions as an optional coverage. The plan was very good insurance covering everything from in-home attendant care, to nursing home care, to hospice. In December, 2005, Dr. Parsons wrote a letter to the company stating that I qualified for long-term care. By April 2006, I was receiving weekly payments. If nothing changed, I would receive payments for 10 years. Approaching retirement at 66, those payments insured that my retirement fund would last and that I would be able to pay for people to help take care of me for a long time to come.

My sister, Judy, was named to the governing board for the Mid-State Technical College where she had graduated with honors in a two-year accounting program. She was the first in our family to hold such a position, and it made me very proud of her.

Terry J. Wenzel, my cousin, was hunting at his lodge in North Dakota on December 27, 2006, when, returning in his Expedition to his lodge at night, he lost control on a gravel road and rolled over, crushing him between the truck and the ground. Terry was not wearing a seat belt and the window appeared to be open. He was 59. His wife, Judy, in Florida, gave no details. Terry was an entrepreneur, master electrician, fishing boat operator, big game guide, resort owner, professional bass fisherman, builder, inventor, and real estate developer. Terry owned Gate Packages, a company making gates for apartment complexes, fences, and entrances for gated communities. He got a patent in 2004 for his Hidden Eyes security system concept. He and Judy were creating a subdivision from his large property on a small lake near Sebring, Florida. Terry married three times and lived the life of Hemingway without writing about it. I miss him and wish I could tell all the stories of his adventurous life. I had grown complacent about trying to contact Terry the last few years and he had not contacted me. I should've picked up the phone and called him. I would have, except that I didn't know that Terry was computer phobic and couldn't or didn't read and answer my emails.

With a shop on every corner, the dry-cleaning and alteration business struggled and many shops went out of business. However, Beh built clientele and worked hard to please her customers so that she could keep the doors open.

The year 2006 was the first I could recall when we didn't go traveling. There were just too many things going on. The old van was up to it, but Beh was worried about all the times I was trying to get the ramp and door fixed. It got so bad that when the sliding door wouldn't open when I got home from work, I would drive around the block and ask people on the street to open the door for me. It was a strange request that some people shied away from, but others quickly realized my plight and helped me out. The battery light stayed on all the time even though the batteries were fine and occasionally something strange would go on that I would have to fix. Otherwise, at 95,000 miles the X1 tires still had plenty of tread and wear left, and, aside from an occasional bad first shift, the engine was running very well.

Still, I looked at my situation and decided that I would try to get a new van after nine years; before I retired and lost my eligibility for Department of Assistive Services (DARS) assistance. Andre at Mobility Plus told me that I could get a "new" used lowered floor van with about 10 to 15,000 miles on it from rental van pools for about $15,000. When we checked into it, there was nothing there that I liked. Mom and Roger advised me to get a Chrysler. But, in spite of the experience I had with my Windstar, I still liked the Fords better, especially because of their larger engines. When Andre checked the vehicles Vantage Mobility had in stock, a 2006 Freestar Limited caught my eye because it had heavy-duty everything as well as some very nice features like automatic headlights and a climate control system. The price was right with rebates for both the Ford and the alteration, so I bought it in June 2006.

Although DARS was willing to fund the modification and waved the required training because I was experienced in the system that was being installed, approvals were a long time in coming because of miscommunication. The van had been purchased from an Illinois Ford dealership and that caused delays as well. It was a good thing that the Windstar was working well and had good air-conditioning because I had to use it all summer waiting for the work on the Freestar to begin. While the driving system, the steering control and the gas-brake lever were essentially the same, the control panel, called a Gold Panel, mounted near my right shoulder, was entirely different. Whereas in the Windstar I had to push and hold every button until the function had completed (like from Park to Drive), in the Freestar I only had to touch the button once in most cases for the full operation to activate. In the Windstar, some of the controls were on the door panel to my left and I could not operate them except when I was stopped and in Park. On the Freestar, all of the controls were on the Gold Panel to my right and could be operated while I held the brake with my left hand. On the Windstar, I operated several functions like the dimmer, horn, and wipers from a head button on a swing away headrest. On the Freestar there was no headrest and these functions were operated by voice commands.

After several delays, the Freestar finally arrived at Mobility Plus. There was more delay while they ordered parts and scheduled the work. Because of the new equipment, five computers had to be placed in the passenger compartment. Three of them went underneath the passenger side removable seat and two were placed in a metal frame between the seats. In the Windstar, we could remove the passenger seat for Beh to drive, and I could pull in alongside on the passenger side in my wheelchair. It didn't look like I'd be able to let Beh drive very much in the new van. While it was easier to switch the steering from mine to the original power steering, there was a switch underneath the passenger seat that had to be thrown and the startup and operating procedures on the Gold Panel were more complicated and difficult for the inexperienced to use. The worst part was that I would not be able to pull in alongside on the passenger side to ride facing forward because of the computers on the floor. I would have to be tied down sideways and that would make it difficult for me to watch where we were going, navigate and get water. Even getting back into the driver's position would be difficult.

Equipment installation went smoothly and was quite well done, unlike with the Windstar eight years earlier. Only one technician, Rick, completed all the work. In early September, I drove the new van for the first time and discovered some problems with the voice control and alarms that were not corrected. I only trained the voice system once and that may have been the problem. The alarms were another matter. The startup procedure required waiting for the computers to go through sequences and if something wasn't right when they booted, the system had to be shut down and the car started all over again. Anyway, we discovered that Andre had not ordered a remote for me to open and close the ramp door like I had on my Windstar. That was on Monday. One would have to be ordered and installed before I could drive the new van.

That Friday, it was a cool morning and my Windstar was idling high when I backed out of the driveway. As I entered the freeway about 3 miles from home, the engine seemed to surge forward more than I was accelerating and didn't back off when I backed off the throttle. In heavy traffic on the way to work on the freeway and in the left lane, I had to use the brakes heavily several times to slow the car down when traffic slowed ahead. The problem bothered me a lot, and I thought about turning around and going home or directly to Mobility Plus several times. But, I stubbornly continued on, knowing that I had a lot of work to do at the office that morning and planned instead to return home early that day to avoid traffic and having to slow down in route.

The exit off 59 to 288 south had its own exit lane and exited downward while braking and then turned sharply to the right upward under acceleration. I always made that curve cautiously because one time I got too far to the right and my wheels ran off the pavement shoulder on a steep downslope where I had to turn sharply to the left to get back up on the lane. I would've surely rolled over if I had not been able to climb back up onto the lane. I chalked that one up to my tricky steering, in a difficult position at 30 minutes with my elbow in my gut while making that turn—making it easy to steer the wrong way—something I did more than once, but recovered from.

This time I made the curve nicely, but had to exit immediately from 288. As I exited the freeway normally to Southmore, the street that I take left over 288 to work, the van was slowing down and everything seemed okay until I tried the brakes *and they didn't work.* I pulled hard on them three times before ramming into the back of an Expedition waiting at the stop light—*hard!* The airbags deployed and kissed my nose and the Expedition rose up in front of me and came back down. I wasn't hurt and the woman driving the Expedition wasn't hurt. However, I couldn't get out of my EZ-Lock and smelled something burning. After what seemed like about 10 minutes, a lot of help arrived and with the help of a police officer, I was able to disengage my wheelchair from the EZ-Lock and leave the van. I had the van towed to Mobility Plus. The Expedition had a very strong back bumper and was barely damaged. Within two weeks, my Freestar was ready, so it was a good thing that the accident occurred when it did. I didn't lose any time at work.

I had planned to gave the Windstar to ADAPT, a national advocacy group for the disabled, and specifically to Michael Thomas, the Houston president of ADAPT who was paralyzed like I was and had to work his way out of a nursing home into more independent living. Michael was quite excited about getting the van after I gave him a ride in it one day. At least that was my plan... before the accident.

The good news was that the Windstar, after the front end damage was removed, turned out to still be completely functional. We bought a front end clip from another Windstar and were putting mine back together to gave to ADAPT as soon as it was ready. All of the high tech driving controls were removed and the EZ-Lock placed so that Michael could ride alongside on the passenger side while his attendant drove the van normally.

Gray Padfield, the acting assistant vice president after JT Glover was fired, told Jim Anderson to form the facilities planning group and develop a budget and job descriptions. Robert Alaniz came to us with skills in AutoCAD and general construction management expertise. Jim took it upon himself to get familiar with the Texas Higher Education Coordinating Board (THECB) and joined the Association of Physical Plant Administrators (APPA) and the Society for College and University Planning (SCUP). After attending some meetings himself, he asked Robert and I to attend meetings and to get certified in SCUP.

President Priscilla Slade, in spite of much criticism from groups like the TSU 3, three TSU students who bravely uncovered and exposed financial wrongdoing and other corruption from a dumpster, was riding high as evidenced by the lavish party that Daisey and I attended at the Post Oak Grill during the Christmas holidays. A short time after that, Slade was showing one of the board members her new home she had just built and expressed pleasure in having the university pay for many of the amenities, including furniture, a security system, maid service, and landscaping.

When the board member brought that information to the Board of Regents' attention, they called for an internal investigation because most of the expenditures were not covered under Dr. Slade's contract. After the board 's initial investigation, the Harris County District Attorney's Office got involved and the entire administration came under a criminal investigation. Jim was subpoenaed for a six-hour deposition and was able to prove that he had nothing to do with all the illegal transactions with state funds. In the end, four people were indicted. Dr. Slade, Quentin Wiggins, her CFO with previous convictions for financial misconduct, Bruce Wilson, SrVP ousted by Slade a year earlier, and Fred Holts, a safety specialist apparently involved in acquiring and installing the security system at Slade's house.

Everyone was ducking and running and some hasty decisions were made as Wiggins and Slade were made to resign, and Gray Padfield, a hired gun, was dropped, leaving us with a rather dysfunctional organization on the physical plant and planning side. I continued to work as usual and provide whatever information people needed. After his brush with the investigators, Jim insisted that we try to bring all the university land, facilities inventory, and energy consumption data up to date and get it verified. Sometime during the early summer 2006, it was determined that the university would have a shortfall in its budget, blamed partly on the fact that utility costs were increasing. Jim and I could prove that we had locked in extremely favorable prices for both natural gas and electricity at fixed rates until 2010, but that fell on deaf ears. Domestic water costs had remained fixed for several years and natural gas prices were low under a contract with the state general land office (GLO). The real culprit was all the jobs that were being made for friends and relatives with the Office of Civil Rights money that had been pouring into the university to bring it up to standard. Most of this money was earmarked for facilities, but ended up being used as salaries for faculty and staff. Jim had brought this fact to the attention of the Coordinating Board and that's why the people leaving targeted him. Scapegoats had to be found.

In his attempt to obtain a budget for facilities planning, Jim tried to find ways to obtain money for equipment and for training. I was scheduled to attend SCUP training in Los Angeles, Minneapolis, Atlanta, and Hawaii in 2005. All of these trips were canceled for lack of funds. The Coordinating Board had asked me to join a discussion group on the facilities inventory and I was turned down twice for meetings with them in Austin. Finally, I wrote a letter to the newly made acting president, Dr. Bobby Wilson, and he allowed me to attend one meeting in August. That was the only trip I took all year. Diann Massingill accompanied me. It was a good meeting and I was glad to finally meet some of the people I'd been talking to over the phone for years. It was also a very long day because I drove from Houston in the morning and then, after returning to Houston, had to drive Diann back to Liberty and didn't return home until 11 p.m.

My Helix databases continued to became more valuable as time passed. Helixtech, or QSA Toolworks, as they were now called, had developed Helix Server 6 for the Macintosh. The server ran on OS X. but the plan was to develop a client that would run on Windows machines so they could access the server. In the meantime, I needed a computer that could run both OS 9 and OS X. Since Apple had rapidly gone to dual Intel processors on all their computers, we had to buy one of the last G5 computers with the Motorola chip available in order to run both the old and new software on one computer. The G5 ran faster and had a huge hard drive capacity compared to the old 7500 PowerMac that I had my brother Tom come and upgrade to a G4. I ran both computers for a time until I got the G5 working like the G4, and then I had the G4 and its monitor taken to the warehouse. However, I quickly found out that my old 20 inch multisync CRT monitor was brighter and sharper than the 20 inch flat-panel wide-angle LED monitor that came with the G5.

While Dragon NaturallySpeaking 8 really helped my productivity on my PC, it was slow

and hard to use while doing correction. Jim decided to update my 2001 Gateway computer, and after several attempts, finally got me a new Gateway. Right out of the box, the new Gateway worked right. My email and applications all worked very well without the constant problems experienced with the old computer. However, when I went to reinstall Dragon NaturallySpeaking 8, I couldn't locate the keys. I discovered the dictation component of Microsoft Office and tried it. I was able to dictate with it, but found the software to be similar to ViaVoice in the way that it acted. And then I got an offer for NaturallySpeaking 9 for $49. I bought the 9 for home use and discovered that its accuracy was much better than 8. So, I also installed my copy of 9 at work and it proved very fast and accurate. The computer upgrades were a long time in coming. Although I had been given three low-quality PCs to work with, my Apple PowerMac 7500 had been in constant use since 1993. It was, perhaps, the oldest working computer on campus. Two of the backup hard drives that served it were even older, circa 1989. One was beginning to scream, making it hard to talk on my speakerphone and giving Jim worries about it failing. I got a new 250 GB SimpleTech back up drive for the G5. The old drives, a 1 GB and a 500 MB that had given yeoman service, were finally retired.

I was having trouble with using FTP (file transfer protocol—used for moving large files between servers directly) to reach my web space for file transferring on the new computers. Fortunately, the techs with our IT service were in love with my Mac and PC computer set up and helped me overcome the obstacles with ports and so on, so that I could reach my personal web space to transfer work to my home computers without using email. Our TSU email was restricted to 8 MB attachments and the backup of my database collections had reached up to 60 MB. The IT guys also set up a backup space on a campus file server so that I could use that to transfer files at work between my computers and create backups.

Talk of decreased enrollment as a result of the bad publicity and budget shortfalls for the upcoming fiscal year resulted in a 10% cut in staff in August 2006. While it was good to see some of the problem people leave the campus, the physical plant lost some key crafts people that were helping the university keep running. They were missed. By the end of the year, there was evidence that some things weren't being maintained as well as they should be.

In order to get a handle on things, Jim wanted an outside firm to came in and determine, in detail, all of our deferred maintenance. He asked several firms to do a preliminary study of campus deferred maintenance. Using this information, Jim determined that some buildings were just too costly to keep up and should be demolished. Some of these were named buildings and some would not be replaced. The biggest problem was that Houston sits on muck from the bayou system that once covered the area and subsoil was always moving and causing structural problems. There were also some ground faults that ran through the campus. Jim also had a preliminary energy audit done that determined that we could reduce energy costs by 10%. The next phase was to conduct a detailed deferred maintenance study and then launch a performance contract by an outside firm with outside funding to eliminate much of the deferred maintenance and pay for it with energy savings from the measures proposed. This was a win-win situation because we would not use any state funds except what we would normally budget for utilities; we would greatly reduce our deferred maintenance; and we would be able to have the advantage of having our staff trained and increased while being supervised by top quality engineers interested in maximizing our savings. Our campus heating and cooling systems would look and run much better and we would be reducing emissions through new and improved technology.

The problem we were faced with was our inept and dysfunctional administration. The combination of established, but unprogressive gatekeepers and the unqualified people brought in by the civil rights money, as well as, favors to the Board of Regents, had brought decision-making to a standstill. The governor brought in a woman consulting CFO and an acting president. These appointments were described as being "rigid" and "what the university needs." The interim president, Major General Boodin, was a retired Korean era Air Force officer. The entire administration was afraid of what would happen with these moves. The former director of human resources resigned with the layoffs. The employment irregularities were high on the list of investigations. Nepotism had been rampant. It was rumored that after the first of the year there would be more indictments and more resignations. Until a new president was named sometime in 2007 and qualified people were hired to fill the spaces vacated in key positions, the university was in trouble. Some outsiders called for the University to be merged with the downtown campus of the University of Houston, a real put down for a senior four-year institution with graduate schools older than the University of Houston. The downtown campus was merely a community college level feeder institution for the University.

The layoffs left the custodial and maintenance staff decimated. And two new buildings, the Science Building and the Public Affairs Building, were coming online. Until the university fully supported the people working at the ground level that took care of the facilities, we would continue to have increasing deferred maintenance and complaints about the state of the facilities. The chiefs had their day and it just didn't work. It was time for the indians.

I continued to write a poem a week, but thought that that may have been slowing me down when I struggled to get one new poem out and posted each weekend. I ended the year on chapter 26 of **American Mole** and was stuck there. While some parts of the book were exciting, I wasn't too happy with the way it was developing and I thought that I probably would have to rewrite more than I did with the other books. Still, I hoped to have the book out by the middle of 2007. I was inspired from time to time to write a short story and wrote two in 2006 that I really liked. *Diabolical Recreation* came to me in a dream and I wrote it very quickly. In response for a request to write a continuing story of *Diabolical Recreation,* I decided to write a story that I had on my mind for 35 years—*Hit and Run.* I received good reviews for both stories and needed to post them where they might get published.

Bookbooters, the publisher of **The Kaleidoscope Effect** and **Alone?**, went out of business in 2006, effectively making those two books, "*out of print." Because* of unfavorable reviews related primarily to editing and character development, I decided to do a revision of each of the books and put them out on Booklocker where I had **Wars End**. I was going to wait until after I finished **American Mole** before the revisions. However, Booklocker.com had a December special with a half-price offer that I couldn't refuse. When I tried to paste the copy into the appropriate format the line spacing went haywire, requiring hand space deletion on every line. I learned later how to do it with just a simple replace command). I did that for **Kaleidoscope**. Thankfully, that was a short book. And also thankfully, I didn't have to do the same for **Alone?**

In November 2006, Everyone's Internet, my long time ISP, decided to go out of the dial up Internet business. I looked everywhere for a fast Internet connection and didn't find one. I settled for a dial-up one with AT&T Yahoo until I could come up with something faster. Since I was the only one on the block without a domain, I finally broke down and bought one. I was shocked to find out that RonHull.com was taken by a realtor in Madison, Wisconsin. I settled for RonHullauthor.com and planned to stay with that for a long time. I had much more space and could triple my web pages and put up my video streams for everyone to watch. After a struggle to set the new website up, I had the process of fixing links in over 500 pages. It took forever. Fortunately, the old site was up for some time before they took it down. So that was how I spent my holiday time, correcting bad links and editing bad English—*yummy.*

Speaking of yummy, Beh started making two or more turkeys every Thanksgiving with all the trimmings, based on a recipe that her nephew, a chef, taught her. From each turkey, I'd get about 20 meals with all the trimmings. I really enjoyed eating turkey all the time and the price was right.

By the end of 2006, most Americans realized that we were in a quagmire in Iraq and our troops should came home. Also, that we would not experience any more devastating earthquakes, tsunamis, or hurricanes. To be realistic, we would. What we must do was everything we could to reverse global warming the way we brought back our birds of prey by stopping the use of DDT, our freshwater fishing by eliminating pollution in the rivers, the ozone layer by eliminating fluorohydrocarbons. To accomplish this would require a major effort, both in the way we develop technology, and in the way we live. It would be a daunting task, but I was optimistic that we would do it justice. We would soon cure cancer and eliminate most major diseases, as well as, repair organs easily through the use of stem cells and gene therapy.

With the Internet, I was able to reconnect with old friends that I thought I would never reconnect with again. Unfortunately, some of them were very old or had already passed on.

Enjoying the Rodeo with Beh and Daisey February 2006

My driving system with gas/brake tri-pin left, EZ-Lock on floor to secure my wheelchair, the steering tri-pin below the Gold control panel.

My 2006 Freestar after 55,000 miles of service. November 2012

# 77

## Reaching Financial Freedom and TSU's Reformation

Roger and I reached 65 on December 21 2007. All of the major predictors of the fate of the world seemed to point to December 21, 2012, as the end of the world. That gave us five years of enjoyable retirement. Since I don't believe that balderdash, I should have many more birthdays ahead. I also reached financial independence. That meant that I should be able to live out my retirement years quite comfortably and give back some that I'd been given. As long as I continued to live *frugally*, that is.

Beh's brother, Bao, got married in Vietnam on January 25, 2007. So, after 15 years away, Beh was excited about going back for the wedding and to visit relatives both in Saigon (Beh hated the name Ho Chi Minh City) and in the north near Hanoi. Her two older brothers lived in Saigon. The oldest was a policeman with a son and daughter who were engineers. The second oldest brother and his wife started a baby products company a few years earlier and were doing very well. Beh was most interested in helping out her relatives in the north. She had been supporting a blind cousin by helping him get the roof on his house replaced and improving his diet so that he could gain some weight and became healthier. Beh's father, who had two brothers and a sister in the north, and Quan, her younger brother, accompanied her on the trip. They also had traveled to a resort area in the middle of the country on the coast with beautiful beaches and a boat tour to mystical islands.

Beh got to see the place where the Communists sent her and her brothers to the forest to farm. They were green city slickers then, but with their mom's advice, raised sweet potatoes and chickens. That's where Beh gained weight and strength and helped rescue starving others by giving them sweet potatoes and chicken. Beh was surprised to see that those who stayed there were rich because the land they occupied had become so valuable. Land in the Saigon area had become ridiculously expensive, but Beh hoped to buy some land on the coast for her and her brothers when they go back to Vietnam in retirement. Paul, Van, Quoc, Vu, brothers, and Tami, an older sister, were unable to take the trip because of their work or school in Houston. Beh was so worried that something would happen to me while she was gone, but I worked up a schedule using four people to help me out. In addition, I knew that I could call Sheltering Arms and get private duty nursing any time if I needed it. Once Beh would see how well I'd done, I hoped that she would think about taking a vacation from me more often.

Daisey Ashley had to spend more time with me during the time Beh was gone to Vietnam, but she was most willing to help out and manage our temporary help. Daisey worked for several clients so it was always important for her to schedule work so she didn't have conflicts Daisey and I were both pleased to see a special showing of *The Great Debaters* honoring Thomas Freeman, a friend of Daisey's and TSU's iconic debate professor still leading, winning debate teams for TSU, after 48 years on campus as a philosophy professor. Freeman personally tutored Denzel Washington and the other stars of the movie. Freeman went on to found the university's honors college and served as its first dean. Freeman retired in 2013, a spry and energetic 96 years old with a building named after him.

When I took possession of the 2006 Freestar in November, it had quite a few nagging problems that were hard to correct. Otherwise, the van seemed to have a much better transmission than the 98 Windstar, stuck in the shop, being rebuilt after the accident. Voice operation reduced stress on my left hand because I only had to press the gas brake lever to the left to activate the microphone and mute the radio. There was no headrest and headrest button, so I used the headrest on my wheelchair while driving. It was difficult to train the computer to understand, *right* "right signal", *left* "left signal", *hazards, dimmer, horn* (a loud, raucous blast), *wipers* (four times to go through the sequence), and *cruise* (was never able to use this). The suspension, with a mechanical kneel for entering and exiting, and standard metal springs and rode and handled better than the Windstar.

I was eager to take some trips to test out the new van's roadworthiness, but Beh couldn't get free from the shop except for her trip to Vietnam. I concentrated on what to do with the Windstar. I had already decided to gave it to Michael Thomas, the local president of ADAPT, a national organization assisting disabled citizens. Bob Kafka, a national leader located in Austin, told me that Michael was not well enough to use the van and couldn't maintain it. I decided not to deed it over to Michael, but to let him use it with me paying for maintenance and insurance. It was a good thing I did that, because soon after I turned it over to Michael, the transmission failed again. And then, Michael entered the hospital because of fluid in his back. He told me that he wanted to write his life story and sent me a first draft. It was interesting and I wanted to read more. Unfortunately, what he had written, was only a couple of pages. So much was left out of his struggle to recover from an accident where he was left for dead and his growing up very poor in Louisiana.

Michael was born to a black woman in Lafayette, Louisiana by a white man he never knew as a father. His uncle sent him to Houston when he was 15. Shortly after he arrived, Michael was doing maintenance for the apartment complex where he lived. Finding Houston full of opportunity, Michael tried several jobs and ended up doing road construction on old 290 near Waller. It was there that Michael had his accident (with heavy road construction equipment. I never asked for details and he never told me) when Michael was 19. Michael was left for dead until his sister discovered that he was moving his fingers where they had placed him in a funeral home. During his recuperation, Michael married a woman who helped him. They had a daughter. From the hospital Michael went to a nursing home. He got out of the nursing home, bought a home, and adopted two boys. After 15 years, the boys were in jail, and his wife, after abusing him, left. Michael had to put himself in the hospital. It was the worst case of physical abuse they had seen. He didn't file charges. Instead, Michael met his second helper, Jocelyn Mosley, and she helped him recover from his sores. Jocelyn drove my van for him. Michael couldn't drive, but he operated his phone and his cell phone very well, moved his mouse cursor with his voice, and dictated all of his work with Dragon NaturallySpeaking 9. Michael was working hard to organize and maintain an ADAPT chapter in Houston. Michael liked the Windstar and he liked to go out to eat. Jocelyn warned him about being out in the cold, but he wanted to be out in the community with the van. He caught pneumonia, more than once. Each time, I visited him in the ICU at Memorial Hermann.

At TSU, the temporary administration that Governor Perry placed on campus began to fire anyone who appeared to have been hired illegally or acted improperly in the eyes of the auditors. Since most of the fiscal activities had been done according to Quentin Wiggins, most of the accountants—mostly his friends, hired with little to do—were let go. The development office and the alumni office were also cleaned out. Kefuss Falls, director of human resources, and nephew of former President Terry, had not completed personnel action forms when people were promoted and was a fraternity brother of Wiggins. So many family members had been hired, making the university reek of nepotism. Morale became quite low and everyone was ducking and running, wondering if they were next.

The grand jury indicted President Slade, CFO Quentin Wiggins, Fred Holts, a safety specialist, and Bruce Wilson, the former vice president for administration, fired with JT Glover in 2004. It was clear that the case against Fred was making him a scapegoat and his trial was dropped in the spring of 2007. After a long trial early in the summer 2007, Quentin Wiggins got 10 years for fiscal misconduct. Former president Dr. Priscilla Slade, after even a longer trial in the fall that ended in a hung jury, went free. She had a good lawyer and the jury believed some of the lies about her building her house for the presidency and not herself. Most of the jury members felt she was guilty, just that a minimum of 20 years in prison seemed to be too harsh. The Harris County District Attorney's Office said that they would retry Dr. Slade. Wilson was not tried and may have cut a deal. There were rumors of other indictments that never came down.

The governor asked the Board of Regents to step down when they tried to interfere with the presidential selection process and appointed a whole new Board of Regents. The former Boards were certainly as much to blame for what happened because of their use of TSU to get jobs for their cronies, poor selection of presidents and poor oversight of campus practices. Auditors found that, "That's the way we've always done it," was common among the administration. Some said that everyone should be fired. That would have included me. There were many long-time employees doing the basic work of the campus, always under pressure from new hires brought in by the administration that had nothing to do with the mess the university was in. To fire them would have been an insult to their faithful and valuable service. On the other hand, there were people at all levels that were not carrying their weight—just collecting a paycheck and having state benefits. But that was true in almost any organization, including private enterprise is.

Gray Padfield, the project manager for the new recreation center, had showed Dr. Slade how to get money for outsourced projects like our on-campus apartments. These were huge deals backed by Fannie Mae using some of the practices that ended up plaguing the entire real estate industry later. Misuse of this money got JT Glover and Bruce Wilson fired. Next, Padfield engineered a deal to build two parking garages for $35 million. Like the money for the apartments, the deal was brokered out of a bank in Crawford, Texas, the chosen home of the sitting president, George W. Bush. As Padfield's reward, Slade put Padfield on an indefinite contract at $20,000 a month. Auditors found that the garages cost $15 million to build and that the remaining $20 million was missing. The only conclusion I could come to was that the missing money was used for "*administration.*" In other words, it was used to grease the wheels politically so that the people pushing for on-campus housing and the parking garages (not economically feasible when land in the area for surface parking lots was so inexpensive) could get what they wanted. Padfield was still working after Wiggins and Slade were fired, but the university stopped paying him in May of 2006 and he left campus like so many others. Sometime during the summer, his young wife divorced him. Gray had only been married to her for a short time after leaving his former wife and children in Tennessee. The newlyweds had purchased a huge home in a southwest suburban upscale neighborhood. No one heard from Gray after he left campus. Sometime before Christmas 2006, Padfield died in his kitchen (he was 53). His decomposed body was found on January 2. Gray Padfield's fate was similar to the vice president of Enron who couldn't deal with what he had done and committed suicide in his car not far from where Padfield lived. From what I knew of Gray, he had a heavy conscience about what was going on, on campus, and probably took a grilling from the grand jury, perhaps pointing a finger, perhaps not. Suicide was not out of the question.

A good friend, Howard Greene, retired about 2005 after being grounds supervisor and assistant director of maintenance for more than 30 years. Howard loved to hunt and fish and we talked a lot about that. He also talked about the land that he and his brothers had inherited from his father in College Station, worth a lot of money. That's what his retirement was all about. Building up the property, hunting and fishing, and enjoying life. In June 2007, Howard took a friend, newly released from the hospital after heart surgery, fishing on Lake Conroe. They started early, but were scheduled to return to the dock at 11 am for lunch. When Howard and his fishing partner turned up missing, friends started searching. Their boat was found circling with the motor on, and the worst was feared. They found his body three days later along with the body of the other man. Howard Greene was 64. Greene was an excellent swimmer. If I were writing a novel, I would say it was a hit because of his strong opinions about how TSU was being run and his testimony to the grand jury. But it was probably just an unfortunate accident. In his haste to save his friend, Howard probably dove in with his clothes on, trying to save the other guy who had fallen overboard without a life vest on, and the boat got away from him, making it impossible to get back to it. Many times, when I ran into trouble related to my disability, Howard came to my rescue and saved my day. Howard Greene was a standup guy. Many missed him.

Jim Anderson was concerned that the grand jury would come after Robert and me, too. So, although he testified for six hours, Jim made sure that I was never called. We spent a lot of time and money verifying the university's land holdings, and appraising what could be sold. We also spent a lot of time verifying the facilities inventory, planning the future course of the campus, and coming up with ways we could solve the problems caused by misappropriation of funds. After an extensive study of our facilities by Carter Burgess, Andersen determined how much deferred maintenance the university had, $52 million, and what it would take to remove it.

Two new buildings were being built, the science building, the brainchild of provost Bobby Wilson, and the public affairs building to house the school of public affairs. The money we were getting from the US Office of Civil Rights funded these projects. Jim found that most of the money from the Office of Civil Rights was earmarked for improving campus facilities, student recruitment and retention, and new housing by way of a dormitory. Instead, most of the money was used to hire mid-level administrators who were friends and relatives of existing administrators and faculty to flesh out the newly reformed school of public affairs. The new science building, while state-of-the-art, did not house all the sciences that the old science building had housed. The technology building and the old science building both had structural problems that the only way effectively to get rid of was to tear them down.

Jim thought that a performance contract from an energy services company, using savings from energy retrofits over 10 years or more, could eliminate deferred maintenance, improve existing operation and maintenance, train our staff, and save energy and emissions. Jim commissioned a study by Direct Energy to determine opportunities for energy cost savings. He also sought a LoanSTAR loan. We met with the interim administration and explained the project to them and had the director of the state's LoanSTAR program there to back us up. Bobby Wilson and some other members of the former Slade administration seemed dead set against the project. While the general, the interim president, seemed to like the idea, he wanted to defer the project until a new president was on board. Jim grew worried that we would lose the money when the state's LoanSTAR funds were threatened to be gobbled up by other state institutions for their projects, Jim grew worried that we would lose the money. When Jim signed a letter of intent for the LoanSTAR loan with the State Energy Conservation Office, he was fired for overstepping his authority. Anderson got a lawsuit underway, and was considering reentering into the nuclear power industry where he worked before on the South Texas Project. After an extended period of unemployment, Jim finally got a job as environmental and energy conservation director for the City of Baltimore's Housing Authority. He was a good man with good intentions, but like so many of us, misunderstood by the powers that be, more politically motivated than interested in providing lower cost education for students.

My just-in-time technology was giving me fits. My new G5 Mac at work was working very well, but I couldn't open it in the classic mode like my iMac at home. I had to open the classic mode separately, taking more time. And, after sending my old 7500 PowerMac, upgraded to a G4, to the warehouse, I discovered that I couldn't open any of my original PowerPoint presentations from over the years. The warehouse had promised to keep my computer around in case I would need something from it. When I got there, they had kept the computer; only the 20-inch monitor, keyboard and mouse were gone. After trying the Internet, and TSU computer support, I found a woman that still had the same computer on campus. I borrowed her keyboard and monitor and discovered that my Power Mac had been damaged in transit. After many coaxes and crashes, I captured the presentations made with the original PowerPoint I received from Barry DuVall on a floppy in 1988, and upgraded them to PowerPoint 4. Bringing the presentations home, I upgraded the PowerPoint 4 versions to Office 2001. I still had to upgrade those to Office 2003 at the office. I cursed myself for not keeping that old computer around. The CRT monitor was far superior to the flat panel monitor. I could have used it for many years after.

My Gateway PC at work was working remarkably well, except for my constant battle with pushing the wrong button on the two-button mouse.

The Gateway's keyboard was very bad, quite clunky, but fortunately, with Dragon NaturallySpeaking 9, I was dictating almost everything. Dragon was lightning fast for answering my email and great for spelling if I didn't get the word right. Using a server in Hannah Hall for backup and transfer, I was able to move files back and forth between computers and provide a backup as well. I also used my web space to FTP (file transfer protocol) files from my computers at work to my computers at home. Security upgrades made some of this process more difficult and I found myself with many multiple usernames and passwords for access to FTP.

After I complained to the Department of Assistive Services (DARS) about not getting the computer equipment and upgrades I needed to do work at both work and at home, they gave me a new printer and a special keyboard with software for multiple key functions. The WiFi wireless HP printer was quite complicated and wouldn't work on the Mac at all, so I had to move it to the work PC where it still gave me trouble. The multiple key keyboard helped a bit, but I rarely used it. I was hoping that DARS would give me a voice system for my Macs. However, the only voice system that supported ViaVoice 8 required Tiger 4.3. I was using Tiger 4.11. If I upgraded to Leopard, I would have to leave the Mac *Classic Mode* behind, along with Helix (I upgraded to Server 6.1 on my own rather than try to get it approved at TSU), MacDraw, and iMovie. These were key applications that I used almost daily.

In the meantime, I had some security problems at home and was getting a tremendous amount of spam on my iMac. My trusty iMac was now six years old and starting to crash when it got warm. The screen no longer showed my backup drive and I couldn't back it up for three weeks. A technical friend of mine told me that the power supply, picture tube, and maybe, the drive were going out. Since I hadn't found a solution to the above-mentioned software problems, I bought a used eMac with twice the speed and drive capacity that would suffice until I could move everything to Leopard. No need to go to Vista. Microsoft promised to support XP for another five or six years.

My complaint remained that all this hardware and software upgrading, except for the voice systems, hadn't improved my computing experience or productivity at all. In some ways, the software was much harder and more complicated to use. Printing became much more difficult, and so was doing artwork. I moved to AT&T for all my computer and telephone services, only to find out that they couldn't provide me with DSL. I moved to Comcast cable and that worked out quite well after the initial setup. High-speed uploading and downloading was wonderful, but I wasn't getting as much work done as I did with 56K dial-up. Something was always hung up, disconnected, dirty, or requiring repair. It's hell to be paralyzed and unable to get my hands in and fix these little hardware problems. My technician/cleaner/courier got upset and I couldn't get anything done. Still, Beh tried and learned, and that was enough. Eventually, she came around and became quite proficient at these things.

I managed to avoid the flus for all of 2007 by making sure I had the flu shot. Something did creep up on me though that I didn't know about. After two episodes where stomach pain prevented me from sleeping at night that were spaced out about two or three weeks apart, on August 8, 2007, I had an episode that forced me to drive to the West Houston Medical Center Emergency room. They checked me into the hospital.

The strange pain that I felt was a one-inch in diameter kidney stone blocking the duct leading to my bladder in my left kidney. The next day, a urologist placed a stent in the duct forcing the kidney stone back so that the kidney could drain. I felt much better and went home. Beh started a home cure consisting of baked pineapple juice and alum. Two days later, I went to Memorial Southwest Hospital and had a lithotripsy on that large kidney stone. A week later, the urologist was surprised to find the large stone *completely gone*—it usually took two or more treatments to break up large stones—so he did a lithotripsy on the smaller stone in the right kidney. Two weeks later, I returned and he removed the stent. I learned that the kidney stones had caused my cloudy urine and distended stomach. I would look for those signs again.

By 2007, I got dehydrated more easily, was more affected by the cold and heat, more muscle spasms, less breathing capacity, more upset stomach, and lost still more abdominal muscles. It was a long decline to where I wouldn't be able to be as active, stay up as long, and eventually, drive my van. After the kidney stone work, we discovered some nasty pimples on the back of my neck. It turned out to be a staph infection. I had planned a trip to Wisconsin the third week in September, hoping to get up there before it got too cold and to see some autumn color. I just wasn't feeling well and couldn't figure out why. Finally, with Diann Massingill coming along to help me, we left on Saturday, September 29. Fortunately, except for some heavy rain in southern Minnesota and some strong cross winds a couple of times, the weather turned out to be beautiful. The fall color was fabulous and I was so impressed at how prosperous everyone in the family was. The trip was so rushed that we only got to see people for a short time. But even that was well worth it.

We were running behind, primarily because Diann had a hard time getting up in the morning and getting us going with all the preparation I needed. After stopping to see my uncle Ed and aunt Marian, Ed directed me to where uncle Don was staying in an assisted living apartment in Thorp. In the background, I could see aunt Marian rolling her eyes, but not saying anything. After going where uncle Ed directed us and finding nothing, we stopped at a famous gas station on the main street and got some directions to two assisted living homes. Uncle Don wasn't in either one, but at the second, an employee looked up Don Marshall in the phone book and told us where he was. We had a nice visit with uncle Don even though he was having trouble at 94 with his vision deteriorating and a frequency problem with his hearing.

We dropped in on Don's son, Keith, and his remote control facility on the old Marshall farm. Everyone stopped flying RC planes to take a look at my vehicle and its controls. Keith got his brother, Wesley, on the line and told him that we were coming. I remembered where the turnoff was off Highway 10 and took that, but it didn't end up going to Wes's place. We drove further east looking when we should have driven west. Finally, it was getting late so we gave up looking. When we got to Mom's place, I asked Diann to knock on the door. Diann knocked lightly, and nobody came. After some time, we went to the local mall and ate and got a motel room nearby. When we called Mom, she had been waiting for us all along, but didn't hear Diann knocking on the door.

The next morning we had breakfast with Mom and she told us to try visiting Jurustic Park by Clyde Wynia. We had a wonderful time there among the creatures that Clyde had constructed out of scrap metal, taking a video. In the afternoon, much of our extended family, including the newly born Kaitlyn, joined us at the motel. After stopping briefly at Jackie and Albert Replogle's for lunch, and later at our friends, Roger and Pat Smith's house, we spent the night in DeForest, having pizza at my brother, Tim's, place and answering questions from my nieces and nephews about family history.

The next day, we arrived at Roger's place and toured the Motorhome Hall of Fame in Bristol, Indiana before taking a relaxing evening boat ride on the St. Joseph River. The next morning we got a late start and had a small lunch on the way to my niece, Kelley's, house where we got lost. Leaving Kelley's, I "hit the wall" while driving in a single lane construction zone and had to pull over because I could no longer push on the accelerator and hold the van at speed—I slowed to about 35 mph and that was way too slow for the traffic behind me. I finally found a place to pull off and let the traffic pass.. As a result, we arrived very late to my friends, Behram and Gool Randelia, who had waited patiently for us at their home in New Albany, Indiana, with a wonderful Indian dinner.

The next morning, we got an early start and arrived at my uncle Bruce's in Kentucky around 10 am, but they weren't home. We pushed on and spent the night in northern Mississippi. I dropped Diann off at her home in Liberty, Texas the next day, and drove home alone, tired but exhilarated by the trip.

When I returned from the trip, I took antibiotics for the staph infection. In the meantime, Michael Thomas was in the hospital again. Three times during the year he went to the hospital with trouble breathing. They would remove fluid from his lungs and he would be able to go back home again. All the while they were having trouble with the Windstar and I would fix it. Michael stayed in good spirits and I visited him in the hospital and home whenever I could. Finally, he went to the hospital again in November, got a staph infection that required an operation on his stomach—twice. Four days later, on December 9, he died. I went to the funeral, attended by his estranged family and his friends in the disabled community. It made me stop and think. That staph infection I had could just as easily have gotten me.

My book writing was bogged down by all of the technical difficulties and things I had to do just to keep up with my life. When I did write, it flowed easily and fast. I liked writing short stories and expected to do more of them; hopefully, enough for a book in a couple of years. I decided to re-edit **The Kaleidoscope Effect**, and **Alone?** and republish them as second editions through Booklocker.com. By the end of 2007 I had about 300 pages of the **American Mole** completed. My hero, Jason Forsythe, was only through about a third of his 20-year service to America. So, I decided to write three novels—a trilogy. **American Mole: The Vespers** would be the first. I intended to follow that novel with two other American Mole novels, as sequels.

While I was pleased to see that the bloodshed in Iraq was declining, I wasn't pleased that the war dragged on and so many innocent civilians had been killed or driven from their homes. The turmoil in Palestine, Iran, Afghanistan and Pakistan continued to grow. Confirming my premonition in my novel, **War's End.** While everyone seemed to be aware of global warming, the government's meager measures to address it seemed too little and too late. Fortunately, the technology we need to make the transition from fossil fuels was already available at prices we could afford. There was just a lot of inertia—left over dependence on fossil fuels—that kept us from moving ahead into these new technologies. There was also immense lobbying by the fossil fuel industries to keep things the way they were—*highly profitable for them.*

With the anticipation that I would have the potential retirement funds, I set parameters for a retirement home with two elements: it must be barrier free and green. I sent these specifications to the deans of the University of Houston and Rice architectural schools with the hope that my ideas could be a student project with students helping me flesh out the plan and come up with alternatives. I never received any response from the two letters that I sent. I didn't follow up either and probably should have, but economic change came and affected my plans.

With friends, Behram and Gool Randelia. New Albany. IN Sept 2007

# 78

# My Economic Downturn

T he year 2008 was the best and the worst. The best was that we were healthy and still working in spite of having reached that grand old retirement age. Everything in the Hull household was positive and productive. I was looking forward to easing out of my work with TSU to devote myself full-time to writing books and volunteering. However, the worst came along and you all know what that was—the economy. The Texas State Teachers Retirement System (TRS) was based on age and years served. My number was 92. One only needed about 65 to retire and many had, but would only receive a portion of their annual salary. With my number, I would receive full salary if I retired. I don't know what the death benefit would be

because I wasn't in the system. I wisely chose the Optional Retirement Program (ORP) in 1981 and built a mutual fund account over the years. Up until 2008 it looked like I had made the right choice. However, with my retirement cut in half by the stock market decline, TRS looked a whole lot better. There was no changing back to TRS—*no return to greener pastures*. Hence, I would be working for a couple more years. In the meantime, I moved about half of my retirement money to a fixed account in March so I wouldn't lose any more of that. I also had good income from my long-term care insurance for eight years more, giving time for the stock market to turn around. Thank goodness for that insurance!

Mom turned 84 January 2, 2008. She had been short of breath for some time and having difficulty walking because of swelling in her legs and her artificial hip. And then, in the fall, she had a spell that scared her, but she waited until a regular appointment to see her doctor about it. Alarmed at her condition, her doctor put her into the hospital to have her arteries checked. The major arteries to her heart were badly clogged and she needed to have a quadruple bypass as soon as possible. The surgery went well and she recovered quickly until she developed arterial fibrillation and had to go back to ICU. She recovered quickly again, and, after a week and a half in a nursing home getting rehabilitation and gaining strength, Mom returned to the hospital with chest pain. The pain turned out to be shingles. Mom returned to her apartment Thanksgiving Day. The shingles were still bothering her.

Roger decided to take his Social Security early in April 2008. His plan was to buy a new Mercedes with the extra money. Unfortunately, his company cut back at the same time and he was out of a job. In semi-retirement, Roger did some contract engineering after that, but never returned to full-time work.

Judy and Paul gave birth to an one acre pond in the summer of 2008. Although the weather didn't cooperate, the pond was partially full and frozen over by the end of the year.

Beh's shop became a Mecca for some of her long-time customers. They told her tales of woe and tried to get her involved in their lives. Beh told me that many men asked her out for lunch or dinner but she didn't have time (she said). As a result, many customers couldn't understand why she didn't take a break after so many hours. Many shops, including some major chains, like Pilgrim, had closed shops, resulting in new customers for Beh.

Of those that I knew of, Beh's celebrity customers included Clyde Drexler, Ilona Carson (Houston Channel 13 four o'clock anchor—formerly from Phoenix and Australia), Elmo Wright (U. of H. football star and former Kansas City Chief and originator of the end zone dance), Chelsea Smith (Miss Texas, Miss USA and Miss Universe, and Yolanda Adams, gospel singer. There were also very rich people who wanted Beh to be their private seamstress. Of course, most of these rich people are only willing to pay slave wages. That's why so many shops were closing—competition had forced them to charge so little they couldn't cover expenses, let alone make a profit.

Beh's father was suffering from lung cancer, congestive heart failure, and had developed diabetes. Beh had to spend nights with him to be sure that he didn't fall or had other problems. Worried about the economy and what she would do after her father died, Beh withdrew part of her mutual fund retirement (in a timely way) and was looking for a way to invest the money that would be safe and help provide her a good life in retirement.

She focused on buying property and renting it out. However, the economy in Houston was still quite good and housing values had not dropped to the point where there were a lot of bargains out there in 2008. Oil money and the immigrants were still pouring in.

Daisey Ashley accompanied me to a reception for UW Stout alumni at Minute Maid Park in August 2008, sponsored by Pam Gardner, a Stout graduate and the COO of the Houston Astros. We watched a game with the Cardinals after. I regret not taking a Louisiana trip in the spring because Hurricane Ike wiped out much of the Bolivar Peninsula that I hoped to travel through on our way up through Louisiana Cajun country.

Edith Concepción rented the upstairs bedroom. Edith helped me out a great deal on weekends when Beh was often at work or out shopping for me.

In spite of having the 2006 Freestar, we did little travel in 2008. By running up and down 59 to work, I managed to put 23,000 miles on the van. After Michael Thomas died, I retrieved the 1998 Windstar and re-donated it to the Houston Center for Independent Living. They were pleased to get it and sold it to their administrative assistant, Maria. Maria was in a push wheelchair, so she strapped herself in, and drove herself with hand controls. Maria had the same problem that I had with the battery getting low all of the time and fixed that with a simple switch that isolated the battery when the van was not in use. Maria was very happy with what she called, "My Baby."

The Freestar had few problems except for an annoying misalignment of the ramp door, occasionally, the failure of the electric driver-side sliding door to close properly, and the voice system for operating nonessential controls. The training of the voice system required training all of the commands in a single session before it was complete. When I tried to improve training of the controls, the training automatically aborted and my voice recognition deteriorated. It came to the point where I could barely use the signal lights and some of the other functions. Fortunately, I was still able to command the wipers to operate in rain, the lights came on automatically when it got darker, and the heat and a/c were on automatic climate control once the temperatures and other settings were set.

I spent three days with Diann as my helper having a good déjà vu of an earlier trip with Beh and Desiree in Corpus Christi. The weather was breezy but beautiful and we enjoyed every minute of it in the sun. The high point of the trip was when we stopped at the Aransas Wildlife Refuge on the high ramp overlooking the Intracoastal Waterway in prime whooping crane habitat. We spotted a troop of javelinas crossing from a marshy island to another in deep water. The largest pigs were in front, but two little piglets, swimming for dear life for the far shore, brought up the rear. I wish we had had our video camera for that one. The battery was dead.

After that, I hired Diann for two nights a week to help relieve Beh so she could stay with her father. Diann had left TSU a couple of years earlier and took her retirement with her after working as a custodian for about eight years. Her new husband promised her the world but didn't deliver and she ended up coming to see me about getting back to work at TSU. Diann was having trouble getting a job because back when she was 18, a man raped Diann. She came to her sister's house and found a gun. She found the guy outside a shopping center and fired one shot attempting to scare him. Instead of scaring him, the shot killed the guy and she served six years for murder. All the time that we traveled together and Diann took care of me day and night, I never once felt threatened by her. So, Beh and I took her in again so she could get started back at TSU.

In August 2008, Diann suddenly stopped coming to work one evening and I couldn't locate her. Eventually, someone called me on a cell phone and told me she was in the Harris County jail. Apparently, she had gotten drunk with her husband, and using the pliers she had to use to start her car—it had been stolen earlier and the ignition ripped out—she hit him over the head with the pliers causing him to bleed a lot, got arrested, and put in jail. Her husband got five stitches and was out of the hospital the next day. Diann got charged with assault with a deadly weapon and put in jail. Because of the prior felony over 30 years earlier, she had trouble, even with a pro bono lawyer, convincing the District Attorney that she was not violent. She was given an offer to take one year, but she refused that. If her case went to a jury trial, I decided to testify and get some others who were willing to come forward to talk about her good character. My hope was, because of jail overcrowding, they would let Diann go free in a couple of months. Ironically, the day before she went to jail, her former custodial supervisor told me that he had a job for her in the TSU cafeteria.

The only other trip was a cruise with Beh and Daisey in April 2008 on Royal Caribbean's Legend of the Seas. While the ship was much bigger and had a mall, ice-skating rink, and rock-climbing wall, I didn't find it as nice as our earlier cruises on the Rhapsody of the Seas. This time, instead of a stop at Key West, we cruised to Jamaica where we enjoyed a bamboo raft adventure on a tropical river. Strong men carried me from my wheelchair to the raft. Beh rode with me, while Daisey followed on a separate raft. Our boatman was very nervous the whole time and not very much fun. On the return trip, we stopped at a seafood restaurant that stunk so bad we declined to eat there, but stopped at a roadhouse down the highway where we got a meal of jerk steak, but I couldn't enter the building because of the large step up at the entrance. The Jamaican owners kindly set up a table in the gravel out front. It wasn't very scenic, but the atmosphere was friendly and the food was good while cars zipped by on the highway.

From there, we returned to the Cayman Islands where I treated the girls to a helicopter ride around Grand Cayman Island. It was a very windy day, while the helicopter operated quite safely in the wind, Stingray City was closed down to tourists. We searched for a large hammerhead shark that frequented the area but only saw stingrays and turtles. We did get an aerial tour of the homes of John Travolta and Morgan Freeman. A retired friend of mine from TSU, Sybil Johnson, told me that her cousin, Colin Powell, took some of the family's land from her on Grand Cayman Island.

When we arrived in Cozumel, I took the girls to the National Park where we viewed replicas of Olmec, Mayan, and Aztec artifacts and watched other tourists play with dolphins. I got stuck in the sand again, but made sure, this time, that I was hydrated. At a Mexican restaurant in town, we were serenaded by mariachis in an authentic, though touristy, Mexican restaurant. We could have eaten much better, for free, back at the ship. When we returned to the ship, the wind caught Daisey's straw hat and dropped it in the water between the ship and the dock. She really missed that old hat.

For some reason, while Royal Caribbean wouldn't let me sell my books this time, they seated us with others in wheelchairs. There were two elderly sisters, one from Denver, and the other from assisted-living right near us in Houston. And there was an elderly gay guy with a black companion from Galveston. The black man, Tommie McNeil, was the life of the party, so I took down his information in case he could help us the future. On ship, we kept running into a family from Anchorage, Alaska. The head of the family, a former muscle builder, had became paralyzed surfing on the beach in Hawaii when he broke his neck at C-2. While he was much more disabled than I, his muscle builder wife and nearly adult kids made sure that he had a good time. I'm not sure I could live through the wet and cold of an Alaska winter.

Our big adventure of 2008 was our brush with Hurricane Ike. Ike came up out of the Gulf as predicted. I arrived home Thursday night and could have gone back to work on Friday, except the university was closed. All of our hurricanes and tropical storms seemed to come on weekends. The president was taking no chances after what had happened earlier with Katrina and Allison. Beh bought us canned goods and a large container to store water, batteries, and borrowed a battery-powered boom box so that we could listen to the radio. We had four cars filled with gas in two garages and ready to go, if necessary. However, when I saw that the storm was traveling much further east than Alicia, I wasn't worried at all.

The mayor rightly called for a staged evacuation, with low-lying areas like Galveston first, followed by areas less in harms way. Unfortunately, everyone seemed to panic at the same time and got out on the freeways, clogging them. While there were stories all around about running out of gas, food, and water, the worse news story was of a bus carrying elderly from a nursing home in Houston that got overheated brakes, caught fire, and burned to death several of the elderly passengers who couldn't get out in time. The nursing home probably suffered little or no damage from the storm. All the unnecessary, panicked people on the highway who shouldn't have been there, probably caused the brakes on the bus to overheat. Resulting in unnecessary tragedy.

Friday night, before time for us to have a hurricane party, the power went out. There was nothing left to do but to go to bed; so we did. The power came on and off until about 3 am and the wind blew, but we awoke to find little damage except a branch in the front yard and our neighbor's fence down. Beh's water tub had split its bottom. I told her to duct tape it and put it out again where our neighbor's roof drained without an eves trough. I showed Beh how, and she cooked my breakfast eggs and bacon in the gas lighter on the fireplace. We were camping out.

Because of the size of Ike, there was widespread power outage, affecting almost all of Houston. Fortunately, we got power back about four o'clock Saturday afternoon, allowing us to have a hot meal that evening. Likewise, Beh's shop had no damage and the power never went out. Sunday morning, it poured, filling Beh's water storage tub. Our neighborhood had no water, but Beh got a cold shower from a downpour, reminding her of her childhood. Likewise, I got a hot shower that evening with that rainwater heated on the stove.

Because of the power problem everywhere, we weren't allowed to go to work until Wednesday. From the freeway signs and awnings to the roofs and trees in the vicinity of TSU, there appeared to be much less damage from Ike than Alicia in 1983. Still, there was a lot of roof damage and tree limbs lost. The damage area was much larger and more devastating for places like Galveston and the Bolivar Peninsula. TSU lost part of a window wall on the new science building, and the technology building, already damaged structurally by subsidence, was declared a total loss because of window leakage.

I was part of a committee to revise the manual for university facility inventories in Austin at the end of the summer, so Beh decided to go along with me for the day, two times. We enjoyed the trips immensely and Beh got to stop both times in Brenham to pick up her favorite sausage. Beh caught up on her reading while I was in the long meetings. The Coordinating Board wanted to adopt the federal guidelines for room inventories. There were some inconsistencies in those guidelines and decoding was not as easily computerized as what the state already had. In the end, conformity won out, and I had to change my database parameters to meet the new rules. This was not difficult, but awkward, something I was trying to remove in my management tools. I detected there was some animosity toward my insistence on a cleaner taxonomy, but most of the players were novices and some were quite politically connected, so I struck a sour note before I left those meetings. If it ain't broke, don't fix it. But change is inevitable even if it isn't pleasant or productive. Most of the changes that I saw installed through that favored word, *outsourcing*, resulted in buying lots of unnecessary equipment and software, as well as having to hire more people to "manage" the process the university no longer had control of. "Hands-off control" seemed to have a Parkinson's rule requiring more "hands-on." And it always entailed training and certification on proprietary systems, creating unsavory public-private partnerships that were always suspect.

When John Rudley was named president of Texas Southern University in 2007, I was pleased and surprised. John was our internal auditor when I first came to TSU in 1981. By 1984, Rudley was named vice president for fiscal affairs and left in 1987. The next time I saw him was in 2002. John had gone back to Tennessee to get his doctorate in education, served in the Department of Education in Washington DC, served the State of Tennessee division of higher education, and had just become the CFO of the University of Houston. I was at a conference at U. of H. and he greeted me warmly and introduced me to the new president at that time. I showed John my books and he was impressed. Three years later, that U. of H. president resigned and went to Auburn. John became acting interim president of U. of H. I had heard that he was in the running for the TSU presidency, but never expected him to come. Rudley failed to get the presidency at the University of Houston and fell back on TSU as a good second.

Upon his appointment, Rudley immediately replaced the Governor's appointed interim people with people from the Houston Community College. I thought that was a bad idea because of our experience with former TSU president JoAnn Horton, a former community college president. Community colleges have always operated with a philosophy dramatically different from 4-year senior colleges. At the time, we were reporting to Lance Ross. Lance Ross was a friend of the interim CFO from Grambling and a former employee of British Petroleum. Lance turned out to be a micro manager who made my life miserable by constantly contradicting my work and coming up with ideas which had very little chance of working at TSU. Lance managed to endear himself (negatively) to almost everyone, and, although he had the title of vice president, when John Rudley put him on his administration organization chart, Lance was described as the "facilities manager." I could see from that change in title that Lance's days were numbered.

President Rudley appointed Gloria Walker as COO, and Tim Rychlec as executive director of facilities and operations. Both came from Houston Community College. Tim, a former submariner, was a breath of fresh air at first. Except for our little planning area, he had everyone resign and reapply for their jobs. The good news was that Rychlec added seven people, including bringing back people that had been unfairly let go in a political layoff during the previous administration. Communication opened up, and everyone seemed to be happier except for a couple of guys who were laid off because they didn't have credentials to reapply and hold their previous jobs. As a result, several other areas of the University went through the process of asking everyone to resign and reapply, effectively weeding out the last of the friends, associates, and relatives that were still working at TSU without proper credentials.

As his first move in office, President Rudley declared that he would tighten admissions so that only those that were qualified to go to college would be able to attend TSU. Everyone praised this action because open enrollment had brought in criminals and non-students who took advantage of federal student funds and never graduated. Fall enrollment dipped a bit but was much better than had been anticipated. Someone sabotaged one of TSU's two electrical feeds and it was suspected that one of the people that were let go had knowledge of high-voltage electricity and was the culprit. Otherwise, the atmosphere on campus was very scholarly, upbeat, and cooperative. This was something that I hadn't felt for many years since the accountants from Arthur Andersen came into the campus and took over, trying to privatize and outsource all of our basic staff functions.

Back in 2007, with a faster, G5 Macintosh, and an upgraded version of Helix, and Jim's approval, I decided to combine all of my databases for land, buildings and rooms, employees, and energy conservation into one database. That process took some time because I had to stop periodically to enter data for various reports into both the old and the new system I was developing. I had also spent over 10 years developing some of the collections and they were becoming quite complex. In some cases, in order to link the collections, I had to change all the links on an entire report. Lots of cutting and pasting. It took about two years to get everything from all the other collections working together as one.

When I was working with Jim Anderson, we had tried to get an outside consulting firm to help us put my database on the Internet. We were unable to get that funded. Tim came up with a novel idea that I should have thought of. He asked the computer science professors to help me come up with a system on the Internet. The previous department head for computer science, Dr. Etta Walker, was angry with me over the lighting controller that I had tried to stop being installed. She would not work with me. The computer science department had ignored Macs in favor of their minicomputers and PCs. With Walker retired, the department was more receptive. They assigned the task of bringing the facilities inventory to the Internet to their fall graduate student classes. In addition, Tim hired three senior computer science students to assist me with collection of data and moving my system to the Internet. With the students' assistance I expected be able to have the system working on the Internet sometime in 2009 and be closer to retirement. Unfortunately, because of other appointments and commitments, I missed key meetings with those professors and students. We started off on the wrong foot. It got worse.

My writing suffered from technical difficulties, primarily with my PCs. The one at work was not well protected and developed problems that required an on-site tech to remedy. It took him a couple of weeks and he had to take my computer and completely reboot it. Finally, he got the Windows 2000 system working right again. Beh's computer, on the other hand, was not as easy. I spent six aggravating weekends working with offshore Microsoft techs from India who continually told me that they had solved my problem and didn't. Finally, taking a clue from the solution at work, I discovered RegEdit, from a firm in Canada that had the highest ranked Registry editor. After I bought that for $40, suddenly, all my problems went away. I also had a Computer Associates suite to keep the evil bugs away from my Internet provider. All that started working quite well again. I was back working on my books again.

In 2007, I was told that Everyone's Internet would no longer support my web space. I moved my web space to The Planet. When I found that my web space there was still limited to only 500 MB, the people at The Planet told me that Host Gator had what I needed. I signed up for Host Gator, but it took me a long time, until September 2008, to get my files moved over. And then, I discovered that there were still many dead links. After nine years on Everyone's Internet, I had so many pages that dead links to that server were inevitable. All I could do was fix them when I found them. It took months.

I still couldn't find a replacement for MacDraw Pro. The old OS 9 Claris application was my mainstay drawing tool and I could not migrate to OS X until I'd found a suitable replacement. Given educational discounts at work, I bought Office 2007 for the PC and Office 2004 for the Mac. After I purchased them, I experienced many problems with navigation, crashes, and incompatibility. For example, I couldn't seem to open any of my PowerPoint presentations. Thank goodness I saved older copies of Office on my Mac. Creating book covers with MacDraw Pro with its memory limitations was a challenge. I couldn't seem to find anything like my old Photoshop 2.5 that worked simply and effectively to get my graphics done. Newer isn't always better. I never learned how to master the copy of Photoshop 7 that I had. Some of the functions I had used often and accomplished easily on 2.5, seemed to be unavailable on 7.

In March, just before our cruise, I managed to finish **American Mole: The Vespers**. The novel was running so long, I decided to break it into three parts. The next two parts were tentatively called, **MS-13** and **The Aryan Nation**. I had not started on either of those from the trilogy because I had been creating second editions of **The Kaleidoscope Effect** and **Alone?** Both books had been out of print since 2004 when Bookbooters went out of business. While I couldn't read my own paperbacks, my reviewers told me that these books were full of errors and needed editing. Toby Endem, publisher and editor-in-chief of Bookbooters, told me that he edited my books. Apparently Toby hadn't (at least not well), and still took forever to have them published originally. As I edited **Kaleidoscope**, I re-wrote several sections and removed as many of the errors as I could find.

The second edition should be much better than the first and available for a very long time at Booklocker, my POD publisher. I decided to produce a book of short stories. So that was to be my next project before returning to the **American Mole** series. Nothing was selling, but that's okay. I expected that one of these days one of my books would be picked up for a movie or television and then I'd have the ride of my life trying to keep up with publicity events.

We endured an era of George Bush's Biblical blunders, Tom DeLay's (originally my Congressman) wild party ploys and inarticulate gerrymandering, and my Republican state representative's fall from grace by trying to take his housekeeper's child. I never could understand why Republicans say the Democrats were for big government when government grew so bloated under Republican administrations. I also cannot understand why they say Democrats were big spenders while Republican administrations had raised taxes and spent so much on themselves and their friends. It was strange how "trickle down economics" touted by Ronald Reagan resulted in the financial crisis we were in. The failure of capitalism was that somehow wealth and power tend to beget more wealth and power, resulting in wider and wider gaps between the haves and the have-nots. The stress and resentment caused by these differences brought down Rome and will, in time, result in social war anywhere that it gets out of hand. Communism was certainly not the answer, either. We must have fair compensation for fair work. Regulation helps, but it was not the answer, either. Until people are truly altruistic and not concerned about wealth and power, the struggle will continue.

I've said it before and I'll say it here, Barrack Obama is the *Abraham Lincoln of the 21st-century*. As a famous civil rights minister, Rev. Bill Lawson, said when I told him that, "*Oh my, I hope not*," was not what I was saying—that Obama would also be assassinated. What I was saying and writing here is that he will be tried by the challenges of the economy and the world the way that Abraham Lincoln had to face our Civil War and slavery. He will also have to be like Franklin Roosevelt in his ability to find the right people to bring our economy and the world economy up from the depths that it is in (in 2008). Obama seemed to have the calmness, patience, intelligence, understanding, and resolve to do this for the people, *all of the people*. Obama was going to be hated, vilified, and loved for his actions. But that is what greatness is all about. Persevering intelligently in spite of great odds.

The economy also postponed my retirement project again—my new retirement home. Although I probably would have great difficulty pulling Beh from her southwestern Houston Vietnamese roots, I planned to move to the country someday. The closest place to the Medical Center in Houston I liked was Lake Houston. Through my foot doctor, I learned of John Paltrow, an engineer developer-real estate agent in the area. John showed me property in the vicinity of the lake that could just do the trick. My plan was for a fully disabled access green home. I would start with a concrete base with radiant plumbing in the floor heated and cooled by a water source heat pump, a geothermal energy source.

The structure would be of aluminum or steel and the walls, straw bales. Oriented to take maximum advantage of passive heating and cooling of the sun and shade, the building would be two stories with a ramp, starting in the garage, that would reach to the second floor so that there would be no need for an elevator to take advantage of the view and warmer second floor. The house would also contain very efficient equipment, solar panels, water recycled and stored from the roof for irrigation, a windmill, and other devices to make the home more comfortable and efficient for my use, including backup power in case of a storm or hurricane. John was somewhat skeptical of my ideas, but I know contractors will join me when I show them how they can work together. I had done it before with great success in 1980, building my solar passive home in Atlanta.

The interior would be designed to be convenient and accessible for my electric wheelchairs and electronics. There was be an intercom, voice controls for doors, windows and vents, and a special bed for comfort and function. An overhead power sling would move me from bed to chair to toilet to shower. Beh would have her large kitchen with convenient appliances. A den for her personal use, and quarters for guests. She would have a garden and fruit trees, but we would limit a lawn or have none like my house in Atlanta. But so far, these were just dreams. There was no money to carry out my plans.

Beh hates snakes. I don't know what she saw in this Iguana. April 2008

I went for the birds. And no, that wasn't the Macaw I kissed.

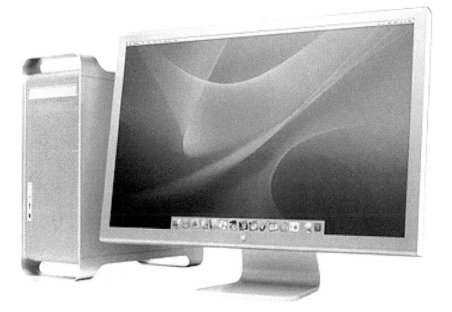

A Macintosh G5 helped me to build a fast, versatile Facilities database.

| DATE | TIME | AMBER | SPEED | PHASE | RTIME | LANE | FRAME |
|------|------|-------|-------|-------|-------|------|-------|
| 9/29/2008 | 9:13:58.1 AM | 3.55 | 17 | R | 0.3 | 1 | A |

HO64-E/B BISSONNET @ SOUTHWEST FWY, W. SERVICE RD.

Running a red light heading to work in light traffic after Hurricane Ike.

# 79

## Postponing Promises

Tim Rychlec came to me one day and flatly asked me to work three more years. He was through discussing transition with me. That was about what I thought I needed to recover from what had happened to my retirement fund and almost everybody else's. I didn't know that it was an order, or I might have retired right then. Instead, like always, I bided my time, knowing that I would have to work much longer just to maintain myself in retirement.

I was told that I would have to transition my work to the very database (TMA-The Maintenance Authority) that I rejected and got me demoted in the first place. While I sensed what many did not, I was naïvely encouraged by signs that our financial system was coming into order, that new rules for controlling greed and excess without productivity were gradually coming into place, that companies had tightened their belts enough and families had scrimped enough for new businesses to form, creating better products, and old businesses to reform and create better jobs. Unless there was a global disaster or a war that extended far beyond human reason, I was optimistic that the recession would be a thing of the past in a couple more years. *I was wrong.*

In spite of the financial situation, my brother Roger reached the point where continuing to look for new engineering opportunities just wasn't in the cards, and he decided to retire. His wife, Sue, continued to work for another year. To kick off retirement, they spent their first January in Florida.

Michael Hull, my nephew, spent two trimesters in the spring of 2009 in the north of England and enjoyed himself very much. He also got to tour Europe thoroughly. Jennifer, his sister, began her college career at the University of Wisconsin-Madison with seven scholarships. Although her mother and her father live in Madison and nearby, Jennifer decided to stay in a dormitory on Lake Mendota and enjoy all that college life had to offer. She chose engineering for her studies, so she needed not to be a commuter.

Whenever he could, my brother Tom explored Native American archaeological sites in Arizona. By the end of the year 2008, Tom was near finishing his log house next to the Coconino National Forest, southeast of Flagstaff. A beautiful house in a beautiful location.

Beh started a new venture after her father died in the summer of 2009. Her brother, Bau, was all alone in the house, so she rented out the two upstairs bedrooms to two Vietnamese guys. Beh became a landlord with my encouragement. A woman that I fired 10 years earlier, May Cole, came to Beh with a business proposition. May and her husband had two residential assisted living homes. Both of them had 4 to 5 elderly or disabled residents. Her business was booming and expanding, but required a major financial outlay to buy a new house and remodel the houses with the attention to detail required to keep them within the law. All that Beh initially considered was to help buy a house and lease it to May. At some point, she would sell the house to May or go into partnership with her as one of May's employees. Whichever way she chose to go, it looked like Beh would make money. I encouraged her to move forward and promised that I would help her with the details.

Rose Hood started working in mid-April 2009 after the guy she had been helping take care of, Freddie Everett, died on April 2 from ALS. Back around 1990, Freddie Everett won the summer Houston citywide talent contest and the Sammy Award (named for Sammy Davis Junior) for his guitar playing two years running. Everett was just becoming successful, well able to support his family in a new suburban house, when he contracted ALS in 2003. Freddie ran through all of his money to provide his care, and eventually held fundraisers to help with the expenses. Near the end of his life, it took someone with skill and strength of Rose to take care of Freddie. Rose worked out well, and will probably work for me a long time.

Travel in 2009 was confined to a trip in June for a training session at The Higher Education Coordinating Board in Austin with Rose and a trip to Fort Worth and Arlington in August with Beh and Rose. Both were a bit eventful. When Rose and I left the THECB headquarters parking lot to come home on the second day about noon, I had to hold the car for some time on a steep incline at a stop sign before we could enter the freeway frontage road. After pulling out on the frontage road, my van struggled and wouldn't shift up or go into reverse. I started out on the highway with hopes that whatever it was would break free, but it didn't, the car just struggled and was very slow, staying in low gear. We stopped 2 miles down the road at a gas stop and I called AAA. I also called Trey Morris at Mobility Plus for assistance if I couldn't drive the van home. The AAA flatbed wrecker hauled us about 5 miles to a Ford dealer. I rode up on the tow truck in my van and Rose rode in the tow truck cab. As I backed my van down off the truck, the reverse worked fine and the brakes were working, everything seemed to be okay, so I tried the gears and everything worked. We were delayed a couple hours by the incident, but made it back to Houston okay.

As soon as I could, I took the van to Mobility Plus to check it out and they couldn't find the problem. A couple of months later, I realized that, with my wheelchair steeply inclined downward like it was, and my foot rest on my wheelchair raised too high, my foot could actually press on the brake pedal and greatly impede forward and reverse progress! After that, I was always very careful not to raise my wheelchair footrests so high anymore. I was lucky that I didn't burn the brakes out. They tested out fine even after being locked on for about 3 miles.

Our trip to Beh's brother's, Quoc, in August 2009, was uneventful except I had to stop and readjust the seat so that my left arm would not get tired trying to hold the throttle at 75 mph on I-45. From Quoc's house, we joined my niece, Tracy, in the Fort Worth Museum District where we toured The Modern Art Museum. After that, we went to the nearby Arboretum and enjoyed a long leisurely tour of all the beautiful places there. I must have covered a couple of miles in my wheelchair. Later, when I wheelchaired into Quoc's garage to get out of the sun (I had no intention of entering the house this time), one of my rear wheelchair wheels *fell off!*

Quoc got out his toolkit and then went and got a neighbor. The neighbor said he wasn't very handy, but tried to figure out what to do. Beh stepped in and figured out how to get the wheel back on. I was happy that the wheel hadn't fallen off deep into the Arboretum and that we were able to go to dinner at a Vietnamese restaurant later, as well as be able to drive back home. On the way home, we stopped at the Dallas Farmer's market. While the variety and freshness of produce was very good, Beh said the prices were high.

My 2006 Ford Freestar reached 30,000 miles without incident by the end of 2009. Because the van was so high-tech, I had to send the control units and some of the computers back to EMC for repair, upgrades, and software upgrades, *often*. I had to take two weeks off in January 2010 to send equipment again for 1000 hours of service maintenance. I couldn't get Michelin X-1 tires again, but bought their HydroEdge model for 90,000 miles of service. Occasionally, I checked in with Maria, the woman that I gave my old van to. She continued to drive the van from her push wheelchair with only seat belts to hold her in place. I don't know how she did that with hand controls. It seems to me that just tying down with seat belts instead of an EZ-Lock would be too unstable to drive with.

When I heard that MacSpeech was available for the Macintosh and that it was the best speech recognition software available, I got excited and asked DARS to help me get a copy. Unlike Dragon, the only array mic supported by Apple was the Acoustic Magic one that I had at work. When I switched microphones and tried to train MacSpeech at home, the Acoustic Magic microphone was too sensitive and picked up every little sound in the house as words, driving me crazy.. When I brought the Andrea Superbeam array microphone back home, MacSpeech would not even train. I had to abandon using MacSpeech on the Mac until it got better and continued to have to open Windows in my iMac so that I could use Dragon NaturallySpeaking with the Andrea microphone. Finally, DragonDictate became available on the iPhone, so I thought it would be only a matter of time before DragonDictate would be available on Macs.

Time continued to take its toll on my spinal cord and I continued to lose torso stability and the ability to grasp with my left hand. This affected my ability to pick up things and feed myself but not my ability to work with the computer. My old hand splint, bent and broken so many times, needed continual adjustment.

The house needed a few things done too, so I hired a young man in April 2009 to do them. Armando worked well for about three days, and then began complaining about his back. I don't know if his back was hurt or not, but I felt sorry for him because Armando was divorced and caring for two young sons. Armando told me that I could get tile installed through a wholesale firm he knew. After talking to the salesman at the wholesale tile store, the helpful man helped me pick out tile and suggested an expert tile installer. The recommended installer, Tin Nguyen, installed floor tile in my bedroom/office and all the traffic areas for my wheelchair in July 2009. I invited Tin back to remove my tub and retile the bathroom in December.

We were very pleased with the look and feel of the tile. It was a big improvement over worn and dirty carpet.

The ingrown right little toenail that gave me so much trouble in 2008, was pulled out by a podiatrist, but grew back and continued to give me trouble, although not as much as before. Beh taped the toenail down every day and shaped its direction of growth. Aside from some spasming, itching, and general irritation from sitting in the same place all day long, I was relatively comfortable. The one thing that I began to notice after all those years of interrupted sleep was finding myself dozing whenever I ate something or tried to read or get some work done on the computer in the afternoon.

The more things changed at work, the more they stayed the same. I finally finished combining all my data into one powerful database for facilities that enabled me to do five major reports annually and keep up with a lot of data on campus that was continually needed for purposes ranging from promotion to proposals, to budgeting, to financial reporting. The students that Tim had hired, worked a year and did a good job, but they were sidetracked so much they weren't anywhere near putting my system on the Internet. It would have been much simpler for Tim to provide me with the resources necessary and everyone would have been much happier. However, that wasn't the way things are done TSU. I was becoming more to blame.

Tim fell into the trap of piece-mealing projects instead of looking at the whole campus and system. As a result, we retained a lot of original deferred maintenance that continued to grow and very few things were getting done—they were just being patched to meet the immediate demands of the administration. Just before the Christmas holidays 2009, I worked on a proposal to get a 2% loan from the federal stimulus money to try to upgrade and improve our energy efficiency with retrofitting and other projects. Our needs were too big to be trying to replace one light bulb at a time. Tim's idea to put emergency generators at the buildings and running them at off-hours probably would end up costing us more money and contributing more pollution than we would want to. It was obvious that with Rudley as president, politics and accounting would determine every project, not good engineering sense. Emphasis was on meeting regulations, not on saving energy or reducing the amount of pollution that heating and cooling the campus caused.

The Rudley administration also brought in friends and relatives that didn't know how a university runs and I found we were repeating some of the same mistakes that were made in the past about how to make things work. For example, John Rudley resurrected the Urban Village idea of former president Douglas and asked him to spearhead the project as executive vice president. This move was an obvious payback for Douglas's part in returning Rudley to campus. Instead of following the existing contract where the new student apartments were leased out to private parties for 30 years, the university used state money to "buy back" those loans and force students to live in the apartments at very high rates so they would, "Stay on campus." The university also acquired the boondoggle parking garages that were so costly that the loan could not be paid back by operation of the garages, alone. Something that I pointed out long before the garages were ever conceived under Fannie Mae loans.

A 3% increase in enrollment was not enough to offset anything except to say that we were growing again.

I still had some autonomy to do what was necessary, provide good data and make accurate reports. However, the liberal working hours that were given to me as an accommodation to help offset my disability were changed by Tim so that I had to work on campus more than 40 hours a week in order to leave work at 4:30 pm and get ahead of traffic three days a week. I was forced to have my helpers get me up much earlier so that I could get to work before 8 am. Apparently, others were jealous of my ability to come and go as I pleased, something I actually always enjoyed as a professional exempt employee. My salary hadn't increased with others on campus. I learned that my status had slipped into a pay scale with hourly, not exempt, employees—and, in some ways was being treated as such, even with all my degrees, experience, and certifications. Texas employment laws are quite regressive, allowing for "at will employment." Basically, what that means is that any employee is always subject to demotion or firing regardless of their status at the whim of an owner or supervisor. While many had won lawsuits against TSU, my superiors would have had to do something particularly a grievous for me to win a lawsuit.

I asked to have my case reopened with the EEOC under the Lilly Ledbetter Act. After some deliberation, it was determined that all the delays in due process at the university had exceeded the statute of limitations. I was given the right to sue although the EEOC did not take action against the university. When I attempted to contact lawyers about my case, they all told me that they couldn't take the case because of the statute of limitations. By giving the administration enough time to respond to my grievances, they had effectively stonewalled long enough until they were not liable.

In 2009, I finished re-editing the second edition of **Alone?** I didn't change much except to remove all the errors left by Tony Endem and Bookbooters and make the book available again. There were a few areas where I had to update information from 2001, but, for the most part, the story remained as it was. I finished the year 2009 by putting together a book of my short stories. After looking at that, I had to write a few more stories before the book would be long enough to publish.

I entered a poetry contest with the Sacramento Poetry Society in the spring of 2009, but never heard if I even got an honorable mention. In the fall, I entered a short story contest with the Mississippi Review. Hopefully, one of my short stories would catch their eye. They didn't, and I received a huge paperback with the winners in it. My poem, *Mesa Verde*, was selected by the Educational Testing Service to be used *in perpetuity* for their testing workbook going to over 500,000 students every year. They paid me $1800. I believe that is the most I will ever get for a poem. My poem, *Autumn Light*, was selected by Elizabeth Kaz as text for a book of paintings and photography to be published in the spring of 2010 by Evergreen press. Some students emailed me and told me they were going to use my short story, *Hit and Run*, in a movie, but I never heard back from them. My poem, *Alienation*, was searched over 7000 times on AuthorsDen.com by the end of 2009 and was being used in high school classes in Australia.

Beh, Ron, and Rose at Forth Worth Arboretum.  August 2009

With my niece, Tracy Hull, associate dean of Texas Christian University
Library at the Fort Worth Arboretum. August 2009

Enjoying the many trails and sights of the Arboretum

# 80

# Recession Depression

The year 2010 saw a continuation of the recession that could only be expected when so much money sat in savings accounts and safe investments rather than being spent on moving the country and the world forward. While banks had an unlimited source of "free" money to lend, they were very unwilling to lend it to small businesses that would create new technology and American jobs. Scientists taking the pulse of the environment and life on the planet were alarmed, but political action and human will were slow to respond. Still, I remained optimistic that we would see the light and move quickly to a hydrogen economy and find ways to save human life and all other life at the same time. All we had to do was compare our time to the Great Depression and we would see *no comparison*, worldwide. There was no comparison between the suffering of that time and the relative abundance, yet financial stress, of ours. Yet, the threat of a Third World War dimmed in the face of the task ahead to make our world whole again.

Judy and Paul drilled a well and finally saw their pond fill with water. The area had undergone drought conditions for a couple of years and there wasn't enough rain for the pond to fill. They lost their year-old Great Dane, Toby, early in the summer after strenuous play and eating grass. Toby twisted his intestines, bloated, and had to be put to sleep. By August, the Woltmann's had found Liberty and Copper. They were brother and sister Great Danes and inseparable.

Beh's business continued to grow, probably because of other businesses' failure. The high point of 2010 for Beh was December 15, when she finally, after 18 years in the United States, earned her citizenship. I got her an iPad for her birthday and she really loved it. All these gadgets and her cell phone made her life more complicated than ever. She got the intuitive part very well, but still had trouble with the working computer part. Didn't know how to downloaded an app and didn't know why she might need to download one. But it was easy for her to find Vietnamese music, movies, and news; she really liked that.

We didn't travel in 2010; primarily, because Beh was working so much. Finally, I talked her into a trip to San Antonio. Diann had just been released from prison, so we took her along. We had a great time at the Natural Bridge Cavern and African Safari nearby. We found many butterflies attracted to flowers planted for them just outside the Cavern. While feeding the animals on the Safari, we ran into an overeager zebra that almost bit Diann. As we left the African Safari, we lost air conditioning. Everyone's mood turned bad in the heat, and it looked like we would be suffering until we got back to Houston. However, after a three-hour repair just up the road at a Ford dealer on I-35, we were on our way again. Beh was pretty upset that my van seemed to want to ruin our trips. She was used to her Corolla running like clockwork. I had to tell her that repairs on the road were just part of travel. She didn't buy it; making it harder for me to persuader her to travel more. We stayed at the historic Emily Baker Hotel overlooking the Alamo—a beautiful place close to everything downtown. We spent some time at the Riverwalk enjoying the food and music. We also got out to Sea World and took in all that was offered. It was strange not to see the trainers riding the Orca anymore. That practice had been outlawed after the accident in 2009 where a trainer was drowned. I noticed that all of the Orca had droopy dorsal fins. I could only take that as a sign of inadequate diet or exercise from being captive. Orca in the wild never have droopy dorsal fins. They probably wouldn't survive in the wild if they were that weak.

And then, Beh broke loose and told me that she wanted to have her family meet us in Corpus Christi over Labor Day. We stayed in the Holiday Inn on Emerald Bay and took in the yacht club with its fine restaurant, Landry's, great music at the hotel, the aquarium, and the aircraft carrier Lexington once again. The original Whataburger was always a great place for breakfast. I bought a painting entitled *Sunrise on Emerald Bay*. My small art collection was growing again.

My continually growing paralysis, my nemesis, for the first time, found my left hand creeping out of the control of the gas-brake function on my Freestar. For a temporary fix we modified the tri-pin, but there may be much more to do for me to continue to drive in the future. I also began having trouble picking up things with my left hand, like my fork, relying more and more on my helpers to feed me. This was all very disconcerting, but necessary, as I adjusted to the changes.

After having several faults in my van's computer system in January, 2010, I was required by EMC to send my steering and gas-brake units in for "routine" maintenance. EMC found nothing wrong with the units but I was charged $2000 anyway. That's when my trouble with the gas-brake unit started. In November 2010, I left work as usual, except that the van would not accelerate on Blodgett Street, only idle. I made a U-turn and idled back to the parking lot and had the car towed home that night. After much delay and consultation with EMC, Mobility Plus determined that a safety device, a clutch, designed to prevent accelerator sticking, the same thing that occurred with my Windstar and caused my wreck, had tripped again. I had to have the van towed to Mobility Plus. A week and a half and $900 later, the safety device was back in place and I was on my way again.

Two days before my Christmas holiday, I was about to leave for work from home and the throttle safety clutch went out again. This time, Mobility Plus had to remove the unit and send it back to EMC before Christmas. The system was back from EMC just after Christmas. They got everything back together for me to go back to work on January 3, 2011.

I bought MacSpeech Dictate 2.02. Dictate was, by far, the easiest and best dictation system I had used so far. However, it took some getting used to. I also upgraded to Dragon NaturallySpeaking 11 at work. Not only did this version have the great features of 10, but it also was very fast and had sidebars that could help with dictation and correction. I continued to recommend DNS 11 for everyone, especially those with carpal tunnel syndrome, those who had never learned to type with all their fingers, or had trouble spelling correctly, like me.

Things remained the same at work. I continued to postpone my retirement because I didn't have enough retirement savings to pay people to take care of me if I lived a long life. Our budget was cut 10% for the two fiscal years 2010-11. However, there was always enough money to add staff even when there was a hiring freeze. And then, I heard that there might be a 25% cut in fiscal year 2012. The president and some politicians on campus claimed that we could save money on energy conservation (something I'd been trying to get the administration to do without success for many years) to pay for the cuts. I pointed out to them that our current energy consumption was just 3.7% of TSU's expenditures. It was impossible for us to cover our expenses with energy savings estimated to be less than 10% of energy expenditures. Still, it would be a good idea to do the energy measures if we could save $370,000 per year, reduce maintenance, and reduce emissions. I never heard after that, but I believe those in the administration and on the board who touted energy savings did not like my poking their political balloons. Those that make illogically formed proposals and get shot down by the facts are quick to come up with ways to circumvent the problem. I expected we would engage in another costly energy conservation effort again, and I would not be included in the process.

The very real problem was that we had, and continued to have, too many staff that did nothing and gave the school a bad reputation. My boss, Tim, was a very practical guy who put out fires continually but didn't appear to be a strategist—just a good soldier carrying out whatever the administration asked for as quickly as possible, regardless of funding. So, they hired an unnecessary assistant vice president who had been fired from the University of Houston to do that job—strategy. All the new man did—I forgot his name—was attack my ability to do my job. Tim wanted my work to migrate to the Internet. My database was very close to being Internet ready, but it already had a very fine client/server component that would do very well for what we needed a database for on our internal network without going to the Internet. Instead of discussing the problem with me, students were told to do the job the way Tim wanted it without working closely with me. As a result, the work wasn't getting done and the students were confused. I was partly to blame, because I missed some key meetings with the computer science faculty who recommended the students, and I was unable to lay out my plan for working with them to Tim. Soon after his second year students arrived, Tim had them reporting to an administrative assistant for their time and pay and to Robert as their liaison with me. It didn't work, and Tim took over dictating to them what work to do. He got very concerned about room utilization and missed the point of the facilities inventory and the broader aspect of my database. While the students admired my work, they weren't allowed to work closely with me, only to work on a way of determining room utilization at the expense of proper coding and all other facilities inventory information.

To kick off the fall term, president Rudley ordered Tim and the physical plant to "clean up the campus" and make all the buildings presentable for the incoming students over the Labor Day weekend. One of Rudley's concerns was the murals that adorned both walls on the east side entrance to Hannah Hall. This entrance had little use off of the plaza in front of the auditorium until one of Dr. Slade's beautification projects built an exclusive circle drive and parking area off Cleburne Avenue on the north side of Hannah Hall for the administration, board members, and other important people to use. Instead of the west side entrances that had traditionally been used, these important people now entered the building on the east side, including the president. Rudley found the murals to be dark and inappropriate for the visitors he saw using the entrance and ordered Tim to have them painted over in white to lighten up the entrance and remove what he considered to be, "Not art."

The murals in Hannah Hall and in some of the other buildings, were painted by the best students of John Biggers, a noted black artist who, until he retired to paint to paint more, was head of the art department at TSU. The murals were a tradition on campus stretching back to the 1950s when Biggers first started granting his best students the opportunity to help decorate the campus. Many of the murals depicted African or African-American history and some had very dark and disturbing sides. My stepdaughter found the paintings so when she visited Hannah Hall in 1982. Still, they were a priceless heritage for the campus and many on campus, including the art department and museum, were trying to come up with ways to restore and preserve the murals damaged by previous renovations, humidity, and age. The two murals painted over, *Mothers of Father and Son*, by Harvey Johnson and, *Han Writin on de Wall*, by another artist in 1969, were both part of John Bigger's legacy and a sign of the times. Harvey Johnson painted in Bigger's style and was a retired TSU art faculty member.

When the staff and faculty came back from the Labor Day weekend, they were surprised to find the murals gone. Rumors traveled fast, and I heard about it in our staff meeting. I was moved to write a poem that I entitled, *Desecrate*. Later that fall during Poetry Day, I read the poem before a small audience using a PowerPoint presentation showing one of the murals being gradually painted over. President Rudley's wife, Docia, a law professor, was present in the audience. Rudley went on television and stated that he had done no wrong. Later, however, under pressure, he set up a fund for helping to restore murals throughout the campus. What I did by writing the poem and reading it publicly on campus did not endear me to him, but Rudley's behavior toward me, in spite of my reaching out to him when he first arrived, had since then been cold and demeaning. I learned that it was part of his personality to act that way, but I suspected that he had heard some of the rumors and lies about me from people as close as former president Douglas because I had criticized the urban village idea as being unworkable because it "forced" students to stay on campus paying high rents and fees.

I didn't want to leave the University with a mess when I retired, but that appeared to be what was going to happen. If that did happen, I would make sure to offer my services as a consultant so that the transition would happen without too much trauma and expense. For example, sometime around 2000, all records regarding real estate were to be maintained by the general counsel. Prior to that, the university comptroller had kept the original deeds to all land in a bank safety deposit box with copies in a well-organized file. During all the reorganizations and firing of individuals that took place, especially after the office of General Counsel changed hands more than once, state auditors who came in during the transitional government could not find any land records and were very upset. Finally, a former general counsel learned of the problem and came to me. I provide her with the complete record of all of the University land that I had at that time. There was very little transition when people left office, and the incoming officer often discarded important records. The university spent an inordinate amount of time and money retrieving or reconstructing information that had been poorly maintained or thrown out by those who did not know its value. That's why I kept all the information I did long after it was not my responsibility. I tried to keep myself available if any of my information was needed in the future.

I spent the good part of the summer of 2010 editing a book about the Civil War exploits of the ancestor of a friend, Johnny Jackson. Johnny's great grandfather, Ben Drake, was a farmer in Ohio who served with the Union Army from 1863 to Appomattox. Johnny had done over 10 years of research locating details of Drake's service and the battles that he was in as a cavalryman. Editing the book was tedious, but rewarding work. Johnny was very pleased with the result.

That work set me back on the short story book I was trying to finish. Over the 2010 Christmas holidays, I wrote two short stories to add to the book. Other than not having enough time to write, the work was going well. I thought that perhaps I wouldn't have as much time in retirement as I hoped because I'd planned to volunteer and would have many projects other than writing to engage in.

In August 2010, Beh and I took a big step and joined with May Cole in a business transaction where we provided capital for the purchase and renovation of an exclusive elderly care facility in the neighborhood. If the project succeeded, and there was every reason to believe it would, we planned to engage in a smaller project for ourselves, eventually leading to the home on Lake Houston that I had long planned to build.

"Emperor and Empress" painting bought from near blind Yonah

583

"Sunrise on Emerald Bay" bought in Corpus Christi. Sept 2010

With artist, Maya Iman Watson and the 2011 Honors painting of the arts
honorees I bid on and won for TSU fundraising. May 2011

# 81

# Drought, Grand Reunion and I Am Out

The year 2011 was an interesting, if not hopeful, year with a glimmer of hope for the economy, our troops coming home from Iraq, Osama bin Laden dealt with, and disasters, large and small, but not too great, to deal with. Texas was marred by drought. Enough of Texas, 2%, was burned, to cover an area the size of Delaware and Rhode Island combined. To top that, the state lost fifty million trees, mostly loblolly pines. Although we had a few rain showers in December, the drought wasn't over and the long-range forecast was for the same weather pattern to continue.

Mom had three mini strokes. The first affected her hands and fingers, and the second, one eye. She recovered from them both quite quickly. However the third, in August, affected her speech and writing, a condition called aphasia, and it was taking a long time for her to recover. Clots thrown out by her heart from poor control by a blood thinner caused the strokes. Hopefully, that was corrected by changing her blood thinner and she would have no more mini strokes. Mom struggled with her hearing, too, and we hoped to find a solution for that. She still lived alone in her apartment and managed an active life, still driving occasionally to Withee and other places. By the end of the year, she announced that she would no longer be driving that far anymore.

Roger and Sue settled into retirement, staying in Florida from after Christmas until March, spending January and February in the Keys and with relatives and friends on the peninsula after. Rocky, their golden

585

retriever, enjoyed going along, running along the beach, swimming, and chasing birds. Roger traded his 2003 Mercedes E320 for a 2004 XJ8 Jaguar and loved it. His golf game was still occasionally quite good. Sue spent her time with charitable events and her favorite pastime, walking. Roger preferred his golf and a bicycle for exercise. Roger had a pontoon boat moored in back of their Bristol, Indiana house on the St. Joseph River. The boat was often on the river with friends and relatives aboard. While most of the banks were fully developed, ducks, swans and geese had returned and were plentiful everywhere. The big event of every year was to decorate the pontoon boat and dress up for the Fourth of July regatta.

All my nieces and nephews were either finishing school or had already graduated and were entering jobs in a very poor job market. I was pleased to see them working in medical fields, maintenance, conservation and eco-friendly work.

Beh was busier than ever in her shop. A man that she had hired for a long time to help her in the morning from 7 am to 10 am, died suddenly of a heart attack. Fortunately, the brother of our business partner, May, stepped in and was a big help. In the fall, Beh got on a garden kick and transformed my backyard by building a trellis and growing a garden. We harvested fifteen tomatoes and about five meals of radishes. We still had snow peas, onions, and Chinese cabbage to harvest before she would start her spring garden.

Thanks to Beh's cooperation, we were able to take a couple of good, long trips in 2011. Before those trips, Beh and I were able to travel to the annual Centers for Independent Living Conference in Austin in April 2011. Besides staying in a fine hotel, I made some contacts with people in the disability community and shared ideas. A large colorful painting by a nearly blind artist caught my eye. The sunflower painting on Masonite hangs directly over the head of my bed, brightening up the room.

Beh told me she wanted to go to the Bahamas because she had heard that others had been there. I received a promotional offer from the city of Palm Beach for some free hotel stays in Orlando, and Fort Lauderdale for taking time to view a timeshare presentation like I had done with Jeanie back in 1989. As a result, I told Beh not to expect much. Fortunately, Diane Crouch (formerly Diann Massingill), who had taken several trips with us before, was available and agreed to accompany me to Florida. It was a rough, two-day drive, but after we checked into a rather mediocre Ramada hotel as part of our free hotel accommodations, we were able to spend the day at Epcot Center where Diane got to try a Segway and we listened to an authentic Beatles band and some colonial Americana singers. Searching for an evening meal, we shared a turkey leg.

The next day, we picked up Beh at the Orlando airport and were able to take in a wonderful airboat ride on a large lake near Kissimmee. Instead of going on a group boat, the crew carried me on to a small boat that was still very fast. Our guide had trouble finding any alligators of any substance, but he did show us a bald eagle nest with baby eagles in it. We saw lots of other birds and came up close to a nest with a sandhill crane sitting on eggs. The ride was fast, and rough, but I enjoyed every minute of it.

The next day, we all went to Animal Kingdom. The high point of that excursion was a front row seat at a performance of the Lion King. Our trip through the African Safari was not as eventful as the one on the ranch near San Antonio. I was disappointed when I wasn't allowed to ride the wild river excursion. That ride could have easily been made accessible for wheelchairs. We got wonderful videos of all of the Disney attractions we saw, and I put them on my website for everyone to see.

The timeshare presentation was quite attractive, and I contemplated for a moment buying a timeshare for Beh and her family to use in Orlando. Before we were to board the cruise ship to the Bahamas, I took the girls to the state park at Palm Beach. There was a boardwalk to the beach and a large wheeled sand buggy that the lifeguards pushed me out on the beach with. They left me in a nice spot, facing the sun and wind, near other people sunbathing, and left. Beh and Diane wandered off looking for seashells. The stress of driving with my gas/brake unit binding and having to deal with heavy truck traffic on I-10 and I-75 had caused a severe case of seborrhea. I had the itchy skin condition most of the time anyway, but this was *bad*. After sitting in the wind and sun for about 10 minutes, the lesions on my face begin to burn. I called out for Beh and Diane, but they had wandered far away and couldn't hear me. Fortunately, a couple was sunbathing near me and came to my rescue. The guy turned the sand buggy around so that my back was to the sun and wind, and the burning subsided. It started to get late, and I was afraid we would miss our 12 noon check-in time on the cruise ship. When Beh and Diane finally came back, I rushed them to get us back to the van. It was only 15 minutes to the ship, so we made it on time and were very quickly up to the check-in point. There was no disabled parking, but I was assured that someone wouldn't park me in so my ramp wouldn't open when we got back the next day.

When I first contacted Diane about going on the cruise, she had lost her birth certificate. I made a special trip to Liberty Texas with her, so that Diane could get a copy of her replacement birth certificate. When asked, we gave the Homeland Security people our documents. Beh's citizenship certificate was with her brother so that she could get a new driver's license. I had made a color copy of the certificate that looked as good as the original. I had my original birth certificates from the hospital, with footprints, and from the county I was born in. Both of us were denied. Previously, my documents had been acceptable for three cruises and Beh had always traveled with her green card, turned in when she got her citizenship. Diane's birth certificate was acceptable, *but we couldn't go!* Beh was very disappointed to say the least. The hospitality people from Palm Beach put us up in a very fine hotel in Fort Lauderdale, a much better experience than in 1989, but that didn't help much. We arranged for Beh to fly home a day early, but it cost her a large fee for changing her schedule.

The next day, Diane and I drove south through Miami and across Alligator Alley to Naples and then north to Tampa for the night. Late in the day, we stopped at my cousin, Sandy's, home for dinner. I really missed being able to stay in people's homes, but at least I was still able to travel; although finding suitable roll-in showers was often difficult. Our trip back was uneventful.

I had been thinking about my high school reunion ever since I missed the 40th in 2001. I wrote a letter to my classmates expressing my regrets that time, but I'm not sure if the letter was read. The only thing I knew was what my twin brother, Roger, who had attended, told me, and the poor pictures I received. Fortunately, the 50th reunion wasn't set until September 10, 2011. After some persuasion, Beh agreed to go if we would take someone else along. Diane had obtained a job taking care of an elderly man in a nursing home, so she was unable to join us. I called Tommie McNeil, the man we had met on the earlier Caribbean cruise who was taking care of his friend in a wheelchair. Tommie was excited and more than willing to go with us. We left on September 4th, just as tropical storm Lee was moving into Louisiana.

As we drove northeast on US 59, the brown and dried out landscape showed the character of the severe drought all of Texas was in. As I fought the severe crosswinds from Lee, I noted that we came across several places where fires had burned up to the highway, but fortunately, had not crossed. By the time we got to Marshall, Texas, Beh was asleep and Tommie was texting as I drove through town. I came upon a house on the left with a brown lawn like every other lawn in town, dried out in the sun. On the vacant lot next door, a fire was burning rapidly in the grass toward the street. I didn't see anyone around, and the way the wind was gusting the situation could get worse very rapidly. We were late and I wasn't in any position to stop the van and go around and find someone to put the fire out. The highway was busy and, hopefully, someone saw the fire like me and reported it or had a fire extinguisher and put it out..

I pushed on to Memphis and it got very late, into night with heavy wind and rain. I missed our hotel exit and had to back track, but finally settled in for the night. The next day, I made the wrong decision and drove to uncle Bruce Hull's via I-40 to Nashville rather than taking US 51 north of Memphis to the Western Kentucky Parkway, a *faster* route. On the way to Nashville, we were buffeted by winds from Lee and occasional rain. But worse, was the "wall" presented by the van's load and the wind in overdrive trying to make the mountains; sometimes, only reaching the summit at 40 mph and then speeding up down the backside to reach 70 mph again. I was glad to get off I-65 and take a long drive on Kentucky 259 to Bruce's homestead—*my downfall.*

I had turn-by-turn directions from MapQuest, but failed to have Tommie take them out and follow them. I turned south, thinking the highway to the right would lead down to uncle Bruce's way too soon, and soon found us in an unfamiliar churchyard. Retracing our steps, we saw a flock of hen turkeys in a yard and stopped to ask directions at a country store. Tommie went in alone and was told to go "straight-ahead for 4 miles before turning." About 2 miles down the road, 259 turned north. I stopped momentarily, but made the mistake of staying on 259 headed north. Before long, we were at the Parkway and 20 miles from Bruce's place! Because I was so stressed from driving in the wind and mountains all day, and it was getting late, I made a horrible decision to go on to Louisville. I called Bruce and apologized but it wasn't enough. That was two times I had missed seeing him and his family in four years.

We got to our hotel in Clarksville, Indiana about 7 pm. We called Behram and Gool Randelia and they took us to the King Fish restaurant on the Ohio River across from Louisville in New Albany. We had great seafood far from the sea, pleasant conversation, and a relaxing end to our stressful day.

We arrived at my niece, Kelley's about noon the next day and both Jeff and Kelley greeted us. Hayley, 17, arrived from school shortly after and Kelley fixed lunch. Soon, Amedee came home from school and Hayley got in her Mercedes and drove back to high school. I tried to straighten out their iMac while Beh and Tommie toured the pool and grounds. Beh was especially impressed with the fence that Jeff made with apple trees by directing the growth of their branches.

We headed for Xenia and arrived in town about 5 pm. We couldn't raise either Bill or my cousin, Debbie, on the phone, so decided to stop at an auto parts store for wiper blades. While driving over to the store, my "low brake fluid" indicator came on. I replaced the windshield **wiper blades** and a store clerk added fluid to my brake master cylinder.

We finally got Bill on the phone and he directed us to their five-acre country estate. Their son, Chris's wife and children were there, but I didn't get to talk to them. Bill had made a long ramp to get me up on their high rear deck and into the house. Debbie made us a wonderful casserole dinner and we talked until it was time to get to the hotel... very late. Just before we left, Bill took a look under the left front wheel and said it was leaking brake fluid. I took note of that and drove us to our distant hotel. The hotel had no roll in shower, so they gave Tommie an extra room and I showered on the toilet and shampooed in the sink.

The next morning, we arrived at Roger and Sue's a little after noon. It was cold and windy and we spent some time trying to figure out how to get my wheelchair into the house. Then we took a look at the cars and Roger showed us how Sue's Volkswagen EOS's cool convertible hardtop operated. We had lunch in the garage, and later, drove over to the Elkhart Arboretum for a cool and windy, but wonderful, walk through the fauna and flora.

Our hotel, a Staybridge Inn, offered free dinner with drinks and breakfast, and a split room (suite) with spacious roll in shower for $95—the least expensive hotel room of the trip. I think they were catering to the Notre Dame football crowd just before football season started. We had free drinks and dinner at Roger and Sue's anyway, so we didn't partake in the freebies.

**The next morning** when I started the car, I got the "brake fluid low" indicator again, so I decided to go to the Ford dealer in Elkhart. Ziegler Ford had angle parking in their service staging area. After requesting brake service, I got back in the van to drive it to the shop for service. When I backed up, the van lurched backward. When I tried to stop, the brakes failed and I ran into a concrete block wall at an angle about 10 mph! Fortunately, there was a tire advertising design on the wall and I hit one tire directly in the center! They popped my plastic bumper out and the rest of the damage was minor—mostly scuff marks and a cracked back up light lens.

Within an hour mechanics found that the front stabilizer bar on the driver's side had worn through the brake line. I contacted Vantage Mobility and they informed me that there had been a recall for the problem in 2008, two years after I bought the van. Ziegler Ford continued to do the repair and finally called me in to check the brakes out because after bleeding the brakes, the computer still told them that the brakes needed further servicing.

We left at 3 pm and arrived at downtown Chicago at 4:45 pm, just in time to be caught in rush-hour traffic. Tommie had to find a restroom and I wasn't sure I could find one in all that traffic. Suddenly, the Des Plaines Oasis appeared in the middle of the freeway and the day was saved! Now I understand why they call these rest stops, *oases*. We did manage to get to the hotel at DeForest Wisconsin about 8:30 pm and over to Tim's for a little while—meeting Stacy, two of her sons, and looking over her Mercedes 450 SL and Tim's TR-6 before retiring—very tired.

The next morning, we had breakfast with friends, stopped at my brother Tim's for an hour or so, where Tom came by. After that we had lunch with relatives, Jackie and Albert Replogle, near Wisconsin Dells. As a result, we got into Marshfield rather late and our hotel had not given me a roll in shower. After some discussion, a room with a roll in shower was found, and we had to switch rooms. Mom had been waiting since noon. When we got there at 5:30 pm, she was quite upset from all the anticipation. I hadn't seen mom in four years. We took her to the World Buffet in the local mall for Chinese food before returning to the hotel.

**My brother,** Roger and Sue treated Mom and us to breakfast. By the time we got back to Mom's place, my sister Judy and her husband Paul joined us. Soon after that, my brother, Tom and his daughter, Angie, arrived with Mom's great-granddaughter Alba. Soon after that, Judy's son, Matt, and Becky arrived with great grandkids Kora and Monty. It was a house full and Mom had some trouble communicating because of her hearing and trouble speaking because of her aphasia. Still it was a great day for her to have me there with all of my brothers and sisters except Tim after so many years.

That evening, Roger and I attended our 50th high school reunion. It was at a local Elks club where there was a wedding going on, so the bar was inaccessible for my wheelchair and the room we were using was quite cramped and crowded with tables so it was hard to get around. The program was very brief and the meal was very good. Afterward I got reacquainted with a few of my classmates after not seeing them for 30 years. I sold some books and enjoyed the brief time I had with the few that I talked to because of the cramped quarters.

In spite of her objection at first, we picked up Mom early the next morning and drove to Thorp where uncle Don Marshall had an assisted living apartment. We caught him at lunch, but he greeted us with, "*Ron, what in the heck are you doing here!*" In spite of very poor vision, he could still read with the help of a special magnifying device and hear with a hearing aid that overcame his frequency problem. At 99 and nine months, he still lit up when he talked about things he enjoyed. Don still cooked and took care of himself with a little help from the apartment staff. When we went to leave, he jumped up from his chair and joined us at the van, marveling at how I could drive with my high tech controls.

We arrived at uncle Ed, 92, and Marian, 86, Hull's and were pleased to see that their adopted son, Jeff, was there helping them out. Both of them seemed to be in good health and spirit. Ed drove everywhere in his new crossover and Marian still preferred her Lincoln Town Car. Ed, a World War II and Korea veteran of the Army Air Corps, emailed me almost daily. His favorite subjects were forwarding me views of the military and of his love—airplanes.

When we arrived at my cousin, Keith Marshall's RC Park, we were surprised to find that his brother, Wes, was there. Wesley was still working for Liberty Homes and worked for Keith as a maintenance man on weekends and when temporarily laid off. The crowd was racing radio controlled cars on a very rough motocross course. Wes, 68, explained that he had just measured the short takeoff run of an ultralight plane that had landed earlier and already left. Keith, 70, had just bought a light plane and told us that he was learning how to fly. If Keith lived as long as his dad, he would be able to fly for another 30 years. We bought a hot dog at the concession stand from Keith's wife, Sandi, and headed on up to the house where she joined us.

Mom and I waited by the car while Beh and Tommie toured the assisted living facility where Sandi cares for five people. And then they toured the little cabin in the trees, filled with antiques that Keith and Sandi use for a retreat. After that, Beh and Tommie enjoyed the chickens and goats that Sandi raises.

We dropped Mom off and, after stopping at the hotel, Beh treated us to a dinner in a fine restaurant. The Sunrise Family Restaurant was the only restaurant on the south side of Marshfield, so we stopped. They had a Sunday buffet, apparently geared to seniors with low prices. The food matched. Tommie had to return his roast pork dinner. The gravy alone was enough to make you gag. I struggled through my chopped steak and couldn't figure out why they used old surplus canned corn when there was so much fresh corn around in season. We had to admit that the salad bar was good. We arrived at Judy and Paul's in the evening to the loud barking of Cooper and Liberty, their Great Danes. Beh and Tommie surveyed the grounds and the pond, while I navigated up to the deck. Andy and his fiancée, Tanya and Judy's little granddaughter, Brooklyn, soon joined us. We chatted while Tanya trained Cooper in the yard.

After breakfast, we stopped off to see Mom one last time. She hated to see us go, knowing that it may be the last time she would ever see me again. We stopped to see my cousin, Lilian, and Shorty (Lawrence) and talked from the car. By that time it was quite late. When we stopped in Neillsville to get gas, a guy came up to the car and talked to me like an old friend. Unfortunately, although I asked his name, it was unfamiliar and I forgot it.

We arrived at Aunt Eleanor's quite late. She and my cousin, Janice Becker, had been waiting for at least three hours and had cheese and sausage for us to eat. Unfortunately, we had too little time there because of our late start in the morning.

Continuing to be late, we arrived in Menominee and UW Stout, my alma mater, about 12:30 pm. Lunch was waiting, so we joined everyone at the lunch table, a beautiful, turn-of-the-19th century inlaid masterpiece that I felt like a rich man sitting at the head of. Sue Pittman, executive director of the Stout Foundation, had invited me to the luncheon with friends. Jeanette Rudiger, foundation director, joined along with my friends and former colleagues, Drs. Lee Smalley, Zenon Smolarek, and Harold Halfin. We discussed old times and had a presentation about the Discovery Center by its director, Robert Daulke. I had set aside and assistantship fund for the center.

Back on the road, we stopped at a Country Inn for the night in Owatonna Minnesota. Tommie was complaining about breathing problems but relaxed after taking a dip in the warm spa. At the same time, Beh enjoyed a swim in the pool. Tommie didn't sleep well at night.

After a long day of driving, we pressed on to make Fort Smith. We looked for tornado damage as we passed Joplin, Missouri on US 281, but didn't see any. Finally, we stopped short, about 60 miles, at Bentonville.

We were very fortunate to find a private hotel called the Simmons Suites. Our room was spacious for wheelchair access and the whole place was beautifully done. Across the road was a restaurant, The Grille, where Beh treated us to an expensive, but elegant dinner. Tommie and I ordered bison tenderloin that was some of the best steak I have ever eaten. It was like filet mignon with a much richer taste. The loaf of bread reminded me of mom 's bread.

The long drive home was uneventful except for a 3 or 4 mile stretch of US 59 south of Atlanta, Texas, that had been burned on the right side. Fortunately, the fire had not crossed 59. I drove past that spot in Marshall too fast to see what had burned, but that fire must have either burned out when it reached the street or been put out, because I didn't see anything.

After fighting a small headwind coming into Houston that was tiring, we arrived too late for Tommie to catch the bus to Galveston. We dropped him off at a place he could stay near the station that night. Later, he got a ride back to Galveston and entered the hospital the next day. Tommie had pneumonia, spent a week in the hospital, but returned home, and recovered.

My writing became an all-consuming quest to do better with each piece I wrote. It was a challenge to write a poem a week, but I willingly took it on to post the poems on both my website and authorsden.com. One of my poems, *Alienation*, was viewed on Authors Den over 20,000 times. Other poems, like *Relaxing*, and *Roaring 20s*, became very popular searches from all over the world on my website. I liked to write the short stories with a twist, or at least, a good ending. I put together a book of 14 of my short stories. **It's in the Water and Other Stories** was published in August 2011. While many readers told me that the stories were very good, the book did not sell well. It may well be because most people could read the stories on Authors Den without having to buy the book.

On August 26, 27 and 28, 2011, I was invited by VSA Texas to sell my books alongside other disabled artists at the Abilities Expo at the Reliant Center in Houston. The show was a very good way for people with disabilities to find products and services they might need. I didn't sell very many books, but I met a lot of people and bought some fine art. Speaking of art, TSU honored faculty and the arts at the Wortham Center in May. While the spectacular, Broadway style, show was going on, a woman was painting an acrylic of the event on the right side of the stage. Later, the painting was auctioned off on eBay. I submitted the highest bid and got the painting . I met the artist, Maya Imani Watson, and had my picture taken with her. My plan was to give the painting back to the TSU university museum in a few years.

I hoped to get back to my trilogy, **American Mole**, the second book in the series that I decided to title, **American Mole: The Cartel.** I initially was going to call it **MS-13**, but after the retaliation MS-13 inflicted on one of my former students, Maria Fernandez, and her husband, I decided not to direct my novel specifically at that gang, but to the whole idea of undermining the United States through the use of drugs.

My software and hardware continued to be a challenge. My trustworthy old eMac kept timing out in the heat during the summer, so I went to Goodwill and bought a G4 with a 20 inch Philips flat panel LED monitor for $180. After that I found out that the machine had only a 160 GB drive just like the eMac, making its hard drive space too limited for keeping my movies. I made a mistake and upgraded from Snow Leopard to the Lion operating system on the iMac as soon as Apple offered it . After I bought Lion, I immediately lost Office 2004. Not only that, but Dragon Dictate began acting up and so did VMware Fusion. I had to upgrade all of those and buy iWork so that I could work with the Office documents I had created in Word, Excel, PowerPoint, and Entourage. Change never ends. Sometimes it can be a real pain in the ass to deal with.

After thirty years, I finally decided that it was time to stop fighting windmills trying to improve operations at Texas Southern University. Three years before, Tim Rychlec had told me that he didn't want me to retire for three years while he developed a Internet based database for the information I collected. Unfortunately, the students he selected to work on the project reported to him and not to me. In the end, he undermined what I was trying to do instead of allowing me to transition what I was doing to the Internet and to an understudy. In April 2011, Tim moved my only assistant, Robert, and me to the old paint shop next to the main shop on the ground floor, declaring that he had given me better access and a larger office. I had some access problems that were never resolved, but I didn't push them because I had applied for retirement with human resources in May without informing Tim. On July 29, thirty-one days before I was due to officially retire, Tim locked Robert and me out of our offices on the premise that a consultant had restructured the area to save money and eliminated our jobs. The move had been planned all along; all that was needed was a cut in the budget to justify doing it. I was a thorn in Tim's side and president Rudley's that they were glad to excise, with a lot of feigned regret.

I immediately filed with the EEOC. It took some time, but finally the agent on the case told me that they were going ahead and offering my charge to the university for response. On December 5, 2011, I was invited to attend a retirement party. I was the only one to RSVP of the sixteen people retired that year. All the others were so upset with their forced retirement that they didn't respond in protest to the president and his actions. TSU canceled the party but sent me my permanent parking decal, 2012 season athletic pass, and a plaque with a clock, barometer, and thermometer on it. I would've preferred an orderly transition of my work. And, a party with other staff like so many others have had over the years after long service and retirement. Already that fall, the office assistants who were given the job to maintain information and to report to the state were struggling with the task. Energy management requires a scientific or technical degree, training, attention to detail, and experience those folks just don't possess.

During 2011, I passed the annual physical like I was in my prime with all my blood parameters in the normal range, but I continued to lose muscle function and that affected everything. I acquired a flu that took me three weeks to get over. Fortunately, I was able to continue my health insurance from TSU with the Employees Retirement System of Texas (ERS) with a Medicare advantage plan from Kelsey Seybold clinic so that I got all of my care without having to pay a co-pay or deductible for anything except medicines. Over the years, I always paid a 20% co-pay. Under the advantage program, ERS paid for the portion that Medicare didn't cover, a benefit for retiring from service to the state of Texas.

By the end of 2011, at 55,000 miles, my 2006 Ford Freestar van was running better than ever. I finally got all the kinks out of the complex, five computer, driving system and expected to be doing a few more tweaks soon so that I could travel with the van without worrying about having trouble on the road again.

Our business arrangement with May Cole had us buying a home in an affluent neighborhood and having her remodel the home to her needs, in a short-term loan paying high interest. The remodeling took over twice as long as was expected, primarily because the neighbors were against the project from the start and forced the City of Houston to use business rules for a residential home. The final inspection took place in early December 2011 and May had ten residents and expected to get her state license as soon as she completed two minor adjustments from the last city inspection. It was a long haul, but Beh and I would realize substantial interest over the next three or four years, allowing me to avoid dipping into my retirement, for the most part, placed in a safe insurance policy earning 7% interest. Fortunately, I sold all my stock before the downturn in 2011 and put it into the project. The result was, in spite of the flat and difficult economy, both Beh and I would be doing very well for the foreseeable future. May was hinting that she wanted to build a new facility on the vacant lot from scratch in two or three years. If we funded that, we would be financially secure for a very long time.

I postponed my thoughts of buying property near Lake Houston and building an energy efficient-disabled access home once again. We had even thought of building in space for two elderly residents that would help pay for their and my care for the future. Property values hadn't increased, so we hoped to be able to buy property in 2012. It would be hard to remove Beh from her attachment to Southwest Houston, but we discussed it and I felt she could make the transition, especially after she sold the shop.

Beh and I joined Tim and Tom at Tim's. Sept 2011

# 82

# Saved by Surgery

In August, 2012, Mom drove to see friends and relatives in Withee. She had time, so she decided to drive to Prentice to see another friend. On the way, a state trooper stopped her for driving too slow. He didn't cite her, but she received a letter requesting that she retest for her drivers license. The year before, she had had an accident at the corner of 1st Street and Central Avenue. It was Mom's first accident in 50 years. After she received a letter from the Department of Motor Vehicles requesting that she retest for her driver's license, Mom was backing out of her garage and caught her driver's side door, damaging it. The handwriting was on the wall. In September, she decided to stop driving and sold her van. She also found out that arthritis in her hip and knees was causing her pain—bone against bone. With one hip already replaced twice years before, replacements were not considered because of her age. Unable to drive out and see friends, Mom felt so isolated and lonely. She wanted to move to an assisted living facility where she would be around people all the time. Instead she got help in her apartment. Meals on Wheels and cleaning. She could get more help as she needed it.

The year 2012 was the only year in memory that I didn't travel. After the trouble we had in restrooms and hotels on my trip to Wisconsin in 2011, Beh stopped us from traveling because she was afraid that she would not be able to transfer me and I would fall and get hurt far from home. However, we developed some new techniques for transferring and I looked at a portable lift, weighing 34 pounds that could help. I was also looking into traveling companions that were much stronger.

My 2006 Ford Freestar reached 55,000 miles by the end of the year and still looked and operated like new. Since my Wisconsin trip, I had several problems with the gas/brake unit, making it hard to accelerate and keep up with traffic on the freeway. Finally, that got corrected after I had the cable replaced one more time and tightened the slack between braking and throttling. My control panel had also lost its backlight, making it difficult to see to make panel selections after dark. I had hoped to change out the panel with a used one, but I was told that I must have one that had been reconditioned by EMC for $1500. With the van parked in the garage for days at a time without me venturing out, the battery quickly ran down because the system continually drew juice. To solve that problem, I bought a battery charger that Beh would connect to the battery on a six-day schedule so that I could start the car when I wanted to leave the house.

In retirement, I left the house primarily for doctor appointments, to tend to the van, visit my dwindling colleagues at TSU and attend various events. The Abilities Expo was one of those events, as well as the Houston Auto Show. I only sold 4 books at the Expo, but had an enjoyable time for three days. It was amazing how quickly the technology for the disabled evolved. I found myself going to more funerals for former colleagues and disabled activists. I was invited to the Woodlands for an open house at a rehabilitation hospital for an evening book signing. I sold one book and had some bad hospital cafeteria food. The Cajun finger food they provided the open house guests with was much better.

In October, I was invited by the Stanford Club of Houston to attend a luncheon and talk by former astronaut, Mae Jemison. I jumped at the chance, and, upon seeing her enter the room, offered to give her my two novels on encountering extraterrestrials. She graciously accepted my books and sat at my right side during lunch. Mae was introduced to speak by her Stanford roommate Linda Lorelle. Linda had been a long time local NBC Houston reporter who had left that job to form her own media firm and produce a weekly show on PBS called *Red, White, and Blue*, discussing political issues. Mae talked about her project, *100YearStarship*. The project, funded by DARPA for $500,000, was to develop a timeline of projects to be able to launch a ship to the stars by the year 2112. Dr. Jemison also talked about the 2nd 100YearStarship Symposium she was holding at the Hyatt that weekend.

I attended the symposium on Friday and Saturday and was amazed at the forward thinking of all the participants. I got my picture taken with Mae and Linda as well as LeVar Burton of Roots and Star Trek, the Next Generation fame. I also met Dr. Jill Tarter, recently retired director for SETI Research, overseeing the Allen Array searching for intelligent life by radio telescopes. .

While attending my 50th high school reunion in 2011, I encouraged Doug Boucher to write his memoir about how he helped save the world from nuclear disaster—twice. When I came home, I wrote a short story, *On the Brink of World War III*. Doug reviewed the story and approved. He gave me an idea for another short story, and I wrote, *Wish upon a Falling Star*.

After that, I got one idea after another and began writing short stories as fast as I could. I put aside writing on **American Mole: The Cartel** at the sixth chapter, and was sidetracked again. Doug sent me his memoir, **Watching from the Edge of Infinity**. I found his contribution to the Air Force and our country fascinating and wrote a review for the book. As far as I know, as yet, Doug's book remains unpublished except for friends and family.

And then, I got a call from Johnny Jackson, a longtime friend and owner of Jackson's Air-Conditioning in Sugarland. Johnny had been researching his great-grandfather, Benjamin Drake's participation in the Civil War with the West Virginia cavalry for 10 years. Johnny told a good story with a lot of humor from the time period. However, I had to correct almost every line for spelling, punctuation, and other errors. It took me several months working off and on. Finally, we had a book ready to publish. Johnny was very pleased with the cover and with the book: **One Man's Journey, the Civil War, 1861-65**.

I found that I had written enough short stories to create another book. All of the short stories were apocalyptic, so I thought of creating a book for the 2012 end of the world theme, since Roger and my 70th birthdays were on 12/21/12. **Verge of Apocalypse Tales** was published in October just ahead of that day.

In the meantime, I reviewed my friend, Jon Michael Willey's book of poetry, **Poets' Designs On Parchment Moons**; a fascinating book of three short stories about World War II by R. David Fulcher, **Trains To Nowhere**; and hilarious London murder mystery by master writer Paddy Bostock, **Two Down**, that was both wonderful and extremely well written.

At Thanksgiving, we took time out to visit our investment in May's elderly care home. It was crowded, but I got a chance to chat again with a Catholic lay pastor who continued to say that May's homes were the best he visits. I'm very pleased with the project's progress after so many problems getting the residence to meet city code and licensing requirements.

I returned to this book, my autobiography, first typed by one finger from 1992 to 1998. I revisited the book in 2001, and again in 2006. Finally, I got started editing again, when Roger sent me his **AUTO Biography**. I switched gears again and thoroughly reviewed the car memoir, making suggestions and corrections. Roger has numerous photos of the cars he wrote about, so the book may be difficult to publish conventionally because of the cost. However, Roger may be able to make a version with the color pictures that can be sent as an attachment to an email as long as the pictures are small enough to keep the file size down.

I was reminded of my mortality when I attended a City Hall meeting October 8, 2012, honoring the Disabled Advocate of the Year. My good friend, Tony Koosis, received the award posthumously. Anne, Tony's wife, also disabled, accepted the award. It was there that I met James Sweatt, a former linebacker for the Arizona Cardinals with multiple sclerosis. James took a picture of me from his wheelchair with Houston Mayor Annise Parker.

I had a physical in April of 2012 and all of my health parameters were in the normal range again, unlike so many people in my age group. However, my long, slow decline continued to take its toll as I got weaker and required more assistance, especially with transferring. I took inoculations for the flu every year, for pneumonia twice, including October 2012, and for shingles. I would recommend that anyone get these immunizations and any others that are required. My leg spasms grew worse and I sought relief by going to my rehabilitation doctors at TIRR. They recommended that I improve my diet to reduce stomach discomfort and an exercise program. Unfortunately, my fabulous Kelsey-Seybold ERS Medicare Advantage insurance, the first certified Advantage program in the country, was reluctant to pay for the recommendations until I appealed several times. The TIRR nutritionist made only one change in my diet, and that was to add nuts and cheese (protein) to my lunch of celery, carrots, radishes and fruit of the day. Otherwise, I was eating healthily, if too much. It was hard to cut back because Beh always came up with new dishes that she wanted me to try and also kept trying to increase portions when I no longer had the ability to burn off the extra calories.

Since I was at my computer in the dining room, dictating long hours each day, I broke it up with sunning and stretching exercises on the front deck. My home office window in my bedroom faces the back yard and all the critters it brings. In the summer of 2012, a pair of Black Bellied Whistling Ducks paraded their young for me twice in the yard and another night the ducklings, alone and scavenging for bugs, invaded the house when Beh opened the sliding glass door from the kitchen to take pictures and a video of them. The pair had three sets of hatchlings that summer in spite of the entire power right of way behind the house being cleared to bare ground in early June. And then, a hawk visited the yard—probably because a sparrow had committed suicide on my window the day before. Many birds did that. Beh's feeding attracted sparrows, starlings, mourning doves, blue jays, cardinals and wrens. Hummingbirds came through in the spring and fall while migrating and stopped at Beh's feeder. Mockingbirds have always been part of the scene and I love their mockery of other birdcalls and their courage in chasing away intruders from their nests.

After several years of trying to get support from my health insurance for an exercise machine, I bought a used Flexarciser from AbleExchange.com. Unfortunately, when I received the machine, the speed control wasn't working properly. I could get it to run at 15 rpm and that was great, but it needed fixing. The next time I tried it, the machine would only run at 65 rpm. That speed didn't hurt me, but my legs were flying like crazy for a minute until I had Beh turn it off. The company sent me a potentiometer and I had my old friend who built my first van, Troy Hamilton, renovate my 1992 Invacare wheelchair and replace the potentiometer on the Flexarciser. The machine worked fine after that and I exercised every day. Only 10 minutes at first, but gradually increased my use in time.

I had the flu in October and missed a doctor appointment at TIRR. I shook the illness off in about a week, but my appointment had been moved to December. As I approached my December appointment, I got a strange fever one Wednesday night. I worked that day, but Thursday night, Daisey told me that I had sweated (I sweated every time I urinated—many times a day) the entire bed wet. By Saturday, I was coughing and feeling a sharp pain in my diaphragm. Trying to decide what hospital to go to was difficult. My insurance had St. Luke's as their primary hospital. But Beh did not know how to get there and it was 20 miles from home. I called TIRR, but their hospital only accepted referrals from doctors. Finally, by Tuesday, December 4, I drove to the emergency room at West Houston Medical

Center with Beh. They diagnosed me with an E. coli urinary tract infection, a blood clot on my left lung, and pneumonia in my right lung. While I was being treated with antibiotics, the pneumonia infection doubled every day and could not be drained. I had to go on oxygen and got weaker each day. Finally, on December 11, I had surgery for a fully involved, collapsed right lung. My lung was scraped clean of the infection, and I awoke in ICU without a breathing tube (a miracle?). Two days later, I was off oxygen and breathing on my own. They told me that was unheard of in my kind of surgery. But I was certainly glad to have the little nostril tubes removed. After a torturous two weeks of being straitjacketed in the hospital, many days without the ability to push a button for a nurse, I survived and was released, to my relief, late on December 26. Through all of this, my little angel, Beh, only a block away in her shop, was by my side whenever I needed her, in 10 minutes. Rose and Daisey worked their usual nights and turned me so that I wouldn't get any pressure sores. Beh was very relieved when she had me home.

I know there was a lot of controversy during the 2012 political season. I think the American people made the right decision. It takes a very long time to come out of a deep recession. Especially when the root causes are systematic and not easily remedied by government action. The initiation, by greedy scoundrels in the mortgage industry and the stock market, most of whom still hadn't been punished, was faced with opposing cures. We were coming out of the recession slowly and on track in spite of the constant hype by the media making small stories large. We may be a bit slow, but we would solve our problems one by one. Next year would be better than the last as it had been the course of history in spite of what some may think who have not remembered or studied how really bad those good old days were. Or lack foresight into the unlimited potential and bright future that we can have if we accept change, embrace it, and go for the stars.

My used Flexaciser with a view of flowers on the deck when I exercise.

# 83

## Life after Pneumonia and Surgery

I didn't feel bad after returning home from surgery except for a persistent pain in my chest that moved around; the same pain that had been with me since I had been told that it was injured ligaments in my rib cage from being transferred over a year before. I was very glad to get on my old meal regimen. In spite of eating everything on my tray in the hospital, I had lost weight. Beh wanted to put some meat on me. And I didn't mind, as long as it wasn't too much. I didn't seem to have as much strength as before and had to have help with eating at first and more help with everything else.

I first had to tackle all the emails that had piled up and ended up not reviewing some. I made sure I found the ones from family and friends and answered those. I finished my annual letter and sent that out to show people that I was back in business and tell them what had happened to me in the hospital.

Once I had caught up with my email, I started writing a poem a week again. A number of the people following me on Authors Den had wondered what happened to me, so I posted a story about my hospital experience that was some good and some bad, but torture for anyone who is quadriplegic like me and unable to move on our own. When you are confined and can't move like I was, it feels like being put in a straitjacket. The confinement not only wears on you, it is damaging to the muscles because they start to atrophy without movement.

Fortunately, I had set up my banking to accept deposits and automatically pay bills, so that was on autopilot while I was gone and Beh did not have to go to the bank for me or pay any bills. It was very easy for me to straighten that out, but much harder for me to tackle my taxes that had become immensely complicated with my disability, retirement accounts, business, rental property, business investment, office use of the home, authorship, paying household employees, and so forth. I had to update many spreadsheets for the calendar year. Fortunately, my bank and my credit card were able to provide me all of the expenditures through downloads that enabled the spreadsheet building process to go quite quickly and well.

For many years, I used TaxAct online for my taxes. Before I went online, I had developed a tax worksheet that followed the 1040 and other forms for doing my annual taxes by hand. I still completed that worksheet every year, mostly in advance, so that it would be much easier to fill in the values during the online tax preparation process; as well as provide some documentation linking all the many spreadsheets of expenditures for the various classifications of deductions. Without TaxAct online, I doubt if I could do taxes by hand using the worksheet any more, it has become so out of date. Still, even using TaxAct online, it is difficult to complete the preparation process. When I finally completed the process in mid February, I had a 1040 with 27 pages and another 65 pages from my brokerage. If it weren't for these online services, I would spend my days like an accountant just trying to keep up with tax information in many physical folders. It makes me wonder how corporate information was kept prior to computers. Accountants had very tedious work back then. I believe I could do my worksheet on Helix RADE, but with tax law changes every year, I would constantly have to be updating. So, I let Second Story and their TaxAct online software do the job for me. The price was right.

Because my attendants were household employees, I did not have to report their earnings quarterly, only annually. That moved all the taxes and withholding to April 15 when I reported them and paid my personal/business taxes. The last few years were quite a hit since I no longer withheld much from my Social Security to cover that kind of the tax year end burden. The good news was that I wasn't handing my money over to the federal government without interest so early like everybody that takes withholding does in some sort of backward savings plan so they can get a "big" refund. I much preferred to use that money during the year in investments and pay all of my taxes at once when they are due rather than too early. I believe that if everybody did that, cash flow to the federal treasury would stop and Congress would go crazy, because the federal government can't wait until April 15 to be paid. They use those quarterly funds from business to stay in business as much as a year in advance of the law.

Driving my van became tricky because I lost some range of motion from the surgery. I found that, even after the adjustment on the previous November, tightening my gas and brake unit, driving was difficult. I decided to take the van to Mobility Plus one more time to see what could be done to fix the problems. As I accelerated out onto the toll road, Beltway 8, and reached the left lane, I suddenly heard a loud "crack" and felt that I had no acceleration. A safety lane was to my left and I had no choice but to roll into it because otherwise fast-moving traffic would have overtaken me. Once in the lane with traffic buffeting me as they passed, I turned off the system and restarted; something that had worked before because it reset the safety clutch. I tried it a couple of times just to be sure, and the engine would start, but only idle. I had two choices: I could stay where I was where it was difficult to get a tow and almost impossible for me to get out of the van, or I could move forward at idle speed. I decided to move forward, turning on the flashers. The Beltway ahead moved uphill slightly and then downhill under the Westpark Tollway. Upon putting the car in drive, it accelerated to about 7 mph, straining to make the slight rise ahead. Once over that, the van reached about 10 mph downhill. At least I wasn't holding up traffic. There was a rather substantial hill ahead coming up out from under the overpass, and I was worried that I would not make it. But the engine power was sufficient to keep me rolling to the crest at about 5 mph. At that point, there was an exit ahead and I started across the lanes as carefully as I could at such a slow speed. Fortunately, there was no screeching of tires or honking of horns as all of the traffic carefully avoided me even though I had no right signal light on, just flashers. I was relieved and continued to work my way over.

When I reached the other side of the freeway just short of the exit, I suddenly saw a truck with emergency lights pull up behind me in the right safety lane and I stopped. Another truck with lights flashing pulled in front of me. A man from the truck from the rear came up and asked me if he could help. I asked him to press on the gas pedal with his hand to see if the engine would rev—it wouldn't. The man told me that he could give me a free tow off the tollway but that was all. I told him that I would, "idle off," and he told me that that was okay. I could've had him call AAA for me, but I knew I would have to wait for them to come and I'd already used up all my free tows for the year. There was no way that I could call anyone myself because I didn't have a cell phone. I asked the guy to call Mobility Plus on his cell phone and tell them that I would be there in about an hour. I'd already idled a couple of miles and figured I had about eight more miles to go. I idled off the tollway and continued along the frontage road until I got to the frontage road for I-10. I had to make a left turn down into a hole and then come up out of that hole. Thankfully, the engine pulled dutifully and I made it past that climb easily. As I turned right onto Upland I saw a white van behind me. I expected the van to pass, but it didn't. Instead its flashers came on and the van followed me all the way to Mobility Plus. I didn't dare stop in the front, but continued on to the service bays and tried to drive up into one of them. I got about halfway in the empty bay, but the slope was too steep. I was about to stop when Chad Strohmatt ran up behind the van to push me in. Chad was the guy who trained me to drive my first van. His office was nearby and he saw me in trouble and heading for the shop, so he followed. Rick, the guy who built my van had been fired, and the new guy there could tell me nothing during the lunch hour, so I left the van there and Chad gave me a ride home in his trainer van.

The gas-brake cable had snapped—*again*. It was the third cable replacement in two years. The replacement cable that came in from EMC was too long. The new guy had difficulty putting it in, and the cost was too much. I called EMC and their service manager at Chad's suggestion. The service manager, Phil, told me that he had a solution for the cable problem that he would provide, *free*. When I told him that the backlighting on my Gold panel was out, he told me that he would replace that, *free*, too. When I told him that since I had the van I couldn't use the voice system (VIC) at speeds above 50 mph, he told me he had a *free* upgrade of that as well. When I called Trey at Mobility Plus, I learned that he had fired everyone and his new people didn't have the capability to make changes to my van any more. Fortunately, Adaptive Driving Access (ADA) had a shop just a few miles further up Beltway 8 and had certified technicians for EMC. When I got to ADA, I learned that they had hired Rick and *he* would be the one working on my van. I left the van there for two weeks and they sent everything to EMC to be upgraded. When the equipment came back, it took a long time to get everything back in and working. ADA cut the labor cost in half, but my free equipment cost over $1000! To top that off, the van wasn't driving very well and I couldn't train the voice system to work properly. The "fix" had replaced the drive cable and clutch again. This time, Rick made an adjustment to the control and I started feeling like I had control of the gas brake again—much better than when the van was new—a welcome feeling. As for the VIC, it was sent back to be repaired to EMC again. After that repair, the VIC would cut out occasionally, just like before. I was seriously considering going back to some other system like the head button system in my Windstar to solve the problem, once and for all.

In the meantime, I had dreams that prompted three short stories. The first story, about a concussion that got very bad, failed to materialize, but I may return to write it later. The second story, *Scanned*, came to me when I learned that brain scanning was getting to the point where doctors were able to diagnose, very specifically, brain diseases and malformations, leading to surgeries that could correct these problems, like Parkinson's disease. I carried this story much further into the realm of Big Brother. My fellow authors liked the story and suggested that I turn it into a novel. The third story, *Hitch Bitch*, hearkened back to my days driving the country and picking up hitchhikers. After writing those two stories, I redoubled my efforts to finish this autobiography, slowed by interruptions and other delays.

But sickness came calling again. Sometime in mid-January 2013, I started feeling a bit feverish and my urine became cloudy again after being crystal clear when I came back from the hospital. I called Dr. Solomos and he gave me an antibiotic. The antibiotic worked, and the cloudiness in my urine disappeared... for a short while. I got an appointment with a neurourologist, Dr. Ben Dillon, and he asked me to give him a sample of my urine for a culture. Dillon suggested that I have a suprapubic tube installed to drain my bladder continuously.

I had been trying to avoid surgery since 1992 when Dr. Rudy suggested a much more invasive procedure using some of my intestine as a tube from my bladder to my stomach wall. That tube would continually drain into a belly bag and that bag would drain into a leg bag. Since my bladder would never get full, dysreflexia would disappear, and the danger of urine backing up into my kidneys and destroying them would also be gone. When I talked to a couple of guys over the years who had had the procedure, they told me that it made things worse. Dr. Dillon claimed that he could install the suprapubic tube in about 8 minutes and easily reverse the surgery if I wanted to later. The idea was tempting, but after looking at all the options, I decided not to have the procedure for now. People online complained of having to drink much soft water so hard water calcium deposits—the reason the tube had to be changed, wouldn't clog the small tube monthly. I worried about snagging the tube and pulling it out while spasming in bed at night—sometimes quite violent, emptying the leg bag, and the affect of tight seat belts on my wheelchair and van on the tube's integrity. Dillon gave me a very strong antibiotic, and, after two weeks, my urinary tract infection, determined by the culture taken earlier, was defeated. I didn't have any trouble with my urine after that.

My psoriasis was another matter. It continued to get worse with time and more stress. And the pimples that had plagued me earlier after my lithotripsies came back on my scalp and neck. I searched around for answers, and eventually, went to a dermatologist, Dr. Dorsey. I'd been told many years earlier by a dermatologist that there was no cure for psoriasis and that anyone with spinal cord injury stress would have a chronic problem with it. I certainly was a candidate in that regard. Dorsey prescribed another strong antibiotic for the pimples and a steroid shampoo for my scalp and cream for my skin. While the antibiotic gradually removed the pimples, the steroid creams put a stop to the flakiness and itching of the psoriasis. It was the first time in a long time—as long as I could remember—when my ears cleared up and I could hear without them being plugged with dead skin all the time. After two weeks, the pimples returned—*worse*. Ever positive, Dorsey prescribed an over-the-counter skin cleanser. After another two weeks, the skin cleanser wasn't working either. Dorsey then prescribed a steroid ointment that seems to have worked—*so far*. At least the psoriasis hadn't returned—*yet*.

One of the first times I left the house after my surgery was in February. Four people were retiring from the facilities and maintenance area of TSU and a party was held in their honor. While they didn't include me in the party, I didn't worry about it because the party was a time to reconnect with several people from our area that had retired as long as twenty years before. I was quite impressed with the way some of earlier retirees had defied aging during their long retirements. Of the formerly retired people who were missing, one was my administrative assistant, Barbara Allen, who had retired early three years before me, at 53, I believe. A short while later, I learned that she had become morbidly obese and died from those complications at 57. In the meantime, I kept up with Norma Fair, a former colleague going through numerous spinal surgeries for bone spurs and other spinal injuries. I also kept in close touch with my friends at HCI L, the Houston Center for Independent Living, so many of whom suffered poverty and early deaths because of their disabilities.

After going to doctor appointments, if I had time, I would drop back to TSU to visit briefly with former colleagues and friends… dwindling now to a very few. On one day, as I was retracing the same shortcut that I often took when I left work, I noticed a squirrel cross the street up ahead. That squirrel reminded me of the story I wrote, *Brian Bushytail and the Urban Forest*. The trees on the esplanade between the massive lanes on 288 had recovered somewhat from the drought, but all of the loblolly pines that had been sticking up beyond the deciduous trees were gone—*dead*. Without some serious planting again, the piney forest would not return there. But squirrels would still love the place, regardless, when the trees got big enough to produce enough food. There were plenty of squirrels in the neighborhood to populate the growing freeway forest. As I turned right at a stop sign onto Wichita and a straight shot to the entry ramp to 288, I noticed a car behind me. I accelerated hard, knowing that I would have to spend time at the stop sign at Dowling, and did not want to hold up the fellow behind me while I set up to cross that busy street. I tried to be courteous to other drivers when I could, especially since I was slower to leave stop signs in traffic.

Just as I reached a speed that was really too fast for the neighborhood with a car parked on the right ahead, a squirrel came from the left out of nowhere under my left front wheel. I pulled on the brake—*hard*—was pushed forward against my belts as I braked, and inertia pushed my steering tri-pin forward causing my steering wheel to turn sharply to the left. The squirrel turned tail under my left front wheel and I let up on the brake. I watched in horror as my van resumed speed instantly and headed sharply left up a high curb and steeply sloped lawn between huge oak trees. I pulled on the brake as hard as I could again and stopped just before reaching the concrete steps leading to the front door, 10 feet off the road and 5 feet higher. As I collected my wits, the guy driving behind me stopped and ran over to see if I was all right. I told him that I was and he helped me back down off that lawn onto the street again.

As I drove off, I felt something drastically wrong and pulled over right away. The same guy came up to my driver's side window and told me that my left front tire was flat. The curb was very sharp and not rounded like most curbs are. My tire was slashed completely through. The good Samaritan, a TSU graduate, told me that he was on his way to the nearby Harris County psychiatric hospital where he had landed a job as a counselor. He was headed over there to have a security screening, but still had time to change my tire. We found that he couldn't lift the cover over the tire behind the rear seat and had to call Adaptive Driving Access for assistance. Once they told us what to do, he was able to pull out my donut

611

tire and put it on the front. I offered him money, but he refused like so many had before whenever I had car trouble on the road. I immediately drove to Discount Tire. They had only one of my tires in stock, but that was enough. I was grateful that there was no damage to the car, the yard, or the house, and that I suffered no injury, except to my psyche, like so many times before.

I put all my illnesses behind me and once again passed my physical with great blood parameters in June 2013. I was exercising every day and gaining my strength back gradually. I began to be more incontinent than ever—probably a combination of spinal deterioration and aging. The pain in my chest finally went away, but then came back and, occasionally, along with headaches and sleepiness as a result of getting up too early. I was putting on weight because I seemed to be given more variety and larger portions that I continually tried to resist. It was very hard to resist yummy food put before me to sample.

For the third year in a row, I sold my books at the Abilities Expo at Reliant Center on August 1, 2 and 3, 2013. I had Tommie McNeil with me on Friday, Diane Crouch with me on Saturday, and Beh once again, joined me on Sunday. This time I took a different tack because my books didn't sell the year before. I offered books free for a donation to those with a disability. Two donors exceeded the retail price of the books by a considerable amount, and the rest did not recoup my cost for the books, but got them out among the reading public. I believe after that experience I will continue to use that approach until I get famous and people will be willing to buy from me regardless what I write. Fame pays, obscurity doesn't.

For the second year in a row, I attended the 100 Year Starship symposium at the Hyatt in Houston. I submitted a proposal for a talk, but it was rejected; probably because my topic was very sketchy and didn't contain any compelling information that the conference organizers thought that they would like me to speak about. That's okay, because creating the presentation would've been quite difficult since my drawing skills have been much reduced by my declining ability to use my hand splint and mouse to draw with. I refuse to present a PowerPoint presentation with only words on it. This topic, about overcoming our Earth-centric biology in the rigors of space travel, like in the movie, *Gravity*, would be difficult to pull off to be creditable with the knowledgeable audience in attendance. But then, who knows what we'll need a hundred years from now. Most predictions are dead wrong, even if only a few years out. Who's to say that my ideas are worse than someone else's. If I can't present them at the symposium, they are in my books. Time will tell.

I look forward to a long-awaited short three or four day trip through Louisiana in fall or spring, but keeps eluding me as I have not settled on the dates or who would go with me yet. That will require another chapter. Christmas is coming again and I have many presents to give in gratitude for what I have been given. So that this story will continue...

James Sweat, former Phoenix Cardinal linebacker with MS, caught me joking with Houston Mayor Anise Parker and my former helper, Jean on his wheelchair camera at an award for Tony Koosis at City Hall.

With Jenny Yeung and LaVar Burton 100YSS. Sept 2012
and Michio Kamu . Oct 2013

Selling my books at the Abilities Expo. Houston, TX. Aug 2013

# Epilogue

## Beyond Comfort

It's safe to say that I've reached a point where I see the future differently than I did when I began writing this saga twenty-one years ago. I can see the light at the end of the tunnel that I couldn't see then. The thread has not broken. Instead, it's been supported and strengthened by good health, improving technology, good fortune and the help of Beh. I still have to face operations and hospital stays and more pain and trauma before I die, but now there is hope that with support, I can live an ever more fulfilling life as I decline physically.

The hardest part was reaching financial independence. With my retirement income more than my need, I can rest assured regardless of the restrictions forced on me by Social Security, Medicare, and the like. Regardless of the stock market's performance, my investments allow a sense of security so that I can be free to write about and work on whatever I like within the restrictions my physical body imposes.

The next thing is staying mobile. My wheelchair can go almost anywhere there are ramps, elevators and a smooth path, up to twenty miles. METROLift can take me almost anywhere in Houston, if I call the day before and schedule the trip before 12:00 noon. METRO buses and light rail can take me anywhere the routes go—free—with my Metro Freedom Pass. My van is expensive and difficult to operate. When the time comes, I'll stop driving and convert the set up so that someone can drive me where I need to go. Airplane flights remain an obstacle as well as hotel accommodations. I need good help to travel great distances.

In the meantime, my banking and taxes still mostly by computer. Cable gives me high-speed connection to the Internet. I expect to be able to communicate more freely with colleagues and associates through email and other means. Voice dictation has sped my work and freed me from physical stress. Miniaturized and touch screen devices are very difficult for me to use and add to my stress. My hope for a voice-operated environment is still off in the future, but I am confident that it will eventually be my primary way of getting things done.

Recent advances in electric vehicles give hope that my chair can become an all weather , all terrain electric vehicle, at least capable of getting me to and from nearby places on a daily electric charge. Other technologies I cannot imagine will come to help me. And perhaps, a cure, a way to regenerate my lost spinal nerves. Stem cells show promise, but that promise recedes with each year a major breakthrough is not achieved. Already there are battery-powered implants that, once embedded in muscles, activate them to accomplish tasks lost to neural damage. Exoskeletal components, operated by impulses in the brain, are adding strength and movement to disabled extremities. These operations are experimental, highly invasive, and provide minimal function, but they are the precursor of electronic systems and techniques that may emulate normal nerve function someday. Unless it is absolutely necessary, my thread is not so stretched that I need to be a guinea pig for surgeries of dubious value. Still, if conditions are right and improved function is expected, especially in the area of bowel and bladder control, I may opt for today's surgery over lost organs or further limitations to my daily life.

One thing is certain. The longer I live, the more likely I will benefit from technological or medical advances, as well as societal understanding. It is my firm hope that the young athlete-scholar that showed so much promise will finally realize full equality of opportunity. After a lifetime of concerted effort to act and live as normally as possible, in spite of the subtle discrimination by those who only pitied and excluded me, I feel the continued need to prove that nothing, especially the ignorance of others, need keep me from a fully productive and fulfilling life. I don't want admiration for what I've done in spite of my disability, I want admiration for what I've done. I don't want others to stand up and speak for me, I want to sit tall and speak for myself. Just as Franklin Roosevelt used his money, power, and influence to appear to be normal and rose to greatness as our longest-serving president in a time of the country's greatest peril, I hope to be valued for my worth as a person, with my disability and apparatus of assistance as invisible as FDR's paralyzed legs in his Fireside Chats.

The threat of the thread is always there, just as the chance that I will get cancer, or struck by a car, or "suffer the thousand slings and arrows the flesh is heir to...." But I am no longer its slave, doomed to a downward spiral of pain, poverty and despair. Instead, I face the new century with renewed hope that I can live a full life and see the day when I am judged for my contribution and not for my overcoming.

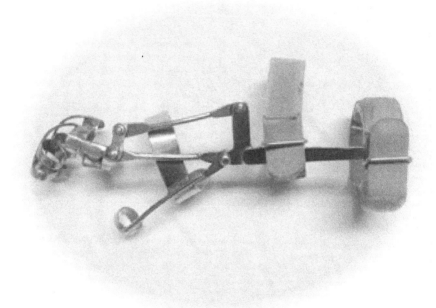

My $200 handsplint built in August 1964 in two days, enabled me to write, draw and type with one finger equivalent to my peers and earn a livelihood. In spite of many band changes and repairs, in daily use for over 50 years.

What I love, riding free out in nature. Fort Worth Arboretum, Aug 2009

# About the Author

# Ronald W. Hull

Ronald W. Hull is a retired administrator at Texas Southern University in Houston, Texas. A spinal cord injury during surgery when he was twenty changed the course of his life, but not his resolve. Determined to be independent, he completed college and learned how to live alone, without assistance. After a brief engineering career, he completed a doctorate and taught in four universities before serving in administration.

Ron is the author of many technical articles, an award winning energy conservation plan, and a poem a week on his website, ronhullauthor.com. Dr. Hull recently completed this, his seventh book. Ron resides in Southwest Houston with his helper and partner, Beh.